ELECTRONIC COMMERCE
Security, Risk Management, and Control

Marilyn Greenstein, Ph.D.
Arizona State University–West

Miklos Vasarhelyi, Ph.D.
Rutgers University

McGraw-Hill
Irwin

Boston   Burr Ridge, IL   Dubuque, IA   Madison, WI   New York   San Francisco   St. Louis
Bangkok   Bogotá   Caracas   Kuala Lumpur   Lisbon   London   Madrid   Mexico City
Milan   Montreal   New Delhi   Santiago   Seoul   Singapore   Sydney   Taipei   Toronto

McGraw-Hill Higher Education

A Division of The McGraw-Hill Companies

ELECTRONIC COMMERCE: SECURITY, RISK MANAGEMENT AND CONTROL Published by McGraw-Hill/Irwin, an imprint of The McGraw-Hill Companies, Inc. 1221 Avenue of the Americas, New York, NY, 10020. Copyright © 2002, 2000 by The McGraw-Hill Companies, Inc. All rights reserved. No part of this publication may be reproduced or distributed in any form or by any means, or stored in a data base or retrieval system, without the prior written consent of The McGraw-Hill Companies, Inc., including, but not limited to, in any network or other electronic storage or transmission, or broadcast for distance learning. Some ancillaries, including electronic and print components, may not be available to customers outside the United States.

This book is printed on acid-free paper.

domestic   3 4 5 6 7 8 9 0 QPD/QPD 0 9 8 7 6 5 4 3 2
international   1 2 3 4 5 6 7 8 9 0 QPD/QPD 0 9 8 7 6 5 4 3 2 1

ISBN 0-07-241081-7

Publisher: *Robin Zwettler*
Senior sponsoring editor: *Stewart Mattson*
Editorial coordinator: *Heather Sabo*
Marketing manager: *Rich Kolasa*
Marketing coordinator: *Melissa Larmon*
Project manager: *James Labeots*
Production supervisor: *Gina Hangos*
Media producer: *Edward Przyzycki*
Designer: *Damian Moshak*
Supplement coordinator: *Susan Lombardi*
Cover designer: *Adam Rooke*
Cover illustration: *Tom White*
Typeface: *10/12 Times Roman*
Compositor: *Carlisle Communications, Ltd.*
Printer: *Quebecor World Dubuque Inc.*

Library of Congress Cataloging-in-Publication Data

Greenstein, Marilyn.
    Electronic commerce : security, risk management, and control/Marilyn Greenstein,
Miklos Vasarhelyi.—2nd ed.
      p. cm.
    Includes bibliographical references and index.
    ISBN 0-07-241081-7 (alk. paper)
    1. Electronic commerce. 2. Risk management. I. Vasarhelyi, Miklos A. II. Title.
HF5548.32.G74 2002
658.8'4—dc21   2001032949

INTERNATIONAL EDITION ISBN 0-07-112340-7
Copyright © 2002. Exclusive rights by The McGraw-Hill Companies, Inc. for manufacture and export.
This book cannot be re-exported from the country to which it is sold by McGraw-Hill.
The International Edition is not available in North America.

www.mhhe.com

Once again, I would like to thank my family, Dan, Jillian, and Cheryl, for their support.

Marilyn

Dumpling—this one's for you.

Miklos

TO THE STUDENT

The area of electronic commerce is an exciting topic to study because of its relative newness and exploding growth rates. The World Wide Web (WWW) was born approximately a decade ago, and it has yet to reach anywhere close to its full business potential. As the Internet and the WWW evolve, so too does the surrounding environment and business applications. Electronic commerce is an area that deeply encompasses many different disciplines of study, such as accounting, business law, information systems, marketing, and management. The finance discipline is also affected because of the manner in which information is disseminated and the new entrants into the brokerage business. Regardless of your field of study, e-commerce is a vital part of the business environment.

Why Study This Text

This text is designed to expose students to the multifaceted aspects of e-commerce. This text will provide a framework for students to use in the analysis and formulation of e-commerce business solutions and strategies. Because of the rapid nature of change in this material, a solid background of the critical issues and methodologies is important to any student facing a business career. Five years hence, the technology will undoubtedly be somewhat, if not markedly, different, but a solid understanding of the important business issues will prove invaluable in moving forward with the unfolding e-commerce environment.

Objectives of the Text

The material in this text is organized and presented with the goal of introducing all facets of the e-commerce environment to students. Because the accounting profession has been and still is in the business of information production and dissemination, one objective of this text is to examine the effects of electronic commerce to members of the accounting profession throughout the text. The large accounting firms also provide many other services, and they hire many students from disciplines other than accounting. These other services have become a large part of the revenue-generating activities of these firms, and most of these services are affected in some fashion by e-commerce. Another objective is to explore these additional services throughout the text.

Understanding the regulatory environment of an *international* infrastructure is another key objective of this text. Because the Internet and the WWW provide another sales and distribution channel, examining the marketing implications of e-commerce is another objective. Unraveling many of the technical "mysteries" of e-commerce security is another important objective.

TO THE INSTRUCTOR

If you have already taught an electronic commerce course, then you know what a joy it is to have such an exciting topic to bring into a classroom. Students easily see the relevance of the material, regardless of the topic, due to the wide coverage of all e-commerce areas by the media. Thus, student motivation is not a challenge; it is a luxury. To take full advantage of this interest, this textbook can be used as a framework for examining the important issues and technologies involved in e-commerce.

If you have not yet taught an e-commerce course, we assure you that you are in for a treat because of the exciting nature of the topic. One problem you will face, however, is information overload. Articles, press releases, and new stories relating to e-commerce are bountiful. This textbook can help you in two important ways. First, it will provide you with an outline of topics and a framework for your course. Secondly, a website will be maintained containing the most recent, important developments organized by chapter. This feature will help you to remain abreast of current events with a minimal amount of effort.

Using the Text

This text is designed to be used for the following purposes:

- As a junior- or senior-level undergraduate electronic commerce course.
- As a supplement to a current accounting or marketing course.
- As a graduate level, general electronic commerce course.

In its first edition, this text was used at many universities for a general MBA-level e-commerce course. It was also used at the undergraduate level for a general e-commerce course. The text is easily adaptable as a supplement to existing accounting information systems or marketing courses. The instructor must decide how much detail to cover. When using the text as a supplement, the basics can be covered. When using the text as the primary or sole textbook, each of the areas can be thoroughly explored. Because of its evolving nature, e-commerce subjects are perfect for generating terrific class discussions and debate. Further, weekly "research" assignments are a natural inclusion for e-commerce stand-alone courses.

Key Features

This text book has the following features:

- *A business strategy approach.* This text includes a chapter on the electronization of business and a chapter on "new economy" business-to-business strategies.
- *A multidisciplinary approach.* The text includes chapters on the regulatory environment, the accounting profession, and Web-based marketing.

• *A discussion of the implications for the accounting profession throughout the text.* The implications faced by the accounting profession for both assurance services and consulting activities are discussed.

• *An emphasis on security and technological features.* The text covers security issues and techniques, such as encryption, digital signatures, certification authorities, and firewalls.

• *Coverage of risks and risk management.* The risks faced by firms engaging in e-commerce are covered as well as procedures for managing such risks.

• *A website containing important updates and current events by chapter.* This feature ensures that the material covered in your course is never outdated.

• *Boxes and real-world examples used to illustrate key concepts through the text.*

• Plentiful *end-of-chapter material* helps students understand the concepts discussed within the chapter. The variety and quantity of review questions, discussion questions, and cases give instructors flexibility in assigning problems.

Supplements

The *Solutions Manual* (ISBN 0072431296), prepared by Marilyn Greenstein, textbook author, and Dr. Diane Hamilton, MIS professor, contains answers to all of the end-of-chapter materials, including review questions, discussion questions, and case materials. For questions that rely on current events, suggestions how to discuss the material are given.

The course *website* contains updates to course materials, and it is organized by chapter for ease of use. Instructors are encouraged to visit the website regularly to view current material. Sample course syllabi are also available at this site, as well as the capability to submit questions to the textbook authors.

The second edition includes *PowerPoint slides* prepared by Margarita Lenk of Colorado State University. The slides are located on the course website: *www.mhhe.com/ greenstein2e*

We would like to thank the following people from PricewaterhouseCoopers for their effort and hard work on the first edition of this text: David Kohl, Jonathan Stearn, Christopher O'Hara, Perry Gentry, Mark Ziskind, Brett Moseley, Royden Hutchison, Jeffrey Zimmerman, Mark Lobel, Keith Sollers, Gregory Smith, Bruce Murphy, and Andrew Toner.

We would like to especially acknowledge the work contributed by Todd M. Feinman to the first edition.

We would like to thank the following professors for their helpful comments and suggestions:

Amelia Baldwin
University of Alabama

Paul Branzina
LaSalle University

Charles Davis
Baylor University

J. Barry Dickinson
LaSalle University

John Dodge
Laurentian University

Richard Dull
Indiana University at Indianapolis

Stephen Fogg
Temple University

Parviz Ghandforoush
Virginia Polytechnic Institute and State University

Diane Hamilton
Rowan University

James Hansen
Brigham Young University

Perry Hildalgo
Gwinnett Technical College

Beth Jones
Western Carolina University

Linda Larson
Texas A&M University at Corpus Christi

Margarita Lenk
Colorado State University

Merle Martin
California State University at Sacramento

Elaine Mauldin
University of Missouri at Columbia

Nancy Melone
Duquesne University

Cheryl Mitchem
Virginia State University

Gary Peters
University of Georgia

Michael Prietula
University of Florida

Amy Ray
University of Tennessee

Alan Sangster
The Queen's University of Belfast

Andy Shinkle
Utah State University

James Tarr
Christopher Newport University

Kerem Tomak
University of Texas

Anthony Wensley
University of Toronto

Alfred Zimermann
Hawaii Pacific University

Marilyn Greenstein, Ph.D.
Arizona State University–West

Miklos Vasarhelyi, Ph.D.
Rutgers University

B R I E F   C O N T E N T S

CONTENTS

1   OVERVIEW OF ELECTRONIC COMMERCE

Learning Objectives

1. To learn the activities encompassed by electronic commerce and the role of the Internet and World Wide Web.
2. To understand the benefits that can be achieved through the use of electronic commerce.
3. To compare various electronic commerce business models.
4. To examine the general nature of security concerns surrounding electronic commerce.

INTRODUCTION

Electronic commerce and the electronization of business processes have revolutionized many industries, such as the travel and financial services industries, and they are shaking up most other industries as well. Electronic commerce and electronic business are two of the most common business terms in use today. In fact, try to find a business periodical or trade journal that does not have several articles discussing how businesses are applying some form of "e" business process or application. So what exactly are electronic commerce and electronic business? Will these terms still be important in the years to come, or will they be two more overused and discarded buzzwords? This chapter examines the definitions of electronic commerce and electronic business and their surrounding environments. The Internet and the World Wide Web (WWW) as enablers of electronic commerce are discussed in this chapter as well as their effect on traditional business models. Security issues relating to electronic commerce are introduced. Finally, an overview of the remainder of this textbook is presented, along with a discussion of the implications of electronic commerce on the accounting profession.

DEFINITION OF ELECTRONIC COMMERCE

One only has to pick up virtually any newspaper or business-related magazine to see a story about some facet of electronic commerce. Businesses are incorporating electronic commerce into strategic plans, business schools have offered new areas of concentration, and consulting and software firms are marketing electronic commerce "solutions." So what exactly is electronic commerce? We define **electronic commerce** as

> The use of electronic transmission mediums (telecommunications) to engage in the exchange, including buying and selling, of products and services requiring transportation, either physically or digitally, from location to location.

Electronic commerce involves all sizes of transaction bases. As one would expect, electronic commerce requires the digital transmission of transaction information. While transactions are conducted via electronic devices, they may be *transported* using either traditional physical shipping channels, such as a ground delivery service, or digital mechanisms, such as the download of a product from the Internet.

Those readers familiar with traditional **electronic data interchange (EDI)** systems may be questioning what makes electronic commerce different from the EDI systems that have been in place for the past 20 to 30 years. EDI is a subset of electronic commerce. A primary difference between the two is that electronic commerce encompasses a broader commerce environment than EDI. **Traditional EDI** systems allow preestablished trading partners to electronically exchange business data. The vast majority of traditional EDI systems are centered around the purchasing function. These EDI systems are generally costly to implement. The high entry cost precluded many small and midsized businesses from engaging in EDI. Electronic commerce allows a marketplace to exist where buyers and sellers can "meet" and transact with one another. Chapter 6 more clearly traces the evolution of traditional EDI to electronic commerce.

The Internet and the WWW provide the enabling mechanisms to foster the growth of electronic commerce. The actual and projected growth rates and uses of the Internet, discussed below, indicate that electronic commerce is no passing fad, but rather a fundamental change in the methods used by businesses to interact with one another and their consumers. One only needs to look at Boeing and General Electric. Prior to its Web-based site, only 10 percent of Boeing's customers used its EDI system to order replacement parts. As early as 1998, Boeing reported that it received $100 million in orders of spare parts through its website. During 1999, GE began the process of combining its plastics distribution business, Polymerland, with its direct supply business. GE's goal: to form a new commercial model for the future that gives its "customers the full advantage of the speed and productivity of the Internet." Internet sales at Polymerland grew from basically zero in January 1999 to more than $5 million *per week* by the end of the year! General Electric has also realized a 50 percent reduction in the purchasing cycle and a 30 percent reduction in processing costs due to its Internet procurement system. Thus, GE is realizing benefits from e-business on both the buying and selling side. Consider the following quote from GE:

> GE is in the midst of an incredible transformation brought on by the Internet explosion. "Our pursuit of e-Business will rapidly change our dealings with our vendors, partners, and most of all, our customers. E-Business represents a revolution that may be the greatest opportunity for growth that our Company has ever seen.
>
> *(GE website–January 2001, www.ge.com/investor)*

Electronic Business

The term *electronic commerce* is restricting, however, and does not fully encompass the true nature of the many types of information exchanges occurring via telecommunication devices. The term **electronic business** also includes the exchange of information not directly related to the actual buying and selling of goods. Increasingly, businesses are using electronic mechanisms to distribute information and provide customer support. These activities are not "commerce" activities; they are "business" activities. Thus, the term *electronic business* is broader. The electronization of business is having significant effects on many businesses and industries. This revolution is so important that we have devoted an entire chapter (Chapter 2) to examine the effects of the electronization of business on business models and on many different business industries. Although the term electronic commerce is used throughout this text, many of the activities described are more accurately classified as electronic business.

POTENTIAL BENEFITS OF ELECTRONIC COMMERCE

For businesses to invest resources to engage in electronic commerce, the benefits must exceed the costs. So what benefits can businesses potentially gain from engaging in electronic commerce?

- Internet and Web-based electronic commerce is more affordable than traditional EDI.
- Internet and Web-based electronic commerce allows more business partners to be reached than with traditional EDI.
- Internet and Web-based electronic commerce can reach a more geographically dispersed customer base.
- Procurement processing costs can be lowered.
- Cost of purchases can be lowered.
- Inventories can be reduced.
- Cycle times can be lowered.
- Better customer service can be provided.
- Sales and marketing costs can be lowered.

The first three benefits are relative benefits of Internet and Web-based electronic commerce over traditional EDI methods. The cost and installation of EDI systems is generally quite high, and it has typically been beneficial only to larger firms that have enough sales volume to justify the costs of developing their own networks or subscribing to a value-added network. A **value-added network (VAN)** is a service to which a firm can subscribe. VANs provide many services, including data transmission, EDI translation, and store and forward messaging of transaction data. VANs and the other services they provide are discussed in greater detail in Chapter 6. Because of the low cost of connecting to the Internet, medium and small businesses can now afford the connection cost. Further, because of software developments that allow Web-based EDI systems to interface with traditional EDI systems, businesses of all sizes can now transact with one another. This vastly expands the number of potential electronic business partners, some of which may be a substantial geographical distance away. The Internet offers a greater choice of global partners with which to conduct electronic commerce.

Procurement costs can be lowered by traditional EDI systems by consolidating purchases, developing relationships with key suppliers, negotiating volume discounts, and better integrating the manufacturing process. Internet electronic commerce offers additional benefits and potential for cost reductions over traditional EDI. Procurement costs can be lowered for all companies, regardless of size, due to the increased ability to transact electronically with one another. Data transmission costs can be lowered. A wider net can be cast when searching for suppliers. Options for partnering with other firms increase. For example, small and mid-sized companies benefit because they are now able to conduct business with the larger firms that are casting the wider nets. The smaller firms also have the opportunity to reduce their processing costs by using integrated electronic processing systems. As mentioned earlier, General Electric realized a 30 percent reduction in the processing costs of its procurement cycle. The cost of the items purchased can also be lowered due to the ability to seek out and negotiate with a greater number of suppliers. Because of this, General Electric was able to reduce its cost of purchases by 20 percent.

A reduction in inventory is desirable because of the associated reductions in storage, handling, insurance, and administrative costs. Internet electronic commerce can help firms to more optimally order the inventories by electronically linking suppliers and purchasers and allowing them to share updated production forecasts and projected inventory levels in order to allow both parties to collaboratively "fine tune" their production and delivery schedules. Businesses can also use the Internet to "unload" unwanted inventory or sell excess capacity very quickly and with extremely low marketing costs. Both American Airlines and USAir determine on a weekly basis which flights have excess capacity and offer last-minute (actually two to three days' notice) deals to Internet subscribers of this service via e-mail. This strategy allows these airlines to reduce the excess capacity on these flights and generate additional revenues.

The **production cycle time** is the time it takes a business to build a product beginning with the design phase and ending with the completed product. Internet electronic commerce is enabling the reduction of the cycle time by allowing engineers and production teams to electronically share design specifications for initial approval and refinement processes. In addition to reducing the design and production phases, lower cycle times also reduce the amount of fixed overhead that needs to be allocated to each unit produced, thus positively affecting the ability to pass cost savings on to the customer or to achieve higher net earnings.

Customer service can be enhanced using Internet electronic commerce by helping the customer to access information before, during, and after the sale. Before the sale is made, customers can electronically retrieve product specifications, quantity, and pricing information. During the product/service fulfillment cycle, customers can electronically check on the status of the order. For example, UPS and FedEx customers can electronically track the status of their packages without the need to speak with a human. Support services for customers are also enhanced by electronic services, such as electronic notification of returned items and the ability to download and print the necessary documentation and shipping labels to return an item for servicing. Convenience and reduced processing costs result for both the buyer and seller.

The omnipresent nature of the Internet allows firms to reach many customers in a very low cost fashion. Some firms are able to shift some of their sales and marketing functions to electronic processes. This shift in communication mediums allows the firm to either reduce their overhead costs or better utilize their human resources to engage in building customer relations rather than performing tedious sales processing tasks. Insight Enterprises Inc. has used this strategy; its sales representatives build relationships with customers and then encourage them to use the Internet to place their orders.

Businesses are not the only benefactors of Internet electronic commerce; consumers may also reap benefits from using the Internet. Some benefits that consumers may expect to receive are

- Increased choice of vendors and products.
- Convenience from shopping at home or office.

- Greater amounts of information that can be accessed on demand.
- More competitive prices and increased price comparison capabilities.
- Greater customization in the delivery of services.

(U.S. Department of Commerce, 1998)

Customers have an increased choice of vendors because they are no longer geographically constrained by a reasonable walking or driving distance. Customers have a greater choice of services they can receive from global Internet companies. For example, a foreign-born resident of the United States may subscribe to an electronic news service from his or her home country and receive an electronic "newspaper" on a daily basis that is sent directly from his or her home country's news service. Regarding product selection, virtual stores such as Amazon.com offer consumers with a choice of more than 28 million unique items; physical stores do not have the actual retail space—nor is it feasible—to stock that many items in each physical retail establishment.

The convenience of shopping at home allows consumers to shop when it is convenient for them and not during prescribed store hours. For handicapped or ill consumers, the ability to shop from home opens up new shopping opportunities and offers greater convenience. The capability of employees to shop online from their office is viewed as a benefit by some and as a detriment by others, and both sides have valid points. Whether the availability to access the Internet for personal use is abused or misused by an employee depends on the employee's personal characteristics and work ethic. For busy employees who work long hours, the ability to take care of some errands may ease tension and allow them to actually devote more, and better quality, time to their tasks. For example, busy workers facing overtime may need to complete some personal errands, including grocery shopping, buying and mailing a birthday present, and retrieving some income tax forms to complete their tax return. While these errands may require a total time of two hours if done physically, they may all be conducted on the Internet in 15 to 20 minutes. Thus, if employees can perform these tasks during their lunch hour, they may still have time to eat, reduce stress regarding their personal life, and feel better prepared to face the rest of the day's workload.

Consumers now have greater access to information that is provided online, and this translates into greater buying power. For example, many consumers are self-educating themselves on car pricing information via the Internet. In fact, one automobile general sales manager, Mike Dobres, claims his profits have declined by about 25 percent. He claims, "People know what you pay for your car, and they don't let you make big profits."

Search engines and intelligent agents, the topics of Chapter 13, are making the process of sorting through information and conducting price comparisons increasingly easier. Information is buying power to consumers, and the Internet is unleashing access to vast amounts of information. How will Internet vendors compete if price comparison is so easy? They are quickly learning that service and reliability are also important. Amazon.com does not just sell books and music, it provides book and music reviews, suggests other books that may be of interest based on the books being examined, and provides sound clips for many of the music titles. It also provides inventory status and expected shipping time.

Internet electronic commerce also offers customers the chance to customize many of the products and services offered by merchants. For example, many online news services allow their customers to "design" the look of their daily newspaper. The Morning Paper (*www.boutell.com/morning*) allows online users to prespecify their favorite websites. Each morning, a "morning paper" is delivered electronically to the user with updates that have occurred on their favorite websites. Customers buying computers over the Internet have the opportunity at many sites to "configure" their own computer easily with pop-up screens and compare prices of alternative configurations, while ensuring that the components selected are compatible with one another.

THE INTERNET AND WWW AS ENABLERS OF ELECTRONIC COMMERCE

The Internet's growth rate has far surpassed the growth rates of any previously introduced electronic information dissemination mediums. Figure 1–1 compares the length of time that it took for radio, television, and personal computer use to reach 50 million people with the time for the Internet to do so. Only four years after it was opened "to the public," the Internet was able to reach 50 million people, which is just a fraction of the time it took for radio, television, and personal computers to reach the same usage rate.

So what is the Internet? The Internet is a very unique infrastructure in that it is "owned" by no one. The most accurate definition of the Internet is admittedly not very informative: The **Internet** is a network of networks. The Internet has evolved over time into its current form, which is still evolving. The Internet came "online" in 1969 as a joint

| **FIGURE 1–1** | *Comparison of transmission mediums* |

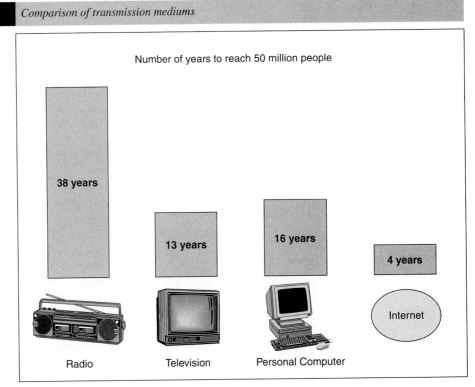

Source: Morgan Stanley U.S. Investment Research: Internet Retail.

project between the Defense Advanced Research Projects Agency (DARPA) and four university host computers. These host nodes transferred data using the packet switching theory first developed by Leonard Keinrock. The same packet switching theory is still the basis of today's data transfer methods. More computer sites were added to the network, and electronic mail was introduced in 1972. Over the next decade, the National Science Foundation (NSF) became involved, and various standard-setting bodies to help structure and develop the Internet were formed. These Internet-related agencies are further discussed in Chapter 9.

In the early 1980s, the commercial sector became increasingly interested in the Internet and began to funnel resources into commercial Internet uses. The WWW was not developed until 1990, when Tim Berners-Lee implemented his groundbreaking concepts and became known as its father. The **World Wide Web (WWW)** incorporates the use of hypertext links, software portability, and network and socket programming. **Hypertext links** allow WWW users to easily and rapidly transport themselves to another site. **Software portability** allows users running previously incompatible platforms to create sites that can be interpreted and easily read by multiple platforms. The transfer of data that occurs from the use of hypertext links is enabled by the network and socket programming concepts developed by Berners-Lee. The ease of use of the WWW has contributed to the Internet's exponential growth rates.

So how important is the growth of the Internet and the WWW to businesses? The following statement concisely describes the importance of the WWW to the information technology field:

> The stage was set for the Web's emergence as the single most dynamic force in the IT [information technology] industry and a historical agent of change during the 1980s when a number of market forces joined and grew to critical mass. This confluence of forces included:
>
> - The advent of increasingly powerful and inexpensive technologies that permitted the use of IT by more and more people and provided the base for scalable systems and applications.
> - The growing availability of telecommunications due to declining costs and increasing bandwidth.
> - The spread of digital information with its incredible flexibility and fidelity.
>
> *(Karl Salnoske, IBM, May 21, 1998)*

The potential benefits that can be reaped by businesses and consumers were mentioned in the preceding section. Forrester Research estimates that global electronic commerce may reach as high as $6.9 trillion by 2004. Figure 1–2 illustrates Forrester Research's projected growth rates for five geographic areas. While North America is forecasted to maintain the leadership share, its percentage of overall electronic commerce gradually declines over the five-year period as other areas' shares increase. Western Europe and Asia-Pacific countries will see a tremendous increase in terms of dollars. Fueling European electronic commerce is the euro currency. Many European sites that hesitated to launch sites due to multiple currency barriers have launched Web-based sites since the euro was phased in. Western Europe and North America are forecasted, however, to have the smallest percentage growth rate over the five-year period. The steepest growth rates are predicted for Asia-Pacific and Latin American countries, which will experience "hyper" growth as illustrated in Figure 1–3. Thus, the growth of the Internet and the WWW is happening so rapidly that businesses are literally caught up in a whirlwind of change. The next section discusses the effect of the growth of the Internet on business models.

FIGURE 1–2 *Forecasted geographic region e-commerce growth rates*

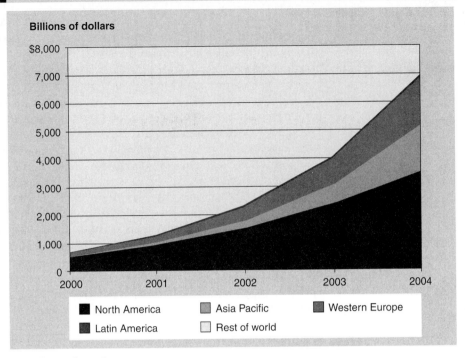

Billions of dollars

Source: Forrester Research.

FIGURE 1–3 *Forecasted growth rates by geographic region*

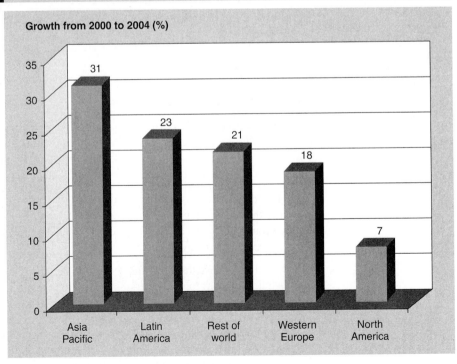

Growth from 2000 to 2004 (%)

Source: Forrester Research.

EFFECT OF ELECTRONIC COMMERCE ON BUSINESS MODELS

Given the astounding growth rates mentioned earlier, electronic commerce is forcing businesses to rethink their traditional business models:

> Today's forward thinking CEO recognizes the challenge of eCommerce as a strategic business issue, not just one more technical issue to be delegated to the IS department, perhaps the existing EDI group. Although a company may have reengineered its internal business process and perhaps painfully installed an ERP system to bring inefficiencies to the back office, eCommerce is about reengineering outward-facing processes—industry process reengineering.
>
> *(Peter Fingar, 1998)*

Thus, electronic commerce is not just a technology, it is a way of conducting business that has the potential to affect every aspect of the firm's value chain. Implementing full-scale, innovative applications of electronic commerce requires management teams to view the marketplace beyond the typical physical boundaries:

> The biggest problem that electronic commerce pioneers encounter is the limited set of mental models that constrain our thinking. We tend to think of the Web in our "industrial age" paradigm—where everything must be described and related to the physical world.
>
> *(Enix Consulting Limited, 1998)*

If electronic commerce applications are not placed in the proper business context and the strategy aligned with the business's overall business strategy, then the electronic commerce application is likely to fail. Thus, new business models are necessary that integrate electronic commerce initiatives with overall business goals. This section first discusses the need to align a firm's online strategy with its overall business strategy. Following that discussion, emerging business paradigms that fully embrace the electronic commerce philosophy are discussed, including a new view of the value chain.

Overall Business and E-Commerce Goal Congruence

Electronic commerce strategies need to be formulated so that they help a business achieve its overall business goals. Figure 1–4 illustrates the relationship between a firm's overall corporate mission and goals and its Web-based electronic commerce plan. Environmental changes may cause a business to rethink or adjust its missions and goals, such as the entrance of "new" competitors into the marketplace. These competitors may arise from previously unknown businesses, unknown perhaps because they are located in foreign countries. Such competitors may launch a Web-based commerce site and have a newly found ability to cost effectively draw customers away from the business.

Once the corporate mission and goals are set, then the information systems and technology group's mission can be set to help accomplish that mission. Ultimately, a Web-based electronic commerce plan can be set. In the box "Air Products Takes E-Business Seriously," one of the overall company objectives is to be a knowledge leader. The launching of the new Product Stewardship section of its website is clearly aligned with this objective.

Unfortunately, various research findings indicate that a disconnect exists between a firm's overall business goals and its Web-based electronic commerce initiatives. A study by the Cambridge Information Network found that more than one-third of firms studied did not believe that their company successfully implemented its electronic commerce

FIGURE 1.4	*Business and electronic commerce goal congruence*

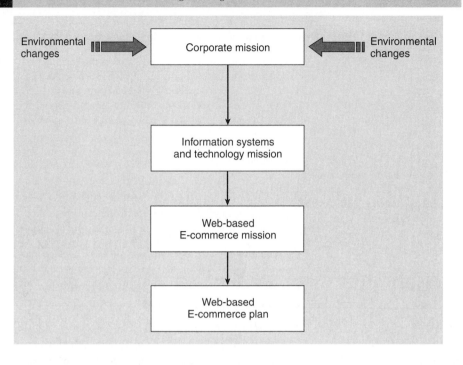

Focus on Air Products

Air Products Takes E-Business Seriously

Air Products and Chemicals Inc., a multinational organization that produces and sells industrial and specialty gases, chemicals and polymers, was founded in 1940. Air Products is a *Fortune* 500 company that generates close to $5 billion in sales annually. It has operations in more than 30 countries and employs 17,000 people worldwide.

Air Products', E-Business Vision

Air Products' director of E-Business, Dave Ashworth, and his "crew" consider themselves to be on a "voyage of discovery through cyberspace, exploring numerous electronic commerce concepts and new business models that have the potential to generate significant new trade—and increased profitability—for the company." The crew consists of 15 cross-functional team members, and they make sure to have a mix of IT specialists and business expertise.

Their Vision is this:

> By 2003, the company would like to shift a sizeable chunk of its revenues to the Internet, generate millions more in new

business on the Web, and realize significant cost savings through global E-Business initiatives.

The team recognizes that to achieve these goals, creativity and willingness to experiment will be required. They are not scared by the new business models, and they embrace the concept that Internet environment brings about wonderful opportunities if your company is willing to adjust.

Air Products has already been doing some experimenting for the past five years. They began their online journey by placing marketing information on the company website. Then they upgraded and split off the site to become a series of interactive sites. The amount of information was increased, but the sites still provided features that allowed visitors to locate the information in an easier fashion. Their interactive sites include such tools as helping customers to assess the feasibility and appropriateness of alternative gas products for specific uses.

The next step was a pilot project for online orders and associated technical information for the packaged gases customers. They relied on assistance from some of their customers to design, implement, and refine the system.

Not to rest with this accomplishment, however, the team now wants to continue its progression and take the company "to a much higher level of business-to-business capability—implementing a wide variety of applications that will add up to additional sales, lower costs, better customer service, and optimal supply chain management."

A Changing Business Environment

According to Steve Cameron, Manager of Communication Programs and E-Business team member: "E-Business gets more sophisticated every day. We now have competitors we never had before—for example, third-party 'aggregators' who put buyers and sellers of surplus and slightly off-spec chemicals together. The key for us is to be active in trying out new E-Business ideas, and to learn and move forward."

Specific E-Business Initiatives

Value-Added Marketing. "Supply interactive electronic information to current and prospective customers to help them make informed buying decisions using the latest Web tools for guided selling."

Selling. "Provide opportunities for current and future customers to purchase company products and services online, 24 hours a day, seven days a week, through our public web site and specific customer Extranets."

New Channels. "Develop new Web-based sales channels that provide company information or transaction capabilities through online relationships, partnerships, auctions, or acquisitions."

Procurement. "Implement companywide initiatives with selected, preferred suppliers that simplify procurement and reduce purchasing costs."

Why Provide Information, "Knowledge" Materials, and Knowledge Tools?

One strategy that Air Products has identified is to be a knowledge leader and provide information to its industry, such as safe handling, distribution, use, and disposal of industrial, specialty, and medical gas products. It already does this on its Product Stewardship site. This site Air Products has been cleverly populated with very useful content for its customers and industry in general. The content includes

- Approximately 100 downloadable Material Safety Data Sheets.
- Safety bulletins.
- Answers to "Frequently Asked" technical questions.
- Conversion tables that calculate formulas when the appropriate data are entered.

Ultimately, Air Products believes that if you serve the industry, the service will eventually pay off in terms of sales. "Our thinking is that if potential customers keep coming to our sites for information, they will eventually turn to us to meet their business needs," says Cameron. "We call it 'guided selling.' We help solve their problem, and that can lead to an immediate online sale."

Storefronts on B2B Portals   Not content to stop at hosting its own website, Air Products launched two sites on VerticalNet, an Internet business exchange that operates almost 50 separate business-to-business sites. Customers go to these types of sites, and Air Products wants to be there in full force.

Source: Air Products and Chemicals, Inc., Winter 2000 Inside Air Products, www.apci.com.

initiative. Approximately one-fourth of these firms attributed the lack of success to a failure to connect the electronic commerce effort with the goals of the business. A study by Jupiter Communications reported that only 24 percent of the top executives of traditional consumer businesses currently measure the success of their online initiatives as an integrated part of their core businesses. Why is it important to integrate the evaluation of online initiatives in a holistic manner with offline initiatives? Isolated measurements, such as online revenues, may not accurately reflect the contribution to the business if the sales would have been made offline (cannibalization of sales). On the other hand, online initiatives may contribute to the overall health of a business, such as increased customer base and cost reductions. These items need to be measured at an overall business level and by the contribution provided from each sales medium, such as Web-based electronic commerce.

The Effect of E-Commerce on the Value Chain

The traditional view of the value chain, depicted in Figure 1–5, is no longer rich enough to encompass the true relationships underlying the flows of information between a firm, its customers, and its suppliers. The **traditional value chain** typically depicts the information system data as flowing sequentially through the processes with inputs/outputs to the supplier at the back-end stage and to the customer at the front-end stage. In reality, firms engaging in electronic commerce may share information with their customers and suppliers at many stages of the value chain. Figure 1–6 depicts a new view

FIGURE 1–5   *Traditional value chain*

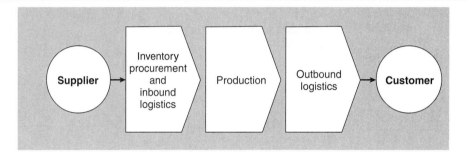

FIGURE 1–6   *Customer-oriented value chain*

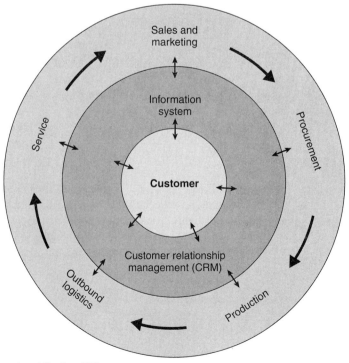

Source: *Greenstein and Hamilton, 1999.*

of the value chain with the customer set as the center of focus to a firm. The firm's information system is the "glue" that links all phases of its processes together. This **customer-oriented value chain** enables the customer to access the firm's (the supplier's) information system at virtually every phase to assess the progress of the order. When firms talk about **customer relationship management (CRM)** systems, they are ultimately talking about the information system that binds the business with the customer and services that customer's need. A customer may link to the firm's inventory data (such as price, quantity, and availability) prior to entering into a sales contract. Further, the customer may be able to electronically receive design and product specifications prior to entering into a sales contract. The actual sales may be placed electronically, and a promised or expected shipping date is given by the supplier's information system to the customer. Once the order is placed, the customer may be able to check the status of the order or service placed.

The customers can also check the shipping status of orders placed with a supplier that have been completed and are in the shipping process. The customer's use of the supplier's information system to help provide better customer service after the sale is complete is another positive use. For example, a customer may wish to return a defective item to its supplier. The customer may be able to access the firm's information system and request a return slip, which the customer can then print out and use to send the item back to the supplier at the cost of the supplier. The supplier benefits by knowing in advance that defective goods were sent to a customer and when to expect to receive them back. These are just some of the many ways in which customers and suppliers may advantageously share the information stored in the supplier's information system.

The customer-oriented value chain illustrated in Figure 1.6 also demonstrates the need to link procurement information systems to those of a firm's supplier. The supplier needs to access its supplier's information system in order to best serve its own customers. The supplier becomes the customer to its suppliers and should be able to interface its procurement systems with its suppliers' information systems to receive the same types of information that it provides to its own customers. The Internet is enabling companies to fully integrate their supply chains, and this integration has a dramatic influence on the structure of participating companies to fully integrate their supply chains:

> In the process of integrating suppliers more closely for efficiency and cost savings, companies are giving rise to **virtual enterprises** in which it is difficult to tell where one organization begins and the other ends.
>
> *(Karl Salnoske, IBM, May 21, 1998)*

A customer may seemingly be ordering from one supplier, for example, Amazon.com, when in actuality it is ordering from one of many virtual bookstores that is independently owned and operated and that seamlessly interfaces with Amazon.com. A model of the virtual operations of an organization is discussed in the following section.

The ICDT Business Strategy Model

A model developed by Albert Angehrn, called the *Information, Communication, Transaction, and Distribution (ICDT)* model, is used as a basis for discussing the Internet strategy of businesses. While the Internet strategy of a business may be the primary or

FIGURE 1–7	*The expanded ICDT model*

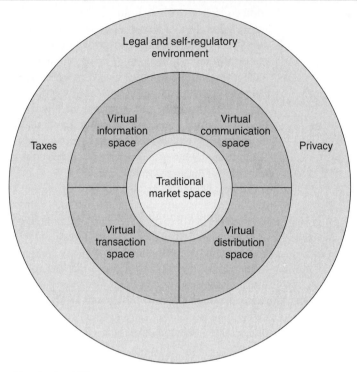

Adapted from Albert Angehrn, 1997.

overriding strategy of one firm, it may be only one component of the strategy of another business. Figure 1–7 illustrates an adaptation of Angehrn's model; the difference between the model illustrated and Angehrn's model is the addition of the outer ring, called the "constraints" ring. Angehrn's model is based on four virtual spaces:

• **Virtual information space.** This space is where a firm displays information about its organization, products, or services. This space is the easiest space for a business to enter and is typically the first step taken toward entering the virtual marketplace. For electronic commerce, major concerns are

- Is the information displayed accurately and currently?
- Is the information displayed only viewed by authorized users?
- Can customers easily find the site and navigate through it once they have reached the site?
- Is the site accessible without long wait times?

• **Virtual distribution space.** This space is used to deliver the product or service requested or purchased by the consumer. For virtual delivery to occur, the products being delivered must be digital (e.g., software) or the service performed digitally (e.g., online broker). Online news services and software companies have been quick to market and deliver their products electronically. For electronic commerce, major concerns are

- Will products and services be delivered only to legitimate, approved customers?
- Will delivery of products and services be reliable?

- **Virtual transaction space.** This space is used to initiate and execute business transactions, such as sales orders. Aside from those companies engaging in the virtual distribution space, most companies have been reluctant to enter this space. The major concern contributing to this reluctance is data security. For those firms entering the virtual transaction space, the major concerns are

- Are data secure?
- Will accuracy and integrity of processing methods be preserved?
- Is the vendor reliable?
- Is the trading partner reputable?
- What are customers' privacy concerns?

- **Virtual communication space.** This space is used to enable relationship building, negotiation, and exchange of ideas such as forums, chat rooms, and virtual communities. Electronic commerce is affected if such a community is a service for which its members pay or if negotiation agents, discussed in Chapter 13, are used.

Businesses, in determining their Internet strategy, need to first determine their overall business strategy and then determine how the Internet can be leveraged, if at all, to help them achieve their business strategy. If a business does determine that Internet technology may serve as an enabler of achieving its business strategy, then it must determine in what fashion the Internet can be best utilized. Angehrn's model is useful for determining which virtual space(s) is(are) appropriate for both the long- and short-term achievement of a firm's business strategy. In the box "CollegeCapital.com," a discussion of how a firm's leader can drive the strategy is presented. Further, the business's specific activities in each of Angehrn's virtual categories are presented.

Firms do face constraints, however, and the decision whether to engage in and how to implement a particular Internet strategy needs to be made with consideration given to the constraints. Two major legal/regulatory constraints faced by businesses engaging in electronic commerce are taxation and privacy. The Chairman of the U.S. House Commerce Committee, Tom Bliley, announced a new electronic commerce initiative in March 1998. He posed the following questions that the committee will address regarding the legal and regulatory environment of the Internet:

- What is the federal government's role in electronic commerce? Should it be a regulator, or should its role be to provide legal certainty, legitimacy, and oversight?
- What real-world laws should apply to the virtual world? Is the Internet going to remain a "Wild West," as some would like, or should we apply today's laws to the Internet?
- Will Americans feel comfortable conducting their daily activities online, or will there be concerns about reliability of service, crime, and invasion of privacy?
- Electronic commerce is conducted globally. How will U.S. laws and policies interact with the laws and policies of other nations?
- What is the future of electronic commerce? Will it develop into a new sector of the economy, or will its prime role be in complimenting existing economic sectors?

E-Commerce in Practice

CollegeCapital.com

 CollegeCapital.com is a business dedicated to education and the allocation of educational-related resources to students, schools, and teachers. The site is probably best known for assisting prospective and current college students to locate the necessary financial aid to fund their education. To understand how an online company such as CollegeCapital.com is driven by the vision of its leader, we need to look at its CEO, Patricia Adams. Adams has a strong background in the financial and mortgage industry. She served as CEO for the Home Mortgage Financing Corporation and has extensive experience in banking and home mortgages. She is not all business, however; she has always been very active in civic duties and has a strong sense of serving the community. When offered the position at CollegeCapital.com, Adams saw a real opportunity to match her banking knowledge with her desire to help the community. She is committed to developing a website that not only matches students with financial aid, but also assists students and their parents before, during, and after the search for college funds. Adams is devoted to creating a holistic virtual space where students can find assistance in choosing a career, choosing a school, dealing with anxieties and stress of a college student, and locating a school abroad if that is a desire of the students. She considers what is best for this virtual community and service in every decision that is made about website content and alliance relationships. Her careful planning is evident in the quality of the content of the website. The site has won 40 awards and has been named the *New York Times* Site of the Day. Adams continues the development of the site, its content, and alliances. She has many philanthropic-related initiatives, where she is pursuing activities that will provide resources back to schools, teachers, athletes, and artists.

The full range of services offered by College Capital.com places it in the category of a portal community that serves as an infomediary. The scholarship and financial aid service that CollegeCapital.com provides is extensive. It has a database with more than 13.5 million different scholarship and financial aid opportunities. The total amount of this financial compensation that is available to students is in excess of $6 billion. The database has 30,000 schools in 179 different countries. Adams believes that if people can just look wisely and efficiently for the opportunities that are available, they will find the funds to support their educational desires. CollegeCapital.com provides such a service by helping students access an incredible database of opportunity. It helps the student filter the database efficiently and focus on applying for the most appropriate financial aid packages.

CollegeCapital.com engages in activities that fall into all four categories of Angehrn's model. Some of the activities (this list is not exhaustive and continues to grow) conducted on CollegeCapital.com's website are categorized into Angehrn's ICDT business strategy model:

Virtual Information Space

- Complete college planning program beginning with the eighth grade.
- Guide to choosing the right college.
- Tips for travel abroad.

Virtual Community Space

- Links to assistance for depression, eating disorders, and many other such problems commonly faced by college students.
- Links to child development and parenting sites.

Virtual Distribution Space

- Delivery of financial aid search service.
- Delivery of internship locator search service.
- Delivery of Educational Calculator.
- Delivery of Kolbe Instinct Assessment Test.

Virtual Transaction Space

- Online payments accepted for services mentioned as delivered in the virtual distribution search.

Each of these topics is covered in detail in later chapters. The legal environment surrounding the Internet is the topic of Chapter 5, including the topics of taxes and privacy. Privacy topics are further discussed in Chapter 7, and encryption techniques are further covered in Chapter 10.

Three Pillars of E-Commerce

Another electronic business model that builds on traditional market spaces is the three pillars of electronic commerce model by Peter Fingar, which is illustrated in Figure 1–8. At the foundation of the model is the existing market space. Three electronic pillars support open market processes: electronic information, electronic relationships, and electronic transactions. Thus, this model builds on the existing market space and utilizes electronic mechanisms as an enabler of supporting open market processes.

The first pillar, **electronic information,** is similar to Angehrn's virtual information space. The WWW is viewed as a "global repository" of documents and multimedia data. Constructing an electronic information pillar is easy: Most word-processing software packages will easily convert documents into a Web-readable format. The challenge is to construct a good, solid pillar that will not crumble, or in WWW terms, the Web page will not freeze up nor will links lead the visitor to a dead-end or have them wandering through a maze of links without easily finding the necessary information. Thus, the construction of the electronic information pillar should not be conducted in a shoddy fashion, or it will not adequately support the objective of an open market. The retrieval of the desired electronic information is the cause of frustration to many Web "surfers." Search engines and other intelligent agents are increasing in popularity to assist users to more efficiently and effectively navigate the WWW. Search engines and intelligent agents are the topic of Chapter 13.

The second pillar, **electronic relationships,** is the central pillar, and it is similar to Angehrn's virtual communication space. The saying "If you build it, they will come" does not apply to website-based electronic commerce. Placing information on products

FIGURE 1–8	*Three pillars of electronic commerce*

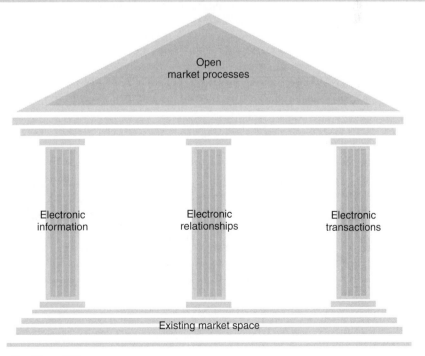

Source: Peter Fingar, 1998.

and service offerings on a website does not mean that potential customers or guests will visit that website a first time, and it especially does not mean that a user will return to the site. The electronic relationships pillar is about building a site that has the feeling of being a "port of entry" into a community. Having entrants pass through this port of entry on a somewhat regular basis is the key to successfully engaging in electronic commerce. To attract users over and over again to a site (which also means *away* from other sites), the site needs to have certain features; it must

- Be innovative.
- Add value.
- Provide information and interaction not otherwise available.
- Create forums for opinion-building activities.

(Peter Fingar, 1998)

A differentiating feature of electronic commerce from other mediums, such as print and broadcasting, is that it is interactive, and users expect to experience interaction when they visit a site. To build good customer relationships, electronic commerce websites need to be designed to give potential customers the feeling of community and interaction they are increasingly expecting. The use of intelligent agents is one way of accomplishing this goal. Electronic business-to-business relationships must be designed somewhat differently than for business-to-consumer relationships, although both are customer-centric. Business-to-business relationships are the topic of Chapter 3.

The third pillar is the **electronic transactions** pillar. This pillar is similar to Angehrn's virtual transaction space, and it also encompasses Angehrn's virtual distribution space. Many businesses have built an electronic information pillar and some have built or are building an electronic community pillar, but substantially fewer have constructed the electronic transaction pillar. Two impediments to constructing the pillar exist: the ability to engage in meaningful and sufficient negotiation processes and security of transaction data. The negotiation process is discussed in Chapter 13, and the security of transaction data is covered throughout the text, but emphasized in Chapters 7, 10, and 11.

ELECTRONIC COMMERCE SECURITY

Companies worldwide are challenged with taking advantage of the business benefits the Web has to offer while minimizing risk to their operations and their bottom line.

(Bruce Murphy, Partner—PricewaterhouseCoopers. 1998)

The issue of security of data transmitted over the Internet is mentioned in previous sections as an impediment to the growth of electronic commerce. How serious is the security problem? To grasp the enormity of the problem, consider the following result of a study conducted by the Computer Security Institute and the Federal Bureau of Investigation (CSI/FBI) Computer Survey 2000: More than 70 percent of the firms studied had detected unauthorized access to their systems. (Of course, the number of undetected unauthorized access is unknown.) Another study, conducted by Information Security, found that

Companies conducting either B2B or B2C e-commerce experience a significantly higher rate of both insider and outsider security breaches than companies not conducting e-commerce.

(Information Security Survey, 2000)

| FIGURE 1–9 | Comparison of security breaches for web-based companies |

Type of Breach	Conduct E-Commerce	Do Not Conduct E-Commerce
Infection of company equipment via virus and malicious code	75%	66%
Abuse of computer access controls	64	51
Physical theft, sabotage or intentional destruction of computing equipment	50	34
Denial of service	42	31
Attacks on bugs in Web servers	33	16
Attacks related to insecure passwords	30	20
Electronic theft, sabotage, or intentional destruction of computing equipment	29	18
Fraud	18	8

Source: Information Security Survey 2000.

Some of the results of the study that are displayed in Figure 1–9 illustrate the increased risk faced by firms engaging in electronic commerce. Those companies studied engaging in electronic commerce have been victims of a greater number of security breaches in all categories reported.

Currently, implementations of enterprise resource planning (ERP) systems are widely occurring. The *1998 InformationWeek Global Information Security Survey* study indicates that businesses with such installations more frequently than firms without such installations have fallen prey to the following types of incidents:

• Revenue, information and data integrity loss.

• Theft of trade secrets or data.

• Infection with a computer virus.

• Manipulation of their internal systems or software applications.

(InformationWeek Global Information Security Survey, 1998)

Given the popularity of the installation of ERP systems, these security breaches are troubling to businesses. Further, ERP software providers, such as SAP, are increasingly investing in the development of electronic commerce modules. ERP systems that use a highly centralized repository of data that are ultimately connected to the Internet must be kept secure, especially since such systems contain mission-critical data.

Regarding security of data, the entire system is only as strong as the weakest link in the chain. Understanding the Internet environment, security risks, and security solutions is considered a key component of conducting electronic business. Consider this quote by Abner Germanow, research manager for IDC's Internet Security research program:

Dealing with security in a reactionary manner is no longer adequate. Security is now a core business requirement, and companies that continue to regard security as a necessary evil will be forced out of business by companies who use security technologies to launch high value applications.

(Abner Germanow, IDC, May 2000)

If businesses are concerned about security, what are they doing about it? Many firms are installing firewalls, the topic of Chapter 11. The answer to security solutions, however, is not in the installation of a single technology, such as a firewall. Good security solutions consist of a well-designed battery of technological devices and good security practices and procedures. The Information Security Survey 2000 study found that approximately 22 percent of the firms studied did *not* have a security policy. For those firms that did have a security policy, 21 percent of them did not feel that their policies were very effective at detecting outside breaches. Needless to say, the best controls may not be effective if they are not implemented or maintained properly. A startling finding from the CSI/FBI 2000 study is that almost one-third of the firms could not assess whether they had suffered from unauthorized access or misuse in the last 12 months. For those firms that did identify incidents, 21 percent of them did not know whether the source of attack was internal or external. Chapters 7 through 12 address security issues, risk assessment, and preventive and detective security devices.

ORGANIZATION OF TOPICS

The objective of this textbook is to familiarize the reader with the concepts relating to electronic commerce and electronic business and the environment in which they operate. New business models and the electronization of business are discussed in Chapter 2. The electronic interaction among businesses is literally reshaping business relations, and this is the topic of Chapter 3.

The accounting profession is profoundly affected by electronic commerce. Historically, accounting professionals have attested to the reliability and integrity of the underlying transactions that form the basis for the information reported in the financial statements. As organizations change and the manner in which these transactions are conducted change, so too must the work of the accounting profession change. Electronic commerce presents new challenges to the accounting profession, as well as many new opportunities. These challenges and opportunities are the topic of Chapter 4.

As mentioned earlier, the legal and regulatory environment poses many constraints to the commerce portion of electronic commerce. To muddy the waters further, the Internet is a global infrastructure unlike any other sales and marketing medium before it. International laws are increasingly important yet difficult to interpret and apply to the ubiquitous nature of the Internet. These issues are the topic of Chapter 5.

Earlier in the chapter, EDI was mentioned as being a subset of electronic commerce. The evolution of EDI into what is now referred to as electronic commerce is considered in Chapter 6. With electronic commerce comes new and even yet-to-be-identified risks. The risks associated with electronic commerce are discussed in Chapter 7, and the management of risks is discussed in Chapter 8.

The uniqueness of the infrastructure of the Internet makes standard setting a formidable task. Because no one owns the Internet, standard setting must occur by collaboration and agreement by many different classes of users worldwide. The topic of Internet standards, with an emphasis on security standards is the topic of Chapter 9.

One method of increased security is to use techniques such as cryptography and authentication. Electronic commerce depends on the use of such techniques because without them, neither consumers nor businesses will have an adequate level of comfort in digital transmission of transaction and personal data. Cryptographic and authentication techniques are presented in Chapter 10. Another popular security technique is the use of firewalls, which is the topic of Chapter 11.

Electronic commerce involving the sale of goods requires that some sort of monetary payment be made between the buyer and seller. Various electronic commerce payment mechanisms are discussed in Chapter 12. Finally, the use of intelligent agents is becoming more prevalent in order to allow both businesses and consumers to more effectively and efficiently navigate the Web and interact with one another. Intelligent agents and their current and potential uses are discussed in Chapter 13. Marketing professionals find electronic business exciting and challenging. The Internet offers to them a rich, new advertising medium, and this is the topic of Chapter 14.

IMPLICATIONS FOR THE ACCOUNTING PROFESSION

Electronic commerce and the change in focus from the traditional value chain to the customer-oriented value chain affects the traditional assurance function performed by the accounting profession. As firms begin to trade data and transact with new trading partners, as opposed to preestablished trading partners, the integrity of both the trading partners and their underlying transaction processing systems must be evaluated. As the various processes and steps conducted in supply chain management, such as inventory requirement planning, purchase orders, sales orders, shipping notification, and cash disbursements, are handled electronically by electronic commerce–based information systems, the ability to monitor transaction data and assess the integrity and reliability becomes challenging. The accounting profession must rise to this challenge and develop new methods of monitoring and reviewing transaction data in real time.

The ability to assess the integrity of information systems in real time is important because of the pressing need for reliable and accurate financial statement data more rapidly than previously tolerated. Companies may need to provide trading partners and other stakeholders with updated financial information in order to conduct their business. In many situations, knowledge about the clients' information systems is not sufficient information; the accountant may also need to assess the reliability and integrity of a trading partner if its system contributes significantly to the processing of its clients transaction processing data. In some situations, ascertaining where one company ends and another begins may be unclear at first glance.

As mentioned in Chapter 4 and throughout this text, members of the accounting profession have to acquire new technical skills to compete in the digital economy. New assurance opportunities are arising over which the accounting profession does not have a protected marketplace as it does over assurance of financial statements. Third-party assurance of websites is an example of a relatively new "product" offering for public accounting firms. Other business professionals, however, may perform similar services as discussed in Chapter 4. In this textbook, both the challenges and the opportunities facing the members of the accounting profession are examined at the end of each chapter.

Summary

Electronic commerce is already proving to be a very powerful business channel. Many "traditional" businesses such as General Electric, Boeing, American Airlines, and US-Air have already successfully implemented successful Web-based strategies. New businesses, such as Amazon.com, are challenging many traditional businesses to rethink the way they conduct business. The success of Amazon.com has prompted many, previously traditional businesses, such as the bookstore retailer Barnes and Noble, to enter the electronic commerce arena.

When implemented properly and when aligned with the firm's overall corporate strategy, electronic commerce can significantly enhance the operations of a firm. The potential benefits of electronic commerce to businesses depend on the extent of implementation and also the industry in which the firm operates. The outlook for Web-based revenues is particularly good for the travel, financial services, and computing hardware and software industries. The primary benefits to consumers are convenience, access to information, and price comparison. All of these benefits to the consumer result in more buying power.

Traditional business models and the value chain are no longer representative of the virtual society in which electronic commerce operates. The value chain of electronic commerce–based companies places the customer as the center of focus with a sharing of data throughout all processes of the value chain and the customer.

Finally, the success of electronic commerce depends on the assurance businesses and customers place on its underlying systems. Security is often cited as the number one impediment to the growth of electronic commerce. A primary objective of this textbook is to present the security challenges that firms face as a result of engaging in electronic commerce and to educate the reader regarding some technological tools and business practices that can be used to mitigate these risks.

Key Words

customer-oriented value chain	software portability
customer relationship management (CRM)	traditional EDI
electronic business	traditional value chain
electronic commerce	value-added network (VAN)
electronic data interchange (EDI)	virtual enterprise
electronic information	virtual communications space
electronic relationships	virtual distribution space
electronic transactions	virtual information space
hypertext links	virtual transaction space
Internet	World Wide Web (WWW)
production cycle time	

Review Questions

1. What is electronic commerce?
2. What is electronic business?
3. What are five potential benefits of electronic commerce for businesses?
4. What is the production cycle?
5. What are five potential benefits of electronic commerce for consumers?
6. How does greater access to information translate into greater buying power?
7. How long did it take the radio to reach 50 million people? The Internet?
8. What is the Internet, and who built it?
9. When was e-mail put into use?
10. What three forces lead to the WWW's emergence as the single most dynamic force in information technology?
11. What is the traditional value chain?

12. What is the customer-oriented value chain?
13. What is customer relationship management?
14. What is a virtual enterprise?
15. What are the four virtual spaces of Angehrn's model? What are the major electronic commerce concerns of each?
16. What are the three major legal/regulatory constraints facing electronic commerce?
17. What are three pillars of electronic commerce?
18. What is a differentiating feature of electronic commerce from print and broadcasting mediums?
19. What are two primary impediments to electronic transactions?
20. What are four security concerns of businesses

Discussion Questions

1. What is one difference between EDI and electronic commerce?
2. How did use of the Internet help General Electric reduce the cost of goods that it purchased?
3. How can electronic commerce help reduce inventory costs? Give an example.
4. How can electronic commerce help reduce the production cycle time? What industries can greatly benefit from this?
5. How can electronic commerce enhance customer service? Give an example.
6. How can electronic commerce help a firm reach its customers in a very low-cost fashion? Give an example.
7. Does Internet access make employees more or less productive? Give an example.
8. Why is it important for websites to differentiate their sites from other similar sites?
9. Why do you think the travel industry's Internet growth potential is so great?
10. Why is it so important to align the electronic commerce strategy with the overall business strategy?
11. Give examples of how the supplier's information system can be used at every link in the value chain by the customer?
12. Why do you think Web-based firms report more security breaches than other companies?

Cases

1. Changing business to business models
   Visit Verticalnet.com and research Food/Packaging markets. Also, research how such business was conducted prior to the Internet.

   a. Write up a summary of how the Internet and the WWW have affected the food and packaging industries.

2. Website comparison
   For each of the following items, locate two websites that sell them:
   - Airline tickets.
   - Personal computers.
   - Compact disks.
   - Clothes.

    a. Mention how you located each site. Did you used a search engine or directory? Mention the search engine and the search terms you used if you used a search engine.

    b. For each item, record the site's URL and company name. Compare the amount of information given and the relative prices.

    c. Mention which site you preferred and why. Would you return to the site or would you continue to look for a better site? Why?

3. ICDT model
   Visit Disney's website (www.disney.com) and, using Angehrn's ICDT model, classify the activities found on the site into the four virtual spaces.

4. Customer relationship management using electronic commerce
   Using the Internet, locate a consulting service or software vendor that claims to help firms better manage their value chains using some form of electronic commerce. *Prepare a report for class that includes the following items:*

    a. The name of the company.

    b. Type of firm—consulting or software vendor.

    c. Potential benefits to customers of services/software.

    d. If a "client list" is given by the consultant or vendor, list the names of three companies that use or endorse the service/software.

References

Cambridge Information Network. *Electronic Commerce Investment: Keeping the Faith—A CIN Member Survey.* 1998. http://cin.ctp.com/Splash/SplashPreviews/Ecommsum.htm.

Computer Security Institute. *Computer Security Issues & Trends 2000.*

ENIX. *Technology Futures for the World Wide Web.* 1998. http://www.enix.co.uk /webtech.htm.

Essick, Kristi. "Euro to Aid E-commerce, Experts Say." *Computerworld On-line.* March 3, 1999.

Fingar, Peter. *A CEO's Guide to eCommerce Using Intergalactic Object-Oriented Intelligent Agents.* July 1998. http://home1.get.net/pfingar/eba.htm.

Greenstein, Marilyn and D. Hamilton. "Electronic Commerce: Re-Engineering the Value Chain to Increase Customer Focus," Proceedings of the 1999 International Academy of Business Administration Conference.

Guglielmo, Connie. "E-Commerce Boom Expected in Western Europe." *ZDNet.* March 9, 1998.

Helm, Leslie. "Web Is Reshaping How Firms Deal with Each Other." *Los Angeles Times.* February 15, 1999.

Hof, Robert, Gary McWilliams, and Gabrielle Saveri. "The Click Here Economy." *Business Week.* June 22, 1998.

IDC. "Security Becomes a Business Requirement for eCommerce Companies," Press Release. May 3, 2000.

InformationWeek. "Global Information Security Survey Reflects IT Professionals Views Worldwide." Press Release. September 9, 1998.

Information Security. Survey 2000.

Jupiter Communications. *MindShare: The Jupiter Senior Executive Program.* http://www.jup.com/research/ms/research.htm.

Leiner, B. M, V. G. Cerf, D. D. Clark, R. E. Kahn, L. Kleinrock, D. C. Lynch, J. Postel, L. G. Roberts, and S. Wolff. *A Brief History of the Internet.* 1998. http://info.isoc.org/internet/history/brief.htm.

Salnoske, Karl. *Testimony before the Subcommittee on Telecommunications Trade and Consumer Protection Committee on Commerce.* May 21, 1998.

U.S. Department of Commerce. *The Digital Economy.* April 1998. http://www.ecommerce.gov/danc1.htm.

WarRoom Research. *Corporate America's Competitive Edge: An 18-Month Study into Cybersecurity and Business Intelligence Issues.* April 1998.

2   ELECTRONIZATION OF BUSINESS

Learning Objectives

1. To understand the nature of the change in corporate processes.
2. To identify potential strategic advantages in these changes.
3. To understand the differences across technologies, processes, and industries.

INTRODUCTION

Some indigenous Internet businesses may have a competitive advantage due to new technologies and business paradigms; however, most traditional firms will not be able to continue to conduct business in the traditional way because of a major change in the basic processes of business. For example, brokerage houses accustomed to charging $90 to $100 a trade will have difficulty surviving charging $8 a trade. Long-distance telephone companies used to 15 to 25 cents a minute will struggle with 3 to 5 cents a minute. Companies accustomed to differential pricing across geographical boundaries will struggle with full information and international comparisons across companies and countries. Organizations accustomed to brand-name differentiation will struggle with the increased commoditization of services and products.

Internet-working and broadband services are altering some basic premises of productivity and production processes. Internal organization networks now providing broadband communications within businesses are changing intracorporate processes by providing a rich information set and enhanced knowledge bases. These more agile processes and the progressive elimination of paper present great productivity improvements and create a new set of trade-offs for performing corporate processes. Revolutionary to these concepts is the idea of sharing processes across organizations and opening information to partners both up and down the value chain (including customers). Organizations now open their inventory files to their suppliers and allow them to manage shelf content. Clients can go into corporate Intranets and order products, interact with suppliers' websites and get customized billing, and instruct intelligent agents to monitor many offers and then choose the most attractive.

The future will bring an entirely new set of processes and players into the electronized business domain. Large current businesses, with strong brand names, will morph into leaner, agile providers. Corporate business-to-business (B2B) auction places will heavily commoditize many markets, where suppliers and customers will interchange roles. New paradigms such as open information and pricing on the Web (prescription drug information), naming your price, also called reverse auction (Priceline.com), and negotiated prices for consumers are already changing the panorama of business.

PRINCIPLES AND AXIOMS

Business has been progressively electronized throughout the industrial revolution. The advent of electric sorters, typewriters, and the early computers has affected **organizational efficiencies,** meaning the most cost-effective processes. The advent of computers has substantially changed the efficiencies of back-office processes, initially focusing on natural applications that replaced manual labor, such as utility billing and corporate payrolls. After labor-saving applications, business started to focus on analytic efforts such as management information systems,[1] decision support systems,[2] and executive information systems.[3] With the advent of personal computers, the productivity enhancements focused on the desktop and white-collar processes that characterized the mid-1980s to mid-1990s.

Parallel to the evolution of computers, organizations witnessed a progressive change in the nature of telecommunications and computer interconnections. These interconnections moved computers first from independent batch processors to time shared machines to parts of corporate networks and finally to the current environment of interconnected networks with symbiotic relationships across a ubiquitous public network.

The business processing and telecommunications evolution has been of major value to businesses by creating the current cycle of revolutionary change that we call the **electronization of business.** Intrinsic to these processes are the transformation of basic corporate processes that compose the corporate value chain. Further, this transformation is causing effects that permeate the organizational arena. Among these effects, which are redefining areas of action and methods of work and efficiencies, are deconstruction, metamarkets, disintermediation, reintermediation, industry morphing, cannibalization, technointensification, and rechanneling. Each of these effects is discussed in the following sections along with a brief discussion of the value chain and bitable goods, and e-commerce.

The Value Chain—Internal and External

The corporate **value chain** links the different processes along the value-creating processes among corporations. Figure 2–1 describes a symbolic view of the value chain process.[4] Less commonly discussed is an **internal value chain,** where several internal processes cooperate with a stated goal of passing or adding value to the corporation by aiming to perform specific functions to fulfill both global and local organizational objectives.

In the value sequence, a series of inputs is provided to the organization through traditional logistics and the Internet. These inputs include raw materials, patents, services,

---

[1]K. C. Laudon and J. P. Laudon, *Management Information Systems: Organization Technology in the Networked Enterprise,* Prentice Hall, November 1999.

[2]E. Turban and J. Aronson, *Decision Support Systems and Intelligent Systems,* Prentice Hall, 2000.

[3]See J. F. Rockart and D. W. DeLong, *Executive Support Systems: The Emergence of Top Management Computer Use,* Dow Jones Irwin, Homewood, IL, 1988; and A. Paller, and R. Laska, *The EIS Book,* Dow Jones Irwin, Homewood, IL, 1990.

[4]M. E. Porter, *Competitive Strategy: Techniques for Analyzing Industries and Competitors,* Free Press, 1988.

FIGURE 2–1	*The interorganizational value chain*

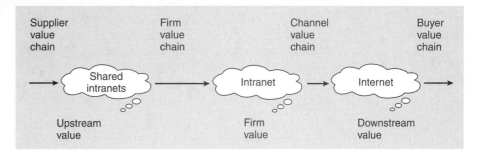

FIGURE 2–2	*Leaping over links in the value chain with Extranets*

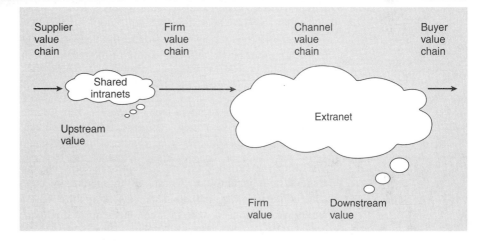

labor (in the form of external service contracts), etc. These inputs are brought into the organization and receive added value or are consumed in the process of providing customer-added value. Ultimately, outputs are delivered in the form of products or services to the clients. While the classic description of value added relates to enhanced products, in reality the **client value** includes products and a series of informational services that are necessary for business activity. For example, if you are selling a radio you must have billing services, warranty services, customer support services, etc.

The "soft" part of the value being delivered can be substantially supported by electronic delivery mechanisms. EDI, voice response systems, and telephone support are technologies progressively supporting these processes. Figure 2–2 illustrates the transformation of the value chain with the utilization of Extranets to enhance value. Extranets are a selective use of the corporate Intranet that is opened to third parties. Extranets are discussed further in Chapter 7.

The internal corporate value chain is composed of many processes such as research and development, production planning, production, financing, accounting, and auditing. These processes managed together create value for the corporation in facilitating and producing its final product regardless of whether it is a service, physical good, or bitable good.

Bitable Goods

A **bitable good,** also called *digital inventory or digital service,* is a good that can be transmitted over the telecommunication network in the form of binary digits, better known as "bits." Among bitable goods are found most financial products (banking products, insurance products, brokerage products), software, music, videos, and information of many types. As the world turns progressively to the typical product mix of more advanced societies with larger portions of the economy turning to services and physical goods having a strong service component, their support is also a bitable item.

E-Commodities

An **e-commodity** is a good that does not need to be seen, touched, squeezed, tasted, or tried on by the consumer to be purchased. Typically meats, vegetables, and high-fashion clothes do not fall into this category because the buyer wishes to inspect these items. On the other hand, canned goods, toilet paper, and napkins are e-commodities and can be purchased easier over remote modes. Today's grocers sell both types of goods, and this distinction may be responsible for the difficulties that are being experienced in e-grocery startups. Factors such as reputation of the vendor, experience by the consumer, distance from the source, and availability of the good may change non-e-commodities to e-commodities. Further, noncommodities, such as music, may be turned into successful online sales items because the customer can try it out online by listening to digital sound clips of the item before purchasing.

Deconstruction

With the progressive advent of e-business, a trend has emerged: the progressive outsourcing or alliancing-out of parts of the internal processes. Furthermore, unorthodox competition is coming into the market attacking the noble points of the chain. Figure 2–3 represents this concept with different elements of the internal value chain and the main organizational elements that affect it.

FIGURE 2–3   *Breaking up the value of content*

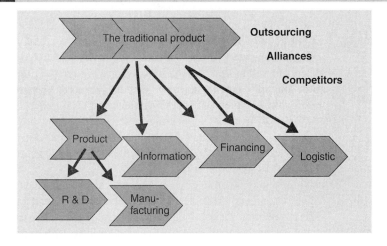

Like other manufacturing concerns, Ford Motor Company has, over the years, provided an integrated set of processes that resulted in the delivery of a car to a dealership that eventually sold it to a consumer. Producing and delivering this product entailed research and development activities, engineering activities, manufacturing processes, generation of information about the car, and development of the logistics process of delivering the car to the dealer. The **deconstruction** of methodology breaks it into discrete components and considers each of these components on its own merits. Modern dot-com organizations have mastered using alliances, outsourcing, and the markets (including competitors) to focus on critical competencies and competitive advantages. For example, Ford may decide that it is better at design and marketing and decide on the outsourcing of manufacturing, financing, and logistics. Alliances can serve to share in the proceeds of any part of the process, such as financing, without having to dedicate any substantive resources to this process.

Metamarkets

Customers do not see their needs the same way a company does. Ford may see a customer as the buyer of a car, while the customer may be trying to acquire a transportation solution that encompasses the car, insurance, chauffeur services, car leasing, gas, and maintenance. A pharmaceutical company may see the client as a buyer of insulin, while the customer would like to see a provider that satisfies diabetic needs. Internet-related technologies have progressively allowed organizations to satisfy metamarket views and needs from clients. By creating value bundles of products and services being offered by **metamarkets** or *meta-organizational entities* (higher level entities that offer integrated service and products from more than one entity), these needs can be satisfied. One modest form of these offerings is through specialized portals that focus on one particular set of metaneeds.

Disintermediation

One of the most remarkable effects of the Internet revolution is the progressive **disintermediation** of many processes. With the advent of advanced network technologies and electronic publishing, many functions are being at least partially disintermediated (eliminated). Some examples include travel agents, insurance agents, pharmacists, and car dealers. In Figure 2–4 the customer initially interacts with the travel agent, who interacts with a reservation clerk at the airline. With the implementation of time-sharing technology and large integrated databases, the airline clerk disappeared from the picture, and the travel agent used a terminal with the airline's reservation systems (e.g., American Airline's Sabre). With the increased usage of the Internet and the Web and improved user interfaces, an entire new industry of automatic airline reservations (e.g., Travelocity) has arisen and is taking market share and jobs from travel agents. Progressively this phenomenon will happen with many professions and job categories and will also be facilitated by the emergence of intelligent agent technology discussed in Chapter 13.

Reintermediation

The Internet has also created a series of opportunities for changing the nature of the elements of the value chain. In circumstances where many clients and many suppliers exist, the economic costs of information gathering and negotiation opened economic opportunities for **information intermediaries (infomediaries).** Customers, using several methods of communication such as the WWW, telephone, and mail, deal with an

FIGURE 2–4	*Disintermediation*

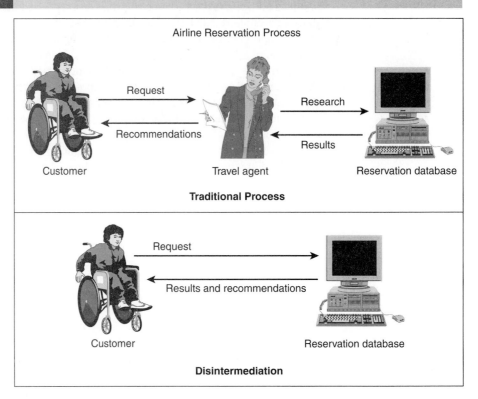

infomediary. The infomediary maintains an e-catalog that contains product descriptions, prices, and availability from many suppliers. Figure 2–5 illustrates this **reintermedia-tion** process. These suppliers are typically transparent to the customer, who only sees the product description, price, availability, shipping and handling charges, and perhaps some form of promotion from the infomediary. Companies such as Amazon.com and CD-Now.com that rate themselves as "stores" often, however, rely very heavily (or fully) on tertiary suppliers who carry all the inventory, packaging, and labels. These suppliers ship the inventory items directly to the consumers. Many infomediaries never have owner-ship or possession of the items sold, which go directly from the tertiary supplier to the client. In a sense, they are a new form of broker.

These changes of the traditional provisioning method are raising havoc with the measurement of business. For example, if a book is sold for $30 but has never been in the possession of an e-bookstore (which pays $26 for the book from a tertiary supplier), what should be the reported net sales: $30 or $4? (Net income before operating expenses will be $4 either way, but firms like to report high sales figures.)

Industry Morphing

One of the key tenants of financial analysis and business strategy has been the concept of industry and industry codes. The Internet and modern e-business have not only cre-ated entirely new types of industries, but they have also greatly confused the concept of industry by deconstructing and reconstructing value propositions. Many businesses do

FIGURE 2–5   *Reintermedication*

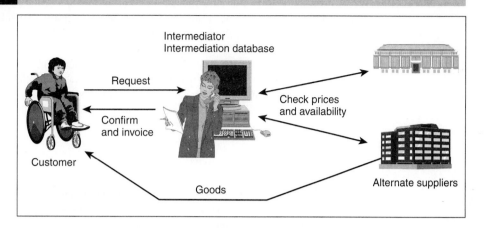

not view themselves as being in the industries in which they should now belong. Businesses are often composed of many parts that belong to different industries, and businesses work on morphing toward the components of their work that are more profitable or in which they have a competitive advantage. **Industry morphing,** then, entails the dynamic changes of the nature of business being performed by a corporation into an existing industry or a sector being created by new market conditions, products, or business models. On the other hand, businesses often maintain parts of their businesses with which they are identified even if these are a small component of all their activities. GE, a leading U.S. industrial entity, still has its refrigerator division, but it is actually a major conglomerate with more than 100 units.

Intuit, the maker of the personal financial software *Quicken,* was to be acquired by Microsoft, but the U.S. Department of Justice blocked the move. Reasons given were the concern of excessive industry concentration in this area of software. Since that date, Intuit acquired Chipsoft and the PC tax software *Turbo Tax,* offered Internet access associated with the use of the QFN (*Quicken* Financial network) portal, and made an affiliation agreement with Checkfree to facilitate payments by customers. Eventually it made agreements with more than 100 banks to connect directly from the desktop to the bank activities, allowing availability of checking information, capability to make payments, and ability to conduct other semi-online activities. It also offers an extensive program of insurance, loans, and market information. Intuit, originally a software developer, is now an integrated financial services provider that carefully chooses which sectors of the financial industry it enters, affiliates, or avoids.

Cannibalization

The Internet and related technologies are rapidly changing the nature of business and often creating the destruction of highly successful businesses. For example,

- IP (Internet Protocol) telephony will rapidly change the nature of telephony, bringing in 2 cents a minute calls instead of 25 cents a minute calls.
- Online brokerage has entered the fray and is offering $8.95 stock trades instead of $100.00 trades.
- Online banks are offering new types of more efficient and cheaper banking.

These changes in the nature of service and products are happening in shorter cycles and are destroying very successful businesses[5] or forcing them to dramatically change their product mixes, strategies, and venues of activity. Consider the following excerpt from an article in *Business Week:*

> Now, PayPal and its competitors may have to fend off the top dog of consumer finance. Citigroup entered the field Oct. 31 with a new service called c2it (www.c2it.com). Citi's stated goal is decidedly ambitious: Make it possible for any person to e-mail a payment to any other person or any business around the globe. That will entail, as Citi freely acknowledges, cannibalizing its own credit-card business. But can it pull this off without killing profit margins on its plastic golden goose?
>
> (*Business Week, November 16, 2000*).

The **cannibalization** of business[6] implies the replacement of an existing set of activities for a new set. The new activity set is often less profitable and desirable, but unavoidable. Cannibalization often works with disintermediation. For example, car dealerships are being cannibalized by sales over the Internet, and traditional brokerage houses are being replaced by online brokers (including software brokerage agents).

Most likely, the major obstacle that management faces is how to deal with **channel conflict** in the evolution of products to the online, digital channel. In the auto industry, both Ford and GM were very slow in going to the online, digital channel because of very overt threats by dealerships. While they were hesitating, a series of Internet plays started (auto.com, cars.com, auto-by-tell, imotors.com), some of which are partially owned by the same resisting dealerships. More recently, both GM and Ford announced direct sales efforts over the Internet. In November 2000, FordDirect started operations in California. Channel conflict is further discussed in Chapter 14.

The other side of the new-product/innovation story is the most common one: changing businesses toward electronic businesses. The story is one of obtaining cost and operating efficiencies through the electronization of different processes. Eventually a good percentage of banks are going to be online banks as the cost structures of online banking are vastly superior to traditional banking. The same will happen with music distribution, brokerage, insurance, and electronic books. More subtle cost structure changes, or operational efficiencies, are discussed later in this chapter through the discussion of the electronization of key corporate processes, such as human resources (HR), supply chain, and customer relationship management.

The problem of managing the decline of a product and introducing a cannibalizing one is a very delicate one. Keeping the income of the traditional product going as long as possible is attractive and desirable, but so is the new product line—even if it is less profitable. Bank One created both WingspanBank.com and Bank One Online to gather the clients migrating to electronic banking and to benefit from the advantages of the cost structures of an electronic bank. A series of problems and very large cost issues arose that led to changes in management and ultimately to merging the two online banking operations. Schwab, a discount brokerage firm, originally established eSchwab, which subsequently ate Schwab—an inspiration for all would-be cannibals and a clear-cut success story.

---

[5]See Clayton M. Christensen, *The Innovator's Dilemma: When New Technologies Cause Great Firms to Fail,* HBS Press, Boston, MA, 1997.

[6]"Internet Defense Strategy: Cannibalize Yourself," *Fortune,* September 6, 1999.

Technointensification

The electronization of business processes has as a basic tenant **technointensification**—the increased use of technology and its consequent increased capitalization and decreased human resource intensity. Most electronization processes focus on decreasing the labor content of its activities through a judicious usage of technology. With this factor, the intrinsic nature of technological processes assumes an important role in e-business. Businesses are progressively

- Having larger and larger capital investment per employee.
- Relying more extensively on third parties for equipment installation, provisioning of software, equipment and software maintenance.
- Hiring more technically proficient personnel.
- Training personnel on technical matters on a continuous basis.
- Producing items with higher value per pound.
- Executing rapid and efficient processes.
- Providing availability $7 \times 24 \times 365$ (7 days, 24 hours, 365 days a year).
- Experiencing highly vulnerable downtime.

Rechanneling

The deconstruction of business implies a breakdown of the different business components of its main processes. Some of these components are then potentially divested through outsourcing, alliances, or competition. **Rechanneling** also implies that businesses change their focus to related products and services. As a result of the atomization (disaggregation) of value-added processes, a company, when delivering a product, may selectively opt to contribute only selected (say, more profitable or critical) processes. Opportunities may also arise in which a business chooses its most promising or expertly run processes and considers them as separate products.

For example, a major European manufacturing concern has a division that manufactures the chassis of trucks and sells these to car manufacturers. Because of quality concerns, they developed great welding experience. The welding process (a subprocess of the assembling and manufacturing) is being launched as a separate product line, thus rechanneling the division's efforts.

Another form of rechanneling is when companies change their methods of distribution or sales to take advantage of the Internet. Most of the disintermediation that is occurring in the brokerage, auto sales, and travel industries (decreasing or eliminating agents) is a change from traditional to electronic channels. The progressive increase of Internet sales by BarnesandNoble.com implies a change from the traditional brick-and-mortar channel to an electronic channel (or a click-and-mortar channel) where customers buy over the net and pick up the product at a physical store. This rechanneling cannibalizes brick-and-mortar stores through rechanneling some sales and may also stimulate the entire market for books or even, in some circumstances, not cannibalize but stimulate traditional channel sales.

Stages of Evolution

The World Wide Web began its growth in the early 1990s and has progressively evolved into different stages. Most organizations go through a set of stages in the maturation of their e-business efforts.

| FIGURE 2–6 | *Stages in the evolution of e-business* |

Stage	Characteristics
Web presence	Informational Web page No contact information No method of user interface Separate from corporate IT
Basic functions	Informational Web page Deeper level of information Methods of contact with the entity CGI scripts Separate from corporate IT
Functional	Extended information set Connected to database Active Web pages Connected to corporate IT by middleware
Competent	Extended information set Connected to corporate main databases Uses Extranets with clients and suppliers Practices one-to-one marketing Many internal processes are electronized Uses extensively knowledge-based tools

The table in Figure 2–6 displays a summary view of the typical evolution of a business toward maturity in its e-commerce activities. Starting from Web presence, the organization evolves to performing some basic functions on the Web and providing some basic services and user interfaces for the public. Stage 3 implies more advanced functionality with some interconnectivity provided by middleware with traditional information technology (IT) functions. Stage 4 (competent) provides mature interconnectivity with internal and external processes, often without the need of handcrafted middleware.

With the evolution of tools and the maturing of e-business, the characteristics of the stages of e-business maturity will change progressively, incorporating new features from a more advanced stage. Companies can jump stages by acquiring more advanced platforms at entry and/or hiring experienced competent personnel. A similar taxonomy of maturity of internal processes can be developed to classify companies' electronization progress.

MAIN EFFECTS ON BUSINESS

E-business is changing the face of commerce and of the processes of administration and production of economic goods. These changes are massive and its nature is progressively becoming clearer. The ensuing changes are likely:

- **Globalization** of markets—In the world of e-business a merchant can set up one electronic shingle and service any place in the world. New provisioning methods and approaches will serve to complement the supra-nationality of a website.

- Dramatic change of business models—Interactive database technologies allow for efficiencies in variable pricing, name-your-price, and group buying, which are changing the economics and the practice of commerce.
- **One-to-one marketing**—This is the ability to direct a message that is very much based on the profile of a particular client and tailored to the perception of that client's needs. This practice will substantially increase the hit ratio of advertising and revolutionize business. Wide-band advertising is giving way to narrower, personalized advertisements and marketing.
- **Customization** (site and product)—Web pages that adapt to the clients' information (my.yahoo.com, my.ebay.com, mySAP.com, myCity.com) as well as products that can be mass marketed, but individually tailored (e.g., custom Levis jeans, custom mountain bikes, custom tires by Pirelli, custom shoes by Nike) will become more common and widespread.
- **Integration of systems with clients**—Companies are linking their Intranets to other companies' systems. For example, they are opening their inventory records and allowing providers to manage inventory and decide on inventory composition, reposition, and changes. Dell, in the provisioning of large orders of computers to its corporate clients, links the client's Intranets to Dell's hardware customization as well as creating middleware to allow for automatic approval, billing, and payment.
- **E-service not even envisaged before**—A new era of service is emerging as many of the production functions are moving to countries where labor is cheaper and plentiful raw materials reside. Also contributing is the sophistication of business processes brought about by the information age that creates complex information management opportunities. This service initially surrounding new e-business ventures will propagate to traditional business, creating new stages of business and expanding the traditional business venue. For example, Dell and UPS are now adding the computer setup service to Dell's provisioning and UPS's logistics.
- **Commoditization of products**—International competition, increased information, comparison websites,[7] and the ability for any firm to globally place itself through a judicious mix of alliances, outsourcing, and physical presence in different markets will bring increasing commoditization to products. **Commodities** are those products with narrow margins and no major brand differentiation in price.

MANAGEMENT ISSUES

The dramatic advent of business-to-consumer results in the emergence of phenomena such as Amazon.com and eBay.com. These firms' loss of value in 2000 and the demise of many similar, formerly highly valued players raises the question of how permanent these entities are and what the management issues are that arise and may be perpetuated in the cyber-age.

Many traditional businesses venturing into e-business will fail during the initiation period. The rate of survival will be somewhat proportional to years of existence.

---

[7]The advent of websites that compare organizations (e.g., Gomez.com) or products (e.g., pricewatch.com, ZD.com) has brought new efficiency to markets.

Consequently, the fact that reality is being played out and many business-to-consumer (young) businesses are failing in the normal Darwinian fashion of the economy should come as no surprise to the business community. Some issues, however, are raised here.

Working with the New Economics

The economics of e-business are potentially quite different. Experienced e-business managers are progressively finding out that

- They should keep away from the excessive promotion expenditures that have plagued dot-coms.
- They will often outsource a much larger portion of their processes than traditional (non-EDI and non-e-business) businesses.
- Often the incremental costs of products are small and the startup costs are enormous.
- Supply and demand laws matter.
- Most businesses should be positioned for growth based on progressive increase in cash flow.
- Earnings matter, but business plans can be designed for progressive (multiyear) entry into profitability.
- Price/earnings ratios often are not the best ratios to evaluate a dot-com, but other ratios (e.g., market value to sales) must also be used.
- Well-known competent management matters.
- Funding is becoming more competitive.

Main Changes in the Business Process

The internal processes that companies must perform are changing dramatically. Some of these major changes are

- Increased pre- and postsale care.
- Increased use of databases and user interfaces.
- Flatter organizations.
- Development of customer profiles.
- Increased reliance on cooperation software.
- Faster product-to-market strategies.
- Increased reliance on third parties.
- Faster turnaround of cash flow.

NEW PARADIGMS AND METAPHORS

A **paradigm** is a pattern, example, or a model. A new business paradigm (terminology overused in the periodicals) is a new way of doing business. New business models (e.g., priceline.com's name-your-price models), new processes to perform traditional needs (e.g., Extranets), and the change of characteristics across industries entail a paradigm change.

A **metaphor** is a figure of speech in which one thing is spoken as if it were another (e.g., all the world is a "stage"). Amazon.com has cash registers and shopping carts, but further examination reveals that it does not have a real cash register or shopping carts but rather has something that acts like a cash register and a shopping cart. Metaphors are important mechanisms to represent familiar items and concepts on the Internet and serve users better by allowing them a frame of reference so they can understand what action is expected from them or what processes they must follow. Listed below are some real-world examples of companies that are forging ahead and entering into paradigm shifts.

Victoria's Secret and Cross Advertising

During the 1999 Superbowl, Victoria's Secret presented a very successful commercial with its "Glam Lounge" advertising its new website. The advertisement caught people's attention with its scantily dressed models illustrating the company's lingerie. Of particular interest was the cross advertising from traditional media to new media that created great interest among male viewers who flooded the site. Actually, both male and female viewers flocked to the site, but a relatively disproportionate number of males went to the site than typically visit the brick-and-mortar stores.

The firm was not quite ready for the level of interest generated, and, for a while, great difficulties provisioning for the Web traffic ensued. However, the number of visits eventually stabilized and led to a substantive number of sales directly through the Web channel from visitors particularly located in areas where Victoria's Secret had no commercial outlets. This cross advertising among channels has become the standard for emerging dot-coms. The 2000 Superbowl was flooded with many fledging dot-coms that spent a significant parcel of their startup dollars on high-profile advertisements. In the recent retrenchment of the business-to-business sector, several of these dot-coms have disappeared either by absorption or pure bankruptcy. However the principle of cross advertising between new and traditional media has been well established and is rapidly becoming the norm.

Financial Instrument Brokerage Industry

Digital or bitable goods and services are the easiest products to sell and deliver using digital or bitable telecommunication devices. Thus, the brokerage industry's being progressively overtaken by online (digital) accounts should come as no surprise. The appeal of the phenomenon is obvious to most. The last decade witnessed a large increase in individual stock ownership, and the advent of the Internet has considerably facilitated the tasks of gathering information, ordering the purchase and sale of stock, and managing the financial tasks. Gomez.com offers many rankings of online brokerage sites. Gomez reviews approximately 79 online brokerage firms. It created a rating method of assigning points for approximately 150 criteria: The higher the number of points, the better rated is the online brokerage. Online brokeraging has completely changed individual investing by disintermediating brokers and facilitating timely stock ownership management.

The information set being offered to investors includes highlights of accounting information, news pieces about the companies, graphs of stock performance, tools allowing the comparison of stocks being considered, and analysts' recommendations and their tabulation. The reality is that before such Web-based services, not only did individual investors not have this information readily available, but even brokers most often could not reach or afford this amount and depth of information.

Online brokeraging is changing the entire face of the industry and the nature of markets. It will eventually lead to global stock exchanges and global regulatory entities and global disclosure on common or at least more similar standards. It is a far superior product from the investor's perspective and will cause brokerage firms that do not adapt to rapidly suffer and ultimately fail.

The Wellness Industry

In the United States more than 12 percent of the gross national product (GNP) is spent on health-related matters, and this places it in sixth place worldwide in terms of average quality of health care. Several countries spending in the 6 to 9 percent range of GNP provide better services in national health care welfare. An entire new set of efforts is going to dramatically change the industry through electronization. Websites and portals of a very different nature are entering this very rich domain and promise to yield very positive effects. Some examples are

- Online pharmacies (planetRX.com and drugstore.com).
- Wellness sites (drkoop.com).
- Disease portals (diabetes.com).
- Pharmaceutical sites (lilly.com and merck.com).
- B2B medical provisioning sites (neoforma.com).

While these sites seem innocuous enough individually, they are signals of drastic change in the nature of health care. Figure 2–7 displays a highly aggregate view of the internal value chain of a pharmaceutical company and the potential changes that are already occurring in the industry.

Several major effects may materialize in the industry as a whole:

- *The disintermediation of the pharmacist.* Electronic pharmacies with clear cost-provisioning advantages will drive the industry toward direct provisioning by high volume e-pharmacists. Potentially this may also stem directly from health portals bundling disease care metamarkets. Consequently, pharmaceutical companies will develop databases on consumers and work on highly effective marketing methods. They will create a bundled set of disease-oriented products and will take shares in e-pharmacies, health maintenance organizations (HMOs), and the like.
- *The democratization of medicine.* The phenomenal quantities of medical information online are empowering patients, and they are acquiring an active voice in their treatments. This is further fueled by the lack of control or management of such medical information by any national regulatory agencies. Educated patients interact very decisively with doctors and will increasingly choose their care regardless of their doctors' opinions by voting with their feet.
- *E-diagnostic.* Related to the democratization of medicine are the numerous websites that now offer some form of simplified e-diagnostics (e.g., *www.nhsdirect.nhs.uk/conditions, www.medical-libray.org/mddx_index.htm).* While many legal and behavioral issues are raised, they provide tremendous pressure on doctors to provide clear and objective diagnostics.
- *Internationalization of medicine.* The abundance of free or low-cost medical information regarding disease care in leading countries will be delivered to all countries. Pressure for the equalization of costs and quality of care will ensue.
- *Doctor comparison and recommendation.* Doctor selection is a very important step in the treatment of diseases. Patients currently rely on primitive methods

FIGURE 2–7 *The health care value chain*

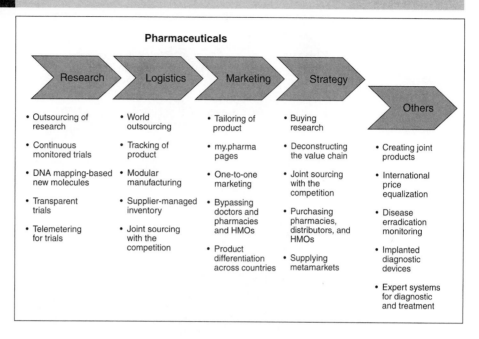

and little, if any, information in the selection process. Many doctor selection sites have been progressively emerging (e.g., *www.doctorquality.com, www.bestdoctors.com*). The consequences are numerous, some of which could be doctors and medical societies attempting to obscure the data to inhibit the attempts of patients engaging in an emerging form of consumer activism.

THE THEORY OF ELECTRONIZATION

"No single force embodies our electronic transformation more than the evolving medium known as the Internet. Internet technology is having a profound effect on the global trade in services."[8] According to Forrester Research, electronic commerce is expected to soar to $1.4 trillion by 2003. As discussed in Chapter 1, electronic business is a broader term than electronic commerce. It describes business activities with associated technical data that are conducted electronically. Further, it encompasses an entire set of different digitally enabled activities that are progressively replacing the more traditional brick-and-mortar commercial functions. While the wider phenomenon of electronization of economic activities encompasses the digitalization of all processes of economic wealth generation (including economic analysis, production, storage, information provisioning, and marketing), the area of sales and related processes facilitated by electronic media has popularly been referred to as **electronic commerce.** Consequently within the more general phenomenon of digitalization of modern life, we find a very important phenomenon—the electronization of business.

---

[8]"The U.S. Government's Framework for Electronic Commerce," The White House, July 1, 1997. *www.ecommerce.gov/framewrk.htm#BACKGROUND.*

| **FIGURE 2–8** | *The Electronization of processes* |

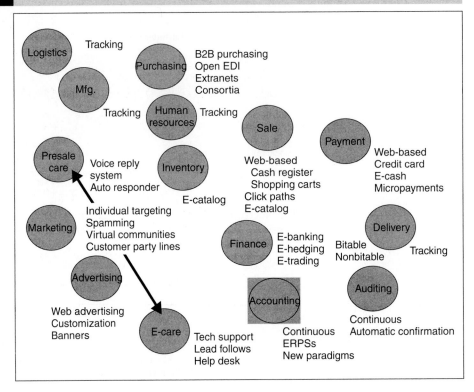

Corporate, not-for-profit, and governmental systems incorporate many related processes of business cycles. The digitalization of many of these processes is resulting in an astounding productivity gain for the world economy.[9] Many processes are changing their essence and becoming less expensive, less time consuming, and more useful. For example, a directory assistance call once required person and operator involvement: manually looking up the listing in paper-based directories in a localized search. Now it involves the caller, a national (or international) computer database, voice synthesis, and automatic connection. Furthermore, the process has been expanded, and reverse searches can be conducted through the Internet that will point to the owner of a listed telephone number, link this number to your telephone, and not involve any individual at the service provider. Thousands of system processes are benefitting from this type of mutation, leading to cheaper, shorter, and expanded types of services. Figure 2–8 describes several components of the business process (e.g., marketing) and e-business tools (e.g., Web banners) that are structurally changing how business is performed.

The marketing, advertising, and e-care triad are the core of the phenomenon. One-to-one marketing (where large customer databases link much information about clients and create very efficient leads) is linked to very tailored advertising mechanisms. The firm knows the client, and when he or she is connected to the Internet it fires off a series

[9]"Why the Productivity Revolution Will Spread," *Business Week,* February 14, 2000. *www.businessweek.com/2000/00_07/b3668001.htm.*

of individually targeted **banners** catering very closely to the client's needs. These advertising banners can explore

- The geography of the client at that moment (e.g., if using a mobile device, the closest gas station, drug store, or sports bar).
- Linkages among products or recent purchase (e.g., if computer was purchased, associated parts and software).
- Linkages among people, termed *social network,* whereby if one member of a group makes a purchase, other members will have the motivation or need to make a purchase. For example, a man buys a cell phone, possibly leading his girlfriend to want to buy one as well, or a listserv, such as one for sharpei enthusiasts and owners, mentions certain pet food as good for the dog's wrinkles, possibly leading many members to desire to buy the product.
- Family factors (e.g., if getting married, wedding dress and florists).

The **electronic care (e-care)** part of the triad is the emerging process of the new organization. Technologically rich products need superior, technologically based support. E-care, which is a mix of e-mail, Web-based support, and (when essential) phone support, is cheaper and more powerful if properly administered than the traditional means. Organizations are finding that the same stringent standards of traditional care must be applied in the e-organization.

The electronic commerce revolution is in its initial phases and will progressively take over all processes either directly or indirectly. The distinction of "snail" commerce and e-commerce will disappear, with all processes being either digital or aided by digital supporting processes. The pace of this transformation is what differentiates winning and losing competitors, industries, and successful investors. The intrinsic nature of the product and processes, as well as the dynamics and resistance to change of corporations and industries, will determine the pace of change and the gains in productivity. Together with the telephone, railroad, and electricity industries, the Internet is one of the major agents of change of modern life. Research predicts a wide range of business expansion on the Internet. The volumes of business-to-business trade are expected to be 6 to 10 times larger than business-to-consumer, but with much narrower margins.

An entire new set of principles of commerce is emerging:

1. The Malthusian physical world is giving way to a place where information is abundant and eyeballs limited.

2. Paradoxes exist due to technology. Giving away goods and services for free, not protecting software against privacy, and paying for users and site visitors may be the paradigms of the e-World.

3. The meanings of the words *competitor* and *industry* are changing. In the faceless world of digital, international trade, your customers and suppliers of today are your suppliers and customers of tomorrow. They are also your competitors and allies.

4. Industries are blending and changing and affiliation agreements allow for the creation of entire product cycles without the ownership of inventory or production facilities.

5. Current pricing models are changing and hybrids of fixed pricing, auctions, variable pricing, contingent pricing, and name-your-price pricing are emerging and creating new business models.

While technology gets most of the credit, in reality, successes are generally based on the triad: technology, business model innovation, and a family of facilitating (profitable) services as illustrated in Figure 2–9.

FIGURE 2–9   *Three key success factors*

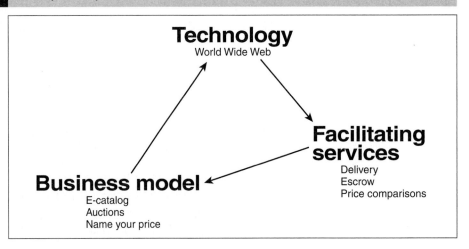

The business-to-business sector of e-commerce will present both vertical and horizontal models. In the vertical model, the firm will focus on an industry and develop great industry expertise to develop its markets. In the horizontal model, the firm will focus on one type of product or service and offer it across industries (e.g., Internet payroll services). The business-to-business sector is intrinsically different from business-to-consumer. Buyers are well informed, possess many resources, and can negotiate based on volume. Brand name is much less of a consideration than price, quality, delivery time, and reliability. Three different models have emerged for business-to-business transactions: (a) the e-catalog model for situations in which many different items are at distributed locations and price is fixed (e.g., auto parts); (b) the auction model in which products are not standardized and great differences exist in the perceptions of value (e.g., auctions of used capital plant products); and (c) the commodity auction model in which few variations are available for the type of product and a large number of buyers and sellers (e.g., natural gas, pork bellies, coffee).

Electronic commerce is progressively and irreversibly changing the facade of many businesses with three dominant phenomena previously discussed: disintermediation, reintermediation, and cannibalization.

The electronic commerce juggernaut is not without its dangers and shortcomings. It is drastically affecting traditional businesses that cannot continue to work the traditional economic model. Examples given earlier, such as the downward price pressure of brokerage fees, illustrate the need for businesses to rethink their business policies and processes. The security weaknesses of the electronic commerce infrastructure have been well divulged. Viruses, security intrusions, and denial of service attacks due to volume attacks are not phenomena that will disappear. They will evolve in a continuous struggle among facilitating technologies, intrinsic technological dangers, and the management of these factors.

Privacy issues present a different set of challenges. The same technology that facilitates business activities and provides wonderful services is also a major threat for individual freedom. Large databases linking dynamic economic activity information from different sources (purchases, banking activity, medical records) provide great economic advantages because marketing is more efficient, loans more targeted, and medical information more ubiquitously distributed. They also create great dangers for privacy and abuse. Doubleclick.com, a marketing analysis technology firm, tracks customer activities in websites. Their click-path analysis allows for firms to understand customer behavior and improve their offerings. However, they have 11,000 clients, and linking the buyers' profiles in these sites together is far too intrusive for the Web privacy advocacy groups. Complaints have been filed with the Federal Trade Commission and boycotts proposed.

Solutions however are not as straightforward as they may seem. Creating illegalities by enacting laws actually creates arbitrage opportunities and extraordinary margins for Internet players. Gambling rules are stricter in the United States than electronic casinos that are created in cooperative havens in the Bahamas. A legal obstacle in the United States is a business opportunity for another country, state, or municipality. Restrictions are placed on the usage and content of databases in Germany, and offshore database havens appear immediately. Website censorship appears in China, then free-Chinese websites are put into place. Telephone systems are monitored and taxed then the creation of supranational satellite telephone networks begins.

Consequently, easy fixes will not exist, and new methods of establishing order, efficiency, and decency will have to be created. Among these, as the Internet is a truly supranational entity, nations need to band together to maintain order and efficiency and reasonableness on the Internet. The same economic factors that allow for arbitrage can also be used for self-policing and monitoring of the electronic commerce environment. To benefit fully from this medium, companies, entities, and nations must have payment clearing solutions, customs solutions, and access to the large markets of the economy. Rogue countries behaving in unacceptable ways can be excluded from the payment clearing chains; such companies can suffer boycotts and be excluded from any affiliation and linking deals. Self-policing seals,[10] inspections, and certificates can be used for monitoring and supervision. International information structures, involving many cooperating organizations, can alert rogue behavior and motivate the creation of reasonable, unbiased rules. Technology can be used to monitor and detect money laundering, illegal product flows, and information trafficking. The same positive monitoring could turn into "big brother watching" type of behavior and must be carefully conceived and supervised. Most important of all is not to succumb to the easy temptation of creating restrictive, not well-thought-out laws that often result because of some local scandal.

E-BUSINESS METHODS AND TOOLS

This section explains some of the methods used and tools that support e-business. The discussion begins with e-catalogs, which are a marketing mechanism as well as a business tool for customers. Other types of marketing tools and methods, such as portal, banners, and sponsorships, are discussed in Chapter 14.

---

[10]AICPA's WebTrust and SysTrust products, TRUSTe, BBBOnline, BizRate, and other seals (discussed in Chapter 4) are examples.

E-Catalogs

E-catalogs are computer databases aimed at presenting a product list directly to buyers. These e-catalogs can have just the seller's item contents or can support the infomediary's role with links to many suppliers. E-catalogs are used both in business-to-consumer and business-to-business settings with little variation in basic technology. Infomediaries (e.g., Amazon.com) will often rely on third-party inventories for much of their sales as well as maintaining inventory in their own warehouses for items with high sales volume. Typically, companies buy turnkey, customizable, Web-based interactive electronic catalogs, such as a21.com. These are some typical capabilities:

- Categorization and parameterization.
- Data collection and normalizaton.
- Data cleansing.
- High-volume scanning and image processing.
- Custom design.
- Dynamic printed output.
- Preprogrammed query capabilities.
- Buying suggestion models.
- Incomplete information search algorithms.

These e-catalogs give buyers the ability to search for products across multiple vendors and to apply complex filters to find items that meet the buyer's exact needs. Moreover, e-catalogs allow sellers to participate in multiple Internet markets without losing control of their pricing, inventory, or discounting models.

One example is Cohera.com's E-catalog system that combines scalable information and broker functionality with complex data abstraction and integration technology. The result is that Cohera can retrieve live data (e.g., pricing and availability) from sellers' sites on demand. It can then join this data with static information (e.g., product or service descriptions) that is maintained at the market hub. Cohera helped LiveListings.com by using Cohera's cataloging software to link LiveListings' thousands of suppliers' products to its own $400 million listing exchange.

With Cohera's e-catalog system,

- Sellers retain control of their key product data and can participate in multiple Internet markets without altering their systems.

- Buyers can perform complex searching across multiple sellers, getting up-to-the-minute pricing and inventory information.

- System users can easily create new catalogs, add or remove sellers, and roll out new functionality without long development times or a proprietary application.

Tracking

E-business enables the merging of separate processes, often from different providers of outsourcing and through affiliation agreements. Competent businesses bring these processes together in a transparent manner aiming to provide a seamless interface for customers to follow the delivery progress of their orders. This is called **tracking.** UPS and FedEx both provide online package tracking sites. Dell and UPS have teamed to provide seamless integration of purchase tracking for Dell computers, meaning that purchasers do not have to go to UPS's website to track their packages, they can do so from Dell's website.

Inventory Management

E-business often implies unorthodox forms of **inventory management.** In addition to the traditional form of inventory management, forms of **joint provisioning** arise where one manufacturer produces inventory for many vendors and labels these parts accordingly. Further complicating the schema, inventory is kept in one common location and many infomediators have "ownership" of these stocks and have to be able to count on their availability.

Database Marketing

Three tools of modern IT and logistics come together in **database marketing** to facilitate the evolution toward one-to-one marketing:[11] data warehouses, tools of data mining, and the ability to profile clients. These tools put together in a judicious marketing plan allow for the improved utilization of the e-business environment by taking advantage of the intrinsic characteristics of the environment. This plan allows for:

1. Geographic focus.
2. Timely reaction.
3. Customer focus.

The click-and-buy approach must use information about the purchasing party (either a consumer or a business) to improve the realization rate. Consider the following example: A customer who lives in South Texas has recently purchased grass seeds and is member of a series of gardening lists. He needs to be offered garden varieties and fertilizers and plant food appropriate for the area. The products suggested should be appropriate based on his income level, in other words, products within a certain price range. Understanding the customer profile will help targeted advertisements to be featured that repeat or complement the purchase and are considered to be within the appropriate pricing scheme for that customer.

Data Warehousing and Data Mining

While a large store of customer data have existed over the last decade in many companies, the rise of the Internet and e-business has allowed, and even required, companies to use these data on a continuous, interactive basis during interaction with the client. Some instances of this use entail

- Credit card companies—approval of a particular transaction at the moment of transaction.
- E-tailers—suggestion models during the moment of purchase (e.g., customers who bought this item also bought these . . .).
- Routing—geographically based suggestion models linking geographical map and wireless communications (e.g., to go to the museum take route 23; by the way, use the enclosed coupon to buy gas on route 23).

---

[11]D. Peppers and M. Rogers, "Is Your Company Ready for One to One Marketing?" *Harvard Business Review,* January 1999.

Data warehouses may link a series of different sources of data or may bring these data into a common receptacle. Traditional data warehouses could contain financial databases (banking, credit card, and credit references), scanner data (from purchases in supermarkets), census data (for building profiles), and more recently, Internet-type data as click paths and accessed websites. **Data mining** allows firms to identify patterns and relationships among the data elements stored in the data warehouse. These patterns and relationships can be used to better serve the customer. For example, the analysis of data has revealed that consumers who buy diapers will also tend to buy beer, but the reverse relationship is not true.

Profiling

By tracking the sites users visit and how they use the sites, marketers can build complex portraits of individual users. This is called **profiling.** Special tools can draw information of particular tastes and tendencies that questionnaires and surveys fail to capture. Amazon.com and LandsEnd.com have websites with tools that enrich the buying experience and at the same time provide interesting and valuable experience to the merchant.

Amazon's music choice model, jaboom.com, presents a creative and dynamic method to entice and motivate the purchase of music. While offering compelling functionality, it also provides very interesting data traces. The visitor is allowed to listen online to new songs and rate them. They can also access the ratings provided by other visitors. The site also matches music with mood and personal tastes.

Another creative approach is Lands' End; it allows a virtual model to try on different clothes. The model can be framed with some of the generic characteristics of the client. This too results in valuable information to be captured for profiling.

Fragmentation is the essence of the Web universe. Too many websites are connected to too many different networks. Most websites use too many different tracking mechanisms and end up ignoring the reports. Technologies and strategies are often at odds. For example, consider the profiling practices of three different online sites: SportsLine.com, LookSmart.com, and Amazon.com. SportsLine is a member of the DoubleClick network of publishers; LookSmart is a contributor to the Engage user profiles database; and Amazon uses its own proprietary system for keeping track of customers. An advertiser depending on Engage's Business Media division is likely not to know that a particular user suffers from high blood pressure; the advertiser looking to reach sports fans on DoubleClick's network will fail to reach the same user; and neither of them will know that he or she is also a Civil War buff, as evidenced by the titles listed among their frequent Amazon purchases. Thus, fragmentation of customer profile data occurs because of the many profiling databases in practice.

Continuous Reporting

During the late 1990s, corporate IT changed dramatically. The causes of change are the following technological enhancements:

1. Interconnectivity of most processes.
2. Widespread adoption of Enterprise Resource Planning Systems (ERPSs).
3. Evolution of user interfaces connected to databases facilitated by the WWW.

When assembled, these capabilities allow for companies to report their financial statements (or a variation thereof) on a semicontinuous basis. For internal management, organizations keep real-time records, most likely of cash, receivables, payables, and inventory. Furthermore, bonds, commercial papers, and other short-term obligations are also managed in a timely manner. Assuming that no liability is involved (which is not the case) and that a desire exists, no obstacle is present to disclose data on a real-time or close to real-time basis. Cisco has often publicly mentioned its "daily book close," but this information is not made public or posted on its website. Progressively more organizations are trying to woo and support investors' and stakeholders' activities by disclosing voluntarily more information. Due to statutory concerns, organizations have started to disclose more nonfinancial information as a way to inform investors, but not to fall into the realm of liability issues. **Continuous reporting** is the real-time disclosure of transaction data.

Continuous Auditing

The speed of business, in particular e-business, has created additional impetus for the continuous monitoring and assurance of online systems, or **continuous auditing.** While certain organizations[12] made efforts in this area in the late 1980s, current realities, such as the speed of business and the preponderance of online activities, have created the need for continuous monitoring and assurance. The American Institute of Certified Public Accountants (AICPA) and Canadian Institute of Chartered Accountants (CICA) have been developing a set of concepts in this area that will eventually develop into another assurance service to add to the already existing Webtrust and Systrust products (these products are discussed in Chapter 4). The latest committee (Continuous Systrust) has designed a blueprint for the service, and is now being relayed to a product development task force.

NEW BUSINESS MODELS

The Internet and the WWW, along with the progressive development of new technology tools, are spawning new modes of performing business. Typically, would-be dot-com entrepreneurs prepare a business plan to specify their business vision and try to understand if the proposed business makes sense. In this business plan, three main factors are specified: (a) the product (value proposition) being advanced, (b) the sources and levels of revenue, and (c) the costs to be incurred. The intrinsic cost structures of the electronic media are different than the traditional ones, consequently allowing some very interesting value propositions, some of which are difficult to understand as a long-term sustainable venture. Several of these strategies are discussed in Chapter 3.

A multitude of new business models have appeared providing great changes in the nature of business. Three of these models are discussed: auction models, reverse auctions or name your price, and buyer's clubs.

Auction Models such as E-Bay.com provide a field of hundreds of thousands of items being sold at any time over the Internet. While they are called auctions, they are somewhat different than the traditional auction model. A physical presence to examine and buy does not exist; it is completely virtual. Further, a longer time period elapses during the auction, and a record of bidding activity is kept.

---

[12]See F. B. Halper and M. A. Vasarhelyi, "Continuous Process Auditing," *Journal of Practice and Theory,* Fall 1991, for AT&T's efforts.

Reverse auctions or **name your price** is a popular business model patented by Priceline.com. It allows for an individual or entity to propose a particular transaction and gives suppliers the opportunity to accept or reject the transaction. For example, a consumer can visit Priceline and ask for a ticket from New York to Los Angeles on August 5 at the price of $300.00. She will be contacted if a provider (say, American Airlines) accepts her offer. Flexibility in travel plans is diminished, however, since the bidder cannot specify the airline or time of day of travel. Reverse auctions are also being used by businesses for bulk purchases. For example, a company may wish to buy 80 personal computers for $2,100 each. It can then submit the request to computer vendors to bid for the job. Each computer vendor would submit "how much computer" they will provide for that price; this would include precise hardware configuration specifications.

The **buyer's club model** is where consumers sign up to buy a particular item (say, a palm personal digital assistant) and manage to get a group discount based on the number of registrants. Examples of this model are mercata.com and mobshop.com.

While these business models are patentable (priceline.com and mobshop.com hold patents for the business model), most e-business models are typically a mix of different forms of income and methods of implementation. While in the early days of the WWW great emphasis was placed on advertising revenues through banner advertisements, current business models tend to focus on many types of revenue generation. E-Bay charges listing and transaction fees for items being sold, but it also has advertising revenue, affiliations, and many other sources of income.

The four most common sources of income[13] for websites are sales over the Internet, advertising fees, subscription fees, and transaction fees. While pure-income models still exist, income is more commonly drawn from a mix of sources.

PROCESSES, THEIR ELECTRONIZATION, AND THEIR TOOLS

This section focuses on the metaprocesses that can be viewed as the most important and as being most affected by electronization. Some of the corporate processes and some aspects of electronization are highlighted.

Marketing and Advertising

Progressive levels of one-to-one marketing are facilitated by several different technologies that bring increased efficiencies to the process. Noteworthy technologies include:

- Adaptation of business strategies to the e-business environment[14] stressing brand, variable pricing, affiliation agreements, bundling, customizing Web presences to the client, customizing products, and adding information value to the product.
- Extensive databases and their mining[15] of client characteristics and profiles.
- Banner provisioning based on knowledge of client characteristics.

---

[13]D. Hoffman, T. Novak, and P. Chatterjee, "Commercial Scenarios for the Web: Opportunities and Challenges," in *www2000.ogsm.vanderbilt.edu.*

[14]E. Schwartz, *Digital Darwinism,* Broadway Books, New York, 1999.

[15]B. A. Kleindl, *Strategic Electronic Marketing: Managing E-Business,* SouthWestern Publishing, Ohio, 2001.

- Suggestion models based on client characteristics.
- Product bundling based on metamarkets.
- Progressive integration of the mobility characteristics of customers for M-commerce (e-business transactions performed on mobile devices such as cell phones or PDAs).

(*Bambury, "A Taxonomy of Internet Commerce," FirstMonday.com.*)

Production and Logistics (Supply Chain Management)

While bitable goods present a very different type of supply chain[16] where logistics are of a different nature, brick-and-mortar companies are progressively benefitting from the power of internetworking. Applying internetworking to the supply chain can bring great efficiencies to corporate production, storage, distribution, and acquisition processes. **Supply chain management** (SCM)[17] has benefited extensively from

- Electronic catalogs that point toward inventory of many provisioners.
- Product tracking through different entities and phases.
- Web processes that manage the distribution of cargo.
- Supplier-managed inventory.
- Shared and distributed manufacturing processes.
- Shared inventory management.

Supply chain management is one of the five core areas of the electronization of business. Brick-and-mortar transformation is slower than in the bitable goods area, so the progressive productivity gain acquirable from this area is just beginning to be realized. The early 2000s will present many opportunities for competitive advantage in SCM.

E-Care

Customer relationship management[18] **(CRM)** has progressively encompassed an increasingly larger importance in the evolution of business. Many organizations in the past have neglected the ultimate consumer by focusing on their immediate customer, an intermediary. For example auto makers focused on the dealers; pharmaceuticals on doctors and pharmacists; and airlines on travel agents. With the progressive disintermediation of many of these intermediaries, business entities are attempting to focus on the consumer through extensive efforts of identification, construction of databases, and creating methods of interface. Simultaneously, products and services are progressively richer in technology.

The three main components of a CRM package—sales force automation, marketing automation, and call-center automation—have been around for a decade. They have been filling corporations' need to collect customer information to better understand their

---

[16] M. Christopher, *Logistics and Supply Chain Management,* Prentice Hall, Upper Saddle River, NJ, 1998.

[17] R. B. Handfield and E. L. Nichols, Jr., *Introduction to Supply Chain Management,* Prentice Hall, Upper Saddle River, NJ, 1999; N. Radjou, "Deconstruction of the Supply Chain," *Supply Chain Management Review,* November–December 2000; M. Hammer and F. J. Quinn, "Reengineering the Supply Chain," *Supply Chain Management Review,* Spring 1999.

[18] S. A. Brown, *Customer Relationship Management,* John Wiley & Sons, Canada, 2000.

user base and to let employees in the front office do their jobs more efficiently. Many smaller firms have been attracted to a wide-open functional niche: Internet-enabled sales, marketing, and support.

With the increase of specific customer information, the offer of a tailored product or service to a client can also be made more specific. Customer information has become essential. The evolution of IT with knowledge systems based on data warehouses, data mining, marketing databases, and profiling allows for an unprecedented targeting accuracy. The market has attracted many actors, including well-known software providers such as Oracle. Most ERP suppliers are adding a CRM module to its products (e.g., SAP). The competition among IT providers is getting tough as the market is expected to drastically increase in the near future. According to IDC, the global revenues from the CRM services markets will increase from $34.4 billion in 1999 to $125.2 billion in 2004.

Oracle Applications[19] v11i offers a free CRM module. This module provides a more efficient set of data about the customer. Oracle also offers CRM outsourcing,[20] the management of the customers for its clients. The information will be made available through WAP (discussed in Chapter 9) and PDA devices.[21] CRM provides not only office-based services but progressively more information and services through mobile devices. These will bring new ways of communicating and servicing customers from the very first stage of the product ideas and research and development through to the offers to the customer and the relationship management. Because acquiring a new customer is, on average, eight times more expensive than keeping a customer, CRM systems are a required and critical layer of any information system.

Finance

Organizational finance departments are substantially benefitting from the technologies that the Internet brings to the platter. Most organizations today will have a finance area that also has accounting responsibilities. On top of an infrastructure of computer systems, typically legacy and ERP systems, new methods and tools exist for corporate measurement, assurance, and financial management, each of which is discussed here.

The Measurement Process (Accounting)

Accounting is the process of business measurement. To provide meaningful measures, a series of concepts must be assumed. These concepts provide a framework of processes around which measurements assume some meaning. For example, the concept of FIFO (first in, first out) is a concept of the physical flow of inventory that assumes that the physical units that were first received were the first sold; while de facto without specific identification, this is not de facto known. Although identifying the actual units may be irrelevant for some particular measurement purposes, it may be very relevant to other such measurement processes, such as the inventory count and value of cars of a specific car dealer. Accounting standard setting has assumed a business model for establishing the principles that allow comparability among financial statements. These standards have, therefore, a business model assumed and some common sense assumptions about their usage.

---

[19]CRM Oracle se met au gratuit: *http://france.internet.com/news.asp?news_ID=1467&Chaine Id=15.*
[20]OracleSalesOnline.com.
[21]"Comment on News Thinque and Aether Systems Partner to Bring Advanced Wireless Infrastructure to New FFA CRM Products," *http://www.thinkmobile.com/Comment/ Default.asp?CTID=1&ID=2221&R=%2FContent%2FDetail%2Easp%3FCTID%3D1%26ID%3D2221.*

Furthermore, measurements are intrinsically costly. Every additional measurement taken has a marginal cost. Particularly in management accounting, managers will make decisions concerning the value of a particular measure and its cost. These same trade-offs were made implicitly by regulators over the years, but the cost and capabilities of information processing have changed. Currently, specific identification serves many more purposes than in the past, including inventory management, analysis of customer buying patterns, and tracking shared inventory.

The role of the accountant, if the profession is to grow and prosper, will involve the measurement of many business functions, including the financial processes. The advent of the Balanced Scorecard[22] exemplifies the need of measurements across many dimensions, most of which are nonfinancial. Figure 2–10 defines some additional measures often used with marketing and Web issues.

The role of the accountant in the electronization of business is that of a measurement specialist who:

- Looks at the different processes.
- Creates measures for them.
- Proposes and evaluates the implementation of measurement schemata.
- Analyzes the measurements and analytics received and incorporates them into software.
- Evaluates and proposes interprocess measures.
- Advises management on the meaning of the outcomes.

FIGURE 2–10	*Web metric definitions*
Abandonment	Incomplete purchase actions
Acquisition	Overt action by customer expressing interest
Attrition	Percentage of customers who stopped buying
Churn	Measure of the turnover of the customer base
Conversion	Turning a prospect into a customer
Duration	Time spent on Web over number of visits
Loyalty	Frequency of customer revisits or repurchases
Reach	Percentage of visitors who are potential buyers
Recency	The elapsed time since a proactive customer action
Retention	Keeping existing customers as measured by their purchases
Unit retention cost	Cost of promotion to retain an average customer
Winback unit cost	Cost of regaining a customer lost to the competition

Adapted from Steve Alexander, "E-Metrics," *Computerworld* communities story, December 11, 2000.

---

[22]R. S. Kaplan and D. P. Norton, *The Balanced Scorecard: Translating Strategy into Action,* Harvard Business School Press, 1996; and "Putting the Balanced Scorecard to Work," *Harvard Business Review* September–October 1993.

The Assurance Process

As a complement of the measurement function, the new economy presents opportunities for a wide range of different assurance services. The AICPA, through the Ellliott Committee,[23] has established several task forces to develop a set of expanded assurance services that includes WebTrust (assurance of websites), SysTrust (assurance services on system reliability), performance measures, and health care, as well as a list of more than 140 other services. The crucial issue to understand is the motivations and causes of the emergence and potential importance of additional assurance services.

Both the annual financial report and the consequent annual audit report are old, maturing products with progressively less added value. Statutory factors are prolonging the products' lives (they are required for a company to be listed), but their actual usefulness for managers and investors has been decreasing progressively. On the other hand, the following factors lead to the need for an entire new set of measurements (metrics), analytics (rules), entities, processes, and alarms to be developed:

- Increase in speed of business.
- Increase in the number of intraday investors.
- Increase in complexity of local and federal laws.
- The ubiquity of e-commerce.
- The participation of several business entities in the life of a transaction.

These new sets of metrics, rules, entities, processes, and alarms are to be based on continuous measurement[24] of a set of internal processes, strategic metrics, and external variables. Continuous measurement leads to internal continuous reporting and monitoring. Eventually some level of external continuous reporting will occur. The structure for process monitoring and assurance is displayed in Figure 2–11.

Corporate metrics are provided by the process management information system (MIS) on a real-time basis. A monitoring structure on top of the MIS links several disjointed systems, selects and filters data, and compares these metrics with standards; if variances surpass discrepancy standards, an alarm is issued. These alarms are issued to operations, auditors, or eventually to other stakeholders.

Corporate Finance

The electronization of corporate finance is still emerging, but it will be one of the most important processes in many corporations. While information production may be viewed as secondary to the primary tasks in areas such as research and development and manufacturing the product, the financial process is purely bitable and will rely on purely virtual processes both internal and external to the company.

In the corporate finance area great reliance will be placed on

- A progressive path to full paperlessness.
- A progressive increase in e-care interaction with internal and external clients.
- Continuous reporting.
- Integration (Extranets) with external entities such as banks, clients, suppliers, regulators, and auditors.

---

[23]*www.aicpa.org/assurance*
[24]M. A. Vasarhelyi, "A Dramatic New Model for Auditing," working paper, Faculty of Management, Rutgers University, Newark, NJ, January 2000.

FIGURE 2–11   *Process monitoring and assurance*

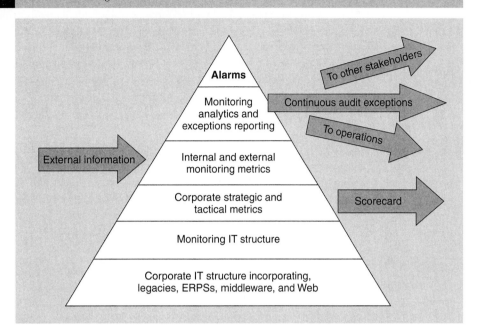

- Extensive use of a variety of assurance products.
- An integrated set of analytic risk management algorithms.
- Continuous auditing.
- Continuous confirmation of accounts, balances, and selected transactions.

Human Resources (HR)

Many organizations with foresight have focused substantive efforts in the electronization of many human resource functions through their corporate Intranets. A traditional labor-and-paper–intensive function has been transformed to a large series of self-service, automatic report function, database-enriched mini-processes. These processes may encompass a series of services such as

- Administrative activities (employee data, company forms).
- Career management (job adds, resume, open positions).
- Value of employment (compensation, benefits explanation).
- Payroll (time reporting, W2, electronic funds transfers).
- Employee services (travel, electronic agenda, calendar, group meeting tools) and
- Health management (donor services, HIP, dental plans).

The area of HR has benefitted extensively in its electronization of ASPs (application service providers), which provide extensive, reasonably priced human resource service providers. This approach of outsourcing IT for HR, or the entire human resource function, has become very popular among startups that do not have the desire or competency to develop these competencies in house.

Research and Development (R&D)

While the area of R&D brings images of individual creativity and physical processes, it will be strongly affected by electronization. Figure 2–7, referred to earlier in the chapter, shows the changes that will affect the R&D area in the pharmaceutical industry with the usage of many tools and features of the electronic revolution. The R&D area, in particular, has been benefitting from

- Groupware for distance work.
- Large databases.
- Telemetering and sensing.
- Powerful databases.
- Visualization software.
- Powerful supercomputers.
- Knowledge management systems.

INDUSTRIES[25] AND THEIR CONTINUING EVOLUTION

Bitable Products

The industries that are focused on bitable products are the ones to be further and faster affected by the electronization revolution. Among those leading the way are the financial sector with online brokerage, electronic banking, and Web-based insurance. While online brokerage has already changed the entire industry, electronic banking is rapidly changing the face of the banking world, while high regulation and industry inertia have slowed inevitable change in the insurance world.

The software and computing industry are a blend of bitable and nonbitable goods, but with a long-term tradition of computer-based purchasing and a large population of customers who are "techies" and not intimidated by the Web. Some software industry members initially stayed away from extensive provisioning of software over the Web because of fear of alienating their channels and bandwidth limitations. This is occurring rapidly, however, and will soon be the main channel of software distribution.

Retail

The evolution of business-to-consumer sales has somewhat slowed, and a large number of spectacular failures of highly touted new ventures (e.g., Boo.com) has created some skepticism in the markets. Several traditional brick-and-mortar entities have stepped in to acquire and support startups in trouble, and click-and-mortar plays have been emerging. Electronic marts have not fared very well, but specialized industry portals have progressively assumed an important role in the panorama of e-business.

Large Manufacturers

While in the preceding areas the emphasis and visibility have been in the sales and customer interface area, the focus in the more traditional industries has been in the many

---

[25]M. Jerome, "The Internet Is Crushing Entire Industries: Is Your Company Next?" *PC Computing,* February 2000.

areas of electronization of the corporate processes. Here, organizations have focused on their areas of critical need and competence (e.g., FedEx in tracking, Pirelli in manufacturing) and are working on methods of increasing market range, reducing costs, and increasing the rapidity and efficiency of their processes.

Services

The area of services presents a series of unusual opportunities that are noteworthy and will eventually change radically the scenario of international competition, methods of performing traditional services (e.g., accounting, auditing, data entry, programming), and the creation of a series of new and creative e-services mainly around new Web-based products.

IMPLICATIONS FOR THE ACCOUNTING PROFESSION

Electronization will affect all corporate processes in different levels of intensity and timing. Because bitable products and information services exist and are on the rise, the accounting and auditing services are already being affected. Both the measurement and the assurance professions, somewhat protected by their own web of statutes and regulations, are going to radically change in order to provide more real value to the client and to obtain the economies that internetworking technology provide. This chapter discussed a series of views of the profession, emphasizing continuous reporting over a much wider area than financial processes and leading to continuous assurance and the development of a much wider set of assurance products. Some of these services may be performed on a supranational basis using broadband channels from lower-cost labor pools, such as India and China. The role of accountants in continuous and other assurance functions is examined in greater detail in Chapter 4.

Summary

This chapter focused on understanding the basic reasons of the internetworking revolution. While the term *e-commerce* has been used extensively, the main phenomenon being witnessed is the progressive electronization of business where its component processes are systematically being changed by e-business tools and processes.

The phenomenon of electronization is a heterogeneous one with firms and industries developing features at different paces. Bitable products and services and suppliers of e-commodities are ahead of the game with substantive focus on improvements. Other industries will observe this focus and piggyback on the developed technology through interindustry emulation and acquisition of competitive economic advantage.

A series of principles of electronization were discussed considering the internal and external value chains of the firm, bitable and nonbitable goods, e-commodities, the deconstruction of business, metamarkets, disintermediation, reintermediation, industry morphing, cannibalization, technointensification, and rechanneling. Based on these concepts, a series of main effects on the future world of business were made that included globalization of markets, changed business models, one-to-one marketing, customization of site and product, integration of systems with clients' systems, new e-services, and the commoditization of products.

A very different business set of models and economy bring in the questions on whether management knows how to work with the new economics and what the major changes in the business process are. New paradigms and metaphors have emerged (e.g., new paradigms in relation to methods of advertising, methods of stock trading, and the entire structure of the wellness industry).

Electronization is enabled by a new series of technological tools, among which we discussed e-catalogs, tracking, inventory management, database marketing, continuous reporting, and continuous auditing. The major elements of the business cycle being electronized are marketing and advertising, supply chain management (production and logistics), e-care, and the financial area (measurement, assurance, and corporate finance). The electronization of business is not just e-commerce; it is much bigger than that. It is the electronization and reengineering of key corporate processes creating e-business!

Key Words

accounting	electronization of business
auction model	e-service
banners	external value chains
bitable good	fragmentation
buyer's club model	globalization
cannibalization	industry morphing
channel conflict	information intermediaries (infomediaries)
client value	integration of systems
commodities	inter-industry emulation
commoditization	internal value chain
continuous auditing	inventory management
continuous reporting	joint provisioning
customer relationship management (CRM)	metamarket
customization	metaphor
database marketing	one-to-one marketing
data mining	organizational efficiencies
data warehouse	paradigm
deconstruction	profiling
disintermediation	rechanneling
e-business	reintermediation
e-care	reverse auction (name your price)
e-catalog	supply chain management (SCM)
e-commerce	technointensification
e-commodity	tracking

Review Questions

1. What is deconstruction?
2. Define a value chain.
3. Explain what is meant by "delegating work" to the computer.
4. Differentiate between internal and external value chains.
5. Differentiate between disintermediation and reintermediation.
6. What are metamarkets?
7. Explain industry morphing.

8. Explain technointensification.
9. What is meant by cannibalization?
10. Explain in your own words the different forms of rechanneling.
11. Internetworking is changing business into e-business. What are the main effects being seen in business?
12. One of the above-mentioned effects is one-to-one marketing. What does that mean?
13. What is the difference between product and site customization?
14. What are the main changes in internal business processes that are occurring?
15. What is M-commerce?
16. Differentiate between a metaphor and a paradigm.
17. Describe a metaphor that represents an e-business activity.
18. Exemplify a major paradigm change that is occurring in one industry due to the Internet.
19. List a set of enabling technologies for the electronization phenomenon.
20. What are the sectors that are most affected by electronization?
21. Explain the three key factors that are bringing e-business to existence.
22. Give an example of the emergence of a set of native Internet businesses relative to the three key factors: technology, business model, and service.
23. List key tools that are helping the transformation of business.
24. What are the five larger areas of electronization?
25. Explain CRM.
26. Explain SCM.
27. List 10 different nonfinancial e-metrics that can be linked to traditional financial measurements.
28. What are the main implications of the electronization of business for the accounting profession?

Discussion Questions

1. What is the electronization of business?
2. How does deconstruction link to outsourcing?
3. Explain how the auto industry is undergoing processes of disintermediation and deconstruction. What are the subprocesses you would keep, and which would you contract out?
4. Focus on the area of e-commerce (marketing) and describe the main effects that compare an e-business to a traditional business.
5. Find and visit sites that discuss one-to-one marketing. Try to define the concept clearly.
6. Visit the AICPA site and find the listing of potential assurance services that were initially proposed by the Elliott Committee.
7. The Internet has been around since the 1970s, and the WWW was originally deployed in 1990 with its Mosaic browser (introduced in 1992). What are the stages of e-business development, and what are its characteristics? How would you modify the stages proposed in this chapter?
8. In a discussion of the pharmaceutical industry, an arrow chart is presented to decompose its processes and discuss the R&D in the industry. Choose an industry with which you are familiar, choose a major area, and create a similar chart. What conclusions can you derive from this chart?

9. Propose 20 different metrics for linking financial and nonfinancial measures using the above arrow chart (developed in Question 8) or any arrow chart (including the one presented in this chapter).

10. Prepare a comparative table of features between traditional brokerage and electronic brokerage. The table should have three columns—one with the nature of the feature, one with e-brokerage, and the third with s-brokerage (old style brokerage).

11. Use the same type of table and nature of features as in the previous question to compare an electronic bookstore (e.g., Amazon.com) with a traditional one.

12. How do continuous reporting and auditing relate to each other?

13. Illustrate the concept of balanced scorecard. How does it relate to the new world of process monitoring?

14. Why is CRM assuming such a large role in the business process?

15. What is the future of e-business? Is it only a fad?

Cases

1. Price comparison sites
   Visit *http://www.pricewatch.com.*
   a. Discuss the nature of the site. What is the business model that guides its development? Discuss this issue.
   b. Does the site make any money? Who pays for the service? What are its sources of income? What would be the other alternatives of revenue for a site such as this?
   c. Is a benefit derived for the users in the utilization of this site?
   d. Comparison sites will have long-term implications to change the nature of business and pricing structures. Speculate about these changes. Find one other price comparison site and compare its business model with Pricewatch's.
   e. Are these types of sites going to contribute to the commoditization of products and to the reduction/elimination of major differences in international pricing?

2. The car industry
   The car industry has been very slow in developing e-models of business mainly for lack of motivation, acceptance of the status quo, and fear of alienating its dealer channels. This stagnation is in the process of evaporating in favor of a series of changes in the industry.
   Visit auto maker sites, as well as sites such as auto-by-tel, Covisent, Edmonds, FordDirect, and Cars.com, to try to understand the types of players and what they are doing.
   a. Break the industry into categories of players, and make predictions of what is going to happen to dealers, what processes the industry will use to deconstruct, and what new players are trying to sneak into the value chain.
   b. What new technologies are to be brought into the traditional car business and how is this going to affect the status quo?

3. How free is free?
   The web is currently full of "free" plays including free Internet access, free Internet phone, free Websiting, free e-mail, free e-commerce site, free fax number, etc.
   a. Identify 20 of these sites.
   b. Try to understand their income model.
   c. Try to understand their future prospects.
   d. Create a classification of these sites.
   e. Make a prediction from these sites about which will succeed (survive) and which will fail. Explain.

4. Disclosure on the Web

Many companies now disclose financial information on the Web at their main corporate website. Choose five companies and examine their financial information in comparative terms to published financial statements, or if those are not available, obtain 10K statements at the Edgar site. Based on your observations:

a. Are companies posting their entire financial statements?

b. Are companies posting any additional or more timely information?

c. What information is not being posted?

d. Is quarterly information being published?

e. Are any tools being given to users at websites that may enhance the traditional data even if no additional information is being provided?

f. Prepare a comparison of the balance sheets and income statements of the companies collected.

References

"Cyberatlas Hardware—CRM Applications a $3 Billion Market,"
   http://cyberatlas.internet.com/big_picture/hardware/article/0,,5921_443211,00.html
"High Customer Expectations to Lift CRM Market,"
   http://cyberatlas.internet.com/big_picture/hardware/article/0,,5921_459191,00.html
"Retek vise le marché de la CRM dans la distribution,"
   http://france.internet.com/news.asp?news_ID=1425&Chaine_Id=9.
"InternetNews—ASP News—CRM Solutions Companies in Cahoots,"
   http://www.internetnews.com/asp-news/article/0,2171,3411_428751,00.html.
"The Evolving World of CRM," *http://sa.internet.com/webbutler/Busapplications/00/08/07.htm.*
"Cyberatlas Retailing—E-Tailers Still Lacking in Customer Service,"
   http://cyberatlas.internet.com/markets/retailing/article/0,1323,6061_435761,00.html.
"Cyberatlas Retailing—Pure Plays Face Trouble in E-Commerce Shakeout,"
   http://cyberatlas.internet.com/markets/retailing/article/0,1323,6061_397301,00.html;
   http://gartner12.gartnerweb.com/public/static/crm/crm.html;
   http://gartner12.gartnerweb.com/public/static/aboutgg/pressrel/pr20000914a.html.
"Customer Retention in On-line Retail," Booz Allen Hamilton, Dr. Gaby Wiegran, Hardy Koth, September 1999.
Annual Reports, Brokat, Siebel, 1999. "Customer Relationship Management Survey," *Financial Times,* March 7, 2000.
"The Demise of CRM," *Forrester,* June 1999, *www.forrester.com.*
CRM case studies, IBM Global Services, *www.ibm.com/services.*
Nikken Speech, KPMG, 1999. "The Internet and Financial Services," Morgan Stanley Dean Witter, August 1999.
"Achieving Business Success through Customer Relationship Management (CRM)," Mosaic Inc., 1999, *www.mosaic.com.*
"Relationship Management," Web Associates, Inc., March 2000, *www.webassociates.com.*
"Viewpoint on Customer Relationship Management," PA Consulting Group, 1999, *www.pa-consulting.com.*
"Why Customer Care Will Drive the Growth of Web-Based Banking," Silknet Software, November 1999, *www.silknet.com.*
"Competitive Brief—Silknet and the New eRM Technology," Silknet Software, November 1999, *www.silknet.com.*
"e-Everything—Technology-Enabled Customer Relationship Management," Web Associates, Inc., March 2000, *http://webassociates.com.*

3   B2B PROCESSES AND STRATEGIES

Learning Objectives

1. To understand the nature of business-to-business (B2B) processes.
2. To identify potential strategic advantages in networks and B2B.
3. To understand the basic elements of traditional strategic thinking and the new variants drawn from "new economy plays."

INTRODUCTION

The early days of e-commerce have focused on business-to-consumer (B2C) transactions and the development of many innovative business models.[1] The wide publicity, the progressive pervasiveness of the Internet, and the steep slope of initial growth[2] of Internet-related companies initially generated an absurd level of valuation for most dot-coms. These B2C ventures fueled a progressive worldwide stampede of high valuation and venture capital investments focusing on B2C ventures with poster children, such as Amazon.com, Priceline.com, and e-Toys.com. In terms of history, market hysteria has followed tulip bulbs in Holland in the 1600s, telegraph stocks around 1880, telephone stocks in the early 1900s, biotech stocks in the 1980s, and until recently Internet stocks. The outcome has been systematically that some key companies survived, prospered, and became scions of the establishment (e.g., Western Union, AT&T, Genetech), and many failed or were absorbed by established companies. This same trend has repeated with the emergence of the Internet; it has however, taken, a dual track. The first track, Internet enablers, such as Cisco, Dell, Oracle, and IBM, were established companies that took additional valuation and substantively more value. The first track is proving, thus far, to be of a relatively enduring nature. The second track, in particular B2C investments, has generated an enormous flurry of startups

---

[1]See L. Applegate, "Overview of E-Business Models," Harvard Business School, August 20, 2000, for a comprehensive and authoritative view of a potential taxonomization of business models.

[2]Note that the larger a company, the more difficult it is to have large slopes in their growth. For example, a company that sells $10,000 a year can double sales easily, but few cases in history exist where a $10 billion company doubled its sales in a year.

and activity, but its outcome has been more modest with a large number of notorious failures[3,4] and many more predicted in the near future.

FROM B2C TO B2B USING CORPORATE NETS

While the B2C wave was beginning its maturity phase, a second and larger wave started to arise, the **business-to-business (B2B)** sector. The B2B market is often rated between 6 and 20 times larger in total dollar sales than B2C. While the volumes of B2B are unquestionably much larger than B2C, the margins per unit are narrower, and the focus is the **electronization** of a narrower sector of the electronic business. Typically the emphasis of B2C is on the Web marketing processes, while B2B focuses on interfaces between (a) the purchasing agent and related process and (b) the tools and methods of market formation. Figure 3–1 compares the focus of B2B and B2C within the electronization framework of the entire business as discussed in Chapter 2.

The second wave of e-commerce B2B has benefitted from wisdom gathered in the B2C movement, namely, more solid business plans, deeper understanding of

| **FIGURE 3–1** | *B2B and B2C electronization focus* |

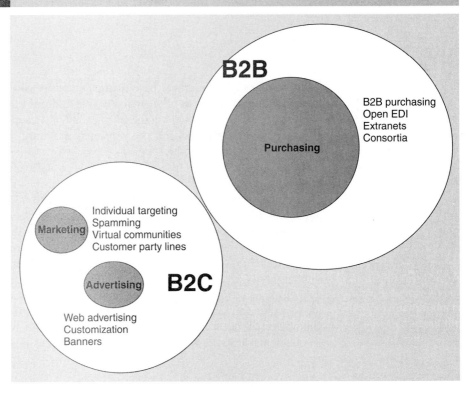

[3]"Autopsy of a Dot-Com," *Computerworld,* January 19, 2001.
[4] C. King, "Study: Dot-Com Shutdowns Are Accelerating," *E-Commerce News,* November 16, 2000, *http://ecommerce.internet.com/ec-news/article/0,1467,5061_513371,00.html.*

methodologies and markets, and increased integration with legacy company applications. As the second wave emerged during the peak of the Internet market euphoria, the same exaggerated valuations emerged in the markets. VerticalNet and Open Markets, at their peaks in 2000, were valued at $160 and $320, respectively. In January 2001, they were valued at $6 and $25, respectively.

Over the last three years the e-commerce scenario has gone from emergent to exuberant and then to a dramatic loss of valuation. This evolutionary path has brought a small, but progressively larger, part of the entire economy to some form of e-commerce execution of transactions. By 2004, a much larger percentage of the economic pie will be flowing through the electronic channel. However, many lessons have been learned from success and failure in both the B2C and the emerging B2B arena. These lessons are leading to entirely new sets of e-commerce–related business strategies. Building on the electronization principles discussed in Chapter 2 that mainly emphasize B2C, this chapter first examines the network infrastructure of corporations that will provide the basis for these new-generation efforts. The emergent and expanding B2B market is then examined, and strategy formulation is discussed.

CORPORATE NETS[5]

The first set of corporate e-business efforts focused outwardly, with companies hanging out their commerce counters as self-contained and independent from corporate information technology (IT) systems. The new generation of e-business efforts, however, is strongly based on a form of **internetworking** that brings the corporate effort closer to the company's internal processes, its electronization efforts, and its rich set of internal networks. Corporate and intra-entity networks are contributing value through their fixed and mobile components. They are increasingly relying on wireless connectivity, and applications are beginning to bring the process to the individual, instead of having the individual or company go to the process. Sawheney and Parikh[6] argue that four high-level value trends exist in the digital economy:

- Value at the ends of the network with highly customized connections with the customer.
- Value in common infrastructure allowing for the sharing of common business function and certain facilities.
- Value in modularity for seamless and quick interconnectivity with other processes.
- Value in orchestration (the most valuable business skill) to coordinate the different elements of the value chain and the introduction of core competencies and unique capabilities in high-value pieces of the chain.

This value will be delivered by several types of networks, and the definitions of these networks increasingly overlap and change in nature over time. First a company's internal IT infrastructure is called its Intranet. Interconnectivity with other company applications occurs through Extranets.

---

[5]B. Liautaud and M. Hammond, *E-Business Intelligence,* McGraw Hill, New York, 2001.
[6]M. Sawhney and D. Parikh, "Where Value Lives in a Networked World," *Harvard Business Review,* January–February 2001.

Intranets[7]

Intranets are a product of the Internet revolution. While technology was developing computer-to-computer communication, companies became wise to the benefits of computer resource sharing. Initially, they pooled resources, such as databases and printers, through proprietary office systems such as Wangs and DECs. Eventually, they started to realize the additional benefits of internal corporate e-mail communications and companywide data sharing from the usage of LANs (local area networks) and their interconnectivity through WANs (wide area networks). The advent of the Internet, its ubiquity, and, most of all, the universality of the TCP/IP protocol made companies progressively drop their proprietary networks and adopt TCP/IP as their internal network protocol. (The TCP/IP protocol is explained further in Chapter 9.) This networking protocol was used along with Internet tools such as Web servers, browsers, and routers. These new internal networks have become key to the life and fabric of corporations. Anghern's ICDT model presented in Chapter 1 also looks at Intranets as the backbone of the corporate space with four main areas:

1. Information space.
2. Communication space.
3. Distribution space.
4. Transaction space.

Figure 3–2 illustrates the use of Intranets for Anghern's virtual spaces.

FIGURE 3–2   *Angehrn's ICDT model and Intranets*

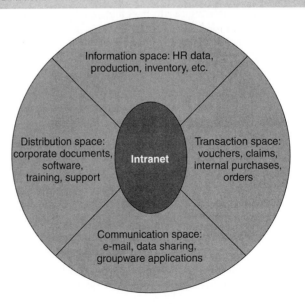

---

[7]A. A. Angehrn and N. Leck. "Intranets: The Backbone of Corporate Market Spaces," INSEAD working paper, 1998.

Extranets

Progressively, the Intranet functionalities became richer and richer, and an obvious extension of great value became apparent: open Intranet access to certain external entities. These Intranets that are shared with external corporations for a particular purpose are called **Extranets**. Figure 3–3 shows a symbolic view of an environment in which company Intranets support a series of applications being used by third parties.

The corporate Extranet is used by Companies A, B, and C through access to a set of applications. For example, Company A may be selling a value-added service or process of goods being manufactured within another company. The tracking system monitors from the moment of sale to the moment of manufacture to the moment of shipping and delivery. Trading partners connect to the company through their relationships with Companies A, B, and C. Often, these trading partners will not be aware that Company A is not the original producer of the item.

In the corporate world, thousands of examples of functioning Extranets performing extremely important services now exist. Some of these examples include

- ARCO[8]—Implemented a secure Extranet to share data and to communicate readily with other oil companies.
- Canadian Coast Guard—Implemented an Extranet to support emergency response exercises related to marine oil.
- Chubb Corporation[9]—Leveraged Extranet technology to give agents, brokers, customers, and business partners access to Chubb's information resources.

FIGURE 3–3   *Angehrn's ICDT model and Extranets*

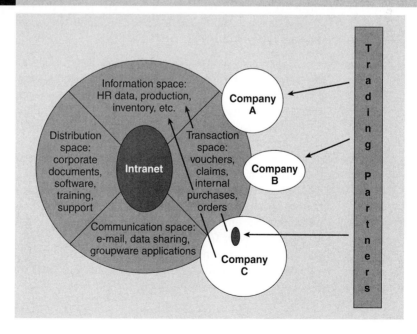

---

[8]P. Watt, "ARCO Surfs Securely," *Network World*, September 28, 1998.
[9]R. Yasin, "Chubb Set for Secure Extranet," *InternetWeek*, July 29, 1998.

- Eastman Kodak—Deployed Aventail ExtraNet Center 3.0 for data sharing, collaboration, and network conferencing solutions.
- Harley Davidson—Uses its Extranet for warranty, recall, and financial information management.
- NN Financial—Uses an Extranet to deliver mainframe data to its partners.
- National Semiconductor—Uses its Extranet for purchasing and customer service support.
- Taco Bell[10]—Linked its Extranet from more than 2,800 franchises to the corporate office using Java-based document sharing software.
- Microsoft—Uses its Extranet to allow its workers to order office supplies and equipment from key suppliers. It cut the staff needed to oversee employee purchase requests from 19 people to 2.
- Texas Instruments—Uses its Extranet to allow employees to order supplies, cutting transaction costs from about $100 per purchase order to $3.50 per order.
- Toro Co.—Uses its Extranet to place its product documentation for dealers. Within the first year, Toro recouped its investment in the Extranet and saved $300,000 by eliminating printing and mailing costs.
- GE Lighting—Used its Extranet to electronically distribute worldwide requests for quotes and bids when buying machine parts. A process that used to take 18 to 23 days was cut in half. Material cost savings were estimated at 5 to 20 percent. All paper and mailing costs were eliminated.
- GE Industrial Systems[11]—Uses its Extranet to provide order processing, custom quoting, and technical information to its customers and delivers it in a dynamic, personalized environment.
- ISIS[12]—Uses its Extranet to provide customers with up-to-date information/downloads relating specifically to their accounts, white papers, online operation manuals, and access to a user group for technical support.
- Communications 2000—Used its Extranet to save thousands of dollars a month to replace mass mailings to 1,100 dealers.

A more complex form of Extranet application is shown in Figure 3–4. A company uses its Intranet to support sales to another corporation as a method to facilitate transactions and to retain business customers. Organizations integrate their sales processes to the clients' purchasing systems, often using tailor-made **middleware**, creating a seamless purchasing process in which the customer configures, orders, obtains electronic approval from superiors, receives invoices, pays automatically, and updates inventory data. A company's legacy system and/or its **Enterprise Resource Planning System**[13] **(ERPS)** are integrated into the firm's front-end (Web-based) systems that interface with the client's. The middleware used for this process is typically tailor-made and evolves over time to create the best form of integrated company view. Sometimes companies, when faced with time constraints, perform this interfacing manually until systems are developed.

Dell Computer Corporation has replaced other microcomputer vendors in sales to corporations by creating special price lists and bulk sales contracts and allowing individual buyers to configure, get electronic approval, and route the orders through both

---

[10]*http://compnetworking.about.com/compute/compnetworking/gi/dynamic/offsite.htm?site=http%3A%2F%2Fidm.internet.com%2Frweb%2Ftacobell.shtml.*

[11]*http://www.geindustrial.com/clnk/default.htm.*

[12]*http://www.isis.co.uk/p.support.extranet.001.asp.*

[13]These are integrated applications to support corporatewide information systems. Among the top software vendors are SAP, PeopleSoft, BAAN, Oracle, and J. D. Edwards.

FIGURE 3–4   *Using Middleware to integrate two corporations' Intranets*

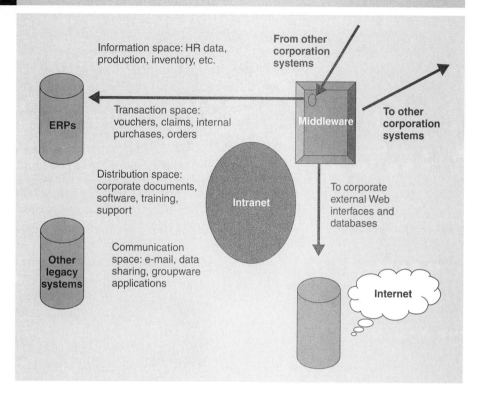

Dell and the client systems. Often this integration may even be semimanual, but from the perspective of the client, systems are integrated, and the purchase process is fluid and well integrated. Integration and facilitation create client loyalties that last for a long time and may transcend price and momentary contingencies.

For many decades, the world of information technology has dictated separated systems with autonomous processes and separate data processing. Internetworking is creating an entirely new set of circumstances where **application service providers (ASPs)** create common platforms that many organizations adopt and companies with intense business relationships share common processes and facilities.

Customer-care Extranets that employ the same documentation and databases used to assist customer support engineers are progressively being made directly available to customers through the Web and other forms of technology such as fax responses and voice response.

Supply chains are being revolutionized by **supplier-managed inventory,** where agreements are made with suppliers that allow suppliers to use just-in-time provision production and sales processes. For example, JCPenney has opened its inventory files to its 2,000 suppliers to keep its stores appropriately stocked with its products. This approach may imply that inventories actually belong to the supplier until a particular item is sold.

These corporate internetworking structures and the opening of internal systems to third parties are important components to the progressive adoption of B2B e-business models with direct electronic dealings, transacting through markets, the formation of consortia, and hub-free peer-to-peer structures.

FIGURE 3–5	*Progressive electronization from fax to EDI*

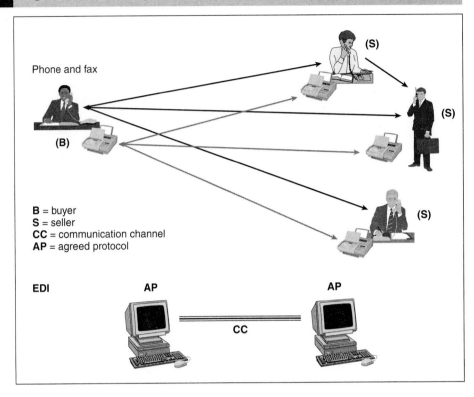

B2B

B2B commerce is defined as business purchases between commercial entities as an intermediate process of value addition until a product, or its derivative, is delivered to the consumer. Business-to-business transactions have evolved from pure manual transactions to electronic data interchange (EDI) transactions, and now to Internet-based purchasing and electronic markets. While electronic marketplaces have received most of the publicity, a progressively substantive electronization of the corporate purchasing processes exists. A substantial number of companies are now migrating to online purchasing, and by 2004, approximately 40 percent of B2B purchases will be made online according to ActivMedia Research.

Manual processes for multiple availability checking and price quoting that had been supplemented by multiple phone calls and faxes are giving way to Internet-intermediated transactions that bring additional efficiencies to the process as illustrated in Figure 3–5.

Market Size Prediction and Top B2B Players

By 2003, B2B e-commerce will draw 90 percent of the projected $1.4 trillion in total Internet-based business. Forrester Research rates the following list of companies as the Top 10 B2B companies for 1999:

- Intel.
- Cisco.

FIGURE 3–6   *Forrester Research's forecasted B2B commerce by sector*

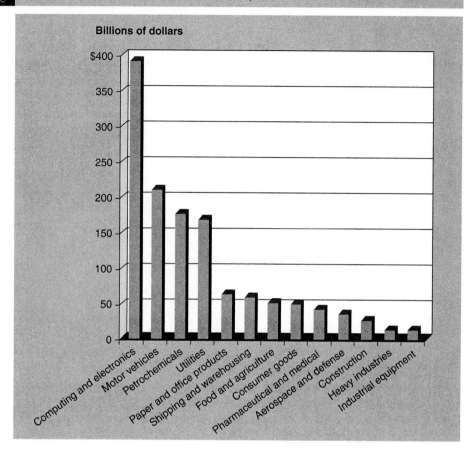

- Dell.
- Boise Cascade office products.
- W. W. Grainger.
- 3 Com.
- IBM.
- Gateway 2000.
- Sabre Group.
- Office Depot.

More than 1,200 ventures have been announced in the formation of B2B markets, and by the end of the year 2000 an estimated 400 of these markets were functioning at some level. Even at this incipient stage, some markets have already folded or have been abandoned by their proponents.

Sector Predictions

Figure 3–6 displays Forrester Research's predictions of sector-based B2B commerce. These numbers are affected by the current size of the market, effect of electronization on the size of these markets, and the expected speed of deployment of the electronization of the industry. The computing and electronics sectors will continue to lead this market, followed by motor vehicles, petrochemicals, and paper and office products.

B2B Characteristics

B2B is intrinsically different than B2C. Typically margins in B2B transactions are much narrower with much larger volumes. While brand in the anonymous international world of the Internet has become very important in B2C as a product differentiator, B2B is of a different nature. B2B buyers, most of the time, are professional purchasing agents and have substantive competency and resources to dedicate to product selection. Consequently, while still important in the B2B arena, brand is less of a factor than in the B2C domain.

In recent years, substantive B2B relationships, while attempting to gather economies of scale and technological leverage, have benefitted from EDI connections that required heavy protocoling of the relationship (with agreement on standards) and private communication links (see Chapter 6). Often the EDI link would depend on EDI providers and proprietary technology, generally leading to expensive solutions. With the rise of the Internet and its TCP/IP infrastructure, progressive development of a series of "open EDI" standards has been sought and continuously developed. The TCP/IP infrastructure has the following characteristics:

- It is very low in incremental costs.
- It has no need for proprietary channels.
- Its environment is very appropriate for transaction processing.

From a proprietary and expensive solution, Web-based EDI businesses now have progressively integrated applications among different entities (see Chapter 6).

When GM started requiring its suppliers to use EDI in its downstream interactions, it often required the might of GM's power to force EDI to come into place as well as substantive investments by the supplier. Today, businesses voluntarily strive to create paperless connections integrating loosely or tightly with their clients. The B2B environment has evolved into a series of characteristics that explain and determine today's environment.

The traditional EDI interface can be represented by Figure 3–5, which illustrates the relationships among a buyer (B), a seller (S), a communication channel (CC), and a set of agreed protocols (AP) that allow form equivalents to travel between the two entities. The EDI formal schema is an evolution of a paper-based system where, for example, B performs its internal processes to generate a purchase order. The purchase order in EDI is formalized into a set of electronic records that is the form equivalent. This form equivalent is transmitted over the CC to S, which captures the records, extracts the relevant fields, and inserts these into the order database that controls its processes. Eventually, shipping confirmation, invoicing, and confirmation of payment order through a bank may flow in the opposite direction to complement the transaction while goods are shipped and received. Even shipping receipts and adjustments may be entered by B's receiving department into B's databases and also transmitted to S.

Even in this formal model some variations may occur. For example, the EDI CC may only be a channel for the transmission of electronic documents (say, Word images), and humans are necessary on both sides to extract the information and enter it into the legacy systems of the B and S. Or B has rather sophisticated mechanisms to receive a set of records (obeying AP) that painlessly are routed to the appropriate applications. The modern B2B environment expands on many of these elements in both technological solutions and business processes that constitute a wider set of activities.

Buyer and Seller will use the Internet to replace the proprietary solution of EDI and will deal with each other in a progressively expanding set of forms of behavior. B and S may participate in a market where transactions are executed according to different business models. For example, B may bid for an article presented by another entity in an auction marketplace, and use a peer-to-peer method of payment (e.g., PayPal) to settle the transaction. On the other hand, S may be part of an organized market with fixed prices that are placed in an e-catalog. A third alternative is that they participate in a commodity market where transactions are agreed when bid and ask prices meet. These scenarios add another element to the puzzle—the market (M), which also has its own characteristics. Figure 3–7 introduces markets in the B2B scenario and market attributes.

Markets present many dimensions of characteristics such as ownership, business model, visibility of entities, degree of IT integration, settlement arrangements, revenue sources for the market makers, and the nature of the market platform as illustrated in Figure 3–8. While the discussion following tries to present an organized rational taxonomy or schemata that represent markets, the essence of the B2B evolution is the progressive engineering of markets that have supposedly improved models for satisfying the need for added value to customers. Consequently, competition drives versatility, experimentation, and development of hybrid models.

Vertical and Horizontal Markets

Markets can be classified as vertical and horizontal markets. **Vertical markets** focus on one industry and provide an environment for not only transactions but for job postings, industry news, technical advice, and other information services. For example, ALTRA, a very successful liquid gas exchange, is considered a vertical market.

Horizontal markets offer one type of service or product across industries benefiting from less industry specialization and more economies of scale. For example, MRO.com offers services to many different industries.

FIGURE 3–7   *Markets and market attributes*

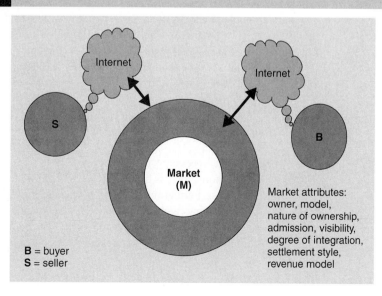

B = buyer
S = seller

Market attributes:
owner, model,
nature of ownership,
admission, visibility,
degree of integration,
settlement style,
revenue model

FIGURE 3–8	Dimensions of market attributes

Who owns the market (or market maker)?
- A corporation that is a big player in the market
- A consortium from players in the market
- A corporation that specializes in setting up trading markets

Business model of the market
- E-catalog market
- Auction market
- Barter market
- Reverse auction market

Nature of the ownership of the market
- Owned by independent entrepreneurs
- Owned by a small number of large market players (closed ownership)
- Owned by industry players with open ownership

Criteria for admission of players
- Any business may buy or sell (no screening)
- Sellers are scrutinized and approved; often pay membership fees
- Buyers and sellers are scrutinized
- Only buyers are scrutinized

Visibility of the entities of the transaction
- Buyer and seller are identifiable
- Buyer or seller are identifiable
- Double blind market: the market does all the intermediation and assumes some liability (maybe through insurance) over the transaction

Degree of integration with the IT of the players
- No integration: buyers and sellers use Web forms to activate transactions and capture their information through manual middleware
- Sellers can post and update information in the market maker system while buyers use manual methods of collection

Settlement style
- Buyers and sellers are left to fend for themselves
- Market maker serves as a settler
- Hybrid model

Revenue source of the market maker
- Transaction fees
- Storefront rental for sellers
- Information services for participants
- Market activities on their own behalf
- Capture of valuable market information sold elsewhere
- Banners on market pages
- Subscription fees
- Hybrid

Nature of the market platform used
- Vendor (e.g., Commerce One, Arriba)
- Single model (e.g., auction)
- Multiple model (e.g., direct and inverted auctions)

Necessary Technology

Many players have evolved in the software support markets to support B2B. These software models tend to be focused on a singular type of approach, such as an auction, commodity market, or e-catalog. The next generation of software platforms will support hybrid models or joint platforms of companies that cater to more than one approach of market making. A trend is emerging by the big B2B players (e.g., Dell Computer) to customize middleware that smoothly integrates internal systems with client systems to create strong company bonds and process interconnection. The subsequent generation of market software will provide a rich toolset to facilitate this integration, in particular with ERPs and widely adopted e-commerce platforms.

New Processes and Necessary Technologies

The e-business phenomenon has brought in a series of new technologies on top of the internetworking process. Furthermore, several new emerging technologies are going to substantially change the panorama of industry. The emergence of a large number of small startups having no experience with controls, mediocre competence, and little commitment to traditional IT processes has harnessed the emergence of a new set of players, the application service providers (ASPs). Also, peer-to-peer computing offers the opportunity of the formation of shared markets without a centralized market or exchange. Furthermore, the development of technologies for intelligent agents may be automated and accelerate some of the basic changes proportioned by the emergence of e-businesses.

Application Service Providers

ASPs are a new form of the old data centers. With the progressive popularization of ASPs, a new form of process sharing has emerged: ASP host applications that many organizations use. Consequently, they share the economies of common developing, platforming, and managing applications. This is a popular solution for outsourcing processes, in particular those that do not provide competitive advantage or are core competencies. On the other hand, rapid product deployment, low capitalization business deployment, and the ability to have businesses with little residual onus are three components any one of which can be very important in the development of a sustainable advantage or competitive competency. Consequently, the mixing of the methods to obtain these processes may be, by itself, a competitive advantage that may be larger than owning and producing a core competence. ASP utilization must be considered in the framework of business objectives, timeliness, immobilization of resources, and the virtual nature of the indigenous Internet businesses. Modern internetworking technology, with its dimensionally improved communications, allows companies to divide their value chains into small pieces and dispose of the pieces for which no core competency or competitive advantage exists.

Peer-to-Peer Models

"When companies can complete complex transactions among themselves through peer-to-peer networks, the need for centralized exchanges decreases dramatically.[14] As mentioned earlier, B2B e-business models started with the automation of the purchasing process and creating channels between the company and some of its suppliers. After this start, the markets have been flooded with proposed markets and consortia. Many of these are going to survive and prosper, but an alternative will emerge where companies pool together in a peer-to-peer method (such as Napster) with or without a central directory and directly create methods of trading without intermediation. This approach will tend to emerge in technologically savvy atomistic sectors that have the most to gain from the approach. Very likely, supporting software will initially be freeware, and eventually businesses will opt for paying to obtain a common standard, some security, and some commonality of standards.

Agents

The current stage of Internet technology has users employing brute force or information aggregators deriving value from the discontinuities of the Internet information. To compare prices, a user has to visit numerous websites and compare items and pieces of information that are difficult to compare. Alternatively, the user may visit a price comparison site put together by a third party (e.g., *www.pricewatch.com*) to perform this task. A new class of software called **intelligent agents** is emerging that will change the status quo as discussed in Chapter 13. Of particular interest are three classes of agents:

- Price comparison agents.
- Buying or selling agents.
- Fraud detection agents.

These software agents, when perfected and operational, will notably change the scenarios of B2B and B2C.

---

[14]A. McAfee, "The Napsterization of B2B," *Harvard Business Review*, November–December 2000.

EMERGING B2B PROBLEMS

B2B ventures and markets have been touted as a panacea for the future and have received a fair share of negative publicity. However, a point should be considered—after the shakeout of startups and the growth of business models to some degree of maturity and stability, a cadre of more permanent problems, not unique to B2B, will emerge and will be permanent features of this sector. Among these problems are

- Antitrust issues.
- Control issues on the market sites.
- Virus and security problems in the sites.
- Privacy of data issues in relation to the markets.

These problems will permeate the environment, likely with greater severity than traditional business enterprises, due to the multiplicity of players.

ELECTRONIC MARKETS

This section illustrates how three industries are affected by electronic markets: auto, airlines, and professional services.

Auto Industry

The success of exchanges will be determined largely by how well high-profile examples perform. Covisint, the auto industry's parts and supplies exchange, has had a very slow start. The big three auto makers got together in the spring of 2000 to automate their procurement processes and reduce costs. They had an expectation of cutting about $100 of processing costs per order. They could collaborate in the supply chain and communicate through just-in-time delivery of parts, collaborative design, and engineering. The expectation is that 30,000 suppliers will have lower inventories, better design, and better communication with their customers.

Ultimately, the electronization of the purchasing process will facilitate built-to-order cars, reduce the lag of manufacturing, and decrease costs for all parties. Covisint started very slowly and had difficulties finding an appropriate CEO. After the Big Three (Ford, GM, and Daimler Chrysler) activated the exchange, Renault and Nissan joined the exchange, but by the end of 2000, they had only 35 of the desired 30,000 suppliers signed up.

Airline Industry

The airlines and some independent players have announced a series of plans to form marketplaces. In April 2000, six airlines—American, Continental, Delta, United, British Airways, and Air France—announced plans to form an Internet marketplace. The marketplace would facilitate the buying and selling of fuel, fuel-related services, engine components, and the like. The amount of goods to be transacted in this marketplace was forecasted at $32 billion per year. The investment cost to build this market is $50 million. British Airways said it plans to reduce the number of its suppliers from 14,000 to 2,000 and to significantly cut transaction costs. By 2002, British Airways' goal is to place 80 percent of its orders online.

The Professional Services Firms

The professional services firms (CPA firms) are in a major transition phase, where consulting arms are being potentially jettisoned. These firms have seen the B2B markets as an opportunity, and they have jumped in with gusto.

Accenture (formerly Andersen Consulting), iPlanet, and Sun Microsystems are investing $300 million to set up a system to provide electronic buying services for businesses. The goal is to help businesses lower their costs on frequently purchased items, such as travel and office supplies. They hope to facilitate in excess of $200 billion of such spending by 2004. They already have $20 billion in spending commitments from firms in the financial services, chemical, automotive, and telecommunications sectors.

PriceWaterhouseCoopers and Informatica have joined forces to jointly develop, sell, and support analytic solutions for the B2B e-commerce market. Their goal is to help e-businesses thoroughly evaluate their performances across key operational areas and ultimately make better-informed strategic decisions. Specifically, they will focus on customer-relationship management and B2B procurement processes.

STRATEGY

The triad—technology, business model, and service—has served to spark the e-business revolution through the B2C and B2B waves. The failure of many startup companies may at first glance appear to announce unsuccessful strategies; however, this is not necessarily the case. Consider the entrepreneur who started a business with a dream out of his garage and $20,000 in cash. The entrepreneur went through a series of angel financing rounds, issued an IPO, and, at its peak, had a company valued at $1 billion in the market. Six months later he went bankrupt. Perhaps in the process, he sold some of his stock before it plummeted. In the end, he was left with a richer résumé, a few million dollars in the bank, and a wealth of experience to share about e-business. He also had offers of new jobs as manager in dot-coms, as advisor for investment banks, and for board of director positions. The firm's strategies were great to *start* the business, at that point in time, and to provide very rapid growth but, ultimately, not particularly good ones to *mature* the business. While the result may have both successes and failures for the entrepreneur, the investors in the company are the ones financially damaged by the ultimately poor business strategy. While some generalities may be postulated that are applicable to many situations, in general, the organization has many contingencies, and strategies are applicable subject to these contingencies. Among these dimensions we find

- Type of entity (individual versus corporate).
- Stage of the business (startup, rapid growth, mature, declining or dying).
- Sector of the economy.
- Product pricing strategy.
- Income and prestige objectives of management and their exit strategies.

Startup businesses will often plan to operate in the red for a while. The obscene valuations of the early Internet days that financed much of their growth with equity created very bad habits in some dot-coms. More sober days are bringing dot-coms back to the reality that profits must be realized and the company must save to grow. Companies with rapid market share growth and/or creation of their own markets have very different economics. Very often, while traditional strategy does not recognize it, share acquisition is justifiable and will eventually be justified by across-the-value-chain plays. Mature companies follow traditionalist strategies. To rejuvenate, often such companies work on the acquisition of dot-coms to shake their cultures and forcefully bring in new thoughts and talents.

While often neglected in the discussion of strategy, the sector of the economy has substantive influence on strategy and the processes of electronization. Capital-intensive entities will behave very differently from service organizations and bitable-goods companies. This parameter influences very strongly the speed and methods of electronization.

The first wave of e-commerce generally focused on replicating traditional business models onto the Internet using static pricing schemes. The second wave of e-commerce is driven by dynamic commerce applications that use the Internet's intrinsic capacity for continuous activity to create new types of fluid, market-driven environments.

Exit Strategy

Unfortunately, some dot-coms have had **exit strategies** that upon profitable exit of the entrepreneur leave a dying entity and its investors holding an empty bag. Corporate objectives tend to include sustainable growth and shareholder retention and return, but poor strategies may not deliver the fruition of these objectives. Figure 3–9 displays a view of the life cycle of an Internet venture. After the initial idea, Internet entrepreneurs will typically gather a core of associates who help in the procurement of initial resources. While some of the initial resources are typically from the originator(s), the prototypical

FIGURE 3–9	Startup initiation processes

Financing Round	*Definition*	*Typical Amounts*	*Who Typically Plays*
Seed	Proof of concept	$25,000–$500,000	Individual angels Angel groups Early-stage venture capitalists
Startup	Complete product development and initial marketing	$500,000–$3,000,000	Select individual angels Angel groups Early-stage venture capitalists
First	Initiate full-scale manufacturing and sales	$1,500,000–$5,000,000	Venture capitalists
Second	Working capital for initial business expansion	$3,000,000–$10,000,000	Venture capitalists Private placement firms
Third	Expansion capital to achieve breakeven	$5,000,000–$30,000,000	Venture capitalists Private placement firms
Bridge	Financing to allow company to go public in 6–12 months	$3,000,000–$20,000,000	Mezzanine financing firms Private placement firms Investment bankers
Going public	Obtaining equity capital from public markets		

Adapted from M. J. Roberts, H. J. Stevenson, and K. P. Morse, "Angel Investing," Harvard Business School, 9-800-273.

venture will rapidly have to resort to "angels" who will come in the form of friends, relatives, acquaintances, or venture capitalists. At this stage a substantive set of concessions must be made in terms of giving up control, share of the company, and freedom of movement. Typically after a couple of rounds of financing, progressively further diluting originator ownership, the business is at a more mature stage ready for a potential initial public offering (IPO) or acquisition. **Venture capitalists (VCs)** will often drill the entrepreneurs on their exit strategy, which means how they are going to realize value. Of course, for the VCs, this is a very important issue that often determines their willingness to invest. On the other hand, many entrepreneurs do not contemplate exit, but sustainable growth.

The Business Plan of a Dot-Com

A startup will begin with the idea of a group of entrepreneurs and their initial setup efforts. Very early in the process they will procure support, financing, facilities, credit, or other business-related elements. For that purpose, a **business plan**[15] will be written that encompasses at least a generic description of the idea, a plan of action, an assessment of the markets, a pro forma set of financial statements, and a description of the management team and its backgrounds and skills.

The statistics on the survival of startups are astounding. In the first year of existence only 15 percent of the ventures survive, while only 35 percent of the startups that make it to the end of the first year make it to the second. While these numbers are very low, they may be exaggerated because many firms do not survive in their current form but morph by acquisition, merger, acquisition of assets, or other organizational transformation. This **organizational morphing** includes primarily companies that are merged or acquired. Actually, a surprising phenomenon is that more companies do not take this path instead of just closing the doors. Webmergers.com conducted a survey and interpreted the reasons more companies do not bail out through mergers. Here are some of the findings:

- Some Internet companies do not have a sustainable business model or built-up set of assets.
- Many rapidly ran out of money before other strategies could be considered.
- Venture capitalists are too busy to play "matchmaker."
- Internet expertise does not need to be purchased via a company anymore; other talent outlets have grown.
- Many brick-and-mortar companies are taking a wait-and-see strategy.

Parameters of Strategy

Strategies in the Internet domain have been rather different than in the traditional domain. As discussed in Chapter 2, the main issue is not e-commerce, but the electronization of business. Indigenous Internet companies have an intrinsic advantage in electronization because no existing traditional (snail) processes exist. Kanter[16] calls these

---

[15]Stanley R. Rich and David E. Gumpert, "How to Write a Winning Business Plan," *Harvard Business Review*, May–June 1995.

[16]R. M. Kanter, "The Ten Deadly Mistakes of Wanna-Dots," *Harvard Business Review,* January–February 2001.

electrolyzing traditional companies **wanna-dots** and prescribes a series of rules to avoid. Based on some of these anti-rules, the following principles can be postulated to facilitate electronization:

1. Relax corporate standards vis-à-vis budgets, controls, return on investment, and corporate compensation. These are very different in emerging businesses. To attract mature Internet talent and to create the passion needed, a more "Silicon Valley" set of rules must apply. Growth, innovation, incentive options, and ownership are highly prized and increase personnel retention.

2. Revisit the perception of the entity's competition and understand that the components of business are being reconstructed with unknown companies invading profitable parts of the **internal value chain.** Constantly understand that highly performing elements of the internal value chain can also be treated as a new product capable of invading another industry's value chain (the **external value chain**). Constantly search for expanded services to be sold to clients along the value chain. For example, Dell and UPS, allied in the logistic of delivering PCs to consumers and integrating their tracking systems, found that a profitable service of assembling the computer for the consumer could be introduced.

3. Focus on a few visible and responsible electronization efforts. These efforts must have crisp objectives and short-term deadlines. Cisco prizes itself that all projects must not exceed six months and must have clearly determined savings and investments.

4. Take the electronization revolution seriously. Do not dismiss certain efforts as a passing fad. While many dot-coms have had difficulties, many will be permanent fixtures of the corporate panorama, and pioneering methods may forever change some processes of business. Gone are the days when industrial concerns could lack a thorough understanding of the client. An essential feature is to have good client information and use it to provide product customization and directed marketing.

5. Find vendors who are attuned to the organization's morphing efforts and take this change seriously, not just as an opportunity to sell services. Find vendors who commit to your objectives and will keep long-term relationships and adapt with the morphing of your organization.

6. Electronization is not just replicating corporate processes with the use of the Internet, it entails serious rethinking and reengineering of a company's processes. Examine the seriousness of these vendors by reviewing their own competence in internal applications. If they cannot do it for themselves, they are either technically unable or insincere about the needs.

7. Offer incentives for joint cooperation among departments in the cyber efforts. Create joint targets with rewards and penalties that depend on joint efforts.

8. Focus on the customer by putting in place extensive mechanisms to collect customer data; to respond to pre-, during, and postsales; and to potentially have a channel directly to the consumer.

9. Create easy-to-use tools to electronize simple processes and distribute these among the different parts of the organization. Efforts of creating paperless environments, corporate human resource databases, electronic signatures, automatic order approval, automatic error correction, and early problem warning fall into this category.

10. Create new benchmarks to evaluate corporate performance in its electronization. The process of industry morphing has created unusual competitors along the different internal value chain processes. Benchmark each module and create metrics of intermodule cooperation and synergies.

Traditional Strategic Thinking and Core Competencies

> In the 1990s companies will be judged on their ability to identify, cultivate, and exploit the core competencies that make growth possible—indeed, they'll have to rethink the corporation itself. (*Prahalad & Hamel, 1990*)

The concept of **core competency** drove much of the strategic thinking of the nineties. Companies strove to develop competencies that allowed them to gain unique positioning in markets, compare positively with the competition, and grow the business in a sustainable long-term path. Companies built the divisions and products around the core competencies as depicted in Figure 3–10. A core competence can be identified by three attributes:

- It provides potential access to a variety of markets.
- It should make a significant contribution to the perceived customer benefits of the end product.
- It should be difficult for competitors to imitate.

These core competencies are still relevant in the Internet age. However, they now assume new facades, with rapid change and constant morphing, bringing some of the old postures to new situations.

Low-Cost Providers

Traditional strategic thinking states that sustainable growth and success are contingent on organizations managing to be **low-cost providers.** Cost inefficiencies in the long term are not sustainable in traditional thinking. On the other hand, this may not be as relevant in Internet thinking. The new economy, and digital products in particular, have substantially different economics than traditional business. For example, the new economy is full of emerging firms that provide their main (digital) product for free and

FIGURE 3–10	*Core competencies*

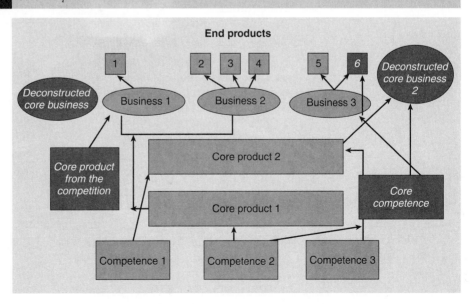

do not have an obvious revenue path. Netscape gave its browser to consumers at no charge; Dialpad, a telephony-over-IP firm discussed later in this chapter, provides free net-to-phone minutes; freePC (now defunct) provided PCs for free. In particular, bitable products have very different cost curves where, for example, the initial production of software is very expensive but the incremental cost of distributing a piece of software is negligible. Consequently, provisioning certain bitable goods has big initial fixed costs and negligible incremental costs. Unusual strategies follow these cost structures.

The Effects of Competition

The traditional emphasis of strategy studies deal with competition. Porter[17] states that "The essence of strategic formulation is coping with competition. Yet it is easy to view competition too narrowly or too pessimistically. While one sometimes hears executives complaining to the contrary, intense competition in an industry is neither coincidence nor bad luck." He proceeds to state that market competition is rooted in the industry economics, market forces, substitute products, and other factors. Figure 3–11 presents an adaptation of the Porter competitive framework picture.

In the new economy, dot-coms—when creatively formulated—have no competition . . . for a while. Their economics entail staying viable and building market share and morphing rapidly to avoid the emergence of competition. Yahoo, a superb success story, has evolved from a search engine to a location and advertising play to a brilliant dynamic multiplay company with e-mail, customization of plays, affiliations, alliances, and other Internet strategy moves that, unlike other content/advertising plays, is prof-

---

FIGURE 3–11   *Competitive factors and forces in an industry*

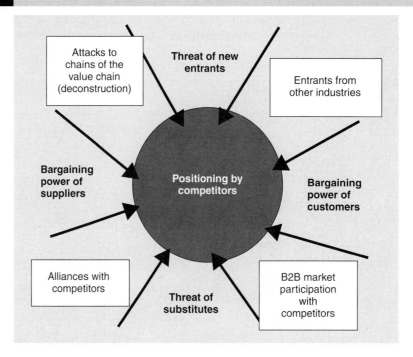

---

[17]M. E. Porter, "How Competitive Forces Shape Strategy," *Harvard Business Review,* March–April 1979.

itable and clearly has sustainable value. No company in the current Internet scenario can be labeled as a real competitor for Yahoo because of its unorthodox sector play and its constant morphing.

New Economy Thinking—Deconstructing the Value Chain

Strategically, **deconstruction** functions as an offensive weapon, where the firm examines its core competencies and chooses attractive links of the competition's or other industry's value chain to place a competitive offer. At the same time, deconstruction is the classic tool through which startup dot-coms tend to threaten the value chain of established businesses. Indigenous Internet businesses starting from zero have the luxury of choosing areas of action and not having to carry baggage of statutory and historical actions of the past. Consider the following questions:

> What will happen to category killers such as Toys "R" Us and the Home Depot when a search engine on the Internet gives the consumers more choice than any store? What will be the point to having a supplier relationship with GE when it posts its purchasing requirement on the Internet and entertains bids from anyone? What will happen to health care providers if a uniform electronic format for patient records eliminates a major barrier for patients to switch hospitals and doctors?[18]

Ultimately, deconstruction is the force that will make organizations reengineer their applications, choose core competencies to compete out of context across industries, and cause entire industries to morph into very different forms and contexts, developing **synergies across the value chain.**

Judo Strategy

Competition on the Internet[19] is creating a new scenario of divergence in which small-scale startups are competing with later-entrant industry giants. Smart startups bypass these conflicts by rapid movement and turning the dominant players' strengths against them. The three principles of **Judo strategy** are rapid movement, flexibility, and leverage.

The **rapid movement principle** implies that small companies are more agile and do not have the structural restraint of established businesses. Consequently, they can change and adapt at a pace that traditional (in particular, brick-and-mortar) companies, cannot. For example, both IBM and Microsoft are tied to existing software architectures and when new/upgrade products are announced, they must maintain compatibility so as not to alienate their existing customer base. If they were to abandon their architectures, they would create a situation that would force customers to leave large software investments and have to make choices. Choice time is dangerous for established companies because it forces customers to rethink their strategies and look at the competition.

The **flexibility principle** implies that small companies cannot tackle face-to-face competition with their established competitors. Consequently, they must give way when faced with frontal attack and morph their strategies and products. The **leverage principle** implies small companies cannot exert the kind of leverage that large established businesses can with their PR, advertising, and multimillion-dollar lines of credits. But

---

[18]C. W. Stern and G. Stalk, Jr. *Perspectives on Strategy from the Boston Consulting Group,* John Wiley & Sons, New York, 1998.
[19]D. B. Yoffie and M.A. Cusumano, Judo Strategy: The Competitive Dynamcs of Internet Time," *Harvard Business Review,* January–February 1999.

once large leverage is applied, established companies move as steamrollers and have little mobility. The same leverage that helps large companies also creates a lack of mobility that can be exploited by smaller, more agile dot-coms. These principles are true to Internet companies and progressively are being used to retain position in the confrontation between brick-and-mortars and dot-coms.

Corporate Strategic Plays

Corporations understand that the electronization of their processes is an inevitable and essential step. They are also, however, confronted with an array of conflicting news, advice, and contingencies provided by the public media and consulting firms. Electronization—for improving existing processes, creating a new channel (electronic), or creating new products—is inevitable and its speed may yield a competitive advantage; however, the strategies for its achievement are not clear. Overall, a company can achieve an electronic channel through four main ways:

- Acquire it from an existing (maybe bankrupt) venture.
- Develop it from scratch.
- Use deconstruction, niche product/service.
- Create alliances and affiliation.

While no cookie-cutter solution exists that offers a better approach, traditional strategies must be complemented with intense use of e-thinking. This thinking must go along the following dimensions, illustrated in Figure 3–12.

Acquiring Strategy (Pac Man)
The acquisition of existing e-entities is a step of small resistance. With proper inducements, entities can be purchased with facilities, strategies, and competent, motivated personnel that may have run out of funding or options, but with good potential to complement an existing brick-and-mortar business with resources, brand, and a traditional management. Among the recent examples of this **acquired strategy** we find a series of moves with brick-and-mortars buying faltering industry businesses that need a piece of the value chain that is not available. Drugstore.com sold a 37 percent share to Rite Aid

FIGURE 3–12	*E-thinking strategies*

Stage of the business	New business Established business Industry leader
E-objective	New channel Process improvement New e-product De-(re)construction
Strategy of electronization	Create entity Acquire existing business (bankrupt, in trouble, viable, and active)
Alliance and affiliation	Buy part of the company Create joint income targets Use joint platforms

in order to use the drug prescription reimbursement mechanism of the brick-and-mortar establishment. CVS acquired SOMMA instead of building an e-commerce channel. Successful e-commerce ventures are the ones that gobble up pieces that help make them whole (Yahoo, Microsoft, Gateway, and Amazon.com have used their mighty market valuations to acquire complements) and avoid being absorbed into the traditional mainstream.

Build Independently

As mentioned in Chapter 1, Air Products and Chemicals built its online market information and sales site for its gas products, and Boeing created a site to sell its spare parts. By trying to **build independently**, both of these extensions have been very successful for the B2B companies. Air Products, however, is choosing alternative routes as well, such as using VerticalNet, to ensure that it can reach all of its customers.

Subdivide and Conquer

The same attribute of size and might that makes giants such as IBM, Microsoft, and now Cisco the leaders of their industries and larger than several of their closer competitors is also their Achilles' heel. Startups can find a nice niche and then **subdivide and conquer.** Companies, while never able to meet IBM head to head, have traditionally found a place in the deconstructed value chain and concentrated all their efforts (and patents) on finding a niche. The start of Sun (large workstations), Apple (microcomputers), Microsoft (microcomputer operating systems), Adobe (graphic display standards), and Hewlett Packard (laser printer division) consisted mainly of niche plays of great vitality, taking advantage of the structural difficulties and lack of agility of a multibillion-dollar company.

Adopting Internet thinking (deconstruction) and niche product thinking can be associated with understanding the value chain and placing competitive efforts in a promising product niche at a place on the value chain that is not an established industry.

Meet Your Enemies

In the modern world of megacorporations, the concept of competition has evolved, and many new phenomena can be observed. Companies morph industries as corporate strategy. For example, Intuit, a personal financial software maker, became a powerful Internet-based financial service provider through a judicious mix of divisional startups, **affiliations**, and **alliances.** Companies buy and sell capacity in B2B exchanges, and the trading partners are mainly their competitors. Companies join B2B **consortia** with their competition to jointly benefit economies of scale or the economies of electronization. Companies pool with the competition to create capacity. For example, AT&T has created joint ventures with its fiercest long-distance competitors (MCI and Sprint) to build underwater fiber networks across seas and oceans. Companies jointly source commodity products and sell them at different brand names. For example, a major producer of canned fruits markets under its own name and then produces, in the same facility, private brands for grocery chains. These are then sold at substantially different prices. To sell globally, companies will resort to joint sourcing and joint inventorying in smaller markets with labeling (of the same product under different labels) occurring after the moment of sale. These effects eventually will reduce international price differences for the same product and bring in a great degree of **commoditization** of many products. Furthermore, companies will struggle to create unique factors about their offers to identify their offers for their buyers. Amazon.com sells the same books as all other bookstores, but it has invested enormous amounts of money in advertising its huge catalog and creating a world-class customer service organization. All of these efforts are known as **meet your enemies.**

Free Play Strategies

Strategies for dot-com startups are of a very different nature than for traditional brick-and-mortar companies. The **free plays** are the ultimate reflection of this fact. Cost structures for Internet businesses imply reasonably low setup costs and low or close to zero incremental costs in providing the services, access, or siting. Depending on the nature of the business, very different cost structures may be implied, but overall, the parallel curves of revenue and expense do not occur as in physical goods. Consequently, the provisioning of services has a different nature and cost structure. Overall, in many of the free plays mentioned below, the expected model is the exponential expansion of the services with its implicit value, and, in parallel, the potential immediate revenue from banners, subscriptions, and referrals. In the early stages of these plays, the free service has dominated. Some examples include

- *Free web hosting.* Homestead.com is among a few ventures that offer free website hosting. Others include *www.netfirms.com, www.prohosting.com, www.atfreeeweb.com,* and *www.freeservers.com.* These sites tend to rely on the traffic brought in to draw banner, sponsorship, and other anciliary income.
- *Free commonware space.* Zkey.com allows users to place information for free on the Web. Among this type of information can be calendar, address book, chat (zroom), e-mail, and, most interesting, the ability to post files on the Web and share with authorized parties.
- *Free e-commerce platform. www.bigstep.com* allows users to build a free e-commerce site with very easy-to-build tools. Its revenue model waits for site sales to charge transaction fees once the site is operating.
- *Free internet telephony.* Both Dialpad.com and Net2phone.com offer free Internet-to-phone telephone calls within the United States. IP telephony (or telephone over the Internet) has been a much-touted innovation. Industry experts forecast[20] universal telephone connectivity in 5 to 10 years for about 2 cents a minute over the Internet, regardless of distance. Dialpad.com has done better; it provides free telephone calls throughout the United States and free inbound calls. Dialpad is an expansion success story. It boasts more than 11 million accounts and has progressively incorporated several income models to its website. Dialpad's website has many banners and logos displayed, and when a call is being made it creates an interstitial window where advertisements are displayed. Dialpad is a private company and is progressively trying to incorporate international long distance in its offerings, now entailing 39 countries at deep discount rates ranging from 4 to 49 cents a minute. The quality of the calls is low, but it is usable and improving. A regular long-distance call, U.S. to U.S., will pay an access charge outbound, a long-distance charge, and an access charge on the receiving side. An idiosyncrasy exists that no outbound access charges are present for Internet calls, and if the Internet is used for long distance, the company still has to pay the receiving inbound charges. An expensive endeavor if 11 million users are active! Understanding the ultimate revenue model of Dialpad is somewhat difficult unless it is an across-the-value-chain termination play, where it would sell off its 11 million accounts to a regional phone company trying to become national. At this point, the free U.S. calls play must be a very expensive one since termination fees exist (approximately 2 cents a minute) for each call.[21]

---

[20]F. Caincross, *Death of Distance,* Harvard Business School Press, 1998.

[21]Visit *www.dialpad.com.*

Currently we find these sites full of secondary revenue sources and maturing toward a sustainable model. Some sites, such as Dialpad, have matured into keeping its free U.S. calls model and attempting to draw income from international calls through selling merchandise, banners, and affiliations. While some free plays have disappeared (e.g., FreePC.com), the general category has shown remarkable resilience with survival rates better than certain categories of B2B and B2C ventures.

A SCHEMATA TO ANALYZE E-BUSINESS STRATEGY

While dot-com startup proposals are of great value in the evaluation of startup businesses, having a generic methodology—complete with key questions to ask that help the comprehension of the scope, value, and sustainability of the proposals—is important and useful. The ensuing discussion addresses these particular issues.

The Source of Income

Dot-coms, even those that serve the B2B sector, have a tendency to be unclear on the actual expected source of the income and long-term trends. In general, Internet-based companies have found that advertising (using the many forms related to the Internet) is not sufficient as a source of income. Consequently, the following items should be addressed:

- Is the model sustainable?
- Is this an across-the-value-chain play?
- Is this an exit strategy with no residual value?
- Is this an information play where value is acquired through collecting individual, corporate, or market information?

Size the Markets

A Web-based proposal must typically be considered in terms of the size of a particular market being proposed and under some assumptions of market share growth and comparability with the traditional service/products. Just by estimating the existing market for the product through overall estimation, segmentation, and acquisition rates, the analyst develops a reasonable feeling for the maximum that can be obtained.

Identify and Assess the Existing Market

In the case of an existing market, market estimation is easier, but the analyst must consider the fuzziness of cyber tools and assessment methodologies in assessing Web-based market value. For example, the analyst can rigorously study the size of the market for business use of mobile commerce devices in the southwestern United States. However, offering an enticing and well-trafficked electronic channel of B2B sales and related wireless services may conceivably increase the size of the market by drawing some otherwise noninterested businesses to purchase these devices on behalf of their employees. If this increase is noteworthy, it can be said that the e-market is stimulative to the market, not purely cannibalistic of the market.

E-Markets and New Plays

On the other hand, new B2B Internet plays are particularly difficult to position in terms of new revenues, market size, and cannibalization of products. When VerticalNet was launched, it was very difficult to estimate the size of the market volume, and whether trading partners would repeatedly come back for their B2B purchases. For example, a purchaser of gas products may match up with Air Products via VerticalNet. Over time, however, as the business relationship becomes stronger and the customer becomes aware of the other services available on Air Products' own website, would they continue to purchase via the market or directly from Air Products' own Web-based system?

Ventro's Chemdex market was highly acclaimed and cited as the example of B2B markets to come. While its demise by itself cannot be taken as a definite indictment of the model, it is an indication of the difficulties independent markets that do not belong to a cabal of major suppliers or customers may face. The last two years has displayed major creativity of the markets with the creation of a large set of alternative business models trying to cater to the multitrillion-dollar B2B market.

Regarding B2B electronic auctions, market size is easier to estimate than B2C because of industry purchasing data. However, estimation of market size is still complicated due to competitive forces and the possibility that multiple auctions may crop up that compete for sales. Markets are progressively being formed either by infomediaries or by industry consortia. In general terms, the most likely markets will be dominated by the sparser set of large players. Figure 3–13 describes three scenarios:

- Few suppliers and many consumers (suppliers tend to dominate the value chain).
- Few buyers and many suppliers (buyers tend to dominate the value chain).
- Many suppliers and many buyers (tends toward the emergence of infomediaries).

For example, in the auto industry few players exist in the car manufacturers' arena, while many parts suppliers and intermediaries exist, and even more ultimate consumers. Figure 3–14 illustrates part of the value chain in which the large auto makers will tend to control both the parts supply markets[22] and the sales markets to the dealers or to the consumers.

The Cost Structures

New ventures have very difficult cost structures to estimate. Many of the first-generation e-businesses focused on unmitigated growth, which obscured their real cost structures. Furthermore, because such businesses subcontract many of their basic processes, these structures may be expensive, but flexibility on their disposition and change exists. This flexibility is exactly what companies want in a morphing, flexible, evolutionary journey. Analysts, to evaluate cost structures, must go to independent provisionaries of services and price these activities. The difference between startup (inexperienced) entrepreneurs and experienced management brought in at more mature stages of the venture is the ability to manage these processes efficiently.

---

[22]Ford and GM, later joined by Chrysler, Toyota, and other auto makers, have created the Covisint, a car market estimated to be worth more than $500 billion. While the FTC had major concerns about the effect (dominance) of the markets, it allowed its continuation, but promised the public to monitor Covisint's activities.

FIGURE 3–13   *Industry concentration and market dominance*

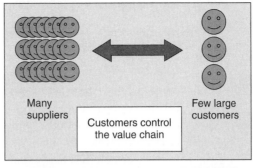

Many suppliers

Few large customers

Customers control the value chain

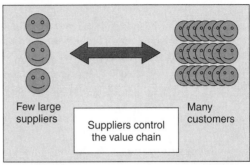

Few large suppliers

Many customers

Suppliers control the value chain

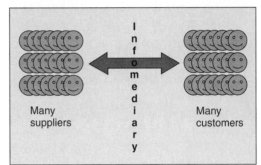

Many suppliers

Infomediary

Many customers

FIGURE 3–14   *Auto industry value chain*

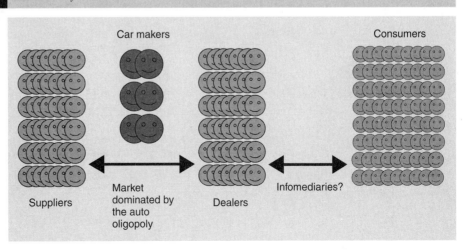

Car makers

Consumers

Suppliers

Market dominated by the auto oligopoly

Dealers

Infomediaries?

Consider the Type of Product Sold

While many theoretical considerations can be made about optimal market structures, the intrinsic nature of the product(s) being sold is of great importance. For example,

- Large bulky products with low value density (dollars per pound of the product) tend to be sold within narrow geographic areas due to large transport costs.
- Perishable goods, in particular bulky generic ones (not specialties), are also narrow geographic area products.
- Products for which the final/intermediate stage results in a greatly reduced weight and bulk from the basic raw material will tend to be manufactured around the source of its raw materials.
- Products with rapid and continuous engineering changes will tend to be manufactured and distributed from one location close to where the human capital for R&D can be found.
- Products with valuable or secret intellectual property rights will tend to be manufactured and distributed only where IP protection is offered by the environment.

Innovation along the Value Chain

Innovation is the key to e-business thinking. While research and development and innovation ultimately propelled traditional business, the dire consequences of lack of innovation appeared at a much slower pace. Often noninnovative firms managed to survive and prosper on the force of their managerial core competencies and competitive might. In the e-economy, these factors are exacerbated.

IMPLICATIONS FOR THE ACCOUNTING PROFESSION

Probably the biggest challenge to the assurance side of the accounting profession is acquiring the expertise to examine the reliability and integrity of the electronic marketplaces in which its clients engage and the security of the transaction processing systems that interface with such electronic marketplaces. If the interaction with the marketplace is initiated and guided by a human, then this is not as critical. However, if the firm's ordering system automatically interfaces with an online marketplace and initiates and approves transactions, then understanding the underlying program code, operating systems, Internet protocols, encryption methods, and firewall configurations becomes crucial to protecting both asset custody and asset record-keeping functions.

Summary

This chapter focuses on the new phenomenon of B2B e-business and the strategic implications of the electronization of business. It also reviewed the progressive evolution of Intranets toward Extranets and a rich environment that is based on the TCP/IP protocol and internetworking applications that are served to a companywide environment and eventually opened up to the world.

The B2B electronic markets are an evolution of the traditional B2B efforts. While some companies exist that use automation to continue their traditional processes, many companies are resorting to different forms of B2B activity with vertical and horizontal markets using auctions, e-catalogs, exchanges, and barter markets to conduct business and lower their costs.

Dot-com companies have refreshed and activated market strategies and, by their intrinsic nature, created new markets and attacked the status quo. While the traditional concepts of core competency, low-cost provisioning and competitive advantage continue to determine strategy, the new Internet economy brought deconstruction, synergy across the value chain, and judo strategies as forms of new thinking. Consequently strategic plays such as acquiring, building independently, subdividing and conquering, and meeting your enemies have been introduced.

Companies now live in a world in which components are being attacked and changed with a constantly evolving scenario of players, methods of operation, business plans, IPOs, stock options, and so forth. To have success in this new strategic world, Web-based thinking and methodologies need to be considered and reevaluated in terms of basic values of income, growth, and stability.

Key Words

acquiring strategy
affiliation
alliances
application service providers (ASP)
B2B (business-to-business)
B2C (business-to-consumer)
build independently
business plan
commoditization
consortia
core competency
customer-care Extranet
deconstruction
electronization
Enterprise Resource Planning System
  (ERPS)
exit strategy
external value chains
Extranet
flexibility principle
free plays

horizontal market
industry morphing
internal value chain
internetworking
intelligent agent
Intranet
Judo strategy
leverage principle
low-cost provider
meet your enemies
middleware
morphing
peer-to-peer
rapid movement principle strategy
subdivide and conquer
supplier-managed inventory
synergy across the value chain
venture capitalist (VC)
vertical market
wanna-dot

Review Questions

1. What are Internet enablers?
2. What is the relative potential size of B2B versus B2C markets?
3. Define B2B.
4. How did B2B benefit from the problems with B2C?
5. Explain the evolution of corporate purchasing processes.
6. How large are the B2B markets expected to be?

7. What are the larger B2B sectors expected to be?
8. What are the characteristics of the B2B markets?
9. What is the effect of industry concentration on the emerging electronic markets?
10. What is the effect of the type of product being sold on the formation of markets?
11. What is the value of brand in B2B markets?
12. Find examples of vertical and horizontal markets.
13. What are ASPs? Why are they becoming an important element of e-business?
14. Explain peer-to-peer.
15. What types of problems will eventually emerge as important considerations in the B2B markets?
16. What are the three main dimensions of strategic thinking?
17. What is the exit strategy?
18. State the major elements of a dot-com business plan.
19. Define corporate core competency.
20. How do you identify a core competency?
21. What is a low-cost provider? How does this strategic issue translate into the Internet age?
22. What are the strategic issues in deconstructing the value chain?
23. Explain synergy across the value chain.
24. What is Judo strategy?
25. What is the Pac Man strategy?
26. What are the strategic issues and trade-offs for a company that wants to start an e-channel/business and that can create or acquire one?
27. Explain the subdivide and conquer strategy.
28. What has changed in a corporation's interface with its competition?
29. What are the strategies implied in the Internet free plays?
30. What are the sources of income for free plays?
31. What are Intranets?
32. What are Extranets?
33. What are ERPSs?
34. What is middleware?
35. What are the four dimensions of Intranets as the backbone of corporate spaces?
36. List some potential functionalities of Extranets.

Discussion Questions

1. How does the concept of B2B markets relate to the electronization of business?
2. Why is outsourcing such an important phenomenon in the strategies of dot-coms?
3. Explain how the auto industry is working on the creation of B2B markets. What are regulators concerned about in relation to Covisint?
4. Focus on the area of strategy, and describe the main effects that compare an e-business with a traditional business.
5. Find and visit sites in which brick-and-mortar B2B companies created separate e-businesses. Evaluate ownership and strategy.
6. Identify some intent strategy plays that imply deconstruction of the traditional value chain.

7. Search the Internet for B2B marketplaces in the airline industry. Try also to find announcements relative to these plays and company plans.

8. Propose 10 different metrics to evaluate the quality and strategies that a particular dot-com is adopting.

9. Identify grocery store–type plays in the Internet. Compare their strategies and business models.

10. Use the same type of table and nature of features to compare features of Yahoo.com with another firm. How good is the comparison? Can insights be gathered?

11. Use the Internet to identify five different companies that are using Extranets to accomplish their business objectives. Prepare a table comparing these efforts.

12. Illustrate the concept of core competency and competitive advantage in the world of Internet company strategies.

13. Internet banking is becoming an important field. How does Internet banking differ from traditional banking? What are large banks doing as their Internet strategy? What is Bank One doing?

14. What is the future of B2B e-business? Is it only a fad?

15. Casinos are moving progressively toward the Internet. What is their strategy? What are the issues? Is that a natural Internet play?

16. Identify customers-care plays that use an Extranet. Create a drawing that represents the elements of this play. How does this compare with traditional customer care?

17. Find a B2B exchange that allows you to see how it works either through a temporary access number or through a simulated test drive. Describe the components of this exchange.

Cases

1. Price comparison sites
   Find five price comparison sites that could be used by businesses and explain the business model that they use.
   a. What are the sources of income? What is the purpose of the site? What is the site's relationship with the sites being evaluated?
   b. How long have the sites been in existence?
   c. What will be the effect of these sites being around?
   d. Comparison sites will have long-term implications to change the nature of business and pricing structures. Are these type of sites going to contribute to the commoditization of products and to the reduction/elimination of major differences in international pricing?

2. Customized products
   Most Internet users are aware of Dell Computer's website, where the customer can customize his or her computer in terms of hardware and software components as well as to buy extra items. Today's world of e-commerce is progressively developing many products that are customizable one way or the other.
   a. Identify some instances of customization.
   b. What is the effect of customization upon price?
   c. How does customization play with the organization's Internet strategy?
   d. What is the future of product customization?
   e. "Imagineer" and describe three customized products that would appeal to you as a businessperson.

3. How can free plays become profitable?
   The web is currently full of free plays, including free Internet access, free Internet phone, free websiting, free e-mail, free e-commerce site, free fax number, etc. Choose one of these plays for an in-depth analysis of its current and future B2B strategies as well as potential alternatives for the future.

   a. Explain its income model.

   b. Identify affiliations and alliances.

   c. Estimate the best you can its cost structure.

   d. Identify any potential across-the-value chain plays.

   e. Forecast its future.

4. How do networks add value?
   Visit a company with a mature Intranet and Extranet and work on identifying the four components proposed by Anghern and how value can be (or is being) added along the four value trends proposed by Sawhney and Parikh.

References

ActivMedia Research. "Real Numbers behind Transactions, Fraud & Security 2000." *www.activmediaresearch.com*

Blackwell, Roger D., and Kristina Blackwell. "The Century of the Consumer: Converting Supply Chains into Demand Chains," *Supply Chain Management Review*, Fall 1999.

Collins, Michael, and Phil Schefter. "The Narrow Path to Victory for B2B Exchanges," *Harvard Business Review*, 2000.

Eppinger, Steven D. "Innovation at the Speed of Information," *Harvard Business Review*, 2001.

Fahey, L., and R. M. Randall, *The Portable MBA in* Strategy, Wiley, 2001.

Geary, Steve, and Jan Paul Zonnenberg. "What It Means to Be Best in Class," *Supply Chain Management Review,* July–August 2000.

Kaplan, Robert S., and David P. Norton. "Using the Balanced Scorecard as a Strategic Management System," *Harvard Business Review*, January–February 1996.

Kelly, K., *New Rules for the New Economy,* Penguin Group, New York, 1998.

Montgomery, C. A., and M. E. Porter. *Strategy: Seeking and Securing Competitive Advantage*, Harvard Business School Press, 1991.

O'Connell, B., *B2B.com: Cashing-in on the Business to Business E-Commerce Bonanza,* Adams Media Corporation, Holbrook, MA, 2000.

Ovans, A., "E-Procurement at Schlumberger: A Conversation with Alain-Michel Diamant-Berger," *Harvard Business Review*, May–June 2000.

Papowsm J., *Enterprise.com: Market Leadership in the Information Age,* Perseus Books, Reading, MA, 1998.

Prahalad, C. K., and G. Hamel, "The Core Competence of the Corporation," *Harvard Business Review,* May–June 1990.

Raffoni, Melissa. "Managing Your Virtual Company: Create a Communication Plan," *Harvard Management Communication Letter*, April 2000.

Reichheld, F. F., and W. E. Sasser. "Zero Defections: Quality Comes to Services," *Harvard Business Review,* September–October 1990.

Reichheld, Frederick F., and Phil Schefter. "E-Loyalty: Your Secret Weapon on the Web," *Harvard Business Review*, July–August 2000.

Shapiro, C., and H. R. Varian. *Information Rules,* Harvard Business School Press, Boston, MA, 1999.

Sinha, Indrajit. "Cost Transparency: The Net's Real Threat to Prices and Brands," *Harvard Business Review*, March–April 2000.

Sliwotzky, A. J., C. M. Christensem, and R. S. Tedlow. "The Future of Commerce," *Harvard Business Review,* January–February 2000.

Stern, C. W., and G. Stalk, Jr. *Perspectives on Strategy from the Boston Consulting Group,* John Wiley & Sons, New York, 1998.

Stopford, John. "Should Strategy Makers Become Dream Weavers?" *Harvard Business Review*, January 2001.

Sviokla, Sr., John Julius. "Four Questions for the Acid Information Age," *Supply Chain Management Review*, Summer 1999.

Tapscott, D., D. Ticoll, and A. Lowy. *Digital Capital: Harnessing the Power of Business Webs,* Harvard Business School Press, Boston, MA, 2000.

Ward, S., L. Light, and J. Goldstine. "What High-Tech Managers Need to Know about Brands," *Harvard Business Review*, July–August 1999.

Werbach, Kevin. "Syndication: The Emerging Model for Business in the Internet Era," *Harvard Business Review*, May–June 2000.

Wise, Richard, and David Morrison. "Beyond the Exchange: The Future of B2B," *Harvard Business Review,* November–December 2000.

4 ELECTRONIC COMMERCE AND THE ROLE OF INDEPENDENT THIRD PARTIES

Learning Objectives

1. To identify new service opportunities for the accounting profession and the underlying forces initiating these changes.
2. To understand the importance of auditor independence for accounting firms providing e-commerce consulting services.
3. To examine the necessary skills needed by the accounting profession for providing e-commerce services.
4. To examine the underlying need for third-party assurance providers of Web-based e-commerce systems and the potential value added by such providers.

INTRODUCTION

Electronic commerce presents many new risks to businesses and consumers alike, and as a result, a number of new opportunities for independent third parties. This chapter explores these opportunities, and the role of the independent accountant, along with the role of other independent industry monitors. This chapter also covers a number of new assurances third parties are being asked to provide and the e-commerce business and technology skills required in order to deliver these assurances. The highlighted concepts and skills are the basis for a number of discussions appearing in later chapters in this textbook. In addition, although this chapter is primarily focused on the accounting profession, distinctions are made where other independent bodies can play a role.

Before this topic is introduced, answering a fundamental question is important: Why is the accounting profession providing e-commerce assurance services? Perhaps a comparison to the brick-and-mortar world is appropriate. In traditional business models, certified public accountants (CPAs) and chartered accountants (CAs) have been regarded as independent, objective third parties who make honest assessments and evaluations of certain business functions. Accountants are well known for opining on the accuracy of financial statements. But they also play a crucial role in assessing risks and reporting on the system of internal controls surrounding business systems and processes. In the brick-and-mortar world, when an entity wants to go public or when a venture is seeking investment capital, not only do CPAs conduct an in-depth review of the financial statements and projections, they also perform a vital due diligence function. This function is intended to give the prospective investor comfort that the business does what it says and can be trusted to perform as disclosed. This same function applies well in the new e-commerce environment. The same accountants who deliver risk analyses in traditional business can provide similar assurances in the electronic world. Objectivity and independence are attributes of the accounting profession that are considered to be its foundation. This chapter examines the importance of these concepts to e-commerce–related services.

CONSULTING PRACTICES AND ACCOUNTANTS' INDEPENDENCE

The **American Institute of Certified Public Accountants (AICPA)** was established in 1887 to serve the accounting profession and to act as a standard-setting body within the industry. The AICPA serves as the accounting profession's national advocate in promoting the interests of CPAs before government agencies, regulatory bodies, and other organizations. The AICPA has more than 330,000 members and estimates that three out of four CPAs are members of the AICPA.

Accountants are required by the AICPA's **Principles of the Code of Professional Conduct** to be independent and perform their duties with integrity and objectivity. Specifically, the Principles of the Code of Professional Conduct defines integrity and objectivity as follows:

• **Integrity** is an element of character fundamental to professional recognition. It is the quality from which the public trust derives and the benchmark against which a member must ultimately test all decisions. Integrity also requires a member to observe the principles of objectivity and independence and of due care.

• **Objectivity** is a state of mind, a quality that lends value to a member's services. It is a distinguishing feature of the profession. The principle of objectivity imposes the obligation to be impartial, intellectually honest, and free of conflicts of interest. Independence precludes the relationships that may appear to impair a member's objectivity in rendering attestation services.

The concept of independence is not as clear. Independence is referred to in the Statement on Auditing Standards (SAS) No. 1, and specific examples of situations that impair independence are illustrated in the AICPA's Interpretation 101-1. For purposes of discussing **independence** in this text, we define it as a relationship between a client and a professional services firm where the professional services firm does not have *any* vested interest in the client firm. This definition precludes any member of the professional services firm or the firm itself from having any claim to assets or income from the client firm. However, the Securities and Exchange Commission (SEC) has recently acknowledged that the independence rules may be outdated, and in 1997, it created an **Independence Standards Board (ISB)** to review the concept of independence and update the definition and examples if necessary.

The ISB issued its first standard, "Independence Discussions with Audit Committees," in January 1999.[1] The standard applies to any accountant who intends to play an independent role in a relationship with another entity within the context of the SEC's

---

[1]The ISB subsequently issued two additional standards: "Certain Independence Implications of Audits of Mutual Funds and Related Entities" and "Employment with Audit Clients."

Federal Securities Acts. Specifically, the standard requires that on an annual basis (at a minimum), the auditor shall

- Disclose to the audit committee of the company (or the board of directors, if there is no audit committee), in writing, all relationships between the auditor (and its related entities) and the company (and its related entities) that, in the auditor's professional judgment, may reasonably be thought to bear on independence.
- Confirm in the letter that, in the auditor's professional judgment, it is independent of the company within the meaning of the acts.
- Discuss the auditor's independence with the audit committee.

Why might standards be necessary? Over the past decade, the services performed by accounting firms have changed dramatically. During the mid- to late 1990s, the revenues from computer consulting practices grew at an annual rate of up to 50 percent for some Big Five accounting firms. A hotly debated topic is whether a firm has a vested interest in a client if it has assisted the client in an advisory role. Prior to issuing its first standard, the ISB contracted with a research company, Earnscliffe Research and Communications, to research many of the independence issues. The results reported to the ISB indicated that, historically, auditors had met a high standard of independence but that most of the individuals interviewed (except auditors) "believe that the pressures on objectivity and independence are growing over time, and are becoming somewhat worrisome." The Earnscliffe Report indicated that the following pressures on independence are growing:

- More aggressive culture of the financial marketplace.
- Multidisciplinary service offerings by audit firms.
- Loss-leading audits.
- Changes in audit firm culture.
- Increased scrutiny.

(Earnscliffe Research and Communication, 1999)

Interestingly, the auditors that were interviewed "maintained that audit functions and consulting services can co-exist indefinitely, perhaps inelegantly, but without causing an erosion, or perceived erosion, of objectivity and independence." As discussed later in this chapter, the accounting profession continues to broaden the range of services it provides to clients.

Some critics assert that an accounting firm can no longer be independent or objective in evaluating the adequacy of the system or in issuing an independent report if the same firm's consultants designed and/or installed the system. Accounting firms assert that their involvement in the design and installation of the system helps them to know the system better and thus enables them to better assess the adequacy of the system. To address the issue of independence, accounting firms often have different teams perform the different stages. The team(s) performing the design and/or installation of the system are segregated from the team performing the assessment of the adequacy of the system, particularly if an official opinion report is to be issued. Roughly half of the chief executive and chief financial officers (CEOs and CFOs) interviewed by Earnscliffe Research and Communications, however, said they like "to use their audit firms for non-audit assignments . . . the audit firm would be motivated to do a good job and charge reasonable fees, knowing the client was a long term, important relationship." This kind of relationship has the potential to reduce the auditor firm's independence as other seemingly dependent relationships are formed that produce greater revenues than the audit.

FIGURE 4–1	*Segregation of functions for firewalls*

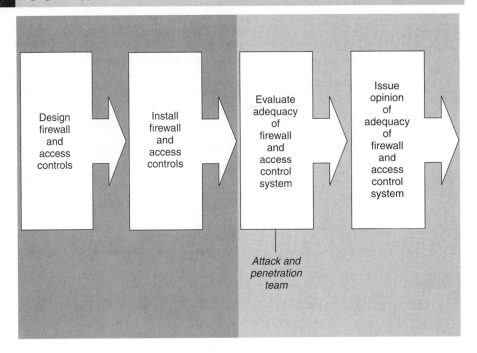

With respect to e-commerce, security auditors are often assigned to assess the adequacy of security controls, such as firewall configurations and network- or system-level security configurations. As illustrated in Figure 4–1, an attack and penetration team should be a separate group of individuals reporting to a different manager from the team that designed and/or installed the firewall. Thus, accounting firms maintain that this segregation of functions within the firm helps it to preserve the concept and appearance of independence.

CPA VISION PROJECT

In 1997, members of the CPA profession banned together and held a series of Future Forums. Primarily led by leaders from state CPA societies, 170 forums were conducted. Participating in these forums were a combination of educators, students, and practicing CPAs. The information gathered from this forum was reviewed and synthesized, and ultimately, a report containing CPA vision elements was released in 1998. This report is described as a comprehensive and integrated vision of the profession's future. The vision statement issued by this group is as follows:

CPAs are the trusted professionals who enable people and organizations to shape their future. Combining insight with integrity. CPAs deliver value by:

- Communicating the total picture with clarity and objectivity.
- Translating complex information into critical knowledge.
- Anticipating and creating opportunities.
- Designing pathways that transform vision into reality.
  (*CPA Vision, 1998*)

This vision statement reflects the trend toward providing a broader range of services. Further, the statement heavily leans toward providing business solutions. The top five core services provided by the CPA profession identified by this group are:

- Assurance and information integrity.
- Management consulting and performance measurement.
- Technology services.
- Financial planning.
- International services.

Where does e-commerce fit into these five core services? Each category is directly affected by electronic commerce. The effect of e-commerce on the assurance function is examined in the following section of this chapter. As discussed in Chapter 1, management consulting is affected because many firms are adjusting their missions and strategy to incorporate electronic commerce initiatives due to the changing technological environment. Because technology is an integral component to the deployment and maintenance of e-commerce initiatives, this core service is probably affected the most. Technological issues, such as system integrity and security, are discussed throughout this text. Finally, international services are fueled by e-commerce, and solutions provided to clients in this area generally have an e-commerce component.

NEW ASSURANCE SERVICES IDENTIFIED BY THE AICPA

The revenues from one of the primary services offered by the accounting profession, and for which it has a monopoly, is the assurance, or attestation, of financial statements. Revenues, however, from such services have remained relatively stagnant over the past decade, while revenue from consulting services has grown exponentially. In 1996, the top 100 accounting firms in the United States reported for the first time that their consulting practices provided more revenues than their tax, auditing, or other accounting revenues.[2] For 1997, the top 100 accounting firms reported that technology-oriented consulting services were the driving force behind their firms' growth.[3] Further, the nature of the traditional assurance task has become increasingly technologically oriented, allowing smaller audit teams to perform the same tasks performed by much larger teams a decade ago, thereby increasing the efficiency of such services, while not continually growing revenues.

The combination of stagnant audit revenues, the requirement of smaller audit teams, and the advancing technological environment with an emphasis on information sharing among nontraditional business partners has led the AICPA to identify new service opportunities for the accounting profession as illustrated in Figure 4–2. Two AICPA appointed committees have been formed to address the need for new service identification: the Elliott committee and the ASEC committee.

The Elliott Committee and the ASEC Committee

The first special committee formed by the AICPA was the **Special Committee on Assurance Services (SCAS)** chaired by Robert Elliott. As might be expected, its effort culminated in a report known as the **Elliott report.** The SCAS was formed in 1994 to

---

[2]Rick Telberg, "Top 100 Firms Propel Consulting Past Tax, A&A," *Accounting Today,* March–April 1997.
[3]Rick Telberg, "The Top 100: Scorching Growth, but for How Long?" *Accounting Today,* 1998.

| FIGURE 4–2 | *Forces initiating changes in accounting profession* |

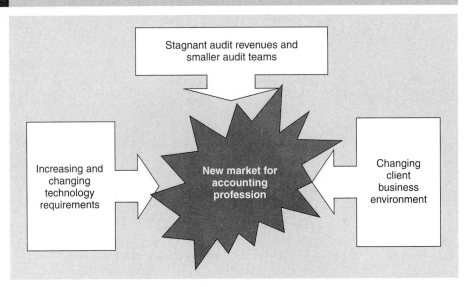

develop a strategic plan to expand the **third-party assurance services** offered by the accounting profession. In identifying new assurance service opportunities, the AICPA identified three important factors that must be considered:

- A customer need.
- A CPA who can fill that need.
- The customer's perception that the CPA's service is worth more than its costs.

A strong presence of each of these factors is extremely important to the success of any new service offered by the accounting profession. The Elliott report identified a shortlist of six new services that have a potential for very high revenues and that can be performed by accounting firms of all sizes as long as appropriate training and expertise are applied:

- Electronic commerce.
- Elder care.
- Health care performance.
- Systems reliability.
- Entity performance.
- Risk identification and impact analysis.

The AICPA asserts that each of these services offers potential revenues of more than $1 billion, which can double or triple the current annual accounting and auditing revenues of accounting firms. Three of the areas listed are directly related to electronic commerce and are more thoroughly discussed in the following sections. The obvious first area is e-commerce, and the other two areas are systems reliability and risk identification and impact analysis.

In providing new assurance services, members of the accounting profession must be aware of the different market environments in which they operate. Unlike traditional

| **FIGURE 4–3** | *Competitive market for technology services* |

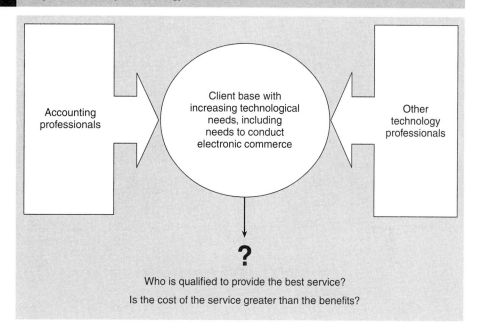

financial statement audit services, the accounting profession does not have the luxury of having the sole right or ownership to perform these services. Figure 4–3 illustrates the new market in which the accounting profession competes for these new services. The accounting profession is now offering services that other nonaccounting professionals may offer as well. Thus, the customer will undoubtedly be approached by competing professionals and will ultimately have to make two decisions:

- Which professional is best qualified to provide the best service?
- Can the professional provide the service at a cost that is less than the expected benefits?

In responding to the first question, the accounting profession must have members who are at the forefront of technology, and they must be recognized for having such skills. Particularly because many accountants are mired by their traditional stodgy images, the Elliott report recognized the need for members of the accounting profession to considerably increase their technology skills and savvy. Specific skill-sets mentioned in the report that were viewed as requirements to compete as an independent assurance body in an electronic commerce environment included an in-depth understanding of the risks related to

- Intentional attacks.
- Transmission failures.
- Lack of authentication.
- Loss of trust.
- Theft of identity.
- Encryption.

- Risks associated with electronic cash.
- Software agents.
- Sensors.
- Preventive and detective controls.
- Systems reliability.

(Elliott Report)

Technology has become such an important component of the accounting profession that the AICPA now issues its list of Top 10 Technologies each year. The Top 10 Technologies and the Emerging Technologies given by the AICPA are listed in Figure 4–4. Yearly updates to this list are posted on the AICPA's website. All of these topics are covered in detail in this or subsequent chapters.

After the completion of the Elliott report, the SCAS was disbanded and a new committee was formed, the **Assurance Services Executive Committee (ASEC),** led by Ronald Cohen. This committee is charged with developing services and providing guidance regarding how to offer the services identified in the Elliott report and listed above. This committee is also charged with identifying whether standards are needed and, if so, initiating a standard-setting process.

Three Waves of Electronic Commerce

Three waves of e-commerce are mentioned in the Elliott report and illustrated in Figure 4–5. The three waves as named by the Elliott report are:

- Traditional EDI
- Electronic commerce
- A new electronic society

Each wave is illustrated as getting progressively larger because with each wave comes more widespread use of e-commerce technologies and practices. The first wave, primarily the electronic data interchange (EDI) practices of the 1980s and early 1990s, has given way to the second wave, and firms are well on their way to catching the third wave. Chapter 6 explores the systems of the first and second waves in greater detail. A key difference between the first and second waves is that in the second wave, electronic transactions can occur between virtual strangers, while in the first wave, electronic transactions only occurred for preestablished business partners. The second wave requires that access to company information be provided to a much larger body of individuals (pre-

| **FIGURE 4–4** | *AICPA's 2001 Top 10 Technologies and Emerging Technologies* |

2001 Top 10 Technologies	*2001 Emerging Technologies*
1. Security technologies	1. Government regulations dealing with technology
2. XML	2. Business service providers
3. Communications technologies—bandwidth	3. E-learning
4. Mobile technologies	4. Electronic evidence
5. Wireless technologies	5. M-commerce
6. Electronic authentication technologies	
7. Encryption	
8. Electronic authorization	
9. Remote connectivity tools	
10. Database technologies	

FIGURE 4–5	*Three waves of electronic commerce*

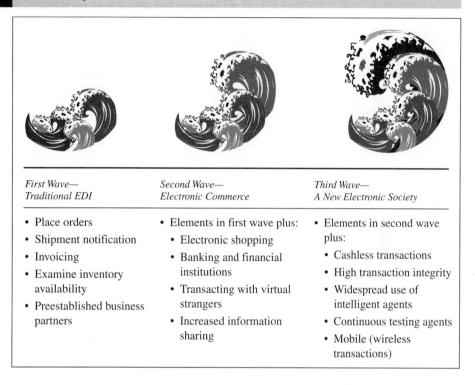

First Wave— Traditional EDI	Second Wave— Electronic Commerce	Third Wave— A New Electronic Society

• Place orders
• Shipment notification
• Invoicing
• Examine inventory availability
• Preestablished business partners
	• Elements in first wave plus:
	  • Electronic shopping
	  • Banking and financial institutions
	  • Transacting with virtual strangers
	  • Increased information sharing
		• Elements in second wave plus:
		  • Cashless transactions
		  • High transaction integrity
		  • Widespread use of intelligent agents
		  • Continuous testing agents
		  • Mobile (wireless transactions)

sumably potential buyers). The challenge is to provide that openness, while still protecting company information and encapsulating sensitive corporate data from unauthorized users. These new system requirements provide a challenge to system designers and administrators, and they necessitate new control methods.

Because in the second wave of e-commerce information not protected from the public can easily be deleted or altered, well-designed security controls are necessary. In addition, methods to solve trading partner disputes are also necessary. Methods for achieving dispute resolution, such as nonrepudiation, digital signatures, and integrity checks, are topics covered in Chapter 10, but are highlighted here as yet another control area that needs to be addressed.

The second wave of e-commerce brings with it the opportunity for third parties, such as independent accounting firms, to provide businesses and customers with the assurance that business transactions conducted electronically, including Internet and Web-based transactions, are safe, secure, and backed by the appropriate controls. With the proper technical training, accounting professionals are well positioned to examine the controls outlined above and render an opinion on their effectiveness. Some of the elements categorized in the third wave are already in their infancy stage and being implemented by a few pioneering organizations. The topic of cashless transactions is covered in Chapter 12, while continuous (intelligent) agents are discussed in Chapter 13. Systems with high integrity are a goal of second-wave e-commerce installations, but they will be in place on a much wider scale during the third wave. Continuous testing agents are vital to continuous monitoring and continuous assurance services discussed later in this chapter. We have added a final item to the list in Figure 4–5: wireless and mobile transactions. **M-commerce,** as it is known in Europe, is rapidly being implemented and new security challenges are arising. M-commerce is covered in subsequent chapters throughout the text.

E-Commerce in Practice

Confidential Messages and Data Placed in the Public Domain

Hallmark. Hallmark accidentally left the door open to confidential data stored on one of its Web servers. The snafu happened when it upgraded its servers in December 1998 and a "programming error" occurred. The glitch left open a data file containing private messages sent by users of Hallmark's electronic greeting card services.

The file, on a public site accessible by its search engine, was left open for approximately eight weeks. The data contained confidential messages sent from as long as 18 months prior to the incident. In the whole scheme of things, Hallmark claims that fewer than 1 percent of all messages were in that data file.

H&R Block Exposes Confidential Data. H&R Block unknowingly exposed the confidential tax return data of 26 of its Internet clients' data during the 2000 tax season (1999 tax returns). The unfortunate incident was caused by an upgrade to the system that was supposed to enhance the site's performance. Instead, the erroneous implementation caused the site to be shut down for a week while H&R Block identified and fixed the problem.

The confidential data were exposed when users logged off to the system and a subsequent user logged in. The previous users' data were imported into the current user's tax preparation documents and screen views.

Electronic Commerce Integrity and Security Assurance

The AICPA discusses a number of categories of assurance that can be provided for e-commerce systems, two of which are integrity and security. **Integrity assurance systems** ensure that (a) the data elements captured in an electronic transaction are the agreed-upon elements and (b) the processing and storage procedures maintain the integrity of the data elements and do not alter them in any unauthorized fashion. **Security assurance systems** ensure (a) the authentication of the transacting parties and (b) that electronic data are protected from unauthorized disclosure. Examples of two lapses in security that occurred as a result of human error are discussed in the box titled "Confidential Messages and Data Placed in the Public Domain."

The response by the accounting profession to these control assurance functions is two relatively new assurance offerings, *WebTrust* and *SysTrust*. These services are discussed more thoroughly later in this chapter. The Elliott report states that although most members of the accounting profession may currently lack all of the necessary technological skills, they are better positioned than their nonaccounting competitors to provide such services because of their existing competencies in systems and control environments, such as their skills in

- Evaluating evidence.
- Planning the extent of validation as a function of the effectiveness of the system of internal controls.
- Reporting to third parties on the results of their work.

(AICPA)

Thus, accounting firms wishing to provide e-commerce assurance services need their accountants to acquire and master the necessary additional technology skills. The AICPA's Top 10 Technologies is a good starting place for a checklist of necessary knowledge.

Electronic Commerce Systems Reliability Assurance

Data integrity and security controls are integral features of any e-commerce transaction. With the proper technology training, the accounting industry can apply traditional control evaluation methodologies and can opine on the effectiveness of data integrity and security controls. Systems reliability control is yet another important part of the transaction and, thus, should be considered when entering into an electronic trading relationship.

Figure 4–6 illustrates a general overview of the customer's need for high-quality information from its trading partners. It also shows the need for server and information reliability of the information systems that contain the desired information. Information is **accessible** if an authorized user can retrieve it. Accessibility of Internet data is affected by two primary components: user privileges and system availability. Authorization procedures should be employed to ensure that data are only accessed by authorized users. Chapters 10 and 11 discuss user authorization procedures. Authorized users need assurance that the system they want to access is available when they need it; this is called **server reliability.** A customer needs the telecommunications links and the remote server to be properly functioning so that the desired information is accessible when it is needed. Further, the server's links to both the underlying databases and processing systems within the organization and the Internet need to be reliable.

Once the customer has gained access to the server, the information provided may be used to make decisions. For the decision-making process, the customer needs assurance that the data *provided at that point in time,* and upon which the decision is based, are

FIGURE 4–6	*Reliable information systems*

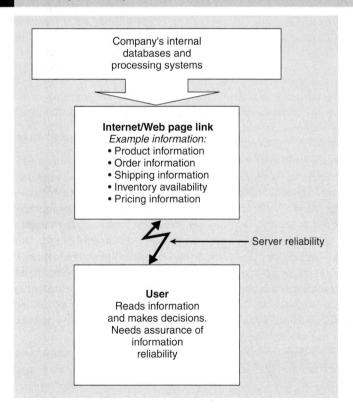

reliable. **Information reliability** requires that the information provided by a system be both accurate and current. To understand the concepts of server and information reliability, consider the following example. Many individual stock market investors transact with online brokerage houses. An investor that hears news that the market is rapidly deteriorating may wish to check his or her stock positions. If the investor cannot rapidly log on to the system or if the server is temporarily offline, the investor will not be able to access his or her account and relevant market information. This scenario reflects an unreliable server. (In most cases, the investor can go offline and telephone the brokerage house, but the phone lines may be flooded at that point.) If the user is able to log on to the system and request real-time quotes, but the download time is two or three minutes, then the quotes are no longer accurate by the time the online investor views them. This scenario reflects unreliable information. Customers need to have assurances that the systems of trading partners are both server and information reliable. The box titled "Recent Outages Show Risks of Online Service Failures, Benefits of Spare Capability" discusses the problems of server reliability that have plagued some online brokers. Another box, "Fictional Merger Posting Causes Trading Activity," gives an example of the importance of information reliability.

E-Commerce in Practice

Recent Outages Show Risks of Online Service Failures, Benefits of Spare Capability

For online brokerages such as ETrade Group Inc. that have suffered embarrassing computer outages recently, the issue boils down to whether it's worth the money to safeguard system uptime.

"You can spend a lot of money on systems redundancy for the days you have huge [trading] volumes, but the question is, how much are you willing to spend and how much risk are you willing to take that you'll have an outage?" said Octavio Marenzi, research director at Meridien Research Inc. in Newton, Mass.

February probably seemed like the longest month to ETrade and Ameritrade Inc. ETrade suffered systems glitches because of a problematic server upgrade on Feb. 3, 4, and 5; Ameritrade customers were shut out by computer outages for 28 minutes on Feb. 8. On Feb. 24, Charles Schwab & Co.'s website went down during a mainframe install.

Online brokerages "have been the victims of their own success," said Patricia McGinnis, an analyst at Mainspring Communications Inc., a Cambridge, Mass.–based research firm.

Although ETrade, Schwab and others have bolstered their capacity and backup capabilities in the past few years, "they simply haven't done enough," McGinnis said. To its credit, Schwab is simplifying its application architecture so trades don't make as many network hops to reach its IBM and Hitachi Data Systems mainframes [*Computerworld,* Feb. 22].

While overly complex IT architectures contribute to online brokerages' reliability problems, bureaucratic business processes also are plaguing investors. A simple online stock trade has to go through a series of confirmations and approvals within a brokerage before it can be executed.

That's one of the reasons retail investors often have to wait hours before their trades are executed—and by then, rarely at the price at which they had hoped to buy or sell a stock.

Executives at organizations that process online trades for institutional clients had one key message for retail brokers: Bulk up on capacity, big-time.

The New York Stock Exchange, for example, can handle 600 messages per second (MPS), even though it has reached only 365 MPS at its peak, or 60% of capacity. NYSE is upgrading its systems capacity to handle 1,000 MPS in about five months and 2,000 MPS in the next year.

"There's no tolerance" for not being able to get an order through, said William Bautz, chief technology officer at NYSE, who gave a speech at IT for Wall Street '99, a conference that was held here last week. "If [investors] think they're getting bad pricing, they'll go somewhere else," he added.

Source: Thomas Hoffman Computerworld Online, March 1, 1999.
© Computerworld, Inc.

Internal Control Framework

The characteristics of good information practices illustrated in the preceding example and in Figure 4–6 are specified in an important internal control framework for the accounting profession, the **Committee of Sponsoring Organization of the Treadway Commission (COSO)** report, issued in 1992. The primary internal control components contained in the COSO report are incorporated into SAS No. 78. The COSO report emphasizes that these elements affect the ability of management to make appropriate decisions in managing and controlling a company's activities. Because of the increasing need for online, real-time access to information, the underlying systems need to provide continuously reliable information. Figure 4–7 illustrates the time lag that occurs between data collection and information compilation and information dissemination to stakeholders. The time lag occurs because of the assurance processes that must be conducted to verify the integrity and reliability of the information produced by the underlying processes. Users of information are becoming less willing to accept much of a time lag between events and the related information about them. Not all companies, however, have a long time lag between engaging in transactions and then recording and reporting them. Cisco Systems Inc. has set a new industry standard by creating a system that enables it to close its worldwide financials within 24 hours!

The Elliott report asserts that the accounting profession must shift from an error detection and correction model to a before-the-fact prevention strategy. Such a strategy is particularly useful in reducing the time lag between events and the dissemination of related information. This strategy requires that the evaluating controls must be both manual and computer based and designed into the overall functionality of the system and

FIGURE 4–7   *Time lag in information dissemination*

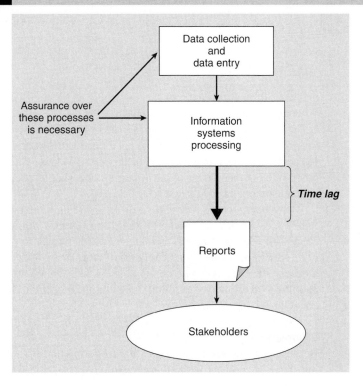

E-Commerce in Practice

Fictional Merger Posting Causes Trading Activity

On February 17, 2000, a hacker broke into Aastrom Bio-sciences Inc.'s website and posted a fictional press release stating that the company was merging with a rival company, Geron Corporation. The trading activity of the two companies' stock nearly doubled on that day as indicated in the chart accompanying. As soon as the false press release was noticed by Aastron Biosciences, it pulled the posting and both companies posted messages to investors that the merger news was a farce.

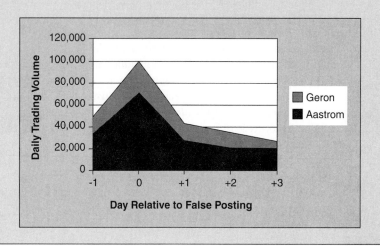

process. The accounting profession must be prepared to help design reliable systems and processes that encompass state-of-the-art technological evaluating controls, such as software agents and electronic sensors and human interactions that monitor system stability and overall "health." Some of the applicable technologies are discussed in Chapter 13. Although the accounting profession certainly has the opportunity to design proprietary agent and sensor systems that can be sold or licensed to clients, the basis for the COSO report is that accountants should be positioned to evaluate the effectiveness of the internal controls surrounding a system or process. The system or process should be continuously reliable, should maintain integrity, and should adequately protect information from unauthorized access and modification.

How does e-commerce data integrity and security assurance differ from systems reliability assurance? According to the Elliott report, integrity and security assurance is concerned with the "security and integrity of networks involved in the public exchange of information," while systems reliability assurance is concerned with "the reliability of an entity's internal database on which an outsider might rely." In reality, overlap exists, and if true assurance of e-commerce systems is desired, the engagement will have to encompass both areas.

Competition

Because accountants do not enjoy market permissions to solely provide these services, they have to compete with other technology professionals. The Elliott report suggests that accountants, in addition to expanding their information technology skills, will have to leverage three competitive advantages:

- Their access to client personnel and the relationship that already exists with the client.
- Their reputation for independence and objectivity.
- Their familiarity with controls integrated in financial reporting systems.

Risk Assessment Assurance

Another assurance function that the Elliott report identifies as a good opportunity for the accounting profession is risk assessment. Risk assessment has been performed by the accounting profession for decades. **Risk assessment** is the process of identifying, analyzing, and managing risks that affect the achievement of management's objectives.[4] The identification of risks associated with managing and reporting financial activity is already a staple of the annual financial audit. In fact, because financial information has been provided by information systems since as far back as the 1960s, accountants are already accustomed to assessing system-level risks and determining the effectiveness of the controls that are designed to mitigate the risks. Therefore, risk assessment assurance in the e-commerce environment is an extension of the methodologies already established by the accounting profession.

By applying the appropriate technical and industry skill-sets, accountants can identify control weaknesses, map them against business and technical risks, and determine whether the risks are being reasonably mitigated. The accountant can then provide assurances based on findings about the risk-mitigating controls that the e-commerce systems, transactions, or processes will function as intended. As an independent third party, such an opinion can hold a lot of weight in determining the real risks associated with particular e-commerce systems and transactions.

EFFECT OF E-COMMERCE ON THE TRADITIONAL ASSURANCE FUNCTION

The preceding section discussed new assurance opportunities, but e-commerce also affects the scope and methods of traditional assurance engagements, which are currently guided by the AICPA's **Statement on Auditing Standards (SAS) 78.** This standard details the relationships between

- The organization's internal control mechanisms.
- The auditor's assessment of risk.
- The audit planning procedures.

Any financial transactions conducted using e-commerce fall under these guidelines. Thus, accountants must have the appropriate technology skills to understand e-commerce–related control mechanisms and to be able to adequately perform an assessment of any risks related to e-commerce transactions.

Because the paper trail virtually disappears in e-commerce systems, the assessment of risk in e-commerce systems is crucial. Further, understanding how to follow and

---

[4]V. O'Reilly, P. McDonnell, B. Winograd, J. Gerson, and H. Jaenicke, *Auditing,* 5th edition, John Wiley & Sons, New York, 1998.

verify an electronic trail is crucial. Chapter 7 examines many of the risks present in electronic systems. Because e-commerce is conducted using telecommunication links, serious vulnerabilities must be protected against. Risk assessment of e-commerce systems is at the forefront of many corporate management teams' minds.

For financial transaction e-commerce systems, those risks identified in Chapter 7 must be fully understood by the traditional assurance team working on a financial electronic commerce engagement. One such risk, for example, is associated with unauthorized access to electronic information, such as credit card information or sales history.

Continuous Auditing

In their more traditional audit roles, accountants typically combine an examination and evaluation of internal controls and some form of substantive testing. For example, the auditor might first examine the systems that support the sale of a product to gain comfort that they will always work as intended. If, in this example, the transaction integrity controls in the system were found to be weaker than hoped, the auditor might choose to perform **substantive tests,** which involves selecting a sample of transactions and tracing the transactions' flow through the system. Certainly, if a lot of these substantive tests are necessary, having an automated means for performing them is beneficial. The concept of continuous auditing addresses this need.

Continuous process auditing allows the auditor to specify transaction selection criteria and perform tests, and the performance of these tests is performed at some prespecified interval, such as daily, hourly, or as they occur. Auditors need to be integrally involved in the design of such systems so that they can place the necessary reliance on the continuous monitoring procedures and outputs. The outputs of a system may be in the form of exception reports or alarms. The use of such reports or alarms may involve auditing *around the computer* techniques, such as following up on the report by investigating the transactions in question by examining logs and data files. Some investigative work, however, will inevitably need to be done by auditing *through the computer* to determine precisely

- How data are electronically collected and transmitted.
- From what parties the data originated.
- The authentication techniques employed.
- From what network address the party originated.
- From what networks the message traveled through.
- How the data are processed and protected once in the system.

This list is not exhaustive, but it gives an idea of the nature of the audit tasks that need to be performed on e-commerce transaction data.

Control agents are auditor-defined heuristics that are periodically applied to transaction sets. The agent, upon finding unusual activity, may first search for similar activities in an attempt to understand the activity pattern.[5] If the activity cannot be explained, the control agent alerts the auditor. These types of control agents are not in widespread use yet, especially for real-time applications.

The security demands placed on transaction processing systems as a result of e-commerce require that improved auditing techniques, such as control agents, be de-

---

[5]A. Kogan, F. Sudit, and M. Vasarhelyi, "Some Auditing Implications of Internet Technology," *http://www.rutgers.edu/Accounting/raw/miklos/tcon3.htm.*

veloped. Once in place, these continuous process auditing agents can help auditors shift from a reactive to a proactive audit model. They also foster more timely assessment of the overall integrity of e-commerce systems, which in turn, leads to a narrower gap between the occurrence of events and the dissemination of related information.

The COVC and Accounting Information Systems

In Chapter 1, the customer-oriented value chain (COVC) was presented. In Figure 4–8, the COVC is presented with an accounting information system (AIS) focus. Electronic commerce activities are accounting activities that fall under the jurisdiction of the traditional assurance function and attestation of financial statements. Specific activities that can trigger a financial transaction in the COVC are identified in Figure 4–8. The items listed are just examples and are not meant to be exhaustive. Each of these e-commerce activities is discussed within the context of their potential effect on the financial statements. The following sections discuss the relationship between e-commerce and internal controls.

Sales and Marketing Activities

The e-business world has spawned and continues to spawn new revenue-sharing arrangements. Traditionally, businesses pay advertisers for space in printed mediums, such as newspapers, magazines, and roadside banners or air time on radio and television. Initially, Web-based advertising began in a similar format, but very rapidly

FIGURE 4–8	*AIS activities within the COVC*

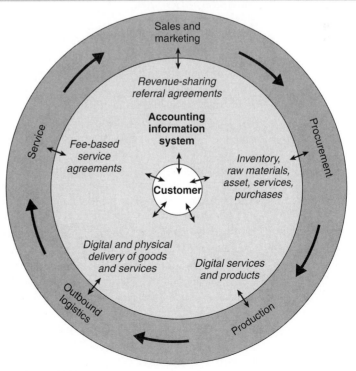

Greenstein and Ray, 2001.

FIGURE 4–9   *Revenue generating advertising techniques*

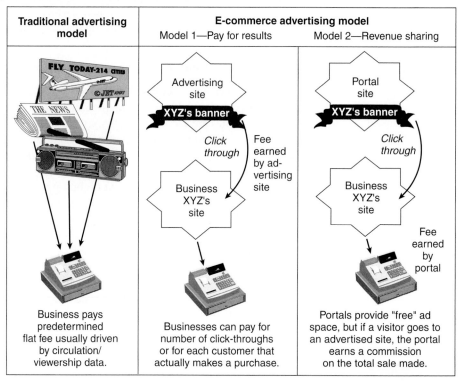

Traditional advertising model	E-commerce advertising model	
	Model 1—Pay for results	Model 2—Revenue sharing
Business pays predetermined flat fee usually driven by circulation/ viewership data.	Businesses can pay for number of click-throughs or for each customer that actually makes a purchase.	Portals provide "free" ad space, but if a visitor goes to an advertised site, the portal earns a commission on the total sale made.

Greenstein and Ray, 2001.

evolved into a "pay for results" model. This evolution was natural because of the ease of tracking online advertising results. Tracking the "success" of a specific advertisement in a magazine is difficult, if not impossible. Tracking the "success" of an electronic banner advertisement as the customer "clicks-through" is easier and generally cost effective. Thus, new advertising expense and revenue calculations are evolving. Figure 4–9 illustrates the challenge to e-commerce firms in accurately recording the advertising revenue and expense amounts. In the traditional advertising model, recording the advertising revenue or expense is straightforward. After the advertisement is placed and run, an invoice is sent. Upon verification of the accuracy of the advertisement, the invoice is paid, the expense is recorded for the business, and the revenue is recorded for the advertising firm.

In an e-commerce environment, two models are presented in Figure 4–9. The recording of the accounting transaction in the first model—the pay for results model—is straightforward for both the business and the advertising site; if a customer is delivered to the site, the business pays a fee to the site that delivered the customer. The advertising expense is incurred immediately when the customer is delivered to the site if the fee is based on number of customers delivered. Both sites can track these data, so information asymmetry and monitoring of the other site are not issues.

Another pay for results model that can be negotiated in model 1 of Figure 4–9 is to pay only for customers delivered who actually make a purchase. Obviously, this fee would be higher than the fee in the previous example.[6] In this case, the recording of the accounting transaction is straightforward for the business if the terms of the fee are clearly predetermined. The terms can be (a) payable upon delivery of a purchasing customer to the site, (b) payable upon receipt of payment by a delivered customer, or (c) payable upon delivery of good or service to the delivered customer. Most advertising sites choose option 1, but then the cancellation of an order becomes an issue in fee payment. In any case, the advertising firm does not directly observe the browsing or purchasing activity of the customer delivered to the site. In this case, the advertising site has to rely on the information reported by the business regarding the number of purchasing customers delivered to the site. If the revenues earned by an advertising site are material in aggregate from *all* of its businesses that advertise on its site, then this monitoring issue becomes a significant accounting process that must be examined in the traditional assurance function.

Model 2 illustrates a very different type of model referred to as a revenue-sharing advertising model. In this scenario, an advertising site (portal) exchanges advertising space to a business in exchange for a commission on all items purchased when the customer visits a business's site via the portal. The same revenue/expense recognition options exist as previously listed for model 1. This model, however, has information asymmetry and monitoring issues as well for the portal. The portal does not observe what is purchased by the customer and must "trust" the information reported by the business. This model can become even more convoluted when businesses, nonprofit agencies, and so forth, outsource their own portal operations. The verification of revenue information requires the verification of the unobservable actions of the portal and the many merchants.

Procurement Activities

Businesses using traditional electronic data interchange (EDI) have been purchasing physical goods, such as inventory, raw materials, and supplies, for several decades. The increased affordability of Web-based EDI is allowing more and more trading partners to engage in online procurement activities. For example, Cessna was able to increase its number of electronic suppliers from 10 to 1,300 by using Web-based EDI. Unfortunately, many businesses offering Web-based EDI services do not have their webfronts integrated with their back-order processing systems. This lack of integration can lead to inventory commitments that cannot be met, such as the 1999 Toys "R" Us debacle. Many organizations still use a "print-and-tear" ordering system whereby when a Web-based order form is received, it is printed out and then the data are reentered into the back-office order processing system. In these cases, the inventory availability cannot realistically be kept up to date on the website. One may arguably conclude that unreliable inventory information being provided to customers is not technically under the jurisdiction of the traditional assurance and attestation function. However, once these data are used by customers to make a purchase decision, a nonreversible economic event may happen—a fee or commission may have to be paid to an advertising site or portal regardless of whether the order is fulfilled. Incorrect transactions that trigger material, unnecessary costs (advertising expenses) are items that should be considered in the scope of the traditional assurance function.

---

[6]Sometimes firms will pay solely for the number of banners that are displayed to visitors (cost per impressions), but this is not a very popular model anymore since it does not consider results.

FIGURE 4–10	*Digital assets versus physical assets*

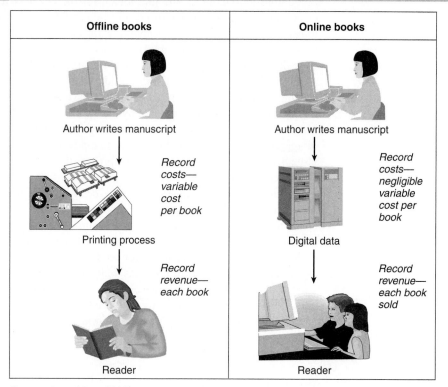

Greenstein and Ray, 2001.

Production Activities

Digital services, such as software updates and stock quotes, and products, such as software, news, and music, provide a challenge to accountants because of the "slipperiness" of the inventory. Figures 4–10 and 4–11 contrast the inventory issues for the production of offline and online books, such as Stephen King's recent novella, *Riding the Bullet,* although this example easily transfers to the hotly debated online digital distribution of music and movies. With traditional offline books, the physical production of the product is more costly, and a variable cost per book produced exists. Revenue is recorded for each book sold. In the online book example, the news stories are stored digitally and no significant variable cost per electronically distributed book occurs.[7] The customer gains access to a digital version of the book. Again, the revenue is recorded for each online book sold.

    The obvious difference between these two methods, the digital versus physical nature of the inventory, raises significant custodianship issues. In the offline example, a specific number of inventory items is determinable. Unsold books are counted and compared against production and sales numbers, and any discrepancies determined. The inventory of books on any given day is an asset under which the custodial responsibilities

---

[7]For news services, different threshold levels exist that will cause an online news provider to increase server capacity if online viewership exceeds certain levels, thus raising costs.

| FIGURE 4–11 | *Verifying digital assets versus physical assets* |

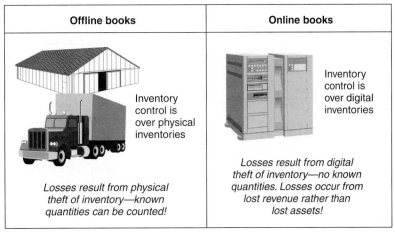

Greenstein and Ray, 2001.

fall under the traditional audit. As the inventory is sold, the assets are expensed against the revenues received from purchases. The custodian of the assets needs to ensure that inventory is not pilfered or stolen. If it is pilfered or stolen in the offline situation, then a write-down of the assets (the inventory) must occur, resulting in an expense. In the online situation, the digital master version of the book is made available to be copied and read by the paying viewer, generally password-protected to only allow authorized, paid customers to view the asset—the book.

The question of stolen or pilfered inventory becomes more difficult to handle from an accounting perspective. The first issue is determining whether unauthorized users are accessing the assets—the books. If they are viewing the online books without paying, then revenues are clearly lost. Assuming that one can determine whether unauthorized access has occurred, how is this treated? A physical hardcopy book with a variable cost attached to it has not been taken; however, the firm's most crucial assets—its writings—have been viewed, which is the same as pilfering or stealing a hardcopy. Clearly, the loss to business is the lost revenue. On the cost side, the amount is negligible, unless the amount of traffic from the unauthorized users crowds out legitimate subscribers. The custodianship of this very important asset—the digital master version of the book falls under the jurisdiction of the traditional audit. Financial accounting standards, however, have not been able to keep up with the technological developments and digital inventory issues.

The unauthorized copying of hardcopy books has always been a concern, but these concerns are intensified by digital products for two reasons: (a) they are easier and cheaper to reproduce, and (b) the "copy" is nearly or the exact quality of the original. In some cases, an authorized subscriber may be able to download stories to his or her own computer. If unauthorized subscribers are able to make a digital copy while they are accessing the digital master file, then the level of stolen assets multiplies. How should digital reproductions of an asset be treated? Again, lost revenues are the damage suffered by a company, but can it be accurately measured? In March 2000, a 66-page electronic novella by Stephen King was released by Glassbook Inc. The electronic book was encrypted with "loose" encryption, and shortly after its release, unencrypted, pirated versions of the book began showing up on websites. The pirated versions were identical in form to what a paying customer would get from Amazon.com. From an accounting standpoint, one must ask the question, was inventory stolen? If so, how can accountants help to prevent this, and how do they record the loss, if at all? Even if a dollar amount is not calculated for an expense charge, should the opportunity cost of lost sales be required to be disclosed in notes to the financial statements? Is this important to the going-concern assessment? How does one value the opportunity costs?

Somewhat similar issues arise regarding other digital intellectual properties, such as software. One viewpoint regarding such products is that frequent upgrades must be purchased, and these will render "bootlegged" copies obsolete after a fairly short period of time. This reasoning does not apply well to the arts, however. Books and music are typically written (recorded) once, and upon that event their value/contribution is determined. A bootlegged digital copy of Pavarotti's Greatest Hits has a much longer (indefinite) useful life than Microsoft's *Office 2000.* The answers to these questions need to be addressed by the financial accounting profession. Only then can guidance be given to the audit profession.

Outbound Logistics

Digital goods and services purchased over the Internet can be delivered either online or offline. Nondigital (physical) goods and services must be delivered through traditional offline mechanisms. For goods sold online, but delivered offline, no unique accounting situations occur. Some questionable business practices, such as booking revenues minus cost of goods sold for inventory items that were never in the possession of the selling firm, are coming to the attention of regulators. But these scenarios are not unique to e-commerce. Digital goods and services that are delivered online, however, are important for accounting purposes. Services, such as online brokerage firms, need to reliably deliver the service. If a firm generates revenues through digital products and services, such as Internet Service Providers (ISPs), then the subscriber should only pay for these goods and services if they are accessible and delivered reliably. Customers who do not get reliable delivery of goods and services may have a reasonable claim against the firm to recover any payment made in advance for services or for a reduction in their bill. Thus, the reliable delivery of digital goods and services is part of the revenue-earning activities; hence, accountants need to monitor these activities and make sure that they accurately portray the reported and billed revenue.

Service

Service and customer care are very important aspects of electronic business. Service is considered in this model to be the after-the-sale customer care. For e-commerce purposes, only those service situations that are fee-based or contractual, such as warranties, are examined because of their potential financial statement implications. Similar to the previous discussion regarding the importance of reliable delivery of products in the revenue-earning stream, so too is its importance in the service revenue-generating stream. Customers may pay technical support for a product, and to the extent that portions of that support are delivered online, then the reliability of that service is important. For example, a security consulting firm that sells firewall products and that also sells remote diagnostic checks must have the services available when the customer requests them, or the revenue will not be legitimately earned.

Some service arrangements may be configured on a per-use basis. In that case, the system must appropriately record all requests for services so that bills can be generated. Also, if 24/7 service is advertised as "part of the reason" to purchase a good or service, then the company becomes responsible for providing that service to the owners of the product. Thus, when accountants are attesting to the assets and cost of goods sold, they cannot neglect to examine whether services promoted with a tangible or digital product are available as promised. If they are not, a material amount of goods may be returned or future sales may be lower, affecting the probability of the entity's being a going concern.

THIRD-PARTY ASSURANCE OF WEB-BASED E-COMMERCE

Security risks faced by businesses engaging in Web-based electronic commerce are raised in Chapter 7, and security techniques to control these risks are presented in subsequent chapters. While recognizing that current security solutions are not perfect and must continue to evolve, at any given point in time cost-effective solutions can be identified. From a consumer or business partner perspective, five categories of concerns arise. These categories are illustrated in Figure 4–12 and discussed next.

FIGURE 4–12   *Major concerns of consumers and business partners*

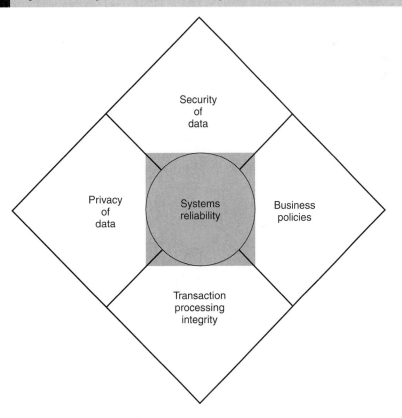

Categories of Concern

Security of Data

The level of protection that is provided is called **data security.** The underlying security questions are

- How secure are the data *maintained* by this business?
  - Personal/business entity data?
  - Website's data used by consumer or trading partner to make transaction decisions?
  - How secure are the data as *transmitted* to and from this business?

Data that are maintained by a business need to be protected from unauthorized access and tampering, as well as unintentional harm. Data stored on a web site server are generally considered to be less secure than data stored internally behind a firewall. (Firewalls are discussed in more detail in Chapter 11.)

Business Policies

The **business policies** of an organization refer to its stated practices. A concern is whether a firm publicly lists its business policies in an easy-to-find place and understandable format. Also of importance is whether a business actually follows its stated policies. Some of the more common business policies that businesses share with trading partners are:

- Billing and payment policies.
- Shipping policy.
- Return policy.
- Tax collection policy.
- Additional policy information.

Transaction Processing Integrity

Transaction processing integrity refers to the precision with which transactions are processed according to agreed-upon methods. In traditional EDI systems, such processing methods may be clearly stated in formal trading agreements. With Web-based e-commerce, trading partners should be able to receive some level of assurance regarding the integrity of transaction processing. Some underlying transaction processing integrity issues are

- What is in place at the company to ensure that transactions are handled as disclosed?
- How does the company ensure that it does not "lose" orders placed?
- How does the company ensure that it accurately processes bills and account information?
- What controls exist to ensure that the company accurately posts payments in a timely fashion?
- Does the company have controls in place to ensure that it ships the right inventory items and quantities?

Privacy of Data

The **privacy of data** refers to the confidentiality of data collected by businesses about their customers. For websites, the data collected about visitors who are not "customers" and how the data are used is also an issue. Privacy issues are further examined in the following chapter, but the main underlying issues are

- What is the privacy policy of the business?
- What information does the business keep?
- How will any information collected be used by the business?
- Will this business share or sell customer data without the customer's permission or knowledge?
- Can the customer verify data and change or delete it?
- What ensures that the company's privacy policies are observed and practiced on a continuous basis?

Another issue is whether a business has stability in its stated privacy policies or changes them at the discomfort of its customers. In September 2000, in an effort to ward off negative feelings by its customers toward a change in its privacy policy, Amazon.com sent an email to all its customers stating:

> Dear Customer,
>
> We have just updated Amazon.com's privacy policy and, because privacy is important, we wanted to e-mail you proactively in this case and not just update the policy on our site, as is the common Web practice. Thanks for being a customer and allowing us to continue to earn your trust.
>
> To read the updated Privacy Notice, visit: *http://www.amazon.com/privacy-notice*
>
> Thanks again for shopping at Amazon.com
>
> Sincerely,
>
> Amazon.com

Systems Reliability

In e-commerce, a critical concern of trading partners is the reliability of the system underlying its electronic transaction processing systems. To some extent, **systems reliability assurance** is embedded in the other categories of concern just discussed: security of data, business policies, transaction processing integrity, and privacy of data. The concept of reliability, however, encompasses critical attributes that are not solely covered by these areas. A reliable system is available when needed and performing procedures and processes as designed without exceptions. In e-commerce, server reliability is an important issue. Customers need the telecommunications links and its trading partners' servers to be properly functioning so that the desired information is accessible when it is needed. Also, the server's links to the underlying databases and processing systems within the trustee's organization and the Internet need to be reliable.

Trust in Electronic Relationships

During the past four years, the accounting profession has launched two new assurance services embedded with the word *trust*—**WebTrust** and **SysTrust.** An understanding of the meaning of trust is a precursor to understanding and evaluating these new product lines. In this section, an electronic business model designed by Greenstein and Vasarhelyi[8] is

---

[8]Greenstein, Marilyn and Miklos Verschelyi. "Trust du Jour: The Development of an Assurance Trust Model and Examination of WebTrust and SysTrust," presented at the Annual American Accounting Association Meeting, 2000.

presented that represents the third-party assurance function. The e-business trust model is developed from Mayer, Davis, and Schoorman's[9] model of organizational trust. Their model is presented in this section and adapted.

Definition of Trust

Mayer, Davis, and Schoorman provide a definition of trust that translates well to the assurance profession:

> Trust is the willingness of a party to be vulnerable to the actions of another party based on the expectation that the other will perform a particular action important to the trustor, irrespective of the ability to monitor or control that other party.

Implicit in this definition is the requirement that a party incur some risk. The risk stems from the vulnerability resulting from being unable to observe or control the actions of the other party. The amount of trust in the other party is a key factor in determining whether the party will engage in a course of action that is perceived to be risky. Thus, trust is only necessary for those situations that are perceived to be risky. The two new assurance initiatives offered by the accounting profession that are examined in this chapter, *WebTrust* and *SysTrust,* were developed in direct response to new risks facing consumers and businesses as a result of e-commerce.

Mayer, Davis, and Schoorman's definition of trust is customized to represent the vulnerability inherent in electronic commerce transactions:

> Trust, in the context of electronic commerce, is the willingness of a trading partner to be vulnerable to the actions performed by the system of another trading partner based on the expectation that the other trading partner will perform a particular action or sequence of actions important to the trustor, irrespective of the ability to monitor or control the other trading party.

This definition is slightly different. The parties are specifically defined to be external entities. Trading partners can mean either business-to-business or business-to-consumer parties.[10] Implicit in this definition is the downtime of trading partners' servers due to overcapacity and maintenance. This definition reflects that the actions will be performed by the trustee organization's "system," which generally refers to its electronic system but does not preclude a system that has manual processing components. For example, some Web-based ordering systems are electronic in the interaction with the trading partner but may actually result in back-office manual processing. Because of the nature of systems and their incorporation of a sequence of actions, this terminology is added to the definition of system trust.

The Trust Model and Its Components

A model that relates e-commerce, trust, and third-party assurance services is illustrated in Figure 4–13. Two trading partners are represented in the model. Trading partner A is the trustee and trading partner B is the trustor. In a business-to-consumer relationship, the business is the trustee—trading partner A. The consumer is the trustor—trading partner B. In a business-to-business relationship, many different scenarios can result, and reciprocal relationships can occur; for example, two companies can buy and sell from one another. For descriptive purposes, trading partner A represents the supplier of goods/services, and trading partner B represents the purchaser of goods/services.

---

[9]Mayer, Roger C., James H. Davis, and F. David Schoorman. "An Integrative Model of Organizational Trust," *Academy of Management Review,* Vol. 20, No. 3, July 1995, pp, 709–734.

[10]The term *external entity* does not preclude a business from transacting with other segments/divisions of its own business. If the business segment transacting with another business segment uses the same mechanism as external trading partners, then they are considered equivalent in this definition of trust.

| **FIGURE 4–13** | *E-commerce, trust, and third-party assurance* |

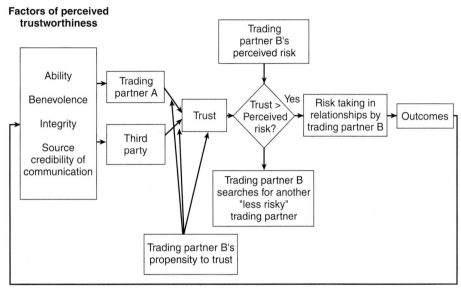

Based on Mayer, Davis, and Schoorman's 1995 model of organizational trust

Trust is described by Mayer, Davis, and Schoorman as a function of four factors: ability, benevolence, integrity, and the trustor's propensity. Ability, benevolence, and integrity are perceived characteristics of the trustee, while the trustor's propensity is a characteristic of the trustor. The characteristics are not the actual or true levels, but rather the level as *perceived* by the trustor. Each of these factors are defined and then discussed within the context of electronic commerce and third-party assurance services.

Propensity is considered to be the general willingness of the trustor to trust in others. Propensity varies from individual to individual,[11] and in the context of organizations being a nexus of people, from organization to organization. In addition to the trustor's propensity to trust, the level of trust is also impacted by the **perceived trustworthiness** of the trustee. Four characteristics of trustworthiness of the trustee are included in the model. Three of the characteristics are given by Mayer, Davis, and Schoorman: ability, benevolence, and integrity.

Ability encompasses the appropriate skill level and competencies for a specific domain. The perception of the trustee's ability or expertise level is viewed as task and situation specific. With regard to e-commerce systems, the ability of the trustee encompasses the specific tasks of data processing, security of data during transmission and storage, and capability of providing the required goods/services in a timely fashion. Trading partner A is the party that either directly maintains these systems or indirectly does so by outsourcing. The third-party assurance provider examines the capabilities of the underlying systems and the management of them.

Benevolence represents the degree of positive attitude of the trustee toward the trustor. In e-commerce, the benevolence of both trading partner A and the third-party assurance provider are important in building and maintaining customer relationships.

---

[11]Mayer, Roger C., James H. Davis, and F. David Schoorman. "An Integrative Model of Organizational Trust," *Academy of Management Review,* Vol. 20, No. 3, July 1995, pp. 709–734.

Integrity incorporates the principles of the trustee. The perception by the trustor regarding the trustee's level of integrity is generally formed from knowledge of prior actions, such as consistency between delivered actions and promised actions, and references from credible other parties, such as other clients/trading partners and third-party assurance providers. In e-commerce, integrity not only reflects the general character of the trading partner and the third-party assurance provider; it also reflects the integrity of the underlying systems that process the transactions. According to the AICPA, **integrity assurance systems** ensure that all of the data elements captured in an electronic transaction are the agreed-upon elements and that the integrity of the data elements are maintained during processing and storage procedures. Thus, integrity is a characteristic that measures many facets: character of both trading partner A and the third-party assurance provider, and the integrity of the underlying systems.

The fourth characteristic is put forth by Tinsley[12] and refers to the signals or messages sent by the trustee, called **source credibility of communication.** Ability is a precursor to source credibility, but source credibility does not necessarily follow ability. These messages should be perceived as accurate, complete, and timely so that the trustor can rely on them for making decisions and engaging in risk-taking actions.

Perceived Risk, Level of Trust, and Risk-Taking Action

At any given point in time, a party will only engage in risk-taking actions if the level of trust is greater than the perceived risk. In this model, the trustor's problem-domain context affects the necessity of trust and the evaluation of trustworthiness. For example, the level of trust necessary for a trading partner to engage in the purchase of a relatively small dollar amount purchase of office supplies may be vastly different from the level of trust necessary to engage in the purchase of raw materials for a just-in-time production line.

As illustrated in Figure 4–13, if the perceived level of trust is greater than the perceived risk, trading partner B will agree to take the risk and, for example, order some raw materials from trading partner A's website. However, if the perceived risk is greater than the perceived level of trust, trading partner B will search for another less risky trading partner. If trading partner B has a very low propensity to trust, it may not find another online site with which it is comfortable. In any case, trading partner B may choose to transact offline, and trading partner A may once again become a viable option.

Outcomes and Future Levels of Perceived Trustworthiness

The trust model is dynamic and allows for outcomes to affect future perceptions of trustworthiness as illustrated by the feedback loop in Figure 4–13. Intuitively, one would expect positive outcomes to strengthen the perceived trustworthiness in the future and undesirable outcomes to weaken the perceived trustworthiness, although not necessarily by similar factors. For example, positive outcomes may somewhat strengthen future levels of perceived trustworthiness, while negative outcomes may strongly weaken future levels of perceived trustworthiness.

Positive outcomes, such as orders placed and the appropriate goods delivered in a timely fashion with no billing problems, can strengthen future levels of perceived trustworthiness. Early in the relationship, these positive outcomes may have a greater effect on revisions of perceived level of trustworthiness. After a fairly stable relationship has developed over time, however, just one significant negative outcome—for example,

---

[12]Tinsley, Dillard. "Trust Plus Capabilities," *Academy of Management Review,* April 1996.

a lost order—can significantly reduce the perceived level of trustworthiness in the trustee by a significantly greater amount than the trust built up over several previous outcomes.

An important issue regarding the effect of negative outcomes for sites that bear a third-party assurance seal is whether their impact transfers to other sites bearing the same seal. Negative outcomes of trusting behaviors at one site bearing a seal will likely lead to less weight being placed on the third-party assurance seal at other sites. Thus, the third-party seal will have less influence on the trustor's assessment of risk for a given site that bears a "tarnished" seal.

Third-Party Assurance Contracting

Contracting with a third-party assurance firm to provide an extra signal of trustworthiness to the market has costs. A trustee firm has many issues to consider. One consideration entails identifying the alternatives of third-party assurance providers that are available. Secondly, the strength of the signal sent by the third party must be considered. The translation of the strength of the signal into tangible benefits, a positive outcome, is another important consideration. Finally, the total cost of purchasing the signal must be compared against the positive outcomes generated. Thus, various providers of third-party assurance bear the burden of convincing potential clients of the strength of the signal being purchased relative to costs as well as delivering the outcomes so that the signal will continue to be purchased.

WEBSITE SEAL OPTIONS

The posting of privacy policies has increased dramatically over the last few years. In 2000, the Federal Trade Commission reported that 88 percent of all firms examined posted at least one privacy disclosure and that 76 percent of the firms linked to it from their home page. Regarding cookies, however (discussed in the following chapter), 54 percent of all firms were silent on the issue. Regarding the security of personal data that are collected, the site did not report as high marks. Only 39 percent state that they take steps to protect data during transmission, and an even lower 29 percent state that they protect data after collection.

In response to consumers' reluctance to transact with websites with which they are not comfortable about these and other issues, various organizations are offering seals or insignias for businesses to place on their websites to help instill consumer confidence and sort out the varying policies. In order to bear these seals, the company or website must demonstrate its ability to maintain certain capabilities, policies, or controls. In this section, six such seal options are reviewed and compared: Better Business Bureau (BBB), TRUSTe, Veri-Sign, BizRate, *WebTrust,* and *SysTrust* by the American Institute of Certified Public Accountants (AICPA) and the Canadian Institute of Chartered Accountants (CICA). These seals are displayed in Figure 4–14.

Better Business Bureau

The **Better Business Bureau (BBB)** is a private, nonprofit organization that has been promoting ethical business standards and voluntary self-regulation of businesses since 1912. The BBB also provides a mechanism for tracking consumer complaints about its member organizations, currently numbering more than 250,000, and helping to resolve consumer disputes. As many businesses migrate portions of their operations to the Internet and new Internet businesses enter the marketplace, a natural, logical extension of

| FIGURE 4–14 | *Website assurance seal options* |

the BBB's service is to promote ethical business practices on the Internet. The BBB's initial response was to launch its BBB*Online* seal. The seal is administered by a wholly owned subsidiary of the BBB, called BBBOnline, Inc. BBB*Online* has expanded and now offers three different seals: Reliability Seal Program, Privacy Seal, and Kid's Privacy Seal. The requirements of the reliability seal are:

- Become a member of the appropriate local BBB.
- Provide the BBB with information regarding company ownership and management, street address, and telephone number at which they conduct business, which is verified by the BBB in a visit to the physical premises.
- Be in business a minimum of one year (with limited exceptions).
- Have a satisfactory complaint handling record with the BBB.
- Agree to participate in the BBB's advertising self-regulation program, and correct or withdraw online advertising when challenged by the BBB and found not to be in compliance with its children's advertising guidelines.
- Respond promptly to all consumer complaints.
- Agree to binding arbitration, at the consumer's request, for unresolved disputes involving consumer products or services advertised or promoted online.

Membership in the local BBB requires payment of a fee. Additionally, a license fee is charged for participation in the BBB*Online* program. The fees are variable, depending on the number of employees in a company. As of mid-2000, more than 5,000 websites bore the BBB*Online* seal.

What assurances does the seal provide the consumer? Referring to Figure 4–12, the BBB*Online* program touches lightly on the business policies issue to the extent that it "vouches" for the business's advertising ethics and response to consumer complaints. It does not, however, mean that the business policies have been reviewed by the BBB.

Regarding transaction integrity, the BBB*Online* seal does not directly verify the integrity controls supporting electronic transaction processing, but it does track customer complaints, and it reserves the right to revoke the seal if too many complaints are received and/or are not satisfactorily handled. The issue of privacy is handled with the additional Privacy and Kid's Privacy seals. As of late 2000, 500 privacy seals had been issued by BBB*Online.* The privacy seal requires that the business

- Post privacy notices telling consumers what personal information is being collected, how it will be used, and choices they have in terms of use.
- Verify security measures taken to protect this information.
- Commit to abide by their posted privacy policies.
- Agree to a comprehensive independent verification by BBB*OnLine.*
- Participate in the programs' dispute resolution service.

The Kid's Privacy seal is a little more stringent, it requires that the website

- Obtain parental consent before any personally identifiable information is collected, used, or disclosed.
- Obtain parental consent before children are allowed to post or communicate directly with others.
- Provide warnings and explanations in easy-to-understand language.
- Avoid collecting more information than necessary when offering children's games and activities.
- Be careful in the way they provide hyperlinks.
- Follow strict rules when sending e-mail.

TRUSTe

TRUSTe is another nonprofit organization issuing a seal. In 1996, TRUSTe was championed by the Electronic Frontier Foundation, a nonprofit civil liberties organization working to protect privacy rights. The objective of TRUSTe is to build users' trust on the Internet and increase consumer confidence on the Internet. Thus, this product addresses only one of the four concerns illustrated in Figure 4–12: privacy. As of late 2000, more than 1,400 websites bore the TRUSTe "trustmark." The requirements of the TRUSTe seal are

- Sign a license agreement agreeing to follow TRUSTe privacy policy disclosure standards.
- Post an easily understandable privacy statement disclosing
  - What information is being collected.
  - Who is collecting the information.
  - For what purposes the information is collected.
  - With whom the information is shared.
- Post the choices available to users regarding collection, use, and distribution of the information. The site must offer users an opportunity to opt out of internal secondary uses as well as third-party distribution for secondary uses.
- Post the security procedures in place to protect users' collected information from loss, misuse, or alteration.
- Post how users can update or correct inaccuracies in their pertinent information.

- Satisfactorily respond to customer complaints within a reasonable period. TRUSTe may provide input for complaint resolution.
- Agree to site compliance reviews by TRUSTe or other independent third parties (under certain situations), including
  - Review of privacy statements.
  - Regular "seeding" of personally identifiable information to test adherence to stated privacy policies.

An annual license fee is required, and it is based on revenue. TRUSTe also has specific children's site criteria and a separate seal associated with the more restrictive privacy practices it requires of children-focused websites. For sites that are directed at children under 13, the following requirements must be met:

The site must NOT

- Collect online contact information from a child under 13 without prior verifiable parental consent or direct parental notification of the nature and intended use of this information, which shall include an opportunity for the parent to prevent use of the information and participation in the activity. Where prior verifiable parental consent is not obtained, online contact information shall only be used to directly respond to the child's request and shall not be used to recontact the child for other purposes.
- Collect or distribute personally identifiable offline contact information from children under 13 without prior verifiable parental consent.
- Give the ability to children under 13 to publicly post or otherwise distribute personally identifiable contact information without prior verifiable parental consent. The site must make its best efforts to prohibit a child from posting any contact information.
- Entice a child under 13 by the prospect of a special game, prize, or other activity to divulge more information than is needed to participate in such activity.

The site must also place prominent notice wherever personally identifiable information is collected requesting the child to ask a parent for permission to answer the questions.

For either program, TRUSTe requires that the privacy policy be easily found. Further, it must be written so that it can be understood by the average consumer. TRUSTe requires that the stated policy be followed by the business bearing the insignia. Further, TRUSTe provides a mechanism for customers to post complaints about any of its members' privacy policies or practices. If a site is found to be in noncompliance with its own stated privacy policy, TRUSTe can revoke its trustmark.

Veri-Sign Inc.

A for-profit corporation, Veri-Sign Inc. was established in 1995 as a spin-off of RSA Data Security Inc. Veri-Sign's mission is "to provide digital certificate solutions to enable trusted commerce and communications." Specifically, **Veri-Sign** provides products that allow websites to transmit encrypted data and to provide authentication about the source and destination of the data. Authentication and encryption are ways that consumers and business partners can gain confidence about the integrity of the source and destination parties engaging in data transmission. As of late 2000, Veri-Sign had issued more than 340,000 website digital certificates and more than 3.9 million individual digital certificates.

The products offered by Veri-Sign address only one of the four concerns presented in Figure 4–12: security. The security it provides is over data transmission to and from the website; it does not provide security over data maintained in databases that reside on

Internet-connected systems. Veri-Sign offers three levels of security certification products. Class 1 and Class 2 certificates are only issued to individuals, not businesses or organizations. Class 3 certificates are issued to individuals, businesses, and organizations. Class 3 certificates issued for the purpose of authenticating a business site must meet the following requirements:

- A third-party confirmation of business entity information, including the business entity's
  - Name.
  - Address.
  - Telephone numbers.
  - Any other industry-deemed information appropriate to the business.
- Domain name confirmation.

BizRate

In a very different model of third-party signals, the customers provide the ratings of businesses on 10 different dimensions with **BizRate.** This information is collected, aggregated, and provided to potential customers. The websites are monitored at two points: the point of sale and after the expected delivery date of the good/service. BizRate does not charge any of its participating firms a membership fee to participate in the survey process in order to remain as independent and objective as possible. BizRate earns its revenues from its online marketplace but maintains that the survey results are independent and objective. BizRate claims that it has ratings on thousands of stores and tens of thousands of online customers who complete its surveys every day. It updates the store ratings weekly. The dimensions of service ratings are

- Ease of ordering (convenience and speed of ordering).
- Product selection (breadth/depth of products offered).
- Product information (information quantity, quality, and relevance).
- Price (prices relative to similar stores).
- Website navigation and looks (layout, links, pictures, images, and speed).
- Shipping and handling (charges).
- On-time delivery (expected versus actual delivery data).
- Product representation (product description/depiction versus what you received).
- Level and quality of customer support (status updates and complaint/question handling).
- Privacy policy (online store's efforts to inform you).

Also, BizRate will not post any ratings until a certain (not stated) minimum number of surveys are conducted so that they are not unfairly representing just a few consumers. Businesses that choose to participate in the program at no cost are identified as a BizRate gold star store, and filling out the survey becomes an automatic option after the purchase. Other stores followed by BizRate that do not agree to participate are monitored and surveyed by its research panel of more than 200,000 online buyers. BizRate also provides company profiles that include items such as ordering methods supported, delivery methods available, payment methods accepted, and other special features. It also indicates whether or not the site uses Veri-Sign.

AICPA/CICA WebTrust Programs

The AICPA/CICA initiated the *WebTrust* program to address the concerns of customers regarding security and privacy issues. In 1997, the AICPA commissioned Yankelovich Partners to survey Internet users and assess their attitudes toward online purchasing. The number one reason given by participants for not buying goods and services on the Internet was the perceived lack of security. After being briefed on the *WebTrust* program, nearly one-half (46 percent) of the participants indicated that the presence of the *WebTrust* seal would increase the likelihood that they would purchase a good or service from that website.

Initially, the *WebTrust* seal was one service offering. The services are currently being divided, however, in multiple, disparate e-commerce service offerings in the following areas:

- Business-to-consumer e-commerce transactions.
- Online privacy.
- Internet service providers.
- Certification authorities.

Additionally, the AICPA has developed another offering, *SysTrust,* which is a systems reliability assurance for business to business. *SysTrust* is examined in the following section.

In order to obtain a *WebTrust* Seal, a CPA, or chartered accountant (CA) in Canada, must perform an examination of the site's business practice disclosures, transaction integrity controls, and security and privacy practices. The examination must be performed according to the AICPA's **Standards for Attestation Engagements No. 1** (also known as AICPA Professional Standards Section AT 100) or the *CICA's Standards for Assurance Engagements* (also known as the CICA Handbook Section 5025). To provide this service, CPAs or CAs must attend a special AICPA-administered training session and be approved to issue *WebTrust* seals. Once the seal is issued, a potential customer shopping on the Internet can visit a trusted third-party service organization, currently Veri-Sign, to verify the authenticity of the *WebTrust* seal. The *WebTrust* seal itself indicates that a specially licensed *WebTrust* CPA or CA has examined the website's compliance with specified criteria. The seal also indicates that the website was fully compliant with the *WebTrust* 2.0 criteria in the three focus areas: business and information privacy practices, transaction integrity, and information protection.

WebTrust Seal for Business-to-Consumer E-Commerce Transactions

The process for issuing a seal is illustrated in Figure 4–15. One key component is the demonstration by the firm or organization to the accountant of at least two months' worth of transaction data that have been processed in accordance with the stated business policies. The review and verification of stated business policies and the integrity and reliability of processing methods differentiate the *WebTrust* seal from the other seals. Websites bearing the *WebTrust* seal must apply for and use a Class 3 digital certificate from Veri-Sign. Digital certificates and their various classes are discussed in Chapter 10.

Initially in version 1.0, the seal had to be refreshed at least every 90 days; in version 2.0 that has been relaxed somewhat by leaving it up to the judgment of the CPA or CA. The individual CPA may also use judgment as to how much and what type of testing must be conducted for seal refreshment. A key component in the maintenance process is the documentation and justification of any changes in policies or transaction methods.

FIGURE 4–15   *AICPA WebTrust seal issuance process*

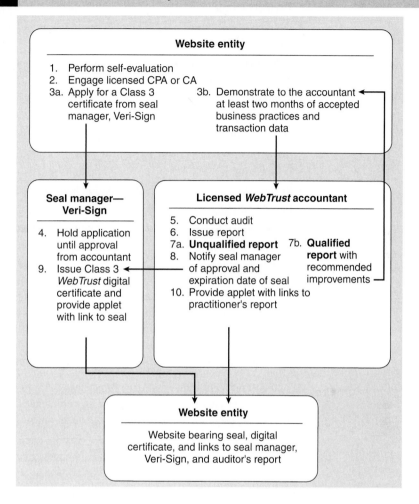

The three categories of risk as defined by the AICPA/CICA are explained below. The information protection category includes the security of data category mentioned in Figure 4–12. Thus, the *WebTrust* 2.0 program covers all four categories of risk. Version 3.0 is slated to have four new principles: availability, confidentiality, nonrepudiation, and customized disclosures. Because these principles have not yet been disclosed, they will be updated to this text's website when they are released.

Business and Information Privacy Practices.   The customer is informed about the business policies of the organization represented by the website, such as delivery policies, privacy policies, return of merchandise, and warranties. The customer can feel assured that the website does not change its business policies at random and that the business has an established history of maintaining such business practices. Some examples of business practices disclosure criteria as listed by the AICPA/CICA include

- Time frame for order fulfillment.
- Time frame for backorder notification.

- Delivery methods.
- Payment terms.
- Payment mechanisms, including electronic payment methods and any related charges to the customer.
- Cancellation procedures of recurring charges.
- Product return policies.
- Condition of good being sold (i.e., new or refurbished).
- Full description of services.
- How information presented was gathered and compiled.
- Location of warranty, service, and support information.
- Information regarding how to file complaints and ask questions.
- Specific kinds and source of information being collected.
- Possible distribution of personal information to third parties.
- Choice given to customers about their personal information collected.
- Method of using cookies, if at all, and consequences to customer of not accepting a cookie.

Transaction Integrity.   The customer gains assurance that he or she will be shipped the goods or services ordered in the time frame disclosed and that he or she will be billed the appropriate agreed-upon amount. Trading partners that have credit card agreements can be assured that billing disputes will be minimized. Some examples of transaction integrity disclosure criteria as listed by the AICPA/CICA include

- Controls are maintained to provide reasonable assurance that
  - Orders are checked for accuracy and completeness.
  - The customer acknowledges the order before it is processed.
  - The sales prices along with all other costs are clearly displayed to the customer before they are required to acknowledge the order for processing.
  - The correct goods and correct quantities are shipped in the time period agreed.
  - The agreed-upon services and information are provided to the customer.
  - The customer is promptly notified about backorders and order exceptions.
  - The billing of orders is processed as agreed, and payment mechanisms are implemented as agreed (i.e., recurring charges or not charging the customer's credit card until the goods are shipped).
  - Prompt correction of any processing, billing, or settlement errors.
- Monitoring procedures are maintained to ensure
  - That the business's practice disclosures on its website remain current.
  - The transaction integrity controls remain effective.
  - That reports of noncompliance are kept and promptly addressed and remedied.

Information Protection.   Consumers can gain assurance that the business uses appropriate data encryption and firewall mechanisms to protect sensitive information, such as credit card data, both during transmission of such data over the Internet and during storage of the data by the site's Internet-connected server. Information protection controls also cover the policies and controls surrounding the protection of personal information. This may include name, address, and phone number, and buying habits, browsing habits, and personal preferences. Some examples of information protection disclosure criteria as listed by the AICPA/CICA include

- Private customer information is protected by controls during transmission over the Internet.
- Private customer information obtained from e-commerce transactions residing in a corporate database is protected by controls from outside access.
- Private customer information is not intentionally disclosed to third parties without notifying the customer prior to collecting the data or receiving customer permission.
- Private customer information obtained for e-commerce operations is used only by the necessary employees of the entity.
- Customer permission is received before storing, retrieving, or altering information stored on the customer's computer (i.e., cookies).
- Customer permission is received before personally identifiable information is used for any other purpose other than processing the transaction, including internal secondary uses.
- Prevention techniques are used against transmission of viruses to customers.

Report Issuance.   Upon the completion of a comprehensive examination, assuming the website demonstrates compliance with the *WebTrust* criteria, the accountant will issue a report that clearly states the time period for which the review was conducted. The report also broadly defines the scope of the review. An AICPA illustrative example of a sample report is given in Figure 4–16. The purpose of the report is not to give specific information about practices; rather it is to indicate that the business practices have been reviewed. If consumers want information about specific practices, they should be able to find this information on the website. The accountant's report provides assurance to consumers that the business practices disclosed on the website are indeed followed by the website entity.

WebTrust Seal for Online Privacy

This seal of assurance is covered by the version 3.0 *WebTrust* principles (currently in exposure draft form) for assurance of business transactions. Thus, the online privacy program 3.0 is a subset of the program just discussed. It is provided as a modular offering. In version 3.0, the AICPA/CICA define privacy as

> . . . the protection of the collection, storage, and dissemination of personally identifiable information. Personally identifiable information is defined as any information relating to an identified or identifiable individual.

To earn a *WebTrust* online privacy seal, the business must demonstrate that

- It complied with its disclosed privacy practices for at least two or more months.
- Its controls over privacy operated effectively.
- It maintained a control environment that is conducive to reliable privacy disclosures and effective controls.
- It maintained monitoring procedures to ensure that such privacy practices remain current and such controls remain effective in conformity with the *WebTrust* privacy criteria.

The criteria for each of these components are comprehensive and rigorous as outlined in Figure 4–17.

FIGURE 4–16   *Illustrative independent accountant's report*

AICPA/CICA Illustrative Example of Practitioner Reports—
Use in the United States Independent Accountant's Report

We have examined the assertion **[hot link to management's assertion]** by the management of ABC Company Inc. (ABC) regarding the disclosure of its e-commerce business and information privacy practices on its website and the effectiveness of its controls over transaction integrity and information protection for e-commerce (at www.abc.com) based on the AICPA/CICA WebTrust Criteria **[hot link]**, during the period Xxxx xx, 1999, through Yyyy yy, 2000.

These e-commerce disclosures and controls are the responsibility of ABC Company's management. Our responsibility is to express an opinion based on our examination.

Our examination was conducted in accordance with attestation standards established by the American Institute of Certified Public Accountants and, accordingly, included (1) obtaining an understanding of ABC Company's e-commerce business and information privacy practices and its controls over the processing of e-commerce transactions and the protection of related private customer information, (2) selectively testing transactions executed in accordance with disclosed business and information privacy practices, (3) testing and evaluating the operating effectiveness of the controls, and (4) performing such other procedures as we considered necessary in the circumstances. We believe that our examination provides a reasonable basis for our opinion.

Because of inherent limitations in controls, error or fraud may occur and not be detected. Furthermore, the projection of any conclusions, based on our findings, to future periods is subject to the risk that (1) changes made to the system or controls, (2) changes in processing requirements, or (3) changes required because of the passage of time, such as to accommodate dates in the year 2000, or (4) degree of compliance with the policies or procedures may alter the validity of such conclusions.

In our opinion, during the period Xxxx xx, 1999, through Yyyy yy, 2000, ABC Company, in all material respects—

- Disclosed its business and information privacy practices for e-commerce transactions and executed transactions in accordance with its disclosed practices
- Maintained effective controls to provide reasonable assurance that customers' orders placed using e-commerce were completed and billed as agreed
- Maintained effective controls to provide reasonable assurance that private customer information obtained as a result of e-commerce was protected from uses not related to ABC's business based on the AICPA/CICA *WebTrust* criteria.

The CPA *WebTrust* Seal of assurance on ABC's website for e-commerce constitutes a symbolic representation of the contents of this report and it is not intended, nor should it be construed, to update this report or provide any additional assurance.

This report does not include any representation as to the quality of ABC's goods or services nor their suitability for any customer's intended purpose.

[*Name of CPA firm*]

Certified Public Accountants

[*City, State*]

[*Date*]

FIGURE 4–17	*AICPA's online privacy criteria*

Disclosures

The entity discloses on its website its information privacy practices. These practices include, but are not limited to, the following disclosures:

1. The specific kinds and sources of information being collected and maintained; the use of that information; and possible third-party distribution of that information.
2. Individuals should be given the opportunity to opt out of such use, by either not providing such information or denying its distribution to parties not involved with the transaction.
3. Sensitive information needed for the e-commerce transaction. Individuals must "opt in" before this information is gathered and transmitted.
4. The consequences, if any, of an individual's refusal to provide information or of an individual's decision to opt out of a particular use of such information.
5. How individually identifiable information collected can be reviewed and, if necessary, corrected or removed.
6. If the website uses cookies or other tracking methods (e.g., web bugs, middleware), the entity discloses how they are used. If the customer refuses cookies, the consequences, if any, of such refusal are disclosed.
7. The entity discloses information to enable customers to contact it for questions or support.
8. The entity discloses any additional privacy practices needed to comply with applicable laws or regulations or any self-regulatory programs in which the entity participates.
9. The entity discloses the process used to resolve disputes.
10. The entity discloses changes or updates to its practices.

Policies, Goals, and Objectives

1. The entity's policies, goals, and objectives regarding the protection of personally identifiable information consider but are not limited to the following items:
   - Notice to the customer regarding the information collected.
   - Choice to the customer regarding the type(s) of information gathered and any options the customer has regarding the collection of this information.
   - Access by the customer to his or her private information for update and corrective purposes.
   - Security of the customer's private information.
   - Enforcement and consumer recourse policies regarding customer privacy.
2. The employees are aware of and follow the entity's published privacy policy.
3. Accountability for the privacy policy has been assigned.
4. The entity provides for adequate security of the programs and data during the backup, offsite storage, and restoration processes.
5. Documented privacy objectives, policies, and standards are consistent with disclosed privacy requirements.

Security Criteria That Relate to Privacy

1. The entity has procedures to establish new users.
2. The entity has procedures to identify and authenticate authorized users.
3. The entity has procedures in place to allow users to change, update, or delete their own user information.
4. The entity has procedures to limit remote access to the internal network to only authorized personnel.
5. The entity has controls in place to prevent customers, groups of individuals, or other entities from accessing other than their own private or confidential information.
6. The entity provides encryption capability for sensitive or private information that is passed across an unsecured electronic network.
7. Systems that retain private information obtained as a result of e-commerce are protected from unauthorized outside access.
8. Private information obtained as a result of e-commerce is not disclosed to parties not essential to the transaction unless customers are clearly notified prior to providing such information.

(continued)

FIGURE 4–17   *AICPA's online privacy criteria—continued*

9. Private information obtained as a result of e-commerce is used by employees only in ways associated with the entity's business.
10. The entity maintains procedures so that individually identifiable information collected, created, or maintained by it is accurate and complete for its intended use.
11. The entity maintains procedures to determine the adequacy of information protection and privacy policies of third parties to whom information is transferred.
12. Customer permission is obtained before storing, altering, or copying information in the customer's computer, or the customer is notified with an option to prevent such activities.
13. In the event that a disclosed privacy policy is changed or deleted to be **less** restrictive, the entity maintains procedures to protect personally identifiable information in accordance with the privacy policies in place when such information was collected. Clear and conspicuous customer notification and choice are required to allow the entity to follow the new privacy policy with respect to their personally identifiable information.

Monitoring/Performance Measures
1. The entity maintains procedures for monitoring the security of its e-commerce systems.
2. The entity has procedures in place to keep its disclosed privacy policy current with laws and regulations and to monitor adherence to its current privacy policy practices.
3. The entity has procedures in place to test its security incident policy and update it as needed due to technology changes, changes in the structure of the e-commerce system(s), or information gained from tests of its plan.
4. The entity has procedures in place to effectively monitor and follow up on security breaches.

WebTrust Seal for Internet Service Providers (ISPs)

This seal of assurance is covered by the AICPA/CICA's "Principles and Criteria for ISPs in Electronic Commerce," version 2.0. The term ISP is used to represent a wide range of services that may be provided by a bandwidth provider of Internet connectivity. A few examples of the many services listed by the AICPA/CICA are

- Ongoing Web server and related technology configuration and maintenance.
- Tailoring of an ISP's proprietary order-taking and fulfillment software to enable the client's specific e-commerce activities over the Internet.
- Web server acquisition, configuration, and implementation.
- Telecommunications security.
- Internet firewall configuration, maintenance, and monitoring.
- Web hosting.

To earn a *WebTrust* ISP seal, the business must demonstrate that it complied with the following principles and their related criteria for at least three or more months for the initial issuance:

• *Business and information privacy practices principle*—The ISP discloses its business and information privacy practices for e-commerce services and provides such services in accordance with its disclosed business practices.

• *Availability principle*—The ISP maintains effective controls to provide reasonable assurance that the ISP's network access point and related e-commerce services are available as disclosed by the ISP.

• *Security and privacy principle*—The ISP maintains effective controls against unauthorized physical and electronic access to the ISP's e-commerce operating systems and applications, and to private customer information obtained as a result of e-commerce activities, to provide reasonable assurance that access to systems and customer accounts is restricted to authorized individuals and that such private customer information is protected from uses not related to the ISP's business.

• *Service integrity principle*—The ISP maintains effective controls to provide reasonable assurance that customer messages and transactions, service requests, and responses are processed accurately and completely.

Each of these principles has numerous criteria that are illustrated in the AICPA/CICA's *WebTrust* document for ISPs, version 2.0.

WebTrust Seal for Certification Authorities

An assurance program for certification authorities was officially issued in August 2000 as version 1.0. The AICPA/CICA expects this program to evolve as the underlying technology evolves. Certification authorities provide the bases for the use of encryption key pairs. Basically, certification authorities provide a way to authenticate entities. Encryption and certification authorities are explained in further detail in Chapter 10. In an explanation of the business issues surrounding certification authorities, the AICPA/CICA state that

> . . . certification authorities may use different standards or procedures to verify the identity of persons to whom they issue certificates. Thus, a digital signature is only as reliable as the CA is trustworthy in performing its functions.

To earn a *WebTrust* certification authority seal, the business must demonstrate that it complied with the following practices for at least two or more months:

• *Business practices disclosure*—It discloses its key and certificate life-cycle management business and information privacy practices and provides its services in accordance with its disclosed practices.

• *Service integrity*—It maintains effective controls to provide reasonable assurance that subscriber information was properly authenticated and the integrity of keys and certificates it manages is established and protected throughout their life cycles.

• *Environmental controls*—The subscriber and relying party information is restricted to authorized individuals and protected from uses not specified in the certification authority's business practices disclosures; the continuity of key and certificate life-cycle management operations is maintained; and its systems development, maintenance, and operation are properly authorized and performed to maintain systems integrity.

The AICPA/CICA's *WebTrust* Program for Certification Authorities, version 1.0, gives a very detailed and illustrative list of criteria that is too lengthy to cover in this chapter. Many of these issues are examined, however, in Chapter 10, where certification authorities are discussed.

AICPA/CICA SysTrust Programs

This assurance service is oriented toward business-to-business trading relationships. The first version of the *SysTrust* exposure draft was released in July 1999 and the version 2.0 Exposure Draft was released in 2000. This assurance service is based on the concept of reliability as indicted in the logo displayed in Figure 4–14. The *SysTrust* Exposure Draft defines a reliable system as "one that is capable of operating without material error, fault, or failure during a specified period in a specified environment."

The *SysTrust* engagement is based on the evaluation of four principle areas:

- *Availability*—The system is available for operations and use at times set forth in service-level statements or agreements.
- *Security*—The system is protected against unauthorized physical and logical access.
- *Integrity*—System processing is complete, accurate, timely, and authorized.
- *Maintainability*—The system can be updated when required in a manner that continues to provide for system availability, security, and integrity.

Initially, a firm had to meet all four principle areas; however, in version 2.0, an engagement can be undertaken based on the individual components, either in isolation or in combinations. The *SysTrust* criteria are fairly detailed, providing 58 specific criteria for the four principles. In assessing a company's system, the examination is for a specific period, and the assertions made by management are in reference to this historical, specific period covered by the report engagement. Specifically, the *SysTrust* Exposure Draft, version 1.0, states that

> . . . management's assertion that during the period covered by the report and is based on the AICPA/CICA SysTrust criteria for system reliability, the entity maintained effective controls over its system to provide reasonable assurance that—
>
> - The system was available for operation and use at times set forth in service-level or agreements.
> - The system was protected against unauthorized physical and logical access.
> - The system processing was complete, accurate, timely, and authorized.
> - The system could be updated when required in a manner that continued to provide for system availability, security, and integrity.

For those engagements encompassing a subset of the four principle areas, the assertions by management would cover only the relevant principles. The assurance firm is not responsible for examining subsequent events that occur after the examination period. The AICPA/CICA recognizes that the profession would like to forge ahead toward continuous assurance. Version 2.0 is but one step toward that goal.

| **FIGURE 4–18** | *Comparison of seals* |

Product	Cost	Privacy of Data	Security of Data	Business Policies	Transacton Processing Integrity
BBB*Online* Suite of seals	Low	Yes	No	Lightly covered	No
TRUSTe	Low	Yes	No	No	No
BizRate	Very Low	Yes	No	Yes	No
Veri-Sign	Low to medium	No	Yes: data transmittal No: data storage	No	Lightly covered
WebTrust	High	Yes	Yes	Yes	Yes
SysTrust	High	Yes	Yes	Yes	Yes

Comparison of Seals

The seals reviewed in this section compete to some extent with one another. Some seals are more specialized, such as the TRUSTe and Veri-Sign seals. Further, the AICPA *Web-Trust* seal incorporates the Veri-Sign digital certificate. Figure 4–18 compares the seals according to the four categories of concern and their relative costs. *WebTrust* and *SysTrust* appear to be the most comprehensive assurance seals; however, they are also the most costly. The lower cost seals have enjoyed greater market penetration thus far. Referring back to the model of trust in Figure 4–13, the contracting organizations must feel that the value of purchasing a signal, such as the seals discussed in this section, outweigh the cost. An important issue is whether consumers and business trading partners can differentiate between the lower- and higher-cost seals.

IMPLICATIONS FOR THE ACCOUNTING PROFESSION

Business practices, transaction processing integrity, information protection, and supporting internal controls are areas of expertise demonstrated by accountants historically. Electronic commerce provides many new opportunities for both accounting and other technology professionals. The accounting profession is affected in many ways:

- It must incorporate e-commerce technology skills in the performance of traditional assurance engagements.
- It has the opportunity to perform continuous assurance functions.
- It has the opportunity to provide e-commerce business solutions that help firms compete aggressively in international markets.

Because of competitive forces, the accounting profession must convince the marketplace that it is the best candidate to perform such services. To convince the marketplace, accountants need to

- Increase their ability as technology specialists.
- Continue to maintain their existing roles as independent, trusted third parties.

Skill-Sets

The technological skills-set bar continues to be raised for accountants who perform traditional assurance functions. Because the accounting profession has chosen to enter the e-commerce assurance business, it is also raising the level of knowledge necessary by accountants to diligently perform the website's e-commerce practices review process. In Chapter 6 an example of fully integrated EDI is given, and in this situation, humans are not involved in most of the transaction processing activities. The tasks are performed digitally, and auditing *through the computer* is a must. Add to this scenario Web-based e-commerce transaction processing systems, and the required technical skill-set increases to include tasks such as knowledge of programming, operating systems, networking (local and Internet), authentication, firewalls, and other security techniques. These skill-sets are also crucial to the effective performance of the *WebTrust* assurance functions.

Not surprisingly, accounting firms are heavily recruiting and hiring computer science and computer engineering majors. Employees working for accounting firms with accounting degrees are important because they bring a knowledge base of the business environment and accounting skills, and they qualify to sit for the CPA exam. This group of employees, however, is liable to become less in demand if it does not increase its technological skill-set. The hiring practices of accounting firms already reflect this trend toward hiring fewer accounting majors and hiring more individuals with technology skill-sets. Traditional accounting programs need to enhance their technology skill components. This curriculum change will most likely occur if the CPA exam is revamped to more accurately reflect the new knowledge base and skill-set required by the accounting profession.

Certified Information Technology Professional (CITP) Designation

In 2000, the AICPA launched a new technology-related certification for its CPAs. The **Certified Information Technology Professional (CITP)** program has four objectives:

- To achieve public recognition of the CPA as the preferred IT professional in the business community.
- To promote members' services through compilation of the CITP Expertise Database and the development of appropriate marketing materials.
- To enhance the quality of IT services that members provide.
- To increase practice development opportunities and advance the careers of CPAs employed in business and industry, education, government, and other areas.

A point-based system is used to qualify individuals to be CITPs. A total of 100 points must be earned to qualify. Business experience and life-long learning may qualify the individual. If enough points are not earned in these categories, then a test may be taken. Basically, the requirements are

- *Business experience in relevant areas* (defined by the AICPA)—A minimum of 15 points and a maximum of 75 points can be earned for a given three-year period. Up to 25 points per year can be earned for each of the past three years in which the applicant had 800 or more hours of relevant experience.
- *Life-long learning in relevant areas* (defined by the AICPA)—A minimum of 30 points and a maximum of 70 points can be earned for a given three-year period.
- *Examination*—A computer-based exam worth 40 points is only necessary if 100 points cannot be reached from the business experience and life-long learning.

Expansion of Assurance Services

The terms *assurance* and *accounting* go hand in hand because of the accounting profession's long-standing reputation and experience of performing traditional financial statement assurance. The well has started to dry up in this area, however, as competitive pressures have driven fees down and this area has matured. Other assurance opportunities have been identified in the Elliott report, however, and new opportunities can be expected to continuously develop. Electronic commerce initiatives are directly related to several new assurance service opportunities. Most notably, systems reliability, risk identification and impact analysis, and website assurance are the areas that accountants are best equipped to embrace in the short run. To gain the necessary technical expertise, as mentioned earlier, many firms are hiring individuals outside of the accounting discipline. Furthermore, large firms have the resources to retrain existing personnel. Accounting firms need to feel comfortable with the assurance services they perform. As illustrated earlier in the chapter in the box titled "Confidential Messages Placed in the Public

Domain," security lapses are bound to happen. This security lapse lasted eight weeks. What if such lapses occur once a firm bears a seal by an independent third party, such as accounting firms performing the *Webtrust* or *SysTrust* seal review? Litigation by injured parties may result if they can prove negligence.

As demonstrated in this chapter, accountants are not alone in providing these expansion assurance services. Consulting firms are aggressively competing in the marketplace for these services. Some industries are developing services that are in direct competition with some of the assurance service opportunities identified by accountants, including the marketing of individual accounting firm seals. The accounting profession must continue to actively survey the marketplace and identify new opportunities.

Consulting and International Services

With electronic commerce comes a complete new set of business "problems." Such problems include international tax issues and other laws, alignment of business and e-commerce strategy, and integration of internal systems, such as enterprise resource planning systems, with e-commerce systems. These problems cause firms to seek the advice of experts, such as accounting firms. Other markets that the Elliott report identifies as potential nonassurance or consulting services that the accounting profession can potentially enter include

- Performing high-integrity electronic transaction processing for firms wishing to outsource this function.
- Developing, authenticating, and storing the digital signatures used in electronic transactions.
- Providing certificate authority services.

The latter two functions are discussed more thoroughly in Chapter 10. Accounting firms can also develop software products that enable companies to quickly implement e-commerce applications.

Summary

This chapter explains the importance of having third-party assurance services performed by an independent entity. It also explores the new assurance services that are open to the accounting profession. Three accounting industry efforts to identify new opportunities are reviewed: the CPA Vision Project, the Elliott committee, and the ASEC committee. The effect of e-commerce on the traditional assurance function is briefly examined, and continuous process auditing as a vehicle for performing real-time audits of e-commerce systems is discussed.

The desire by consumers to receive a signal indicating that (a) a website is reputable, (b) their private information is securely transmitted, and (c) their private information is securely stored electronically has created a market for Web-related assurance products. The products offered by the Better Business Bureau, TRUSTe, BizRate, Veri-Sign, and the AICPA/CICA are reviewed and compared against four categories of security issues: privacy of data, security of data, business policies, and transaction processing integrity. The AICPA/CICA's business-to-business assurance offering, *SysTrust,* was also discussed. Finally, the implications of the opportunity for the accounting profession to provide new assurance services and the competitive marketing place in which it operates were discussed.

Key Words

ability	M-commerce
accessible	objectivity
American Institute of Certified Public Accountants (AICPA)	Principles of the Code of Professional Conduct
Assurance Services Executive Committee (ASEC)	perceived trustworthiness
	privacy of data
benevolence	propensity (to trust)
Better Business Bureau (BBB)	risk assessment
BizRate	security assurance systems
business policies	server reliability
Certified Information Technology Professional (CITP)	source credibility of communication
	Special Committee on Assurance Services (SCAS)
Committee of Sponsoring Organization of the Treadway Commission (COSO)	Standards for Attestation Engagements No. 1
continuous process auditing	Statement on Auditing Standards (SAS 78)
control agent	substantive tests
data security	systems reliability assurance
Elliott report	*SysTrust*
Independence Standards Board (ISB)	third-party assurance services
independence	transaction processing integrity
information reliability	TRUSTe
integrity	Veri-Sign
integrity assurance systems	*WebTrust*

Review Questions

1. What is the AICPA?
2. What did the ISB's first standard seek to accomplish?
3. Identify three forces that are creating potential new markets for the accounting profession.
4. Why was the Special Committee on Assurance Services formed?
5. What are three important factors that must be considered in identifying new assurance service opportunities?
6. Identify three new services related to e-commerce that are identified by the Elliott report.
7. What new skill-sets are necessary for accountants providing the e-commerce assurance services?
8. Why was the Assurance Services Executive Committee formed?
9. What are the three waves of e-commerce assurance?
10. What do integrity assurance systems ensure?
11. What do security assurance systems ensure?
12. What is systems reliability assurance?
13. What are the characteristics of reliable information systems?
14. How does e-commerce assurance differ from systems reliability assurance?
15. What is continuous process auditing?
16. What tasks performed by accounting firms should be segregated in order to maintain independence?
17. What is meant by "trust" in e-commerce?
18. What are the four components of the trust model?
19. What are the four categories of concerns to consumers of transacting on the Internet? Give an example of each.

20. What is BBB*Online?* What categories of concern does it address?
21. What is TRUSTe? What categories of concern does it address?
22. What are the requirements of the TRUSTe trustmark?
23. What types of products does Veri-Sign provide?
24. What requirements of authentication must a business site meet in order to receive a Veri-Sign Class 3 certificate?
25. What security does a Veri-Sign Class 3 provide?
26. What is BizRate? What categories of concern does its program address?
27. What is the AICPA/CICA *WebTrust* seal? What categories of concern does it address?
28. What are the three categories of risk defined by the AICPA/CICA? Give three examples of each.
29. What is the AICPA/CICA *SysTrust* seal? How is it different from the *WebTrust* seal?
30. What is the CITP designation? Who can qualify for it?

Discussion Questions

1. Why are smaller audit teams able to perform more technologically complex audits?
2. Why is the AICPA forming task forces to identify new markets for accountants?
3. Why are accountants facing unprecedented competition for new service offerings?
4. In which wave of e-commerce are we?
5. What three competencies does the AICPA assert that accountants possess that give them a market edge in providing e-commerce assurance services? Do you agree?
6. How does systems reliability assurance differ from traditional assurance services? Are there any similarities, or does an overlap exist?
7. Distinguish between auditing around the computer and auditing through the computer. Which becomes more important in e-commerce applications? Why?
8. Why does the accounting profession need to shift from a detection and correction model to a before-the-fact prevention strategy?
9. How can accounting firms leverage their knowledge of internal controls to position themselves as a good provider of systems reliability assurance?
10. What are the current issues related to independence and objectivity?
11. Discuss the various seals and their signals with reference to the model of trust presented in this chapter.
12. Why might an organization be reluctant to agree to binding arbitration for customer disputes by the BBB?
13. Does the TRUSTe seal present on a website indicate that the customer data are not shared with or sold to third parties?
14. How can "seeding" of websites be used to test a website's privacy policy?
15. Since the *WebTrust* seal uses a Veri-Sign Class 3 certificate, then why not just contract with Veri-Sign directly?
16. Why must the *WebTrust* seal be "refreshed" every 90 days?
17. Why is a key component in the maintenance process of the *WebTrust* seal the documentation and justification of any changes in policies or transaction methods?
18. How many different offerings of *WebTrust* are available? Why have different offerings?
19. What is the purpose of the independent accountant's report issued by the *WebTrust* program? Is this where the consumer should look for business policies, such as its privacy policy?
20. Does *SysTrust* provide an assurance about system reliability?
21. How, if it all, can the CITP designation help the accounting profession?

Case

1. Trust model from an international perspective

   Discuss the trust model from an international and cultural perspective. Discuss any similarities or differences you would expect for both business-to-business and business-to-consumer. Give examples from countries other than the United States.

2. AICPA's Top 10 technology issues

   a. Visit the AICPA's website and locate its Top 10 technology issues for 2001. Rank-order the list according to which technologies you are most comfortable with (1 being the most comfortable and 10 being the least comfortable.) Bring your rank ordering to class.

   b. Identify the three strongest weaknesses you have, and outline a plan for enhancing your skills in this area. Be prepared to share your plans with fellow students.

3. Privacy policy disclosure: To regulate or not?

   Below are some excerpts from articles about Internet privacy policies:

   > . . . another problem has emerged, a conflict between the U.S. view of personal privacy, and the more stringent one adopted in Europe.[a]

   > The EU *(European Union)* has adopted a directive requiring the creation of independent privacy commissions in each country and notification to those commissions before data can be processed. The U.S. wants its industry to develop a far-reaching self-regulatory regime.[b]

   > The problem for the U.S. is that not only does the directive toughen liabilities, it also gives them a global reach . . . data identifying any individual gathered from any equipment in European Union territory is covered by the directive. So, U.S. firms must comply or risk a lawsuit in Europe.[a]

   > The EU directive requires that companies with an international presence must ensure that personal data on the Internet is
   >
   > - Processed fairly and lawfully.
   > - Collected and processed for specified, explicit legitimate purposes.
   > - Accurate and current.
   > - Kept no longer than deemed necessary to fulfill the stated purpose.[a]
   >
   > Users also have the rights to
   >
   > - Access.
   > - Correction, erasure, or blocking of information.
   > - Object to usage.[a]

   > Unless industry can demonstrate that it has developed and implemented broad-based and effective self-regulatory programmes by the end of this year, additional *(U.S.)* governmental authority in this area would be appropriate and necessary . . . but in an effort to head off any legislation, the Online Privacy Alliance, a group of prominent companies and trade associations working on the internet, including Microsoft, Netscape, and America Online, yesterday announced an alternative programme of electronic "privacy seals."[c]

---

[a]David Bicknell, "They Want to Be Safe," *Computer Weekly,* June 18, 1998.

[b]Nancy Dunne, "US-EU in 'Productive' Talks on Internet Privacy," *Financial Times (London),* July 30, 1998.

[c]Mark Suzman, "FTC Chief Warns of Internet Privacy Action," *Financial Times (London),* July 22, 1998.

     a. Do you think market forces will prevail in the United States (demands by consumers), or will the desires by business organizations in an unregulated environment prevail?

     b. Since this is an emerging issue, find two articles within the last month on this topic.

     c. How can the U.S. policy and EU policy be reconciled?

     d. If the U.S. does initiate additional Internet privacy regulation beyond that of children's issues, what will happen to products such as TRUSTe's trustmark?

4. Seal comparison project

    Visit 10 websites that sell products or services and record their URL and note:

     a. Any seals they bear.

     b. Their privacy policies and whether they reserve the right to trade or sell customer information.

     c. Their security procedures for transmission of personal data. Are the data encrypted?

     d. Whether they gave you a cookie.

References and Websites

Aggarwal, Rajesh, and Zabihollah Rezaee. "EDI Risk Assessment," *Internal Auditor,* February 1996.

AICPA/CICA. *WebTrust Principles and Criteria for Business-to-Consumer Electronic Commerce, Version 1.0,* December 23, 1997.

American Bankers Association. "ABA Introduces Web Site Validity 'Seal'; SiteCertain Seal Will Promote Electronic Commerce," *PR Newswire,* September 28, 1998.

American Institute of Certified Public Accountants. "The CPA *WebTrust* Seal Initiative." *http://www.cpawebtrust.org/ developer/details/det_seal.htm.*

_____. *New Assurance Services. http://www.aicpa.org/assurance/scas/newsvs/index.htm.*

_____. "AICPA and SEC Create Independence Standards Board for Auditors of Public Companies," *http://www.aicpaorg/pubs/cpaltr/jun97/independence.htm.*

BBB*Online. http://www.bbbonline. org/standards.htm.*

Bicknell, David. "They Want to Be Safe," *Computer Weekly,* June 18, 1998.

CPA Vision. *About the Process. http://www.cpavision.org/project/project_a.cfm.*

Earnscliffe Research & Communications. "Report to the United States Independence Standards Board: Research into Perceptions of Auditor Independence and Objectivity," November 1999, *www.cpaindependence.org.*

Federal Trade Commission. "Privacy Online: Fair Information Practices in the Electronic Marketplace: A Federal Trade Commission Report to Congress," May 2000.

Gray, Glen. "New Assurance Service: The Electronic Frontier—Boldly Going Where No CPA Has Gone Before?" *Journal of Accountancy,* May 1998.

Gray, Glen, and Roger Debreceny. "Electronic Commerce Assurance Services and Accounting Information Systems: A Review of Research Opportunities," *Advances in Accounting Information Systems,* 1998.

Greenstein, Marilyn, and Miklos Verschelyi. "Trust du Jour: The Development of an Assurance Trust Model and Examination of WebTrust and SysTrust," presented at the Annual American Accounting Association Meeting, 2000.

Helms, Glen, and Jane Mancino. "Wave Good-bye to the Paper Trail," *Journal of Accountancy,* April 1998.

Hofstede, G. "Motivation, Leadership, and Organization: Do American Theories Apply Abroad?" *Organizational Dynamics,* Vol. 9. No. 1, pp. 42–63.

Independence Standards Board. "Standard No. 1 Independence Discussions with Audit Committees," January 1999, *www.cpaindependence.org*

Information Factory. "Introduction to TCP/IP," 1998, *http:/www. informationfactory.com/ifc3.htm.*

International Computer Security Association. *http://www.ncsa.com/services/certification/wcpr.htm.*

Johnson, Everett C. "Testimony before the House Committee on Commerce Subcommittee on Telecommunications, Trade and Consumer Protection," June 25, 1998, *http://aicpa.org/belt/johnson.htm.*

Kegley, Tami. "IT Consulting: Is Integrity at Stake?" *AccountingNet,* December 7, 1998.

Koreto, Richard. "In CPAs We Trust," *Journal of Accountancy,* December 1997.

Mayer, Roger C., James H. Davis, and F. David Schoorman. "An Integrative Model of Organizational Trust," *Academy of Management Review,* Vol. 20, No. 3, July 1995, pp. 709–734.

Ohslon, Kathleen, "Glitch Exposes Customer Tax Records," *Computerworld Online,* February 16, 2000, *www.computerworld.com.*

Petersen, Melody. "Computer Consulting by Accountants Stirs Concern," *New York Times on the Web,* July 13, 1998.

PricewaterhouseCoopers LLP. "PricewaterhouseCoopers Announces Further Expansion of Its Network of Associated Law Firms," Press Release. January 6, 1999.

Richtel, Matt. "Private E-Mail Greetings Are Made Public by Mistake," *New York Times,* February 25, 1999.

Sliwa, Carol. "Outsourcing Rouses Firms to Make Switch to EDI," *Computerworld Online,* April 26, 1999.

Tinsley, Dillard. "Trust plus Capabilities," *Academy of Management Review,* April 1996, pp. 335–337.

TRUSTe. *http://www.truste.org/ webpublishers/ourprogram.htm.*

Veri-Sign. *http://www.verisign.com/ products/sites/datasheets/index.htm.*

5   THE REGULATORY ENVIRONMENT

Learning Objectives

1. To identify the primary legal issues surrounding Web-based electronic commerce.
2. To understand the effect an international environment has on a country's domestic legal framework.
3. To understand privacy issues.
4. To understand the trademark and copyright laws in electronic environments

INTRODUCTION[1]

Regulation of electronic commerce and the Internet is slowly evolving. As businesses flock to the Internet and as private citizens, including children, increasingly use the Internet, its environment is facing scrutiny by government agencies, consumer groups, and business coalitions. Depending on the issue, some groups want lawmakers to intervene, imposing and enforcing "laws of the land." On other issues, the very same group can vehemently oppose any legislative acts and prefer self-regulation. For those issues in which intervention is desired, the problem is to decide what law for what land in this global environment. Each country has three categories of Internet users to serve:

- Government and law enforcement agencies.
- Businesses.
- Private citizens.

The primary issues faced by these three groups are

- Encryption key escrow regulation.
- Privacy rights of citizens.
- Inappropriate web linking practices and protection of copyrighted material.
- Domain name disputes.
- Tax policies.
- Electronic agreements.
- Content responsibility of online auctions.

---

[1]Daniel P. Jensen, Esq. of Peskind, Hymson and Goldstein, Phoenix, contributed to this chapter.

Trying to balance the needs of the three user groups (which are not always homogenous) on these issues proves to be a daunting task. Add to the equation that the Internet is global and involves a multitude of very different cultures and governments that clash on many of these issues, and the legal environment of the Internet can appear untetherable. Despite the overwhelming nature of the legal environment, legal disputes are arising and bringing attention to specific issues, and case law is slowly beginning to set precedents. Governments are enacting worldwide Internet legislation, and industry consortiums are proposing self-regulatory programs. This chapter explores some of the legal issues that the Internet poses. In all areas, the legal framework is evolving, and where possible, legislative efforts to date and legal precedents are mentioned.

CRYPTOGRAPHY ISSUES

Cryptography is a method of mathematical encoding used to transform messages into an unreadable format in an effort to maintain confidentiality of data. Various cryptographic methods are presented in Chapter 10. For now, the important point to understand is that the encryption process transforms a cleartext message into a nondecipherable form known as **ciphertext. Encryption** and **decryption keys** are necessary to transform cleartext into ciphertext and vice versa. Good encryption methods mask the underlying message, and deciphering a well-encoded message should be virtually impossible without the decryption key. The strength of the encryption process is largely dependent on the **key length.** The larger the key size, the stronger the encryption process. Because of the inability to decipher well-encoded messages, government bodies and law enforcement agencies are very concerned with issues surrounding the length of the key. Two very controversial legal issues arise regarding cryptographic keys:

- Whether a government allows cryptographic software to be used domestically, to be imported into the country, or to be exported outside the country.
- What kind of access privileges, if any, to decryption keys law enforcement agencies should be granted, and whether the decryption key should be required to be held in escrow.

These issues are considered in the following sections.

Government Agency Concerns[2]

Government bodies and law enforcement agencies have been concerned with two primary issues:

- The use of "unbreakable" cryptographic methods by domestic criminals.
- The use of "unbreakable" cryptographic methods by terrorists, potentially hostile governments, or governments that have not enacted sufficient anti-money-laundering policies.

---

[2]Much of the information in the section regarding cryptographic regulations in non-U.S. countries was gathered from Bert-Jaap Koops's continuing Crypto Law Survey. This site has been updated regularly, and is a good source of information. *http://cwis.kub.nl/,frw/people/koops/cls2.htm#prc.*

In the past, law enforcement agencies relied on the ability to obtain a court order, when they provided the appropriate justification, to allow them to either wiretap a telephone line or place a listening device in a room to eavesdrop on suspected criminals in an effort to catch the criminal(s). With computers, e-mail, and encryption algorithms, criminals can communicate confidentially with one another by encrypting their messages so strongly that a court order allowing the agency to read the message is basically worthless since the message cannot be decoded. The following quote summarizes the sentiment of many law enforcement agencies:

> We can count on the fact that the spread of strong encryption is going to mean that lives are going to be lost. People are going to be at greater risk because it is going to compromise law enforcement's ability to investigate [criminal acts].

> (*Robert Litt, Principal Associate Deputy Attorney General, at the 1998 EPIC Cryptography Conference*)

Computer crime is becoming more and more commonplace with the continued growth of the Internet and other computer-related tools. The government, in attempting to keep the "dirty" side of computers in line, originally felt the need to impose strict regulations regarding encryption techniques, often at the expense of American business interests and public venues. The government, however, found itself between a rock and a hard place. Both the U.S. and French governments yielded to the pressure they were receiving from businesses that were both providing and using cryptographic products. By gradually relaxing export laws in 2000, the United States finally eliminated all export restrictions, except to terrorist countries.

Not all government officials believe that encryption will weaken that capabilities of law enforcement agencies. In June 1999, the German government released its "Corner points of the German Cryptography policy." One of the five cornerstones was (translated)

> The spread of strong cryptography should not erode the government's interception powers. Developments will therefore be closely monitored, and a report will be issued after two years. Besides, the government will make an effort to enhance the technical competence of law-enforcement and security agencies.

> *According to translation by Bert-Jaap Koops*

Domestic Use and the Import and Export of Cryptographic Products

Domestic Use and Import Laws
For the most part, most countries do not restrict domestic use of or the importation of encryption products. A few exceptions are mentioned later in this section. Although unrestricted domestic use of encryption products is allowed by most countries, law enforcement agencies and privacy advocacy groups have been pitted at opposite ends of a heated debate over key escrow and key recovery plans. In a **key escrow** system, all decryption keys would be required to be kept in a central repository that could be accessed by law enforcement agencies with proper authorization. **Key recovery** systems do not necessarily escrow the actual key in a central repository, but some mechanism allows law enforcement agencies with the proper authorization to recover and use the key. The following quotes summarize the sentiments of privacy advocacy groups regarding both key escrow and key recovery systems:

> A secret between two is a secret of God; a secret among three is everybody's secret.

> (*French Proverb*)

> Mary had a crypto key,
>
> She kept it in escrow,
>
> And everything that Mary said,
>
> The Feds were sure to know.
>
> (*Sam Simpson, July 9, 1998*)

Many variations of key escrow or key recovery plans have been proposed, but none have yet to be accepted or enacted. One example of a proposal was the highly unpopular Oxley-Manton amendment to a House of Representatives' bill that, if it had been passed, would have required encryption software vendors to accommodate law enforcement agencies by providing immediate access to requested information stored electronically on a computer or network without the permission or knowledge of the owner or user of the computer. This proposed policy, like many others, was looked upon as a "Big Brother" effort by opposing privacy groups. The U.S. government used to require (but no longer) that firms file a key recovery business plan to gain approval to export encryption software.

The required implementation of a key escrow or key recovery scheme does not appear on the near horizon, at least for the United States, but from a global perspective it is not completely ruled out. If a key escrow or key recovery scheme is going to be used, then controls over law enforcement agencies are desirable. To gain any support for a key escrow or recovery system by privacy groups, law enforcement agencies should not be able to obtain any key they desire at any time. Proposed compromises include requiring the agencies to go through strict and proper channels before being offered the key. If a trusted third party is used, it too requires strict rules and regulations regarding releasing keys. The International Criminal Police Organization (INTERPOL), however, has issued a statement indicating that it favors a key recovery mechanism.

Export of Cryptographic Products

The U.S. government grappled with the legal export of cryptographic methods for the past eight years. It finally gave up and lifted the restrictions, except to terrorist countries. The final humiliation to the U.S. government occurred in January 1999, when RSA Data Security Inc., in a move to circumvent U.S. export laws, announced the opening of its first overseas development center in Australia. In a press release, RSA announced:

> RSA's global expansion enables the company to offer the rapidly expanding international marketplace products from a non-U.S. source that are fully compatible with its industry-standard, award-winning encryption products.
>
> (*RSA Data Security, Inc. January 1, 1999*)

RSA was able to structure this international operation within legal boundaries by hiring two non-U.S. citizens (they are Australian citizens) to head the Australian subsidiary. Thus, RSA found a loophole that allowed it to circumvent U.S. export laws.

China

A 1999 State Order ("Commercial Use Password Management Regulations") strongly restricts domestic use of cryptographic products. Manufacturers of cryptographic software products must receive an "official designation" from the State Encryption Management Commission (SEMC). Organizations and individuals are restricted from distributing foreign encryption products. Individuals may not use commercial encryption products developed by themselves or produced abroad. If they desire to use their own products or foreign products, they must get approval from the Commission. Foreign diplomats and consulates are exempted from these approval requirements. Apparently, foreign business travelers going to China with "built-in" encryption devices, as opposed to specialized hardware and software, are not subject to these regulations either. The import and export of encryption products requires a license by the SECM as well.

Belarus, Kazakhastan, and Pakistan.
Kazakhastan requires a license from the Committee of National Security to develop, manufacture, repair (including technical support), advertise, or sell (including use and advertising) cryptographic products domestically. Approval is required in both Belarus and Pakistan in order to domestically sell or use encryption hardware or software. A license is also required to import or export cryptographic products to or from Kazakhastan and Belarus.

PRIVACY ISSUES

Because of the vast amount of data that can be collected on the Internet and because of its global nature, private citizens worldwide have expressed concerns over their rights to privacy. Shoppers browsing through various stores in a physical shopping mall, stopping to glance at a specific item in a specific store, do not have to worry that their every move is recorded. The available technology, however, used in e-commerce and Internet sites makes it perfectly feasible for data to be recorded about every item "clicked-on" by a user browsing through an electronic shopping mall or visiting a website. Privacy groups have formed around the world in the interest of protecting the privacy rights of individuals. A few of these groups are

- Center for Democracy and Technology.
- Electronic Frontier Foundation.
- Electronic Privacy Information Center.
- Privacy International.
- Privacy Rights Clearinghouse.
- Online Privacy Alliance.

We define **information privacy** very generally to be the right to have one's personal or business data kept confidential. The **Federal Trade Commission (FTC)** identified five core principles of privacy protection that are generally widely accepted in the United States, Canada, and Europe:

- **Notice.** Consumers should be made aware of an entity's information practices before any personal information is gathered.
- **Choice.** Consumers should be given the opportunity to consent or deny any secondary uses (uses other than the processing of a transaction) of information. Secondary uses include mailing notices or transfer of data to third parties.
- **Access.** Consumers should be able to access their personal data and review it without significant delays. Further, consumers should be able to easily correct inaccurate personal information in a timely manner.
- **Integrity** and **Security.** The data regarding consumers' personal information should be processed in a fashion so that the data are accurate. Further, the data need to be kept confidential when is transmitted, processed, and stored by the entity.
- **Enforcement.** Consumers should have recourse if any of the above core principles are violated.

Several categories of concerns arise relating to information privacy. The first category is concern over the security of electronic data when transmitted, which is directly related to key length issues discussed in the previous section. The second category of concern is over the unauthorized reading of one's personal information, such as encrypted messages. This concern is directly related to the key escrow issues mentioned in the previous section. Because these two categories of concern were discussed in the previous section, these issues are not explored further in this section except to say that strong encryption without key escrow or key recovery policies attached allow individuals to enjoy the greatest amount of digital privacy.

The third category, consumer's privacy rights regarding electronic data stored about them by businesses, is another widely debated issue. Although the U.S. government has maintained a strong position of cryptography regulation, it has tried to avoid electronic data privacy protection regulations. As mentioned in the previous section, the United States is beginning to relax some, but not all, of the cryptographic regulations, and as is discussed in this section, it is beginning to increase regulation regarding the Internet privacy rights of children.

Regarding the privacy rights of adults, the U.S. government is still willing to allow private industries the opportunity to devise sufficient privacy rights policies, but thus far these efforts have fallen short of expectations. The U.S. government is facing pressure from privacy advocacy groups and the European Union's (EU's) new privacy regulation. As a result, U.S. lawmakers are increasingly "threatening" the business sector that they may soon introduce privacy regulations if industry efforts are not satisfactory. In July 1998, the FTC announced to Congress that new privacy laws for adults should be instituted if the efforts made by industry do not improve by the end of the year.[3] The FTC's 2000 report findings are discussed in the next section.

FTC's 2000 Privacy Online Report

> . . . a majority of the Commission finds that self-regulation alone, without some legislation, is unlikely to provide online consumers with the level of protection they seek and deserve. Accordingly, a majority of the Commission recommends that Congress consider legislation to complement self-regulation. Despite this conclusion, I want to emphasize that there will continue to be an important role for self-regulation in ensuring the protection of privacy. The private sector has every incentive to engage in effective self-regulation so that electronic commerce reaches its full potential.
>
> (*U.S. FTC, Chairman Piftofsky, May 2000*)

The FTC, in its diligent ongoing monitoring of the online environment, conducted another online privacy practices survey in January and February 2000. It systematically selected a random sample of 335 U.S. business sites that had at least 39,000 monthly visitors. It also chose the 100 most popular business sites according to Nielsen/Net ratings and surveyed them as well. Pornographic sites, children's sites, and inaccessible sites were excluded from the survey. Nine of the most 100 popular sites were excluded from the survey, leaving 91 sites. Here are some of the findings of the percentage of sites that

- Collect personally identifying information—97% random sample; 99% most popular sites.
- Collect personally identifying information other than e-mail—87% random sample; 96% most popular sites.

---

[3]FTC, 1998.

Figure 5–1 illustrates some somewhat comforting results regarding the top 100 sites, but some not-so-great results regarding the random sample. Almost all of the most popular sites provide a privacy policy and link to it from the home page. Roughly two-thirds of the random sites provide a privacy policy and nearly three-quarters of those sites link to it from the home page. However, all five core principles of privacy are far from being met. Figure 5–2 illustrates the percentage of sites that collect personally identifying information that engage to some extent in the FTC's fair information practices of notice, choice, access, and security. The most popular sites fare better than the random sample. Roughly one-half of the random sample firms provide the visitor with either notice,

FIGURE 5–1	*Percentage of U.S. sites that post privacy polices and link from home page*

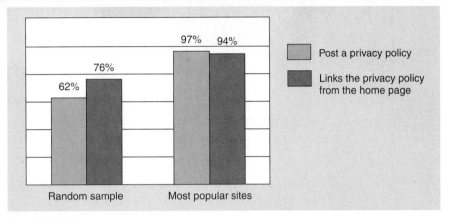

Source: FTC, 2000.

FIGURE 5–2	*Percentage of U.S. sites that collect personally identifiable information that implements to some extent fair information practice principles*

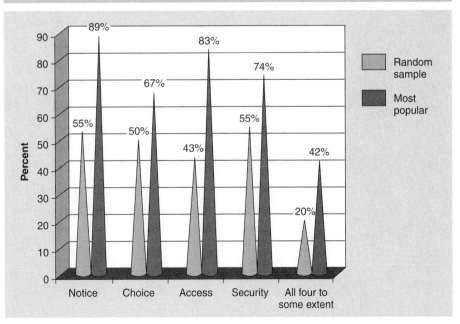

Source: FTC, 2000.

| FIGURE 5–3 | *Percentage of U.S. sites that collect personally identifiable information that implement and offer choice; mechanism used to offer choice* |

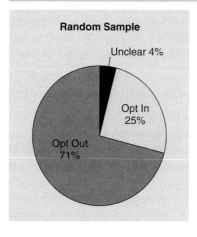

Random Sample

Unclear 4%
Opt In 25%
Opt Out 71%

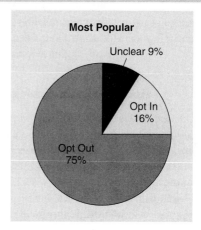

Most Popular

Unclear 9%
Opt In 16%
Opt Out 75%

choice, access, or security practice statements, but only 20 percent provide all four. The most popular group ranged from 67 to 89 percent in its delivery of these items, but only 42 percent of them practiced all four.

Caution needs to be used when interpreting the security figures because these numbers represent firms that make a statement that its site takes *any* steps to provide security, not an analysis of the quality of the security. The following statistics reveal that the security precaution quality is actually much lower than the statistics in Figure 5–3 may illustrate:

- Sites that claim to take steps to provide security during transmission—39% random sample; 54% most popular sites.
- Sites that claim to take steps to provide security after receipt—29% random sample; 48% most popular sites.

Remember that these statistics are for those sites that collect personally identifiable information. If these statistics are any indication of data security practices, they are not very comforting.

Privacy seals continue to be the "hope" of businesses desiring to escape privacy legislation. However, the FTC's 2000 report indicates that only 8 percent of all of the random sample sites and 45 percent of the most popular group sites display some kind of privacy seal. Privacy regulation in the U.S. is on the horizon, but as mentioned in the box, "Privacy Legislation Raises Questions," we will have to wait and see what occurs.

Children's Privacy Regulation

The results of the FTC's 1998 survey of children's sites, however, was so startling that even industry representatives admitted that regulation was necessary for this sector of the population. An overwhelming 89 percent of the 212 children's sites surveyed in 1998 collected personal information. The personal information collected varied widely from site to site including such information as

- E-mail address.
- Postal address.
- Telephone number.
- Social security number.

| **E-Commerce in Practice** |

Privacy Legislation Raises Questions

Pending Federal, State Laws May Be at Odds

For companies worried that the potential approval of new privacy laws could affect their data collection practices, it may not matter who wins tomorrow's presidential election. The reason is simple, said attendees at a privacy conference here: The push for privacy legislation is coming from all sides of the political spectrum.

The U.S. Congress and individual state legislatures next year are all but certain to consider a wide range of legislation that could affect many industries, said privacy experts and corporate officials at last week's Privacy2000 conference here. And while e-commerce companies and industry groups have urged the government to favor self-regulation over new rules, that sentiment may be changing because of potential conflicts between federal and state privacy laws.

The ability of the federal government to override state law is one of the reasons why Walt Disney Internet Group in North Hollywood, Calif., backs a bill proposed last summer by Sen. John McCain (R–Ariz.) and two other senators. The bill, which isn't expected to win approval this year, would require Web sites to disclose what they plan to do with the personal data they collect and compel them to give customers a chance to limit how the information is used.

"We're supporting that legislation more because of business predictability than . . . the fact that we don't think self-regulation is working," said Alden Schacher, privacy director at the Walt Disney Internet Group, an independent company that manages the Internet businesses of Burbank, Calif.–based The Walt Disney Co.

The proliferation of proposed state-level privacy bills "creates a very unpredictable environment," Schacher said. Federal legislation preempting state laws would make the privacy issue less complicated for companies to manage, she added during an interview.

But federal laws don't automatically preempt state legislation: Congress has to choose to include that provision in the bills it passes. The Gramm-Leach-Bliley Act, a financial deregulation bill that was approved last year, wasn't preemptive—which is creating problems for companies looking to follow its provisions.

For example, Kirk Herath, chief privacy and public policy officer at Nationwide Financial Services Inc., said 17 states have prohibitions on data sharing among financial services firms that remain in force after the passage of the Gramm-Leach-Bliley Act. Included on the list is Ohio, the corporate home of Columbus-based Nationwide Financial.

Complying with conflicting sets of state and federal law isn't easy for companies, Herath said. "You can't create two different systems," he noted. "It's not easy to take your customer base and segment it 50 different ways, or even two or three different ways." As a result, Herath said, the most restrictive state laws often become the de facto national standard.

Companies that have spent most of their attention focusing on federal privacy legislation are going to have to start paying more attention to state legislatures, said Emily Hackett, the state policy director at the Internet Alliance, a trade group in Washington.

Privacy legislation at the state level is "going to be very active," Hackett said. "Any company that is interested in the privacy issue cannot ignore the states."

Hundreds of State Bills

At least two-thirds of the 50 states are considering an aggregate total of privacy bills numbering in the hundreds, according to estimates made at last week's conference, which was organized by the Technology Policy Group of the Columbus-based Ohio Supercomputer Center. And data privacy has become an issue that cuts across party lines, attendees said.

"If you're in business and you think that one party is going to help you on this issue . . . I think you are sorely mistaken," said Steve Emmert, director of government affairs at London-based Reed Elsevier PLC, which owns the Lexis-Nexis information service and other businesses.

Source: Patrick Thibodeau ©, Computerworld Online, November 6, 2000.

- Age or date of birth.
- Gender.
- Education.
- Interests.
- Hobbies.

For those sites that collect a child's name and/or e-mail address, the FTC found that

- 48 percent collect an additional three or more pieces of information.
- 21 percent collect an additional five or more pieces of information.

Oftentimes, children are enticed to give such information in order to enter a contest, play a game, or enroll in a pen pal program. In response to the FTC's report, a law was passed, entitled the **Children's Online Privacy Protection Act (COPPA),** that went into effect April 21, 2000. The box, "Website Operators Must . . . ," explains the general compliance features for websites. Infractions can result in civil penalties of $11,000 per violation. The FTC reports that it currently has a number of nonpublic investigations under way.

E-Commerce U.S. Privacy Regulation in Practice

Website Operators Must . . .

Post Their Privacy Policy.   Websites directed to children or that knowingly collect information from kids under 13 must post a notice of their information collection practices that includes

- Types of personal information they collect from kids—for example, name, home address, e-mail address, or hobbies.
- How the site will use the information—for example, to market to the child who supplied the information, to notify contest winners, or to make the information available through a child's participation in a chat room.
- Whether personal information is forwarded to advertisers or other third parties.
- A contact at the site.

Get Parental Consent.   In many cases, a site must obtain parental consent before collecting, using, or disclosing personal information about a child.

Consent is not required when a site is collecting an e-mail address to

- Respond to a one-time request from the child.
- Provide notice to the parent.
- Ensure the safety of the child or the site.
- Send a newsletter or other information on a regular basis as long as the site notifies a parent and gives them a chance to say no to the arrangement.

Get New Consent When Information Practices Change in a "Material" Way

Website operators need to notify parents and get consent again if they plan to change the kinds of information they collect, change how they use the information, or offer the information to new and different third parties. For example, new parental consent would be required if the website decides to

- Send information from children to marketers of diet pills instead of only marketers of stuffed animals, as covered in the original consent.
- Give a child access to a chat room if the parent's original consent covered only sending a newsletter.

Allow Parents to Review Personal Information Collected from Their Children.   To do this, website operators must verify the identity of the requesting parent.

Allow Parents to Revoke Their Consent, and Delete Information Collected from Their Children at the Parents' Request.   Parents can revoke their consent and ask that information about their children be deleted from the site's database. When a parent revokes consent, the website must stop collecting, using, or disclosing information from that child. The site may end a child's participation in an activity if the information it collected was necessary for participation in the website's activity.

Source: Text taken for the FTC's website, *http://www.ftc.gov/bcp/conline/edcams/kidzprivacy/biz.htm.*

Adults' Privacy Rights and the EU's Directive

The EU passed a privacy directive that went into effect at the end of 1998. The EU directive requires that

- Personal data on the Internet be
  - Processed fairly and lawfully.
  - Collected and processed for specified, explicit legitimate purpose.
  - Accurate and current.
  - Kept no longer than deemed necessary to fulfill the stated purpose.
- Users have the following rights:
  - Access.
  - Correction, erasure, or blockage of information.
  - Object to usage.
  - Oppose automated individual decisions.
  - Judicial remedy and compensation.

(*David Bicknell,* Computer Weekly, *June 18, 1998*)

This directive affects many U.S. companies. Millions of data transfers occur every day between the United States and Europe, and the EU directive gives its member countries essentially "a global reach" with an attached liability for noncompliance. Basically, non-European companies have to meet the EU's directive if they want to conduct electronic commerce in Europe or risk legal action. In response to the EU's directive, the U.S. Department of Commerce and the European Commission developed a "safe harbor" framework in July 2000 that allows U.S. organizations to satisfy the requirements and ensure that personal data flows to the United States are not interrupted. The safe harbor framework "bridges the differences between the EU and U.S. approaches to privacy protection and ensures adequate protection for EU citizen's personal information." Many U.S. privacy advocates are upset that the implementation of safe harbor provisions by U.S. firms will result in greater privacy rights for foreign citizens than for the U.S.'s own citizens. Firms began signing up in November 2000, but by March 2001, only 30 U.S. firms had applied. The basic requirements of the safe harbor provisions are as follows:

- *Notice.* Individuals must be informed about the purposes for which data about them are collected and used. Individuals must be provided with contact information for the organization where they can place inquiries or complaints. Specifically, the types of third parties to which their information may be disclosed must be disclosed.
- *Choice.* Individuals must be given the opportunity to opt out of having their personal information disclosed to a third party. They must also be able to opt out of having their personal data used for a "purpose incompatible with the purpose for which it was originally collected or subsequently authorized by the individual." Individuals must be asked to opt in when the information is considered "sensitive."
- *Transfers to third parties.* The notice and choice principles must be applied. When transferring information to a third party that is acting as an agent, the organization may do so if
  - The third party subscribes to the safe harbor principles.
  - The third party is subject to the directive or another adequacy finding.
  - The third party provides at least the same level of privacy protection as is required by the relevant principles.

- *Access.* Individuals must have access to personal information about them that an organization holds and be able to correct, amend, or delete that information where it is inaccurate, except where the burden or expense of providing access would be disproportionate to the risks to the individual's privacy in the case in question, or where the rights of persons other than the individual would be violated.

- *Security.* Organizations must take reasonable precautions to protect personal information from loss, misuse and unauthorized access, disclosure, alteration, and destruction.

- *Data integrity.* Personal information must be relevant for the purposes for which it is to be used. An organization should take reasonable steps to ensure that data are reliable for the intended use, accurate, complete, and current.

- *Enforcement.* To ensure compliance with the safe harbor principles, the organization must have
  - Readily available and affordable independent recourse mechanisms so that each individual's complaints and disputes can be investigated and resolved and damages awarded where the applicable law or private sector initiatives so provide.
  - Procedures for verifying that the commitments companies make to adhere to the safe harbor principles have been implemented.
  - An obligation to remedy problems arising out of a failure to comply with the principles.

Sanctions must be sufficiently rigorous to ensure compliance by the organization. Organizations that fail to provide annual self-certification letters will no longer appear in the list of participants, and safe harbor benefits will no longer be assured.

Enforcement is probably going to be the most difficult if the EU decides to take action against noncomplying U.S. firms. Assistance from the United States will be necessary, but applying differential international laws regarding privacy of foreign citizens greater than that afforded to its own citizens will probably result in another media circus event.

Third-Party Sharing/Selling of Data

The FTC and EU directives both require that individuals be notified and given a choice about the transfer of their data to third parties. The year 2000 saw many fledgling dot-com companies being purchased by other companies. Transfer of customer lists to the purchasing companies raised the eyebrows of many concerned individuals, privacy groups, and legislators. The first suit to get a lot of media attention was Toysmart.com, which was allowed by the FTC to sell its customer list to a "successor company" if it purchased the entire company, including its website. The sale of a customer list alone was not sanctioned. At question was Toysmart's posted privacy policy bearing the TRUSTe seal of privacy that stated that the consumer's data would not be shared with third parties. Privacy advocates claimed that this "promise" should not be overlooked or discarded when the company is sold. In July 2000, Disney, a 60 percent owner of Toysmart, made an offer to buy and destroy the customer list for $50,000. Toysmart turned down the offer, claiming that it was too low. After the FTC's intervention requiring that the list could only go to a successor company, a better offer did not come, nor would it have been allowed. In January 2001, Disney made the made offer again and it will probably be accepted.

Another case, that involved more "sensitive" data than that stored by Toysmart.com, involves the data kept by defunct More.com. More.com was an online drugstore that was purchased by HealthCentral.com. Privacy advocates got upset when they learned that the customer data would be passed on, especially since the database includes prescription information. The FTC's position that it is acceptable to pass on data if the entire business is purchased was in disagreement with the attorneys general of 39 states who assert that a successor company is a third party. More.com traffic is currently being forwarded to HealthCentral's online pharmacy, WebRx, which also claims in its privacy policy that "We will not rent, sell, trade, disclose, or loan any personally identifiable information we obtain from Web orders or customer registrations to outside companies or third parties unless we are legally required to do so."

Carnivore

The U.S. government has received a lot of concern during the past year regarding the Federal Bureau of Investigation's (FBI) Internet sniffing software called Carnivore. An ISP provider, EarthLink, resisted the installation of the software in April 2000, and at that point the existence of the software became known to the general public. EarthLink was concerned that the monitoring activities would cause it to be in violation of its own privacy policy as shared with its customers. EarthLink was concerned because it was not able to perform an examination of the software and its code to determine exactly what activities could and would be performed.

Carnivore, as the general public has learned, is a software program that can monitor and track packets of data passing through an Internet service provider's (ISP's) network. Government officials claim that the software will only be used in those instances in which a court order has been obtained to monitor a specific, alleged criminal act. Privacy advocates do not trust the intent or use of the software, and worry that widespread monitoring of e-mail contents will occur. A research team from the Illinois Institute of Technology Research Institute conducted a review of the software and gave it a favorable review. This review is seriously being questioned by five independent researchers and privacy groups as mentioned in the box "Is Carnivore Dangerous? Controversy Continues." Again, the issue of privacy versus law enforcement raises its head again. This saga will continue to unfold.

WEB LINKING

The Internet is built on the concept of **hypertext links** (commonly called links). A hypertext link is an item, such as text or an image, that has the address or location of another Web page attached to it. When a user clicks on the hypertext link, they are instantly transported to the attached location, and the associated Web page is automatically loaded. The links frequently connect to Web pages that reside on another site. Thus, a user who clicks on the hypertext link at one site may "jump" to another site. This ability to place, at no cost other than very simple programming, a link to any website in the world allows users to traverse the Internet, following paths that will hopefully lead them on a useful voyage. Legal issues arise, however, as businesses, organizations, and individual websites begin to insert links to sites from their websites. Some practices that have already caused disputes include

- Inappropriately referencing a linked site.
- Retrieving and displaying information from a linked site without proper reference.
- Retrieving and displaying information from a linked commercial site with advertising frames without displaying the site's advertisements along with the retrieved document.
- Unauthorized use of trademarks in metatags.
- Unauthorized display of registered trademarks.

E-Commerce in Practice

Is Carnivore Dangerous? Controversy Continues

Researchers Claim Review of Program Doesn't Go Deep Enough to Say for Sure.   The researchers who first identified technical issues that they said should be studied regarding the FBI's Carnivore e-mail surveillance system told the U.S. Department of Justice (DOJ) last week that they have "serious concerns" about the controversial technology, despite a generally favorable draft report by the independent team that reviewed it.

The five researchers, from organizations that include AT&T Labs and the University of Pennsylvania, said the review done by the IIT Research Institute (IITRI) in Chicago "appears to represent a good-faith effort at [an] independent review" of the surveillance system. But, they added, the "limited nature of the analysis described in [IITRI's] draft report simply cannot support a conclusion that Carnivore is correct, safe or always consistent with legal limitations."

The researchers recommended that the government release Carnivore's source code for public review to create more public confidence in the software.

Carnivore is a program that monitors packets of data passing through an Internet service provider's network. Officials at the FBI and the DOJ have said the surveillance system can be legally deployed only to monitor alleged criminal activity under a court order, but privacy advocates have said they're worried that the software could lead to widespread and random surveillance of e-mail messages.

The draft of IITRI's report, released three weeks ago, concluded that the software essentially does what it was designed to do: track specific digital communications, under court order. The final report was due last Friday.

But the researchers took particular issue with what they said are vague and changeable audit trails within the Carnivore system. Without a definitive audit trail, they said, it would be impossible to determine who had monitored what.

The researchers also claimed that IITRI didn't spend enough effort investigating "operational and 'systems' issues."

In addition, the report stated, "It is simply not possible to draw meaningful conclusions about isolated pieces of software without also considering the computing, networking, and user environment under which they are running."

One of the researchers, Peter Neumann, a principal scientist at Menlo Park, Calif.–based SRI International's Computer Science Laboratory, said Carnivore could be misconfigured to monitor almost anything.

A DOJ spokeswoman said the document prepared by the researchers will be submitted to the U.S. attorney general's office by the end of this month, along with the IITRI's report and all other Carnivore-related submissions.

The suggestion to release Carnivore's source code is also backed by the Electronic Privacy Information Center (EPIC) in Washington. "If the FBI really wants to provide any type of public assurance as to what Carnivore can and can't do, there is no substitute for releasing that source code," said David Sobel, general counsel at EPIC.

Source: Michael Meehan, © Computerworld Online, December 11, 2000. *www.computerworld.com.*

Defamation and Inappropriately Referencing a Linked Site

Establishing guidelines for defamation and inappropriately referencing a linked site is difficult. Case law will most likely set the parameters of what references associated with linking are acceptable. If linked individuals feel that the link is a defamation of their character, then a legal battle may ensue. **Defamation** occurs when an individual makes a false statement about an individual or business that is damaging to their reputation. The issue is whether a website "owner" likes or dislikes the context in which another site links to its website. If the website owner dislikes the link reference, whose rights prevail: (a) the right to free speech by the site owner placing the reference or (b) the right not to be a target of unwelcome comments that may be considered damaging or harassing by the targeted site owner? What about websites that contain critical or unflattering comments regarding services or products and then provide a link to the company's or organization's website? For example, consider the situation in which a former employee posted on her personal website a statement such as "This product is a piece of overpriced garbage" with a link to her former employer's website bearing sales information for the product. Is this a true or false statement, or merely an opinion? Do opinions count as defamatory? If product sales are hurt by the comments, will the individual posting the negative comments be the target of a costly lawsuit?

Imagine if Oprah Winfrey had made her negative comment about beef in a written statement on her website with a link to a report about mad cow disease on the National Cattleman's Beef Association's website rather than making a casual remark on her television show about her fear of eating beef because of mad cow disease. Ultimately, she won the case, but only after hefty legal fees and six weeks of legal hearings in Texas. One can only wonder if the outcome would have been different had she made a written statement on her very popular website.

Displaying Information without Proper Referencing

This issue involves displaying images or documents without appropriately referencing them. One of the first cases publicized, in which a company issued a cease-and-desist order, involved the improper use of a Dilbert comic strip image. A user linked to the image directly and attached his own header without identifying the source. After receiving the cease-and-desist order, the user began to appropriately link to the comic strip's source and home page. Thus, this dispute was solved without being brought before a court. The two parties were able to work out the situation. The future may involve treating cases similar to this one as plagiarism cases are currently treated.[4]

Linking Using Framing

This issue has resulted in lawsuits involving some big companies. The issue is the use of framing techniques by one company to link to another company's website. A Web page is often divided into different viewing zones called **frames.** Each frame has its own program code and linking capabilities. By using frames, a website can place its own advertising banners, for which it earns advertising revenue, in one frame and then link to a document from another site, placing the contents of the document into another frame. The problem arises because the linked document originates from a site that also uses frames and places advertisements in these frames; however, the advertisements of the site from which the document resides are not seen.

A highly publicized case was a suit filed against TotalNews based on multiple claims:

1. Copyright and trademark infringement.
2. Unfair competition.
3. Wrongful interference.[5]

TotalNews had used framing techniques to place its own advertisements in one frame and placed linked articles from *The Washington Post* and several other news sources in another frame. The suit settled out of court, but it was widely publicized, and the Internet environment has changed as a result. For example, websites that use such framing links know that they may be forced to defend a lawsuit that is costly and may bring negative publicity. Website developers that use frames for advertising have learned to

---

[4]See Kristi Vaiden, 1998, for more information regarding this dispute.

[5]*Washington Post* v. *Total News,* No. 97 Civ. 1190 (S.D.N.Y., complaint filed February 20, 1997).

protect sites by changing the program codes to prohibit the retrieval of that site's documents by other sites without also retrieving its advertising frames. Another preventive technique is for websites to block access from prespecified sites identified as "threats." Thus, as suits are filed, Internet users and programmers become more knowledgeable about what behavior will be tolerated and how to better protect the content of websites.

Linking Using Trademarks in Keyword Metatags

One technique used by web search engines to locate "matches" for queries is to search a previously created index. The index is built by periodically searching websites, assessing important words on the site and adding them to the index. One widely used method of obtaining keywords is to look at **HyperText Markup Language (html)** metatags that are labeled as keywords. Programmers of websites have placed other sites' trademarks in its **keyword metatags** with the intention of attracting users looking for that trademark to its own site. Numerous lawsuits have been filed against those sites, claiming trademark infringement and/or unfair competition. In one civil case, *Insituform Technology Inc. v. National Envirotech LLC.,* National Envirotech was ordered to delete Insituform's trademarks and service marks from its metatag keywords.[6] Further, it was required to resubmit its keywords, along with the court's order, to five major search engine companies: AltaVista, HotBot, Infoseek, Lycos, and Webcrawler.

Unauthorized Display of a Registered Trademark or Copyrighted Material

A trademark includes words, names, and symbols, including logos and graphical designs. Trademarks may be registered at the federal and/or state level. When conflicts arise, federally registered trademarks preempt state trademarks. **Federally registered trademarks** bear the sign®. An image that is also a registered trademark is considered to be "owned" by the company. Links to logo images can be considered a trademark infringement if only the image is displayed on the website without explicit permission granted by the owner of the trademark *and* if the trademark is displayed in a fashion that either:

- Causes a likelihood of confusion.
- Dilutes the value of or tarnishes the trademark.

Likelihood of confusion can be caused by many factors, including the following:

- Similar appearance, sound, or meaning to the trademark.
- Similarity of goods or services by an entity using another entity's trademark.
- Malicious intent by an entity in using another entity's trademark.
- Actual evidence of consumer confusion.

Dilution by tarnishment is also considered to be caused by many factors, some of which are

- Associating the trademark with another entity's trademark with inferior quality goods.
- Altering the trademark.
- Representing the trademark in an "unsavory" attack.

---

[6]*Insituform Technology, Inc. v. National Envirotech Group, L.L.C.,* Civ. Action No. 97-2064, (E.D. La. Complaint filed July 1, 1997.) The case settled August 27, 1997, and a permanent injunction was ordered by the court.

Bearing the trademark on a link to the owner of the trademark's website, if not done in one of the above manners, is generally acceptable. In fact, in 1998 a federal judge in Georgia, in the case of *ACLU* v. *Miller,* allowed a "right to hyperlink" using registered trademarks. Some critics argue, however, that visitors to the site may erroneously assume that the site has permission or some type of alliance with the site. In 2000, Mattel won a case based on the Anti-Cybersquatting Consumer Protection Act, passed in 1999. A pornographic site was ordered to cease and desist from using Mattel's trademark "Barbie" as part of its domain name. Mattel argued that this could tarnish the "Barbie" trademark. The **Anticybersquatting Consumer Protection Act** prohibits "bad-faith" registration of or use of a domain name when it is a registered trademark. This includes domain names that are identical or confusingly similar to the registered trademark. The Act also helps to define "bad faith" of a domain name holder.

Linking to Illegal Files

Unfortunately, the ease of scanning images and digital recordings of music and video make it easy for "bootlegged" copies of music and pictures to reside on the Internet. The **Motion Picture Experts Group audio layer 3,** better known as **MP3,** is one such compression technique that has made it technologically feasible to upload and download digital audio files that were otherwise considered too large to transmit. The compression results in near-CD-quality music files. MP3 compression software to create and play back MP3 files is widely, freely available, and thus the unauthorized sharing of copyrighted music began to occur on the Internet at enormous rates.

The Recording Industry Association of America (RIAA) has waged some battles against pirated music clips illegally placed on the Internet for downloading. Not only do they want to stop the individuals posting the material, they want to stop parties that lead visitors to the sites containing the material. One such battle includes the ongoing lawsuit against Napster. Napster claims that because it only provides links to other sites containing music files and does not store the files, that the practice is acceptable. An attorney for RIAA claims that the 1998 Digital Millennium Copyright Act makes it illegal to lead an Internet user to a site with pirated material. Not only does Napster provide the location of the digital music with a link to it, it provides a download shortcut, a player to listen to the music, and software that searches users' hard drives for additional music to list on its site. The box entitled "Napster Ruling Reaches Beyond Music Industry" discusses the implications of the ruling against Napster in July 2000. Napster lost at the trial stage, but it appealed. In making an argument to have Napster shut down during the appeal process, the RIAA claimed that every day, Napster fosters the infringement of 12 to 30 million copyrighted works. On March 5, 2001, a preliminary injunction was issued against Napster requiring it to block access to copyrighted material once notified of such material. Shortly thereafter, the following statement appeared on Napster's website:

> The Court has issued its injunction in the record industry's case against Napster. Napster is following the Court's order. Record companies and other rights holders are required to certify that they hold the rights to specific songs that are available on Napster. When we receive notices from them, Napster will take every step within the limits of our system to exclude their copyrighted material from being shared. We will continue to work for a resolution that preserves the Napster community and the file sharing experience.

> (*http://www.napster.com/ March 8, 2001*)

Emusic immediately submitted a list of approximately 30,000 copyrighted songs.

E-Commerce in Practice

Napster Ruling Reaches Beyond Music Industry

Court Order Has Implications for All Online Copyrighted Works, Experts Say

Last week's legal blow against online music distributor Napster Inc. is still reverberating among music lovers. But the federal court order also has serious implications far beyond the music business, according to intellectual-property experts.

Some said U.S. Judge Marilyn Hall Patel's ruling last Wednesday ordering Napster to halt the trading of copyrighted material over the Internet helps shut the door on the free exchange of all copyrighted content online.

"If you are a Web site that plays a role in the exchange of any kind of copyrighted materials—whether it's film, books, or audio—you should study the Napster preliminary injunction very closely," said Rich Gray, an intellectual-property attorney in Menlo Park, Calif.

Like other observers, Gray said he believes the Napster ruling and the planned appeal are merely the first in a string of legal battles over copyrights that will ensue between traditional media companies and Internet file-sharing software and services companies such as Gnutella.com and Warpster.com.

The Motion Picture Association of America in Encino, Calif., has already filed a copyright infringement suit against Scour Inc., an Internet company in Beverly Hills, Calif., that offers a Napsterlike file-sharing service for movie buffs.

Sending a Message

The ruling against San Mateo, Calif.–based Napster stems from a lawsuit filed last December by record companies represented by the Recording Industry Association of America (RIAA) in Washington. The association charged the 14-month-old music company with violating federal and state laws through "contributory and vicarious copyright infringement."

Napster software allows users to log on to its servers and make their personal MP3 collections available for download by other users. Since the company's launch late last year, an estimated 20 million people have used Napster software to download MP3 music files.

But Patel's ruling specifically enjoins Napster from "assisting or enabling or contributing to the copy or duplication of all copyrighted songs and musical compositions of which the plaintiffs hold rights."

Cary Sherman, the RIAA's senior executive vice president and general counsel, said that record companies are pleased with the ruling.

"This once again establishes that the rules of the road are the same online as they are off-line and sends a strong message to others that they cannot build a business based on others' copyrighted works without permission," Sherman said in a statement.

What the ruling doesn't change and can't stop is the availability of free music on the Internet, according to Doug Milles, an executive at online music company New York–based EverAd Inc.

EverAd's approach differs from Napster's in that it embeds banner ads in digitally encoded music it licenses from record labels and then distributes the music free of charge—but with advertising—at its site, www.playj.com.

"Napster was saying early on in its mission statement things like 'We're going to take down the labels.' It's hard to backpedal off of that," Milles said. "If they had kinder, gentler goals, they might have had a kinder [court] settlement today."

Source: Julia King and Kim S. Nash, © *Computerworld Online,* July 31, 2000. *www.computerworld.com.*

Meanwhile, Napster has formed a business alliance with Bertelsmann AG. According to a Napster press release, they have developed "a business model for a membership-based service that will provide Napster community members with high-quality file-sharing that preserves the Napster experience, while at the same time providing payments to rightsholders, including recording artists, songwriters, recording companies, and music publishers."

In a different type of music copyright infringement, MP3.com was legally challenged by the recording industry for its jukebox services. Basically, a user can load a purchased CD-ROM into their hard drive and using MP3.com's Beam-It software, the MP3.com site recognizes the CD and places listening rights to it in that individual's listening account. Anytime that individual logs into MP3.com with his user ID and password, he can listen to that CD without having to carry the CD with him. As a result of the dispute, an agreement was reached between music publishers and MP3.com that requires MP3.com to pay $30 million over three years, which covers MP3.com's past use of copyrighted music and provides royalty payments for future use of approximately one million songs. The royalty agreement calls for one-quarter of a cent royalty each time a consumer accesses a song, as well as a one-time fee each time a user stores a song on My.MP3. (MP3.com did lose a lawsuit against Universal Music Group as well, and was ordered to pay $53 million, which it did not expect to appeal.)

Domain Name Disputes

Prior to 1992, the U.S. government directly handled the administration of top-level domain names, such as ".com" (commercial) or ".org" (organization). In 1992, the U.S. government contracted with a private corporation, Network Solutions Inc. (NSI), to administer the top-level domains. The actual registration service is called **InterNIC,** which is located at NSI and funded in part by the National Science Foundation. In October 1998, the U.S. government intended to hand over this task to an international, nonprofit corporation, **Internet Corporation for Assigned Names and Numbers (ICANN).** NSI is now one of many domain name registrants that operates ICANN.

As many business entities and service organizations have expanded their entities to the World Wide Web, the assignment and use of top-level domain names has resulted in turf battles, or **domain name disputes,** many of which involve the use of trademarks. Initially, domain names were to be issued on a first-come, first-serve basis, but this method posed some problems:

- Companies with similar or identical trademarks for different products, both wishing to use the same domain name.
- Individuals or businesses registering for domain names of competitors to use as a marketing device.
- Individuals or businesses registering domain names for which they personally have no use and holding them "hostage" for a ransom.

Because of the high volume of domain name registration applications, a background check of registered trademarks is not conducted for each application. This first-come, first-serve, no-questions-asked policy contributed to some of the conflicts discussed in this section. ICANN does provide specific information about dispute resolution on its website. Here is some general information:

> In general, the policy provides that registrars receiving complaints concerning the impact of domain names they have registered on trademarks or service marks will take no action until they receive instructions from the domain-name holder or an order of a court, arbitrator, or other neutral decision maker deciding the parties' dispute. There is an exception in the policy, however, for disputes involving domain names that are shown to have been registered in abusive attempts to profit from another's trademark (i.e., cybersquatting and cyberpiracy). In these cases of abusive registration, the complaining party can invoke a special administrative procedure to resolve the dispute. Under this procedure, the dispute will be decided by neutral persons selected from panels established for that purpose. The procedure will be handled in large part online, is designed to take less than 45 days, and is expected to cost about $1,000 in fees to be paid to the entities providing the neutral persons. Parties to such disputes will also be able to go to court to resolve their dispute or to contest the outcome of the procedure.

(*www.icann.org FAQs*)

Similarly Named Companies or Products

To understand the nature of this problem, consider that in 2001, a search of the online Pennsylvania Yellow Pages yielded 323 companies beginning with the word "ace," yet in the *entire world,* only one "ace.com" can exist. Companies with federally registered trademarks have tended to receive preferential treatment over other types of trademarks.

A dispute that arose for similarly named domains that was settled between the two parties was between a magazine entitled *Wired* (wired.com) and a women's issues computer network called WIRE (wire.com). The issue of domain names that were too similar was raised by *Wired* Magazine. The two parties reached an agreement that WIRE would change the domain name to wwire.net. The two parties shared the cost of changing the name, and *Wired* Magazine agreed to run some advertisements for Women's Wire. Thus, this case was also resolved without a court decision.[7]

Another case, somewhat different from the one just discussed, involves a dispute between Tiger Electronics Ltd., the manufacturer of Furby toys, and David Matteo, owner of a website called furbynation.com. The site has a chat room for visitors to discuss Furby toys, and Matteo also resells the toys. Tiger Electronics is demanding that Matteo relinquish his domain name because it contains within it the trademark Furby. Further, it claims the site itself creates a likelihood of confusion such that visitors may think they are at an official Furby site. Matteo's site does indicate that the site is not affiliated with Tiger. As of 2001, Matteo still has his site in operation under the name furbynation.com. On it, Matteo displays the letter he received from Tiger's attorney and the response from his attorney.

Registering and Using a Competitor's Name

A widely publicized case in 1994 between two competing test preparation companies brought the problem of unfair use of domain names on the Internet to the public's attention.[8] Princeton Review applied for and received the domain name "kaplan.com." Stanley Kaplan only learned of this website when it applied for the same domain name and was rejected. Meanwhile, Princeton Review was using the site to advertise the relative strengths of its own test preparation services as compared to Kaplan's, and oftentimes used disparaging remarks about the quality of the Kaplan courses. Further, Princeton Review did not notify visitors that it was administering the site and its contents. Kaplan filed a lawsuit for trademark infringement against Princeton Review. In an effort to settle the case, Princeton Review informed Kaplan that they had only registered the domain name and administered the site as a joke, and then offered to sell the domain name to Kaplan for a case of beer. Kaplan refused the offer, and the case went to an arbitrator, who ruled that Princeton Review must relinquish the domain name to Kaplan.

Domain Names Registered and Held Hostage

The low cost (approximately $35 for one year) and ease of domain name registration has allowed individuals to register domain names of well-known companies. The intent by many registrants was to hold these domain names hostage until a company would

---

[7]See Gayle Weiswasser, 1997, for dispute details.
[8]Ibid.

E-Commerce in Practice

Automakers Race After Alleged Cybersquatters

Ford, Nissan in Domain Name Disputes

Ford Motor Co. recently filed suit and won a temporary injunction against an alleged cybersquatter who Ford claims attempted to infringe upon its trademarks, in one of several Internet domain name disputes involving automakers.

Dearborn, Mich.–based Ford contends that Ohio resident Cory Czech attempted to sell 52 domain names, including Ford-quality.com and Lincoln-quality.com, on eBay Inc.'s auction website last month. The automaker won a temporary restraining order from the U.S. District Court in Northern Ohio to halt the domain name sales. Ford is also suing another individual to gain the rights to www.sporttrac.com, the name of a Ford utility vehicle.

Citing the federal Anti-Cybersquatting Consumer Protection Act passed last fall, Ford officials claim that by attempting to hawk the domain names on eBay, Czech meets the bad faith intent stipulated in the act. The act protects trademark holders from individuals who purchase domain names with bad faith intent.

Czech also holds domain names that include the trademarks of automakers such as General Motors Corp. in Detroit and DaimlerChrysler in Stuttgart, Germany.

Czech's attorney, Vince Ruffa of Oakar Ruffa and Abood in Broadview Heights, Ohio, declined to comment on the case.

Legal Battles Possible

GM spokeswoman Kelly Cusinato said she applauds Ford's "activism in protection of its trademarks." Cusi-nato said GM plans to investigate instances where it may be able to recover domains that use the company's trademarks.

Bob McAughan, a partner and intellectual property attorney at Howrey Simon Arnold & White LLP in Washington, said he expects the anticybersquatting law to help resolve domain name disputes quickly. But the law could also spark legal battles over Internet trademark issues where the interests of the parties aren't clear-cut.

One such case involves Nissan North America Inc. in Gardenia, Calif. In December, the company brought suit against an alleged cybersquatter to gain the rights to Nissan.com and Nissan.net. Unlike in typical cybersquatting cases, these domain names are registered to the owner of a business with a similar name: Uzi Nissan is president of Nissan Computer Corp. in Raleigh, N.C.

Uzi Nissan registered the names in 1994 for what he described as Internet service provider and computer reseller businesses. Officials for the automaker claim that the company's case meets the bad faith provision of the anticybersquatting act because Uzi Nissan offered to sell the domain name for $15 million.

But he contends that the high figure was offered in jest. "They want to crush me and get it for nothing. I feel that they are pressuring me to give it up," he said.

Source: Lee Copeland, © *Computerworld Online*, February 28, 2000. *www.computerworld.com*

offer to buy the rights to use the domain name. Dennis Toeppen registered more than 200 domain names, including panavision.com and americanstandard.com. Mr. Toeppen repeatedly lost cases filed against him by companies defending their right to use their trademark name.[9] The box entitled "Automakers Race After Alleged Cybersquatters" discusses incidents involving Ford and Nissan. Registrations are approved on the basis of the assumption that no other entity has a legal right, such as a registered trademark, to use that domain name. If that assumption proves to be false, ICANN reserves the right to reexamine the registration of that domain name and generally gives preference to entities with a federally registered trademark.

---

[9]For example, *Panavision Int'l., L.P. v. Toeppen*, 945 F. Supp. 1296 (C.D. Cal. 1996).

INTERNET SALES TAX

Federal, State, and Local Tax Issues

The taxation of Internet-related goods and services has been and continues to be another widely debated topic. For services delivered over the Internet, determination of the geographic location of the source of the sale and the destination of the service provided is oftentimes difficult. Local tax authorities are very interested in levying taxes on any services provided by servers located in their geographical jurisdiction. Many members of the U.S. government believe that state and local taxing of Internet services is not feasible and could hinder the growth of the Internet and even result in multiple taxation. Congress reports that consumers and businesses engaging in Internet services could be subject to more than 30,000 different taxing jurisdictions in the United States if left to local taxing authorities. The state and local taxing authorities, however, complain that they need these revenues to fund education and other services in their communities.

The **Internet Tax Freedom Act** became law in October 1998. This Act establishes a three-year moratorium on new state and local Internet taxes on:

- The Internet or interactive computer services.
- The use of the Internet or interactive computer services.

In providing rationale for this Act, Congress states the following:

> Even within the United States, the Internet does not respect State lines and operates independently of State boundaries. Addresses on the internet are designed to be geographically indifferent. Internet transmissions are insensitive to physical distance and can have multiple geographical addresses.

> Because transmissions over the Internet are made through packet-switching it is impossible to determine with any degree of certainty the precise geographic route or endpoints of specific Internet transmissions and infeasible to separate intrastate from interstate, and domestic from foreign, Internet transmission.

> (*S. 442*)

During the three-year moratorium, the Act recommends that the issue of Internet taxation be closely studied and that policy recommendations for both domestic and international Internet taxation be made. Thus, the tax moratorium is meant to be an interim measure that addresses and promotes fair and consistent tax measures while the issue is further studied. Several states have already taken actions that inconsistently tax Internet-related activities.

This Act does not, however, exempt entities that provide these services from net income taxes; it only exempts the receiver of the service from having to pay sales tax. Nor does the Act exempt entities from having to pay business license taxes.

Further, if the Internet is used as a vehicle to sell a good that is physically delivered offline (similar to mail-order businesses), the sale may not be exempt from state and local taxes under this Act. The determination whether the sale is taxed depends on whether the buyer and seller reside in the same state. For the seller, this means having a **corporate presence,** which is generally believed to be a physical building. If the seller has a corporate presence in the state in which the buyer resides, then the sale is subject to sales tax. Retail stores count as a corporate presence, so if an online retailer has a traditional retail store in the same state as the buyer, it must charge a sales tax. This is an existing law, so the three-year moratorium does not apply. At this point in time, most people believe that merely using a server located in a state, without having a physical building, does not qualify it as a corporate presence, although nowhere is this stated in law.

If the seller does not have a corporate presence in the state in which the buyer resides, the sales tax does not apply, but a use tax does. A **use tax** is a tax that theoretically goes to the state and/or local government in which the buyer resides. For years, state and local governments have looked the other way in collecting this tax from mail-order firms. The cost of compliance is high because businesses would potentially have to collect and remit taxes to possibly every state and numerous local governments. Because of this compliance cost, some tax reformers advocate eliminating the local and state sales and use taxes and replacing them with a federal tax that can be allocated to state and local governments. With the end of the three-year moratorium rapidly approaching, these topics will be hotly debated.

International Tax Issues

The Internet Tax Freedom Act declares its opinion that "the Internet be free of foreign tariffs . . . . " It also encourages the President to seek international consensus on such a policy. Japan is currently leaning towards a similar no-taxation of Internet-based services similar to that of the United States. The EU has not, however, agreed with differential tax policies for Internet services. It had delayed its introduction of value-added tax (VAT) on online transactions until June 2001. For the EU, the big hurdle is determining how to apply the VAT to online transactions from sellers outside the EU to EU purchasers. One proposal would have all foreign seller "operators" register in just one EU country and have the revenue shared among all 15 members of the EU. Unless a uniform rate is charged, however, all operators would probably register in the country with the lowest VAT.

China has indicated that it will also impose Internet taxes. In August 2000, China's State Administration of Taxation (SAT) asserted that e-commerce was essentially no different from selling a product or service in physical stores and should not be exempted from taxes.

Not yet adequately addressed by Internet tax laws is the geographic location of the source of the sale (i.e., when the sale is placed on the Internet, but delivered offline), such as through a freight company. If a company has its corporate headquarters and warehouse in one state, but has its electronic commerce transaction processing system located on a server in another state (or even in the same state, but different city or county), where is the location of the sale for tax purposes? This scenario can be expanded to an international basis. What if a German-based company sells a product or service in the United States and places its Web page on a server in New Jersey, but has no office or warehouse located there? Will the item be taxed as a locally sold item, a foreign item, or both? Currently, a safe interpretation is that the German-based company does not have a **permanent establishment** in the United States and thus would not be subject to tax. Any country with which the United States has a tax treaty is only subject to U.S. tax *if* the company has a permanent establishment in the United States.

The big question for foreign businesses wishing to sell their goods in the United States over the Internet and avoid U.S. taxation is this: What qualifies a business to have a permanent establishment? Basically, if the company has a physical place of business or a dependent agent in the United States, it is considered to have a permanent establishment. Most businesses located in another country that want to use the Internet just to interact with the customer, sell the good, and then ship it from a country outside the United States will have no problem avoiding the physical presence criteria. If the business has a warehouse in the United States in which it stores inventory, the firm may be treated as having a permanent establishment.

What if the business contracts with a U.S.-based value-added network to market the site, accept orders, and process them on behalf of the business? Because this may be interpreted as a dependent agent, the business may be treated as having a corporate presence and be required to pay taxes. U.S. firms selling their goods and services face these same issues abroad and will have to carefully study the tax laws of each country in which their buyers reside.

How foreign countries treat the location and use of a server is different. For example, Portugal and Spain do not consider physical presence in a country to be necessary to qualify as a permanent establishment. The United Kingdom, on the other hand, takes the position that servers or websites do not constitute a permanent establishment.

The **Organization for Economic Cooperation and Development (OECD),** an organization with 29 member groups that "provides governments a setting in which to discuss, develop, and perfect economic and social policy," is examining international Internet tax issues. The OECD considers the topic to be so important that it placed it as one of its top four projects. The group is specifically considering the definition of permanent establishment and how ISPs, Web servers, and websites relate to the definition.

ELECTRONIC AGREEMENTS AND DIGITAL SIGNATURES

Traditionally, legal agreements have been made in a written, hard-copy format that bears the handwritten (or equivalent, such as a thumb or footprint) signatures of the parties involved. Transactions conducted on the Internet typically occur in real time. The process of utilizing hard-copy agreements negates many of the desired attributes of e-commerce, such as speed and reduced paperwork. Thus, new methods of delivering enforceable legal agreements (contracts) and producing valid signatures in a digital format are necessary for most aspects of completing electronic sales transactions.

The delivery of electronic legal agreements on the Internet is typically via an electronic form with a delivered statement that the user (signer) reads and "clicks" on an "I Accept" button. This type of agreement has been upheld in a few court cases. Another form of **electronic contract** is being entered into by computer programs, called **electronic,** or **intelligent, agents.** The computer-programmed agents are essentially "authorized" to contract on behalf of the party owning and operating the program. Programs such as these that have the capability to locate potential transaction partners and negotiate with their computer programs necessitate new legal guidelines for enforceable agreements. The topic of intelligent agents is more thoroughly discussed in Chapter 13.

The clicking of an "I Accept" button is not considered to be a sufficient legal signature by many members of the legal profession because it lacks some formal requirements necessary for a signature to be enforceable in a court of law, especially for negotiated contracts that may be reasonably expected to go through a few iterations of revisions before final signing. The American Bar Association (ABA) discusses some important attributes of signatures:

• **Signer authentication.** A signature should indicate who signed a document, message, or record and should be difficult for another person to produce without authorization.

• **Document authentication.** A signature should identify what is signed, making it impracticable to falsify or alter either the signed matter or the signature without detection.

- **Affirmative act.** The affixing of the signature should be an affirmative act that serves the ceremonial and approval functions of a signature and establishes the sense of having legally consummated a transaction.
- **Efficiency.** Optimally, a signature sense of having legally consummated a transaction; its creation and verification process should provide the greatest possible assurances of both signer authenticity and document authenticity, with the least possible expenditure of resources.

(American Bar Association—Digital Signatures Guidelines, August, 1996)

The ABA contends that the use of digital signatures, when performed correctly, not only meets these attributes, but can surpass the handwritten signatures on paper technology. Digital signature technology is covered in detail in Chapter 10.

E-Sign

In response to the growing demand for action by both businesses and consumers, the United States enacted the **Electronic Signatures in Global and International Commerce Act (E-Sign)** in mid-2000. The law went into effect October 1, 2000. E-Sign sets forth a structural outline of how business may be performed in electronic form. The statute essentially provides that a signature, contract, or other record relating to a transaction may not be denied enforceability solely because it is in an electronic form or because it contains an electronic signature. Although E-Sign *allows* the use of electronic records and signatures, it does not *require* their use. In fact, E-Sign specifically states that it does not require any person to agree to use electronic signatures.

Furthermore, E-Sign requires a company to electronically retain any contract that it is otherwise required to retain by statute, regulation, or other rule of law (a large number of contracts entered into in a business context require a written document to be enforceable). The electronic record of the document must: (a) accurately reflect the information set forth in the written document and (b) remain accessible to all persons entitled to access.

Software applications are available that attach electronic signatures and ensure the accuracy of any electronically signed document. However, the specific requirements for retention and accuracy have yet to be defined. How, and if, any particular software package complies with the security requirements of the statute can be difficult to determine without thoroughly investigating the software and underlying infrastructure. The technology that supports digital signatures is discussed in Chapter 10. Additionally, different software packages do not necessarily interact with each other, creating additional difficulties.

In addition, E-Sign does not apply to all documents. For instance, wills, changes to wills, or testamentary trusts may not be signed electronically. Contracts relating to adoption, divorce, or other matters of family law are not governed by E-Sign. Substantial portions of the **Uniform Commercial Code (UCC)** are not governed by E-Sign. Also, additional exceptions are given, for example, transportation of hazardous materials, recall of products, and cancellation of certain insurance benefits. Finally, E-Sign preempts only certain state laws and is effective only for those contracts relating to interstate commerce; specifically, it does not apply if a state has adopted the Uniform Electronic Transactions Act (UETA) discussed next.

UETA

The National Conference of Commissioners on Uniform State Laws (NCCUSL) adopted the **Uniform Electronic Transactions Act (UETA)** in 1999. It has been adopted, in one form or another, in at least 22 states, with several others currently in the legislative process. UETA is similar to, although more detailed than, E-Sign. However, UETA is also only a framework under which to do business electronically, and it deals primarily with electronic signatures and documents. Highlights of UETA follow:

- UETA only applies if all parties to a transaction agree to conduct it electronically.
- Parties may agree to waive some, or all, of the requirements of UETA.
- UETA's purpose is not to create new legal principles but to ensure electronic transactions are equally as enforceable as standard, written transactions.
- UETA primarily provides that electronic signatures or electronic records may not be denied enforceability simply because they are in electronic form.
- UETA governs when an electronic record is sent or received for enforceability determinations.
- UETA governs when an electronic signature is enforceable.
- UETA does not require the use of electronic signatures but is technologically neutral.
- UETA provides for a standard to transfer documents, to ensure their accuracy and integrity.
- UETA validates contracts sent by electronic agents.

Because UETA is technologically neutral, its widespread use may take a while due to interoperability issues. Each participant to a transaction must utilize compatible technology to transfer documents and verify signatures. Many vendors offer their own technology to compete in this arena. Until a few top contenders prevail, electronic transactions may not become commonplace.

UETA, like E-Sign, exempts itself from applicability to certain transactions such as wills, changes to wills, and so forth. UETA does not revolutionize how business is performed, but rather ensures that electronic signatures and transactions cannot be denied validity just because they are in electronic form. Thus, UETA helps in the evolutionary migration toward e-business.

UCITA

The NCCUSL also abandoned its efforts to bring the UCC in to the digital age through means of newly proposed Article 2B. NCCUSL decided to draft the proposed revisions as a stand-alone uniform law entitled the **Uniform Computer Information Transactions Act (UCITA).** NCCUSAL states that UCITA's purpose is to

- Support and facilitate the realization of the full potential of computer information transactions in cyberspace.
- Clarify the law governing computer information transactions.
- Enable expanding commercial practice in computer information transactions by commercial usage and agreement of the parties.
- Make the law uniform among the various jurisdictions.

(UCITA, Preferatory Note)

UCITA was approved by NCCUSL on July 29, 1999, and at least two states have enacted it into law, with revisions (Virginia and Maryland).

International Initiatives

Many countries have enacted or begun the process of enacting digital signature laws. Listed here are some international digital signature acts passed into law:

- Australia (Commonwealth) Electronic Transactions Bill 1999.
- (Argentina) Presidential Decree No. 427/98—Digital Signatures for the National Public Administration.
- Austria Federal Electronic Signature Law 2000.
- Canada Bill C-6 (the Personal Information Protection and Electronic Documents Act) 1999.
- Columbia Draft Proposal of Law on Electronic Commerce, Digital Signatures and Certification Authorities 2000.
- Estonia Digital Signatures Act 2000.
- European Union Directive 1999/93/EC of December 13, 1999, on a Community Framework for Electronic Signatures 2000.
- Finland Act on Electronic Service in the Administration 2000.
- Germany Digital Signature Act 1997.
- Hong Kong Electronic Transactions Ordinance 2000.
- Ireland Electronic Commerce Bill 2000.
- Japanese Law Concerning Electronic Signatures and Certification Services (2000).
- Malaysian Digital Signature Bill 1997.
- Philippines E-Commerce Act of 2000.
- Singapore Electronic Transactions Act (1998) and (1999).
- Switzerland Decree on E-Certification Services 2000.

> (*McBride Baker & Coles International Database for E-Commerce and Digital Signatures, www.mbc.com/ecommerce/international.asp*)

This list is not meant to be exhaustive. Many countries also have digital signature acts pending that may be passed by the time this is printed.

SPAM MAIL

Junk mail sent electronically has many ISPs, businesses, and individuals frustrated, annoyed, and even angry at this tactic. **Spam mail** is the sending of unsolicited e-mail advertisements to massive recipient lists of individuals or businesses that have never chosen to receive such e-mail, or many times never even visited the spammer's site. The e-mail addresses may be purchased or traded with another business. Another method of obtaining e-mail addresses is the use of software robots to scan the Web and collect addresses from public sources such as Usenet postings. Once a database of e-mail addresses is created or obtained, the cost of sending spam is very low to the sender. It can, however, be costly to businesses and ISPs that have their e-mail services clogged with traffic from junk mail. Some case law provides support for the notion that ISPs own their servers and, therefore, can deny the use of their servers to abusers, such as spammers. One example is the case of *AOL* v. *Cyber Promotions Inc.*

Many federal and state legislators are proposing anti-spam bills. In July 2000, the U.S. House of Representatives passed a bill that, if passed into law, would make it illegal to send e-mail messages to recipients who asked not to receive such mail. The European Union is considering similar regulation.

E-Commerce in Practice

Yahoo Told to Block Nazi Goods from French

Yahoo Inc. must prevent French customers from gaining access to the portions of its auction site that sell Nazi-related goods, a judge in France ordered in a precedent-setting decision that will reverberate throughout the Internet industry.

The decision handed down late today reinforced a preliminary opinion delivered by Judge Jean-Jacques Gomez in May instructing Yahoo to put filtering systems in place. Yahoo had long contended that filtering systems don't work, while plaintiffs such as the League Against Racism and Anti-Semitism, or LICRA, and the Jewish student group UEJF had advocated that a partial solution is better than none.

Gomez ruled that Yahoo must put a three-part system in place that includes filtering by IP address, the blocking of 10 keywords, and self-identification of geographic location. The system follows the recommendations of an expert panel appointed by the court to investigate such technologies. Yahoo will have three months to put the system in place, after which time the company would be subject to a fine of 100,000 francs, or $13,000, a day if the system has not been implemented.

The case has raised questions about the jurisdiction of national courts over international Internet companies and has sparked a widespread debate over whether local laws should apply to foreign Internet companies. Yahoo believes its U.S. parent company should not be subject to French law, and that it already complies with the French law forbidding the sale of Nazi-related goods on its French website, Yahoo.fr.

"Our reaction [to the decision] remains what we've said thus far in the case," said Yahoo spokeswoman Sue Jackson, leaving the courthouse in Paris this evening. Yahoo doesn't believe that a U.S. company should be subject to individual laws around the world, she said. "Does one country have jurisdiction to regulate companies in another country?" she asked.

But the French courts—as well as the French public, which in increasing numbers sees Yahoo as an insensitive American invader—obviously see things differently.

"The French justice system has heard us," said Marc Knobel, a member of the board of LICRA. "It is no longer OK for online retailers to say they are not affected by existing laws." Global Internet companies should put "ethics and morals" first, Knobel claimed. "If they won't do it themselves, they have to be forced."

Yahoo said it is currently reviewing the decision and will decide how to proceed in the coming weeks. The company can appeal the decision in French courts and may end up fighting the battle in U.S. courts, as well, said Jackson. "Given the free-speech implications, there are strong questions whether a U.S. court would agree to the decision," she said.

LICRA will continue its fight if Yahoo decides to appeal, said Knobel. "It's stubbornness until the end with Yahoo, but we will continue to the end as well."

Whether Yahoo decides to comply or not, the verdict has already had an impact on the Internet industry, which remains fearful of a highly regulated Internet controlled by many different governments at the same time. The repercussions will grow if the case ends up in U.S. courts.

"This case has sparked off the issue of cultural differences and national sovereignty," said Jean-Claude Patin at Juritel, a Paris-based legal research firm. Internet companies are going to come under increasing fire if they don't comply with existing regulations, he said. "We will definitely see more of the of these cross-border cases."

Source: Kristi Essick, © ComputerworldOnline, November 20, 2000. *www.computerworld.com*

ONLINE AUCTIONS AND CONTENT FILTERING

Online auctions have flourished, and hundreds of thousands of consumer-to-consumer sales are occurring daily; as a result, the diversity of items being sold is increasing. Prior to the 2000 U.S. election, mail-in proxy votes showed up on eBay.com's website. Selling election votes is illegal in the United States, thus it was a relatively easy decision for eBay to remove the item from auction after being contacted. Yahoo is now involved in a situation in which it has been ordered by the French government to install filtering technology so that French citizens cannot gain access to portions of its site that contain Nazi items. Selling these items in France is illegal. The proposed filtering technique would examine the IP address to determine whether the user trying to access the site is from France. Yahoo does not agree with the court order, as mentioned in the box "Yahoo Told to Block Nazi Goods from French." This conflict continues as Yahoo plots its course of action.

TEXAS SHUTS DOWN FORD'S PREOWNED AUTO SITE

You just have to see this one. The following text was taken from the Ford Motor Company's website (*http://www.fordpreowned.com/houston.html*) in January 2001:

Citizens of Texas Denied Access to This Website

Please be advised that the Ford Pre-Owned Showroom is temporarily closed due to actions taken by the Texas Department of Transportation, Motor Vehicle Division—Enforcement Section (TMVD). As a result, citizens of Texas are not able to utilize this convenient alternative to shop for previously owned vehicles.

We are concerned and deeply disappointed by this disservice to the citizens of Texas. The TMVD's action prevents consumers and automobile dealers in Houston from accessing the Ford Pre-Owned Showroom Internet website—a site that citizens in many other large metropolitan areas are currently enjoying. We believe this is an unfair attempt to regulate the Internet and are troubled by this decision and its implications.

The Texas Division of Motor Vehicles (DMV) asserts that a state law prohibiting manufacturers from serving as dealers and engaging in direct sales was violated by Ford. Ford placed its inventory of preowned cars on the Internet along with the prices. Deposits could be made on the Internet, but the sale had to be completed at the dealer actually holding the car. The DMV claimed that because it was a fixed price, it was a direct sell to a consumer. Ford contends that the sale is not complete until the purchaser goes to the dealer and completes the transaction. The DMV threatened participating Ford dealers with $10,000 fines. This case continues.

IMPLICATIONS FOR THE ACCOUNTING PROFESSION

The evolutionary nature of the international legal environment facing firms engaging in e-commerce presents a challenge to members of the accounting profession, but with that comes an increasing opportunity set of services that it can provide. Some of these opportunities are discussed in this section.

Liability Exposure and Risk Assessment

Estimating a firm's exposure to risk elements and developing techniques to mitigate and control risk is an important function traditionally performed by accountants. The expanding nature of business functions performed electronically expands the scope of the risk assessment function. Correspondingly, the role of the accounting profession is expanding as a result of the changing business environment in which its clients operate. Estimating a firm's exposure to legal liability is an important factor of risk assessment, and accounting professionals must clearly understand the potential legal implications of actions performed by its clients and their computer-based information systems. Website design issues become important as improper procedures; such improper Web linking can result in the client's being faced with a costly lawsuit. As mentioned in this chapter, the legal framework for governing Internet actions is evolving, which makes this task more challenging to accountants and systems consultants.

Expansion of Legal Resources and Services

Accounting professionals must be well aware of the regulatory and legal environment in which their clients operate. Clients of all sizes may be venturing into uncharted waters merely by posting a Web page from which customers may order goods. This marks immediate international exposure for them, whereas before they may have only operated in their state or country. E-commerce applications that allow firms to have a corporate presence site from which it may collect data about its visitors and/or conduct business transactions must be designed while considering the following international laws of *each* country from which the visitor/customer resides:

- Taxation.
- Privacy.
- Intellectual property.
- Cryptography.
- Digital signatures.
- Acceptable business practices.

Accounting firms need to have expertise in these areas readily available to them by either in-house counsel or by outsourcing them to a law firm. Clients will expect their accountant to understand the legal, most secure way data can be transmitted, as well as the international taxes for which they are responsible. Further, if the accountant is involved in third-party assurance of the client's website, then he or she should be able to advise the client if they are in danger of a lawsuit, either at home or abroad. For those clients that serve as ISPs or online auctions, the accounting professional needs to be able to assess the exposure the firm may face due to varying international libel and sales laws and be sufficiently trained to offer guidance.

Digital Signatures and Certificate Authorities

As computer programs begin to engage in transaction negotiations and commitments (electronic agents), accounting professionals need to understand the underlying program code and legal exposure of such systems. Digital signatures attached to e-business transactions and agreements need to be secure and included in the systems design and risk assessment functions; the accounting professional should be integrally involved in both these functions. Further, accountants need to understand the underlying infrastructure upon which digital signatures are based—certificate authorities. Digital signature validity rests heavily on a trusted certificate authority. This topic is discussed more thoroughly in Chapter 10. Serving as a trusted third party, certificate authority is a service that accounting firms may choose to provide in the future.

Summary

The Internet and the Web have been and will continue to be in a high-growth phase for at least the next three years. During this high-growth period, some growing pains are to be expected as government and law enforcement agencies, businesses, and private citizens struggle to tame this new, exciting, yet "wild" frontier. Policies need to be set that harmonize a country's domestic needs with the needs of the international Internet community. Culturally diverse countries make the world exciting and interesting; however, these differences also impede the development of internationally uniform policies.

The Internet, given its globally ubiquitous nature, necessitates a congruent legal environment among varying nations. Unfortunately, nations are currently struggling with their own domestic legal policies. As they debate domestically, most nations are keeping one eye open and focused on international legal developments. Law-making bodies are quickly learning that legislation and regulation affecting Internet policies cannot effectively be formulated and administered by focusing narrowly on the internal demands of one's own country. Thus, the legal framework of the Internet is evolving and will be shaped into more concrete policies over the next few years.

Key Words

access
affirmative act
Anticybersquatting Consumer Protection Act
Carnivore
Children's Online Privacy Protection Act
  (COPPA)
choice
ciphertext
corporate presence
cryptography
decryption key
defamation
dilution by tarnishment
document authentication
domain name disputes
efficiency
electronic (intelligent) agents
electronic contract
Electronic Signatures in Global and
  International Commerce Act (E-Sign)
encryption key
enforcement
Federal Trade Commission (FTC)
federally registered trademarks
frame
hypertext links

HyperText Makeup Language (html)
information privacy
integrity
Internet Corporation for Assigned Names
  and Numbers (ICANN)
Internet Tax Freedom Act
InterNIC
key escrow
key length
key recovery
keyword metatags
likelihood of confusion
MP3 (Motion Picture Experts Group
  Audiolayer 3)
notice
Organization for Economic Cooperation and
  Development (OECD)
permanent establishment
security
signer authentication
spam mail
Uniform Commercial Code (UCC)
Uniform Computer Information Transactions
  Act (UCITA)
Uniform Electronic Transactions Act (UETA)
use tax

Review Questions

1. Identify the three categories of users served by each country.
2. What is cryptography?
3. What are two legal issues regarding cryptographic keys?
4. Define key escrow policy.
5. Define key recovery policy.
6. Identify six privacy advocacy groups.
7. What are the five core principles of privacy protection identified by the FTC?
8. Explain the main provisions of the Children's Online Privacy Protection Act.
9. What is Carnivore, and who developed it?

10. What rights should users have regarding personal data under the EU directive?
11. What is a hypertext link?
12. How can framing techniques be used to infringe on another company's trademark or copyright or to engage in unfair competition?
13. How can a website developer protect a site against unwanted framing techniques used by other sites?
14. What factors may cause the "likelihood of confusion" of a trademark?
15. What factors may cause a dilution by tarnishment of a trademark? Why was Mattel upset about its Barbie trademark?
16. Identify several types of disputes that have arisen over domain names.
17. Explain what is meant by holding a domain name "hostage."
18. What is the resolution guideline for domain name disputes?
19. Distinguish the difference between sales and use tax.
20. What is an electronic agent?
21. List four important attributes of signatures.
22. What is E-Sign?
23. What is spam mail?

Discussion Questions

1. From the viewpoint of law enforcement agencies, give the reasons for a key escrow/key recovery policy.
2. From the viewpoint of private citizens, give the reasons for a key escrow/key recovery policy.
3. Has the United States responded appropriately to the EU's privacy directives?
4. What privacy issues are raised because of the prevalence of the Internet and the Web?
5. Why has the government actively pursued regulation of cryptography, but only recently considered the regulation of privacy-related activities?
6. How can defamation be exasperated because of the Internet?
7. How can hypertext links be used in such a way as to cause disputes between owners of websites?
8. Why isn't it acceptable to include the name or trademark of a competitor in one's own keyword metatag?
9. Why did the RIAA not approve of Napster's website? Explain your answer fully.
10. Should a company that operates only locally (within a city or country) bother to obtain a federal trademark if it already has a state trademark?
11. Should a federally registered trademark, such as Ford, have the right to more than domain name with that trademark?
12. Why does the Internet Tax Freedom Act only go into effect for three years?
13. Why are many local government agencies opposed to the Internet Tax Freedom Act?
14. Why can digital signatures surpass the legal validity of a handwritten signature?
15. Why might marketing firms be angry with software that labels them as "spam" when they have an opt-in mailing list?
16. Why does the use of the Internet raise potential international conflicts regarding sales restriction laws?

Cases

1. Value-Added Tax (VAT)
   Research the European Union's VAT.
   a. Discuss why e-business with business-to-business trading partners external to the EU makes a financial difference to firms.
   b. Make a recommendation as to how the VAT should work with external-EU trading partners.

2. Digital Signatures and XML
   Locate the product specifications for InternetForms by PureEdge Solutions.
   a. Explain how this product supports digital contracts and signatures.
   b. Discuss interoperability issues with this product.

3. Unauthorized Sharing of Copyright Materials
   Visit the following sites: Gnutella, Aimster, and Freenet. Also visit Napster and MP3.com and complete the following:
   a. Determine what kind of music can be downloaded. If payment must be made for any music or services, indicate the payment fees.
   b. Discuss any differences or similarities found and how what you found supports and infringes of copyright laws.

4. Litigation Risk of Financial Information Disseminated via the Internet and the SEC Information Requirements
   Research the following legal cases:

   Jaillet v. *Cashman,* New York, 1921.

   Daniel v. *Dow Jones & Co., Inc.,* New York, 1987.

   Then go to *www.computerworld.com* and read "New SEC Rule Pushes More Firms to Web." Discuss how the decisions reached by the courts may be used as a basis for judgement for cases involving financial information that is erroneously misreported via the Internet.
   a. Discuss the potential implications for members of the accounting profession.
   b. Discuss the international issues.

5. Liability Insurance for Copyright/Trademark Infringement and Libel
   a. Using the Internet, locate an insurance company that offers liability coverage to companies with websites for copyright or trademark infringement or libel. Summarize the coverage policy and per incident limits.
   b. Discuss how such a policy may affect the design of websites.

6. ISP Liability Relating to Offensive Material
   Felix Somm, former manager of CompuServe Germany, was convicted by a German court of distributing online pornography. He was held responsible for pornographic material that was posted by third parties. However, the case is under appeal, and a new law has been passed relieving German ISPs from the responsibility of the content put on its servers by third parties.
   a. Using the Internet, research this case and determine the status of the appeal.
   b. What issues are raised by the initial case and Germany's new law?
   c. Develop a policy statement for what you believe should be the legal responsibility of ISPs regarding online pornography.

References and Websites

American Institute of Certified Public Accountants. "Computer-Disseminated Information," *http://www.aicpa.org /assurance/scas/comstud/asl/cdi.htm.*

Akdeniz, Yaman. "UK Encryption Wars," *Wired News.* May 25, 1998.

American Bar Association. *Digital Signature Guidelines.* August 1, 1996.

Barbeiri Montgomery, Susan, and Robin Maisashvili. "UCC 2B Could Result in Ambiguous IP Rights," *The National Law Journal.* May 18, 1998.

Beer, Matt. "Web Address Pact Extended," *Chicago Sun-Times.* September 30, 1998.

Bicknell, David. "US Firms Spark Encryption Confusion," *Computer Weekly.* July 16, 1998.

Center for Democracy and Technology. "Senators Introduce Pro-Privacy Encryption Bill, In Stark Contrast to Administration Position," *http:// www.cdt.org/press/051298press.html.*

_____ . "They Want to Be Safe," *Computer Weekly.* June 18, 1998.

Boreham, Gareth. "Government Gets Tough on Net Privacy," *The Age.* June 16, 1998.

Bracken, Mike. "Bridging Britain's Crypto Gap," *Wired News,* May 29, 1998.

Bridis, Ted. "Clinton Pushes for Internet Privacy," *AP Online,* July 30, 1998.

Clausing, Jeri. "Commerce Chief Calls U.S. Encryption Policy Flawed," *The New York Times,* April 16, 1998.

_____ . "House Panel Votes to Strengthen Export Controls on Encryption," *CyberTimes,* September 10, 1997.

_____ . "Control of Domain Names Draws Alternative Proposal," *The New York Times.* October 5, 1998.

Corcoran, Elizabeth. "U.S. to Relax Encryption Limits," *The Washington Post,* September 17, 1998.

Craddock, Ashley. "Rights Groups Denounce UK Crypto Paper," *Wired News,* May 30, 1997.

Crowe, Elizabeth Powell, " Legislating Spam," *ComputerUser.com* July 21, 1998. *www.computeruser.com.*

D'Amico, Mary Lisbeth. "German Court Ruling Another Blow to U.S. Encryption Standard," *The Industry Standard.* September 22, 1998.

DiSabatino, Jennifer. "Carnivore Not as Selective as FBI Said, Privacy Group Charges," *Computerworld Online.* November 17, 2000. *www.computerworld.com.*

_____. "Mattel's Barbie Wins Case Against CyberSquatters," *Computerworld Online.* July 20, 2000. *www.computerworld.com.*

Ditchburn, Jennifer. "Canadian Sued over Newsgroup Squabble," *The Edmonton Journal.* June 11, 1998.

Dunne, Nancy. "US-EU in 'Productive' Talks on Internet Privacy," *Financial Times (London).* July 30, 1998.

Electronic Frontier Foundation. "RSA Code-Breaking Contest Again Won by Distributed Net and Electronic Frontier Foundation," Press Release. January 19, 1999.

Federal Trade Commission. *Privacy Online: A Report to Congress.* 2000 and 1998.

Glave, James. "Crypto Kills—Really, It Does," *Wired News,* June 8, 1998.

Global Information Infrastructure Commission. "A Comparison of U.S., EU, MITI and GIIC Reports on Electronic Commerce: Part I of III," *http://www.gii.org/egi00256.htm.*

Grossman, Wendy. "Rules, Britannia," *Wired News,* July 7, 1998.

_____. "Encryption Proves a Slithery Beast to Control," *The Daily Telegraph (London),* January 21, 1999.

Hardesty, David. "Internet-Based Sales to the United States," *AccountingNet,* March 8, 1999.

Haring, Bruce. "Lycos Decides to Work with Record Industry," *USA Today,* February 2, 1999.

InterNIC. "About InterNIC Registration Services," *http://rs.internic.net/ about,rs.htm.*

Kaplan, Carl. "English Court May Test U.S. Ideals on Online Speech," *The New York Times,* June 5, 1998.

Koops, Bert-Jaap. "Crypto Law Survey," *http://cwis.kub.nl/.frw/people/koops/lawsurvy.htm.*

Lawson, Stephen. "China to Tax E-commerce," IDG.net, August 4, 2000. cnn.com.

Lehman, Dewayne. "Ford Battles Texas over Internet Sales," *ComputerworldOnline,* April 14, 2000. *www.computerworld.com.*

Licken, Eoin. "US Eases Encryption Control," *The Irish Times,* September 18, 1998.

Macavinta, Courtney. "EU Report Seeks Net Privacy Laws," *CNET News.* July 1, 1998.

Machlis, Sharon. "Key Recovery Is Needed, Interpol Exec Explains," *Computerworld Online,* March 9, 1999. *http://www.computerworld.com.*

Markoff, John. "U.S. Fails in Global Proposal for Internet Eavesdropping," *CyberTimes,* March 27, 1997.

McConnell, Bill. "U.S. Easing Curbs on Exports of State-of-the-Art Encryption," *American Banker.* July 8, 1998.

Meller, Paul. "EU Postpones Decision on Online Taxation," *Network World,* November 29, 2000. *cnn.com.*

Murphy, Kathleen. "Law Group Formulates Uniform Rules for Online Transactions," *Web Week.* March 17, 1997.

Niccolai, James. "Court Rules Against Net Censorship," *Computerworld Online,* February 2, 1999. *http://www.computerworld.com*

Ohlson, Kathleen, "Ticketmaster, MicroSoft Settle Linking Dispute," *Computerworld Online,* February 17, 1999.

Olbeter, Erik, and Christopher Hamilton. "Finding the Key: Reconciling National and Economic Security Interests in Cryptographic Policy," *Economic Strategy Institute,* April 1998. *http://www.econstrat.org/ECONSTRAT/crypto.htm.*

Post, David. "The Link to Liability," *The American Lawyer.* July–August 1997.

Radding, Alan. "Encryption and You," *Computerworld.* June 29, 1998.

Reuters. "Crypto Battle Continues in New Congress," *CNET,* February 1, 1999. *http://www.news.com/News/Item/0,4,31751,00.html.*

Rodger, Will. "Marketers Concede that Some Privacy Laws Needed," *ZDNet,* September 23, 1998.

_____. "AmEx, EDS May Face European Privacy Lawsuits," *Inter@ctive Week Online.* July 1, 1998.

_____. "Europe Presses Electronic Privacy," *Inter@ctive Week Online.* June 15, 1998.

Rosencrance, Linda. "Sale of More.com's Customer List Raises Privacy Concerns," *Computerworld Online.* October 26, 2000. *www.computerworld.com.*

_____. "Music Publisher Reach Preliminary Agreement with MPS," *Computerworld Online.* October 18, 2000. *www.computerworld.com.*

RSA Data Security. "RSA Provides Security Solutions to Worldwide Markets Through New Operation in Australia," Press Release, January 6, 1999. *http://www.rsa.com.*

S.442. 105th Congress, 1st Session. March 13, 1997.

Sandburg, Brenda. "Commercial Code Upgrade May Fall Apart," *The Recorder.* September 28, 1998.

Sergeant, Jacqueline. "Tangled in the Web," *Home News Tribune,* February 9, 1999.

Simons, John. "Rules on Exporting Encryption Products Are Relaxed in Boost to High-Tech Firms," *The Wall Street Journal,* September 17, 1998.

Simpson, S. "Crypto Related Quotes," *http://www.hertreg.ac.uk/ss/Quotes.htm.*

Suzman, Mark. "FTC Chief Warns of Internet Privacy Action," *Financial Times (London).* July 22, 1998.

Stykes, Rebecca, and Margret Johnston. "SAFE Act Clears First Legislative Hurdle," *Computerworld,* March 11, 1999. *http://www.computerworld.com/home/news.nsf/CWFlash/990314safe.*

Taylor, Paul. "Europe 'Must' Act to Spur E-Commerce," *Financial Times (London).* September 24, 1998.

Tedeschi, Bob. "Despite Reprieve, Tax Laws Complicate Internet Retailing," *The New York Times on the Web,* February 9, 1999.

Terry, Paul. "Uniform Legal Code for Electronic Contracts and Licensing Issues," *The Metropolitan Corporate Counsel.* March 1998.

Thorel, Jerome. "As French Hang a Leash on the Net, Military Interests Surface," *TIS,* June 14, 1996.

_____. "TicketMaster Sues over Weblink," *Computerworld Online,* April 30, 1997.

Uhlig, Robert. "Connected: Americans Fail to Keep PGP to Themselves," *The Daily Telegraph.* September 17, 1998.

Vaiden, Kristi. "A Discussion of Some of the Recent Developments in Cyberlaw," *The Metropolitan Corporate Counsel.* July 1998.

Varney, Christine. "You Call This Self-Regulation," *Wired News.* June 9, 1998.

Voorhees, Mark. "Roadrunner to Network Solutions: Shame on You," *InfoLaw Alert.* June 19, 1996.

_____. "Network Solutions Says Name Policy Is 'Not Subject to Review' by Courts," *InfoLaw Alert.* May 17, 1996.

Watt-Morse, Peter. "Electronic Contracting: Update on Agreements, Encryption and Digital Signatures," *Internet Law Update.* Pennsylvania Bar Institute. 1998.

Weiswasser, Gayle. "Domain Names, the Internet, and Trademarks: Infringement in Cyberspace," *Santa Clara Computer and High Technology Law Journal.* February 1997.

Welch, William. "Internet Sales Tax Moratorium Is Likely," *USA Today,* September 29, 1998.

Wilf, Frederic. "Trademark Law on the Internet," *Internet Law Update.* Pennsylvania Bar Institute. 1998.

Zitner, Aaron. "Software Leaders, Reno discuss Encryption Impasse," *The Boston Globe.* June 10, 1998.

"Child Online Protection Act" (H.R. 3783). *http://epic.org/free_speech/house_cda2.htm.*

"European Union Rejects TTPs," *Intelligence Newsletter.* April 2, 1998.

"Internet Tax Freedom Act Clears House Committee," *TechMall,* May 14, 1998. *http://www.techmall.com/techdocs/TS980515-5.htm.*

"Syria's on Net, and on Guard," *Wired News.* July 10, 1998.

"The White House: Fact Sheet—Administration Updates Encryption Policy," *M2 Presswire.* September 18, 1998.

U.S. Department of Commerce—Bureau of Export Administration. "Commerce Updates Export Controls on Encryption Product," Press Release, December 30, 1998.

"U.S. Relaxes Data Encryption Controls," *The Scotsman.* September 23, 1998.

"U.S. to Ease Rules on Encryption Exports," *Chicago Sun-Times.* September 18, 1998.

6   EDI, ELECTRONIC COMMERCE, AND THE INTERNET

Learning Objectives

1. To understand the evolution of EDI from traditional systems to fully integrated Web-based systems.
2. To differentiate EDI from financial EDI.
3. To identify the potential benefits of EDI.
4. To understand the role of trading partners, VANs, and the necessity of standards in EDI.
5. To understand the effect of XML and XBRL on Web-based EDI.

INTRODUCTION

For more than three decades, some pioneering businesses have been using electronic mechanisms to exchange transaction data. Most firms currently engaging in electronic data interchange (EDI), however, entered the electronic movement during the last decade. According to the Electronic Commerce Research Group, EDI volume increased 30 percent per year in the early 1990s and is currently growing at about 15 percent per year. Giga Information Group predicts that EDI transaction value will rise from $3 trillion in 1999 to $4 trillion by 2003. The methods of data exchange between firms have evolved over time, and EDI standards have emerged and continue to emerge as new Web-based standards evolve. This chapter illustrates how traditional EDI systems operate and explores the enhanced capabilities that Internet-based e-commerce systems offer.

TRADITIONAL EDI SYSTEMS

Electronic data interchange (EDI) refers to the exchange of electronic business documents, that is, purchasing orders, invoices, and the like, between applications. The exchange involves no paper, no human intervention, and takes place in a matter of seconds. EDI documents are formatted using published standards. These standards were developed by large businesses during the 1970s and are now under the control of the ANSI (American National Standards Institute) X12 subcommittee, which sets EDI standards in North America. EDI requires a network connection between the two companies exchanging business documents, called **trading partners.** Traditionally, this has required a dedicated leased line or a connection to a value-added network (VAN). The services provided by VANs are discussed later in this chapter. In theory, EDI allows all vendors and their customers to link their computing infrastructures without worrying about the differences in their respective organizations and systems. In practice, however, EDI has been difficult to use efficiently or inexpensively.

Initial successes with EDI were in captive supplier markets such as the auto industry. In these cases, large purchasing companies chose to invest in proprietary systems that permitted them to raise barriers to entry and exert control over other industry participants. The dominant purchasers dictated to the dependent suppliers that all transactions would use EDI, in essence saying, "If you want to do business with us, you'll use EDI." The automobile industry is an example of mandatory use of EDI by its trading partners. But for many small and medium-sized companies, the investments in EDI hardware and software, as well as monthly VAN connection fees, have rendered EDI cost prohibitive. Unfortunately, EDI has existed in a high-end level of the market where large players send and receive large numbers of EDI documents on a regular basis over a VAN, doing a large enough volume of transactions to justify the cost.

The Origin of EDI

In 1964, an innovative sales manager at American Hospital Supply Company (AHSC) created a system to assist a local hospital experiencing inventory problems. The salesman gave the hospital a stack of prepunched cards. The cards, a unique one for each item purchased from AHSC, were inserted in a box of supplies to indicate when the item should be reordered. At that time, the cards were collected and fed into a card reader provided to the customer. The data were sent across a standard phone line to a punch machine at AHSC, where an identical set of cards was duplicated. The order fulfillment was then processed as usual. This electronic data interchange greatly improved accuracy and efficiency for many hospitals when ordering supplies. Immediately, inaccurate orders disappeared, delivery times decreased, and inventory shortages were eliminated.

Over the years, this imaginative invention grew into a legendary strategic information technology application now known as EDI. EDI has resulted in significant competitive advantages, including lower costs, tighter links to customers, and increased product differentiation. Over time EDI has evolved from the one-to-one system first used by AHSC into complex electronic markets consisting of a community of industry suppliers, producers, network facilitators, and customers.

EDI has provided great value to trading partners, especially those in certain EDI-enabled industries, such as retail, automotive, and petroleum. Unfortunately, these larger firms have been prevented from doing business with much smaller companies that cannot afford the complexities of EDI. However, the advent of the Internet has created a common information and communications platform upon which business can be conducted. In fact, the Internet provides the communications capabilities of EDI over a value-added network at a much lower price. EDI can be rolled out to small companies, provided that an Internet connection is present. What exactly does the future hold for EDI? Even for the largest, most demanding EDI users, the future seems to be "Webward."

Non-EDI Systems

EDI today is most widely used in large businesses and by smaller companies trading with larger businesses. To illustrate the benefits of EDI, let us compare a typical pro-

| **FIGURE 6–1** | *Non-EDI system* |

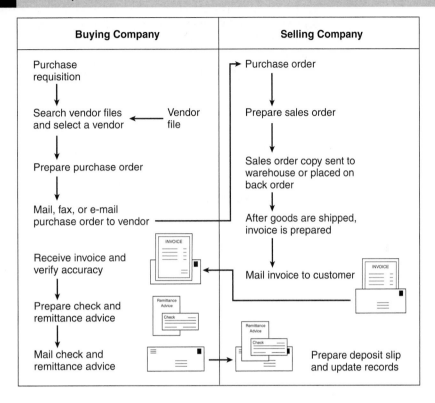

curement function in a large business. Figure 6–1 illustrates how a typical **non-EDI system** works for the example procurement function. A purchase requisition is completed by the production planning department or any other department needing equipment or supplies. A purchasing agent then reviews the purchase requisition. If other similar requests have been received, then the requisitions may be combined to take advantage of quantity discounts. The purchasing agent then manually reviews the available vendors for price by combing through product catalogs and price lists and calling vendors to inquire about inventory availability. Once a vendor is selected, the purchasing agent completes a purchase order. The purchase order is then mailed to the vendor.

Once the vendor receives the purchase order, a sales order processing clerk transcribes the necessary information onto a sales order form. A potential interim step not shown on the diagram is a credit-checking process. A copy of the approved sales order form is sent to the warehouse where the goods are pulled. If the goods are not available, they are placed on back order, which usually involves further clerical work. Available goods are shipped, and an invoice is prepared and sent to the customer. The customer then checks the invoice for accuracy and processes it for payment. If no discount is offered for early payment, the invoice may be held for a time period up until the appropriate due date. The customer's cash disbursements department prepares a check and remittance advice and mails them to the vendor. The vendor's cash receipts department, upon receipt of the check, prepares the deposit slip, and the accounts receivable department updates the accounts receivable records. The vendor may not have access to the funds for several days after the deposit has been made while the checks clear the bank.

The entire non-EDI process requires the use of multiple clerks by both the customer and vendor to complete the transaction. The typical clerks involved in the buying cycle are inventory control, purchasing, receiving, accounts payable, and cash disbursements. The typical clerks involved in the selling cycle are sales order processing, credit, warehouse, shipping, accounts receivable, and cash receipts. In this example, as many as 11 clerks are involved in the process from start to finish.

Value-Added-Networks and Preestablished Trading Partners

The EDI scenarios described earlier employ third-party network services, generally called **value-added-networks (VANs).** The services provided by most VANs include EDI translation software; security assurances of data; reliability of service due to multiple, alternative telecommunication links; EDI systems development assistance; and employee training sessions. The role of an EDI VAN is to execute only authorized transactions with valid trading partners. To enable the VAN to distinguish authorized transactions and valid trading partners, the exact **trading relationships** between parties must be explicitly expressed in signed contracts.

Companies engaging in EDI transactions may choose to subscribe to a VAN in order to reduce the technical complexities and cost of implementing their own connections with a multitude of trading partners. Some large companies have developed their own private networks, but this has proven costly to implement and unnecessary with the growth of the Internet. Increasingly, companies view **EDI messaging** as a function to be outsourced to a specialist. VANs provide this outsourcing function and serve as a messaging station for trading partners. Trading partners do not have to subscribe to the same VAN; messages can be transmitted from one party's VAN to the other party's VAN.

Sometimes a business partner may wish to examine data, such as current price lists and inventory availability, before placing an order. A trading partner may place data that are relatively constant, such as price data for some firms, on the VAN's system. As illustrated in Figure 6–2, an authorized trading partner can send a request for price information, and the VAN is able to transmit the price data immediately back to the requesting partner without needing to contact the vendor. If the authorized trading partner requests data that do not reside on the VAN's system, such as inventory availability data, then the VAN will have to request the inventory availability data from the vendor before it can transfer the data back to the requesting trading partner. The transaction data exchanged between business partners are likely stored in different formats by the trading partners, and the transaction messages must be converted to a standard format as discussed in a later section.

Partially Integrated EDI Systems

In a **partially integrated EDI system,** illustrated in Figure 6–3, the process begins the same as in a non-EDI system: A purchase requisition is completed by the requesting department and submitted to the purchasing department. A purchasing agent reviews the purchase requisition. Again, if other similar requests have been received, then the requisitions may be combined to take advantage of quantity discounts. The purchasing agent then reviews the available vendors for price and inventory availability. Once a vendor is selected, the partially integrated EDI system differs from the non-EDI system as highlighted in the shaded area of Figure 6–3. The purchasing agent logs onto a computer system that displays a computerized purchase order form. The agent keys in the appropriate data and submits it. Because the purchasing agent does not manually fill out a form

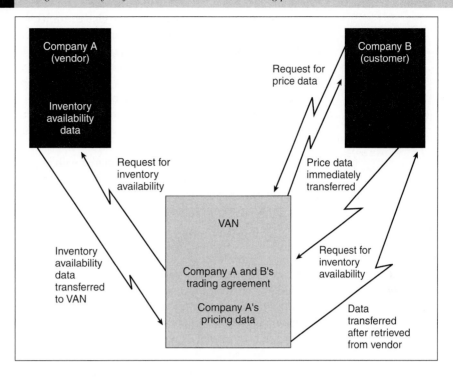

FIGURE 6–3   *Partially integrated EDI system*

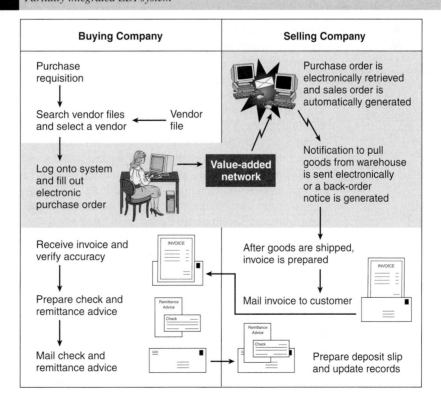

and then submit it to data processing, the chance for a clerical error in data entry is reduced. Once the electronic purchase order is submitted, the data are transferred to a VAN and then channeled from there to the appropriate vendor's mailbox. The vendor retrieves its orders from the VAN, and a sales order is automatically generated. Because another data entry step is removed, the chance for a data entry error to occur at this point is eliminated since no additional data entry is required to convert the purchase order to a sales order. A credit-checking procedure is most likely conducted by the EDI system at this point. The electronic system notifies the warehouse personnel to ship the goods from the warehouse.

Because many EDI systems are integrated with inventory, the EDI system can automatically generate a back-order notice for out-of-stock goods. Data entry errors are further reduced because the back-order notice is generated by the computer system. After the goods are shipped, the rest of the process resembles the non-EDI system for invoice processing.

The time from approving a purchase order to receipt of the purchase order and preparation of the sales order by the vendor is typically reduced by as much as three to seven days. The time reduction can be traced to the elimination of traditional methods of delivering purchase orders, such as via the postal service. If the goods are available, they may be shipped on the same day the order is received. The turnaround time from recognition of a need for goods to receipt of the goods can potentially be reduced by an additional three to seven days. The number of clerks required to perform the entire cycle is reduced from eleven, in our first example, to 9 due to the elimination of the sales order and credit clerks. The possibility of clerical errors is also reduced, as is the amount of paperwork generated by duplicate copies.

Fully Integrated EDI Systems

Fully integrated EDI systems encompass electronic data sharing throughout all aspects of the purchasing and payments cycles. The processing of the actual payment and remittance advice is called *financial EDI* and is discussed later in this chapter. Fully integrated EDI, including financial EDI, provides firms with the greatest benefits in terms of speed and accuracy, but they also have the greatest cost. Figure 6–4 illustrates ways in which our example transaction could be performed in a fully integrated EDI model. Note that nearly all processes involve the computer, and the human element is eliminated except for pulling the goods from the warehouse, loading the goods onto the trucks, receiving the goods, and recording receiving data into the system. Additional features can be included, such as distribution tracking, to allow for greater purchaser assurance that the product is en route and for checking its location during the transport process.

The fully integrated EDI system allows the purchaser's computer system to electronically check inventory levels and production schedules to determine whether the requested item is in stock or when it is scheduled to be produced. Assuming that the computer programs running the systems and the data files upon which it makes its decisions are accurate, the error rate should be virtually eliminated. The recorded data allow the vendor's system to determine the appropriate time and amount to electronically bill the customer. The customer's system automatically compares purchasing data with receiving data and pricing data to determine if the billed amount is appropriate. If not, it is flagged for review by a human accounts payable clerk. If the amount is appropriate, then the system automatically prepares an electronic transfer of funds and remittance advice. The remittance advice may be sent through a separate channel from the actual electronic payment. The notification of receipt of funds is virtually instantaneous, and

FIGURE 6–4	*Fully integrated EDI system*

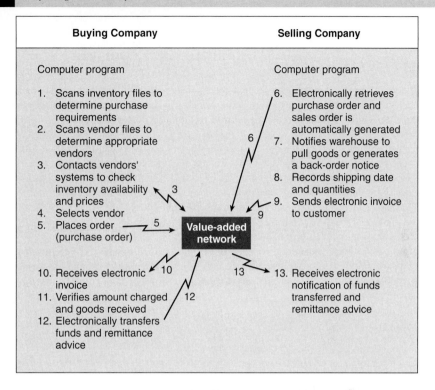

the vendor's access to the funds is not delayed due to the processing of cash receipts and waiting for checks to clear the banks. The number of clerks required to perform this cycle is reduced from 11 for the non-EDI system to 3; warehouse, shipping, and receiving clerks are still needed to physically handle the goods and for document shipping and receiving information.

Benefits of EDI Systems

Most firms with EDI systems fall somewhere between partially integrated EDI systems and fully integrated EDI systems. Firms engaged in the process of just-in-time (JIT) raw materials inventory systems typically use some form of integrated EDI systems to ensure that the supplies necessary for the production process arrive at the desired time. If the goods arrive too early, the production plants have costs associated with maintaining the inventory; if the goods arrive too late, the production stops, which costs the purchasing organization money.

The most widely recognized benefits of EDI are

- Reduced lead time from placing the order to receiving the goods for manufacturing and retail firms and reduced lead time in processing claims for insurance and medical professions and other service organizations.
- Reduced errors in producing manual documents and data entry.
- Reduced processing costs.
- Increased inventory supply and claim processing information for customers.

E-Commerce in Practice

Why Electronic Reporting?

If you're looking for an example of successfully reinventing government look no further than the Wisconsin Worker's Compensation Division's groundbreaking electronic reporting project. Using innovative electronic data interchange (EDI) technology, Worker's Compensation has become more efficient and more responsive to the needs of its customers.

In 1995, the number of first reports of injury received electronically by the Division was 9 percent. As of early 1998, the Worker's Compensation Division receives about 41 percent of these reports electronically, reaching and slightly exceeding their initial goal of 40 percent.

Electronic reporting is an exciting concept that provides the perfect win-win opportunity. Insurance carriers, employers, and injured workers all come out ahead with electronic reporting.

Electronic Reporting Saves Time

It takes about four minutes for an experienced worker to key in one first report of injury paper claim, or about 15 an hour. This same person can process 50 to 60 electronic claims an hour. With EDI, a carrier or self-insured can transmit claims immediately. There are no delays because of the post office, the weather, or handling in the mailroom. EDI speeds the exchange of information so claims are reviewed more quickly and managed better. This enables injured workers to receive proper care sooner and to return to work faster.

Richard Bagin, director of worker's compensation and medical services for Briggs & Stratton, a self-insured company, said EDI has helped the company meet state reporting requirements.

Electronic Reporting Saves Money

Frank Gates Service Co. of Columbus, Ohio, a third-party administrator, has estimated it costs them $3.50 to key a first report of injury claim, compared to only 20 cents to receive the same document electronically.

Major savings are realized with EDI relating to litigation. Prompt reporting and processing can cut the need for costly litigation. If claimants see that progress is being made on their claim, they are less likely to file for a hearing. The benefits get triggered for workers more quickly when EDI is used, Briggs & Stratton's Bagin said.

Electronic Reporting Increases Accuracy

If information is keyed in once instead of two or three times, keying errors are reduced. Under a paper-intensive system, the employer keys the information, then sends paper to the carrier. The carrier then keys it again and sends it to the State, where it is keyed a third time. EDI reduces this to one step and reduces keying errors accordingly.

Electronic Reporting Enhances Data Flexibility

As an added bonus, when using EDI employers and carriers automatically build a versatile database. This allows users to access a rich claims database and to extract a wide variety of information from the data to suit their individual needs.

The Division currently offers two types of electronic reporting. One utilizes a national electronic bulletin board and a system designed to handle large amounts of data. The second option is the ANSI format, which is the format of choice for many commercial vendors.

Wisconsin is a national leader in the effort to advance EDI. The State is working closely with the International Association of Industrial Accident Boards and Commissions, a group striving to develop national EDI standards.

Source: Ken Brady, Wisconsin Worker's Compensation Division.

The box entitled "Why Electronic Reporting?" discusses the achievement of these benefits by the Wisconsin Worker's Compensation Division as a result of the implementation of their EDI system. The extent to which a firm reaps these benefits depends on the degree of integration of their EDI system into their operations and the quality of the system employed. EDI systems based on the philosophy of replacing manual documents with electronic documents will reap some benefits; however, EDI systems based on the philosophy of sharing mission critical data with key trading partners will reap the most benefits.

Data Transfer and Traditional EDI Standards

The discussion thus far has mentioned the exchange of data between two firms; however, firms generally capture and store data internally in incompatible styles and formats. As a result, **translation software** that converts the data to a format that can be appropriately interpreted by all trading partners is necessary. The **American National Standards Institute (ANSI)** served as a guiding body to help develop EDI standards. More recently, the **Accredited Standards Committee (ASC)** coordinates the standard setting process. The accepted standard set in North America is the **ANSI ASC X12 format,** hereafter referred to ASC X12. Multinational firms face the difficulty of different international standards. The United Nations' **Electronic Data Interchange for Administrators, Commerce and Transport (EDIFACT)** is a single standard, different from ASC X12, that is used in the European Community. An international effort is being made to merge ASC X12 and EDIFACT into an international standard, which is an important precursor to a global EDI network. This effort is further discussed in Chapter 9.

Figure 6–5 illustrates the translation process necessary to exchange business data. Firms using different hardware and software platforms with different data formats for their internal applications can exchange data by translating the information into a common format, such as ASC X12. Company X may send EDI purchase orders to hundreds of vendors. Each vendor may have vastly different data formats. If a common communication method were not available, these firms would not be able to exchange data. Each company transmitting data, such as Company X, must perform an **outbound transformation** of its internally generated data into the common format, ASC X12. As each company retrieves the purchase order, such as company Y or Z, it must perform an **inbound transformation** from the ASC X12 formatted data into its own format.

FIGURE 6–5	*ANSI ASC X12 translation*

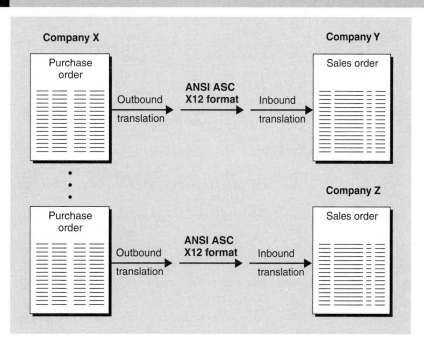

The outbound and inbound translation processes may be performed either by the firm's translation software or outsourced to a firm's VAN. The startup cost of EDI for small businesses with personal computer–based systems is declining substantially as translation software is becoming more available, affordable, and easier to use. A small business with a personal computer, modem, EDI translation software, and a subscription to a mailbox messaging service with store and forward capabilities[1] can engage in EDI trading relationships with relative ease.

The ASC X12 format requires that data be organized in a specific fashion. Figure 6–6 illustrates the levels of data organization necessary for a firm to transmit two purchase orders and one invoice to a trading partner. The entire transmission includes three documents of two different types. An **electronic envelope** that contains the entire message (the three documents in the example) is used for data transmission and is identified by an **interchange control header.** The interchange control header identifies the sender and the receiver and defines the procedures to be used in transmission of the message, message receipt acknowledgment, and underlying formats of the message.

Following the interchange control header is the first **functional group header** which defines the type of business data to be transmitted. In the example in Figure 6–6, the first functional group header represents purchase orders. Following the functional group header for purchase orders is the **transaction set header** representing the first purchase order, A1001 in the example, to be transmitted. The transaction set header defines the type of electronic document represented using a three-digit number corresponding to the ASC X12 document definition coding scheme. Next, each electronic document may have various **data segments,** and each segment defines the order in which the following data elements flow. The actual **data elements** for purchase order A1001 follow the transaction set header. Each data element refers to a data element dictionary that maintains a unique, standard identifying code, such as alphanumeric, numeric, date, time, telephone number, etc. The data segments can contain loop segments that allow multiple items to be entered. Purchase order A1001 lists the date, time, and terms of sales only once, but the detail data segment is a loop that allows multiple items to be recorded. Thus, a one-to-many data relationship can be represented by this format.

Following the **transaction set footer,** which indicates the end of that transaction item, for the first purchase order is the transaction header for the second purchase order, A1002. Again, data segments and data elements are defined for the second invoice followed by data segment and transaction set footers. Upon completion of the two transaction sets representing the two purchase orders, a functional group footer signals the end of purchase orders. The second functional group header represents invoices, and the above process is repeated to transmit the invoice 990100. At the end of the transmission of all documents, an interchange control footer signals that the entire envelope of electronic data has been transmitted.

Data conversion and deconversion into and from the ASC X12 format happens seamlessly in a well-designed EDI system, and it allows trading partners' data to be stripped down to their elements and standardized so that the information may be shared. The transformation software also performs the function of converting the stripped-down data into the unique formats used by the receiving organization. The airline industry coordinated its work with the petroleum industry so they could coordinate the purchase of jet fuel as described in the box entitled "International Cooperation and EDI Bring Advantages to Petroleum and Airline Industries."

---

[1]*Store and forward* is a term used to describe a mailbox feature of a VAN. It means that messages are received on an organization's behalf and stored by the VAN until the messages are retrieved by the organization.

FIGURE 6–6	ANSI ASC X12 formatting

Interchange control header—electronic envelope
   Functional group header—purchase orders
      Transaction set header—purchase order A1001
         Data segment header—source
            Data element—terms of sale
            Data element—date
            Data element—time
         Data segment header—details looping
            Data element—item number
            Data element—description
            Data element—quantity
            Data element—price
      Transaction set footer—purchase order A1001
      Transaction set header—purchase order A1002
         Data segment header—source
            Data element—terms of sale
            Data element—data
            Data element—time
         Data segment header—details looping
            Data element—item number
            Data element—description
            Data element—quantity
            Data element—price
      Transaction set footer—purchase order A1002
   Functional group footer—purchase orders
   Functional group header—invoices
      Transaction set header—purchase order 990100
         Data segment header—source
            Data element—invoice number
            Data element—terms of sale
         Data segment header—details looping
            Data element—item number
            Data element—description
            Data element—quantity
            Data element—price
      Transaction set footer—invoice number 990100
   Functional group footer—invoices
Interchange control footer—electronic envelope

Department of Defense Transaction Example

The U.S. Department of Defense, along with many other government branches, are significantly affected by the **Federal Acquisition Streamlining Act of 1994.** The objective of this act is to streamline the procurement process of the federal government. The **Federal Acquisition Computer Network (FACNET)** was established by this act. FACNET requires the federal government to shift from a paper-driven acquisition process to an EDI-based process. As mentioned in the previous section, transaction sets are defined by

E-Commerce in Practice

International Cooperation and EDI Bring Advantages to Petroleum and Airline Industries

Using the experiences of several industry implementations, four critical areas were identified as keys to the success of an AVNET, or any EDI implementation: management support, application programs, control procedures, and industry standards.

Airlines purchase millions of dollars of jet fuel annually, their largest expense after labor, and a necessity in order to operate. So when the petroleum industry approached their airline customers about the benefits of implementing electronic data interchange (EDI) for the fuel procurement cycle, it was a natural fit. And due to the global scope of the airline industry, the use of both U.S. and international EDI formats was an essential business requirement.

In a unique approach to EDI standards, petroleum and airline industries jointly developed a comprehensive guide for applying EDI to the sale and delivery of aviation fuel, using both ASC X12, the U.S. national EDI standard, and UN/EDIFACT, the United Nations–backed international EDI format. The global scope of AVNET, the Aviation Network project, dictated the use of both standard protocols. The coordinated AVNET effort maintained comparability of the business information contained in the two standards, with the aim of making execution of EDI in one or both formats straightforward and nearly transparent to the user.

AVNET Document	ASC X12 Transaction Set	UN/EDIFACT Message
Fuel invoice	**810** Commercial invoice	**INVOIC** Commercial invoice
Delivery ticket	**856** Ship notice/ manifest	**DESADV** Espatch advice
Price notification	**832** Price/sales catalog	**PRICAT** Price/sales catalog

Implementation Benefits

Once EDI messages start flowing between carriers and their oil suppliers, the benefits can be substantial. Although the financial benefits may be difficult to quantify, operational benefits range from increased productivity to reduction of paperwork errors to greater ability of airlines to plan and deal with their fuel expenses.

A key benefit for the AVNET implementation is the availability of better, more accurate information for decision support. According to the airlines, petroleum companies are sometimes slow quoting prices to them when jet fuel prices are low. When an oil company begins to quote its pricing information in a more timely manner through EDI, customers view the suppliers as a more positive source for its jet fuel.

An original pilot of the Price Notification was taking place during "Desert Storm." Due to the nature of the Iraqi conflict, petroleum prices were fluctuating not just on a daily basis, but sometimes on an hourly schedule. The data the airline [were] receiving via EDI [were] invaluable as a source of information to help the carrier plan for and deal with fuel expenses during the crisis. As a result, the airline increased its confidence and reliance on the fuel supplier.

Another tangible benefit for the airline participants involves better cash management. One major carrier was finally able to take advantage of terms discounts already contractually negotiated with their petroleum vendors. Prior to EDI, the airline seldom benefited from a 10-day payment discount because they simple could not process the paperwork in a timely enough fashion. Since they began receiving the AVNET fuel invoice, they've never missed a discount—a savings of hundreds of thousands of dollars a year. In fact, the AVNET implementation is far and above this airline's most successful dollar project on EDI.

The coordinated AVNET effort worked to maintain comparability of the business information contained in the two standards, with the aim of making execution of EDI in one or both formats straightforward and nearly transparent to the user.

International Implementations

Another U.S.-based oil company has successfully implemented the AVNET EDIFACT invoice. A long-time user of the X12 standard, the company found that the AVNET EDIFACT formats easily met their complex business requirements. In fact, working across multiple time zones; language and cultural differences; and varying tax, legal, and business requirements [was] more of an issue than the technical aspect of the implementation.

An opportunity for the oil company to pursue an implementation with a foreign carrier offered many benefits—potential increased sales of product to the airline, as well as a springboard to implement EDI with other airlines. Challenges included the opportunity to use the EDIFACT standard, Value-Added Tax (VAT) and currency issues typically not addressed in U.S. domestic uses, as well as the applications integration difficulties. These integration problems included the fact that the internal applications were not developed with EDI in mind, and that trading partner requirements and application layouts were different. Although their current implementations are with European trading partners, the oil company is confident that it can also use the EDIFACT messages with domestic trading partners.

Government Activity

In supporting the U.S. military, the Defense Fuel Supply Center purchases more light petroleum products than any other single organization or company in the world. DFSC purchases over 148 million barrels of petroleum products annually—enough to fill the Pentagon, one of the world's largest office buildings, seven times. Naturally, they are a key player in the AVNET arena.

To date, DFSC has implemented the fuel invoice and price notifications with over more than 20 fuel suppliers, domestic and international. As for the delivery ticket, they no longer need to even receive one. By improving the quality of their invoice and price data, they have been able to eliminate a step in the fueling cycle, asking the fuelers to store the delivery ticket data only for audit purposes. And through the success of their AVNET program, DFSC has been recognized as a catalyst for other federal government EDI initiatives.

Widespread management support is vital to a successful rollout of EDI.

Lessons Learned

Using the experiences of several industry implementations, four critical areas were identified as key to the success of an AVNET, or any EDI implementation: management support, application programs, control procedures, and industry standards.

Management Support. Widespread management support is vital to a successful rollout of EDI. Many of the petroleum companies involved in the AVNET project had several years of EDI experience prior to this implementation. During this time, they had established general EDI policy, purchased translation software and provided man-

agement training and awareness. For many of the airlines, these activities needed to be undertaken prior to implementing the AVNET documents. This made the need for management support all that more critical.

Support grows in importance when a project involves several functional groups, as was required by AVNET. In addition to EDI staff, accounting, administration, fuel purchasing and marketing personnel from both the oil and airline industries were involved. Using the concept of a "Virtual Team," most AVNET implementors have recognized the importance of having not only the right internal staff on the project, but the absolute necessity of including your trading partners as an integral part of the planning.

Moreover, given the long-term nature of EDI, it is important to obtain management support for allocating funds for training and travel to participate in industry work groups. Where management support is limited, it may be necessary to adjust the implementation timetable.

Application Programs. As with most industries, many of the airline and oil companies' internal application programs were written prior to EDI's conception. Consequently, they lack EDI functionality or file interface capability.

Modifications needed included the addition of EDI control screens and pass interface files, identification and exercise of EDI transmission selection/trigger events, and development of a procedures to handle transaction corrections. Such changes are complex and required development of a thorough acceptance plan.

Control Procedures. Lack of strong control procedures slows problem identification and correction. To strengthen control on the project, many companies assigned a business coordinator with responsibility for reviewing daily control reports and solving all problems. The business coordinators also played a key communication role between companies. By talking to responsible people on both sides, better solutions were uncovered. Also, many of the AVNET implementors simplified problem identification by implementing one delivery location at a time, starting a second location only after the previous was error free.

Another audit and control issue faced when implementing with an international trading partner is the lack of a functional acknowledgment. Generally recognized as a standard business practice in the U.S., international companies do not automatically accept the use of an EDI functional acknowledgment, an issue which can lengthen trading partner agreement negotiations and eventually require changes to standard operating procedures.

(continued)

E-Commerce in Practice–continued

Industry Standards. The first step in undertaking this project was to define the business requirements, independent of the EDI transaction sets or messages. Part of this definition cycle included the development of an AVNET Business Model.

Lack of EDI industry standards can bring project development to a standstill. When industry implementation guidelines don't exist, companies have the option of waiting for industrywide standards, or helping to establish them. In order to facilitate development of industry standards, the AVNET project was formed as a joint effort of the Air Transport Association of America, the American Petroleum Institute, and the International Air Transport Association.

The project deliverable was the AVNET Implementation Guide. Published in 1992, the document is a comprehensive guide to applying EDI to the sale and delivery of aviation fuel. It includes technical mapping for the X12 and

EDIFACT documents, as well as detailed sections covering the AVNET business model and information requirements.

Once the business information requirements were identified, the data was easily mapped into the corresponding ASC X12 and UN/EDIFACT formats.

More than a dozen petroleum companies and airlines, as well as four fixed-base operators worldwide, have put the AVNET messages into production and are already benefiting from their use. In summary, the aviation/oil industry collaboration demonstrates that the two EDI standards are compatible, and that, for those users [that] began with an X12 implementation and are now moving to the EDIFACT format, the changes are not insurmountable.

Source: Kendra L. Martin, *EDI Manager American Petroleum Institute.* *http://www.api.org/faeb/pidx/members/committees/usergroups/avnetfiles/avnetarticle.htm.*

a three-digit ANSI ASC X12 coding scheme. Many of the transaction set codes used by the Department of Defense are listed in Figure 6–7.

The Office of Management and Budget asserts that e-commerce is helping reduce costs in the following ways:

- E-commerce helps *government* buyers make more informed decisions faster, more easily, and with less burden and fewer resources. It also helps them ensure accurate and prompt payment to sellers.

- E-commerce helps *sellers* learn about and access contracting opportunities more easily and transact more quickly, effectively, and inexpensively.

- E-commerce helps *taxpayers* realize greater return for their investment through better and more responsive agency decision making and lower government operating costs.

FINANCIAL EDI

The Bankers EDI Council defines **financial EDI** as

> The electronic exchange of payments, payment-related information or financially related documents in standard formats between business partners.

> *(Bankers EDI Council, http://www.nacha.org/bedic)*

Financial EDI is a key distinguishing feature between partially and fully integrated EDI systems. In partially integrated EDI systems, the payment and related information may be produced in hard copy form and sent through the postal system. Some firms may transfer the funds electronically and produce the remittance advice in hard copy form

FIGURE 6–7   *Department of Defense example transaction sets*

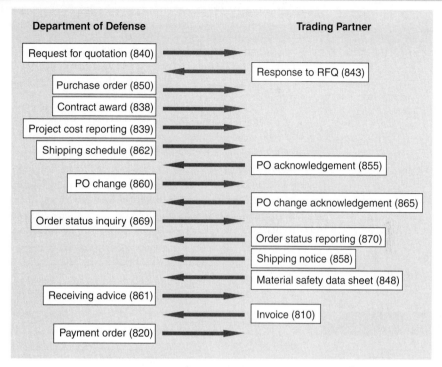

Source: *Introduction to Department of Defense Electronic Commerce: A Handbook for Business,* Version 2.

that is sent through the postal service. Fully integrated EDI systems encompass financial EDI and both payment and remittance information is transferred electronically.

Financial institutions exchange their customers' payments and remittance information over a network called the **Automated Clearing House (ACH).** The types of payment made by these financial institutions include business-to-business payments; government payments to contractors; direct deposit payroll checks; pensions and Social Security checks; and automatic payments of mortgages, car loans, and utility bills. Firms and government agencies have an economic incentive to migrate away from hard-copy checks. In 1999, the cost to the Federal Reserve to process each check (3.8 cents) is more than twice as much as the cost to process each ACH transaction (1.7 cents). The volume of transactions traded electronically is increasing steadily each year as illustrated in Figure 6–8. The dollar amount of ACH transactions more than quadrupled from 1990 to 1999.

The relationship between financial institutions and ACH is depicted in Figure 6–9. Both the payor and payee of a transaction must have an account at a financial institution with EDI capable software that can transmit the data to the ACH network. The ACH network is overseen by the **National Automated Clearing House Association (NACHA).** The NACHA estimates that more than 10 billion checks per year are sent to remittance locations and lockboxes. One Federal Reserve study estimates that if "just half the check volume in this country is converted [to electronic payments], the U.S. economy would save over $30 billion a year." NACHA is diligently working toward meeting this goal.

FIGURE 6–8	*Trend in financial EDI*

Electronic Payments Statistics for the 1990s

- Automated Clearing House (ACH) payments increased fron 1.5 billion in 1990 to 6.25 billion in 1999.
- Debit card payments for purchases increased from 188 million to almost 7 billion.
- Direct deposit of payroll increased from about 10 to 56 percent of workers. In 1999 there were more than 3 billion direct deposits made, saving the country more than $6 billion.
- In 1999, almost 2 billion consumer bills were paid automatically by direct payment, saving consumers more than $600 million in postage costs, and countless more in late fees that were avoided.
- The federal government made 96 percent of payroll payments and 76 of Social Security benefits by direct deposit in 1999. The Electronic Federal Tax Payment System has more than 3 million businesses enrolled, and in fiscal year 2000 has collected more than $1.3 trillion.
- 90 percent of the dollars that move through the payments systems do so electronically.

Source: NACHA.

FIGURE 6–9	*The ACH network*

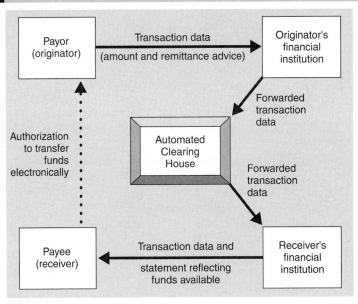

Source: Greenstein, 1998.

Financial EDI is in a high-growth phase, and significant enhancements to the infrastructure over the next 5 to 10 years are expected. In 1998, NACHA required for the first time that financial institutions furnish the means to transmit and receive electronic remittance advices. Their implementation of the requirement is aided by the Federal Reserve's FedEDI software. Beginning in July 1999, NACHA started a pilot program to test telephone authorizations of debits. During the month of July 2000, 110 companies originated almost half a million transactions.

EDI SYSTEMS AND THE INTERNET

The EDI systems described thus far require a network connection between the two organizations exchanging documents. Typically, this requires a dedicated line running between the two companies or a connection to a VAN. As mentioned before, these connections often have high startup and annual costs, thus isolating EDI systems to the largest of trading partners. However, the advent of the Internet has created a common information and communications platform upon which business can be conducted. In a sense, we now have a network to which everyone is connected, provided the necessary hardware and software is in place. Smaller suppliers are now transacting electronically with larger customers. For example, IBM claims to have cut its paper invoices by 90 percent from 12,000-plus smaller suppliers using XML, or Web-based EDI. This universal connectivity as provided by the Internet allows multitudes of additional parties, particularly small and mid-sized businesses and consumers, to utilize EDI technology at a lower cost. This section covers the additional security concerns of Web-based EDI and the benefits of Web-based EDI and XML-based EDI.

Security Concerns

One of the Internet's greatest benefits, increased connectivity, is also at the root of a business's greatest fear. We must remember that the Internet, originally called the ARPANET, initially began as a research project of the Department of Defense (DOD) to develop a communications backbone for which it could survive hostile, battlefield conditions in times of national crisis. Later, the ARPANET was segmented into the DOD-related and non-DOD-related networks. Eventually, the National Science Foundation assumed control of the civilian segment of the research network, evolving into a community of academic researchers whose use was limited to academic research. By 1992, the National Science Foundation removed its restriction on commercial Internet traffic. Consequently, businesses began to consider the Internet for financial transactions.

The Internet was not created with the intention of using it as a communications network to conduct sensitive transactions securely and reliably. A public network by its very nature is susceptible to information being viewed, copied, or altered while in route to its final destination. Consumers have long heard horror stories about hackers intercepting credit card data and personal information on the Internet. Certainly this fear consumers have about secure payment processing has been somewhat of a stumbling block for Internet commerce thus far. We take the stand that while security is perhaps the most important enabler of Internet commerce, this fear has been exacerbated. With the use of encryption technology and digital signatures, consumers can be assured that the risk of credit card details being intercepted are less than the risks many cardholders run today when they hand over their card to a waiter in a restaurant.

Many different interested parties are developing and implementing the security and reliability measures that will make the Internet a more secure and reliable communications network. The **Electronic Data Interchange—Internet Integration (EDIINT)** standard, now in draft form, defines the standards for using encryption and digital certificates to secure EDI transactions over the Internet. In addition to these drafts, many industries are developing their own industry-specific protocols for using EDI over the Internet. For example the Gas Industry Standards Board and the Automotive Industry Action Group have each developed their own set of standards above those specified in the EDIINT. The security, encryption, and authentication issues will be revisited many times throughout this text, and specific solutions are offered in later chapters.

Security of Data during Transmission

Trading partners subscribing to a VAN and transmitting data over private lines can be relatively comfortable that an EDI document will be routed to its recipient without any modifications. However, this level of assurance is not provided when connecting to the Internet via an ISP. This can be illustrated by performing an Internet network trace. By utilizing a program commonly called Traceroute, any Internet user can follow the route traveled by an Internet Protocol (IP) packet[2] from its source to its final destination. This exercise yields some interesting observations:

1. The Internet does an efficient job of routing packets to their final destination.
2. Between the source and the destination many different intermediate network nodes handle the packet. At any one of these nodes, any individual with a network protocol analyzer, or sniffer, could easily capture, view, or reassemble the packets that make up a data packet. Sniffers are discussed in more detail in the following chapter.
3. A technical glitch occurring at any one of the hops in the route could cause the packet to be dropped or discarded.

If the information contained in the packets contains sensitive information, measures must be taken to prevent such threats from occurring when an EDI document is sent over an open network such as the Internet.

Audit Trails and Acknowledgments

VAN subscribers also have the capability to track an EDI document through the VAN. An example of this involves notifications sent to the trading partner upon the download of the EDI document by the recipient from its VAN mailbox. A second example is a functional acknowledgment sent by a VAN to the sender that indicates the receipt of a transaction by its recipient. Document tracking and functional acknowledgments offered by the TCP/IP protocol suite or supplied by an ISP do not meet the level of service provided by a VAN. This tracking information is very important in designing any online application, as well as in meeting the approval of financial auditors and legal counsel.

Authentication

The process of determining that a trading partner is indeed who he or she claims to be is called authentication. It eliminates the possibility of spoofing the identity of a trading partner while a document is in transit on a public network, such as the Internet. In the case of a VAN, a trading partner can only send or receive documents after they have been authenticated by the VAN. This process usually consists of the user logging into the network with the appropriate user ID and password. Authentication is covered in more detail in Chapter 8.

Benefits of Web-Based EDI

According to Forrester Research, global business-to-business and business-to-consumer e-commerce will reach $6.9 trillion by 2004. However, the growth will not be a painless, smooth journey. John R. Patrick, IBM Corporation Vice President, Internet Technology, likens the growing information superhighway to a real highway under construction: "All the lanes have not yet been paved. There are a few exit ramps that do not go anywhere,

---

[2]See Chapter 9 for an explanation of IP packets.

and you will encounter occasional accidents." Among committed business users, however, the overriding view is that the commercial benefits of the Internet clearly outweigh the risks. EDI Internet systems are capable of providing the following benefits:

- Universal connectivity.
- Lower entry cost.
- Greater sharing of information.
- Greater tracking of market data.

For consumers, the increased sharing of information and reduction in entry costs result in greater shopping power; knowledge is power. Not surprisingly, consumers and business customers are beginning to demand greater access to product and pricing information. The Internet enables firms to deliver this requirement, and Web-based EDI systems allow firms to "close the sale" in addition to marketing product information. The reduction in entry costs is a direct result of the proliferation of Internet service providers during the mid- to late 1990s and the accompanying competitive pricing strategies of these service providers.

Figure 6–10 illustrates various system configurations and their degree of **connectivity** and **data sharing** with other businesses and consumers. Degree of connectivity refers to the number of entities with which an entity can electronically reach. Data sharing refers to the ability to transmit and receive electronic data. Partially integrated EDI systems have more connectivity and sharing of data with business partners than do non-EDI systems. Fully integrated EDI systems have substantially more sharing of data and, in some cases, more connectivity with business partners than do partially integrated EDI systems.

Partially integrated Web-based EDI systems have more connectivity than fully integrated non-web-based EDI systems because more suppliers and customers, and even the ultimate consumer, can be reached via the Internet connection. Partially integrated

---

FIGURE 6–10   *Comparison of EDI systems*

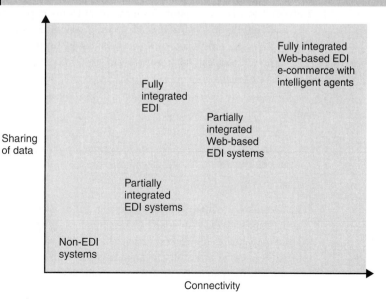

Web-based EDI systems, while they offer more connectivity, do not typically facilitate the sharing of greater amounts of information than fully integrated EDI systems. For example, a partially integrated EDI Internet system may allow a greater number of customers to view product information and submit an order but provide no other information to the consumer. However, while non-Internet, fully integrated EDI systems may connect to fewer customers, they may share more information, such as production schedules, with their trading partners.

Ultimately, **fully integrated Web-based EDI systems** provide the greatest amount of connectivity and sharing of data. Many companies are integrating or have plans to integrate their enterprise applications onto the Internet. Supply chain management and support can be greatly enhanced via Internet technology. Vixel Corporation, a manufacturer of high-speed fibre channel storage products, is using an Extranet-Internet model to allow it to electronically share revisions of manufacturing diagrams and engineering drawings with its subcontractors. Web-based EDI systems that employ intelligent agents have even greater ability to locate the best product at the best price. **Intelligent agents** allow customers' computers to conduct sophisticated price and delivery comparisons. These agents are not yet widely used for these purposes, but their potential and growth is great. Intelligent agents are more fully discussed in Chapter 11.

Not all businesses are interested in connecting with every possible supplier or customer, however. Reduced set, private data exchanges are the choice of some industries as indicated in the box entitled "Quietly, Private E-Markets Rule."

EDI-Web Browser Translation Software

Web browser EDI services that allow low-cost connectivity and EDI translation software for Internet usage are available from many vendors. For low-volume users of EDI, a low-cost mechanism is imperative, and the packages available provide a new opportunity for small and medium-sized businesses to play on par with larger businesses in the EDI arena. Figure 6–11 illustrates the transformation necessary from a forms-based Web browser page to ASC X12 formatted data. **The EDI Web browser software packages** easily allow firms to connect with EDI trading partners. The easiest way to do this is by using a VAN that provides the translation service seamlessly to the partners involved. The EDI translation from the Web forms is performed by low-cost packages such as Harbinger's Harbinger Express. Companies that offer Web-based EDI platforms provide a repository of forms that can be used by the trading partners in a Web-based format, and they also provide the translation to and from the Web-based form to ASC X12 format.

XML and EDI

> XML is looking like a magic elixir in a cloudy bottle these days: cheap data exchange, document structure, and a proven cure for warts.
>
> *(Uche Ogbuji, SunWorld, 1999)*

The **eXtensible Markup Language (XML)** is an extension of the World Wide Web Consortium's (W3C) Standard Generalized Markup Language, SGML. What makes XML so adaptable for Web-based applications is its *extensibility*. By having the ability to create custom (extensible) tags, XML allows the flexibility necessary to represent and name whatever data tag is necessary for online documents. The use of such customized

E-Commerce in Practice

Quietly, Private E-Markets Rule

Public and industry-sponsored business-to-business marketplaces that boast access to thousands of new buyers and sellers are grabbing all the headlines. But behind the scenes, tens of thousands of companies are opting for private digital exchanges to electronically link a deliberately reduced number of key suppliers.

Take Nypro Inc. The $600 million injection molding company buys the bulk of its raw materials from prequalified suppliers it has brought together over a private digital exchange built with software from Commerx in Chicago.

"I'm clearly on the side of paring down and creating better relationships with my existing suppliers, because it's by integrating with your suppliers and sharing forecasts that you can get the economies everyone is talking about," said Mike MacKenty, director of information technology at the Clinton, Mass.–based manufacturer. "I think that's where the movement will be long term." So does Gartner Group Inc. in Stamford, Conn., which estimates that some 30,000 private exchanges are in various stages of development, compared with some 600 public exchanges now in operation.

Public exchanges, however, won't disappear altogether, experts say. Instead, they will likely be tapped by users for spot buys and commodity purchases.

But not all of them, according to Tom Koulopoulos, an analyst at The Delphi Group in Boston. "Right now, B2B is an incredibly convoluted marketplace," he said at Delphi's business-to-business executive summit last week. "One-half of the B2B exchanges out there will go under in six months."

Meanwhile, eMarketer Inc., a New York–based Internet research firm, reports that 93 percent of all business-to-business commerce is currently transacted through private or so-called proprietary exchanges, many of which have generated huge and well-documented supply-chain efficiencies.

Think Bentonville, Ark.–based Wal-Mart Stores Inc. and Round Rock, Texas–based Dell Computer Corp. Even some public business-to-business marketplaces are embedding private exchanges within their Web sites.

GoFish.com Inc., a seafood exchange based in Portland, Maine, has what it calls a pipeline feature. The feature lets big corporate buyers like the Pleasanton, Calif.–based Safeway Inc. grocery chain do business privately on the site with preferred suppliers.

"Safeway doesn't wake up wondering where they'll buy shrimp," said GoFish CEO Neal Workman. "What our model starts to morph into is what their business relationships already look like."

Several managers at last week's executive summit said they agreed that what's driving the explosion in proprietary exchanges is companies' long-standing preference to do business with tried-and-true suppliers.

Public exchanges, they said, may be a good place to make spot purchases or to buy commodity items, like paper or janitorial services, on the cheap. But commodity items aren't what most companies are looking for to keep their production lines rolling.

J. Tyler Welch, a materials director at Northrup Grumman Corp. in El Segundo, Calif., estimates that less than 10% of the direct goods the airplane manufacturer buys are so-called standard items.

"There are very rigid specifications and huge liabilities associated with aircraft parts," Welch said. "You can't afford to have Radio Shack parts you bought online show up in an airplane."

Still other companies, such as Anheuser-Busch Cos., have strict specifications on even their indirect goods. For instance, Anheuser-Busch buys pallets, which must be of a certain size and contain a certain number of screws, from prequalified vendors.

"We have unique packaging requirements, so why would we want to put them on a [public] exchange when we've already [got] qualified suppliers?" said Jennifer Coop, director of e-commerce at the St. Louis–based beer maker.

Wary of Consortia

For now, Welch said he's equally leery of doing business on any of the aircraft industry consortia exchanges. He said Northrup Grumman has looked into MyAircraft.com and another exchange announced by The Boeing Co. in Seattle.

"But there are costs, such as transaction costs, involved in participating," Welch said. After poking into these things at Northrup Grumman, "we're not finding a lot of substance, at least in our industry."

Source: Julia King, © *Computerworld Online*, September 4, 2000. *www.computerworld.com*

FIGURE 6–11   *Web-based EDI translation and VANs*

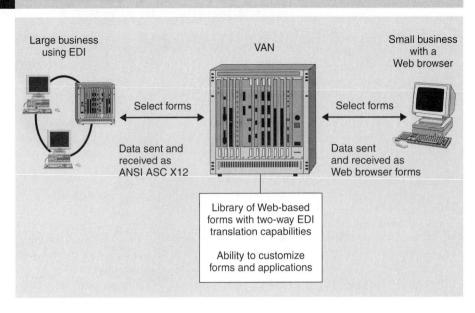

tags is illustrated in Chapter 9. What is important for EDI is how XML will affect and integrate into traditional EDI systems. This issue is explored in this section.

First of all, a list of what XML ultimately does is a good place to start. The following list is a synopsis:

- Provides a universal data format.
- Allows data objects to be serialized into text streams.
- Is fast to parse, so that it can be used to pass data between processes.
- Produces documents that can be passed easily over a variety of network protocols.
- Has companion standards to support browser presentation, hyperlinks, and querying.

(Jonathon Rich, Cambridge Technology Partners, June 1999)

According to the XML/EDI group (a large consortium of business professionals working together to promote and guide the future of XML/EDI standards), the combination of XML and EDI provides the benefits exhibited in Figure 6–12. An important aspect in implementing XML/EDI is the use of standardized **Document Type Definitions (DTDs),** which is a schema that defines what data elements should be on standard documents, such as purchase orders and invoices, and the names for the tags that contain the data.

The W3C has been diligently working on a fomal schema specification, and in October 2000, it announced that it had developed an XML, DTD schema, called **Xschema,** that was close to being an official specification. In vertical industries, this works well. However, for firms that transact across industries, the various DTDs that are being developed can present a problem for data transfer. For example, a supplier of office supplies may sell to the automobile, oil and gas, financial institution, and transport industries. Each of these industries has begun to develop its own XML DTDs. Some examples of industry-specific XML DTDs are

FIGURE 6–12	*XML/EDI*

XML	+	EDI	=	XML/EDI
Tagging standard		Business language		A standard framework to exchange different types of data (e.g., an invoice, health care claim) so that the information— be it in a transaction, exchanged via an application program interface, Web automation, database portal, catalog, a work flow document, or message—can be searched, decoded, manipulated, and displayed consistently and correctly by first implementing EDI dictionaries and extending our vocabulary via online repositories to include our business language, rules, and objects.
Script attachment		Business practices		
Transaction validation		Trading partner profile		
Search techniques		Logging and archiving		
Linking and reference		Acknowledgments		
Multimedia		Application APIs		
Wide World Web		Transaction expertise		
Authoring tools		Message standards		

Source: The XML/EDI Group.

- adXML—to automate online advertising market.
- AIML—astronomical instrument markup language by NASA.
- cmdXML—for construction and manufacturing distribution data exchange.
- RIXML—Research Information Exchange Markup Language for financial services firms to share data.

These are but a few examples. The XML organization has list of more than 200 organizations known to be developing industry-specific or cross-industry XML specifications. Also, Enterprise Resource Planning (ERP) vendors, such as SAP, are incorporating XML specifications into their e-commerce applications.

XBRL and EDI

One of the specifications listed by the XML Organization is **XBRL,** which stands for **eXtensible Business Reporting Language,** and it is based on XML. The XBRL specification is being developed by the XBRL Organization, which is an impressive list of more than 65 international companies, standards organization, and accounting firms. The initial goal of XBRL is to

> Provide an XML-based framework that the global business information supply chain will use to create, exchange, and analyze financial reporting information including, but not limited to, regulatory filings such as annual and quarterly financial statements, general ledger information, and audit schedules.

> *(The XBRL Organization.)*

XBRL is used to report highly aggregated data in financial reports, not to record individual transactions. Thus, XBRL is an extension of Web-based EDI into Web-based reporting of aggregated data. In July 2000, the first taxonomy and set of specifications was published and is currently being field tested by six global *Fortune* 1000 firms.

The following components of XBRL are defined by the XBRL Organization:

• *XBRL specification.* Explains what XBRL is, how to build XBRL instance documents, and XBRL taxonomies. It explains XBRL in technical terms and is intended for a technical audience.

• *XBRL schema.* The core low-level components of XBRL. The schema is the physical XSD and DTD files that express how instance documents and taxonomies are to be built.

• *XBRL taxonomy.* A "vocabulary" or "dictionary" created by a group, compliant with the XBRL specification, in order to exchange business information.

• *XBRL instance document.* A business report, such as a financial statement prepared to the XBRL specification. The meaning of the values in the instance document is explained by the taxonomy.

Figure 6–13 illustrates one potential use of XBRL to highlight and compare highly aggregated financial figures on a website. The XBRL Organization is expected to unfold additional specifications in 2001 and 2002 to cover regulatory and tax filings, including filings for the Securities and Exchange Commission's EDGAR System. The use of such XBRL coding schemes will also facilitate the use of such data by intelligent agents, a topic discussed in Chapter 13.

Insight's EDI and Internet Systems

In the third quarter of 2000, Insight Enterprises Inc., a direct-sales firm of hardware and software, achieved its phenomenal 21st consecutive quarter of increased sales and earnings! Insight was named by VerticalZOOM as one of the "100 Best B2B Internet Suppliers" in 2000. Insight's unassisted Web sales increased from $33.8 million in the third

---

FIGURE 6–13   *Sample XBRL page*

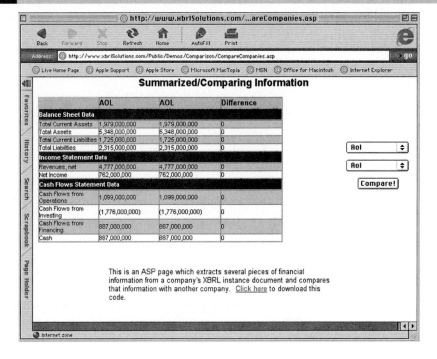

quarter of 1999 to $57.5 million in the third quarter of 2000. It turned its inventory over 68 times just in the third quarter of 2000. How has Insight achieved such growth in a highly competitive market? They developed an intricate and well-run logistics system.

Real-Time EDI Inventory Links with Suppliers

Insight uses EDI to connect to 20 of its suppliers. The system allows inventory pricing and availability data to be retrieved in real-time from the supplier's system directly into Insight's own inventory system. This link to its suppliers is a critical success factor for Insight because it only stocks in its warehouse a small portion of the 110,000 inventory items it offers to its customers. By developing reliable, integrated inventory systems with its suppliers and developing excellent distribution channels, Insight is able to provide an extremely large inventory offering to its customers without having to invest in costly physical inventories.

Integrated Delivery Links with Federal Express

To properly track shipments, Insight has integrated its sales order processing, labeling, and tracking systems with FedEx. Customers who order one of the nonstocked items do not experience any additional delays in receiving their merchandise as a result of Insight's alliances with its suppliers and FedEx. The items are ordered by Insight's customers via the real-time EDI link with Insight's suppliers and are shipped directly from the supplier's warehouse to the customer. All of these interfaces are transparent to the customer.

Web-Based Sales

In addition to phone-in orders by customers, Insight is dedicated to serving its customers via the Internet. Figure 6–14 illustrates Insight's Web-based system. The entire inventory of items offered by Insight is offered to its Internet customers. Customers are

| **FIGURE 6–14** | *Insight's Web-based ordering system* |

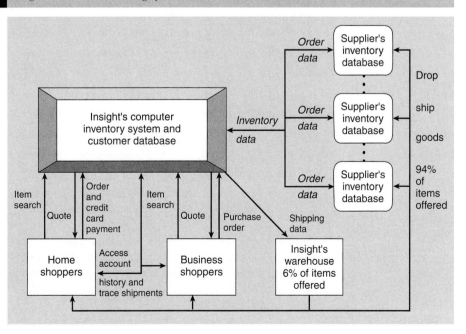

encouraged by their sales representatives to use the Internet to place their orders. Insight serves both home shoppers and business customers via the Internet. Initially, the majority of the Internet shoppers were home shoppers, but the business customer base is steadily increasing. Insight's Internet shoppers ask for a quote for a specific inventory item and receive the best price quote available from Insight's database, including the nine suppliers linked to the EDI system. The website also allows Insight's customers to access account histories and trace shipments.

The Internet business customer base is increasing as customers find that they appreciate the ability to peruse inventory items offered, compare prices, and order the desired items by themselves at the website. If at any time they wish to speak to their sales representative, all they have to do is pick up the phone and call. Business customers with a preestablished trading agreement may order their goods via the Internet and be billed with net 30-day terms. Home shoppers pay for their items online with credit cards. Business shoppers may, of course, use business credit cards.

Business shoppers who wish to negotiate a preferred customer pricing arrangement must first speak to a sales account executive over the phone. After their pricing agreement is negotiated, they may order their items from Insight's Web page. Their log-in procedure identifies the customer and provides real-time quotes for the customer based on the negotiated pricing agreement stored in a database. Insight is committed to the fostering of Internet relationships with their customers. To encourage its sales account executives to fully support the Internet ordering of items by their customers, their commission compensation is based on their customers' total orders, both phone and Internet.

EFFECT OF EDI INTERNET APPLICATIONS ON THE ACCOUNTING PROFESSION

The use of electronic transmission and exchange of transaction data require that accountants have a thorough understanding of the risks surrounding such processes. Specifically, accountants need to understand encryption of data for confidentiality during transmission. Also, authentication of transaction partners, digital signatures and nonrepudiation are core concepts of e-commerce that dramatically affect the security features of transaction processing systems. All of these techniques are covered in Chapter 10. The security of a company's network servers is also a key component to a well-protected system. The topic of firewalls, an important network server security measure, is discussed in Chapter 11. Additional issues regarding the necessity of accountants to deeply understand the digital elements of fully-integrated EDI systems are discussed below.

Increased Complexity of Auditing through the Computer

Large and medium-sized accounting firms have been performing thorough, computerized audits of traditional EDI systems for quite some time. One might even say that this audit technology is in a mature state. However, as firms progress toward Web-based fully integrated systems, most, if not all, of the paper trail is eliminated. The proverbial "black-box" of auditing through the computer becomes larger. The accounting profession must possess the knowledge and expertise to perform the through-the-computer audits of the Web-based fully integrated EDI systems. Several issues are raised in auditing these types of operations.

Integrity and Reliance in the VANs

Because many important features may be performed by a VAN, such as message acknowledgment, time stamping, and message routing, the integrity and reliability of the VAN become an integral component of the audit. A transaction processing system is only as good as its weakest link. Auditing through the computer of a firm's own internal system is not good enough. The audit must be extended to assess the processing procedures of the VAN. Taking them for granted is not acceptable. Thus, accounting firms need to understand the technologies used by VANs and be able to examine the digital operations performed by them on behalf of their clients.

Extension of Audit to Trading Partners' Systems

As corporations open up their systems to their trading partners and rely on them, certain features of the trading partners' systems may need to be assessed for a couple of reasons:

- Integrity of data being provided by the system.
- Reliability of the system if it is integral to the operations of the client.

The incoming data in a manual system can be checked for accuracy and validity; likewise digital data can be checked in a computerized system. The underlying programs that check the data need to be thoroughly investigated by the audit team. In some cases, with closely aligned business partners, reliance on the checking procedures made by the trading partners' systems may occur. In this case, the auditor needs to identify these situations and periodically assess the adequacy of these systems. This validation procedure may occur by performing an audit of the trading partners' relevant systems or by a collaborative work with the trading partners' auditors. If the operations of a trading partner or service provider, such as a freight company that delivers goods on one's behalf, are crucial to the success of the firm, then an audit of the reliability of the relevant systems may also be necessary in performing risk assessment procedures. Again, the assessment may be performed either by the client's audit team or collaboratively with the trading partner's auditors.

Increased Technological Skills of Smaller Accounting Firms

With the building of a strong financial EDI infrastructure and lowered barriers to entry into EDI via the Internet, smaller businesses are beginning to electronically transfer documents. Small public accounting firms typically audit smaller businesses. These small public accounting firms need to gear up to perform audits on electronic paper trails, similar in nature to the services performed in the past by smaller and medium-sized accounting firms. Undoubtedly, these firms will look to hiring new college graduates with a strong background in accounting, information systems technology, and electronic commerce.

Summary

EDI has evolved over the past four decades. Businesses worldwide are at various stages of adoption of EDI technologies. As efficient supply chain management becomes an increasingly important goal, firms are discovering that fully integrated EDI systems are an enabling and necessary mechanism.

The widespread infrastructure of the Internet and the increasing number of ISPs are greatly increasing connectivity. The low-cost connectivity to the Internet along with an increasing supply of EDI Web-based software packages offer a tremendous opportunity for businesses to finally get involved in EDI.

The XML platform is breathing new life into traditional EDI and is proving to be a useful mechanism for increasing the transfer of Web-based data. XBRL while not directly related to the processing of individual Web-based transactions, is an important specification for the sharing of highly aggregated financial data.

Key Words

Accredited Standards Committee (ASC)	Federal Acquisition Streamlining Act of 1994
American National Standards Institute (ANSI)	financial EDI
ANSI ASC X12 format	fully integrated EDI systems
Automated Clearing House (ACH)	fully integrated Web-based EDI systems
connectivity	functional group
data elements	header
data segments	inbound transformation
data sharing	intelligent agents
Document Type Definitions (DTDs)	interchange control header
EDI messaging	National Automated Clearing House
EDI Web browser software packages	Association (NACHA)
Electronic data interchange (EDI)	non-EDI system
Electronic Data Interchange for	outbound transformation
Administrators, Commerce and Transport	partially integrated EDI systems
(EDIFACT)	security
Electronic Data Interchange—Internet	trading partners
Integration (EDIINT)	trading relationships
electronic envelope	transaction set header
eXtensible Business Reporting Language	translation software
(XBRL)	value-added network (VAN)
eXtensible Markup Language (XML)	Xschema
Federal Acquisition Computer Network	
(FACNET)	

Review Questions

1. What is EDI? What functions did EDI initially serve?
2. What are the typical clerks involved in a non-EDI system for procurement?
3. Do partially integrated EDI systems use financial EDI?
4. Do computers perform *all* tasks in fully integrated EDI systems?
5. What are the benefits of EDI?
6. What is a VAN?
7. What is EDI messaging?
8. What services are provided by VANs?
9. Why is translation software necessary for EDI to work properly?
10. What are the components of an ANSI ASC X12?
11. What is financial EDI?
12. Why haven't more firms engaged in EDI in the past?
13. What purpose does the Automated Clearing House serve?
14. What are the benefits of conducting EDI over the Internet?

15. How are EDI Internet–based systems driving selling prices down?
16. What are intelligent agents' role in EDI?
17. What are the two primary deterrents to rapid EDI Internet growth.
18. What functions do EDI Web browser translation software perform?
19. What is XML, and how does it affect EDI?
20. Explain the purpose of XBRL.
21. What are the four components of XBRL?

Discussion Questions

1. Why has EDI evolved over time from a manual document replacement tool to a mission critical function?
2. How is e-commerce helping society?
3. Why do you think the Department of Defense has informed its contractors that it will be increasingly difficult for them to compete if they do not become e-commerce/EDI capable?
4. Why do you think any businesses are still completely non-EDI? Give an example.
5. Why is EDI a key element in a just-in-time inventory system?
6. Why might a firm's private network not be as reliable as a VAN?
7. Why must trading partners supply their VANs with explicitly signed contracts?
8. What are the issues surrounding international e-commerce?
9. Explain the Federal Acquisition Streamlining Act of 1994, and discuss whether it has affected EDI.
10. How can Internet EDI affect the balance of power in businesses?
11. Why are connectivity and data sharing considered to be both great advantages and concerns for e-commerce?
12. Why are some businesses opting for smaller, private exchanges?
13. Why do you think business credit cards have become so popular?
14. Why do you think the Social Security Administration halted the activity of giving earnings and benefits information via the Internet?
15. Do you think the services provided by the federal government on the Internet are increasing its efficiency and effectiveness? If so, how?
16. Why are EDI Web browser systems so attractive to low-volume users?
17. What benefits has Insight Enterprises Inc. achieved because of its Web-based operations?
18. Is XML beneficial or does it just add another cumbersome level to EDI?
19. Contrast XML and XBRL.
20. Is e-commerce having a positive or negative affect on the accounting profession?

Cases

1. Internet Research Project
   Locate three vendors that sell Web-based e-commerce solutions to medium-sized businesses, and collect the following information:
   a. Ability to integrate data into existing systems or necessity of purchasing entire platform.
   b. Software that can run on company's own server or a Web-hosting service.
   c. The XML specification used.
   d. Pricing features exclusive of consulting/setup fees.

2. EDI in "The Patch"

The Canadian oil industry implemented EDI to reduce purchasing cost, invoicing cost, and turnaround time from the ordering to receipt of goods. Several major oil companies, such as Amoco, Chevron, Gulf, Mobil, and Suncor, sent representatives to participate in a joint EDI effort. The group decided on a standard 810 invoice form to be used by all involved parties. Gulf Oil estimates that it processes about 175,000 invoices per year, and check production costs have dropped from $20 to $30 per check to less than $10 per check.

a. Does such a system benefit the suppliers? If so, how?

b. Eventually, approximately 2,500 suppliers will be certified EDI trading partners. What steps do you think a firm would have to take to become a certified trading partner?

c. Approximately how much is Gulf Oil saving a year as a result of the 810 invoice?

3. General Electric Information Services

General Electric Information Services manages a trading community of more than 100,000 trading partners. Visit their website at *www.gegxs.com* and report back on their GE Interchange Services and how what they provide relates to this chapter.

4. Sterling Commerce

Visit *www.sterlingcommerce.com* and select industry solutions. A pulldown menu of many companies will appear. Read the business challenge and solution for the company or companies that your instructor assigns.

References and Websites

Bankers EDI Council. "Financial EDI Facts." *http://www.nacha.org/bedic/fedi.htm.*

Corporate EFT Report. "Head of Federal Reserve EDI Group Outlines Promotion to Boost FEDI." April 1, 1998.

Crosby, Tom. "Striking It Rich in Canada's Oil Country." *Electronic Commerce World.* October, 1997.

Department of Defense Electronic Commerce Office. *Introduction to Department of Defense Electronic Commerce: A Handbook for Business,* Vol. 2. October 1997. *http://www.acq.osd.mil /ec/newhandbook/cover/cover.htm.*

GE Information Services. *Introduction to EDI—A Primer. http://www.support.geis.com/edi/ edipindx.htm.*

Greenstein, Marilyn. "Attestation of EDI-Internet Transaction Systems," *The Review of Accounting Information Systems,* Vol. 2. No. 3, 1998.

Harbinger Corporation. *http:// www.harbinger.com.*

Heywood, Susan. "Winning the E-Commerce Game." *Electronic Commerce World.* March, 1998.

IBM Global Services. *http://www.ibm.com/globalnetwork/edibr.htm.*

Insight Enterprises, Inc. *1997 Annual Report.*

Marlin, Steve. "EDI: An Engine for Electronic Commerce." *Bank Systems & Technology,* Vol. 34, No. 10, October 1997.

Meehan, Michael. "Forrester: E-Commerce to Explode in Asia, Europe, South America," *Computerworld Online.* April 21, 2000.

National Automated Clearing House Association. "Electronic Payments Grew Rapidly in 1990s." September 19, 2000. *http://www.nacha.org/news/pressreleases/PR091900/ pr091900.htm.*

_____. "The Automated Clearing House (ACH) Network." January 22, 1988. *http://www.nacha.org/nacha-info/ach.htm.*

_____. "Appeal of ACH Surges with New Rule Requiring Financial Institutions to Pass Remittance Information to Companies." October 31, 1997. *http://www.nacha.org/ whats-hot/press/ appeal6.htm.*

_____. "NACHA Approves Rules for Consumer Electronic Payments by Telephone." October 2, 2000. *http://www.nacha.org/news/pressreleases/PR100200/pr100200.htm.*

_____. "1995 NACHA Corporate Financial EDI Study." *http://www.nacha.org/bedic/edistudy.htm.*

_____. "1995 NACHA Corporate Financial Study." *http://www.nacha.org/bedic/edistudy.htm.*

Rich, Jonathon. "XML and the IT Architect," *Sun World,* June 1999. *www.sunworld.com.*

Segev, Arie, Jaana Porra, and Malu Roldan. "Internet-Based Financial EDI." *http://haas.berkeley.edu/~citm/EDI-proj.html.*

Shih, Janson, Drummond. "Requirements For Inter-Operable Internet EDI," EDIINT Working Group, Internet Draft, December 1998.

Skylonda. "What Are the ANSI ASC X12 Standards?" *http://www.skylonda.com/skyansi.htm.*

Sliwa, Carol. "EDI Dinosaur Lives—and Grows," *Computerworld Online,* May 1, 2000. *http://computerworldonline.com.*

_____. "W3C Readies Long-Awaited XML Schema Spec." *Computerworld Online,* October 30, 2000. *http://computerworldonline.com.*

Stein, Tom. "Enterprise Risk—Extending Enterprise Applications to the Internet Has Benefits and Dangers, Users Say." *InformationWeek.* October 27, 1997.

Yarbrough, L. "EDI Over the Internet: EDIINT," *EC.COM,* September 1997.

7   RISKS OF INSECURE SYSTEMS

Learning Objectives

1. To identify the risks of insecure systems faced by business trading partners and consumers.
2. To differentiate between Intranets, Extranets, and the Internet and to understand their relative risks and benefits.
3. To understand different categories of malicious code techniques that may harm an insecure system.

INTRODUCTION

The Internet and electronic commerce offer endless possibilities and opportunities to businesses of all sizes as well as convenience to consumers. These benefits are not reaped without risks, however, to both merchants and consumers. Some of these risks have been alluded to in the previous chapters. In this chapter, we begin to investigate the risks faced by merchants and consumers in greater detail. Unfortunately, the fast-paced evolution and exponential growth rates of electronic websites have enticed many enterprises to embrace technology without fully understanding the ramifications and control issues involved. Furthermore, some consumers eager to point-and-click to purchase their desired products have found themselves vulnerable to insecure systems. Media coverage, and sometimes media hype, about these consumer risks have caused many potential consumers to be leery about electronic transactions and to refrain from engaging in such activities.

An Intranet is the private networking technology for intracompany telecommunications. Risks may be solely at the enterprise level if Intranets are in place, or the risks may expand to external perpetrators when both Internet and Intranet applications are present. This chapter presents the different types and levels of risks faced by parties engaging in e-business transactions. Figure 7–1 illustrates the major players involved in e-commerce on the Internet. Unfortunately, legitimate selling agents and legitimate customers are not the only parties connected to the Internet. Other parties lurking on the Internet include various perpetrators, both internal to legitimate buying and selling agencies and external independents, with a multitude of techniques and motives for engaging in fraudulent, harmful acts on the Internet that affect both selling agents and their

FIGURE 7–1   *Agents, buyers, and perpetrators on the Internet*

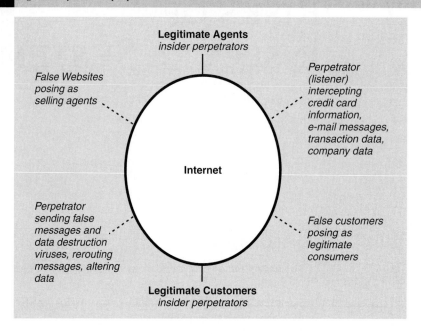

customers. This chapter also explores why businesses facing rapid growth or changes in their corporate information systems may face an increased risk of insecure systems. Thus, the focus of this chapter is on risk identification. In subsequent chapters, security precautions that can be used to reduce these risks are discussed.

OVERVIEW OF RISKS ASSOCIATED WITH INTERNET TRANSACTIONS

This section explores the general risks associated with the Internet. Specific risks will be discussed later in the chapter. What is meant by the term *risk*? The Merriam-Webster dictionary defines risk as the "possibility of loss or injury" or "someone or something that creates or suggests a hazard." Losses or injuries in a digital society may occur in many different ways. Data may be stolen, corrupted, misused, altered, or falsely generated. Attacks on hardware may occur that render systems unable to operate properly. Hardware and/or software may be used without authorization, which may translate into lost revenue or slower response time for authorized users. Programs may be altered to cause systems to perform incorrectly or even to crash. In terms of e-commerce, **risk** is viewed as the possibility of loss of confidential data or the destruction, generation, or use of data or programs that physically, mentally, or financially harm another party, as well as the possibility of harm to hardware.

In 1996, the potential and actual threats to infrastructures critical to the operations of the U.S. government and to the Internet in general caused President Clinton to establish the President's Commission on Critical Infrastructure Protection (PCCIP). The Commission is charged with "recommending a national strategy for protecting and assuring critical infrastructures from physical and cyber threats." Interestingly, the Commission views national security over these critical infrastructures as a shared responsi-

E-Commerce in Practice

Feds Warn Hackers, Then Ask Them for Help

At the opening of the annual Def Con hackers convention, . . . the Pentagon's CIO pleaded with attendees to leave government systems alone and outlined proposed new laws aimed at prosecuting computer crimes more expeditiously. But he also said the government's doors are open to hackers who want to help prevent attacks.

"Some of you are extremely talented, gifted even at what you do," said Arthur Money, Assistant Secretary of Defense and CIO at the Department of Defense (DOD). "If you're thinking about what you want to do with the rest of your life, maybe you should think about this in a different manner. You should think about coming to work for us."

Speaking during a "Meet the FED" panel at Def Con 8, Money said anyone who has been convicted of a felony shouldn't bother applying for jobs with the DOD. But he and other government representatives said half-jokingly that the Pentagon has plenty of technology to offer to hackers interested in going to work for Uncle Sam.

"There's no one here with a level of sophistication that can't be matched by the government," said Dick Schafer, director of information assurance for the DOD. "No one here has a set of toys as neat as what we've got. I hope we have some military recruiters here to handle the onslaught." A uniformed Marine officer in the back of the room raised his hand.

On a more serious note, Money said the proposed legislation for speeding up prosecution of computer crimes also would increase the penalties for malicious attacks and make it easier to investigate suspected crimes by freeing law enforcement officials from restrictive wiretap laws.

Money sounded a similar theme . . . during his closing keynote address at the Black Hat Briefings conference, a precursor to Def Con that features security-related presentations aimed at corporate users. "The laws in the United States are totally arcane and antiquated when it comes to cybercrimes," Money said during the Black Hat speech. But if the proposed legislation passes, he added, computer attacks against the DOD would become a national security violation instead of just a criminal action.

The bill also would give the DOD "the ability to talk back, trace back, and attack back," Money said. In addition, the Pentagon would be able to take over investigations from the FBI more quickly, without having to wait several weeks to get wiretaps for each leg of an attack to prove it was a computer crime.

At Def Con . . . , Money said there were more than 22,000 confirmed attacks against the DOD's systems in the last year alone. "Not pings, but attacks," he said. "This is no longer [fun] and giggles, this is serious stuff."

Source: Tom Mahoney. Excerpt from © *Computerworld Online*, July 28, 2000.

bility between public and private sectors. As discussed in the box entitled "Feds Warn Hackers, Then Ask Them for Help," the U.S. government's computer systems have been the successful target of many hackers and have raised the concern level to one of major importance. The Commission defines a **threat** as

> Anyone with the capability, technology, opportunity, and intent to do harm. Potential threats can be foreign or domestic, internal or external, state-sponsored or a single rogue element. Terrorists, insiders, disgruntled employees, and hackers are included in this profile.

Until relatively recently, most information security breaches were initiated by insiders. However, a 2000 study conducted by the Computer Security Institute and the FBI (CSI/FBI study) indicates that this trend is rapidly changing. The findings indicate that the number of external attacks is growing because of the increased use of the Internet. The 2000 CSI/FBI study found that for frequent points of attack, 59 percent of firms reported their Internet connection as the source, while only 38 percent reported their internal systems as the source. The report also illustrates that this trend of proportionately more external attacks has maintained for three consecutive years. Thus, attacks on the whole are on the rise, and designers of systems need to adequately ensure that controls

FIGURE 7–2   *CSI/FBI 2000 computer crime and security survey highlights*

Security Technologies Used	Percent of Firms
Anti-virus software	100%
Access control	92
Physical security	90
Firewalls	78
Encrypted files	62
Reusable passwords	54
Encrypted log-in	50
Intrusion detection	50
PCMCIA	39
Digital IDs	36
Biometrics	8

Computer Crimes	Number of Firms Reporting Costs	Average Costs for 2000
Active wiretapping	1	$5,000,000
Theft of proprietary information	22	1,136,409
Unauthorized insider access	20	1,000,050
Financial fraud	34	617,661
Sabotage of data or networks	28	535,750
System penetration by outsider	29	172,448
Insider abuse of Internet access	91	164,837
Telecom fraud	19	157,947
Denial of service attack	46	108,717
Virus	162	61,729
Telecom eavesdropping	15	33,346
Laptop theft	174	6,899

are in place to prevent dangers from both internal and external threats. Figure 7–2 highlights some of the other findings reported in the 2000 CSI/FBI Survey.

External hackers enter their targets in a variety of ways and for a variety of purposes. Historically, the most common external breaches have involved probing the system, compromising internal documents and e-mail messages, introducing a virus, and compromising trade secrets. Each of these activities is troublesome, although some activities pose more of a threat than others. These types of security breaches are discussed later in this chapter. As mentioned earlier, more than half (59 percent) of those firms responding to the survey indicated that their computer networks were attacked by external perpetrators.

The average estimated losses due to security breaches is approximately $1 million for the 271 firms that were able and/or willing to report the amounts. These costs are not trivial, and they are *per firm* costs. The U.S. Department of Defense has characterized these attacks "at a minimum . . . a multimillion dollar nuisance." Firms currently connected to the Internet and those firms considering connecting to the Internet need to identify and manage the risks associated with these Internet connections. Management of identified risks is an important step in protecting a firm's assets and critical data, and risk management must be considered from a cost-benefit perspective. The role internal controls play in the management of risks is discussed in the following chapter.

E-Commerce in Practice

Customer Data Exposures

Barclays.com

Customers reported that they were able to view summaries of accounts belonging to other people. (September 2000)

Buy.com

Customers returning merchandise could view names, addresses, and telephone numbers of other customers. (October 2000)

E*TRADE.com

Security researchers report that E*TRADE's customers' passwords were vulnerable to theft by attackers. (October 2000)

H&R Block

Customers' tax data were exposed by erroneously importing their data into other customers' tax returns. (February 2000)

SelectQuote.com

Medical histories and personal data of applicants were exposed to other customers. (March 2000)

WesternUnion.com

A hacker broke into this site and copied approximately 15,000 credit and debit card numbers. (September 2000)

INTERNET-ASSOCIATED RISKS

This section examines the issues faced by firms that have connections to the Internet and that use the Internet for a number of reasons: external e-mail, geographically separated internal e-mail, marketing, and electronic sales and purchasing systems. The risks to both customers and selling agents are also examined. Customers and selling agents who use the Internet are not the only parties at risk, however, and a brief discussion of how an individual not engaged in e-commerce may become a victim of cybercrime is presented. Some of the risks presented in this section can be mitigated by using authentication and digital signatures, which are topics covered extensively in Chapter 10. Threats to business transaction data between trading partners are highly important Internet-associated risks, and an entire section later in this chapter is devoted to the coverage of these risks.

Risks to Customers

The Internet has not been viewed by most users as a safe place to use credit cards to conduct business transactions. This feeling of insecurity is primarily due to the large number of press reports citing story after story about thefts of credit card information and other personal information. The box entitled "Customer Data Exposures" lists some brief examples of the exposure of customer data at online sites. This section covers the many risks faced by customers when they transact online. One note is important, however: Theft of customer data does not only occur as a result of online transactions. In fact, it occurs as well from transactions originating at brick-and-mortar establishments. Customers frequently hand over their credit cards to strangers in retail establishments and restaurants frequently without any preconceived notion of danger. In fact, they are surrendering the same exact information that is reported in the press as stolen credit card information procured by Internet hackers!

False or Malicious Websites

Malicious websites are typically set up for the purpose of stealing visitors' IDs and passwords, stealing credit card information, spying on a visitor's hard drive, and uploading files from the visitor's hard drive. The bugs discussed in the following section are either remedied by the most current version of the browser software, or they can be remedied by recent "patch" files that can be found on the vendors' websites. Unfortunately, new variations continue to pop up as soon as "cures" for the old variations are available. Website assurance should be helpful for assessing the trustworthiness of a website. Website assurance was discussed in Chapter 4.

Stealing Visitors' IDs and Passwords.   This can be accomplished by individuals who set up a malicious website that asks the user to "register" with the website and to give a password. The password is given voluntarily and can only be harmfully used if the visitor uses the same password for many different applications, such as ATM cards, work-related passwords, and home security alarm passwords. The rule to live by here is to always use a different password for various Internet-related purposes.

Stealing Visitors' Credit Card Information.   This can also be obtained by "false" websites being set up and temporarily staged as legitimate businesses, such as a site selling Christmas Gift Baskets to be delivered anywhere in the United States on Christmas Eve. The site could be set up any time prior to Christmas Eve, collect credit card information, and then shut down on Christmas Eve. No one would know to complain until after Christmas Eve, and by that time the site has most assuredly already shut down. This type of scam is not unique to the Internet, however, it is easier to attract a large customer base and then "disappear" from the Internet without having to physically pick up and move from one's domicile.

A more troubling manner in which credit cards, IDs, passwords, and other information, including bank account access codes, may be intercepted by a malicious website is accomplished through the use of bugs that allow all visitors' sessions to be monitored and such information recorded. These types of acts are sometimes referred to as **man-in-the-middle attacks.** Such bugs as "the Bell Labs Bug," the Singapore Bug," and the "Santa Barbara Bug" involve some variation of a procedure that allows JavaScript pages of a malicious website, which must first be visited, to view and capture any information transmitted to subsequent websites visited. The basic manner in which this is conducted is by attaching a virtually invisible window, perhaps 1 by 1 pixel, that remains open as other sites are visited. The most troubling aspect of this type of bug is that information can be stolen even if the site is "secured" with Secure Sockets Layer (SSL), discussed in Chapters 9 and 12.

Spying on a Visitor's Hard Drive and Uploading Files From the Visitor's Hard Drive.
This has been accomplished via bugs such as the "Freiburg bug" that exploit file upload holes in Web browser software. These types of bugs also use a virtually invisible frame[1] generated by the malicious website. As the visitor browses the website, a JavaScript program proceeds to examine the visitor's hard drive, and through file-sharing techniques, any files with known names can then be uploaded to any site desired on the Internet. The file name must be known in advance. Unfortunately for security reasons, many common

---

[1] A Web browser screen may be divided into different areas called frames. These frames have code attached to them.

E-Commerce in Practice

Microsoft Java Machine Could Enable "Attack Applets"

A security flaw in Microsoft Corp.'s Java Virtual Machine could allow a Java applet to wreak havoc on a system if the user simply views a Web page or e-mail message.

The Princeton Secure Internet Programming team, Drew Dean at Xerox PARC and Dan Wallach at Rice University, discovered the flaw in Java Virtual Machines with Internet Explorer 4 and 5 for Windows 95, 98, or NT. The security hole allows hackers to create an "attack applet" that is attached to an HTML page and delivered to Java Virtual Machines that have Internet Explorer and Outlook built in to them.

Such an attack applet could read files, change content, make network connections, set up a listening station or do other actions when it launched, said Gary McGraw, vice president of corporate technology at Reliable Software Technologies Corp., a Dulles, Va.–based software consultancy. McGraw has worked with the Princeton team on other security matters.

"It's Melissa on steroids" by taking control of a victim's computer and performing any kind of action, he said.

According to Edward Felton, a professor at Princeton and a member of the programming team, no computer has been hit by the Java flaw yet.

McGraw said the flaw was discovered a couple of weeks ago but wasn't revealed until this week, when Microsoft issued a new version of Java Virtual Machine at *www.microsoft.com/java/vm/dl_vm32.htm* and a security bulletin. He advised Java Virtual Machine users to download the new version.

"It's pure luck that the major flaws in Java haven't run wild" yet, McGraw said. Attack applets are the worse kind of Java flaw, and like other mobile code, the risks are serious, he said.

Source: Kathleen Ohlson, © *Computerworld Online,* August 31, 1999.

---

files reside on most computers, such as "cookies.txt" that may have voluntarily supplied, unencrypted password information stored in it, although the storing of unencrypted password data is rare. The only types of files that may be uploaded are text, image or HTML files. Through such an attack, files may be scanned and uploaded, but they may not be altered while they are on the visitor's hard drive. The box entitled, "Microsoft Java Machine could enable 'Attack Applets' " explains how such Java applets can attack Internet Explorer 4 and 5 to spy and obtain data.

Theft of Customer Data from Selling Agents and Internet Service Providers

Customers purchasing goods and services on the Internet, including the use of an **Internet service provider (ISP)** to have access to the Internet, typically pay with credit cards. Cyber cash payment methods are another, less popular alternative. This credit card information is stored by the selling agents and ISPs. Unfortunately for the customers, hackers are occasionally successful at breaking into the selling agent's and the ISP's systems and obtaining the customers' credit card data. Little, if anything, can be done by the consumer to prevent this type of exposure other than not using credit card information at all on the Internet. The risk, however, is comparable if you use your credit card for any other purpose since corporate databases containing non-Internet customer credit card information may also be penetrated and stolen.

Privacy and the Use of Cookies

The issue of **privacy** on the Internet is of concern to many people. Many coalitions have been formed to monitor and disseminate information regarding privacy issues on the Internet and to proactively lobby for greater privacy measures. A few of these groups are the Center for Democracy and Technology (CDT), Electronic Frontier Foundation (EFF), Electronic Privacy Information Center (EPIC), Privacy International, and Privacy Rights Clearinghouse (PRC). As mentioned in Chapter 5, the European Union has enacted privacy legislation, including use of cookies, but the United States has not.

So what information is kept about a visitor? The answer depends on how much information the visitor divulges about him- or herself and how he or she configures the Web browser preferences. **Cookies** were designed to allow Web servers to operate more efficiently, provide a better response time to repeat visitors to their sites, and more accurately track how many different users (as opposed to repeat visitors) visit a site. The use of cookies, however, has become a very controversial topic by privacy groups preferring to have no information about Web browsing activities be kept by the websites visited.

Depending on which Web browser is being used, cookies may be placed in a single file or individual files. For many websites, the only information recorded is a unique identification number so that the site may track the number of first-time and repeat visitors. The process is illustrated in Figure 7–3. When a user initially visits a website, the host site may assign a unique identification code to that user and create a cookie that is placed on the visitor's permanent storage device, such as a hard drive. While the cookie file is written to the visitor's hard drive, no files from the hard drive may be read, altered or uploaded from this procedure. In some instances, other information such as user ID and password are placed in this file, but only if the individual offers this information by typing it into a form. This information is encrypted by some sites, but not by all. The cookie file is a text file (.txt) that is easily read. Although rare, if an unencrypted password is placed in this file, the danger of the file being read by some other malicious mechanism is a potential exposure. Even if a password is unencrypted in a cookie file,

FIGURE 7–3   *Illustration of cookies*

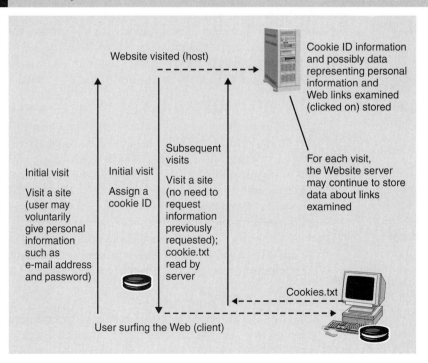

E-Commerce in Practice

Group Decries Use of Web Bugs

Companies and online advertisers that use information-gathering "Web bugs" on their websites should clearly disclose the presence of the technology to users, according to a Denver-based privacy group that proposed a set of standards to address the issue last week.

The proposal was detailed at the Global Privacy Summit in Washington by the Privacy Foundation, which claimed that many websites are using Web bugs to track the activities of visitors without their knowledge. Users "don't have much control over" Web bugs, said Stephen Keating, the foundation's executive director.

Web bugs are similar to the Internet cookies that are widely used to track the online movements of Web users and store information about them, but the bugs are invisi-ble to users. Cookies can be turned off or controlled through a Web browser, but Keating said there are no such management features for Web bugs because they're embedded within the HTML code on a Web page. That means they "can be much more insidious," he added.

The Privacy Foundation's proposal calls for standards under which Web bugs would be clearly shown as visible icons on a computer screen, rather than as small, dot-size images that are nearly impossible to see. The group also supports a requirement that the icons be clearly labeled with the names of the companies that have placed the Web bugs on a site.

Source: Todd R. Weiss, © *Computerworld Online,* September 18, 2000.

it is possible that information passed from it to a server is encrypted, such as during an SSL session.

On the website server side, the assigned user ID number is stored. In many cases, that is all that is stored. In other cases, time visited, length of the visit, items clicked on, and user preference data given by the visitor may also be stored by the website server into a database. Privacy groups are concerned about these types of data repositories being created and sold for marketing or other purposes. The box entitled "Group Decries Use of Web Bugs" describes how a site may collect such data using a **Web bug** much to the chagrin of privacy advocates.

The main reason given for the justification for the creation of cookies is one of efficiency. On subsequent visits to this website, once the cookie is read, the server can obtain any information stored about the visitor without having to ask for it again. For example, cookies can process multiple advertisements sequentially so that one is not repeated until a cycle is complete. Also, the website server does not have to store any of the visitor preference data on its computer, and thus the potential to push data storage to the visitor exists.

How long do cookies last? Just like edible cookies, computer-generated cookies have expiration dates assigned. Most sites either set their expiration dates for a very short (a couple of hours for shopping carts) or a very long (several years) time period depending on the site's objectives.

Unbeknown to the website visitor, he or she may be inadvertently linked to a marketing firm, such as DoubleClick, which also issues a cookie to the visitor. This linking mechanism is the subject of hot debate, and privacy advocacy groups are trying to make these types of unsolicited links illegal. A general overview of how a marketing firm may issue cookies is depicted in Figure 7–4. When the user visits one of the websites included in the marketing firm's network, the requested Web page is loaded into the visitor's Web browser. However, embedded in the page are **image tags** that graphically link the visitor's browser to the marketing firm's server, and a link is established directly between the visitor and the marketing firm. The marketing firm can then issue its own cookie,

FIGURE 7–4   *Privacy, cookies, and marketing firms*

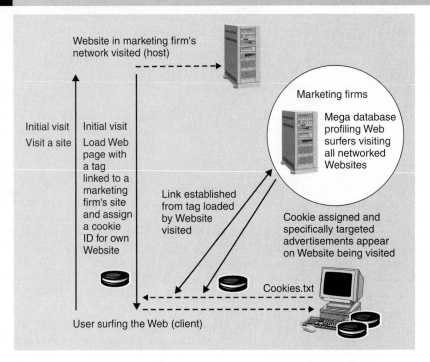

with a unique ID number. With this link established, the marketing firm has the potential to capture any information provided by the visitor. Considering that the network size of some of the marketers exceeds half a million sites, the amount of data that can potentially be gathered is staggering.

The purpose of assigning these cookies is to send customized advertising images and links to the website being visited. These cookies contain a specific user's buying patterns and preferences, which can be used to lure the user into clicking on an advertisement. This customized advertising is the product sold by these marketing firms. One of the larger of these marketers, DoubleClick, initially asserted that it did not gather any personally identifiable information in its cookies. DoubleClick claimed to collect only data regarding the ads that it sends to the Web browser so that it can either eliminate redundant advertising or purposefully repeat advertising messages. In 1999, DoubleClick came under public scrutiny and litigation when it purchased a direct-mail marketing company, Abacus Alliance. The merger of these businesses gave DoubleClick the capability to link user profiles to personally identifiable information.

As users' demands for privacy continue to increase, so too will the demand for privacy attestation reports by independent assurance firms. Increasingly, firms are providing disclosure about privacy policies. In the box entitled "Disney Cookie Policy," Disney explains its cookies policy and why it uses them.

In response to users' demands for privacy, recent versions of Web browsers have the enhanced capability for users to customize their preferences to either refuse the receipt of a cookie or to require permission before a cookie is accepted. Many websites will not allow the user to access the site, however, if its cookie(s) is(are) not accepted! Further, the cookie files may be edited by the user to judiciously remove cookies so that websites can be revisited anonymously.

E-Commerce in Practice

Disney's Cookie Policy

Use of Cookies

What are cookies? Cookies are pieces of information that a website transfers to an individual's hard drive for record-keeping purposes. Cookies make Web surfing easier for you by saving your preferences while you're at our site. We never save passwords or credit card information in cookies. The use of cookies is an industry standard—you'll find them at most major websites.

By showing how and when Guests use a site, cookies help us see which areas are popular and which are not. Many improvements and updates to the site are based on such data as total number of visitors and pages viewed. This information is most easily tracked with cookies. We use the information from cookies to provide services better tailored to our users needs.

Disney Online and the GO Network have two primary uses for their cookies. First, we use them to specify unique preferences. For example, in GO Network's News Center, users can specify keywords across several news categories. This way you don't have to tell us over and over again about the kinds of news stories you want to see. Secondly, we use cookies to track user trends and patterns. This helps us bet-

ter understand and improve areas of the Disney Online and the GO Network service that our users find valuable. While both of these activities depend on the use of a cookie, visitors to Disney Online and the GO Network always have the option of disabling cookies via their browser preferences. Information from cookies is sometimes attached to messages sent to our Customer Service department.

Most browsers are initially set up to accept cookies. You can reset your browser to refuse all cookies or indicate when a cookie is being sent. However, note that some parts of the Disney Online and the GO Network service will not function properly or may be considerably slower if you refuse cookies. For example, without cookies, you will not be able to set personalized news preferences or you may have difficulty completing shopping transactions, entering contests, or playing games.

You may occasionally get cookies from our advertisers. Disney Online and the GO Network do not control these cookies. The use of advertising cookies sent by third-party servers is standard in the Internet industry.

Source: © Disney. *http://www.disney.com* Excerpt from online privacy policy—11/2000.

Risks to Selling Agents

When people think of Internet-related risks, they typically think of the risks to the consumer; however, selling agents also face risks, and that is why many organizations have not taken the leap from advertising on the Internet to allowing sales transactions to be completed on the Internet. Overall risks to the selling agent are covered in this section, while a more detailed discussion of transaction data–related risks are covered in a later section in this chapter.

Customer Impersonation

One risk to the selling agent is that the customer is not the entity he or she claims to be, also called **impersonation.** How can false customers wreak havoc on a selling agent's system? If they can misrepresent themselves as legitimate customers, they can order goods and services for a variety of reasons. One reason may be to obtain a free service or product, such as to purchase and download software paid for with a false credit card number. Another reason may be to have goods shipped with no intention to receive or to pay (the perpetrator must be disguised as a trading partner with credit terms approved). In the second case, the intent is purely malicious and not for personal acquisition of the good. Malicious use of false ordering techniques may be conducted for a number of reasons: (a) the intrinsic satisfaction to the hacker for accomplishing such a feat, (b) to target hurtful acts against companies with social policies not in agreement with the hacker's own personal philosophies, or (c) to hurt corporate profits and customer relations of a competitor or former employer.

Unfortunately for big businesses, the Internet is a relatively new frontier, and it allows new mechanisms, due to loopholes in security, to fall into the hands of the "little" guy to wage personal battles and vendettas. The Internet and e-commerce also allow a new playing ground for "dirty" competitive acts to be conducted among those business people with mean, competitive spirits. The vast majority of businesspeople do not fall into this category, but the few that do can inflict a great deal of damage.

Denial of Service Attacks

Selling agents, among other website servers, may be the target of malicious attacks called **denial of service attacks.** A denial of service attack is used by an individual to destroy, shut down, or degrade a computer or network resource. The goal of such attacks is to flood the communication ports and memory buffers of the targeted site to prevent the receipt of legitimate messages and the service of legitimate requests for connections. These types of attacks are on the rise as methods and program code for conducting such acts are publicly available on hacker websites. The 2000 CSI/FBI survey revealed that 27 percent of the firms studied had detected a denial of service attack of some sort in the last year. These attacks are extremely difficult to trace back to the perpetrator because of address hiding techniques used such as IP spoofing, discussed later in the chapter, and the ability to obtain an IP address easily through the plethora of Internet service providers (ISP).

Many different variations of denial of service attacks exist, and new ones continue to be created. One example of a denial of service attack is known as *SYN flooding.* The attacker requests the establishment of a new connection with the target via a SYN (*synchronization*) packet. The receiving site, the target in this case, responds with a SYN/ACK (*synchronization/acknowledgement*) packet. At this point, the connection is half-open. The target computer's memory buffer maintains the information while it waits for the initiating server to respond with an ACK (*acknolwedge*) packet and complete the connection. The final ACK packet is never sent and the connection remains half-open. If enough of these SYN packets are sent to the targeted site, the memory buffers become

---

FIGURE 7–5   *SYN flooding illustrated*

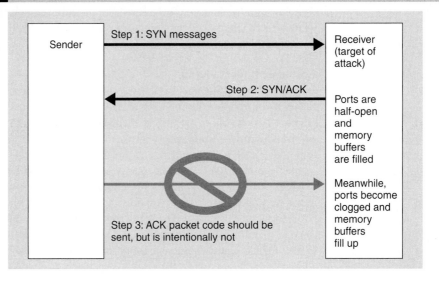

full, and legitimate users' SYN packets are unable to get through. The SYN flooding process is illustrated in Figure 7–5.

Distributed denial of service (DDoS) attacks were numerous during the first and second quarters of 2000. DDoS attacks are launched through a master-slave configuration and are much more difficult to detect, and thus to prevent or thwart. The reason they are more difficult to defend against is because the attack is launched through a network of hacked and hijacked (slave) computers that send out the illegitimate requests for services. A very troubling aspect is that many home and business PCs connected to the Internet were commandeered, and the owners are for the most part unaware of their use in these attacks. Because the incoming illegitimate requests for services are not from a central IP address, but rather from hundreds or even thousands of slave computers, the firewall detection software cannot easily, if at all, discern good from bad requests. Many large sites have either had their services severely degraded or even shut down by DDoS attacks, such as Amazon, CNN, eBay, E*TRADE, the FBI, and Yahoo. The prevalent form of DDoS attacks in early 2000 was a method called Trinoo, which was publicly posted on the Internet in late 1999. Unfortunately, variants of this attack continue to merge, such as Tribal Flood Network and Trinity.

Other denial of service scenarios include the deletion of the startup files on a computer, rendering it unbootable, or deleting Web pages from a Web server. Why would anyone launch any of these types of attacks? After all, they are not gaining access to sensitive data. Attacks have been launched for various reasons ranging from political reasons to being an integral part of a larger attack. One such attack was launched by attackers protesting a site maintained by the Institute for Global Communication that hosted a site promoting Basque Independence. Another attack was launched against a spam mail firm, Cyber Promotions, in protest to its cyber space junk-mail operations. A denial of service attack might also be used to bring down a server that a hacker wants to spoof. For example, a hacker may attempt to spoof a bank to obtain PINs or credit card numbers.

Denial of service attacks are extremely hard to prevent. Even Sun Microsystems has conceded that these types of attacks are "by far, the most prevalent security concern." They do point out, however, that the primary loss is downtime and the system can usually be easily recovered by rebooting it. For many businesses on the Internet, however, lost time can mean lost sales and, therefore, lost revenue.

Data Theft

Important data, such as customer lists and engineering blueprints, used to be kept under physical lock and key. If an individual wished to steal files from a company, he or she would have to physically travel to the building and gain access to it, as well as any file cabinets containing the desired information. Acts such as this require some degree of nerve, especially if security guards are posted at the building. The perpetrator must consider whether he or she will physically encounter someone or be chased by an armed security guard. However, data files that are stored digitally and connected to public telecommunications lines can potentially be accessed by an unauthorized user without the perpetrator ever having to leave the comfort of home. Furthermore, the perpetrator may be miles or oceans away from the site from which the data are stolen. Additionally, if perpetrators suspect exposure, they can quickly disconnect and likely not be traced. Thus, theft of electronic data is a serious concern of many companies. According to the 2000 CSI/FBI study, 24 percent of the firms reported the digital theft of proprietary information, and the average value of loss per firm was $1 million.

Because many firms' assets are digital, such as books, music, and videos, the theft of data results in the theft of the firm's inventory. This problem is exacerbated by the problem of identifying the data; hence, revenue loss is extremely difficult as mentioned in chapter 4. The risk of theft of data can be reduced by preventive techniques, such as firewalls introduced in this chapter and more thoroughly discussed in Chapter 11. Encryption, discussed in Chapter 10, can be used as a second line of defense to render stolen data useless.

INTRANET-ASSOCIATED RISKS

This section examines issues concerning risks to organizations that employ **Intranets.** Some Intranets are extremely large; the Chase Manhattan Bank NA reportedly had 15,000 browsers and 50 Intranet servers as of the end of 1997 and was expecting an expansion of about 20 additional servers during 1998.[2] These Intranets may or may not be connected to the Internet. The intracompany telecommunication links may connect workers within one building, in adjacent buildings, or in geographically separate buildings, including workers connecting from roving laptop computers. The applications employed on these Intranets may be as simple as e-mail, or they may encompass client/server applications including electronic trading between subsidiaries. In fact, as Intranets grow to include sister companies of large corporations, the exact distinction between the Internet and Intranets becomes blurred as ISPs may be used to connect geographically separate intrafirm entities. This section focuses on the risks inherent to traditional Intranets. Once the Internet is entered into the equation, the risks are added to the previously mentioned risks for agents trading on the Internet.

The maintenance and security of corporate Intranets is becoming an unwieldy beast for some very large organizations. In some of these organizations, merely keeping abreast of the number and actual location of its Intranets is proving to be a challenge. Boeing Co., in an internal discovery search of its own Intranets, located in excess of 1 million pages that were hosted by at least 2,300 major Intranet sites, and the possibility exists that all Intranets, servers, and pages were not found in that search.[3] The U.S. Postal Service has 10,000 local area networks in its Intranet, connecting approximately 35,000 locations and 800,0000 employees. This proliferation of Intranets is fostered by low cost and relative ease of implementation. Unfortunately, many of these Intranets are exposed to serious security risks because they are not supported by the information technology department. Some companies are becoming vulnerable because of individual group decisions to implement low-cost Intranet technology, yet sufficient resources may not be available to support the fragmented infrastructure.

Thus far, the discussion in this chapter has focused on malicious acts performed by individuals external to the firm. Internal hackers are troubling because they potentially have a wealth of information from which to proceed in designing malicious schemes. Many of the inside abuses are covered up by large, publicly traded organizations that do not prosecute internal perpetrators caught in the act of malicious and harmful computer acts. This lack of prosecution is often blamed on the fear of negative public perception regarding the management of internal controls. Regardless of source of attack, however, firms are typically squeamish about reporting intrusions. The 2000 CSI/FBI study found that only 25 percent of the firms that experienced a computer intrusion reported it to a law enforcement agency; 55 percent of the firms decided that civil remedy was best; and 52 percent cited fear of negative publicity as the reason for not reporting the intrusions to law enforcement officials; 39 percent did not report the intrusion because of the fear that a competitor could use the information to its advantage.

---

[2]Paula Rooney, "Imposing Order from Chaos." *Computerworld Online,* November 24, 1997.
[3]Carol Sliwa, "Maverick Intranets a Challenge for IT," *Computerworld Online,* March 15, 1999.

This section focuses on malicious acts that may be conducted by both inside workers and nonemployees who gain access to the Intranet. Specifically, employee sabotage of data and networks is discussed. According to the 2000 CSI/FBI survey, 28 percent of firms experienced such attacks, with an average annual cost of $535,750 per firm.

Sabotage by Former Employees

Do former employees really launch vindictive acts against former employers and their computer systems? The 2000 CSI/FBI study revealed that 81 percent of the firms felt that an attack launched by a disgruntled employee was likely to occur. One only has to look at this headline to see it can happen:

> "Jury Convicts IT Manager of Crippling Company's Systems" (*Computerworld, May 10, 2000*)

The employee, an engineer and network administrator who was recently fired, allegedly posed as the network administrator at Omega Engineering. He launched a logic bomb that wiped out all of the firm's software and caused approximately $10 million in damages.[4] The loss of 80 jobs due to layoffs is blamed on this incident. In a case such as this, protection is difficult. This employee worked for the company for 11 years and helped to design the very systems he is accused of destroying. Would a policy of changing passwords for terminated employees help? Yes, but only if the employee has not left any unknown backdoors into the system. This particular employee had far too many responsibilities. He had the job of maintaining, securing, and backing up the company's critical programs that ran its manufacturing facilities. Prior to his termination, this company, at a minimum, should have had another party create backups and store them in an unknown, offsite storage facility.

Former employees who leave under bad circumstances are very troubling because of their knowledge. They have the ability to collect a multitude of information about the company. In many of the cases reported, the employee becomes suspicious or even paranoid about losing his or her job and begins collecting internal information in advance, and they are frequently found with company documents they had no business possessing.

Threats from Current Employees

Current employees can also wreak havoc on a company's computer system. As mentioned previously, the 2000 CSI/FBI study found that 38 percent of the firms studied experienced internal attacks, and 71 percent experienced unauthorized access from employees. The security issues discussed earlier regarding former employees also apply to current employees. The difference is the motive. Instead of vengeance, the motive may be the thrill of breaking into unauthorized data. The motive may be a scheme to earn additional income by selling customer data to underground agencies or to competitors. Another motive may be the direct embezzlement of assets.

Does corporate espionage only happen in the movies, or does it really occur? According to a U.S. Department of Justice lawyer, the losses attributed to trade secret theft amount to more than $24 billion a year, and most of these crimes are committed by insiders. The 2000 CSI/FBI study found that 44 percent of the likely sources of attack are from U.S. competitors, and 26 percent said they were motivated by the likelihood of attacks from foreign corporations. The reported dollar amounts of the losses due to thefts of propriety information came to an average cost in excess of $1 million.

---

[4]This case is still in court. The first jury found the perpetrator guilty, but this decision was later overturned by a judge on appeal. The plaintiffs are appealing that decision.

At what level are these crimes committed? A common myth is that this type of crime is conducted by low-level employees. In fact, mid-level managers are the most frequently prosecuted.[5] The strongest control mechanisms, however, are typically targeted at low-level employees. Figure 7–6 illustrates the relationship between internal controls, management override capability, and organizational hierarchy. Managerial-level employees are sometimes given access to too much user ID and password information and are also given internal control override permission. Properly segregated functions and internal control mechanisms become useless if the prescribed procedures are not followed or are allowed to be too easily overridden or ignored without the proper authorization.

Financial problems are a well-known motivation for fraud, embezzlement, and corporate espionage, and, in many cases, an individual's financial troubles are easily spotted by examining his or her credit records. One way companies can protect themselves from employees is to routinely conduct background checks, especially for information systems personnel. A 1997 survey conducted by Computerworld Inc. found that 19 out of 104 firms were victims of theft and fraudulent acts committed by the firms' own information systems' employees. Surprisingly, only 25 percent of the businesses in the survey conduct criminal history checks on their applicants for information systems personnel, and only 11 percent routinely conduct credit checks to establish whether the applicant has any financial problems. The issues surrounding background checks are further elaborated on in the box entitled "What You Don't Know about That New Employee Can Hurt You!"

FIGURE 7–6   *Internal controls, override capability, and organizational hierarchy*

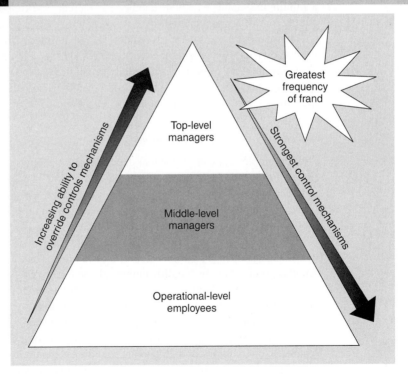

[5]Financial Executives Institute, "Safety Nets: Secrets of Effective Information Technology Controls," An Executive Report, June 1997.

E-Commerce in Practice

What You Don't Know about That New Employee Can Hurt You!

Recently, a bookkeeper, with a criminal file a foot thick, was arrested for stealing at least $2.5 million from his employers. Over a 12-year period he victimized 15 to 20 businesses. His resumé listed two prior long-term employers who did not exist. An accomplice, whom he met while doing time for fraud, gave glowing recommendations to anyone who called the phone numbers listed on his resumé.

Each of these businesses could have avoided being duped if they had done a basic employee background check costing as little as $30. Employers who background their employees significantly reduce their hiring risks. Background checks help avoid workplace violence, protect against lawsuits and damages, reduce employee theft and fraud, uncover application falsification, make the first-time right hire, and—as a result—improve the bottom line.

Employee backgrounding is simple, inexpensive, legal, and ethical when properly done.

Application Verification

A background check is sometimes called an application verification. A background check validates a candidate's job application using independent sources such as prior employers, educational institutions, criminal and civil court records, and credit records. A background check starts where reference checks leave off.

Costs for a background check are typically between $40 and $100 per candidate. The fees vary based on the number of information sources checked and the cost of accessing the sources. For example, a typical background check for a production position would include a Social Security number check, a criminal record check, and prior employer verification. Whereas, a background check for an accounting manager would also include a college education verification and a credit check.

Turnaround time is usually under a week and is determined by the information sources checked. Some information sources, such as credit reports, are online and immediately available. At the other extreme, some state and federal agencies only respond to requests by mail and may take weeks to respond.

Negligent Hiring Liability

A major driving force behind employee backgrounding is the relatively new legal doctrine of negligent hiring liabil-

ity. Negligent hiring liability effectively requires that an employer check a prospective employee's background. Courts hold employers responsible both for what they do know and *what they should have known* about their employees. While it may seem unfair, the courts have repeatedly found employers responsible for the criminal actions of employees on the job, and in some cases, off the job. The average award in security (personal safety) negligent hiring cases is more than $1 million. Essentially, the courts see a background check as cheap insurance against repeated criminal acts.

The laws and the courts generally recognize and support an employer's need to hire competent and safe employees. For example, the FCRA (Fair Credit Reporting Act) specifically identifies employment as a legitimate use of credit reports.

New Laws Protect the Providing of Information on Former Employees

In many states employers now have more latitude when giving employment references because of new laws that have changed the rules for providing information about former employees. In the past, fear of legal action has caused most employers to limit the information provided on former employees. These new laws protect the sharing of former employees' work performance and qualifications with prospective employers. Typically, the new law protects a former employer if (a) the inquiry is made by a prospective employer, (b) the communication is based on credible evidence, and (c) the information is given without malice.

Employers should reconsider how they respond to work performance and qualification inquiries from prospective employers. A basic no-comment policy may no longer be the best policy. For example, it is not hard to see how a jury could hold a company liable for a former employee's actions if it can be shown that a violent crime could have been prevented by an open, honest, and now-protected answer to a prospective employer's inquiry.

Today, employee background checks can be simple, inexpensive, legal, ethical, and extremely useful when properly done.

Source: Glenn Hammer, Founder and President of A Matter of Fact.

Perhaps the most troubling case of neglect in performing background checks occurred in 1999 when the U.S.'s Federal Aviation Administration (FAA) did not perform background checks on programmers hired to fix Y2K problems:

> The FAA allowed foreign citizens—including 36 Chinese nationals, as well as citizens of Pakistan, Ukraine, Britain, and Ethiopia—access to 15 of its 153 critical computer systems, according to a report issued by the General Accounting Office (GAO), the investigative arm of Congress. (*Computerworld Online, January 5, 2000*)

The FAA has policies and procedures, they just did not follow them.

Recent **negligent hiring** laws enacted in approximately 30 states allow firms to be held liable for actions their employees take after-hours if the firm could have prevented the act. This prevention includes knowledge of the employee's past offenses. For example, if an employee steals customer data stored by the employing firm, such as credit card information, and sells it to an underground source, the damages incurred by the customers (e.g. losses due to fraudulent credit card charges) can potentially be collected by the employer if it did not do a background check that would have revealed the employee's previous criminal background.

Sniffers

Most Intranets are configured so that the computers connected to it share a communication channel. This communication channel serves as the passageway by which all data are transmitted, including, but not limited to, messages, documents, user IDs, and passwords. If this information is sent over a shared channel, it has the potential to be intercepted, called *sniffing,* by another computer station. This situation becomes even more troublesome as open Internet connection cables can increasingly be found in office buildings that are wired to accommodate laptop computers and future growth, and in areas with minimal to no physical security.

Sniffer software can be easily downloaded from the Internet for free, or it can be found in popular commercial software. A user who has such software and is able to connect to one of the many cables commonly found in office buildings can potentially sniff, or capture and view, unauthorized data. The perpetrator's own work computer, with the right software, may do the trick.

Once the perpetrator has the connection to the Intranet and the appropriate software, all he or she needs to do is sit back and wait for co-workers to begin sending sensitive files. Some of these data are in clear-text form, such as File Transfer Protocol (FTP) and TELNET passwords, and of course some text files. How many firms are sending unencrypted passwords? According to the 2000 CSI/FBI survey, only 50 percent of the firms studied are using encryption log-ins, meaning that the other 50 percent are potential targets of password theft through sniffing techniques.

If all data is transmitted in a **virtual private network (VPN),** which is an encrypted telecommunication tunnel, then the data are secure unless the **session key** is obtained. A session key is the encryption/decryption algorithm used to encode/decode a specific message. The perpetrator may have the capability to decrypt encrypted messages if he or she can locate the session key from earlier data. Some sniffers only allow the user to sniff data passing through his or her computer, while other sniffers allow the perpetrator to see all data being transferred across the physical subnet. Switched networks that distribute packets along different routes can prevent against successful interception of all packets. How many firms use VPNs? According to the 2000 CSI/FBI survey, only 38 percent of the business-to-consumer and 56 percent of the business-to-business firms are using VPNs.

E-Commerce in Practice

Tool Helps Sniff Out Network Snoopers

Some organizations worry that techies armed with network analyzers can snoop on any packet to extract passwords, eyes-only memos, and other sensitive data.

Now Network Associates Inc. in Santa Clara, Calif., is attempting to allay those fears with security options for its Distributed Sniffer System (DSS).

New software for this shared protocol analyzer will limit capabilities for three levels of users. The help desk can view only performance statistics, for example, while troubleshooters and administrators get more power to peek inside packets.

The package also adds an authentication step, requiring a password for access, and then tracks user activity.

"Right now, we can't tell who is running the DSS software," said Brian Leafe, senior technical analyst at Liberty Mutual Insurance Co. in Portsmouth, N.H.

That situation raises "massive concerns" by auditors in financial institutions and the human resources departments of most large corporations, according to Ray Paquet, a management analyst at Gartner Group Inc. in Stamford, Conn.

Controls in the new DSS software "can alleviate some of the paranoia," Paquet said. But the safeguards don't apply to the stand-alone Sniffer, the market-leading protocol analyzer found in nearly every network operation center. Someone could still plug that analyzer directly in to the network and decode any packets, Paquet said.

Source: Patrick Dryden, "News," © *Computerworld Online,* January 12, 1998.

Sniffers do have legitimate uses by network administrators in monitoring a network's activity, and this commercial network software continues to be available to perform these tasks. Much concern has been raised, however, to the possible risks firms may face as a result of the unauthorized use of such products. As a result, some sniffer detection software is on the market. However, these sniffer detectors are not foolproof. In the box entitled "Tool Helps Sniff Out Network Snoopers," the concerns raised by organizations regarding sniffers are mentioned. Some of the more common commercial network sniffers can detect whether other installations of the same software are running. While this is helpful in detecting some users, hackers with other network sniffers cannot be detected. Unfortunately, because networks were designed to foster the sharing of information and peripheral devices, controlling the unauthorized interception of shared data is proving to be a difficult feature for software companies to deliver. Because sensitive data is held and transmitted on these networks, auditors are becoming increasingly concerned. As mentioned in the box, new software can alleviate *some* of the paranoia, but ultimately, it cannot prevent a determined user from capturing data. Systems with single use password devices might deter hackers from using sniffers to capture passwords since the intercepted data is encrypted. Further, if the password itself is intercepted, it cannot be used after a very short period of time, e.g., a matter of seconds.

Financial Fraud

Access to data and programs by insiders have always been a primary concern to auditors. The internal control devices were easier to implement and monitor in centralized, traditional processing environments, where physical access to programs and data was more easily guarded than in distributed processing and client/server applications.

In one recent, extremely large financial fraud case, city employees in Brooklyn, New York, used electronic databases to defraud the city of New York of $20 million. Collusion between several workers, including the former Deputy Tax Collector, occurred. This collusion allowed the electronic elimination and reduction of $13 million in property taxes and $7 million in accrued interest. What motivation did the workers have to engage in such acts? They received bribes from taxpayers to wipe out or lessen their tax bills. Some property owners would pay the workers involved in the scheme anywhere from 10 to 30 percent of their tax bill to have the tax bill reduced or eliminated.

Employee access to highly sensitive databases allowed the city employees to become "computer hackers and [they] used city computers to electronically pickpocket the city of New York out of millions and millions and millions of dollars."[6] As in many cases like this one, the fraud scheme was uncovered by a tip from a fellow employee. The Deputy Tax Collector had previously been terminated by the city for receiving city contracts for which he was not eligible. After his termination, he continued his involvement with the fraud scheme by working with his former employees, staff members who updated computerized property tax information and received tax payments.

Properly implemented control devices at the operational level may have helped in this situation, but the key elements were "computer glitches," the involvement of management, the Deputy Tax Collector, and the tempting opportunity to exponentially increase earnings. As mentioned earlier, internal controls must be in place at all levels, not just the operational level. The role of the internal auditor with a need for technical expertise in network technology is becoming increasingly important. The internal auditors are the company's guards over all types of assets and resources, and they should have a direct reporting line to the board of directors or equivalent.

Downloading of Data

Intranets that allow connections between employee computers and centrally located databases increase the risk of unauthorized access and copying of data by employees. As mentioned earlier, some employees with malicious intent may download sensitive data because they fear the loss of their job. Employees may also download data for the resale value, such as employee Social Security numbers, customer credit card information, customer lists and preferences, recipe formulas, design specifications, financial data, etc.

Properly designed **user access control tables** that define the access, read, and write privileges of every user, or class of users, should help to prevent employees from accessing unauthorized data. Employees, however, often share passwords to assist one another for various reasons. A trusting employee who shares his or her password may be opening a door for another employee to access and download a combination of data elements that may have trade-secret or financial value. Single-use passwords and other strong authentication techniques are a good preventive measure to this type of scheme and are discussed in Chapter 8. Further, logs should be kept of all sensitive and mission-critical data that are accessed, downloaded, or printed. A good detective policy is sending employees a summary of such activity at certain intervals and requesting that they verify the performance of such acts.

---

[6]Lynda Richardson, "29 Arrested in Tax Fraud Scheme Described as New York's Largest," *The New York Times,* November 22, 1996.

E-mail Spoofing

E-mail spoofing occurs when a perpetrator, either from inside the Intranet or externally from the Internet, poses as another valid Intranet user. E-mail spoofing is relatively easy to do in many networked environments; one only needs to change one's identity in many e-mail packages to trick the recipient into thinking the sender is someone else. Most individuals will believe the name and user ID information in the header section of the e-mail message.

One disturbing reason for posing as another user may be to pose as the system administrator and obtain sensitive information, a method known as *social engineering.* The masquerader a.k.a."administrator" sends a message:

Return-Path: Robert.Kendi@yourcompany.com

Organization: Your Company, Inc.

Subject: Urgent account information

References: 29347kdjfid987384@book.dfjkl.com

To: "kkc@yourcompany.com" <kkcyourcompany.com>

Date: Fri, 31 Oct 2001 07:00:02

Return-Receipt-To:"Robert.Kendi"

Karen,

Last night I was installing an upgrade to the network operating system and during the conversion process some files were corrupted. The file containing your password is unreadable. You will probably encounter trouble accessing some files. I must re-enter your account information in order for all applications to function properly. Please e-mail your password to me as soon as possible. Thanks.

Bob

Assuming the user hits the reply key, the response containing the password information could be sent back to the masquerader, not the true network administrator. The masquerader now has the password or password file and can gain access to the targeted user's data and application programs. E-mail spoofing can be prevented and detected with digital signatures, which are discussed in Chapter 10.

Both internal and external users may engage in these types of actions. External users may be more easily thwarted if a firewall is in place that has a router that rejects external message packets that have an internal network source address.

Social Engineering

Another mechanism to help break and enter into computer systems is called **social engineering.** Social engineering is a method used by intruders to obtain passwords, network operating system, and firewall configuration data from employees willing to help others do their jobs. Human beings are considered by social engineers to be the weakest link in security controls. They play on the general trusting nature of humans and their natural instinct to help others do their jobs. In other scenarios, the social engineer may use anger or play on the employee's sympathy to get information.

Recall the example given in the previous section where the perpetrator poses as the network administrator, except this time the tone of the message is changed:

Return-Path: Robert.Kendi@yourcompany.com

Organization: Your Company, Inc.

Subject: Urgent account information

References: 29347kdjfid987384@book.dfjkl.com

To: "kkc@yourcompany.com" <kkc@yourcompany.com>

Date: Fri, 31 Oct 2001 02:00:02

Return-Receipt-To:"Robert.Kendi"

Karen,

Good morning . . . I hope you had a better evening than I did last night. I was here until the wee hours of the morning installing an upgrade to the network operating system. (You'll notice I am sending this to you at 2:00 a.m.!) During the conversion process some files were corrupted (just my luck). The file containing your password is unreadable. You will probably encounter trouble accessing some files . . . Oh no! I just spilled coffee all over the manual! This is definitely not my week :—(

Anyway, the only way I know to fix it is to re-enter your account information in order for all applications to function properly. I know you are busy, but I really need to get everything working properly or well, I don't even want to think about that. Would you please e-mail your password to me so I can get the system back on track?

Thanks a million,

Bob

The same information is requested, but the tone is warm and fuzzy and meant to draw sympathy from Karen so that she will be eager to help "poor Bob". The perpetrator in this case can be either an internal or external spoofer. E-mail addresses and titles of employees are increasingly easy to find on corporate websites. Titles and e-mail addresses are very valuable pieces of information to the social engineer. A corporate phone book containing all employee listings is probably the single most valuable piece of information. Names of technical support personnel, executives, and lower-level employees are at the social engineer's fingertips.

Most commonly, the social engineer uses the telephone to gain information by calling and posing as a service person, posing as a much higher level executive than the immediate supervisor or requesting information from the "help" desk. Different types of telephone rings for inside and outside calls and internal caller ID systems are a good way to warn employees whether the call is an inside or outside call. A policy of never giving sensitive or classified information over the phone is important. In addition, users should never give passwords to other users, even if they claim to be administrators. No problems require an administrator to obtain a user's password. Firms should design computer security policies to clearly educate employees regarding the definition of sensitive and classified information.

RISKS ASSOCIATED WITH BUSINESS TRANSACTION DATA TRANSFERRED BETWEEN TRADING PARTNERS

Electronic data interchange (EDI) systems are the predecessors to Extranets. Pure EDI systems are still in existence, but many are being revamped to leverage the opportunities offered by the Internet. Extranets are another type of network in addition to Intranets and the Internet. In this section, Extranets are introduced, and their relationship to other networking concepts is explored. Also included in this section is a discussion of the risks associated with sending important business transaction data over Extranets and the Internet.

Intranets, Extranets, and Internet Relationships

An **Extranet** is a group network that uses Internet technology to connect business partners, including suppliers, customers, distribution service providers, or any other businesses engaging in collaborative ventures. One may argue that Extranets are merely extensions of EDI that include Internet channels and the trading of a wider variety of information other than inventory, ordering, and payment data. Extranets may be designed to allow authorized trading partners to link together portions of their Intranets. A single firm may be a member of several Extranets.

How do Extranets differ from the Internet? A clear answer is not easy to derive. Extranets may use Internet routes and ISPs to transmit their data. An ISP is a for-profit company that provides access to the Internet. One clear answer can be given about Extranets: Although it is admittedly ambiguous, Extranets are wider in scope than Intranets, but are only a subset of the Internet. The relationship between Intranets, Extranets, and the Internet is depicted in Figure 7–7. The entire network depicted is the Internet. Three

FIGURE 7–7   *Intranets, Extranets, and the Internet*

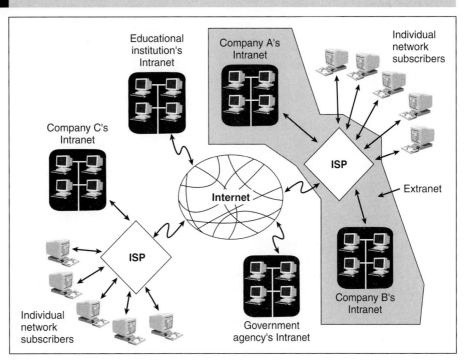

E-Commerce in Practice

Moving from Intranet to Extranet Not Easy

External Links Need Better Security and Interfaces

Converting an Intranet into an Extranet isn't as simple as flipping a switch.

Just ask St. Onge Co., a materials handling consulting firm in York, Pa. Having created a homegrown Intranet, the company wants to make its information available to customers on an Extranet.

"We offer a very focused subject matter and content other firms don't have, and we think we have a great service to offer," said Paul Evanko, a vice president at St. Onge, who sponsored the portal project. "The knowledge we have at St. Onge is unique, and we realized that this was a good medium to make that information known to our customers."

Yet starting with an existing portal often requires scaling hardware for higher Web traffic, adding slicker user interfaces for external users and implementing airtight security.

"Security concerns are the No. 1 reason companies are not doing this," said Wayne Eckerson, an analyst at Patricia Seybold Group Inc. in Boston.

Eckerson recommends implementing session management techniques to shut down Web sessions if activity ceases, thereby limiting exposure to unauthorized users.

Loancity.com Inc., an online residential mortgage financier and services company, originally developed an internal portal based on InfoImage Inc.'s Freedom software to give its employees access to reports and loan processing data. Bruce Maurier, vice president of internal systems at Loancity in San Jose says he plans to give mortgage brokers information about in-progress loans.

"The traditional model involves making phone calls and chewing your fingernails waiting for an answer. Now, in a matter of seconds the broker gets status on where the loan stands in our pipeline," he said. "We still have to be selective about what information we give our affiliates access to."

In addition to offering self-service, companies should offer buying opportunities along the way, says analyst Phil Russom at Hurwitz Group Inc. in Framingham. Mass. "Savvy IT shops will offer self-service, plus an opportunity to purchase their service or product right along with that information," he said.

St. Onge wants to do just that when it debuts its Intranet-turned-portal by year's end, hoping the information turns browsers into paid customers. "We think there is more value than the potential danger that people will do their own consulting" using information they gained from the site, said Art St. Onge, president of the company that bears his name. "We hope there might very well be a desire to get more knowledge on the part of a warehouse operator to confirm a conclusion he came to, and we would be the natural ones to contact."

Some firms find that large customers demand access to their Intranets.

Landing the U.S. Postal Service and the Department of Defense as customers meant that DHL Worldwide Express needed to provide broad access to corporate information about shipment timetables, costs, and tracking. The Redwood City, Calif.–based international package delivery firm extended special Extranet privileges to the Postal Service and the Defense Department last year to handle shipments from U.S. bases to Bosnia.

"They required a single Extranet location that gives them visibility into our shipment process," said Barney Sene, director of e-commerce systems at DHL. "So we provided it."

Source: Lee Copeland, © *Computerworld Online,* November 8, 1999.

company Intranets, one educational institution Intranet, one government agency, and numerous individual network subscribers are all parties connected to the Internet via different sources in this depiction. Obviously, this is only a very elemental representation of the vast numbers of parties connected to the Internet. The multiple routes connecting the Internet illustrate that the Internet is itself a network of networks. As can be seen in this figure, Company A and Company B may "connect" their applications and data to form what is called an Extranet. If Company C is a supplier to Company B, then Company C could also enter into another Extranet with Company B.

Why are firms beginning to invest in Extranets? One reason that interest and investment in Extranets is on the rise is the ease with which firms' systems can be interfaced with the Internet. In the box entitled "Moving from Intranet to Extranet Not Easy," DHL Worldwide Express explains that if it wanted the US Postal Service and the Department of Defense as customers that it had to make the move. Another business, St. Onge, discusses the security challenges in moving from an Intranet to an Extranet. Open standards, the ability to use different database systems and Web browser software on different hardware platforms are big advantages to businesses wanting to develop and improve their telecommunication links with other businesses.

In the box entitled "Extranets Put IS in Risky Position," Fruit of the Loom Inc. opened up their Intranets to include distributors in the design process. General Electric Co. asserts that they are less expensive and easier (in theory) to build. Both General Electric and Fruit of the Loom ran into typical systems implementation problems that have plagued internal end user satisfaction levels for a long time—unhappiness with the restrictions of the system and the feeling of being excluded by some parties. The only difference is that the end users are now parties external to the firm. GE had to revamp its Extranet to have longer bidding deadlines and blind bids by vendors. Fruit of the Loom had to expand its Extranet to include additional distributors that felt neglected and somewhat slighted by being excluded from the Extranet design process.

The data being exchanged by both GE and Fruit of the Loom with their Extranet partners is very sensitive, as well as mission critical. This includes contract bids and design specifications. In general, the Extranets need to have well-designed security controls. This may involve connecting partners via a leased line or a VPN that encrypts data to maintain confidentiality. Other Extranets may only rely on firewalls. By implementing an Extranet, the entire network becomes as vulnerable as the most vulnerable link. End-to-end security measures are a crucial factor for Extranet members, and these security issues and techniques are discussed in Chapter 11.

Data Interception

Regardless of whether the data being transferred over the Internet are between two firms connected via an Extranet or whether it is between an individual user and an online merchant or service provider, the interception of data is a serious concern. Figure 7–8 illustrates the risks faced by firms sending data over the Internet. Because the message is broken into packets and the individual packets may travel over different routes to their destination, the most vulnerable points of interception are the points of entry to, and exit from, the Internet. Each of the concerns presented in Figure 7–8 is discussed and the security remedies are presented in greater detail in Chapters 10 and 11. Strong encryption is a recommended method of sending and storing data. However only 62 percent of the firms studied in the 2000 CSI/FBI study use some form of data encryption for at least some of their data files.

Message Origin Authentication

The recipient of the message needs to be sure that the message he or she is receiving is really from the party the message claims is the sender. Spoofing techniques discussed earlier are a concern. How can forged messages be a danger to a company? They can be used to simulate bogus orders and cause production schedules to be erroneously altered. They may be used to request classified information from a seemingly valid source. They may be used to issue false directives to employees of a firm. For example, if a malicious intruder sends e-mail messages to the sales force of a company and makes the message

E-Commerce in Practice

Extranets Put IS in Risky Position

General Electric Co. says it halved its 14-day purchasing cycle by communicating with suppliers over an Extranet instead of the old-fashioned trio of phone, fax, and postal mail.

But there is a secret behind that success story: The first version of the application upset GE's suppliers so much, they demanded that it be redesigned.

"Nobody liked it," said Rich Wilson, operations manager at Matrix Tool & Machine, Inc., a GE supplier in Mentor, Ohio. The problem was that the open online bidding process meant suppliers were constantly undercutting one another's bids.

Extranet builders face various delicate business issues when they create a World Wide Web application for business-to-business electronic commerce. Some question whether information systems departments can be trusted to run Extranet projects that, if handled poorly, could hurt relations with critical trading partners.

"If it's done wrong, an Extranet is potentially much more damaging" than a simple informational website, said Troy Eid, executive director of InfoTest International in Denver. InfoTest is developing a massive Extranet for the manufacturing industry.

Extranets are applications that let outsiders, such as suppliers or customers, into internal information systems via specially secured websites. They are less expensive than electronic data interchange (EDI) systems and, in theory, easier to build. But even savvy GE, which runs one of the most highly touted Extranets, tripped on a land mine. Besides letting suppliers who were chasing contracts see and undercut one another's bids, the forerunner to the company's Trading Process Network allowed bidding only during certain hours of the day.

"You would see vendors online bidding against you at 5 o'clock. At 5:10, they cut it off. During that 10-minute time frame, you'd be frantically putting in prices," Wilson said. GE learned that suppliers must be included in the Extranet design process. Now bids are blind, and deadlines are revealed days in advance. And Wilson is happy.

Other potential Extranet pitfalls include the following:

- Business partners that aren't included in the Extranet design team may accuse the company of playing favorites with other suppliers.

- The selection of certain Extranet technologies could exclude businesses that can't or won't use those technologies.

- The Extranet operator may be liable for the loss of business operations at other companies if the Extranet crashes.

- Training Extranet users at other firms is a never-ending chore.

It's also dangerous to put IS workers who are inexperienced with business issues in charge of creating an Extranet. Decisions about an application that could become a critical money-moving channel "are not to be made in isolation by the IT department," Eid advised.

That's because Extranets, more than other technology projects, put IS in a position to possibly sour business relationships, said David Annis, vice president of information technology at ITT Hartford Group, Inc. in Hartford, Conn. "This is more sensitive than it's ever been," Annis said.

The fear is that zealous tech-heads will create an Extranet that may be technologically sound but is shot through with legal or business problems. For example, a site that forces users to run fancy Java applets to get at needed information may upset companies that have banned Java.

Some companies have recruited business-side managers to, in part, prevent business snafus in their electronic-commerce projects. For example, Mark Gallagher, first vice president of technology administration at Chicago-based First Chicago NBD Corp., is a former investment banker. John Rudin was promoted to chief information officer at Reynolds Metals Co. in Richmond, Va., after 30 years of distinctly nontechnical jobs at the aluminum unit.

Meanwhile, Fruit of the Loom, Inc. had to play politics when it put up an Extranet for its highly competitive clothing distributors last March. The Bowling Green, Ky., company wanted to include distributors in the design process, but it also wanted to avoid the "too many cooks" syndrome. When the company limited the number of participants, some excluded distributors felt slighted, said Patrick Flynn, vice president of systems development at Fruit of the Loom. The excluded distributors worried that chosen collaborators influenced the Extranet's design in their own favor. To soothe raw feelings, Flynn said he wants to get as many partners online as quickly as he can. Twenty-three are up so far, and another 12 are in the works.

When choosing a supplier or customer to collaborate with on Extranet design, look for an "average Joe," Eid advised. "An Extranet built with your most savvy technical partner in mind will likely be difficult or plain impossible for others to use," he said.

Source: Kim Nash, *Computerworld Online News*, May 27, 1997. © Computerworld, Inc.

| **FIGURE 7–8** | *Risks faced by messages sent over the Internet* |

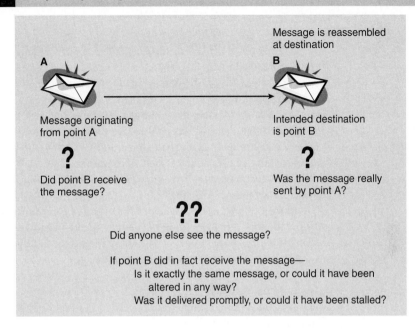

appear as if it is coming from the vice president of sales, he or she may be able to affect the sales strategy being promoted by the sales force. If the intruder is a competitor, he or she could maliciously use this act to his or her advantage. The intruder could also send e-mail messages changing meeting times with customers so that the sales force arrives late, if they arrive at all. Another example would be a client who sends his or her stockbroker an e-mail to buy stock. After the stock plummets, the client attempts to deny ever sending the e-mail message.

Thus, ensuring that the message received was sent by whom it claims to be sent by is extremely important. In electronic commerce transactions, **nonrepudiation** is a key element. Nonrepudiation is the provision of proof of the origin, receipt, and contents of an electronic message. For example, the trading partner who receives a purchase request wants to be able to prove, if necessary, that the seller placed an order. This proof may be necessary in the event that the purchasing partner refuses receipt of goods or refuses to pay for the goods by claiming that he or she did not order them. Authentication techniques to verify the sender, digital signatures, and nonrepudiation services are techniques available to ensure the sender is who he or she claims.

Proof of Delivery

The sender of the message needs **proof of delivery** to be assured that the message was received by the intended recipient. If purchase requests or product information requests are intercepted, a company's customer relations and profitability can suffer. Consider the example given earlier. If the actual vice president of sales issues a valid directive to lower the price on a certain product line and push its sales to reduce storage and spoilage costs, and the intruder intercepts the message and prevents the intended recipients, the sales force, from receiving the message, the directive will not be carried out. By the time the sales force is informed of the directive, precious time may have been wasted and large amounts of inventory may have been spoiled. Enhanced message protection services, such as proof of delivery or return receipts, nonrepudiation services and time stamping, are techniques available to ensure the sender that its message was received by the intended recipients.

Message Integrity and Unauthorized Viewing of Messages

If the intended recipient does in fact receive the message, is it exactly the same message as the one originally sent? In other words, was the original message altered in any way? Was **message integrity** upheld? If the valid message from the vice president of sales is altered so that the product line to be put on sale is changed, the message is still from the VP of sales and it is still received by the intended recipients. The message origin and proof of delivery techniques may appear to be in order, but the contents of the message have been altered. Techniques such as digesting, digital signatures, and encryption are available to maintain integrity, authenticity, and confidentiality, respectively. These techniques are explained in Chapter 10.

Another related issue is whether the message was viewed by anyone else, even if it was not altered. The prevention of the viewing of messages containing sensitive information, such as contract bids is extremely important. Strong encryption techniques are useful to help provide confidentiality of messages.

Timely Delivery of Messages

Messages may flow through various service agents before reaching their destination. They may also be placed into a store-and-forward mailbox. The length of time the message is stored before it is forwarded is a key issue for applications that require immediate receipt of messages. A devious perpetrator may stall certain messages for a matter of minutes, hours, or even days. For the case of GE, where bids for contracts are received electronically, stalling one of the bids for even a few minutes can determine whether that bid is received by the deadline. A digital **time-stamp signature** is a detective device that may be used to determine the actual time a message was sent.

RISKS ASSOCIATED WITH CONFIDENTIALLY MAINTAINED ARCHIVAL, MASTER FILE, AND REFERENCE DATA

Except for the discussion of Intranet-associated risks, the risks discussed thus far have dealt with data that are transmitted, such as transaction data, over the Internet. This section discusses the risks to data that are stored by a site that is connected to the Internet. When a firm has archival, master file, or reference data stored on a site computer that is connected to the Internet, it must consider the fact that perpetrators may penetrate the firewalls erected to prevent unauthorized users from accessing data.

As firms begin to embrace the concepts of the Internet and Extranets, the issue of controlled sharing of data becomes a challenge. **Firewalls** are techniques used to limit and control access to hardware, software, and data from users outside of the local network. Firewalls are used to keep intruders out, but if data are to be shared, how does the firewall determine which users are allowed to interact with the data? Imagine a castle with a fortress around it with guards posted at various spots both outside and inside the castle. The initial guard who allows entry into the fortress must determine whether the person wanting to gain entry to the castle is a friend or foe. If a foe is masquerading as a friend and gains entry, they will only get so far in the castle before they encounter another guard. Does the guard inside the castle again question the visitor, or

FIGURE 7–9	*Firewalls*

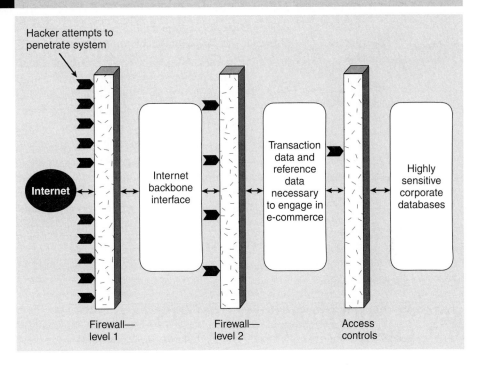

do they assume that if they got past the first guard they must belong in the castle? Firewalls are akin to these guards, and they should repeatedly verify the status of users. Unfortunately, some firms have their tightest controls at the outside firewall level and substantially weaker controls at subsequent levels. This is based on the philosophy that the first line of defense is so strong that they do not need to worry so much about subsequent levels. Penetrating the various levels of firewalls is a challenge to many hackers.

Figure 7–9 illustrates how firewalls work in general. Each firm's exact configuration may vary of course, but a general model such as the one depicted in the figure portrays the separation of different categories of data and applications. The process by which a firm determines what resources need to be protected is called **risk assessment.** The organization classifies resources into sensitivity levels through this process. Once resources are classified, then a security strategy can be crafted. All too often, companies begin securing data, networks, programs, etc., before they understand how sensitive each piece is. This "backward" strategy is usually a waste of time and money.

Each firewall level represents another hurdle that a hacker must overcome in order to get to the sensitive data or programs. Firewalls will be discussed in greater detail in Chapter 11. For now, understanding that different types of data and applications may need different levels of protection is important. The most sensitive and confidential data should be placed at the level behind the most fortresses. These added layers are not without added costs, however, and not just financial costs, but also costs in efficiency and response time. The greater the number of firewalls and security devices, the slower the response time will most likely be for those parties interacting with the firm's site.

Assuming that a hacker does penetrate the system, what damage can they do? The greatest risks are

- *Destruction of data.* A malicious perpetrator may delete important transaction or master file data with the intent of disrupting business operations
- *Alteration of data.* A malicious perpetrator may alter the data. Sometimes these acts may go unnoticed for some time and may cause the firm to incur financial losses. For example, if a perpetrator alters the price file, orders may unknowingly be transacted with trading partners at the wrong price. Because transactions have not been lost, a red flag alerting management that prices are incorrect may not be raised until a human reviews an invoice and questions the transaction price.
- *Unauthorized use of data.* The perpetrator may use the data to gain an advantage over a competitor. Viewing contract bidding data, for example, would allow a company to more accurately anticipate the amount a competitor will bid for a contract and then undercut that bid just enough to win the contract.
- *Alteration of applications.* The perpetrator may alter the program so that it makes erroneous calculations.

Firewall design issues that can be used to reduce these risks are discussed in Chapter 11.

RISKS ASSOCIATED WITH VIRUSES AND MALICIOUS CODE OVERFLOWS

This section covers the risks of infection from viruses, Trojan horses, and other malicious codes. These techniques can result in computer downtime or loss of data.

Viruses

With the increasing use of e-mail and downloaded data and programs from the Internet, virus infections are becoming more prevalent. The 2000 CSI/FBI study found that 70 percent of all firms studied suffered losses from computer viruses in the last year. Further, a study conducted by Computer Economics, Inc. reported that the 1999 economic effect of viruses worldwide was $12.1 billion. In May 2000, a new bug, the "I Love You" bug, hit hard and will likely cause the 2000 losses to soar much higher than 1999. This bug is discussed in the box entitled "Love Bug Throws Crippling Arrows at E-mail Systems."

The greatest reported effects of viruses are loss of productivity and unavailability of personal computers, difficulty reading and saving files, and corrupted files. What is a virus? A **virus** is malicious programming that possesses three characteristics:

- It replicates itself in some form.
- It is incorporated into program code or macro code without consent.
- It performs unrequested and oftentimes destructive acts.

Many different permutations of viruses have been created. Viruses can

- Infect the boot portion of a secondary storage device (memory resident virus).
- Infect executable files.
- Infect any type of file that can have a macro attached (e.g., word processing and spreadsheet files).
- Remain dormant for a period of time before beginning their destruction.
- Slowly destruct files over time.

E-Commerce in Practice

Love Bug Throws Crippling Arrows at E-Mail Systems

In May 2000, the phrase "I Love You" became the most dreaded phrase for IT managers and personnel to see in e-mail headers. The first day the virus hit, it hit hard. It infected a staggering 45 million e-mail users the first day alone.

The losses attributed to this bug are estimated by Computer Economics Inc. to be in excess of $6 billion.

The Love Bug, as it was called, contained a simple message in the subject line, "I LOVE YOU." Apparently not many e-mail users were able to resist the temptation to open the attachment as instructed in the text of the e-mail. Once opened, the malicious visual basic script code sends the same message to everyone listed in the user's e-mail address book. The increased e-mail load degraded and even shut down many businesses' servers for quite a while.

The virus also had the capability to capture e-mail passwords, which if they were stored unencrypted, could be used to access Internet and e-mail accounts.

More flexible and powerful e-mail systems that allow all types of files to be sent as attachments are a serious virus risk since attachments can contain executable applications or documents embedded with macros. Word processing documents and spreadsheets are among such macro-friendly files. A **macro virus** can be embedded in a document. When the recipient opens the document, the macro may be immediately executed and the virus spread.

Virus detection programs, known as **anti-virus software,** can help detect known viruses and sometimes clean them from the drive without any damage being inflicted. A problem with anti-virus programs is that they can only scan for known viruses. Because new viruses are constantly being created, one cannot be absolutely sure that all viruses will be detected. Another detective virus protection software method is to monitor and report any attempts to alter any file with an executable extension, such as ".exe". Detecting viruses embedded in e-mail messages is difficult since most e-mail packages do not scan for viruses. E-mail vendors are beginning to address the macro virus e-mail issue. New versions of software are beginning to help users protect themselves against macro viruses by warning the user when macros are embedded in a file that is requested to be opened. If the user is suspicious, they may choose not to open the file and thus, the embedded macro does not have the opportunity to execute and inflict harm.

While macro viruses are more than twice as prevalent as boot viruses, infections from **boot viruses,** such as Michaelangelo, attack the boot sector of a storage device, such as a hard drive, CD RW drive, or floppy diskette. Typically, the virus displaces the boot information to another location and replaces it with the virus program so that the virus becomes memory-resident upon boot up. The amount of available free memory diminishes and, in some cases, the virus erases portions of the hard drive, including the part that houses the system software, thus making the computer unbootable.

The implementation of good security measures against various forms of viruses is important. Unfortunately, effective measures such as virus scanning software take time to run, and employees may not be willing to comply. Each organization needs to consider the best way to successfully employ the widespread use of virus scanning software. Another issue is keeping the virus scanning software updated. New viruses are continuously being detected. Virus scanning software can only scan for known viruses. Thus, most virus scanning software packages have frequent updates to their packages to include newly found viruses.

Trojan Horses

A **Trojan horse** is similar to a virus in that it can unknowingly infiltrate a computer system and, unbeknown to the user, wreak havoc, but it is dissimilar in one very important manner. Trojan horses do not replicate. Instead, they sneak into the system by attaching themselves to what appears to be a legitimate program or file. An example of this is the "AOL4FREE.COM" program. As the name implies, it gives potential victims the impression that they can download the software for free access to AOL. If a user does download it or receive it as an attachment to an e-mail file and executes it by double-clicking on the file, his or her hard drive will be erased. The program does not attempt to replicate itself from disk to disk or platform to platform; it sneaks into the system as a legitimate software offer and performs its damage, erasing the hard drive. The "I Love You" bug is also an example of a Trojan Horse, tempting users to open the malicious code file and then inflicting its damage upon executing. Trojan horses are more difficult to detect by virus scanning software because they do not replicate.

Hoaxes

Another concern is **virus hoaxes.** These hoaxes are false alarms about viruses sent out via e-mail. The hoaxes do not infect systems, but they are very costly to investigate. The Computer Incident Advisory Capability (CIAC) is concerned with viruses, Trojan horses, and other malicious or detrimental computer activities. The CIAC reports that they "are spending much more time de-bunking hoaxes than handling real viruses." One hoax, the Irina Virus Hoax, was circulated by an electronic publishing company to draw attention to a newly published book with the same name. A few of the many hoaxes that have appeared include the Good Times Virus Hoax, Deeyenda Virus Hoax, Ghost.exe, and Death Ray.

The CIAC has two pieces of evidence that may raise red flags that a warning received is really a hoax:

- The warning urges you to pass it on to others.
- The warning indicates that it is a Federal Communication Commission (FCC) warning—the FCC asserts they never have, and they never will, issue a warning.

Valid warnings are typically issued by authoritative sources such as the CIAC and the Computer Emergency Response Team (CERT), which are digitally signed messages using pretty good privacy (PGP).

Buffer Overflows

Hackers may cause **buffer overflows** by exploiting known or suspected holes in the resource handling section of operating systems. The perpetrator basically crashes the system or "smashes the stack" by writing too many characters into a word buffer array. The extra characters, the overflow, may be placed in an unauthorized root section of the system. The extra characters may form machine language code that can contain some very potent bugs, which may crash the system or give unauthorized access to the system. Numerous support groups are on the Internet sharing their fixes and patches to these bugs. Unfortunately, hackers also share their techniques and can actually learn from the posted "fixes" to such problems and use the knowledge to launch an attack on a platform that has yet to patch the system's hole.

IMPLICATIONS FOR THE ACCOUNTING PROFESSION

At the heart of a firm's financial reporting system are its underlying transaction processing systems. The information compiled by the financial reporting system is only as good as the underlying data. A primary responsibility of the traditional assurance function performed by accounting firms is to assess the integrity of the transaction processing systems. To adequately perform this role, accountants must understand the entire environment in which the system operates. Further, accountants provide services beyond the traditional assurance function, such as website assurance, and the provision of these services requires accountants to thoroughly understand the risks posed by networked systems. Only after risks are identified can they be adequately managed; the following chapter explores risk management.

Intranets and Internal Controls

For years, accountants have been aware of the risks imposed by employees. Prevention against and detection of embezzlement schemes and sabotage by insiders are key tasks performed by the traditional assurance function. Internal controls, such as segregation of functions, are designed to prevent adverse events from occurring. The evaluation of the adequacy of internal controls is conducted during every assurance engagement. This assessment must include the controls over Intranets if they contain any data or processing systems that either directly or indirectly affect the financial statements or other mission critical data. As mentioned earlier, Boeing Co. identified more than 2,300 major Intranet sites in its organization, and they were not sure that all Intranets had been identified and included in that estimate. If an accounting firm is to properly conduct its internal control analysis function, it must:

- Know the exact number of Intranets and servers.
- Be aware of the data and processing methods contained on each Intranet.
- Decide which Intranets contain data and processing methods within the domain of the audit engagement.
- Understand the configuration and internetworking infrastructure.
- Assess the security methods employed over data accessible by the Intranets, including protection methods and policies against malicious programming code.

Internet and Internal Controls

Firms that engage in Internet-based e-commerce operate in an environment with significantly greater risks than firms with internal transaction processing systems that have no public Extranet or Intranet connection. As with Intranets, if the Internet-based systems either directly or indirectly affect the financial statements or mission critical data, then the analysis of the adequacy of related controls falls under the traditional assurance function. Specifically, accountants must

- Know the exact number of Internet entry points (gateway servers).
- Know the location of firewalls and their exact configurations.
- Know the location of other security devices and their exact configurations or procedures.
- Understand thoroughly the network configuration of any internals systems that are linked in any fashion to the gateway servers.

- Understand the data access methods for data linked in any way to the gateway servers.
- Assess the security of data and processing methods linked in any way to the gateway servers, including protection methods and policies against malicious program code.
- Understand the processing methods of systems with which the company shares data over the Internet, as well as the integrity and reliability of such systems.
- Understand the processing methods and configurations of any ISPs or VANs used, as well as the integrity and reliability of such systems.

Website Assurance

In Figure 7–1, six categories of risk were illustrated, many of which affect customers. Two major concerns of customers are transacting with false websites posing as legitimate businesses and theft or misuse of information. As mentioned in Chapter 2, accountants are performing a website assurance function that is designed to assess the adequacy and legitimacy of the many facets of Internet business. Because the specifics of this assurance function were discussed in detail in Chapter 4, they are not reviewed here. However, a major issue for accountants is assessing the adequacy of server reliability of sites that perform any kind of online service.

Summary

Electronic commerce is an exciting and relatively new frontier, but like all frontiers explored and developed throughout history, new risks are hurdles that must be overcome. The open nature of the Internet, Intranets, and Extranets and the sharing of data makes security a serious challenge. Private interest groups, major corporations, and worldwide government agencies are devoting resources to develop a safer e-commerce environment. Until cost-beneficial solutions are found and properly implemented, parties engaging in e-commerce may continue to experience growing pains until a plateau is reached on the learning curve.

The risks of e-commerce affect both buying and selling agents. The perpetrators may be internal to a firm or an external hacker. The risks faced include theft, destruction, interception, alteration, stalling or rerouting of data, as well as forged messages. Stolen data may be used to defraud credit card companies of money or to learn trade secrets of competitors. The motives of perpetrators vary widely including, financial gain, revenge by former employees, or for the intrinsic satisfaction of hacking or cracking the system.

Perpetrators sometimes use what many security specialists consider to be the weakest link in information systems—humans—to gain access to the system by conducting social engineering. The information necessary to penetrate a security system is often obtained by asking targeted employees the right questions in the right fashion.

Key Words

anti-virus software	cookies
boot virus	denial of service attack
buffer overflow	distributed denial of service (DDoS) attack

e-mail spoofing
Extranet
firewall
image tags
impersonation
Internet service provider (ISP)
Intranet
macro virus
malicious website
man-in-the-middle attack
message integrity
negligent hiring laws
nonrepudiation
privacy

proof of delivery
risk
risk assessment
session key
sniffer
social engineering
threat
time-stamp signature
Trojan horse
user access control tables
virtual private network (VPN)
virus
virus hoax
web bug

Review Questions

1. What is meant by e-commerce risk?
2. What are the most popular security breaches conducted by external hackers?
3. What are the most costly security breaches?
4. What are the Internet risks to customers?
5. What are the Internet risks to selling agents?
6. What is a man-in-the-middle attack?
7. What are three privacy groups?
8. What is a cookie?
9. What is a denial of service attack?
10. What is an Intranet?
11. What percentage of firms studied by the CSI/FBI experienced unauthorized access of their system?
12. What level of employees are most frequently prosecuted?
13. What is a negligent hiring law?
14. What is a sniffer? Do they have any legitimate uses?
15. What kind of corporate data may have resale value?
16. What is e-mail spoofing?
17. What is social engineering?
18. What are frequently used tools of social engineers?
19. What is an Extranet?
20. What are the risks faced by messages sent over the Internet?
21. What is nonrepudiation?
22. What is a firewall?
24. What is a virus?
25. What type of damage can a virus inflict?
26. What is a macro virus?
27. What is a boot virus?
28. What is a Trojan horse?
29. What is a buffer overflow?

Discussion Questions

1. Why did President Clinton establish the PCCIP? Shouldn't the private sector respond to the infrastructure?

2. Explain the difference between a denial of service and a distributed denial of service attack. Which is more difficult to prevent? Why?

3. Has the increased use of the Internet increased internal or external threats more?

4. How can a virtually invisible window or frame be placed on a Web page?

5. Explain how your credit card number might be stolen if you browse the Web but never purchase any products at any websites you visit?

6. Can cookies serve any good legitimate purpose? Can they be used unethically?

7. How does a marketing firm, such as Doubleclick, make money using cookies?

8. Why do most firms not report computer intrusions to law enforcement officials? Is the reasoning rational? Why?

9. Are employee background checks important? Ethical?

10. Devise a plan to prevent external perpetrators to use e-mail spoofing and social engineering to obtain passwords.

11. How can the untimely delivery of electronic messages hurt a firm?

12. Extranets are designed to allow companies to share data among themselves. How can a firm share data over their Extranet and the Internet and still restrict access to hackers?

13. Why are macro viruses so troubling? How can they be prevented?

14. Why are hoaxes a problem if they are not destructive to data?

15. Electronic bulletin boards are very helpful for programmers who exchange solution to security problems. Why can these bulletin boards be dangerous?

Cases

1. FAA and Employee Background Checks
    Use the Internet to research the negligent practices in hiring the Y2K programmers without background checks by the FAA as mentioned earlier in the chapter. Do the following:
    a. Determine whether they have finished performing the retroactive background checks.
    b. Identify the possible problems that could have or still can result from this situation.

2. Virus Calendar Bulletins
    Visit the McAfee website (*www.mcafee.com*). Go to the anti-virus center and then the virus calendar and do the following:
    a. Explain the purpose of this calendar.
    b. Report the number of viruses posted for the upcoming week.
    c. Choose four viruses and detail the specifics of the virus. Be prepared to report this to your class.
    d. Discuss the implications that the viruses you selected can have on a business.
    e. Go to the virus hoax page and choose two hoaxes; detail the specifics of the hoaxes. Be prepared to report this to your class.
    f. Discuss the implications that the hoaxes you selected can have on a business.

3. Starwave
    "Online credit card scare an inside job."
    "Starwave says two separate but chilling messages were sent to people who purchased items online from ESPNet or the NBA Store this week."

The first anonymous e-mail told shoppers they had been the victims of careless security and that their credit card numbers and addresses were easily available.

The second message, sent by E-mail and regular mail by the World Wide Websites' host, Starwave Corp., alerted 2,397 online shoppers that their credit card information might have been misappropriated.

Starwave said the credit card information was in a secure, encrypted area that was accessed by an intruder who had the proper password information. "This was not done by a hacker," said Jennifer Yazzolino, a Starwave spokeswoman. "They knew how to get in to the system and unlawfully used classified information." The area that the intruder broke in to was an order processing system that sends shoppers' orders from each site to 1-800-PRO-TEAM, a Florida fulfillment company.

Following the break-in, Starwave called in the FBI and the U.S. Secret Service to investigate. It has also implemented a new encryption process and changed all system passwords. "We think this is a matter of a password either being used directly by someone involved with the system or passed along directly by someone involved in the system," Yazzolino said. "We relied too much on human integrity."

Stewart Deck, Computerworld Online, July 10, 1997. (http://www.computerworld.com)

a. Who do you think sent the first e-mail message, and what could be the motive for the message?

b. The intruder is believed to be an insider who used a password. What are the possible ways the intruder obtained the password?

c. Will the new encryption process and changing all system passwords prevent this from happening in the future?

References and Websites

Aleph One. "Smashing the Stack for Fun and Profit." *Phrack,* Vol. 7, Issue 49.
   http://www.fc.net/phrack/ files/p49/p49-14.

Anderson, Heidi. "The Rise of the Extranet." *PC-TODAY Online Report.* 1997.
   http://www.pc-today.com.

Anon. "Hackers Crack Defense Computers," *Science News.* June 9, 1996.

Berg, Al. "Cracking a Social Engineer." *LANTimes Online.* November 1995.
   http://www.lantimes.com.

Bort, Julie. "Liar, Liar." *Client/Server Computing,* Vol. 4, No. 5. May 1997, p. 40.

Bowman, Lisa. "Netscape to Post Bug Fix." *PCWeek Online.* September 2, 1997.
   http://www.zdnet.com.

Brown, Carol. "Electronic Sabotage." *http://www.bus.orst.edu/faculty/brownc/lectures/virus/virus.htm.*

CERT Coordination Center. "Spoofed/Forged Email." *http://www.cert.org.*

Chicago Tribune. "Former Employee Charged; One Computer Company Deleted."
   December 19, 1996, p. 3 Zone N.

Client/Server Computing. "Social Engineering: The Biggest Threat." Vol. 4, No. 3, March 1997,
   p. 64.

CNET, Inc. "It's a SYN." *http://www.cnet.com /Content/Features/Dlife/Crime/ss02a.html.*

Cole-Gomolski, Barb. "Hackers Hitch Ride on E-mail; Lack of Security Opens Door."
   ComputerWorld Online. April 28, 1997. *http://www.computerworld.com.*

Computer Security Institute. "Computer Security Issues and Trends—2000 CSI/FBI Computer
   Crime and Security Survey." Spring 2000.

Cookie Central. "Shaking the Cookie Jar." *http://www.cookiecentral.com/dscprop.htm.*

_____. "Find Out How You Are Traced While Surfing on the Web."
   http://www.cookiecentral.com/dsm.htm.

Cox, Howard. "Neither Rain, nor Sleet, nor . . . Hackers." *InfoSecurity Magazine,* November, 2000. *www.Infosecuritymag.com.*

Damar Group Ltd. "AOL4FREE-Trojan horse program deletes user's files." *http:// www.dgl.com/dglinfo/1997/dg970418.htm.*

Dow Jones News. "Fired Worker Accused of Computer Sabotage." November 25, 1997, p. A40.

Felten, Edward, Dirk Balfanz, Drew Dean, and Dan Wallach. "Web Spoofing: An Internet Con Game." Technical Report 540-96, Department of Computer Science, Princeton University. February, 1997.

Garceau, Linda. "The Threat of Social Engineering." *The Ohio CPA Journal,.* Vol. 56, No. 1, February 1997, p. 42.

ICSA Net and Global Integrity. "2000 Information Security Survey." September 2000. *www.infosecuritymag.com.*

Institute for Global Communications. "IGC Responds to Destructive Emailbombing and 'Denial of Service' Attacks." *http://www.igc.org/igc/about/ehj_pr.html.*

Internet Security Systems. "Security Policy vs. Practice." *http://www.iss.net/vd/ presentations/asac/sld010.htm.*

_____. "Network Packet Capture FAX." *http://www.iss.net/vd/packcapt.htm.*

Klaus, Christopher. "Sniffers FAQ." *http://www.faqs.org/faqs/computer-security/sniffers.*

Lee, Elizabeth. "Junk E-mail Hit with More Backlash." *The Atlanta Constitution,* May 8, 1997, p. 7G.

McCarthy, Linda. "Intranet Security—Stories From the Trenches." *http://www.sun.com/970923/ cover-security/chap1.htm.*

Microsoft Corporation. "IE Buffer Overrun Bug." *http://www.windows95.com/bugs/bufferrun.htm.*

Nash, Kim, and Julia King. "IS Employers Skip Background Checks." *Computerworld Online.* October 27, 1997. *http://www.computerworld.com.*

National Computer Security Association. "1997 Computer Virus Prevalence Survey." 1997. *http://www.ncsa.com.*

Network Associates, Incorporated. "Remote Explorer." *http://www.nai.com/products/ antivirus/remote_explorer.asp.*

Partridge, Chris. "Keeping Out Criminals." *The Times.* October 1, 1997.

Porter, Darrell. "Michaelangelo Report." *http://galaxy.tradewave.com/editors/david-hull/ porter.htm.*

President's Commission on Critical Infrastructure Protection. "About Privacy and Security." *http://www.pccip.gov/ gov-sys.htm.*

Rapoport, Michael. "Former Forbes Employee Accused of Hacking Forbes Computer," *Dow Jones News,* November 24, 1997.

Smith, Nathan. "Smashing the Stack." *http://millcomm.com/~nate/machines/security/.*

Sullivan, Eamonn. "New Form of Attack Unleashed on the Internet." *PCWeek Online.* September 16, 1996. *http://www.zdnet.com.*

Sun Micro Systems. "Secure Computing with Java™: Now and the Future." *http://java.sun.com/ security/javaone97-whitepaper. htm.*

TechWeb. "It is 11 pm. Do You Know How Secure Your Network Is?" *http://techweb. cmp.com/intranet-build/2f2.htm.*

U.S. Department of Energy—CIAC. "Internet Hoaxes." UCRL-MI-119788. *http:// ciac.llnl.gov/ ciac/ciachoaxes.htm.*

_____. "H-67: Red Hat Linux X11 Libraries Buffer Overflow." May, 30, 1997. *http:// ciac.llnl.gov/ciac/bulletins/h-67.shtml.*

WarRoom Research LLC. "1996 Information Systems Security Survey." *http:// www.warroomresearch.com/ wrr/SurveysStudies/1996ISS_Survey_SummaryResults.htm.*

Weiser, Benjamin. "Ex-employee Accused of Engineering Forbes Computer System Crash." *The Arizona Republic.* November 29, 1997, p. A29.

8　Risk Management

Learning Objectives

1. To understand the risk management paradigm and methodology.
2. To differentiate between control weakness and control risk.
3. To understand the role of internal controls in risk management.
4. To understand the objectives of disaster recovery plans.

INTRODUCTION

The previous chapter identified many of the risks faced by firms engaging in electronic commerce. The number and types of risks may appear overwhelming at first, and perhaps even insurmountable. Good risk management programs, however, provide a systematic process for evaluating the security environment and implementing appropriate security devices. This chapter introduces the concept of risk management. The role of internal controls in assessing and reducing risks is presented, as well as the importance of good disaster recovery planning techniques.

In Chapter 7, *risk* was defined as "the possibility of loss or injury." The methods used to reduce the possibilities of loss or injury are known as risk management. We adopt a modified version of the Software Engineering Institute's (SEI's) definition of risk management.

Risk management is a methodology for

1. Assessing the potential of future events that can cause adverse affects.
2. Implementing cost-efficient strategies that can deal with these risks.

Several key elements are inherent in this definition. The first element is the assessment of future events. Oftentimes, the proverbial crystal ball must be used to predict unknown, maybe even unknowable, events from happening. Once a cadre of potential future events is identified, then prevention and detection strategies may be proposed. A careful analysis of the potential risks, and the probability that they may occur, must be weighed

251

against the cost of implementing associated prevention and detection devices. In e-commerce, **business interruption** is a major concern. Consider the following events:

- MCI's unexplained frame-relay congestion causes hundreds of corporate users to experience slowdowns and shutdowns, including outages experienced by the Chicago Board of Trade.
- eBay experiences 20 hours of unplanned downtime during a five-month period. During such outages, customers cannot access the site.
- During a "routine upgrade," ADP's system crashed. This unplanned event left five of its customers without services, such as matching buy-and-sell stock orders and sending online traders confirmations of their transactions.

Clearly, businesses do not desire that these types of event occur, but they must realize that in e-commerce, such possibilities exist and sometimes happen. The goal of risk management is to systematically plan for undesirable events. Before proceeding with a discussion of how much risk reduction is desirable, the following quote views risk in a somewhat different light:

> Risk in itself is not bad; risk is essential to progress, and failure is often a key part of learning. But we must learn to balance the possible negative consequences of risk against the potential benefits of its associated opportunity.[1]

Unfortunately many firms do not conduct a thorough analysis of their computer-related risk. As mentioned in the box entitled "Risk Management Still a Wild Frontier," only one-third of business executives have methods to assess information technology risks. The 1998 CSI/FBI survey indicates that only 16 percent of the firms studied had conducted a risk analysis of the downstream civil liability they may face from:

- Customers and clients.
- Business partners.
- Stockholders.
- Any other party negatively affected by a network intrusion or the misuse of their computer systems.

Risk management is typically conducted as either a reactive or proactive strategy. Firms that have experienced litigation, substantial losses due to downtime of technological resources, or security breaches may become more sensitive to the need to engage in effective risk management practices. Other firms may witness, either directly or indirectly, these same events occurring to other firms and realize the need to avoid such situations. Firms that face business interruptions from their service providers may experience litigation from their own customers, not to mention loss of customer confidence and loyalty. Trading partners are becoming less forgiving to interruptions of services due to increased website traffic and denial of service attacks. The next section discusses some key components of risk management.

CONTROL WEAKNESS VERSUS CONTROL RISK

Control weakness is a term that is used to represent a situation in which the cost of implementing the controls is less than the expected benefits. A **control risk** is a term used to denote a situation in which the expected benefits of additional controls may

---

[1]Roger L. Van Scoy, "Software Development Risk: Opportunity, Not Problem," Software Engineering Institute, CMU/SEI-92-Tr-30, ADA 258 742. September 1992.

E-Commerce in Practice

Risk Management Still a Wild Frontier

In the rush to deploy client/server and Web-related technologies and perhaps gain competitive advantage or generate higher revenue along the way, few companies stop to consider that those systems expose them to some operational and financial risks.

Hardly any companies have a fully integrated approach to managing all their information technology and business risks together, said Paula Sinclair, a senior editor at The Economist Intelligence Unit based here.

And most companies that do manage and monitor their IT risks do so with a "fragmented" approach, said J. Russell Gates, a managing partner at Arthur Andersen & Co.'s Computer Risk Management practice in Chicago.

Gates, who announced the results of a survey on the topic at a conference here, added that most of those companies use products such as Computer Associates International, Inc.'s Unicenter TNG systems management software to identify operational malfunctions.

The survey, which examined management of IT risks, found that more than two-thirds of the more than 150 CEOs, chief financial officers, and chief information officers at global companies surveyed by Arthur Andersen and The Economist Intelligence Unit admit that IT risks aren't well-understood at their companies. Meanwhile, only one in three executives said their companies have methods to determine risk.

Firms represented in the report include J. P. Morgan & Co. in New York, Capital One Financial Corp. in Falls Church, Va., and Mitsubishi Corp. in Tokyo.

One common problem is that few companies have made any effort to anticipate problems that may arise following systems deployment.

For example, security is an oft-mentioned threat to electronic-commerce initiatives. Yet few cyber-ready companies can determine what impact faulty connections and inaccurate data might have on customer retention, Gates said.

Both Gates and Sinclair were unable to estimate the total dollar value companies jeopardize with lax risk management practices. However, one frequently cited example in financial services is London-based Barings PLC, which nearly went bankrupt in 1995 after rogue trader Nicholas Leeson circumvented the bank's risk management monitors and lost hundreds of millions of company dollars in the Asian markets.

Barings and other high-profile trading frauds in the mid-1990s prompted Fidelity Investments in Boston to launch an integrated, companywide risk-management program in 1995.

As part of its three-year effort, orchestrated by chief risk officer James C. Lam, Fidelity is beta-testing an intranet-based "push" technology system that will send electronic warning flags to the company's top 100 senior executives whenever trading losses pass predetermined thresholds, Lam said.

Lam wouldn't say how much privately held Fidelity has spent to develop the push-based risk management systems, which are expected to be fully deployed by June.

Although the homegrown systems were "not inexpensive" to build, continuing efforts to integrate the company's information systems division and 40 business units have led to a decline in the company's loss-to-revenue ratio, Lam said.

Crisis management, he said, "is a lot more expensive and embarrassing" than risk management.

Source: Thomas Hoffman, © *Computerworld Online,* February 16, 1998. © Computerworld, Inc.

---

not exceed their implementation and maintenance costs. A commonly accepted notion is that all risk can never be eliminated. The **residual risk,** or risk that will always be present, is due to situations such as completely unpredictable events or massive acts of collusion against which protection is generally not available. This residual risk is often termed *inherent control risk.* The relationship between risks and cost is illustrated in Figure 8–1. The inherent risk base in the figure represents that an additional investment in controls will not eliminate this type of risk. The amount of inherent risk is a judgment, and it may vary from firm to firm. The section of the diagram representing the control weakness illustrates high risk relative to the cost of controls in place, indicating that from a cost-benefit perspective the additional investment in controls to reduce risk is worthwhile.

| FIGURE 8–1 | Risk levels and related costs |

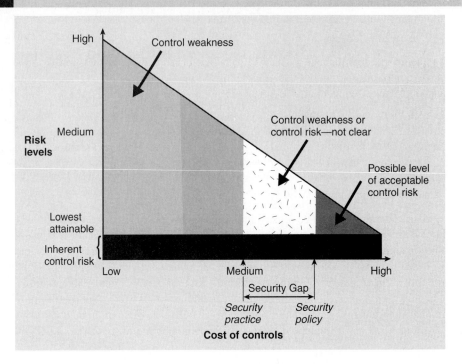

The section of the diagram labeled control risk represents the section in which costly controls are already in place, risk has been substantially reduced and minimized, and the marginal utility of additional controls is diminishing. The section between the control weakness and the control risk is the "gray area," where the relative benefits of additional controls are not clear. Controls within this domain clearly require much analysis and judgment. Different firms possess different risk perspectives and philosophies, and thus, they may treat control issues in the "not clear" area and control risk area differently from one another.

Security Gaps

A **security gap** may occur when firms develop control policies and procedures, but they are not followed in practice. The sharing of passwords, using diskettes from a home computer without first scanning for viruses, not immediately reporting a suspected intruder on the system, or performing maintenance to a Web server without disabling the Internet connection are examples of what may seem like small infractions against a firm's policies, but they may amount to costly disasters. Security gaps may occur because of poor or outdated policies and procedures, poor culture management, or not enough resources to properly implement a plan. In Chapter 7, we observed that the Federal Aviation Administration (FAA) ignored its own security policy of conducting background checks of its programmers. This security gap results in unchecked foreign nationals, as well as unchecked U.S. citizens, having access to the program code of many critical FAA systems. Not only did they have access, many of these individuals had the ability to change the code to solve Y2K issues. The repercussions of such a security gap is still being considered by government agencies.

Culture Management

Controls over the human factor are called **social controls,** and managing these controls is called **culture management.** The human element of managing risk is the most troublesome aspect to many information technology professionals. The major risks of the human factor are

- Bad judgment.
- Honest errors.
- Fraud.
- Virus damage.

Policies and procedures that are well thought out, clearly articulated, and backed by top management are a good mechanism for setting the cultural tone regarding information technology risks. Employees should be informed of appropriate and inappropriate actions and periodically reminded of these policies. Some firms have their employees read policies and sign statements indicating that they understand them and will follow them. Some firms have negative consequences inflicted on an employee found violating the policies.

Password sharing by employees in a reusable password environment is an example of poor culture management coupled with a low-strength security device—a dangerous combination. In this situation, to counteract the use of reusable passwords, frequent, strong reminders against sharing passwords should be sent to the employees and signed by them.

Excessively Tight Controls

The diagram in Figure 8–1 indicates that some level of control risk may be acceptable. After considering the multitude of risks and threats previously discussed in Chapter 7, extremely tight controls may seem to be the ultimate goal. These do have their downsides, however, some of which include

- Inefficient operations.
- Reduced flexibility.
- Excessive control costs.
- Negative culture.

Designing strong controls that do not tax the efficiency of the system and do not affect the flexibility of use of the system is the challenge faced by system designers. Firms want "more open" systems to interact with the external environment and greater flexibility in retrieving data. At the same time they want to "beef up security." Thus, the paradox of the desire for more open systems with tighter security results. Good risk management techniques need to address the strategic needs of business enterprises, and these needs are constantly changing and evolving. Further, if a firm is too militaristic in its deployment of policies and procedures and related sanctions, poor employee morale may result. Figure 8–2 provides a list of characteristics of the best controls for risk management.

FIGURE 8–2   *Characteristics of good risk management controls*

The best controls are

- *Redundant*—Combining passive controls with active and formal controls with informal (e.g., passwords plus audits, policies plus shared values)
- *Consistent*—(e.g., policies are modeled and reinforced by top managers' behavior; verbal prohibitions are accompanied by physical barriers to prevent the prohibited behavior)
- *Clearly written policies*—Widely communicated and enforced, and necessary for successful litigation
- *Fair*—perceived that way and applicable to everyone in the organization

- *Neither too detailed nor too restrictive*—Either of which raises control costs, interferes with effective operations, and promotes distrust and unethical behavior
- *Not a replacement for trust in employees*—Should complement a culture in which good performance is valued and rewarded and in which risk management is viewed as everyone's job
- *Helpful*—Not adversarial or punitive
- *Two-way channels*—Providing communication about risks, incidents, and opportunities for improved control
- *Supportive of valid organizational learning*—From past experience

Source: Financial Executives Institute, "IT-Related Risks-Myths and Realities," *Safety Nets: Secrets of Effective Information Technology Controls,* 1997.

FIGURE 8–3   *Risk management paradigm*

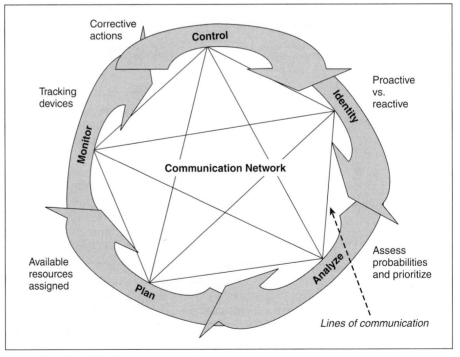

Source: Adopted from SEI's risk management paradigm.

RISK MANAGEMENT PARADIGM

A **risk management paradigm** is illustrated in Figure 8–3. This paradigm is a continuous process that recognizes that risk management is an ongoing process, not an annual or biannual event. The first step is to scan the internal and external environment and identify information technology risks *before they become a problem.* The key is to be proactive rather than reactive. In some cases, launching a reactive solution may be unavoidable; however, one objective of this paradigm is to minimize reactive solutions and seek out proactive designs. In the box entitled "Amazon Opens Book on Website," the management of high growth is discussed. Amazon's Director of Enterprise Management, Kim Rachmeler, explains how they are moving toward a more proactive approach of managing its server capacity and connectivity to its customers. They are trying to shift away from serious capacity situations in which most internal staffers could not run their own reports and operations during peak periods of the business day, not to mention rushing to Home Depot for a tarp to protect its servers from a leaky roof.

E-Commerce in Practice

Amazon Opens Book on Website

Peek Behind Scenes Reveals How Retailer Scaled Hardware During Dramatic Growth

The world's largest online bookseller once protected its precious database servers from a leaky Seattle roof with a piece of blue tarpaulin that a staffer rushed out to buy at Home Depot.

Amazon.com Inc. has come a long way since attaching that tarp to the fourth-floor ceiling of its downtown Seattle nerve center two years ago. Today, the retailer is building a second data center in Virginia that will have four times the capacity of its current one, Kim Rachmeler, director of enterprise management, told a Retail Systems 2000 audience here last week.

Amazon is typically tight-lipped about its information technology. So Rachmeler's speech provided a rare glimpse into the behind-the-scenes technical challenges, and sometimes dramatic solutions, that staffers devised on frenetic Internet time to cope with traffic levels that grew 30 percent each month during the company's first 18 months in business.

"Survival is absolutely the same thing as scaling for us," Rachmeler said. "Scaling is the most important thing we do. It is our No. 1 strategic initiative."

And it has been driving Amazon's Web architecture decisions. As traffic soared the first few years, Amazon opted for bigger and bigger boxes because it had the money but not the time or the staff to optimize systems, Rachmeler said.

When Amazon opened shop in July 1995, IT staffers set up a bell to ring every time a book order reached Ernie, the sole Sun Microsystems Inc. SPARCstation V box that served Amazon's Web site. But they might have gone deaf if they had left that system in place. The next year, they relieved Ernie in favor of a Digital Equipment Corp. Alpha 2000 and later added another one because it was "the biggest box out there," Rachmeler said.

"By changing vendors, we were going to give ourselves more room to expand in the long run," she said.

By the spring of 1997, Amazon eased the strain by substituting two DEC 8400s as it launched the second version of its Web site. More significant architectural changes would come later as the company made plans to link up with major portals and to add features such as recommendations and one-click shopping.

"We were scared," Rachmeler said. "We were about to drink from the fire hose, and we had no idea the kinds of traffic that we were going to get from those situations."

The solution: It removed one of the DEC 8400s in favor of redundant DEC 4100s serving Web pages at the front line. "What it allowed us to do is expand the capacity of the Web site only by buying new machines. Instead of

(continued)

Amazon Opens Book on Website—*continued*

spending human power to get more capacity, we could simply use our credit cards and increase the front line," Rachmeler said, noting that Amazon had fewer than 30 IT staffers at the time.

"It also meant that any one of these online machines could be taken off-line for maintenance or if it had hardware problems, and the store would stay open," Rachmeler said.

But Christmas '97 was coming, "and that shouldn't have been a surprise, but it was," she said. The taxed database server was already running on the biggest machine available, so Amazon couldn't put in another box. Instead, a SWAT team launched Project Database Headroom to squeeze out 30 percent more performance.

"We would go to executives of the company and ask them not to run their reports during the day. We would tell the financial teams not to execute billing programs during peak periods of time. We sent out messages to the entire Amazon staff that if they had programs accessing the database, they needed to talk to this SWAT team," Rachmeler recalled.

Big Iron for Christmas

When the Christmas rush was over, Amazon brought back its idle DEC 8400 as a hot standby, and then over the next two years began cracking off pieces of the main database to run on separate machines. In time for last Christmas, staffers brought in big iron—a Hewlett-Packard Co. V-class machine—to anchor the system. They also split up the Web database from one to four machines and increased the number of online servers.

But in the future, Amazon knows that hardware won't be able to solve every problem. Rachmeler noted that the online retailer's focus will shift to modular software systems, which will help ease development and maintainability.

Giga Information Group analyst Mike Gilpin said Amazon took the right approach to expansion, given its circumstances. Now the company will experience the "classic set of growth pains" encountered by early adopters as they grow to be large companies, he said.

Amazon will need to take a "more controlled approach to software architecture" and do "more separation of function between different layers of the architecture. There never is an easy time to make those changes," he said.

One challenge, for instance, will be solving a "contentious" middleware issue, since the company now uses software from several vendors, according to Rachmeler.

"Moore's Law is not going to save us anymore," she said. "We're going to have to get smarter about the way that we use our systems, not just increasing (capacity and availability) by steroids."

Source: Carol Sliwa, © *Computerworld Online,* April 24, 2000. *www.computerworld.com*

Once the risks are identified, the second step is to analyze these risks. The probability of occurrence and their potential effect must be studied. All identified risks should be classified according to type of risk (risk to disruption of operations, theft of data, loss of data) and prioritized as to urgency. With a monthly growth of 30 percent during its first 18 months of operations, server capacity to accommodate customers was the biggest risk item identified by Amazon. Once risks are classified and prioritized, the firm's available resources must be evaluated and a plan developed. In many cases, controls for systems may require that top management allocate additional resources. Fortunately, firms are beginning to see the importance of systems and information technology projects during capital budgeting decision processes.

Once a plan is in the implementation and operations phase, its progress must be monitored at every stage. Risk indicators should be monitored. Any deviations in implementation or operations from the plan should be tracked. The final phase is to use the data from the **monitoring** stage to evaluate the risk management plan and control for any deviations. Great monitoring systems can be developed that track important deviations from a plan or standard, but if the monitoring data are not used to remedy a deviation, then the efforts of the monitoring phase are in vain. Thus, deviations should be thoroughly investigated and explained. For example, in the earlier box, "Risk Management Still a Wild Frontier," the situation described a system that is being designed to send electronic warning flags to a company's top 100 senior executives each time certain trading thresholds are reached. This is an example of a monitoring step. If the senior executives act on the information they receive, this is called a control procedure.

Most importantly, this process is iterative, the results found in the tracking and evaluation phase may help to identify new risks and the existing plan may need to be modified. Open lines of communication should be established so that feedback is constantly channeled to the risk management team and can be used in refining the plan during all phases. Risk management plans need to be continuous and adaptive. Flexibility is extremely important in order to fine-tune the plan or even make radical adjustments if necessary.

DISASTER RECOVERY PLANS

Even the best-designed system cannot control the prevention of a natural disaster. All firms should have a **disaster recovery plan,** which is a contingency plan for resuming operations for those situations in which operations are interrupted for any reason, including when an unforeseen man-made or natural disaster occurs. **Natural disasters** include incidents such as fires, smoke, floods, tornadoes, earthquakes, and high wind and electrical storms. **Man-made disasters** include incidents such as viruses, hardware failure, sabotage, and error. The incident described in the box entitled "Cable Cuts Ground Northwest Flights" describes an unexpected, man-made disaster in which a construction crew laying new telecommunication cables severed existing fiber-optic and copper lines. Both the main telecommunication and redundant lines for Northwest Airlines were cut. As a result, Northwest Airlines had to cancel 130 flights. The disaster could have been

---

E-Commerce in Practice

Cable Cuts Ground Northwest Flights

A cut cluster of cables left thousands of airline passengers across the country stranded yesterday and Northwest Airlines Inc. officials wondering why their backup system was also disabled.

The problem began at 2 P.M. CDT, when a subcontractor laying new lines bored through clusters of cables, cutting 244 fiber-optic and copper telecommunications lines. The lines included ones that link Northwest's Minneapolis–St. Paul hub to the rest of the nation.

What Northwestern officials soon discovered was that their redundant system lines apparently run alongside the lines they are backing up.

"What we don't understand is why the redundant system was also affected," said Kathy Peach, a spokeswoman for Northwest. "It does seem odd that the redundancy is so near the main lines. Because the cut was so severe, it also affected the redundant lines."

A spokesman for Denver-based US West Inc., the local phone provider whose lines were cut, did not return phone calls immediately. But a worker who did not want to be named blamed the problem on the "reckless abandon" of the subcontractor who was laying new cables for a US West competitor when the lines were cut.

According to Peach, Northwest had to cancel 130 of its 1,700 daily flights because of the problem, which disabled the airline's system for 3.5 hours. The cut cables also knocked out some local phone service.

Source: DeWayne Lehman, © *Computerworld Online,* March 22, 2000. *www.computerworld.com*

avoided, however, if a proper review of telecommunications and power sources had been conducted and the parallel paths of the primary and backup power sources discovered. Had the undesirable situation been identified, perhaps an acceptable disaster recovery plan could have been formulated.

A trend in recent years has been to outsource contingency and disaster recovery planning functions to specialists. Good specialists can offer a lot to a firm in the way of hardware, software, and service. They can perform the analysis of risks and design solutions that they stand ready to deliver in the case of an interruption of service or disaster.

A firm may choose, however, to assess, plan, and maintain its own contingency and disaster recovery plan solutions. The cost to do so can be quite high. Maintaining multiple hardware/software sites can be expensive. If a firm has geographically separated sites with similar platforms, however, they may be able to develop a cost-effective plan for switching their processing from the disaster location to another division of the firm.

Disaster Recovery Plan Objectives

Good planning involves considering the following objectives:

- Assessment of vulnerabilities.
- Prevention and reduction of risk.
- Creation of cost-effective solutions.
- Minimization of business interruption and assurance of business continuity.
- Securing alternative Internet access modes.
- Recovery of lost data.
- Providing disaster recovery procedures.
- Training employees for disaster recovery scenarios.
- End-to-end recovery for e-commerce applications.

In designing a plan, the primary goal is to reduce the interruption of business and to ensure business continuity. For firms that have e-commerce as a mission-critical application, alternative ISPs, Web servers, and necessary databases and Web-based programs must be readily and rapidly available. Disaster recovery plans, in order to be conducted properly, need support from top management because these plans can use substantial firm resources, both financial and human. Further, disaster recovery plans should be updated continuously as the operations change that they are intended to replace or supplement. An outdated plan may have been brilliant when it was created, but if it no longer reflects reality, it will be useless or less than sufficient when a disaster strikes. Because availability of services is a key component to success in an e-environment, planning for reliable, continuous end-to-end computing between trading partners is crucial.

Second Site Backup Alternatives

The continuation of services is a key element to good disaster recovery planning. If the original site is unserviceable, then a second site needs to be available to continue operations. Comdisco Inc., a firm that specializes in disaster recovery solutions, claims that firms can no longer wait 48 to 72 hours for recovery plans to kick in. In today's environment, 47 percent of its businesses want recovery in less than 24 hours, and some businesses need almost instantaneous recovery.

Focus on Air Products

Air Products Plans Ahead

The world headquarters of Air Products and Chemicals Inc. is located in Trexlertown, Pennsylvania, on a 550-acre campus. This campus consists of several office, research and development, and support buildings. Included in these buildings are two main administration buildings: Admin 3 and Admin 5. Each administration building contains a data center. The main data center is located in the Admin 3 building, and the secondary data center is located in the Admin 5 building. These two buildings are approximately one-third of a mile apart.

The diagram below graphically illustrates the primary backup and recovery mechanisms. Located in the Admin 3 building are an IBM mainframe, approximately 300 servers, and some Tandem processors. Located in the Admin 5 building are approximately 150 servers. The telecommunications between the buildings are made through a fiber distributed data interface (FDDI) ring.

Backup of Data

Data is backed up daily and moved to an offsite storage facility. Data is backed up from the mainframe, all servers, and the Tandem processors.

Disaster Plan

In the event of a disaster, Air Products has contracted with a vendor to quick ship a mainframe. For the servers, Air Products assumes that both buildings will not be affected. Air Products self-insures by using its own servers as backup for the servers. The plan calls for the decommissioning of servers with low priority to take over the tasks performed by higher priority servers in the building affected by the disaster.

Source: Jack Fekula, Air Products and Chemicals, Inc. ©Air Products and Chemicals, Inc.

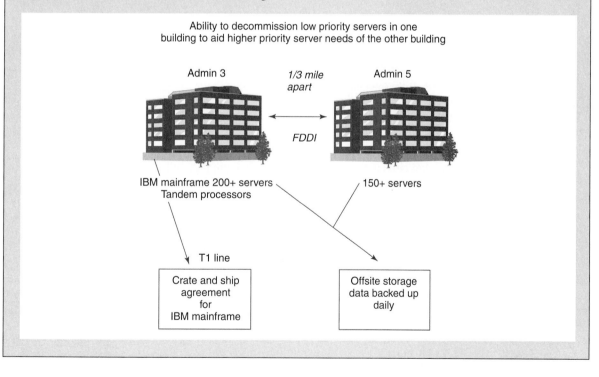

Some firms may be able to switch the disrupted business operations to another division for a short while. Air Products relies on this method for its servers, but not its mainframe as mentioned in the box entitled "Air Products Plans Ahead." Switching services to another in-house facility is not always an available or desirable option, and other available alternatives are discussed in this section. In each of the options discussed here, data loss recovery and transfer of data to the new site are serious issues that must be addressed.

Mutual Aid Pact

A **mutual aid pact** involves an agreement between two or more organizations to share resources with one another in the case of a disaster. For this to work properly,

- Each organization must have excess capacity or be able to drop the level of their operations while they are assisting one of the other parties.
- The organizations must have compatible platforms.
- All of the parties in the agreement must not be affected by the disaster.
- The organizations must have a high level of trust in one another.

This method can cause unforeseen problems integrating the operations of two or more companies and is becoming less popular.

Cold Site (Shell Site)/Crate and Ship

In a **cold site** configuration a firm, or maybe a group of firms, lease space in a building site and design it to hold computer equipment. The computer equipment is not actually stored on the site. In the case of a disaster, a previously negotiated agreement with a **crate and ship** vendor allows the hardware and software to be shipped immediately to the cold site, usually within 12 to 24 hours. This option costs more than the mutual aid pact, but can be less troubling to implement if the crate and ship vendor is reliable. If multiple firms share a site, trouble can result if a natural disaster occurs that affect multiple parties and the space parameters cannot accommodate the equipment and personnel for multiple operations. For example, if three firms in the Seattle area share a site and all three firms are affected by an earthquake, they will all need access to the cold site. Further, in choosing a crate and ship vendor, the disaster recovery planning team needs to investigate the number of customers the vendor has in any given region and determine whether the vendor can accommodate all customers in the case of a regional natural disaster.

Hot Site and Remote Mirroring

In a **hot site** configuration, a completely equipped, fully functioning disaster recovery operation center is available. A firm may build its own hot site or subscribe to a hot site service, such as those provided by Comdisco Inc. Hot site services typically maintain a variety of platforms. The same concerns regarding natural disasters discussed for cold sites apply to hot sites. If an outsourced vendor is used for the hot site, the disaster recovery planning team needs to assess the number of customers the vendor serves within the same geographic region. Mirroring data is a technique used to back up data, and when used in conjunction with a hot site can be a very effective defense against a disaster. As data are processed in a **remote mirroring** production environment, they are also processed in a backup environment. If a disaster occurs, the mirrored site is ready to go.

Conducting a Dress Rehearsal

Testing the disaster recovery plan is often thought of as unnecessary or even impossible, but it can be done in different degrees. Testing the plan should be conducted similar to a fire drill; it should be unexpected. The employees should be tested to see if they know the appropriate procedures and how efficiently and effectively they carry out the procedures. If a crate and ship scenario is used, the service should be tested to see if it delivers the appropriate hardware and software within the given time frame. The vendor will have to agree to participate in such a plan "spur of the moment" and re-stocking fees associated with the delivery of the equipment should be negotiated in advance. Mutual aid pacts are the most difficult to test because most trading partners will not want to reduce their processing capacities to allow the other partner to test the system. Cold sites and hot sites are easiest to test, but not without additional costs from the vendors.

IMPLICATIONS FOR THE ACCOUNTING PROFESSION

Assessing internal controls and performing risk management are skills that accounting professionals have been performing for many years. This time-proven experience and technical expertise is a knowledge base against which the accounting profession is uniquely in a position to leverage. The accounting profession strongly values effective internal controls and has conducted many studies on this subject and issued guidelines and standards. Firms engaging in e-commerce must have their internal controls expanded to include all facets of the transaction processing systems that interface with other systems, including Web browsers, and trading partners. Further, firms must have faith in the internal control systems of the business partners with which they trade data. Accountants have an incredibly strong background for performing internal control assessment and risk management of e-commerce systems. Members of the accounting profession need to enhance this skill-set by strengthening their Internet technology skills. As illustrated in the box entitled "The Corporate Netspionage Crisis," Pricewaterhouse-Coopers is actively assessing the risk factors associated with network break-ins and identifying some countermeasures that can be taken by its clients. This box reinforces the necessity of technical skills, such as cryptography (discussed in Chapter 10) and firewalls (discussed in Chapter 11).

Evolution of Internal Control Framework

The guidance for the internal control framework was initially provided by Statement on Auditing Standard (SAS) 55 in 1988. The original definition was eventually viewed by the accounting profession as being too narrow in focus. In 1997, SAS 78 superceded SAS 55. SAS 78 broadened the definition of internal control structure to reflect the definition given by the COSO (Committee of Sponsoring Organizations of the Treadway Commission) Report: *"Internal Control—Integrated Framework."* The definition of **internal control** is

> A process—affected by an entity's board of directors, management, and other personnel—designed to provide reasonable assurance regarding the achievement of objectives in the following categories: (*a*) reliability of financial reporting, (*b*) effectiveness and efficiency of operations, and (*c*) compliance with applicable laws and regulations.

Internal control is defined as an ongoing process. The elements of internal control as set forth by SAS 78 and the COSO report include the control environment, risk assessment, control activities, information and communication, and monitoring. These key elements are the same elements presented earlier in the risk management paradigm. To engage in the successful design, implementation, and maintenance of internal controls and effective risk management practices for e-commerce, an understanding of the internal control framework is important.

E-Commerce in Practice

The Corporate Netspionage Crisis

PricewaterhouseCoopers Investigators Reveal 11 Factors That Put Companies at Risk— And 10 Steps to Effective Protection

Over 59 percent of companies with significant Internet presence suffered break-ins during 1998 (Information Week study fielded by PricewaterhouseCoopers), demonstrating that corporate "netspionage" is now a major threat to corporate Americas' intellectual property, reported PricewaterhouseCoopers Investigations LLC, a wholly owned subsidiary of PricewaterhouseCoopers, the world's largest professional services organization.

To help companies deal with this burgeoning problem, PricewaterhouseCoopers investigators examined 11 risk factors—the combination of which can help determine a company's exposure to network break-ins—and produced a 10-point checklist to help them evaluate their protection measures.

"Most companies will find themselves with several of these risk factors. Unfortunately, as computer technology continues to get more sophisticated and available, we can expect more assaults. While these lists are very broad, realizing potential risk and knowing the steps necessary to take is critical to developing effective protection," noted Mr. William C. Boni, former federal agent and current director within PricewaterhouseCoopers Investigations' cybercrime practice.

Risk Factors

Top 10 percent industry rank Recent attempts in the industry to steal business secrets Extensive reliance on computer technology/Internet connectivity	Some risk
Large R&D efforts as percentage of revenues National/international media profile Substantial multinational operations	Significant risk
High margin products High technology products Breakthrough product(s), process(es) or service(s) Recent or projected merger or downsizing Extensive and overly expedited Y2K remediation measures	Dangerous Exposure

Strategic Countermeasures

Operational Measures	*Technical Protection Measures*
• Identify the "crown jewels" (the most significant intellectual assets) • Obtain valuation for critical intellectual assets via rigorous intellectual assets management program • Assign an individual responsible for protecting intellectual assets • Integrate physical and other security measures • Respond to incidents and investigate anomalies	• Periodically test firewalls and other security systems • Monitor the Intranets, Extranets, and Internet for indicators of theft • Deploy strategic cryptographic systems • Implement intrusion detection technology • Establish electronic evidence recovery capability

Source: Press Release by Doug C. Wilson, Manager—Financial Advisory Services—*Americas Theater Marketing*, Pricewaterhouse Coopers, March 22, 1999. *http://www.pwcglobal.com*

The Control Environment

The control environment reflects and affects the culture of the organization and is the foundation for the other four internal control elements. The control environment elements in the COSO report and sample information technology assessment questions include:

Integrity, Ethical Values, and Competence

How involved is top management in establishing and evaluating the effectiveness of the tone at the top?

Does the entity have an adequate information technology and security personnel in numbers and experience to carry out the firm's mission? If not, has the firm adequately screened the competence level of outside consultants?

Board of Directors or Audit Committee Directives and Attention

Has the board ever issued directives to management detailing specific information technology or security actions?

Management's Philosophy and Operating Style

Does management move cautiously, proceeding only after carefully analyzing the risks and potential benefits of proposed information systems and security plans, or does it jump impulsively into uncharted waters?

Assignment of Authority and Responsibility

Are established reporting relationships, formal or informal, direct or matrix, effective? Do they provide managers with information appropriate to their responsibilities and authority?

Does management periodically evaluate the information system department's organizational structure in light of changes in the business or industry?

Human Resource Policies and Practices

Are candidates with frequent job changes or gaps in employment history subjected to particularly close scrutiny?

Do hiring policies require investigation for a criminal record?

(Excerpt from the COSO report)

This list is just a sampling of assessment issues for investigating the nature of the control environment for a firm. Firms may conduct in-house assessments, but those firms needing an independent audit opinion must also have external assessments conducted. The amount of external assessment can be reduced if done properly by an internal audit team that reports directly to an audit committee or the board of directors.

Risk Assessment

Definitions of risk and risk management were discussed in Chapter 7. The assessment of risk is a key component in the design and evaluation of internal controls. Risks should be identified at both the enterprise level and business activity level. The risks to be considered at the enterprise level are

External Factors

- New technological developments.
- New marketing strategies of competitors.
- Unfavorable regulatory changes.
- Natural disasters.
- Unfavorable economic environment and foreign markets.

Internal Factors

- Disruption in information processing operation.
- Ineffective personnel hiring and training practices.
- Change in management responsibilities.
- Inadequate access controls to assets by employees.
- An unassertive or ineffective top management or audit committee.

At each business activity level, risks of downtime or security breaches need to be considered. For example, the effect on sales processing if the server that processes incoming sales orders is down due to an unforeseen event is a specific risk that must be considered.

Control Activities

The COSO report and SAS 78 discuss two broad groupings of information systems controls - **general controls** and **application controls.** Figure 8–4 lists the controls that fall under these categories. The list of application controls is not intended to be an exhaustive list. The number and types of applications will vary by firm and industry. In reality, these two groupings of controls are intertwined. If the general controls are not adequate, then the reliability of the applications is questionable. General controls are necessary to support the reliable and accurate functioning of the applications. In e-commerce, well-designed general controls are essential for reducing risk. More and more applications are being connected to e-commerce networks every day. Control techniques relating to e-commerce for the data center, system software, access security and application development, and maintenance are presented in the remaining chapters of this text.

FIGURE 8–4   *Information system controls*

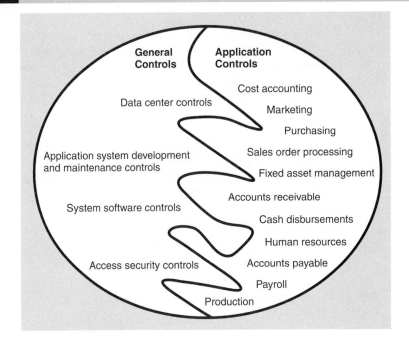

Information and Communication

Information technology personnel can tend to get bogged down in a current development project and forget to monitor systems that are currently in the operations or maintenance phase. Good communication channels need to exist so that the feedback gets distributed and digested by the appropriate personnel. The risk management paradigm previously presented in Figure 8–3 illustrates lines of communication between all levels of security assessment, planning, and implementation phases. The benefits of the model diminish if communication is not present or sufficiently engaged.

Monitoring

To be effective, monitoring should be an ongoing process and not an event. A security gap between policy and practice can occur if information is generated, but the designated personnel are too busy to read and respond to it. To be effective, the implementation of response reports may be necessary. Response reports require that personnel log their response actions to reports. If a "management by exception" philosophy is used, then response actions would only be necessary for reports that indicate that some process is outside of a preset boundary. For example, if the average wait time for a visitor to a website is 3 seconds with a standard deviation of 0.3 second, a report would be generated and sent to the website administrator if the average wait time is 4.2 seconds. The website administrator should file a **response action form** to indicate that he or she is aware of the problem, and he or she should list the corrective actions taken or a plan of corrective actions that will remedy the problem.

The Role of Internal Controls in Risk Management

Internal control guidelines have guided accountants in the financial accounting attestation role for years. As firms reengineer their practices and information technologies toward an enterprise approach, the scope of the internal control attestation role is expanding to include the entire enterprise information system. What used to be referred to as the "Big Eight," then the "Big Six," and now the "Big Five" accounting firms are currently referring to themselves as professional services firms. The traditional financial accounting audit function is shrinking in size in comparison to other services provided by these firms, such as business and management advisory services. The internal control structure is important to each of the services performed by accounting or professional services firms. Regardless of whether the services are performed by in-house professionals or a consulting firm, the internal control framework should be at the core of the construction of an e-commerce information system plan.

Summary

While the risks presented in Chapter 7 may seem insurmountable to the novice, a good process of risk analysis and risk management can help reduce the risk to a manageable and acceptable level. A thorough understanding of both good internal control issues and technical knowledge is necessary to conduct a good security audit. Once an assurance of the current controls and risk assessment is conducted, then a risk management plan can be formulated and implemented.

Risks can be managed, but even the best-designed system may be a victim of a natural or man-made disaster. Every organization should have a contingency planning process and a formal disaster recovery plan. The critical business operations need to survive a disaster or the firm itself may be a casualty.

Key Words

application controls

business interruption

cold site

control risk

control weakness

crate and ship

culture management

disaster recovery plan

general controls

hot site

internal control

man-made disasters

monitoring

mutual aid pact

natural disasters

remote mirroring

residual risk

response action form

risk management

risk management paradigm

security gap

social controls

Review Questions

1. What is risk management?
2. Distinguish between control weakness and control risk.
3. Explain the term *residual risk.*
4. Identify the major risks of the human factor of information systems.
5. What is culture management?
6. List the five stages in the risk management paradigm.
7. What is internal control?
8. What are SAS 78 and the COSO report?
9. Explain the term control environment.
10. Identify the types of risks that should be considered at the enterprise level.
11. What are general controls?
12. What are application controls?
13. Explain what a disaster recovery plan encompasses.
14. Identify three disaster recovery plan objectives.
15. What is a mutual aid pact?
16. Distinguish between a hot and cold site.
17. What is meant by end-to-end recovery?

Discussion Questions

1. What types of civil liability can a firm face from inadequate control over its computer systems? Give two examples.
2. Can a control risk become a weakness? How?
3. Is the security gap preventable? How?
4. Why may firms treat control weaknesses differently?
5. If money is not an issue, should controls be designed to be as tight as possible?
6. Why aren't quarterly risk management reviews adequate?
7. Explain the importance of good communication procedures in adequately maintaining a system. Give an example.
8. How can an action response form be considered a documentation device from the perspective of assurance teams or internal auditors?

9. Conducting a dress rehearsal for disaster recovery plans is often considered to be unnecessary and a nuisance by the companies for which they are designed. Comment on why you think these businesses resist performing what appears to be a vital task.

10. What are some factors to consider in selecting a crate and ship vendor and cold site partners if you live in an active flood zone?

11. Is a 24-hour computer downtime period more of a financial threat to an online retailer than to a traditional manufacturing firm? Explain.

Cases

1. Condisco, Inflow and E-business Continuity Plans
   Visit Comdisco's and Inflow's websites and determine what specific products and services they offer for business continuity planning as service availability. Contrast the two companies in a one-page report. Specifically identify whether they are competing or complementary services.

2. Internet Research Project—Disasters and Prevention
   a. Search the Internet and find two "disasters" (either natural or man-made) that either disrupted service or exposed a firm to risk of litigation. The articles should be within the last four months.
   b. Describe each disaster in a paragraph or two.
   c. Determine how good risk management and internal control procedures could have helped to prevent these events.
   d. Discuss how a disaster recovery plan helped each firm to recover or how it could have helped if only it had been prepared in advance.

3. Management Philosophy
   Using online databases, search for an article that discusses a specific company's philosophy, as determined by top management, toward ethical behavior and internal controls. Print a copy of the article to hand in with this assignment.
   a. What is the company's philosophy toward ethical behavior and internal controls?
   b. Is the company portrayed in the article in a favorable light? Why *or* why not?
   c. Is the market rewarding, punishing, or not affected by this policy?
   d. Does such a policy cost the firm? Explain.

4. Ice Storm Freezes Operations
   Cold temperatures are supposed to boost computer performance. But the massive ice storm that recently blasted parts of New York, New England, Quebec, and Ontario put a freeze on many computer operations in those regions.

   That's because one- to two-week power failures forced many businesses to operate with skeleton staffs, shut down, move to remote disaster sites, or rely on generators that in some cases are being used beyond their normal capacity.

   There are cold, hard lessons to be learned for IT. Disasters can occur without major physical damage to computers, and you can never have enough generators, backup power systems, and staffing strategies in place. The best plan should include building relationships with generator makers and disaster recovery vendors so you are in priority order when disaster strikes, IT managers said.

   Early estimates of overall residential and business losses are at nearly $1 billion in Canada and $200 million in the United States. The most pressing issue for many companies was the lack of information technology staff to keep computers and applications running because of the number of roads closed by fallen trees, power lines, and utility poles.

   In Montreal, some downtown companies closed or ran on reduced power, while others let workers bring their families into the office for warmth because most of the outlying communities were still without power.

   "Most of our problem was just getting people in," said Richard Cox, a project manager at Air Canada in Montreal. "We had a very high absentee rate. A lot of our technical support came to a screeching halt for a solid week." To cover for the number of employees trapped at home, Cox set up a 24-hour coverage plan for the remaining staff to oversee Air Canada's applications and to make sure company operations ran smoothly across the country, even if Montreal's Dorval Airport was socked in.

IBM Canada closed its Bromont, Quebec, plant, which assembles most of the chips IBM sells. IBM wanted to save electricity in the fragile power grid and protect its 2,000 employees, most of whom live in communities that were blacked out.

The Inspector Generale for Financial Institutions, a Canadian government agency, shifted some of its computer processing to its Quebec City headquarters because its Montreal offices had been closed since Jan. 9, a spokesman said.

Hydro-Quebec, the province's power utility, doubled the number of technical staff on duty to maintain its computer network, which is crucial to tracking repair progress and customer service calls.

Many businesses relied on a combination of uninterruptible power supplies (UPSs) and diesel generators to ensure that the computers kept running even when the power lines toppled.

At Kennebec Valley Health in Augusta, Maine, such a scheme worked well, though the hospital's Waterville, Maine, offices didn't have enough UPSs in place to keep all its servers running, said Bill Terrell, Kennebec's chief information officer. That put a crimp in computer applications, Terrell said, but the hospital had power. Medical staff were able to provide normal care and get caught up on related computer work when the power came back on.

Other companies weren't so lucky. Five Canadian firms opted to run their operations at Comdisco Inc.'s disaster recovery sites in Montreal, Toronto, and New Jersey. Seven other companies put Comdisco on alert status, said an official of the Rosemont, Ill., disaster recovery firm.

The long outages resulted in breakdowns and a shortage of parts for the many ride-through diesel generators that companies depend on for power. The generators are typically designed to run for a couple of days, not a couple of weeks.

At Domco Inc., a floor coverings maker in Farnham, Quebec, backup generators failed after three days. Closed roads and the loss of all telephone service meant Domco's headquarters was cut off from its two other plants in the United States. So IT staff switched operations to SunGard Data Systems Inc.'s disaster recovery site in Philadelphia. But Domco's U.S.–based plants also had to shut down computer operations for three days until the hot site was online, because order and shipping applications are normally centrally managed from Farnham's AS/400.

Domco, like many other firms in the region, had a disaster recovery plan in place but hadn't considered an ice storm.

"You can plan for a disaster when a building is destroyed, but we never figured on a disaster where we couldn't communicate with our Farnham offices" via roads, phone lines, network lines or cellular connections, said Guy Chamberland, Domco's IT director.

Net Cuts Through

Rescue workers in upstate New York and Vermont were able to ring up New York state disaster relief officials even after conventional phone service was completely cut off by the recent ice storm that has brought the region to a near standstill.

The isolated communities are linked to the state's disaster recovery headquarters via an advanced communications network, the Adirondack Area Network (AAN), that relies on frame-relay and Integrated Services Digital Network (ISDN) communications links.

The system provides direct voice and videoconferencing contact among state officials in Albany coordinating cleanup operations, and hospitals and schools acting as command centers in the outlying communities.

According to the network's developers, combining underground ISDN lines and IP networks that don't use regular phone lines helped to keep the system running, even in places where electricity and phone service had failed.

Most similar high-speed networks use such a strategy, but AAN's community-oriented effort and focus on an area with limited infrastructure is a departure from the norm. Because of its current geographic limits, the network won't be used for more distant areas in New England and Canada, which were also hard hit by the storm.

(Source: Tim Ouellette and Thomas Hoffman,© *Computerworld Online News, 1/19/98.*
http://www.computerworld.com)

a. Computers were not actually destroyed during the ice freeze, so why did so many business operations get interrupted?

b. How did the Canadian Financial Institution government agency respond to the disaster to be able to continue processing business applications?

c. Why did some of the equipment used in the disaster recovery plan work initially and then ultimately fail?

d. Domco Inc. switched its operations to a disaster recovery site. Why did it have to shut down business operations for three days? Do you think the disaster recovery plan included a three-day business closure?

e. How did advance communications networks help the New York state disaster recovery headquarters?

f. Should this disaster have caught so many businesses off-guard? Was it that unpredictable?

g. Overall, what worked well and what did not? What can be done to improve disaster recovery planning for this region?

References and Websites

American Institute of Certified Public Accountants—Special Committee on Assurance Services. "Assurance on Risk Assessment." 1997. *http://www.aicpa.org/assurance/scas/newsvs/ risk/index.htm.*

———. *"Consideration of Internal Control in a Financial Statement Audit: An Amendment on Auditing Standards No. 55."* Statement on Auditing Standards No. 78. December 1995.

Anon. "Disaster Recovery Firms Shift Focus to E-Commerce," *Computerworld Online,* May 22, 2000.

Committee of Sponsoring Organizations of the Treadway Commission. *"Internal Control— Integrated Framework."* 1992.

Computer Security Institute. *"Computer Security Issues and Trends—Information Security Market for 1998."* Winter 1997/1998.

Computer Security Institute. *"Computer Security Issues and Trends—1998 CSI/FBI Computer Crime and Security Survey."* Spring 1998.

Financial Executives Research Foundation—Bashein, Markus and Finley, authors. *Safety Nets: Secrets of Effective Information Technology Controls.* June 1997.

Franckowiak, Dave. "Risk Management and Internal Control." January 30, 1998. *http://www.colybrand.com/industry/banking/ias/publications/risk_management.htm.*

Frazier, David, and Scott Spalding. "The New SAS No. 78." *CPA Journal,* May 1996. *http://www.luca.com/cpajournal/1996/0596/features/f40.htm.*

Sliwa, Carol, David Orenstein, and Kathleen Ohlson, "Outages Plague Irate MCI Users," *Computerworld Online,* August 16, 1999. *www.computerworld.com.*

Software Engineering Institute. "SEI Risk Management Paradigm." *http://www. sei.cmu.edu/technology/risk/Risk_General/paradigm.htm.*

Vijayan, Jaikumar, "Transaction Loads Sack eBay Hardware," *Computerworld Online,* May 24, 1999, *www.computerworld.com.*

Weiss, Todd. "Update: Online Trading Problems Caused by Upgrade Glitch at ADP," *Computerworld Online,* November 8, 2000. *www.computerworld.com.*

9 INTERNET STANDARDS, PROTOCOLS, AND LANGUAGES

Learning Objectives

1. To understand the necessity of standards.
2. To understand the effect that the global environment has on standard setting processes.
3. To identify the seven layers in the Open Systems Interconnections Model.
4. To identify common Internet protocols and languages.

INTRODUCTION

The Internet is a complex infrastructure, technically governed by no one, that electronically links together the entire globe. Considering the enormity of the Internet, its high growth rate, the interconnection of multiple cultures and languages, and its lack of designated ownership, one may marvel at how well it works. This relatively smooth Internet ride taken by the vast majority of its users has not resulted accidentally. Standard-setting and protocol development bodies have been involved in Internet development since its inception (some bodies existed prior to its inception), and others have emerged as a result of its birth. This chapter introduces the major standard-setting bodies, discusses the issues facing standard-setting bodies, and introduces the major protocols and computer languages in use on the Internet.

STANDARD-SETTING ISSUES AND COMMITTEES

For users to communicate with one another in a meaningful fashion on the Internet, they must send messages in a manner that can be interpreted by the receiving entities. Both the message content and its delivery mechanism need to follow agreed upon methods referred to as **standards.** The problem that has arisen during the past two decades is that two widely used, yet different methods have emerged internationally. The resulting situation is not unique to the Internet. Throughout time, different groups have developed standards that conflict or are incompatible with one other. Probably the first such development is the agreed-upon methods of oral communication, known as languages.

Geographically close groups of people developed their own representations of things, actions, thoughts, etc., and called them words. When different groups met, they could not easily communicate because of the different standards of speech that had emerged. In many cases, communication was conducted—and still is by some foreign travelers— through sign language when people spoke different languages.

Another example of the development of different standards is the metric system and the old-fashioned units of measurement, hereafter called "old units." The conversion from the old units to the metric system worldwide has occurred rather slowly given the strong, and almost unequivocal, superiority of the metric system as a measurement device. The United States is still largely using the old units, but the metric system is gaining ground.[1] Yet another example is the different electrical standards that are used in different countries. Travelers visiting foreign countries with different electrical standards must use converter devices to operate electrical devices, such as hair dryers and electrical razors, that are from their home country. Many times, the converters do not work that well, sometimes destroying the electrical devices. Similar to the operation of electrical devices in foreign countries, data conversion between two electronic systems that do not have the same standards must be conducted. If the conversion process is not conducted properly, the data can become garbled and unusable, just like the malfunctioning or destruction of electrical appliances used in incompatible foreign countries.

In an effort to develop uniform methods of Internet communication and commerce, numerous groups have formed around the globe. Untangling the web of seemingly similar standard-setting bodies, both in the United States and abroad, is a daunting task. This section introduces only some of the more influential committees that study and recommend Internet standards, and it discusses the move toward a single international standard. A time line illustrating the inception dates of the primary committees and many of the events discussed in this chapter is found in Figure 9–1.

| **FIGURE 9–1** | *Time line of major standard setting bodies and internet societies* |

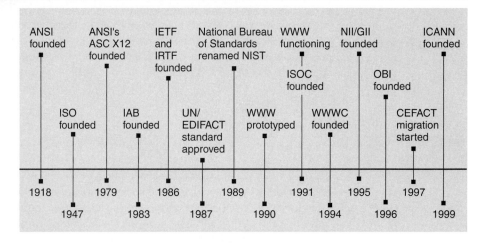

---

[1]According to the Unites States Metric Association, the vast majority of U.S. state Departments of Transportation currently use the metric system; the Food and Drug Administration requires that both old units and metric labels be placed on customer products.

ANSI

The **American National Standards Institute (ANSI)** was founded in 1918 by five engineering societies and three government agencies. Although government agencies were involved in its creation, ANSI has always been a private, nonprofit organization that is supported by both private and public sector organizations. ANSI was setting standards long before the first digital computer was created, much less networked. For example, ANSI sets standards for exact sizes of sheet film for cameras. During the past 71 years, the essence of ANSI's primary goal has remained unchanged despite the monumental technological changes occurring during this period. Its primary goal is the enhancement of global competitiveness of U.S. businesses by promoting and facilitating voluntary consensus standards and promoting their integrity. The key concepts of ANSI's primary goal are standards that are voluntary and agreed upon by consensus. Voluntary means that the standards put forth by ANSI are not mandates. However, companies wishing to interact with other businesses understand the need for conformity and willingly adhere to such standards in most cases.

ANSI does not develop the standards by itself. It serves as a facilitator for standards development by providing channels for consensus building. Why is consensus building important? In an unregulated environment in which standards are allowed to voluntarily emerge, the greater the agreement by major producers and users of the standardized items, the greater the acceptance of the standard. The more acceptance a standard receives, the more it will be adopted, and the greater amount of interoperability between items and products sold by the industries.

In a very important act for U.S.-based EDI, ANSI chartered the **ANSI Accredited Standards Committee (ASC) X12** in 1979 to develop uniform standards for interindustry EDI. ASC X12 membership is open to anyone and currently meets two to three times a year. To date, the ASC X12 committee has developed in excess of 275 standard transaction sets.

UN/EDIFACT

While the United States' ANSI ASC X12 was working diligently to develop widely accepted standards, parallel efforts were being made abroad. A very popular standard messaging format for business and government communications was developed called the **Electronic Data Interchange for Administration, Commerce, and Transport** (EDIFACT). The United Nations has repeatedly endorsed EDIFACT standards and recommended that all governments use the EDIFACT format. This widespread support of the **United Nations EDIFACT** (UN/EDIFACT) standard has challenged the ANSI ASC X12 standard. Note that this is only a recommendation by the United Nations, not a mandate, and hence, adoption of the standard is voluntary. As firms globalize, the need arises to share data with entities in various countries worldwide, and they rapidly begin to understand the need to have one international EDI standard. Thus, the adoption of standards is theoretically voluntary, but to stay in the game, the adoption of a standard that is meaningful in all countries fosters voluntary support of one international standard as a basic necessity of international commerce.

ANSI's ASC X12 Alignment Task Group Leading the Migration to UN/EDIFACT

ASC X12's parent, ANSI, is guided by the philosophy of promoting U.S. standards internationally. However, it also champions the adoption of international standards as national standards in situations where such adoption is considered to be appropriate. Although somewhat reluctant at first to merge with the UN/EDIFACT standard, the need for United States' businesses to use globally accepted standards has caused ASC X12 to commit to the migration to UN/EDIFACT syntax.

> We need to apply our skills at the standards development level to meet the challenges of the global marketplace. To encourage integrated electronic exchange, we are working to represent X12 semantics in an XML format to support the data transfer needs of a broad base of users, including small and medium-sized enterprises. We must also continue to synchronize the functionality across X12 and UN/EDIFACT as we work to build common solutions.

(David Barkley, Message from the ASC X12 Chair, 2000)

A standing task force, the Alignment Task Group, is in place to plan for and lead the UN/EDIFACT migration. This task force has been working diligently to integrate EDIFACT syntax into the currently defined transaction sets. The ASC X12 has updated its philosophy to state that it develops, maintains, interprets, publishes, and promotes the proper of both ANSI and UN/EDIFACT international data standards. The ASC X12 still strongly dominates the United States' EDI market, and thus both of these standards currently co-exist. However, the EDI community predicts that ASC X12 will fade out and be completely replaced with UN/EDIFACT. The first agreement to connect an ANSI ASC X12 system with a UN/EDIFACT system was initiated at the end of 1997 by CoreStates Bank and the Royal Bank of Scotland. In the future, these types of initiatives are likely to become common as the integration is better facilitated by an increasingly common syntax between ASC X12 and UN/EDIFACT.

Another important development in EDI is the use of the **eXtensible Markup Language (XML)** to exchange EDI data through Web browsers. XML is discussed later in this chapter, but at this point an important feature of XML is that it allows customized tags to be created in defining fields of data. The customized tags, however, need to be the same from firm to firm. A logical progression is to use the X12 and UN/EDIFACT data definitions in the XML-based tagging systems. A set of specifications that are being developed to enable a modular electronic business framework is called **ebXML.** It is a joint initiative of the United Nations (UN/CEFACT) and OASIS.[2] In December 2000, the group announced that it was two months ahead of schedule in its 18-month project to deliver the core technical infrastructure of ebXML:

> The ebXML specifications for transport, routing and packaging, trading partner agreements, and registry/repository are stable and ready for evaluation and early adoption. This is great news for Web developers who want to get a jumpstart on creating electronic commerce applications built on global standards.

(Klaus-Dieter Naujok, chair of ebXML and member of the UN/CEFACT Steering Group)

MAJOR STANDARD-SETTING STRUCTURES AND INTERFACES

This section discusses several standard-setting infrastructures and processes. Understanding the interrelationships of these organizations is important when attempting to assess why standardization and interoperability continue to be unsolved issues. For the most part, these complexly related infrastructures work quite well.

---

[2]OASIS is another international, not-for-profit consortium that advances electronic business by promoting open, collaborative development of interoperability.

FIGURE 9–2   *Relationships among major standard-setting bodies*

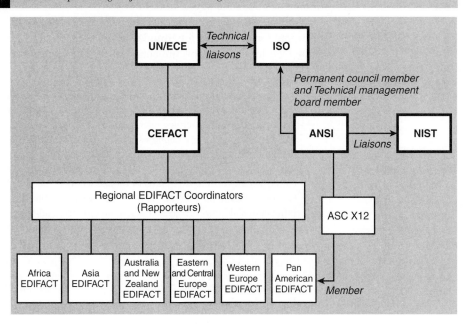

U.S. and International Standard-Setting Bodies

Figure 9–2 illustrates the relationships among major U.S. and international standard-setting bodies. The organizations in the boldly outlined boxes represent standard-setting organizations that encompass a much broader realm of standard-setting issues in addition to Internet and e-commerce–related topics. The subgroups illustrated, EDIFACT and ASC X12, are just subsets of the many other standard-setting and technical groups housed under these organizations.

ANSI and one of its subgroups, ASC X12 were introduced earlier in the chapter. ASC X12 has two standing task forces to specifically address alignment with UN/EDIFACT standards and another to address its regional integration issues via the Pan American EDIFACT group that coordinates the efforts of North, Central, and South America. As previously mentioned, ANSI's ASC X12 committee is committed to promoting UN/EDIFACT compatible standards, and these two task forces aid in this endeavor. Thus, the United States has one input mechanism into the UN/EDIFACT via the Pan American EDIFACT group.

The entire UN/EDIFACT effort is currently housed under the **United Nations Centre for Facilitation of Procedures and Practices for Administration, Commerce, and Transport (CEFACT),** which is housed under the **United Nations Economic Commission for Europe (UN/ECE).** The strategic objective of CEFACT is "to support international commerce, transport, and administration in the simplification of their business processes and procedures." The UN/EDIFACT group falls under one of CEFACT's six permanent working groups—electronic commerce policy. CEFACT is the streamlined result of a two-year engineering process aimed at separating technical development from policy making and also empowering technical bodies. Reorganization of standard-setting bodies is imperative in order to allow them to become more responsive to changing needs and technological developments and to reduce the standards development implementation cycle time.

ANSI has input into the UN/ECE indirectly through its strong ties with the **International Organization for Standardization (ISO).** The ISO was established in 1947. It is a worldwide, nongovernmental federation of national standard bodies from more than 120 member countries. The ISO's vision is given here:

> ISO sees a world in which global trade between nations continues to grow at a rate three to four times faster than national economies; a world in which the design, manufacturing, marketing, and customer service operations of a growing majority of individual enterprises are distributed across many countries; and a world in which electronic communications have dramatically increased human collaboration in every field and between all countries. . . In this rapidly evolving scenario, globally applicable standards will pay a key role. Such standards, whether developed by ISO or others, will become one of the primary driving forces to support international commerce. In this context, ISO intends to be recognized globally as an influential and innovative leader and as an effective and responsive producer in the development of globally applicable international standards which meet or exceed the expectations of the community of nations. . .

(ISO in the New Century, www.iso.ch)

The ISO has approved approximately 12,000 international standards. Its standards are developed according to the following principles:

- Consensus, which requires approval by 75 percent of all members.
- Global industry wide solutions.
- Market-driven and voluntary involvement by market participants.

The standards approved by the ISO are referred to as ISO xxxx. For example, ISO 8879, the Standardized Generalized Markup Language, is an international standard that received consensus approval by the ISO.

ANSI is a founding member of ISO and is active in its governance. It is the United States' sole representative to the ISO. U.S. standards are frequently proposed as international standards via ANSI's membership in the ISO. The ISO is not part of the United Nations, but it has technical liaisons with U.N. agencies. Domestically, the National Institute of Standards and Technology (NIST) was established by Congress to facilitate the rapid commercialization of products based on new technological developments. In relatively recent years, the NIST has realized the importance of voluntary standards by nongovernmental entities and has asked ANSI for assistance as reflected in the following statement by ANSI:

> A strong U.S. position in the global marketplace requires a strong partnership between the private sector and the federal government. Government is relying more on the use of private sector voluntary standards for acquisition, regulatory reform, and conformity assessment. The NIST has a major leadership role in coordinating the activities of federal agencies in the transition to voluntary consensus standards. NIST has asked ANSI to assist in this activity, an activity that will benefit all business sectors and consumers. Greater government reliance on voluntary standards should result in more government and private-sector participation in the ANSI-accredited standards development process.

(Chairman's Overview—ANSI's 1997 Annual Report)

ANSI has responded to this call for assistance by preparing a National Standards Strategy for the United States that it presented in testimony regarding standards to Congress in November 2000.

Internet and World Wide Web Specific Committees

The parent organizations mentioned thus far originated prior to the inception of the Internet and the World Wide Web (WWW). They have since adapted their organizational structures to the changing environment and created new task forces to address these changes. Even so, new organizations continue to appear on the scene to specifically deal with Internet and WWW matters.

Internet Committees

Several of these groups are illustrated in Figure 9–3. The **Internet Society (ISOC)** has several groups considered to be under its umbrella. It is a nongovernmental, international, not-for-profit organization. The ISOC was actually formed long after the creation of some of its groups, such as the **Internet Architecture Board (IAB)** and the **Internet Engineering Task Force (IETF).** The ISOC asserts the principle rationale for its formation was to provide financial support for the Internet standard-setting process and to give it a home. One reason given for the necessity of a home was to provide a legal umbrella for the IAB and the IETF. The IETF develops the standards and is comprised of international members with eclectic backgrounds, such as network designers, operators, vendors, and researchers. The common thread among these members is that they are concerned with facilitating the smooth evolution of the Internet's architecture and its operations. In 1994, the IETF was accredited by the ISO as an international standards board. The **Internet Engineering Steering Group (IESG)** considers the standards put forth by the IETF and approves the formal standards actions. The IESG members are technical specialists.

FIGURE 9–3   *ISOC, IAB, and related committees*

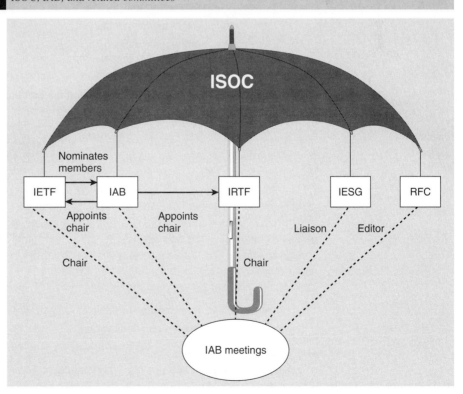

Internet Research Task Force (IRTF) as its name implies, is comprised of research groups working on short- and long-term issues. They are also charged with setting research priorities. They cover a wide spectrum of topics, such as protocols, applications, architecture, and technology. The IRTF chair is appointed by the IAB.

Requests for comments (RFCs) are a series of notes on a wide variety of technological topics. RFC documents are documents submitted by the IETF Working Groups or they can be from an individual or organization. The IAB publishes the RFCs. Some examples of RFCs on topics discussed later in this chapter are

- RFC 791—the IP protocol.
- RFC 793— the TCP protocol.
- RFC 822— the SMTP protocol.
- RFC 2068— the HTTP protocol.
- RFC 2948— the Telnet encryption protocol, DES3 64-bit output feedback.

Until mid-1998, the U.S. government outsourced the management of **domain names** to Network Solutions Inc., commonly referred to as the Internic. NSI coordinated the assignment and maintained a register of unique values for Internet parameters, such as Internet addresses and domain names. In 1998, the **Internet Corporation for Assigned Names and Numbers (ICANN),** a nonprofit, international organization, was formed to manage many of the Internet's primary domain registration functions. In November 2000, it approved seven new domain name extensions, .biz, .info, .name, .pro, .museum, .aero and .coop. Also in November 2000, ICANN started using multilingual characters in domain names. ICANN performs the following functions:

- IP address space allocation.
- Protocol parameter assignment.
- Domain name system management.
- Root server system management.

World Wide Web Committees

The WWW was created long after the inception of the Internet. As explained in Chapter 1, the WWW was originally prototyped in 1990 and operationalized at CERN (a French acronym) in Switzerland led by Tim Berners-Lee. By the mid-1990s, the WWW was greatly embraced by users worldwide. The WWW is based on the concepts of hypertext links, software portability, and network and socket programming.

W3C.   Not surprisingly, new groups of WWW committees began to pop up immediately after its acceptance. The most prominent committee, the **World Wide Web Consortium (W3C),** was founded in 1994. Initially, it was connected with CERN, but much of the seed funding came from the **U.S. Defense Advanced Research Project (DARPA)** and the UN/ECE. The W3C's charge is "to lead the WWW to its full potential by developing common protocols that promote its evolution and ensure its interoperability." Specifically, some of the services provided by the W3C include:

- A repository of information about the WWW for developers and users.
- Reference code implementations to embody and promote standards.
- Prototype and sample applications to demonstrate the use of new technologies.

Individuals may not join the W3C, but membership is open to any organization for a fee. Software products developed by the group are made available for public use, and reference software is made available free of charge. Currently, the W3C is an international collaborative effort, hosted jointly by the Massachusetts Institute of Technology's laboratory for computer science, INRIA in Europe, and Keio University in Japan.

OBI.   To promote easier Internet purchasing systems, a group of *Fortune* 500 companies self-organized and formed an Internet Purchasing Roundtable, which in turn set up an **Open Buying on the Internet (OBI)** consortium in 1996. The OBI is a nonprofit organization charged with providing a forum for developing open standards for business-to-business Internet commerce, as well as providing education and compliance certificates. It issued its first standard in May 1997 and has gained some support from business organizations, as well as some technology organizations, such as Microsoft, Netscape, and Oracle.

Global Information Infrastructure Commission

Standard-setting groups formed before the Internet, for the Internet, and for the WWW are discussed in the previous sections. This section discusses one last, relatively new group, the **Global Information Infrastructure Commission** (GIIC). This group was founded in 1995 in response to the perceived failure of traditional institutions and regulatory frameworks to meet the challenges posed by today's complex environment and global networks. Some standard-setting bodies, such as ANSI and the UN/ECE, have admitted that their structure and processes need to be streamlined and more responsive to the changing environment's impact of societal needs, and they have made significant strides in restructuring.

The mission of the GIIC does not have standard setting as an explicit objective, but it does attempt to generate change by having liaisons disseminate the GIIC's opinions to such bodies as the national information infrastructures of various countries, international standard-setting committees, and other public interest groups. The opinions and messages sent forth by the GIIC are determined at numerous international meetings at which participants examine what is working well and why, what issues need to be addressed, and which problems need to be fixed. The GIIC has strong ties with the World Bank, which hosted its inauguration, and it consists of industry leaders from more than 45 countries. The GIIC is particularly interested in including both developing and industrialized countries in its initiatives and agenda. The GIIC was organized with a three-year mandate of producing results by the end of 1998; however, the committee continues to work past that date on its digital divide project. This initiative seeks to close the digital divide that exists between various countries and socioeconomic groups. Figure 9–4 highlights some data provided in October 2000 by the GIIC regarding the digital divide between countries.

SECURITY COMMITTEES AND ORGANIZATIONS

Security on the Internet is a primary concern to all parties connected. This section introduces some of the primary groups working toward a safe Internet environment. Located at the **Software Engineering Institute (SEI),** which operates at Carnegie Mellon University, the **Computer Emergency Response Team Coordination Center (CERT)** is a highly visible organization that provides a great service to the Internet community. CERT was founded in 1988 as part of SEI's Networked Systems Survivability Program (NSS). It was organized to operationalize the goals of the NSS by helping prevent, detect, and resolve Internet security incidents. In response to what it viewed as a software

FIGURE 9–4	Levels of access to technology by region				
	GNP per Capita	Net Hosts per 10,000	PCs per 1,000	Mobile Phone per 1,000	Phone Lines per 1,000
Sub-Saharan Africa	$1,440	2.0	8	5	14
South Asia	1,940	0.2	3	1	19
East Asia and the Pacific	3,280	2.0	14	25	70
Middle East and North Africa	4,630	0.4	10	8	81
Europe and Central Asia	5,510	15.0	34	23	200
Latin American and Caribbean	6,340	15.0	34	45	123
United States	20,314	1,509.0	459	256	661
European Union	20,440	608.0	311	230	514

Source: GIIC October 2000 PPT Presentation on Digital Divide, *ww.giic.org.*

crisis, the U.S. Department of Defense (DOD) sponsored the SEI in 1984. The goal of the NSS is to promote and ensure practices that help to resist attacks against networked systems. In cases of successful attacks, minimalization of damage and continuity of critical services is the primary concern.

CERT is probably best known for its alert archives, incident report telephone hotline, and e-mail report services. The **alert archives** are advisories that specifically address Internet security problems. The advisories explain the cause of the problem and offer solutions to fix the problems. In many cases, remedial program code, called **patches,** to fix the problems can be downloaded from CERT's website. These advisories are disseminated via a mailing list, USENET, and the CERT's homepage. Since its inception, CERT has published more than 300 security alerts and handled more than 18,000 phone hotline calls and more than 300,000 e-mail messages.

CERT does not operate in a vacuum. For example, its staff members regularly attend IETF meetings. CERT has periodically been asked to testify before Congress about security issues. During 2000, a representative from CERT provided various testimonies to the U.S. Congress a total of six times. CERT also interacts in some fashion with the other security groups mentioned in this section. CERT organizations exist worldwide for similar purposes and are typically funded by some branch of each country's national government.

An international consortium of computer incident response and security teams is the **Forum of Incident Response and Security Teams (FIRST).** Most of the worldwide CERT organizations are members, along with many business organizations. The mission of FIRST is similar to that of CERT, but with a greater focus on sharing information globally between geographically separated security and incident response teams facing similar problems and issues.

The **International Computer Security Association (ICSA)** founded in 1989, is an organization that is structured very differently from all of the previously mentioned entities in that it is an independent, for-profit organization. It has paying members and sells services. The ICSA certifies products, systems, and people and disseminates information by issuing alerts, white papers, studies, and other guidelines.

Not mentioned yet in this section are the numerous governmental security agencies. Understandably, governments worldwide are extremely concerned about security and are among the first to organize security-related agencies. In many cases, much of the work they conduct is shared with nongovernmental committees in an effort to promote a safer Internet environment. The following governmental agencies work toward creating a safer networked computing environment:

- NIST's Computer Security Resource Clearinghouse (CSRC).
- Computer Security Technology Center (CSTC).
- Computer Incident Advisory Capability (CIAC).
- Federal Computer Incident Response Capability (FedCIRC).
- Advanced Security Projects.
- Secure Systems Services.

SECURITY PROTOCOLS AND LANGUAGES

In the previous section, the primary standard-setting committees were discussed. This section discusses the major Internet and WWW protocols and languages. **Protocols** are agreed-upon methods of communicating and transmitting data between telecommunications devices. A **computer language** is also an agreed-upon method of communicating, but the focus is on communicating with the computer and its operating system. Internet protocols and languages are constantly evolving in response to an ever-changing and growing environment. Further, new protocols and languages continue to surface. To stay on top of this topic, as with all technology topics, one must constantly monitor the environment and update one's knowledge base!

OSI

Interoperability is a necessary condition for Internet data sharing. The NIST defines interoperability as "the capability for applications running on different computers to exchange information and operate cooperatively using this information." A general reference model for the standardization of data communication procedures that support interoperability is the ISO **Open Systems Interconnections (OSI) model** released in 1984. The OSI model consists of seven layers, illustrated in Figure 9–5.

- *Application layer.* This layer is a "service" used to communicate with the actual application in use. It performs such tasks as converting messages into the necessary format for use by the application.
- *Presentation layer.* This layer negotiates the syntax (format) of the data transferred.
- *Session layer.* This layer is responsible for establishing and maintaining communications channels. It negotiates packet recovery and provides synchronization checkpoints for data packets transmitted.
- *Transport layer.* This layer provides data reliability and integrity checks of the data received by the ultimate end node. It also performs error detection and control functions.

FIGURE 9–5   *OSI reference model*

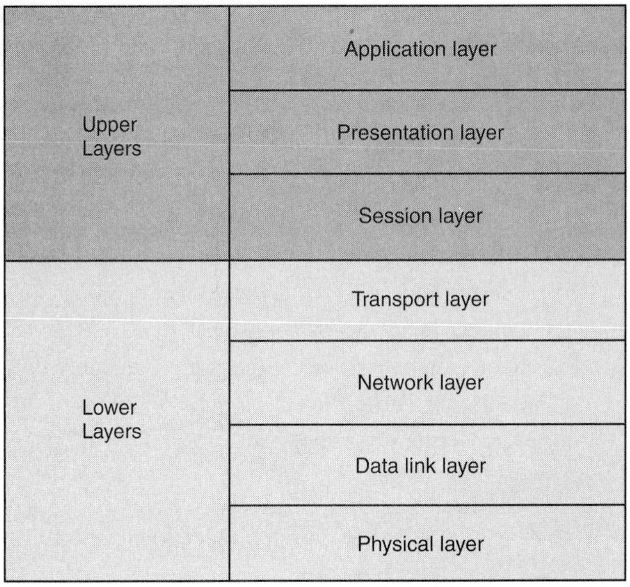

	Application layer
Upper Layers	Presentation layer
	Session layer
	Transport layer
Lower Layers	Network layer
	Data link layer
	Physical layer

- *Network layer.* This layer performs data routing and delivery across multiple (intermediate) nodes.
- *Data link layer.* The layer performs the transmission of data and error control from one node to another node (a single communications link).
- *Physical layer.* This layer performs the physical transfer of bits to the transmission medium; it is the data communications interface with the hardware.

The first four layers are typically called the lower layers because they deal with the physical data transfer. The last three layers are called the upper layers because they deal more with message handling of the data packets transferred.

The data link and network layers can operate in one of two nodes. The first mode, **connection-oriented,** transmits the entire message in a data stream. The connection is established, the data are transferred, error checks are performed and receipt of data is confirmed, and the connection is closed. The second mode, **connectionless,** splits the message into packets or datagrams and sends them intermittently to the destination. At the destination, the datagrams are collected and reassembled and any lost packets are identified. The transport layer basically masks the underlying transport mode and handles data reliability and integrity checks. Thus, the OSI model is a reference model that is useful for understanding the underlying data transport methodologies employed by the protocols discussed in this section.

TCP/IP

The most widely used protocol on the Internet, although it may be transparent to many WWW users, is the **Transmission Control Protocol/Internet Protocol (TCP/IP).** This set of protocols was developed in the early 1970s and, as will be discussed later, continues to evolve. This is called a reliable protocol because delivery of all data is guaranteed.

If packets get lost along the way, they are automatically resent. Basically, it is a communications protocol used to connect Internet hosts. This set of protocols is built into the UNIX operating system. The Windows-based interface for TCP/IP is called a **Windows socket,** more commonly referred to as **Winsock.** TCP operates at the transport layer of the OSI model, while IP operates at the network layer. The TCP/IP protocol is further described in Chapter 9.

IP Addresses

When a message is sent, an **IP address** for both the sending and receiving nodes must be known. Currently, the IP addresses are 32 bits under the IPv4 classification (4-byte packets) in length. The IP next generation **(IPng)** or **IPv6,** expands IP addresses to 128 bits to accommodate more website host addresses. Currently, IPv4 is still is use, and the decomposition of IP addresses varies according the assigned class. Figure 9–6 illustrates the components of an IPv4 IP address and each of the classes is discussed in the following sections.

IPv4

Class A.   This class is reserved for organizations or groups with very large networks, such as IBM, and they are set up so that they can accommodate a large number of hosts (or user computers). A zero in the first bit represents this class. Only 126 Class A addresses exist (128 numerical possibilities exist, but the values 0 and 127 are reserved for special purposes). The next seven bits represent the network identifier. The remaining 24 bits identify the specific host. This class has the ability to represent the greatest number of host computers on a network, more than 16 million.

Class B.   This class is used for medium-sized networks. A one-zero in the first two bits represents this class. The next 14 bits represent the network identifier. These are almost exhausted and difficult to get; an example is the ISP America Online. The other 16 bits represent the hosts on each network. This class can represent close to 66,000 host computers on a network.

FIGURE 9–6   *The IPv4 protocol*

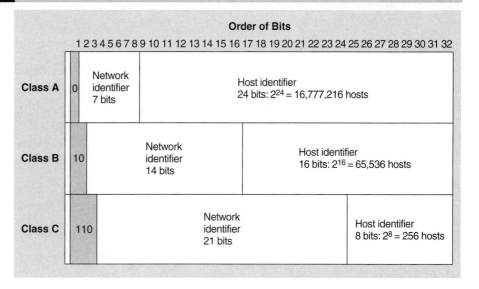

Class C.   This class is used for small networks. A one-one-zero in the first three bits represents this class. The next 21 bits represent the network identifier. The other 8 bits represent the hosts on each network. This class can only represent 256 host computers on a network.

Class D and Class E.   These classes are reserved for special and experimental purposes. Figure 9–7 illustrates how an IP address may be used to track the source of a message. By backtracking from the IP source and using a domain name service to locate the registered domain name, the source can be identified, such as Lehigh University's business faculty network. The challenge at that point is pinpointing the exact computer from which the message originated. If designated nodes are used, then pinpointing the computer is possible. If the computer is a shared computer, and password logs are not available, then identifying the exact person who sent the message may not be possible.

IPv6

The IPv4 addressing scheme will eventually exhaust itself as the number of Internet users grows exponentially. A new version of the Internet Protocol, IPv6, will eventually replace the old IP protocol, IPv4. The IETF has examined this protocol and chosen it as the next standard. RFCs 1883 and 1884 explain the IPv6 protocol, which uses a 128-bit address, rather than a 32-bit address. In the next couple of years, firms will begin to migrate their systems to IPv6. Aside from using a larger address, and thus being able to accommodate more networks, IPv6 has some additional enhancements such as more optimal processing, simplified autoconfiguration, and enhanced standard features.

Domain Names

The top-level domain names are managed and maintained by ICANN. Initially, the main categories were

.edu	Four year colleges and universities
.com	Commercial organizations
.net	Network providers
.org	Nonprofit organizations

FIGURE 9–7   *IP address tracking*

A suspicious message is received and an investigation reveals that the true IP address of the sender is 128.180.94.102

A domain name service that maintains a list of registered domains determines that this message was sent by a business department server at Lehigh University—computer node 102

If Lehigh can track a specific computer assigned to node 102, then they can pinpoint the computer from which the message was sent.

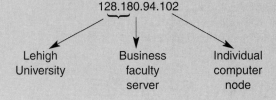

Other top-level domain names managed by the U.S. government are .gov and .mil. Foreign country code top-level domains are defined in ISO 3166. Some examples are

.es	Spain (Espana)
.uk	United Kingdom
.ca	Canada
.de	Germany (Deutschland)
.mx	Mexico

Increased demand for names both domestically and internationally is creating host name conflicts and shortage problems. The demand for additional **global top-level domains** has been great. As a result, a new governance framework emerged, the **Generic Top Level Domain Memorandum of Understanding (gTLD),** to provide an international governance policy for administering and enhancing the domain naming system. So far, at least seven new generic top level domains have been set: .biz, .info, .name, .pro, .museum, .aero, and .coop.

One noticeable change is that the extensions are not restricted to three letters as they have been in the past. This new structure will not make it as easy to guess an entity's Web address. Different extensions will be assigned based on the type of business. A classification problem for some entities that sell goods, provide information, and also have some form of entertainment activity will undoubtedly result.

FTP and TELNET

A popular method for uploading and downloading files is the **File Transfer Protocol (FTP).** FTP is a common tool used for uploading Web documents to a server. A Windows version of FTP, WinFTP, makes file transfer procedures trivial. After giving the remote host, user ID, and password information to the software, it will log onto the desired system and show the local directory in one window and the remote directory in another window. To transfer files, all one has to do is point-and-click. Some remote host computers allow anonymous log-ins for retrieval of non-private data files. TELNET allows a remote user with a valid ID and password to log-in to a system. Once the user is logged in, it is as if he or she is sitting at the console of the remote system. TELNET is appropriate for information perusal and data entry. FTP is appropriate for data uploading and downloading. Both of these applications run on top of TCP/IP.

NNTP

One of the great benefits of the Internet is the ability to easily share information. The **Network News Transfer Protocol (NNTP)** is an IETF standard that is explained in its basic form in RFC 977. NNTP is designed as an open Internet protocol to facilitate the distribution, inquiry, retrieval, and posting of news articles. This protocol allows users to search for specific topics of interest. Some collaborative workgroup software, such as Netscape's Collabra, is built to be compatible with NNTP-compliant servers so that interactive discussion group sessions can be held.

HTTP and HTTP-NG

The protocol that underlies the WWW is called the **HyperText Transfer/Transport Protocol (HTTP).** This protocol runs on top of the TCP protocol. This is a stateless protocol. When a user clicks on a link to a Web page, the connection is opened, data are transferred (the Web page is displayed), and the connection is broken. It began as a request-response protocol that allowed different platforms and applications to exchange documents. In its original form, its primary purpose was to

- Define message formats.
- Define message transmissions.
- Define Web server and browser commands.

The IETF has an HTTP working group on improving HTTP specifications. HTTP 1.1, which is an upward compatible version of HTTP 1.0, provided the benefits of decreasing the load of HTTP on the Internet, and thus related congestion, and providing more efficient caching. An extension mechanism for HTTP is the **Protocol Extension Protocol (PEP)** that accommodates the need for dynamic interactions for transaction-based applications. In 2000, the IETF issued another HTTP extension framework experimental document, RFC 2774. The types of extensions proposed in the framework are

- Extending a single HTTP message.
- Introducing new encodings.
- Initiating HTTP-derived protocols for new applications.
- Switching to protocols that, once initiated, run independently of the original protocol stack.

SGML and HTML

Standard Generalized Markup Language (SGML) is a data encoding system that promotes document sharing. It is an internationally accepted standard (ISO 8879) used for organizing and tagging elements in a document. SGML is hardware and software independent. The information in SGML documents is divided into three categories:

- Data—full multimedia capabilities, as well as hidden data capabilities.
- Structure—the relationship among the data elements, such as headings, subheadings, bullets, and illustrations.
- Format—the appearance of objects, such as boldfaced text, or a centered paragraph.

The rules for the structure of a document are contained in a hierarchical model, called the **document type definition (DTD).** For example, a DTD may specify that a document must have an e-mail address immediately following a person's name and title. These structure definitions are especially useful for sharing documents among many business organizations.

The **HyperText Markup Language (HTML)** is sometimes referred to as the offspring of SGML. This is currently the most popular language for authoring Web pages. HTML is similar to SGML, but it does not have as many application capabilities as does its forefather. HTML is also hardware and software independent, and it is a language for encoding and recognizing electronic documents. HTML code is easily generated by many popular word processing, spreadsheet, and graphics packages. HTML code begins and ends with an HTML tag represented as <HTML> and </HTML>, and it is divided into two sections. Formatting commands, or tags, used on the illustrated HTML documents are shown here:

        <B></B>   Bold

        <I></I>   Italics

<Font Size=n> </Font>	Font size
<P> </P>	Paragraph beginning and end
<P Align="CENTER"</P>	Center
<HR>	Horizontal line

XML

A similar markup language, in concept, is the eXtensible Markup Language (XML). One very important distinction between HTML and XML, however, is that XML allows the creation of customized tags, rather than requiring the use of standard tags. Figure 9–8 illustrates some very simple XML code for a customer file. Much of it looks similar to HTML, except that the tags are customized. Thus, the designer has much more flexibility, as with SGML. The ASC X12 is actively pursuing the use of XML in EDI applications because of its relative ease of translation. An example of General Motors Corporation's use of XML in its Web commerce initiatives is given in the box entitled "GM to Implement Web-Based IT Ordering System."

Bert Box of the W3C offers the following explanations of XML:

1. *XML is a method for putting structured data in a text file.* For "structured data" think of such things as spreadsheets, address books, configuration parameters, financial transactions, technical drawings, etc. . . XML is a set of rules, guidelines, conventions, whatever you want to call them, for designing text formats for such data, in a way that produces files that are easy to generate and read (by a computer), that are unambiguous, and that avoid common pitfalls, such as lack of extensibility, lack of support for internationalization/localization, and platform dependency.

2. *XML looks a bit like HTML but isn't HTML.* Like HTML, XML makes use of *tags* (words bracketed by '<' and '>') and *attributes* (of the form name="value"), but while HTML specifies what each tag and attribute means (and often how the text between them will look in a browser), XML uses the tags only to delimit pieces of data and leaves the interpretation of the data completely to the application that reads it.

FIGURE 9–8	*XML code*

```
<customer>
    <name>Cosmic Graphic Inc.</name>
    <billing-address>
        <street>1317 Star Blvd.</street>
        <city>Kemah</city>
        <state>Texas</state>
        <zipcode>77571</zipcode>
    </billing-address>
    <credit-limit>2000</credit-limit>
    <type-of-business>wholesaler</type-of-business>
    <contact>
        <first-name>Cynthia</first-name>
        <last-name>Barker</last-name>
    </contact>
</customer>
```

E-Commerce in Practice

GM To Implement Web-Based it Ordering System

General Motors Corp. today announced plans to scrap the manual, paper-based ordering system it uses for buying standard IT commodities, such as computers and help desk support, with a Web-based procurement system from Ariba Technologies Inc.

GM hopes to reduce costs by more closely controlling spending and better leveraging the company's buying power.

Also yesterday, GM discussed plans to use the Extensible Markup Language (XML) to share data throughout the corporation. GM will use DataChannel Inc.'s XML Framework product to help Web-enable the data in its legacy-based infrastructure, as well as create new XML-based applications.

XML tags help companies better organize and categorize information for search purposes or sharing data between applications.

GM will undertake several extensive XML pilots in engineering, quality control, manufacturing, finance, and electronic commerce over the next few years. The company also hopes to use XML to enhance customer service, a company official said.

Source: Carol Sliwa, *Computerworld Online,* March 15, 1999. © Computer-World Inc.

In other words, if you see "<p>" in an XML file, don't assume it is a paragraph. Depending on the context, it may be a price, a parameter, a person,

3. *XML is text, but isn't meant to be read.* XML files are text files, because that allows experts (such as programmers) to more easily *debug* applications, and in emergencies, they can use a simple text editor to fix a broken XML file. But the rules for XML files are much stricter than for HTML. A forgotten tag, or an attribute without quotes, makes the file unusable, while in HTML such practice is often explicitly allowed, or at least tolerated. It is written in the official XML specification: applications are not *allowed* to try to second guess the creator of a broken XML file; if the file is broken, an application has to stop right there and issue an error.

4. *XML is a family of technologies.* Around XML 1.0, there is a growing set of optional modules that provide sets of tags and attributes, or guidelines for specific tasks. There is, for example, Xlink (still in development as of November 1999) which describes a standard way to add hyperlinks to an XML file. Xpointer and XFragments are syntaxes for pointing to parts of an XML document. (An Xpointer is a bit like a URL, but instead of pointing to documents on the Web, it points to pieces of data inside an XML file.) The DOM is a standard set of function calls for manipulating XML (and HTML) files from a programming language. XML Namespaces is a specification that describes how you can associate a URL with every single tag and attribute in an XML document. What that URL is used for is up to the application that reads the URL, though.

5. *XML is verbose, but that is not a problem.* Since XML is a text format, and it uses tags to delimit the data, XML files are nearly always larger than comparable binary formats. That was a conscious decision by the XML developers. Disk space isn't as expensive anymore as it used to be, and programs such as "zip" and "gzip" can compress files very well and very fast. Those programs are available for nearly all platforms (and are usually free). In addition, communication protocols such as modem protocols and HTTP/1.1 (the core protocol of the Web) can compress data on the fly, thus saving bandwith as effectively as a binary format.

6. *XML is license-free, platform-independent and well-supported.* By choosing XML as the basis for some project, you buy into a large and growing community of tools (one of which may already do what you need!) and engineers experienced in the technology. Opting for XML is a bit like choosing SQL for databases: you still have to build your own database and your own programs/procedures that manipulate it, but many tools are available and many people who can help you. And since XML, as a W3C technology, is license free, you can build your own software around it without paying anybody anything. The large and growing support means that you are also not tied to a single vendor. XML isn't always the best solution, but it is always worth considering.

(W3C.org)

DOM and DHTML

The **Document Object Model (DOM)** specifies the representation of objects in a Web page. Standardization of DOMs is being examined by the W3C to ensure that the DOM is interoperable among Web browsers and is scripting-language neutral. DOM allows programs and script to access and dynamically update a document's content, style, and structure. The specification of DOM is in a language and implementation-neutral interface, the **Object Management Group Interface Definition Language (OMG IDL)**. **Dynamic HTML (DHTML)** relies heavily on DOM. DHTML allows a visitor to a website to view differing images or text. A visitor from a French server may see the page in French, while a visitor from a Spanish server may see the page in Spanish. If cookies are used, a repeat visitor may see a different page than a first-time visitor. DHTML needs the DOM to make changes to the website's appearance on an as-needed basis.

XHTML

A significant advancement in HTML is a progression toward reformulating it to look and act more like XML. **XHTML** 1.0 provides a document type that can be shared across communities, such as personal digital assistants, mobile phones, vending machines, desktops, and televisions. It is also capable of allowing simple content authoring.

Java

So far, protocol and language names discussed in this chapter have been acronyms with an underlying meaning. Java, however, is not an acronym. The **Java** programming language, primarily developed by Sun Microsystems, was originally called Oak. After a trademark search revealed this name was not available, the programming language was renamed Java. Given all the caffeine-related adjectives attributed to Java-related products and comments, any other name is hard to imagine for this product. Java is an object-oriented programming language that is platform neutral. Sun Microsystems formally introduced Java in 1995. It supports graphical user interfaces and client/server applications. Java is very similar to C++, which may help account for its popularity and widespread adoption. Java is well-suited for the WWW, and Web browsers have been quick to accommodate the running of Java programs.

The advantage of being platform neutral results in less efficient processing of Java programs due to an extra processing layer. Figure 9–9 illustrates the extra step involved in processing compiled Java program code. The computer on which the program is to be executed interprets the Java program in a manner that the microprocessor can understand.

FIGURE 9–9   *Java virtual machine applications*

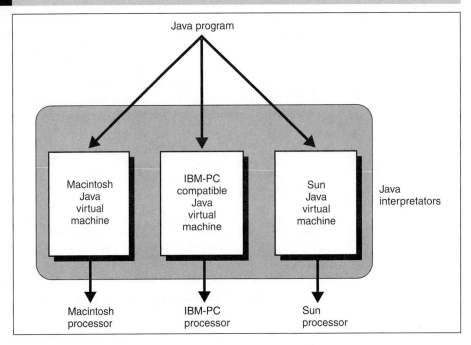

These Java interpreters on the client's computers are commonly referred to as **virtual machines,** which today are available for Sun, IBM-PC compatible, and Macintosh computers. Certain security checks can be performed by the virtual machine before the program code is executed.

The portability of Java programs, because of the virtual machine component, made it a natural and popular tool for designers of Web-based applications. This portability feature of Java is commonly referred to as **write once, run anywhere.** A Web browser, called **HotJava,** was soon designed and written by Sun Microsystems in the Java programming language. The HotJava browser was the first browser to incorporate the virtual machine component, enabling the retrieval of a special type of Java program that can be executed locally from a Web page, called an **applet.** HotJava was soon followed by other browser programs, and now Java-enabled browsers are an expectation of consumers. HotJava is no longer sold; it can be downloaded free of charge from Sun Microsystem's Web page. Sun MicroSystems has now announced a wireless Java profile called **Mobile Information Device (MID).** This technology allows mobile content creators to develop highly differentiated and personalized products and services by providing dynamic and interactive content.

MESSAGING PROTOCOLS

This section introduces the protocols that have evolved to enable the electronic transmission of messages over the Internet. First, basic e-mail store-and-forward and remote server protocols are discussed, and then the security-related protocols are introduced.

| FIGURE 9–10 | *Basic mail protocols* |

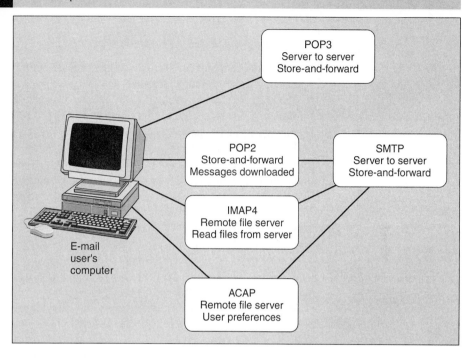

Basic Mail Protocols

Four mail protocols are discussed in this section. The relationships among them are probably best described graphically in Figure 9–10. An e-mail user may send his or her message to either a **store-and-forward** Internet server or to an Internet server to which he or she has read, write, and delete privileges. The store-and-forward protocol is the **Post Office Protocol (POP). POP2** acts as a central clearing house for storing messages until they are retrieved and downloaded. A more recent version of POP, **POP3** can send messages without the need to move through a SMTP server (discussed below). According to RFC 1939, POP3 is not intended to provide extensive manipulation operations of mail on the server. Basically, mail is generally downloaded and then deleted. POP3 is used by many popular e-mail products, such as Netscape e-mail.

Another method is the **Internet Message Access Protocol (IMAP). IMAP4** allows the user to access and read mail directly from the server without having to download it. The mail can be managed directly on the server by having a remote file server connection. For example, messages can be searched using keywords while the messages are still on the mail server. Similar to IMAP, but recently developed by the IETF, is an e-mail protocol, **Application Configuration Access Protocol (ACAP),** that allows the user to store his or her mail preferences and address books directly on the server. For users who wish to retrieve mail using many different physical computers, this protocol eliminates the need to maintain multiple preferences and address book files.

Regardless of whether POP2, IMAP, ACAP, or some other Internet server protocol is used, another protocol must be used to store-and-forward messages from server to server as the message travels from its source to its destination. The **Simple Mail**

Transfer/Transport Protocol (SMTP), developed by the IETF, is the protocol used to transfer messages from server to server.

Security-Enhanced Mail Protocols

Many businesses are not comfortable using e-mail services that send messages over unknown paths. Some commercial e-mail services use a protocol called **X.400** that requires that e-mail be sent along paths with only known, trusted e-mail carriers, such as AT&T and MCI.

Another protocol, **privacy enhanced mail (PEM),** was put forth by the IETF and the IRTF in late 1980s. PEM was an explicitly designed, security-minded messaging protocol to provide basic message protection features. During its implementation it became a public key method. The primary security features of PEM are as follows:

- Origin authentication and nonrepudiation.
- Message integrity.
- Message confidentiality.

These terms were discussed in Chapter 8. PEM was incompatible with the rapidly emerging multimedia Internet protocol, **Multipurpose Internet Mail Extension (MIME),** and this incompatibility seriously impeded PEM's commercial success. Now, PEM is widely considered a historical relic.

In an effort to overcome PEM and MIME's incompatibility, the IETF proposed the **MIME Object Security Services (MOSS)** protocol to complement the MIME protocol. MIME, another IETF specification, provides the formatting specifications for both ASCII and non-ASCII Internet messages, and thus enables the transmission of multimedia files. MIME and MOSS are used conjunctively to provide messaging security features. **Secure MIME (S/MIME)** evolved as an alternative to MIME and MOSS and was developed by private industry, RSA Data Security Inc., based on its own cryptographic standard, **Public-Key Cryptography Standards (PKCS).** S/MIME, perhaps because of its private-enterprise development, has gained the greatest acceptance among commercial vendors.

In 1997, RSA Data Security requested that the IETF designate S/MIME as the preferred standard for e-mail. In an effort to increase universal interoperability, these same vendors are actively working with U.S. government agencies toward integrating S/MIME with the **Message Security Protocol (MSP),** the mail protocol of the U.S. government.

Figure 9–11 illustrates the communications problem between U.S. Department of Defense (DOD) workers and civilians. The gateway computer that sends the message from the DOD computer to the Internet strips the message of its security encoding. Under the integrated protocol, different levels of security are available for the DOD workers and messages can be encoded appropriately. If the security level is approved, then alternative, acceptable encoding algorithms can be used and maintained until the non-DOD worker receives the message. Thus, messages leaving the gateway computer and traveling to a non-DOD user can remain secured.

A popular and free-of-charge method to secure personal messages is **Pretty Good Privacy (PGP).** While freeware, PGP is good for personal use, but it is not intended for commercial use without registering and paying for upgrades. PGP is based on its developer's, Philip Zimmerman's, public-key method. It uses both encryption and digital signatures. PGPv.6.5 is currently available for download from MIT's website.

| **FIGURE 9–11** | *Integration of S/MIME and MSP* |

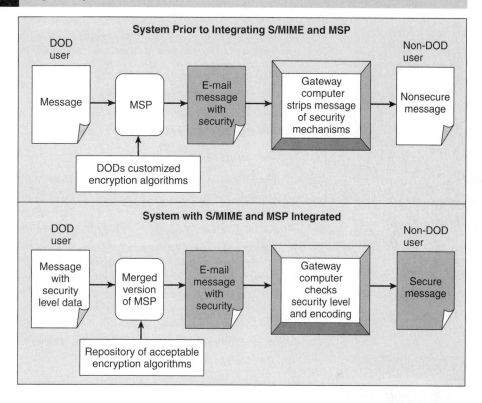

S-HTTP and SSL

To deal with security concerns Enterprise Integration Technologies, a private organization, developed **Secure-HTTP (S-HTTP).** Although it is not as prevalent as **Secure Sockets Layer (SSL),** also developed by a private organization, Netscape Communications, it is sometimes used in conjunction with SSL for combined benefits. Specifically, S-HTTP was developed to transmit individual messages in a secure fashion. It uses a complex algorithm to encrypt the individual message and produce digital signatures. On the other hand, SSL was designed to establish a secure connection using private key encryption. SSL encrypts the communication channel in its entirety, but it cannot produce a digital signature for an individual message. Thus, these two protocols can be combined for enhanced security.

SET

Securing the data transmission of credit card information began as a tug-of-war between two credit card giants in 1995. Visa, in conjunction with Microsoft, announced their standard for secure financial transactions—the **Secure Transaction Technology (STT)** protocol. Meanwhile, MasterCard teamed with IBM, Netscape, GTE, and Cybercash to put forth their own standard—the **Secure Electronic Payment Protocol (SEPP).** These two standards methods were actually very similar in their capabilities, but they were not interoperable. Both standards were reviewed by the IETF, but, initially, neither group was willing to change its specifications to foster interoperability.

Both sides received much criticism from the banking industry, vendors, and the general press. By the end of 1995, both sides agreed to work toward a common standard, ultimately called the **Secure Electronic Transmission (SET)** specification. In response to an increasing need by businesses and consumers to support secure e-commerce, the SET designers set out to design a protocol that would use cryptography to

- Provide confidentiality of information.
- Ensure payment integrity.
- Authenticate both merchants and cardholders.
- Interoperate with other protocols.

(SET Specification, 1997)

Figure 9–12 illustrates the typical steps of an electronic purchase. The shaded boxes are the steps of the transaction process addressed by the SET specification.

At the core of the SET specification is the use of cryptography to protect the sensitive data during transmission. The SET specification uses two widely accepted cryptographic methods. The **Data Encryption Standard (DES)** is used for its secret-key algorithm, and the **Rivest, Shamir, Adelman (RSA) standard** is used for its public-key algorithm. The SET specification and its security features are discussed in detail in Chapter 12. Figure 9–13 compares the features of SSL and SET. Apparently SET has more features, yet SSL has achieved high usage rates not enjoyed by SET. In Europe and Asia, SET has been used somewhat. In excess of 100 banks support SET in 13 European countries. Five countries in Asia have approximately 100 banks support that support SET.

FIGURE 9–12	*The role of SET in the electronic shopping experience*

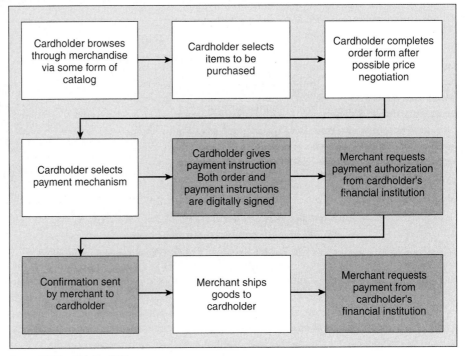

Source: SET Specification, 1997.

FIGURE 9–13	*Comparison of features—SSL versus SET*

Comparison of Features	SSL	SET
Encryption of data during transmission?	Yes	Yes
Confirmation of message integrity?	Yes	Yes
Authentication of merchant?	Yes	Yes
Authentication of consumer?	No*	Yes
Transmission of specific data only on a "need know" basis?	No	Yes
Inclusion of bank or trusted third party in transactins?	No	Yes
No need for merchant to secure credit card data internally?	No	Yes

*Can be done with an additional step; digital certificates can be used in SSLv3.

Source: Greenstein and Hamilton, 2000.

MOBILE COMMERCE AND THE WAP PROTOCOL

Mobile commerce is gaining in popularity, especially in Europe. Handheld devices are being used to send/receive e-mail, download information from websites, and pay for products in vending machines. Protocols are necessary for these devices to work interoperably. In January 1998, some major companies (Ericsson, Motorola, Nokia, and Unwired Planet) joined together to develop a wireless protocol. Together they proposed and developed the **Wireless Application Protocol (WAP).** This protocol is targeted to bring Internet content and advanced services to digital, wireless devices. Developing a wireless protocol presents several challenges:

- Displays are much smaller than a traditional computer screen.
- Memory and processing speeds are limited.
- All HTML tags may not translate well to the smaller screens.
- Data transmission security is a concern.

The third item in the list requires some new procedures to be used since a server sending a message will have no idea about the physical capacity and limitations of the device for which the message/web page is intended. To help with the process, a **Wireless Markup Language (WML)** has been developed as part of WAP; it is based on XML. It is an open language that allows the text from Web pages to be displayed on wireless and handheld devices. Figure 9–14 illustrates in general how a server can send a regular Web page to a wireless, handheld device. Basically, the message has to be recoded into WML based on the type of wireless device that is receiving the message. Many websites, such as Yahoo mentioned in the box entitled "Yahoo Auction, Directory Go Wireless," are currently creating a database setup that allows them to send certain "nuggets" of information to personal digital assistants and digital, wireless phones. One company, TANTAU Software, announced in December 2000 that its mobile commerce platform "successfully completed performance testing confirming its ability to support 10 million users with a sustained load of 100,000 concurrent users executing 10,000 transactions per second." TANTAU's technology supports high-volume wireless transactions, such as

- Money transfers.
- Balance inquiries.
- Bill payments.

The transactions can be sent across wireless, digital phones; pagers, and personal digital assistants. Regarding security, WAP also includes a specification called **Wireless Transport Layer Security Specification (WTLS)** that provides authentication and encryption options.

THE ROLE OF ACCOUNTANTS IN INTERNET-RELATED STANDARD-SETTING PROCESSES

Accountants are affected by the emerging standards that are used in electronic commerce systems. The standards and protocols employed in the transmission of electronic data must be understood by accountants in order for them to assess the adequacy of clients' data transmission techniques in terms of reliability and security. The protocols discussed in this chapter are essential to the performance of electronic data exchange. Accountants must understand these protocols to adequately perform the internal control assessment function when significant amounts of transaction data are transmitted electronically. Further, clients often look to accountants for advice regarding transaction transmission methods.

For the most part, accountants have primarily followed the Internet standards that have been set by standard-setting committees. Noticeably absent from the list of Internet and WWW standard-setting committees are professional accounting organizations, such as the AICPA, FASB, Institute of Internal Auditors, UK Accounting Standards Board, and International Accounting Standards Board. For accountants to become leaders in e-commerce, they must assume an active role in standard-setting activities.

| **FIGURE 9–14** | *WAP protocol* |

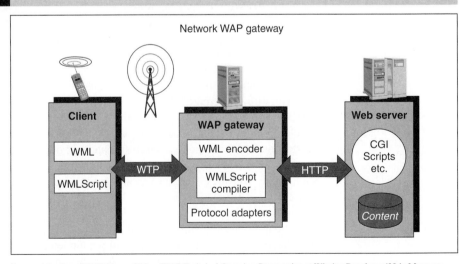

Source: Adaption of WAP Forum Slide—WAP Technical Overview Presentation at WirelessDeveloper '99 in Monterey, CA, USA. May 6, 1999.

E-Commerce in Practice

Yahoo Auction, Directory Go Wireless

Yahoo Inc. yesterday announced wireless versions of its auction, movie listing and Web directory services as part of an effort to strengthen the company's position in the nascent market for delivering Internet content to mobile phones and other portable devices.

The new services can be accessed on any mobile phone or device that supports Wireless Application Protocol (WAP) and add to Yahoo's existing wireless offerings, which include e-mail, stock quotes, news and calendaring, Yahoo officials said yesterday.

There are an estimated 5 million WAP-enabled phones in use in the U.S., and analysts expect that number to grow rapidly as more wireless Internet services become available, Mohan Vishwanath, vice president of Yahoo Everywhere, Yahoo's wireless division, said in an interview.

"Our goal is to make Yahoo's services available to users wherever they are, no matter what type of device they use to access the Internet," Vishwanath said.

Absent from the new services announced yesterday is an application that would allow mobile users to shop online. Yahoo is likely to offer a wireless version of Yahoo Shopping by year's end, Vishwanath said.

The portal company said it hopes the new services will help compete against rivals like America Online Inc. and Microsoft Corp.'s Microsoft Network, which are also battling to take an early lead in the wireless data market.

The auction service announced yesterday, called Yahoo Auctions to Go, lets users make bids and watch the progress of auctions that are under way on the Internet. An alert feature will notify a user when he has been outbid, Vishwanath said.

Yahoo Movies on the Move helps users quickly locate a theater in their local area, read the synopsis of a movie and check show times. The information provided is based on the address provided when a user registers for Yahoo's services, although a different location can be searched if the user is away from home.

Wireless Yahoo Directory Services is modeled after the directory on the company's main online portal and includes a list of Web sites whose content has been reformatted for mobile phones using Wireless Markup Language (WML) or Handheld Device Markup Language (HDML).

A fourth new wireless service announced yesterday allows new users to register for Yahoo's personalized content and services from their phone rather than from their PC.

"These devices might be the first point of Internet access for some users, particularly in other parts of the world, so we wanted to allow people to register for Yahoo through their phone," Vishwanath said.

Yahoo served about 120 million unique users last December and about 100 million people are registered users, Vishwanath said. He declined to say how many users have signed up for Yahoo's mobile services since they were launched last June.

Yahoo has partnered with a number of service providers to distribute its wireless services to users. The partners include Sprint PCS in the U.S., Bell Mobility in Canada, D2 Mannesmann Mobilfunk in Germany, SmarTone and New World in Hong Kong, Radiolinja in Finland and SK Telecom and Hansol PCS in Korea. The company has also teamed up with device makers including Motorola Inc. and Palm Inc.

Source: By James Niccolai, ©*Computerworld Online,* and IDG News Service, March 22, 2000.

Summary

Regardless of whether the topic is standards, protocols, or languages, the common thread in international unification of methods is interoperability and platform-neutral specifications. Technology providers, businesses, consumers, and government agencies all recognize the need for compatibility. The gap that exists between the desired state of truly interoperable systems and the current state of incompatible systems is due in large part to parallel simultaneous efforts in standards development by different entities. Many standard-setting bodies have been criticized for cumbersome processes that do not provide timely solutions. On the other hand, private vendors in a rush to bring their products to the marketplace have developed similar, yet different specifications.

Because the Internet is a truly global infrastructure, the need for international agreement on methods is crucial. Government agencies worldwide connected to the Internet face a double-edged sword—they want increased connectivity and increased security. Meeting the needs of all constituents, public and private, in a timely manner in a continuously changing environment will continue to challenge the standard-setting bodies, technology providers, and government agencies well into the twenty-first century. The quick development and implementation of the WAP protocol is proof that industry consortiums work well in standard developments that can benefit many different vendors.

Key Words

alert archives
American National Standards Institute (ANSI)
Accredited Standards Committee
  (ANSI ASC) X12
applet
Application Configuration Access Protocol
  (ACAP)
Computer Emergency Response Coordination
  Center (CERT)
computer language
connectionless mode
connection-oriented mode
Data Encryption Standard (DES)
Document Object Model (DOM)
document type definition (DTD)
domain name
Dynamic HTML (DHTML)
ebXML
Electronic Data Interchange for
  Administration, Commerce, and Transport
  (EDIFACT)
eXtensible Markup Language (XML)
File Transfer Protocol (FTP)
Forum of Incident Response and Security
  Teams (FIRST)
Generic Top Level Domain Memorandum of
  Understanding (gTLD)
Global Information Infrastructure
  Commission (GIIC)
global top-level domain name
HotJava
HyperText Markup Language (HTML)
HyperText Transfer/Transport Protocol
  (HTTP)
International Computer Security Association
  (ICSA)
International Organization for Standardization
  (ISO)
Internet Architecture Board (IAB)
Internet Corporation for Assigned Names and
  Numbers (ICANN)

Internet Engineering Steering Group (IESG)
Internet Engineering Task Force (IETF)
Internet Message Access Protocol (IMAP
Internet Protocol version 6.0 (IPv6)
IP address
Internet Research Task Force (IRTF)
Internet Society (ISOC)
interoperability
Java
Message Security Protocol (MSP)
mobile commerce
Mobile Information Device (MID)
MIME Object Security Services (MOSS)
Multipurpose Internet Mail Extension (MIME)
Network News Transfer Protocol (NNTP)
Object Management Group Interface
  Definition Language (OMG IDL)
Open Buying on the Internet (OBI)
Open Systems Interconnection (OSI) model
patches
Post Office Protocol (POP2 and POP3)
Public-Key Cryptography Standards (PKCS)
Pretty Good Privacy (PGP)
privacy enhanced mail (PEM)
protocol
Protocol Extension Protocol (PEP)
Request for comment (RFC)
Rivest, Shamir, Adelman (RSA) standard
Secure Electronic Payment Protocol (SEPP)
Secure Electronic Transmission (SET)
Secure HTTP (S-HTTP)
Secure MIME (S/MIME)
Secure Sockets Layer (SSL)
Secure Transaction Technology (STT)
Simple Mail Transfer/Transport Protocol
  (SMTP)
Software Engineering Institute (SEI)
standards
Standardized Generalized Markup Language
  (SGML)
store-and-forward

TELNET
Transmission Control Protocol/Internet
  Protocol (TCP/IP)
United Nations Centre for Facilitation of
  Procedures and Practices for Administration,
  Commerce, and Transport (CEFACT)
United Nations Economic Commission for
  Europe (UN/ECE)
United Nations Electronic Data Interchange
  for Administration, Commerce, and
  Transport (UN/EDIFACT)

U.S. Defense Advanced Research Project
  (DARPA)
virtual machine
Windows socket (Winsock)
Wireless Application Protocol (WAP)
Wireless Markup Language (WML)
Wireless Transport Layer Security (WTLS)
World Wide Web Consortium (W3C)
write-once, run anywhere
XHTML
X.400

Review Questions

1. Why are standards important?
2. What is the prevalent standard for transmission of transaction data?
3. Why are Internet standards voluntary instead of mandatory? Does this impede progress?
4. Explain the purpose of the ANSI ASC X12's Alignment Task Group.
5. How are the ISOs standards developed?
6. What is the NIST, and what role does it play in the private sector?
7. Why was the ISOC formed?
8. Upon what concepts is the WWW based?
9. Who organized the OBI?
10. What is the GIIC?
11. Discuss the role of CERT in the Internet community. Explain its alert archives.
12. What are FIRST teams?
13. What is the ICSA?
14. Explain the importance of protocols.
15. Identify the seven layers of OSI.
16. What is TCP/IP?
17. Identify the different classes of the IPv4 protocol.
18. Define the term "domain name."
19. Give two examples of top-level domain names.
20. Identify a difference between FTP and TELNET.
21. What is NNTP?
22. What was the original primary purpose of HTTP?
23. Define S-HTTP and SSL. Are they compatible?
24. Differentiate between HTML, SGML, and XML. How do they differ?
25. What is a DOM?
26. Why is DHTML important for international applications?
27. Why was Oak renamed Java?
28. Explain what is meant by write once, run anywhere?
29. What is an applet?
30. What is STEP?
31. Explain what is meant by store-and-forward.
32. Differentiate among POP2, POP3, IMAP, and ACAP.
33. What is SMTP?

34. Identify two primary security features of PEM.
35. What are MIME, MOSS, and S/MIME?
36. What is MSP?
37. Define PGS and explain its major drawback.
38. Distinguish among STT, SEPP, and SET.
39. List the four stages of the electronic shopping experience that SET addresses.
40. What are WAP and WML?

Discussion Questions

1. How is it that some of the Internet standard-setting bodies existed before the Internet was even conceived?
2. Why have competing and incompatible standards emerged?
3. Why have government agencies become involved in Internet standard-setting processes?
4. How do some standards developed by U.S. agencies become "international" standards?
5. Why did new standards groups pop-up after the creation of the WWW when numerous Internet committees were already in existence?
6. Why did *Fortune* 500 companies align and form their own consortium?
7. What criticism did the GIIC vocalize toward existing standard-setting committees?
8. CERT's origination can be traced to the U.S. government's DOD. How then can it be affiliated with worldwide security agencies?
9. How does the ICSA differ from organizations such as CERT and FIRST?
10. Why do protocols and computer languages keep changing?
11. How does the IPv6 differ from the IPv4 protocol?
12. Why did the gTLD emerge? Will it make "guessing" domain names easier or harder?
13. Have security-related solutions been developed by mostly public or private organizations? Why do you think this is the case?
14. Why is the W3C examining the DOM specification?
15. How is Java different from C++? Why is it so popular?
16. How can WWW technology help firms share product development documents?
17. Why is the ACAP framework popular with business travelers?
18. Why does the government wish to integrate S/MIME with MSP?
19. By what group was WAP developed? Why did or didn't this method work?
20. What are some challenges of wireless computing?

Cases

1. Wireless Computing
   Without worrying about computer programming, pick a website that sells a product or service over the Internet that currently does *NOT* deliver wireless content. Illustrate how the screens could be redesigned to fit on a wireless device. Specifically, do the following:
   a. Capture a screen shot of the website.
   b. Illustrate (using any computer drawing features) some prototype handheld screens that could, in essence, mirror what the regular website displays.

2. Managing New Top-Level Domain Extensions

   Much controversy has surfaced with the introduction of the new top-level domain name extension. Many business with registered trademarks have successfully prevented other businesses from using their trademark in the dot com domain.

   a. Do you think a company should have all rights to use that name in multiple domains, or should they be opened up to other organizations?

   b. Pick two large companies and research what they are doing or not doing to protect their trademarks.

3. The SET Protocol

   MasterCard, Visa, and American Express have expressed their support of the SET protocol for securing credit card transactions. But will the SET protocol prevail? Because SET has definite advantages over SSL, one would expect that it would win hands down. However, SET has been criticized for being slow in introducing an updated and more sophisticated version. In 1998, a media research analyst for Forrester Research claimed that the whole approach to updating SET "from the technology to the marketing has been bungled." A writer for *The Gazette (Montreal)* claims that

   > The only problem is that SET has been going nowhere fast, even though its technical specifications were published last year, and vendors like IBM and Hewlett Packard rushed SET-compliant electronic-commerce products to market last fall. Despite confident predictions that it would be fully deployed by last Christmas, I have yet to come across a single merchant offering SET transactions—and I've been looking.

   > *(Matthew Friedman)*

   Find some recent articles regarding SET and its usage worldwide. Comment on the longevity of this product.

4. W3C and Controversial Internet Filtering Specifications

   The W3C must consider not only programming and protocol specifications, but international social policies as well. In early 1998, it came under heavy scrutiny for agreeing to a filtering standard. These filtering rules determine what information a user can view. The W3C maintains that they are not applying or endorsing any specific filters. The filters can be set as the user wishes. But civil liberties groups assert that such technology will allow repressive governments to "use the filtering technology as a tool to screen political speech." Further this same group feels that

   > . . . these technologists are acting as an unelected world government, wielding power that will shape social relations and political rights for years to come. In cyberspace, these critics assert, computer code has the force of law.

   > *(Amy Harmon, The Dallas Morning News)*

   a. Research the Carnivore program, and determine if any similarities can be found.

   b. Can you think of any positive uses of such filters?

   c. Do you think such filters should be developed by the W3C? If not, who do you think should develop these rules?

   d. Search the Internet and report on the current state of such filters.

References and Websites

American Parts and Accessories Association. "Standard for the Exchange of Product Model Data (STEP)." *http://www.apaa.org/step.htm.*

ANSI. "About ANSI." *http://www.ansi.org.*

_____. *1996 Annual Report. http://www.ansi.org.*

Application Configuration Access Protocol. "ACAP in a Nutshell."
  http://andrew2.andrew.cmu.edu/cyrus/acap.

ASC X12 Alignment Task Group. "Minutes—February 2, 1998 and March 23, 1998."
  http://www.disa.org/ apps/minutes.

Bank Technology News. "Bringing Smart-Card Style to the Internet." June 1997.

Carpenter, Brian. "What Does the IAB Do, Anyway?" *http://www.iab.org/iab/ connexions.htm.*

CERT. "Meet the CERT* Coordination Center." *http://www.cer.org/.*

CISCO Systems Inc. *"OSI Procotols." http:// www.cisco.com.*

Commerce at Light Speed. "STEP." *http://www.cals.com/step/index.htm.*

_____. "SMGL & HTML." *http://www.cals.com/sgml/index.htm.*

CommerceNet and OBI Consortium. "Management of OBI Consortium moves to ComerceNet;
  CommerceNet to Host Open Buying on the Internet Consortium." *Businesswire.* April 30,
  1998.

Cybercomm. "OSI-Protocols." *http://www.cybercomm.net/ ~bsamedi/osimodel.faq.*

Data Interchange Standards Association. "ASC X12 Eyes Potential Synergy of XML and EDI."
  Press Release. February 23, 1998.

Enete, Noel. *JAVA Jumpstart.* Prentice-Hall. 1997.

ETHOS News. "Open Buying on the Internet (OBI) Standard." *Tagish Ltd.* September 10, 1997.

FIRST. "What Is First." *http://www.first.org/ about.*

Financial Times (London). "Trading Names." June 11, 1998.

Friedman, Matthew. "Future in doubt for SET Protocol." *The Gazette (Montreal).* March 4, 1998.

Gardner, Elizabeth. "Protocol War: Full of Sound and Fury." *WebWeek.* Vol. 1, No. 7, November
  1995.

GIIC. "The GIIC Mission Statement." *http://www.gii. org/egi00181.htm.*

Greenstein, M., and D. Hamilton. "Global Implementation of the SET Protocol for Electronic
  Commerce: A Cost/Benefit Analysis," *International Journal of Business Disciplines.* 2000

gTLD-MOU. "Frequently Asked Questions." *http://www.gtld-mou.org.*

Harmon, Amy. "Internet 'Filter' Draws Fire; Rules May Govern What Users Can See." *The
  Dallas Morning News.* January 19, 1998.

Herreld, Heather. "Merged Standard Could Allow Governmentwide Secure E-Mail." *Federal
  Computer Week.* January, 5, 1998. *http://www.fcw.com/pubs/ fcw/1998/0105/fcw-dms-1-5-
  1998.htm.*

IANA. "Internet Assigned Numbers Authority." *http://www.iana.org/iana/overview.htm.*

ICSA. "General Information." *http://www.ncsa.com/ about_ncsa/general.htm.*

IETF. "Overview of the IETF." *http://www.ietf.org/ overview.htm.*

International Ad Hoc Committee. *"Recommendations for Administration and Management of
  gTLDs." http://www.iahc.org/draft-iahc-recommend-00.htm.*

Internetnews.com. "RSA Makes Move for Standard E-Mail Protocol."
  http://www.internetnews.com/bus-news/1997/10/103-rsa.htm. October 1997.

ICANN. "Governments Endorse Private Sector Internet." Press Release, March 2, 1999.
  http://www.icann.org/icann-pr02mar99.htm.

IRTF. "IRTF Mission." *http:// www.irtf.org/irtf.*

ISO. "Introduction to ISO." *http://www.iso.ch/ infoe/intro.htm.*

ISOC. "All About the Internet Society." *http:// info.isoc.org/isoc.*

_____. "IETF and ISOC." *http://www.isoc.org/ related/ietf.*

Kantor, Brian, and Phil Lapsley. "Network News Transfer Protocol." Network Working Group—
  RFC 977. February 1986. *http:// info. internet.isi.edu/in-notes/rfc/ files/frc977.tx.*

Kessler, Gary. "An Overview of TCP/IP Protocols and the Internet." April 1998.
  http://www.hill.com/ library/tcpip.htm.

Maciag, Gregory. "A Wake-Up Call for Industry Standards." *National Underwriter.* Vol. 102,
  No. 15. April 3 1998.

MasterCard and Visa. *"SET Secure Electronic Transaction Specification."* May 31, 1997.

Millman, Howard. "A brief history of EDI." *InfoWorld.* Vol. 20 No. 14. April 6, 1998.

Moeller, Michael. "MasterCard, Visa Settle Squabble Over Spec." *PC Week.* Vol. 12, No. 50, December 18, 1995.

Netscape Communications. "Netscape Data Security." *http://www.netscape.com/newsref /ref/netscape-security. htm.*

NIST. "NIST at a Glance." *http://www.nist.gov/ public-affairs/ guide/glintro.htm.*

_____. "Interoperability and Portability." *http://www-08.nist.gov/nistpubs/800-7/node10.html.*

PCWebopedia. *http://www.pcwebopedia. com.*

Pierce, Michael, and Donald O'Mahoney. "Scaleable, Cash Payment for WWW Resources with the PayMe Protocol Set." *http://www.w3.org/ conferences/ www4/papers/228.*

Power, Carol. "Credit Card Firms Back Security System." *The Irish Times.* May 22, 1998.

RSA Data Security. "Security in the SET Protocol." *http://www.rsa.com/set/html/ security.htm.*

Segal, Ben. "A Short History of Internet Protocols at CERN." April, 1995. *http://wwwcn.cern.ch/pdp/ns/ben/TCPHIST.htm.*

SGML Open. "Standardized Generalized Markup Language." *http://www.sgmlopen. org/sgml/docs/sgmldesc.htm.*

Sun Microsystems. JAVA. *http://java.sun. com.*

IKCEDIS. "UN/EDIFACT." *http://www.eca. org.uk/ukcedis/edifact.htm.*

UN/ECE. "UN/CEFACT: Ready for Business." *http://www.unece.org /trade/press/97trad8e.htm.*

_____. "United Nations CEFACT and OASIS to Deliver ebXML Technical Infrastructure Ahead of Schedule." December 12, 2000. *http://www.unece.org.*

W3C. "About the World Wide Web Consortium." *http://www.w3c.org/ consortium.*

_____. "DOM." *http://www.w3.org/ DOM. htm.*

_____. "HTTP-Hypertext Transport Protocol." *http://www.w3.org/protocols/activity.htm.*

_____. "XML Activity." *http://www.w3C.org/ XML/Activity.*

Whatis.com Inc. *http://whatis.com.*

10   CRYPTOGRAPHY AND AUTHENTICATION

Learning Objectives

1. To understand and compare alternative encryption techniques.
2. To understand digital signature technology.
3. To understand the role of certificate authorities in key management.
4. To identify important key management tasks.

INTRODUCTION

This chapter explores security solutions to the potential exposures identified in preceding chapters. The term "constant evolution" best describes the necessary environment in which security solutions exist. The "breaking" or invalidation of current solutions at any point in time, because of the nature of security issues, will continue to be the target of scholars, hackers, government agencies, and private organizations offering security solutions. Hackers will continue to find and exploit weaknesses in security solutions in an effort to satisfy their own motivations. Scholars, government agencies, and private organizations, either in isolation or more likely working together, will continue to validate or invalidate current methods both in theory and to patch any loopholes or backdoors before hackers discover them. These groups also have great interest in the continuous development of newer and better security methods. The tremendously high growth rate of computing power in hardware also provides strong motivation for the continuous development of security methods. This chapter discusses the primary security issues and reviews the current technological security solutions.

MESSAGING SECURITY ISSUES

To conduct electronic commerce on the Internet, including the WWW, messages must be electronically transmitted in some manner. As mentioned in the box entitled, "Electronic Signatures in Global and National Commerce Act," the U.S. government is moving toward electronic technology through the use of digital signatures for electronic contracts. A primary concern of electronic business is the nonrefutable linking of message contents to individuals and businesses. This act helps the digital economy move forward by updating contract law.

E-Commerce in Practice

Electronic Signatures in Global and National Commerce Act

Today I am pleased to sign into law S. 761, the "Electronic Signatures in Global and National Commerce Act." This landmark legislation will help ensure that we reap the full benefits that electronic technology offers for the American economy and American consumers....

The Act clarifies the legal validity of electronic contracts, signatures, notices, and other records, and allows contracting parties to choose the technology for authenticating their transactions without government intervention.

It provides the legal certainty necessary for entrepreneurs to invest in electronic commerce. Firms need to know that their contracts and transactions will not be unenforceable solely because they are electronic. They need to know how they can satisfy State and Federal notice and record-keeping requirements with electronic notices and records. They need to know that the same "rules of the road" apply to on-line business disputes as to those in the paper world.

The Act will also ensure that on-line consumers will have legal protections equivalent to those in the off-line world. The Act does not diminish the protections offered by any Federal or State law relating to the rights of consumers, other than to eliminate requirements that contracts and other records be written and signed on paper.

Source: Former President William J. Clinton *The White House,* June 30, 2000.

Several important security services are required to ensure reliable, trustworthy electronic transmission of business messages. The primary security services are divided into five categories, although some of these services are interrelated. As illustrated in Figure 10–1, the five security services are

- Confidentiality.
- Integrity.
- Nonrepudiation.
- Authentication.
- Authorization (also known as access control).

These security issues are not new concepts to business managers. In fact, well-designed manual and traditional computer-based financial accounting information systems have been designed with these issues in mind for decades. For example, in paper-based systems, confidentiality has been accomplished through the use of thick envelopes in which checks or other sensitive documents are placed before mailing. The recent challenge has been to update security measures for Internet-based e-commerce.

Confidentiality

When a message is sent electronically, the sender and receiver may desire that the message maintain **confidentiality,** and thus not be read by any other parties. Analogies can be drawn to traditional mail and phone systems. In regular mail systems, the sender uses an envelope to conceal the inside contents rather than writing the information on a post card. In an office environment, workers wishing to have a personal, confidential phone conversation may choose to place their call from a private phone line rather than a shared phone line accessible by multiple phone stations. With electronic messages, private telecommunication lines are not typically an option, nor are physically sealed envelopes. To give an electronic message the property of confidentiality, the message must be made uninterpretable to everyone except the designated receiver.

FIGURE 10–1	*Primary security issues*

Security Issue	Security Objective	Security Techniques
Confidentiality	Privacy of message	Encryption
Message integrity	Detecting message tampering	Hashing (digest)
Authentication	Origin verification	Digital signatures Challenge-response Passwords Biometric devices
Nonrepudiation	Proof of origin, receipt, and contents (sender cannot falsely deny sending or receiving the message)	Bidirectional hashing Digital signatures Transaction certificates Time stamps Confirmation services
Access controls	Limiting entry to authorized users	Firewalls Passwords Biometric devices

For e-commerce, keeping order details and credit card information confidential during transmission is a major security concern. Further, trading partners sharing design specifications also want to ensure the confidentiality of their messages so that proprietary design specifications can be viewed only by the sender and the intended receiver of the information. The most effective technique for masking a message is encryption. Later in the chapter, popular encryption techniques are introduced.

Integrity

When a message is sent electronically, both the sender and the receiver want to ensure that the message received is exactly the same as the message transmitted by the sender. A message that has not been altered in any way, either intentionally or unintentionally, is said to have maintained its **integrity.** For e-commerce, verifying that the order details sent by the purchaser have not been altered is one major security concern. Trading partners electronically sharing design specifications need assurance that the design specifications sent by the customer to their supplier, or vice versa, have not been altered in any way during their electronic transmission.

An effective cryptographic means of ensuring message integrity is through the use of **hashing,** where a "hash" of the message is computed using an algorithm and the message contents. The hash value is sent along with the message; then, upon receipt, a hash is calculated by the recipient using the same hashing algorithm. The two hash values (received and calculated) are compared, and a match can indicate that the message received is the same as that sent. Hashing is similar to the use of check-sum digits in accounting. Users should be cautioned that hashing is not encryption, but it can be used in conjunction with encryption for added security. The only ISO and ANSI accredited standard hashing algorithm is Secure Hash Algorithm-1 (SHA-1), although others exist, for example, Message Digest-5 (MD-5). The Message Digest-4 (MD-4) hashing algorithm is insecure and should never be used. Other common techniques that can be used with hashing to verify the integrity of the message are check values and digital signatures, both of which are discussed later in this chapter.

Authentication

When an electronic message is received by a user or a system, the identity of the sender needs to be verified in order to determine if the sender is who he claims to be. This is called **authentication.** To identify a user, at least one of the following types of information is generally required:

- Something you have (e.g., a token),
- Something you know (e.g., a PIN).
- Something you are (e.g., fingerprints or signatures).

Three-factor authentication refers to techniques that use all three types of information, while two-factor authentication techniques use two of the three types of information. One-factor authentication techniques use a single piece of information for identification and are most easily defeated. Two-factor authentication is discussed in the box entitled "Two-Factor User Authentication Criminal Information System Successfully Implemented." The authentication process is analogous to a traveler crossing an international border producing a valid passport containing a photograph. To authenticate a customer using a credit card (something you have), a signature (something you are) or personal identification number (something you know) is usually required. Credit card companies are trying to reduce fraudulent use of physically stolen credit cards by encouraging, and in some cases requiring, users to have a photograph on the credit card for verification by the merchant. Electronic authentication methods are designed to detect whether an individual is attempting to impersonate someone else. In some cases, trusted third-party services are engaged to "vouch for," or authenticate, the user. Common authentication measures discussed in this chapter are digital signatures, challenge-response, one-time passwords, smart cards, tokens, and biometric devices.

Nonrepudiation

The term **repudiate** means to refuse to accept as having rightful authority or obligation, as in refusing to pay a debt because one refuses to acknowledge that the debt exists. For business transactions, unilateral repudiation of a transaction by either party is unacceptable and can result in legal action. Well-designed e-commerce systems provide for **nonrepudiation,** which is the provision for irrefutable proof of the origin, receipt, and contents of an electronic message.

Consider the dispute that would arise if Bob sent a message to his stockbroker at 8:00 A.M. ordering her to buy 1,000 shares of XYZ stock as soon as the price per share reaches $65.00. Assume that at 9:35 A.M., the price hits $65.00. Three very different chains of events could happen at that point, each of which could cause a dispute:

Scenario One: The stockbroker executes Bob's order as directed. At 11:30 A.M., a major competitor announces a new product release that renders XYZ's main product virtually obsolete. By 3:00 P.M., XYZ's stock price has plummeted to $45.00. Bob receives an account statement from his stockbroker a couple of weeks later. He denies the purchase of the XYZ stock and demands that his account be adjusted. This is **a proof of origin dispute.**

Scenario Two: The stockbroker neglects Bob's order, and it does not get executed. Very favorable earnings announcements for XYZ are released two days later, and the stock price soars to $76.00 per share. Bob calls his stockbroker immediately, and orders her to sell his XYZ stock at once. Her reply is "What stock? You do not own

---

E-Commerce in Practice

Two-Factor User Authentication Criminal Information System Successfully Implemented

The state of Kansas invested in the technology to place critical information into the hands of its police officers. Mission critical data to law enforcement agencies include background information of criminals they pursue. Allowing police officers to instantaneously access important criminal data files, such as the Federal Bureau of Investigations' criminal database, enables the officer to make quicker and better informed decisions.

Security over such data is critical as well. Only authorized individuals should have access to such highly sensitive data. Thus far, approximately 270 state agencies and 4,000 users have access to the database via the Web. Eventually 750 agencies and 15,000 users will be on the system.

How are these data accessed in a secure fashion? A two-factor authentication process is used. Each officer or law enforcement employee is given two things: a SecurID key fob and a personal identification number (PIN). Thus, they *have* something, the key fob, and *know* something, a PIN. The key fob is a product marketed by Security Dynamics Tech-

nologies Inc. that contains a small, durable token that, in this case, attaches to a keychain. The token is synchronized with the State's network security software, and an algorithm is used to generate a pseudo-random code every 60 seconds. Thus, the key fob and the network security software, because they are synchronized, will generate the same code at any given point in time. The code can only be used within that 60-second time period, or it becomes invalid.

To gain access to the State's system, the officer enters the generated code that is displayed on his key fob. Additionally, the officer enters his unique PIN that is linked to his specific key fob. Thus, only his PIN is valid in conjunction with the code generated by his key fob. This two-factor authentication process allows for strong authentication to gain access to the state and federal criminal records.

What did the system cost? Total cost for the system was about $1 million, including $400,000 spent on a new backup system.

---

any XYZ stock." She refuses to acknowledge that she ever received Bob's order to buy XYZ stock. This is a **proof of receipt dispute.**

Scenario Three: The stockbroker executes Bob's order, but erroneously purchases only 100 shares of stock instead of 1,000 shares. Very favorable earnings announcements for XYZ are released two days later, and the stock price soars to $76.00 per share. Bob calls his stockbroker and orders her to sell all 1,000 shares of XYZ stock. Her reply is "But you only own 100 shares of XYZ stock." She claims the buy order was for 100 shares, not 1,000 shares. This is a **proof of content dispute.**

These three scenarios illustrate potential problems faced by a firm engaging in e-commerce. The most effective way to enable nonrepudiation is through the combined use of hashing in both transactional directions and digital signing. In addition to using such integrity and authentication techniques to guard against such problems, transaction certificates, time stamps, and confirmation services help provide nonrepudiation. These techniques are discussed later in this chapter.

Access Controls

E-commerce systems, particularly those using the Internet and the WWW, require a certain amount of data sharing. Limiting access to data and systems only to authorized users is the objective of **access controls.** Some form of authentication procedure is typically employed in access controls in order to gain entry into the desired part of the system. The emerging attribute certificate or "privilege management" technology promises to be a highly effective form of access control provided it is implemented correctly. Firewalls can also be used to implement additional screening mechanisms. The topics of access controls and firewalls are discussed in Chapter 11.

ENCRYPTION TECHNIQUES

Confidentiality of electronic messages is a necessity of e-commerce applications. The primary method of achieving confidentiality is **encryption.** Messages are initially created in a form that is readable and understandable by the sender and by any other individuals if they have access to the message. The message, when it is in this form is commonly referred to as **cleartext,** or *plaintext.* Encryption is defined as the transformation of data, via a cryptographic mathematical process, into a form that is unreadable by anyone who does not posses the appropriate secret key. The data, while in this unreadable form, are commonly referred to as **ciphertext.** If a message is intercepted and read, it will be useless since the ciphertext message is unintelligible to any party not possessing the secret key. To be able to read and understand the message, the encrypted message (i.e., ciphertext) must be transformed back to its original state—the cleartext state. The process of restoring the ciphertext to cleartext is called **decryption.**

The **key** contains the binary code used to mathematically transform a message. Two types of cryptographic mechanisms can be used to provide an encryption capability: **symmetric cryptography,** where entities share a common secret key, and **public key cryptography** (also known as *asymmetric cryptography*), where each communicating entity has a unique key pair (a public key and a private key). For symmetric cryptography, the key used to encrypt and decrypt a message must be kept a secret. For both symmetric and asymmetric encryption, the relative strength of the cryptography is most commonly measured by the length of the key, in bits. However, it should be noted that the true strength of the confidentiality service may depend on a number of variables associated with the encryption function:

- The security protocol or application used to invoke the encryption function.
- The trust in the platform executing the protocol or application.
- The cryptographic algorithm.
- The length of the key(s) used for encryption/decryption.
- The protocol used to manage/generate those keys.
- The storage of secret keys (key management keys and encryption keys).

The strength of a system usually increases as the key length increases. This is because a longer **key length** implies a larger number of possible keys, which makes searching for the correct key a more time-consuming process. Any key length less than 64 bits is no longer considered to be secure. The box entitled "RSA 512-Bit Key Successfully Factored Collaborative Effort" discusses the hardware and process used to factor the underlying prime numbers of a 512-bit key.

Symmetric Encryption Keys

In symmetric key systems, both the sender and the receiver of the message must have access to the same key. This shared secret key is used to both encrypt and decrypt the

E-Commerce in Practice

RSA 512-Bit Key Successfully Factored by a Collaborative Effort

RSA continues to challenge the public to "crack its code," but this time it wants the underlying key generation ability to be tested. In August 1999, an international group of researchers successfully determined the underlying two prime numbers that were used to generate a single 512-bit RSA key. Why does RSA challenge worldwide researchers to do this? It does so to generate public awareness of the need for longer key lengths. As soon as the international consortium of researchers identified the prime numbers, RSA advocated the use of 768-bit keys for secure encryption.

What resources did the researchers use? They used 292 individual computers, nothing too powerful. They used

- 175 to 400 mHz SGI and Sun workstations (160 total).
- 300 to 450 mHz Pentium II PCs (120 total).

- 250 mHz SGI Origin 2000 processors (8 total).
- 500 mHz Digital Compaq CPUs (4 total).

The computers were spread throughout six countries and 11 sites. It took them approximately eight months including the preliminary computations.

Does it really matter that they determined the underlying prime numbers if it took them that long with that many computers? It does for firms with data that will still be useful to crackers after that period of time. Credit card number, bank account, new product design specifications, and medical histories all have a life much longer than this cracking period. Also, if the stakes are high enough, a very powerful mainframe computer with a bit of distributed processing help can probably do this much faster than such a consortium of relatively weaker computers.

FIGURE 10–2   *Symmetric encryption method*

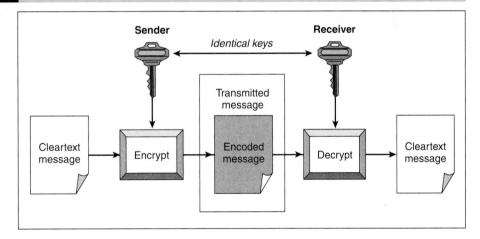

message as illustrated in Figure 10–2. The encoded message—the ciphertext—is unintelligible to anyone intercepting the message. The challenge with symmetric encryption schemes is disseminating the shared key to both the sender and the receiver while keeping this key a secret from everyone else, especially in those instances when the sender and receiver are geographically separated. A mechanism for accomplishing the confidential sharing of the secret key is presented in the following section.

Data Encryption Standard

The primary symmetric encryption algorithm used to be the **Data Encryption Standard (DES),** developed in 1977 by IBM for the U.S. government. DES is a **block cipher–based** encryption technique based on a 56-bit key. The DES encryption process is not as straightforward as Figure 10–2 suggests, however. An encryption process that uses a block cipher technique takes a fixed block of text, 64 bits for DES, and transforms the 64-bit block of text into a 64-bit block of ciphertext. The basic DES encryption steps are

1. Scramble a 64-bit text block one time.
2. Divide the 64-bit block into two 32-bit blocks.
3. Take each of the 32-bit blocks and scramble them 16 times using the secret DES key.
4. Apply the inverse of the initial scramble.

This cipher has been proven over time to be pretty weak in today's computing environment. In January 1999, a consortium of computers cracked a 56-bit DES encrypted message in less than one day. The federal government is replacing DES with its Advanced Encryption Standard (AES) discussed later in this chapter.

Triple Encryption

The strength of DES encryption has generally thought to be increased by using **triple encryption,** and this has been the method of using DES that has been advocated by encryption specialists. The best way to conduct triple encryption is by using three different secret keys in the process as illustrated in Figure 10–3. This process requires that both the sender and the receiver maintain three separate, secret keys. If any of the keys is lost, the ciphertext is unretrievable. Note that while this method provides greater security against attacks, it also requires more computation time to encode the message three times and then to decrypt each message layer. This is typically implemented with an encrypt-decrypt-encrypt, where two keys are used, not three. The message is encrypted with the first key, decrypted with the second, and encrypted again with the first key. The message is decrypted by reversing the procedure. Hence, the name "triple DES" is something of a misnomer. For example, triple DES using 56-bit encryption results in about twice (not three times) the encryption strength of single DES. The encrypt-decrypt-encrypt technique has been proven to be less secure than the technique of using three different encryption keys.

Advanced Encryption Standard

As mentioned earlier, DES is no longer considered to be secure. In 1998, a theoretical weakness in certain implementations of triple DES was also found, thus it was no stronger than regular encryption. Although this evidence is only theoretical, the National Institute of Standards and Technology (NIST) is taking it seriously; they abandoned adopting a new international standard using triple encryption for financial transactions. The NIST spent three years conducting a worldwide search and competition for its new encryption standard, the **Advanced Encryption Standard (AES).** They hope that it will prove to be a stronger encryption mechanism. The chosen algorithm is expected to be very important because it is intended to be used to protect sensitive U.S. federal government data, and it will likely be used in other private sector applications, such as the financial industry.

In October 2000, the U.S. Commerce Department announced the winner of the contest—it beat 15 competing algorithms from 12 countries. Many of the world's best math-

FIGURE 10–3   *Three-key triple symmetric encryption method*

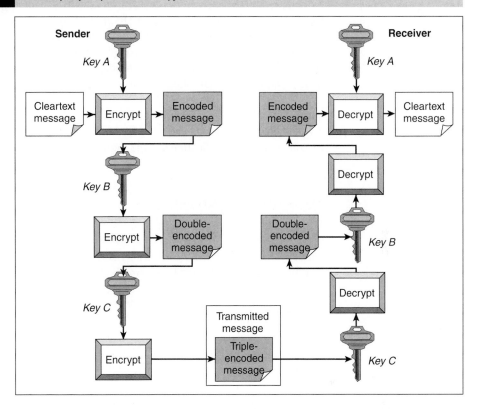

ematicians and cryptographers entered the contest. The winner is an algorithm called **Rijndael.** It was developed by two Belgium cryptographers, Joan Daemen and Vincent Rijmen. The algorithm, as required in the competition rules, supports key sizes of 128, 192, and 256 bits. As noted in an earlier box, RSA considers 768-bit keys to be a necessity for security. Key length is not the only factor involved; however, theoretically a very strong algorithm can make a smaller key length just as strong. Time will tell as the new algorithm is implemented and put to the test of the general public.

Skipjack
The National Security Agency (NSA) designed a stronger encryption algorithm, called **Skipjack.** It is much stronger than DES since it employs an 80-bit key, and instead of scrambling the data 16 times, it scrambles it 32 times. The Skipjack algorithm is placed on the **Clipper Chip.** This chip is based on the concept of a divided, shared, secret key, meaning that an escrowed key would require two escrow agencies to provide a password to recover the escrowed key. The purpose of splitting the recovery key is to ensure that law enforcement agencies go through the proper channels (e.g., court order) before recovering an escrowed key and using it to decrypt a message. The commercial acceptance of Skipjack depends on the commercial success of the Clipper Chip. The details of the Skipjack algorithm have been kept classified. The lack of details about the algorithm may also affect its commercial success.

RC2, RC4, RC5, and RC6

Some alternatives to DES have been developed by private organizations, such as RSA Data Security's **RC2, RC4, RC5,** and **RC6,** all of which are creations of Ronald Rivest. RC2, RC5, and RC6 are block cipher algorithms, and RC4 is a stream cipher. All three algorithms have variable key lengths. RC5 is also a block cipher that has variable block sizes ranging from 32 to 128 bits, a variable key size ranging from 0 to 2,048 bits, and a variable number of scrambling rounds ranging from 0 to 255.

RC6 is a block cipher based on RC5, and it was primarily adjusted to meet the requirements of the AES competition. Although RC6 was not chosen as the new AES encryption algorithm, it made it to the list of five finalists. The two main differences from RC5 are integer multiplication and the size of the working registers, which were changed to comply with the AES competition requirements.

Asymmetric Cryptography

The sharing and dissemination of secret keys presents implementation problems in keeping the shared, secret key confidential. In 1976, a concept referred to as public-key cryptography was introduced by Whitfield Diffie and Martin Hellman, called the **Diffie-Hellman** technique. The public key method allows a sender and a receiver to generate a shared, secret key over an insecure telecommunications line. This process uses an algorithm based on the sender's and receiver's public and private information. Figure 10–4 illustrates the following steps:

1. The sender determines a secret value *a*.
2. A related value, *A*, is derived from *a*. *A* is made public.

FIGURE 10–4   *Diffie-Hellman public key cryptography*

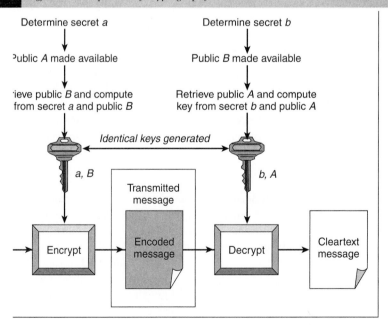

3. The receiver determines a secret value *b*.

4. A related value, *B*, is derived from *b*. *B* is made public.

5. The Diffie-Hellman algorithm is used to calculate a secret key corresponding the key pairs (*a,B*) and (*b,A*).

The sender knows his private value, *a*, and the receiver's public value, *B*. The receiver knows her private value, *b*, and the sender's public value, *A*. The secret key is generated from (*a,B*) and (*b,A*) by an algorithm that makes it computationally infeasible to calculate the secret key from solely knowing the two public values, *A* and *B*. To generate the secret key, one of the secret values must be known. The secret key is shared, thus avoiding the problem of transmitting it over an insecure telecommunications line.

Diffie-Hellman cryptography is still used today, but with some form of authentication procedure because of its vulnerability to a **man-in-the-middle attack.** A man-in-the-middle attack is illustrated in Figure 10–5. The masquerader intercepts both the sender's and receiver's public values, *A* and *B*, and replaces them with his own value, *Z*. The sender then generates the encryption/decryption key using (*a,Z*), and the receiver generates the encryption/decryption key (*b,Z*). Thus, the sender and receiver no longer share a secret key. Any messages sent directly from the sender to the receiver will be undecipherable. If the masquerader intercepts the message encrypted with the (*a,Z*) key, then he may generate a matching key (*z,A*) to decrypt the message, read, and possibly alter the message. The masquerader then encrypts the message with the (*z,B*)-generated key and forwards the message to the receiver, who then decrypts the message with the (*b,Z*)-generated key.

FIGURE 10–5   *Man-in-the-middle attack on public key cryptography*

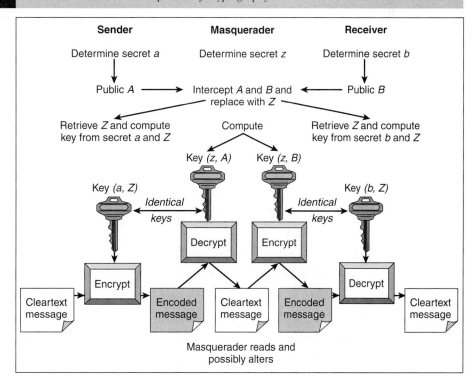

Neither the sender nor the receiver realizes their message has been intercepted, or perhaps altered. Authentication and message integrity techniques become imperative in preventing this kind of attack. These methods are discussed later in this chapter.

Public-Private Key Pairs

Another method for transmitting data using a combination of public and private information is by using a **public key** and a **private key** pair, known simply as **key pairs.** This method differs from the Diffie-Hellman method discussed in the previous section because each individual has his or her own public-private key pair that is used for encryption, decryption, or both. This key pair is not a function of anyone else's public information. Thus, when used correctly it is not subject to a man-in-the-middle attack.

The public-private key pair is a mathematically derived pair from a **one-way function** with an intentional **trap door.** A one-way function is a mathematical problem that is relatively easy to perform in one direction but is extremely difficult and time-consuming to perform in the reverse direction. Key pairs are generated using such a function, but they have a trap door. The trap door makes the reverse computation relatively easy if a precise piece of information is known. This additional piece of information, which serves as the trap door, is the key pair owner's secret password. Thus, one can freely publish his or her public key without fear of the private key being derived from it.

A popular algorithm used for key pair generation was developed by Ronald Rivest, Adi Shamir, and Leonard Adelman, and it is known as the **RSA algorithm.** The mathematical specifics of this algorithm are described in Appendix A of this chapter. The security of a public-private key pair, such as RSA, rests on the difficulty in reversing the computation. The most difficult reverse computation to perform is the factoring of large prime numbers. Factoring large prime numbers can be a very difficult task. Increasingly powerful computers and the continuous development of better factoring algorithms make this difficult task easier over time, but this progress is overcome by increasing the size of the prime number used. However, if someone discovers a rapid and extremely efficient prime numbering factoring algorithm, then this encryption algorithm will no longer be a valid security measure. If an individual or group discovers such an algorithm and does not let their discovery be publicly known, they could potentially calculate private keys and decipher any message encoded by the one-way function. While this is a troubling scenario, most mathematicians believe that this is not probable. That is why the ability to determine the underlying prime number becomes troublesome as mentioned in the box on page 313 entitled "RSA 512-Bit Key Successfully Factored by a Collaborative Effort."

Public-private key pairs can be used in a variety of ways. Figure 10–6 illustrates how the key pair can be used to provide message confidentiality. Consider a student named Penelope with a personal medical condition who needs to disclose this condition to her professor to explain a lengthy absence from class. Penelope may wish to ensure that no one else can read the message and learn of her medical condition. Penelope uses her professor's publicly available key to encrypt the message. The encoded message is then transmitted and ultimately reaches the professor. Penelope can feel comfortable that the only person who can convert the encoded message back into cleartext form is her professor, who possesses the matching private key. Thus, Penelope is able to send a confidential message to her professor. Note that this message provides no assurance to the professor that the message truly is from Penelope; anyone can encode a message with the professor's public key.

Key pairs may also be used to provide assurance to the receiver that the sender of the message is who he or she claims to be. Figure 10–7 illustrates how the key pair can be used to provide such an assurance. This time the professor sends a message to Penelope requesting a conference to meet and discuss course-related items. The professor wants Penelope to be assured that the message is really from him and not from a fellow student playing a joke. The professor encrypts the message with his private key and then transmits the message to Penelope. Upon receipt, Penelope is alerted that the message is encrypted and that the professor's public key is necessary in order to decrypt the message and read it. This step provides Penelope with the assurance that the message is

FIGURE 10–6   *Key pairs used to provide confidentiality*

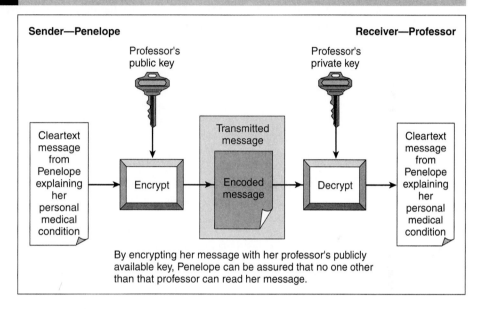

FIGURE 10–7   *Key pairs used to authenticate sender*

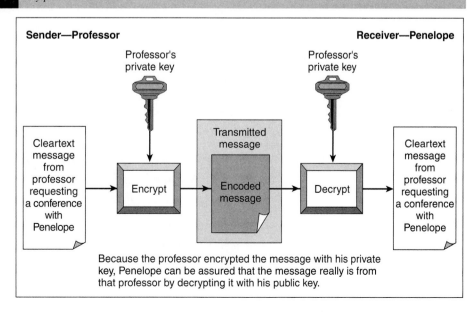

really from the professor. In a properly managed key pair system, this assurance is also called authentication. The transmitted message does not have the property of confidentiality, however, since anyone can decrypt the message by obtaining the professor's public key.

Neither of these scenarios provides both authentication of the sender and message confidentiality. Figure 10–8 illustrates how key pairs may be used to achieve both of these objectives. This scenario employs two key pairs, the professor's key pair and Penelope's key pair. In this message, the professor is not only requesting a conference with Penelope, but he is also disclosing her grade. The professor desires both authentication of the sender and message confidentiality. To assure Penelope that the message is from him, the professor first encodes the message with his own private key. To ensure that only Penelope can read this message, he then encodes it again, this time with Penelope's public key. The professor then transmits the twice-encoded message to Penelope. Upon receipt, Penelope must first decrypt the message with her private key and then decrypt it with the professor's public key. Penelope can be assured that the message is from the professor and that no one else was able to read the encoded message disclosing her grade. The use of the sender's private key for encryption facilitates authentication of the sender, while the use of the recipient's public key facilitates message confidentiality.

The preceding example is theoretically sound for providing authentication and confidentiality. The problem is that public key cryptography is not as efficient as the DES symmetric method presented earlier in this chapter. DES encryption is much faster than RSA public-private key encryption—at least 100 times faster in software and 1,000 times faster in hardware. A combination of symmetric key technology, such as DES, with public-private key pairs, such as RSA, can provide for more efficient, and just as effective, security. Rather than encoding the entire message with the slower public-private key pair, it is encoded with a faster DES algorithm. This process is illustrated in Figure 10–9. The DES key is a randomly generated key. The challenge is to get the DES

FIGURE 10–8   *Key pairs used to provide confidentiality and authentication of sender*

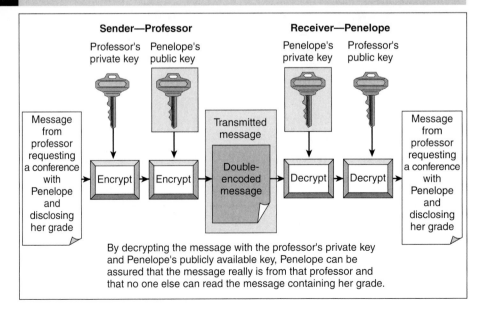

FIGURE 10–9   *Symmetric and public-private key pair combination approach to encryption*

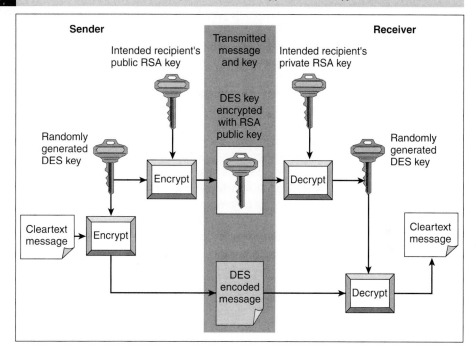

key to the recipient of the message in a secret fashion. Typically, the DES key will be much smaller than the message that it is used to encode. The DES key itself is encoded using the intended recipient's public key. The DES encoded message and public key-encoded DES key are both transmitted to the recipient. No one can read the message unless they can obtain the DES key, and only access to the recipient's private key can facilitate the retrieval of the DES key. Note that the AES will soon replace DES in this example, and efficiency of computation was an important selection item.

Thus, message confidentiality is achieved by using the DES method to more efficiently encode the message and then using the less efficient, but secure method of public-private key encryption to encode the DES key. Note that the scenario discussed provides message confidentiality, but not authentication of the sender. A message signing feature that provides both authentication and a message integrity check is discussed later.

Digital Wrappers

With a public-key infrastructure in place to manage key pairs, digital wrappers around messages become possible. **Digital wrappers** act as gatekeepers around messages. As mentioned earlier, a message encrypted with a user's public key can only be opened by the user who has the corresponding private key. As digital inventories continue to grow, as well as thefts, digital wrappers will play an important role in protecting digital assets. The wrapper that unlocks the message inside, which can be a song, a book, software, etc., can contain instructions as to when the message can be unlocked with the key. The instructions may only let the message be unlocked a specific number of times or may be a period of time.

Elliptic Curve Cryptography

A growing field in mathematics is that of **elliptic curve cryptography (ECC).** Recently used in the proof of Fermat's Last Theorem,[1] these curves have been used by cryptographers in public key cryptosystems since 1987. ECC is based on another one-way function—that of solving the elliptic curve discrete logarithm problem, which is more difficult than solving the discrete logarithm problem employed by RSA RC algorithms. Because the one-way function is more difficult than that contained in other algorithms, the key size can be made much smaller, thus increasing speed and efficiency of the algorithm. Roughly, a 160-bit key offers the same security of the RSA system and discrete–logarithm based systems with a 1,024-bit key. In 1998, RSA began offering its own ECC algorithm as an option to users of its BSAFE 4.0 encryption product.

RSA received a patent in 1999 for a "new, efficient way of converting between two popular but incompatible implementations of elliptic curve cryptography (ECC)." ECC, because of its efficiency has favorable features for small devices with less memory and computing capability, such as handheld wireless devices. However, many of the ways of representing the ECC numbers in multiple systems are not compatible. RSA has developed a cost-effective mechanism for converting between disparate systems.

Integrity Check Values and Digital Signatures

In the previous section, authentication of the sender was achieved by the use of a private key to encode the message. For this method to work properly, the recipient must be able to gain assurance that the related public key of the sender does in fact belong to the sender. Public-private key pairs are generally registered with a trusted third party, called a **certification authority.** Key management and certification authorities are important players in authentication, message integrity, and nonrepudiation security measures. The topics of key management and certification authorities are discussed later in this chapter. This section further explores authentication and message integrity devices.

Integrity Check Values (Hashes)

In order to verify that the contents of a message has not been altered in any way, **integrity check values** can be used. Figure 10–10 illustrates how two users sharing a secret hashing algorithm can verify that the message has not been altered from its original form. The sender hashes the message and produces a checksum or integrity check value based on the contents of the message. A hash takes a variable-length set of data and computes a fixed-length representation. Obtaining the full data set from the hash is virtually impossible. Also, collisions (two sets of data that produce the same hash) are rare enough to be considered nonexistent. The hash is computed with an algorithm that is not secret. No key is used. A hashing algorithm is used such that if the message is altered in any way, no matter how slight, a different integrity check value or hash will result.[2]

---

[1]Fermat's Theorem has been called the world's greatest mathematical problem [Singh, 1997] since it remained unproven or disproven for 300 years. The theorem was finally proven in 1995 by Andrew Wiles. The proof of this theorem and the relationship between modular forms and elliptic equations have caused interest in ECC.

[2]An alternative method, a message authentication code (MAC), does depend on a key. It is a hash combined with a secret key.

FIGURE 10–10   *Integrity check values*

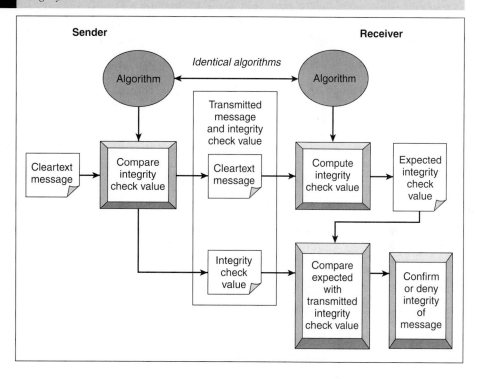

The integrity check value is a one-way function, meaning that it is virtually impossible to reverse the process and produce a message from the check value. Because the check value reveals nothing about the message, it does not need to be encoded. Both the message and the check value are then transmitted to the receiver. The receiver of the message independently recomputes the integrity check value from the message received. If the recomputed check value is identical to the check value received, then the receiver can feel confident that the message received is in its original form.

Note that the process illustrated in Figure 10–10 does not provide nonrepudiation or confidentiality of the message. If confidentiality is also desired, then some form of message encryption is necessary. Message encryption can easily be incorporated by encrypting the message after the integrity check value has been calculated. Encrypting the check value is not necessary since it reveals nothing about the message.

Digital Signatures

What if the sender needs to be specifically bound to a document? Shared keys, because they are shared, do not foster the identification of the originator of a specific message. Binding the sender of the message with the exact contents of the message is a very desirable, if not necessary, feature of many e-commerce transactions. **Digital signatures** are designed to bind the message originator with the exact contents of the message. Public-private keys are used because secret keys can be assigned to individuals, and these keys should never be shared with other users.

The sender uses his or her private key to compute the digital signature. To compute the digital signature, a one-way hashing algorithm may be used to first calculate a **message digest,** as is done by RSA. A hashing algorithm is a way in which a very large message can be represented in a unique way in a much smaller format. Message digest algorithms, such as Ronald Rivest's MD2, MD4, MD5, and MD6, transform messages of any reasonable length into a 128-bit digest. (Note: Of these, only MD5 and MD6 are considered robust enough to be used as a hashing algorithm.) The message digest is an efficient way to represent the message, as well as being a unique number that can only be calculated from the contents of the message. As with the integrity check value, if even one letter of the message is altered, the message digest will be changed.

The sender's private key is used at this point to encrypt the message digest. The encrypted message digest is what is commonly referred to as a digital signature. It is generated from the contents of the message and the sender's private key; thus, it is a unique creation of the contents of the message and the sender's private key. The message, therefore, can be attributed to no one else, and the message content is virtually indisputable. The message and the digital signature are transmitted to the receiver. The hashing algorithm is used by the recipient to recalculate the message digest. The recipient uses the sender's public key to decrypt the message digest. If the recalculated message digest is identical to the decrypted message digest, then the message can be attributed to the sender (authenticated) and its contents considered to be in its original form (message integrity).

The ability to link or bind a message to both its originator and the contents of the message is considered to be a mechanism for providing nonrepudiation of origin and nonrepudiation of content. Some legal experts assert that, in some ways, digital signatures, when used properly, are more trustworthy than handwritten signatures because of the use of the message digest, which provides strong evidence that the original document has not been altered since the signature was made. Because digital signatures are legally binding in the United States and many other countries as mentioned in Chapter 5, one should always carefully read any message to which they attach their digital signature, just like one should do when signing any paper-based document. The scenario illustrated in Figure 10–11 does not provide for confidentiality of the message since the message is sent in its cleartext form. Further, anyone can decrypt the digest, since a public key is used for this process. Thus, any message sent in cleartext form with a digital signature can be read and authenticated by anyone. One way of sending a confidential, digitally signed message ensuring authentication and message integrity is presented in Figure 10–12. Many alternatives to this model are possible.

The U.S. government originally specified the **Digital Signature Algorithm (DSA)** defined by the NIST's **Digital Signature Standard (DSS)** as its digital authentication standard. In February 2000, the U.S. Department of Commerce adopted two additional digital signature algorithms to be included in DSS: X9.31-1, **Reversible Digital Signature Algorithm (rDSA),** and X9.62, **Elliptic Curve Digital Signature Algorithm (ECDSA).** In October 2000, NIST announced plans to incorporate other algorithms into DSS so that federal departments, agencies, and contractors who use digital signatures can have options other than DSA, rDSA, and ECDSA.

DSA, also known as the Federal Information Processing Standard, or FIPS 186, is similar in concept to RSA, but it is based on a different hashing algorithm that produces a digest that, along with the private key, is used to generate a signature with two 160-bit numbers. The public key size can be as large as 1,024 bits, while the private key size must be less than 160 bits. Both of the 160-bit generated numbers accompany the message. The authentication process involves recalculating the digest and then using the public key and one of the 160-bit numbers accompanying the message to verify the value of the other 160-bit number accompanying the message. Thus, this method also provides authentication and a message integrity check.

FIGURE 10–11   *Digital signatures using a hashing algorithm*

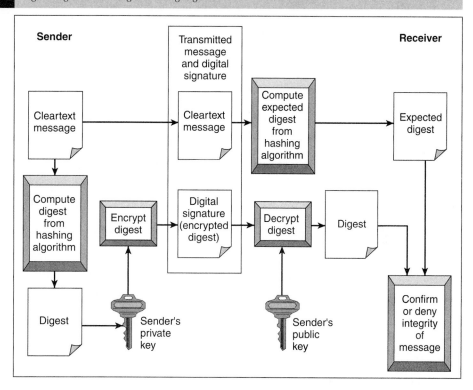

One-Time Pads

Modern cryptography really started in 1917, when Gilbert Vernam was asked to create an encryption scheme that was unbreakable by the Germans. He did one better—he created an encryption scheme that has yet to be broken. It was called the **one-time pad.** Vernam took two long strips of paper tape, one with the message printed on it, the other with the key printed on it. He proceeded to add the characters together. One disadvantage of this scheme, though, was the large amount of key material required—equal to the amount of data needing encryption.

Years later, a gentleman by the name of Lyman Morehouse solved Vernam's problem of the large materials used for the keys. This new cipher was the **Morehouse cipher** and is considered nearly identical to the one-time pad. Instead of a single, large set of key material, the Morehouse cipher uses two shorter groups of key material. These two key materials are used in such a way as to equal the strength of a Vernam cipher.

Why is this one-time pad scheme so important? The algorithm has no "back door." That is, one must have the encryption key if he is to read the message. If a hacker obtains only part of the key, he still will not be able to determine the message. This is currently the only algorithm said to be provably unbreakable.

The Vernam cipher one-time pad works as follows: Sufficient random numbers are generated so that they are the same length as the message. Then the two series of numbers are XORed together (see Appendix B for an explanation of the term XOR). This process sounds simple enough, so what makes it so unique and difficult to crack? The numbers must be truly, physically random and moreover, can only be used once. Thus,

FIGURE 10–12　　　*Encryption techniques providing message integrity, authentication, and confidentiality*

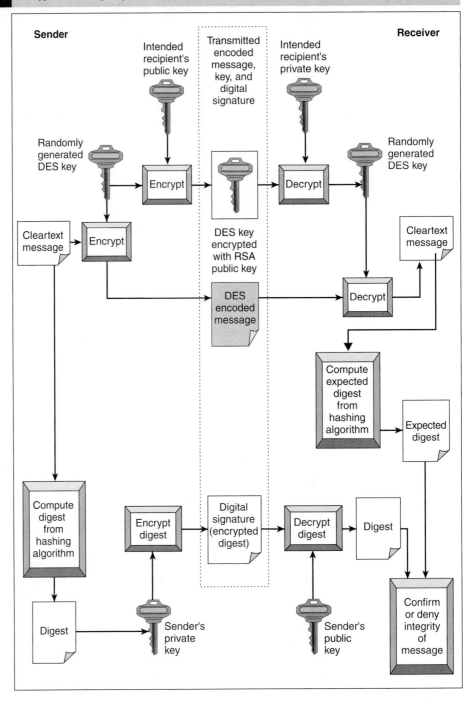

if implemented correctly, no mathematical method exists to decrypt the message without the key. A user of this cryptosystem would then have to concentrate on the physical security—making sure that no one obtains the key.

Regarding the problem of physical security of the key, a problem of key management exists as well, although less today than years ago. Many scholars suggest that because the key must be the same size as the message, the key lengths are difficult to handle. While this may have been true during World War I, this problem is less troublesome given the speed and size of modern computers. This impracticality is precisely what has delayed modern use of this cryptosystem. The Morehouse cipher further helps to solve this problem by reducing the number of key material needed for large data sets.

Good Encryption Practices

The procedures mentioned here provide good security only if certain safeguards and precautions are taken. This section discusses good encryption practices that foster stronger security.

Password Maintenance
First and foremost, one should never share one's secret password. In the United States, digital signatures are legally binding. A password can be used to protect the private key, and therefore the digital signature. If the password and private key are shared and they are used to enter into an undesirable business or contractual transaction by the person with whom you shared your password, you must prove that you are not bound to that transaction. Disputing the claim may prove to be difficult. Another good practice is to frequently change the password and related encryption key. Should the encrypted messages be the target of an attack, the greater the number of ciphertexts available to the attacker encoded with the same key, and the easier his or her job may be to successfully break the code. Passwords should be at least six digits in length, preferably eight, and make use of pseudo-random characters, such as numbers and other nonalphanumeric symbols.

Key Length
Use an appropriate key length whenever possible. As a general rule, the longer the key length, the greater the security. For domestic use, a key length of at least 128 bits should be used since a 64-bit key is no longer considered to provide adequate security. To the extent possible, financial transactions should be encoded with 1,024-bit keys to ensure even greater security.

Key Management Policies
Excellent key management policies and procedures are a precursor to data security. If key management is conducted in-house, the policies, procedures, and software management need to be carefully studied, designed, and monitored. If key management is outsourced, third-party key management agencies should be chosen carefully. Key management issues are discussed in the following section.

Compressed Files
To reduce transmission time, **data compression** is frequently used to reduce the size of a file. Most lossless data compression techniques are based on removing redundancy from the file. Encryption, however, is the process of transforming ordered data into seemingly random data. Therefore, lossless compression techniques will not be effective on encrypted data, but the opposite is still true; because encryption techniques are unaffected by the presence or absence of redundancy, they will still be effective on compressed data. So, when compression and encryption are both to be performed, it is vital that compression be performed prior to encryption. In addition to reducing transmission time, another potential side benefit of using compression with encryption is that the compression-encryption process can often be performed faster than encryption alone

because compression is a simpler mathematical operation than most modern encryption algorithms and therefore can be performed much faster. If an overall system view is taken, balancing how much compression is achieved (more compression = more processing time) versus how much faster the encryption operation can be performed (less data = faster encryption), then significant processing time reductions can be achieved.

Message Contents

For messages encoded with a publicly available key, nothing is to prevent an attacker from "guessing" what is in the message, encoding the guessed message, and comparing the resulting ciphertext with the actual ciphertext. This type of attack is called a **guessed cleartext attack.** In some situations, the message contents may be relatively easy to "guess" in an iterative fashion on a computer. Consider a business that is soliciting contract bids from four top contenders. The strategy from the bidders' viewpoint is to bid low enough to win the contract and still be able to provide a quality product on time and earn a reasonable return. Bids are frequently submitted in a sealed fashion by a specific due date. If one of the bidders knows the bid amount of a competitor, it is in a position to slightly undercut that other bidder. Assume the company soliciting the bid requires the bids to be placed in a predefined format for ease of comparison and then provides a public key for encryption of the bid before it is transmitted. If one of the bidders can intercept the electronic copy of a competitor's bid, it may be able to successfully launch a guessed cleartext attack. It can take the predefined form, and with the use of a computer, try placing various values in the predefined fields, encrypt the "guessed" message with the public key, and assess whether the resulting ciphertext is the same as the intercepted ciphertext. If the attack is successful before the bid deadline, the company can then adjust its bid to appear more favorable in comparison with its competitor. If security is an issue, then extra, meaningless characters should be inserted into the cleartext message before it is encrypted in order to thwart a guessed cleartext attack.

PUBLIC KEY INFRASTRUCTURES

For public-private key pairs to function properly, both the public and private keys must be securely bound to the individual to prevent masquerading and forgery. Key pairs can be used for external authentication as illustrated in Figure 10–14 or for internal confidentiality, authentication, and nonrepudiation functions. The **public key infrastructure (PKI)** is predicted to explode in the next few years. Datamonitor (a research firm) predicts that the PKI market will grow from $70 million in revenue in 1999 to $595 million by 2003. The box entitled "Implementing PKI in SAP R/3 Environments" describes how RSA's Keon PKI products interface with the ERP system. A PKI typically consists of three main functional parts:

- **Certification authority (CA)**—A trusted entity that issues and revokes public key certificates and **certificate revocation lists (CRLs).**
- **Registration authority (RA)**—An entity that is trusted by the CA to register or attest to the identity of CA users.
- **Certificate repository (CR)**—A publicly accessible electronic database that holds information such as certificates and CRLs.

Certification authorities perform the task of managing key pairs, while the verification of the person or entity bound to that key pair is initially ascertained at the time of application by the registration authority. **A certificate** is issued by a CA and links an individual or entity to its public key, and in some cases to its private key. Certification

E-Commerce in Practice

Implementing PKI in SAP R/3 Environments

RSA's Keon family of PKI products joined SAP R/3's Complementary Software Program by providing an add-on security product. Specifically, the Keon Agent will allow users of SAP R/3 to "open new lines of trusted communications and increase cooperative ventures with customers, partners and employees."

The agent software provides security services for all SAP R/3 applications through:

- two-factor authentication.
- digital certificates.
- data encryption.

The security devices are designed for communications that occur between both desktop and applications servers. The two-factor authentication requires that the SecurID smart-card be implemented as well.

The digital certificates are standard X.509 formats. Businesses can choose to issue their own certificates with the Keon Certificate Server or they may choose to outsource it to RSA's partner, Veri-Sign.

Source: Based on information from *RSA Press Release,* June 2, 1999. *www.rsa.com*

authorities can offer different grades of certificates depending on the type of initial identification provided by the individual. To ensure scalability, a distributed hierarchy can be built, with a "root" CA and "subsidiary" CAs and RAs. When a certificate is compromised, or lost, then that certificate is revoked by the CA and added to a certificate revocation list (CRL). This list, along with the valid certificates issued and still in effect, is posted in the certificate repository (CR). The industry standard for certificates and directory authentication is the International Telecommunication Union's **ITU-T X.509** format, which defines the fields contained in a certificate. This format is illustrated in Figure 10–13. This standard is widely adopted and used by most certification authorities. (Note: ISO is currently developing a series of certificate management standards known as **ISO 15782.** These standards will generally replace ITU-T X.509.)

A general verification model using a CA is illustrated in Figure 10–14. In this illustration, both the customer and merchant have certificates issued by the CA; however, they do not necessarily have to use the same CA. The customer may wish to verify the legitimacy of an Internet business. The CA provides a mechanism for verifying that the business is indeed the business it claims to be. The merchant may wish to verify the legitimacy of a customer before it releases a product or performs a service. Again, the CA provides a mechanism for verifying that the customer is who he or she claims to be.

This authentication scenario only works if the CA is trustworthy and secure. Various types of CAs exist, and they must have their own public keys, which also must be trusted. The public key of the CA is used by applications that verify and manage certificates. If the CA's key is compromised, no certificate issued by that CA should be considered secure.

A **certification practice statement (CPS)** outlines a certification authority's policies, practices, and procedures for certifying keys. In the case of a public certification authority, discussed in the following section, this statement should be read and understood before an entity chooses a certification authority with which to contract. In the case of an enterprise or outsourced CA, the CPS must be developed by the enterprise or a third party acting on behalf of the enterprise. Such a CPS cannot be generic, and one should never simply "lift" a prototype CPS document provided by the vendor. An enterprise

FIGURE 10–13   *X.509 version 3 certificate format*

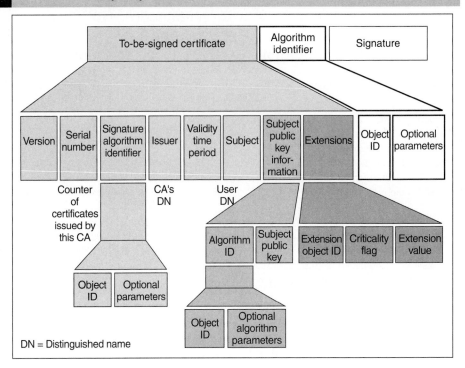

FIGURE 10–14   *General certification authority*

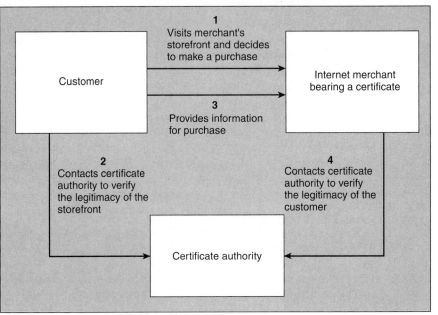

CPS provides the linkage between the vendor's certification solution and the enterprise's business case and systems environment.

A **certificate policy (CP)** is a named set of rules that indicates the applicability of a certificate to a particular community and/or class of application with common security requirements. This defines how, when, and for what purposes certificates are used within an organization. Various methods of key management exist, and three of many possible scenarios are illustrated in Figure 10–15 (scenarios A, B, and C).

FIGURE 10–15	*Key management alternatives*

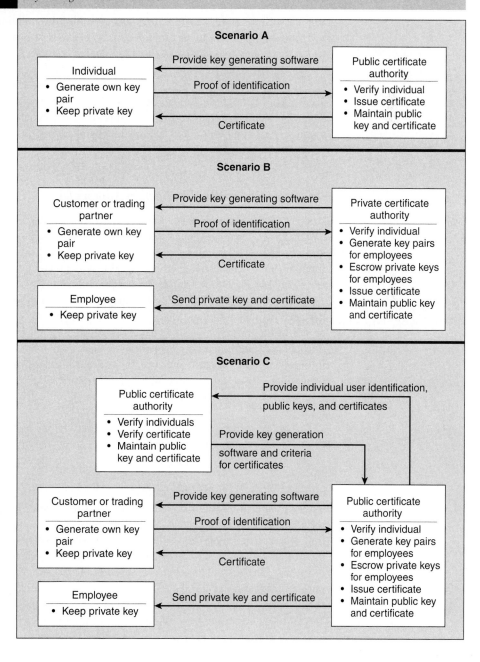

Public Certification Authorities

A *public certification authority* is one in which the enterprise does not control the root CA. For enterprises using such an approach, a certain amount of uncertainty exists regarding identity behind a digital signature outside its own enterprise. Scenario A is representative of an individual who may wish to have a digital signature and contracts with a public certification authority for a key-pair. This scenario could just as easily apply to an organization. Typically, different levels of certificates are issued based on the level of authentication the individual wishes to provide for his or her messages. The greater the security assurance, the greater the amount of information and proof of identity that will be required in order to receive the certificate. The certification authority, after receiving sufficient proof of identification, provides the individual with key-generating software, and the individual generates his or her own public-private key pair. The private key is solely maintained by the individual. The secrecy of the key, therefore, is the responsibility of the user, and nonrepudiation can be achieved. The public key is maintained by the certification authority and is kept in a **trusted directory** considered to be secure from tampering. As mentioned earlier, a successful attack of the certification authority would be catastrophic since the directory would no longer be trusted and massive impersonations could be launched by changing the names associated with certificates in the directory.

Private or Enterprise Certification Authorities

Another option is for organizations to establish their own *in-house certification authority* that issues certificates under the certification authority's root key as depicted in scenario B. This option requires greater in-house technical expertise than outsourcing this function, but it does provide the organization with greater control and flexibility over the certificate issuing policies and key management.

In-house certification authorities can issue key pairs to its employees and trading partners, but they will most likely issue different types of certificates. The individual or organization must provide some acceptable form of identification to a trusted certification authority administrator. Depending on the type of user, key generation is conducted in one of two fashions in scenario B. Trading partners may be provided with key-generation software to generate their own key-pairs, similar to scenario A. Allowing the trading partner to generate and maintain its own key-pair provides nonrepudiation for these users.

The key-pairs for employees, however, may be generated by the certification authority's trusted administrator. This may be done so that the private keys can be placed in escrow with the certification authority. Thus, both the employee and the certification authority have a copy of the private key. Kerberos, a secret-key authentication system, is designed to accommodate **key escrow** and works well for in-house access controls. Why would a company want to keep the secret keys in escrow? Usually, this is done to simplify matters if an employee loses his or her key or forgets his or her password. In addition, when an individual leaves his or her job, either voluntarily or involuntarily, the organization may need to decrypt data that the individual has encrypted. Without a copy of the key, the data would not be recoverable. The private certification authority, like the public certification authority, has its own public key and trusted directory, and in some cases, a private key escrow database. All of these items must be securely maintained. A successful attack could be very damaging to the organization, especially since private keys are centrally stored.

Hybrid Public and Private Certification Authorities

A *hybrid approach* to key management is another possibility since public certification authorities are offering in-house management capabilities for some of their products. A general model of how an organization may use a hybrid approach is illustrated in scenario C. The primary difference between scenarios B and C is that the certificates can be issued at either the public or private level. The public-level certificate authentication provides the advantage of name recognition of the public certification authority for individuals with little knowledge of the security practices of the organization with which they are dealing. A private certification authority provides easier interfaces with major application software because of their embedded root keys.

KEY MANAGEMENT

Regardless of whether the certification authority is public, private/enterprise, or a hybrid, specific tasks need to be performed. The methods for performing some of these tasks may vary, but each task and how it is performed needs to be carefully planned by any certification authority.

Identification and Verification of Users

Specific policies for acceptable proof of identification for each type of certificate issued should be explicitly stated. Adherence to these policies is extremely important for maintaining the integrity of the system. Some types of identification requirements are driver's license, passport, notarized identification form, and fingerprints. Certification authorities should publicly display their identification requirements, certificate issuance, and maintenance policies so users can assess the adequacy of the security provided.

Key Generation

The algorithm used to **generate** the key pairs should be selected and the key length determined. Because of legal constraints, variable key lengths may be necessary for different applications. These available key lengths should be explicitly stated by the certification authority, and the certificates should clearly indicate the key length.

Key Registration

The process of linking a generated key pair with an approved user and placing the public keys in a registry is called **key registration.** This process binds the key to a specific user for nonrepudiation.

Key Escrow and Recovery

If a private key is lost, and no copy of the key exists, then encrypted information may be permanently lost. Public certification authorities generally pass the responsibility of private key maintenance to the end user. Private certification authorities, however, may maintain a backup of the private keys in what is called a *key escrow.* The use of private key escrows is relatively uncontroversial and considered a fair business practice.

Private key escrow by public authorities or the government is very controversial, however, and is a hotly debated topic. The government would like for its law enforcement agencies to be able to gain access to escrowed keys, called **key recovery,** if the need arises and the agency possesses appropriate authorization, such as a court order. The political issues regarding key escrow are discussed in greater detail in Chapter 3.

Key pairs can be categorized into two types: signing and encryption pairs. A **signing pair** is used for the purpose of providing a digital signature. The private key is never escrowed, since having more than one copy makes nonrepudiation and authentication impossible. An **encryption pair** is used for encrypting and decrypting messages. The private key may be escrowed to prevent loss of data if a password is forgotten.

Key Updates and Replacement

Keys should have a limited life to prevent the creation of a library of related ciphertext by a would-be attacker. When keys are retired, they should no longer be used for new encryption or digital signatures, but they may need to be maintained to decrypt previously encoded messages. To avoid further use, the certification authority must manage the public key so that it is not available for encryption purposes, but allow it to remain available to authenticate previously signed messages or decrypt private-key encrypted messages.

Key Revocation and Destruction

A situation may arise where a certification authority may deem it necessary to revoke or destroy a certificate and its associated key-pair before its expiration date. A **certificate revocation list** (CRL) is typically maintained by the certification authority. It lists certificates that have been revoked and the general reason for the revocation. Reasons for revocation include

- Authority level of an employee or individual has changed.
- The key is compromised or reported as compromised.

A compromised key is particularly troubling, since determining the actual date of compromise is difficult, if not impossible. The certification authority should not allow new encryption or signatures to occur. The dilemma is what to do with currently encrypted messages. If the key is destroyed, then no one can decrypt the message. If it is not destroyed, then unauthorized viewing of the message with the compromised key may occur. The certification authority needs to have a policy by which it can determine when **key revocation** or **key destruction** is used.

Another CRL-related concern is the mechanism and speed with which key compromise information is promulgated. CRLs, posted to the publicly available certificate repository, can suffer from abysmal promulgation rates if the CA does not frequently update them, or if the users do not frequently access them.[3]

Cross certification is the process by which two independent CAs agree to recognize the other's authority. This is required when two enterprises become business partners and desire to share information. If the CAs for each enterprise are cross certified to the other, then the process of certificate validation can be supported by either CA. Since this process in essence extends the trust model beyond an individual enterprise's boundaries, a critical requirement is that the involved parties know of, fully understand, and

---

[3]Some alternative methods for promulgating revocation information include DeltaCRLs, use of CRL Distribution Points (CRL-DP), Online Certificate Status Protocol (OCSP), and Certificate Revocation Trees (CRT).

agree to each other's certification practice statement and certificate policies. If the organization's certification statements and policies do not closely match, then the security of both enterprises will be limited to that provided by the "weaker" of the two organization's practices.

ADDITIONAL AUTHENTICATION MECHANISMS

This section explores additional authentication methods that may be used in conjunction with the previously discussed encryption techniques. Well-designed authentication techniques allow the user to identify himself or herself to the host computer without revealing any confidential information, such as a password, to a session eavesdropper. A **one-time password** protects the user from having his or her password stolen during log-on transmission to a remote host computer and then being used by the eavesdropper. Encryption of the log-on password can also prevent the eavesdropper from intercepting and using the password. A combination of one-time, encrypted passwords provides both strong security against eavesdroppers and strong authentication.

How does a user obtain a new password every time he or she logs on to the computer? Smart cards and tokens provide the hardware and program devices for enabling one-time passwords. A **smart card** is a small plastic card that looks similar to a credit card, but it contains a microprocessor and storage unit. Smart cards are popularly used for authentication and payment of financial transactions. The use of smart cards for financial transaction payments is more thoroughly explored in Chapter 12. Smart cards need to be inserted into a reader, which may be a PCMCIA slot, a device that fits into a floppy drive, or an external device that plugs into a serial port. A **token** is similar to a smart card in that it too has a microprocessor and storage unit, but it does not require a reading device. Tokens may be in the form of very small calculator-like pads that are roughly the size of credit cards, pagers, or other palm-held devices. They have either a numeric keypad or biometric input device and a display screen. Many vendors offering smart cards and token products use the terms interchangeably in their product literature, making the differentiation somewhat difficult.

Smart cards are called **two-factor identification devices** because they require both a password and a physical device to be present. With regard to these products, a relatively secure log-on procedure would be to require the physical presence of a smart card in conjunction with input of the corresponding user ID. This requirement prevents hackers from gaining entry into a system by merely guessing a password; they must also physically hold the smart card to gain entry to a system. The box on page 311, "Two-Factor User Authentication Criminal Information System Successfully Implemented," provides an illustration of two-factor authentication. This type of security is similar to an automated teller machine card in which the user must have both the card and knowledge of the user ID in order to conduct transactions.

For greater security, the smart card or token may be synchronized with the host computer to compute a new password at prespecified intervals, perhaps every 30 seconds, after which time the password is unusable. Further, the system may only accept the use of a password once. Because a new password can be generated every 30 seconds, this feature does not pose an inconvenience to valid users. This feature provides security against an eavesdropper capturing a password and then using it later. The typical steps in the authentication process include

1. Entry of memorized password or scan of thumbprint.
2. Calculation of currently valid password by smart card or token.

3. Display of currently valid password.

4. Entry of currently valid password by user.

5. Authentication by host computer of combination of memorized password (or thumbprint) and currently valid password.

This procedure can also be categorized as a **challenge-response technique,** which is an interactive procedure in which one end (the user) must prove something by answering a challenge to the other end (the host computer or authenticator). In the preceding example, the challenge is to provide the currently valid password. The scenario described does transmit both the memorized and the currently valid password in an unencrypted fashion. This is not particularly troublesome because the currently valid password may only be used once and expires in 30 seconds. However, some users transmitting highly sensitive data are worried that their memorized password may be obtained by an eavesdropper and used for some other application. Tokens and smart cards can be used to generate an encrypted password for transmission. Some tokens or smart cards may be used to provide responses to multiple, variable challenges for increased security against eavesdroppers.

Another form of authentication called **biometrics** requires that some physically unique characteristics of the user be used for identification. The use of a thumbprint in the previous example is an example of a biometric device. Voice recognition, face recognition, signature recognition, and retina scans are other biometric devices in use, with retina scans currently considered to be the most secure.

ADDITIONAL NONREPUDIATION TECHNIQUES

This section discusses additional techniques used to provide nonrepudiation. Three types of nonrepudiation were previously mentioned:

- Proof of origin.
- Proof of contents.
- Proof of receipt.

An additional concern is proof of the time when the message was created, when it was sent, and when it was received. Digital signatures help provide proof of origin and proof of contents as previously mentioned. **Confirmation services** and time stamping help to provide assurance of proof of receipt and time. Mail messaging services, as well as certification authorities, can provide additional message services that provide proof of delivery of a message to a specific recipient, as well as proof of origin of a message. The confirmation service can also attest to the integrity of the message through the use of a message digest.

For important paper documents, mail services that require a signature for the receipt of a letter or package provide proof of date sent and received. Electronic documents can also be sent through electronic mail services that provide time stamping features. **Digital time stamping** is used to determine the exact time in which a message was created, while a messaging service can attest to the exact time the message was sent and received. Digital time stamping can be conducted by a messaging service without any need for knowledge of the contents of the message. The digital time stamps are typically computed by an algorithm linking the specific record bits (not contents) to a certain time.

IMPLICATIONS FOR THE ACCOUNTING PROFESSION

The five security issues first mentioned in the beginning of the chapter—confidentiality, message integrity, authentication, nonrepudiation, and access control—have been of concern to accountants for decades. The current challenge to the accounting profession is to not only understand how e-commerce changes the methods by which these control issues are addressed, but to become experts in these fields in order to assess any control risks faced by firms engaging in e-commerce. Accounting information systems must be designed and periodically reviewed for adequate internal controls, and the five security issues mentioned at the beginning of and throughout this chapter fall within that domain.

Confidentiality

Accountants need to understand cryptographic methods that are available to mask data that are stored on systems connected to the Internet and also private networks. This task is an extension of the traditional accountant's role. Accountants have always been concerned with the confidentiality of transaction data. As enterprise systems are becoming common, other types of mission-critical data reside in these repositories, such as design specifications or customer preferences, over which accountants also need to consider the level of confidentiality. Traditionally, the accounting function did not necessarily examine the controls over this type of nonaccounting data. However, as systems become more integrated and open to access by trading partners, accountants realize the need to provide a more holistic approach to internal control assessment that focuses on a broader examination of the confidentiality of crucial data.

Message Integrity

A critical component of a transaction processing system is the validity of data that are received into a system that represent a transaction. Transaction data, such as purchase orders, sales orders, or shipping notifications, must be reliable in that the data received reflect reality. The internal control assessment of a system must include an assessment of the probability that a digital message containing such information can be manipulated to represent inaccurate information. To perform such an assessment, accountants must understand the underlying methods of data transmission and digesting or hashing techniques.

Authentication

Identifying a trading partner as it attempts to engage in a transaction is also an important component to any business transaction. Prior to electronic systems, purchase orders were made on a business's specially printed forms with a logo and signed by a purchasing agent. With e-commerce systems, no means to physically view or examine a source document prior to approval makes the authentication of a trading partner a technological issue. Thus, techniques need to be employed to digitally determine whether a digital transmission is from the professed trading partner. Accountants need to understand the technologies available to support digital authentication. As mentioned in the box entitled "European Commission Contracts to Use Public Key Infrastructure Technology," an accounting firm is involved in not only assessing such methods, but

E-Commerce in Practice

European Commission Contracts to Use Public Key Infrastructure Technology

The European Commission (EC) wants to place approximately one-fourth of its purchases online by 2003, and it wants these transactions to be conducted in a secure environment. In a move to help the achievement of this goal, the EC contracted with two strategically aligned firms, Baltimore Technologies Inc. and PricewaterhouseCoopers, to provide a public key infrastructure (PKI).

A month prior to the announcement of this contract, Baltimore Technologies, a provider of PKI technology, and PricewaterhouseCoopers, a provider of global security and network solutions, announced their strategic alliance to provide global PKI e-commerce solutions. The alliance was forged to aid in the delivery of security conscious end-to-end e-commerce and business solutions. A key component is to provide organizations with the ability to employ digital certificate technology.

The EC is particularly interested in providing companies that reside in its 15 member countries with digital certificates. The businesses register for the digital certificate. The data transmitted by each business can be encrypted and digitally signed. Thus, the business solution provided by Baltimore and PricewaterhouseCoopers supports confidentiality, message integrity, authentication, and nonrepudiation.

providing consulting services to help implement and install such systems. A partner at PricewaterhouseCoopers claims:

> As a Certificate Service Provider in Europe, PricewaterhouseCoopers is setting an immediate precedent for this important service. Our work will speed the adoption of e-business across Europe. . . As a firm, PricewaterhouseCoopers sees the importance of adopting a position of trust and independence to support the current e-business revolution. This contract [with the EC] demonstrates the firm's commitment to be at the vanguard of e-business services.

> (Alistair MacWillson, Partner, PricewaterhouseCoopers, 1999)

Nonrepudiation

Accountants are responsible for assessing the reliability and validity of a firm's reported sales and accounts receivables. Disputed and/or fraudulent sales cause these accounts to be more difficult to audit. As mentioned in the box entitled "Visa: E-Commerce Is Major Fraud Source," roughly half of Visa's disputes and discovered fraud arise from its Internet sales. Proof of a sale becomes the issue in trying to collect earned revenues. The use of certificate authorities and digital signatures is a good method for achieving nonrepudiation. As mentioned earlier, accounting firms are becoming actively involved in the certificate authority activities that help promote authentication and nonrepudiation.

Access Controls

Guarding against unauthorized entry into a firm's transaction processing systems, wherever they may reside, is a critical component of the internal control framework. If they reside on any equipment that is either directly or indirectly connected to public networks, then the level of necessary security controls is heightened. Password techniques

---

E-Commerce in Practice

Visa: E-Commerce Is Major Fraud Source

Although only 2% of Visa International Inc.'s credit-card business relates to Internet transactions, 50% of its disputes and discovered frauds are in that area, a company executive said yesterday.

Consumers are responsible for most of the disputes and fraud, not merchants, said Mark Cullimore, director of emerging technology at Visa International Asia-Pacific, here at the Second Roundtable on E-Commerce in Asia, organized by Economist Conferences.

"This has become a significant issue for our industry over the past six months," he said. "It is all down to the problem of authentication, which has become the most important issue in the financial industry."

Cullimore said that disputes over transactions are more common than outright fraud, a common case being consumers denying they had ordered goods or services from sites, especially so-called brown-wrapper sites—those that at the customer's request disguise their identity on credit-card statements.

Other common complaints include consumers saying they had not gotten what they ordered, that the goods were delivered late, or that there were extra charges.

"Consumers worry too much about fraud on the Internet, and merchants don't worry enough," Cullimore said.

"Some merchants have told us they have had to triple the size of their dispute departments."

Cullimore said that security technologies such as Secure Socket Layer (SSL) could adequately prevent eavesdropping and manipulation of online messages and transactions. But SSL can't help with the authentication problem, he said. The Secure Electronic Transaction (SET) protocol, along with recognized Certification Authorities for issuing digital signatures, could assist in solving the problem, he added.

"There is very little SET use at the moment, and the bulk of the traffic is just encrypted," Cullimore said. "We need laws and technology in this area, and we need governments to stand behind [Certification Authorities]."

Cullimore said that the e-commerce community needs to build trust among merchants and consumers, something which is notably lacking at present. According to Visa research, only 5% of consumers currently trust electronic commerce, compared with 57% who trust PC banking, 62% who trust telephone banking and 77% who trust automatic teller machines.

Source: David Legard, *Computerworld Online,* March 24, 1999. © Computerworld, Inc.

---

are examined by accounting firms in their traditional assurance activities. Enhanced techniques are necessary for remote users (e.g., employees, trading partners, and customers) logging into systems. Accounting firms need to be at the forefront of technology in assessing the adequacy of a firm's access controls. Further, the assessment of the benefits of alternatives must be assessed in relation to their costs. For example, biometric authentication devices, such as a retina scan, may provide the best form of authentication before allowing a user to access a system, but the cost may be unjustified for certain types of firms. Accounting firms can and do provide services for assessing the adequacy of access controls, called penetration testing. To provide such a service, in-depth knowledge of networking techniques and server system software is necessary.

Internal Control and Risk Analysis

A startling figure was reported in a 1998 Computer Security Institute/Federal Bureau of Investigation study of computer security. Only 16 percent of the firms studied reported that they had performed a risk analysis of their downstream liability as result of network intrusions. Risk analysis and the resulting liability of potential risks to information systems fall within the domain of internal control analysis.

Clients are already beginning to look to accounting firms for assistance in developing well-designed and controlled e-commerce systems that encompass their accounting information systems and enterprise systems. Accounting firms, however, do not enjoy the luxury of being the only consultants their clients can turn to for solutions. Security system consulting firms are thriving. Accounting firms have the technical expertise and experience of understanding, designing, and controlling accounting and enterprise systems. This existing expertise and experience is an advantage the accounting profession possesses over other types of consulting services. Accounting firms can leverage this advantage by adding to their e-commerce security systems expertise.

Summary

Providing a technological environment in which secure messages can be sent between trading partners is a crucial aspect of electronic commerce. The methods discussed in this chapter—encryption, hashing, public key infrastructure technology, digital signatures, passwords, smart cards, tokens, and biometric devices—are some of the means to achieving the goal of a safe, business-oriented messaging environment. However, because the potential payoffs are high to hackers that can circumvent controls, existing methods must be tested continually and improved, and new security methods must constantly be explored.

Appendix A—RSA Algorithm

1. Find two very large prime numbers; the larger the numbers, the greater the security provided. Call these two prime numbers, P and Q.

2. Find a number E that has the following properties:
   a. It is an odd number.
   b. It is less than $P * Q$.
   c. It is relatively prime to $(P-1) * (Q-1)$ meaning that E and the result of this equation have no common prime factors.

3. Compute a value D that has the following property:

   A. $((D * E)-1)$ can be evenly divided by $(P-1) * (Q-1)$.

The public key-pair is the pair $(P * Q, E)$.

The private key is the number D.

The public key is E.

Now the encryption and decryption functions can be specified.

T = Plaintext
C = Ciphertext

The encryption function uses the public key E and the modulus $P * Q$:

   Encrypted message = (T^E) modulus $P * Q$.

The decryption function uses the private key D and the modulus $P*Q$:

   Decrypted message = (C^D) modulus $P * Q$.

(Francis Litterio, "The Mathematical Guts of RSA Encryption,"
http://world.std.com/~franl/crypto/rsa-guts.html)

Appendix B—XOR Function

XOR (Exclusive Or) is a mathematical function.

For a binary state: 0 or 1

AND function :
0 and 0 = 0
0 and 1 = 0
1 and 0 = 0
1 and 1 = 1

OR function:
0 or 0 = 0
0 or 1 = 1
1 or 0 = 1
1 or 1 = 1

XOR function:
0 xor 0 = 0
0 xor 1 = 1
1 xor 0 = 1
1 xor 1 = 0

Thus, an EXCLUSIVE OR function says that if two numbers or concepts are exclusive and XORed together, they will be true, if they are the same.

Key Words

access control
Advance Encryption Standard (AES)
asymmetric cryptography
authentication
biometrics
block cipher
certificate
certification authority (CA)
certificate policy (CP)
certificate practice statement (CPS)
certificate repository (CR)
certificate revocation list (CRL)
challenge-response technique
ciphertext
cleartext
Clipper Chip
confidentiality
confirmation service
cross certification
data compression
Data Encryption Standard (DES)
decryption
Diffie-Hellman technique
digital signature
digital wrapper
Digital Signature Algorithm (DSA)

Digital Signature Standard (DSS)
digital time stamping
elliptic curve cryptography (ECC)
Elliptic Curve Digital Signature Algorithm (ECDSA)
encryption
encryption pair
guessed cleartext attack
hashing
integrity
integrity check value
ISO 15782
ITU-T X.509
key
key destruction
key escrow
key generation
key length
key pairs
key recovery
key registration
key revocation
man-in-the-middle attack
message digest
Morehouse cipher
nonrepudiation

one-time pad	Reversible Digital Signature Algorithm
one-time password	(rDSA)
one-way function	Rijndael
private key	RSA algorithm
proof of content dispute	signing pair
proof of origin dispute	Skipjack
proof of receipt dispute	smart card
public key	symmetric cryptography
public key cryptography	token
public key infrastructure (PKI)	trap door
RC2, RC4, RC5, and RC6	triple encryption
registration authority (RA)	trusted directory
repudiate	two-factor identification device

Review Questions

1. Identify the five primary security issues of secure electronic messaging.
2. List two security techniques for ensuring confidentiality. Which one is prevalent in business use?
3. What is message integrity?
4. Discuss two security techniques for ensuring message integrity.
5. List four security techniques for ensuring authentication.
6. What is nonrepudiation?
7. List four security techniques for ensuring nonrepudiation.
8. What is encryption?
9. Differentiate between cleartext and ciphertext.
10. What is a key?
11. Explain what is meant by key length.
12. Explain a symmetric key system.
13. Discuss the challenge of a symmetric key system.
14. What is DES?
15. Explain triple encryption.
16. What is the Advanced Encryption Standard?
17. What is Skipjack?
18. Explain public key cryptography.
19. What is a digital wrapper?
20. Explain a man-in-the-middle attack. How can it be prevented?
21. What is a public-private key pair?
22. Explain a one-way function.
23. What is a trap door?
24. What is the RSA algorithm?
25. Identify the difficult task that must be performed in generating a public-private key pair and what makes that key pair so secure.
26. Which is more efficient, DES symmetric keys or RSA public-private key pairs?
27. What is an integrity check value?
28. Distinguish between a certificate and a certification authority.
29. What is a digital signature?

30. Explain how a hashing algorithm works.
31. What is a message digest?
32. What is the Digital Signature Algorithm?
33. What is DSS? What algorithms does it include?
34. List five good encryption practices.
35. Explain how a guessed cleartext attack is conducted.
36. What is the X.509 format?
37. Differentiate between public certification authorities and private certification authorities.
38. What is a trusted directory?
39. Distinguish between key escrow and key recovery.
40. Identify six key management tasks.
41. What is the Clipper Chip?
42. Define a one-time password.
43. Distinguish between smart cards and tokens.
44. What is a challenge-response technique?
45. Explain what a biometric device is. Give three examples.
46. What services can a confirmation service provide?
47. What is digital time stamping? Why is it important for e-commerce?

Discussion Questions

1. Has electronic messaging seriously affected the confidentiality of messages?
2. Has electronic messaging seriously affected the integrity of messages?
3. Distinguish among proof of origin, proof of receipt, and proof of content disputes. Which is the most troublesome for e-commerce, if any?
4. Is conducting e-commerce increasingly about data sharing or access control of data? Explain.
5. Why were the laws initially different regarding export of cryptographic products for financial institutions? Was this a fair policy?
6. If triple encryption is generally thought to be stronger than regular encryption, why is it not always used?
7. Compare Skipjack with DES. Why has it not replaced DES?
8. How is it possible to generate a shared, secret key over an insecure telecommunications line?
9. Give an example of why a competitor may launch a man-in-the-middle attack.
10. Why are public-private key pairs not generally subject to a man-in-the-middle attack? What would have to happen in order for a successful man-in-the-middle attack to be launched in a situation where public-private key pairs are used? Is this very likely to occur?
11. Why are security firms that sell security products and proprietary algorithms interested in and investing money in both theoretical and applied weaknesses in the very algorithms they sell?
12. Explain how a hybrid approach using both DES symmetric keys and RSA public-private key pairs works.
13. What would you feel more comfortable accepting as legal evidence, a document with a handwritten signature or an electronic legal document with a digital signature? What do you think a typical jury panel would consider the most valid if both were produced in court?

14. Are on line merchants or on line customers more likely to be concerned about certificates and authentication?

15. Why would a company elect to manage keys and certificates in-house? Are any advantages available to firms that use a public certification authority in addition to in-house management?

16. Why are key escrow and recovery so confidential? What do you think the government's policy should be?

17. Do you think smart cards or tokens will be more popular in the future? Why?

18. How do the five security issues mentioned in this chapter, as they are related to e-commerce, affect the responsibility of public accounting firms?

Cases

1. Digital Wrappers and Digital Assets
   Can a digital wrapper succeed in protecting intellectual property, such as music?
   a. Find at least two articles from the last six months related to illegal copying of music and/or the use of encryptions techniques to protect these assets to support your viewpoint.
   b. Turn in the two articles with a one-page explanation of your views.

2. VA PKI Project
   Visit the following site and answer the following questions:
   http://www.va.gov/proj/vapki/
   a. Why did this organization decide to use a PKI? What problems did they think it would solve or benefits would it bring?
   b. What vendor did they choose?
   c. What specific applications use the PKI?
   d. What types of certificates are issued? Is any identification needed to get a certificate? What is the process?
   e. How many certificates have been issued?
   f. What are future plans?

3. Smart Cards
   Research the following questions. A good site to visit is *www.scia.org*.
   a. Why do you think the United States and North America have lagged behind in smart card use? Does this imply that the United States is technologically inferior?
   b. What is the outlook for smart cards? What new products have been offered in the United States in the last year? How are they doing?

4. Certification Authority Licensing
   The purpose of certification authorities is to vouch for the identities of individuals and entities, but who vouches for the certification authorities? This issue has been repeatedly raised and is concisely stated in the following excerpt:

   > There are fewer than 20 certification authorities in the market. But as Internet commerce grows, there could be hundreds. How do you know a certification authority isn't an imposter? What are its credentials? What are its operating standards? What level of investigation did it conduct of a given entity before awarding that seal of authenticity? What level of liability is the certification authority willing to assume? What will be needed is some form of accreditation, certification or licensing of certification authorities themselves.

   (Cornell and Frye, "Who's Vouching for Whom in E-Commerce?", 1998)

France has already implemented a government licensing plan.

   a. What entity should perform this accreditation service of the certification authorities and why?
   b. Research the current state of certification authorities licensing in the United States, Europe (choose any two countries except France), and Australia, and summarize your findings.

References and Websites

Baltimore Technologies Inc. "European Commission to Use Baltimore PKI Technology for Secure E-Business Network," Press Release, February 3, 1999. *http://www.baltimore.ie.*
_____. "Baltimore and PricewaterhouseCoopers Form Strategic Alliance to Provide Global PKI and Consultancy," Press Release, January 18, 1999. *http://www.baltimore.ie.*

Computer Security Institute. "1998 CSI/FBI Computer Crime and Security Survey." *http://www.gocsi.com.*

Cornell, Craig, and Emily Frye. "Who's Vouching for Whom in E-Commerce?" *Computerworld.* February 2, 1998.

Diedrich, Tom. "Smart Cards Are Coming." *Computerworld.* June 29, 1998.

Dunn, Ashley. "Governments and Encryption: Locking You Out, Letting Them In." *CyberTimes.* October 8, 1997.
_____. "Of Keys, Decoders and Personal Privacy." *CyberTimes,* October 1, 1997.

Ford, Warwick, and Michael Baum. *Secure Electronic Commerce.* Prentice-Hall, 1997.

Harrison, Ann. "Commerce Department Proposes Belgian Algorithm as New Encryption Standard," *Computerworld Online,* October 2, 2000. *www.computerworld.com.*

Internet Engineering Task Force—Public Key Infrastructure Working Group. "Public-Key Infrastructure (X.509)." *http://www.ietf.org/html.charters/pkix-charter.html.*

Johnston, Margaret. "OMB Readies Agencies for E-Commerce Requirements," *Federal Computer Week,* February 10, 1999.

Litterio, Francis. "The Mathematical Guts of RSA Encryption." *http://world.std.com/ ~fran1/crypto/rsa-guts.html.*

Markoff, John. "U.S. Group Delays Encryption Standard." *CyberTimes,* March 31, 1998.
_____. "Netscape and Microsoft Are Cleared on Exports." *CyberTimes,* June 25, 1997.

Menezes, F., P. Oorschot, and S. Vanstone. *Applied Cryptography.* CRC Press, 1996.

Rivest, Ronald. "Chaffing and Winnowing: Confidentiality without Encryption." Working paper, 1998. *http://theory.lcs.mit.edu/~rivest/chaffing.tx.*

RSA Data Security Inc. "Answers to Frequently Asked Questions about Today's Cryptography." Version 3.0, 1996.
_____. "RSA Crypto Challenge Sets New Security Benchmark," Press Release, August 26, 1999. *http://www.rsa.com.*

Security Dynamics Technologies Inc. "Security Dynamics Guards Police Database," Press Release, February 10, 1999.

Shipley, Greg. "Certification Authorities: How Valuable Are They?" *Network Computing Online.* March 25, 1997.

Singh, Simon. *Fermat's Enigma: The Epic Quest to Solve the World's Greatest Mathematical Problem.* Walker and Company, 1997.

Wayner, Peter. "FBI Plan Would 'Deputize' Private Sector Companies." *CyberTimes,* July 11, 1997.
_____. "Administration Gets Sour Taste from Own Encryption Medicine." *CyberTimes.* June 18, 1997.

11   FIREWALLS

Learning Objectives

1. To learn the TCP/IP and OSI models.
2. To understand the underlying components of firewalls, including their benefits and limitations.
3. To learn important factors to consider in designing a firewall.

INTRODUCTION

This chapter continues the discussion started in the previous chapter regarding security solutions to potential exposures. One of the primary security issues is access controls. Although some access controls, such as passwords and biometric devices that help to identify authorized users and provide authentication, were introduced in the previous chapter, one final example of access control remains: firewalls. This chapter explains firewalls and how they may be used as a preventive device to keep unauthorized users from accessing networks.

One way a corporate network can be protected is by disconnecting it from external networks. Until a short time ago this was a feasible and common practice. If data only need to be shared among co-workers, then an Intranet is adequate. With the explosion of the Internet, the WWW, and electronic mail, however, most companies find it impossible to completely isolate their networks. Firewalls provide a means to control connections between a company's private network and other networks, such as the Internet.

The 2000 Computer Security Institute/Federal Bureau of Investigation's (CSI/FBI) *"Computer Issues and Trends"* study found that 58 percent of the organizations studied claimed that they had incurred security incidents initiated from outside their organization and that 59 percent reported that their Internet connection is a frequent point of attack. It also reported that 78 percent of the firms surveyed currently use firewalls. The number of firms using intrusion detection devices increased from 42 to 50 percent from to 1999 to 2000, indicating that firms are trying to detect probing attempts before the intruder uncovers a weakness (known or unknown) and penetrates the system. These statistics indicate that firewalls and other such intrusion detection devices are considered by organizations to be very important security measures.

FIREWALLS DEFINED

The term "firewall" is borrowed from the construction industry. Firewalls are built out of fire-resistant material to protect apartments or office buildings. If a fire breaks out in one section of the building, these walls retard the spread of the fire to other locations. In regard to networking, firewalls provide similar controls—they can allow employees on a corporate network to access resources on other networks (such as the Internet) while preventing unauthorized users on these other networks access to systems on the corporate network.

The ICSA defines a **firewall** as a "system or group of systems that enforces an access control policy between two networks." A firewall should possess the following characteristics:

- All traffic from inside the corporate network to outside the network, and vice versa, must pass through it.
- Only authorized traffic, as defined by the local security policy, is allowed to pass through it.
- The system itself is immune to penetration.

(Cheswick and Belloven, 1994)

Firewalls should be used as a *component* of enterprise security, not as the only solution. While firewalls provide a robust set of controls, they are not foolproof, and an organization that relies solely on firewalls for network security is turning a blind eye to many exposures that firewalls do not address.

TCP/IP

To understand access controls and firewalls, a basic understanding of the **Transmission Control Protocol/Internet Protocol (TCP/IP)** is necessary. TCP/IP is a conglomeration of underlying protocols designed to enable communications between computers across networks with four basic layers:

- **Physical/network layer.** This layer is responsible for accepting network packets and transmitting them over the physical network. Physical networking protocols such as Ethernet, Token Ring, Fiber Distribution Data Interface (FDDI), and others run at this layer. Logical protocols such as Address Resolution Protocol (ARP) and Reverse Address Resolution Protocol (RARP) running at this layer are responsible for mapping the physical address of a machine's network interface cards (NICs) to the machine's programmed IP address.
- **IP layer.** This layer is responsible for the routing of packets across the network. Protocols such as Routing Information Protocol (RIP), Open Shortest Path First (OSPF), Border Gateway Protocol (BGP), Interior Gateway Routing Protocol (IGRP), and others run at this layer and determine the method by which packets are delivered from one machine to another. These routing protocols make decisions to get a packet from one system to another using the fastest network path.
- **Transport layer.** This layer manages the virtual session between two computers for the TCP, providing reliable end-to-end communication. For TCP, this layer manages the packets by arranging received packets in the correct order and transmitting acknowledgements (ACK) or retransmitting lost packets. The transport layer also manages the transmission or reception of **User Datagram Protocol (UDP)** packets.

• **Application layer.** This layer manages the networking applications, formatting data for transmission between a source and destination computer system. For example, a user requests a **Universal Resource Locator (URL)** by clicking on a link. The Web browser (a client networking application) formats this request into a HyperText Transport Protocol (HTTP) *connect and get requests* packet for the desired Web document. On the server side, the Web server (a server networking application) receives the request acknowledging the connection and returning the requested HyperText Markup Language (HTML) file.

The layers described, commonly referred to as the **TCP/IP stack,** are implemented through software that interfaces with the systems hardware, operating systems, and application software. Certain systems designed for networking, such as UNIX, Windows NT, and others have the TCP/IP software more tightly woven into the operating system. Other systems, such as DOS, require add-on software to support networking.

OPEN SYSTEMS INTERCONNECT

Another way of looking at networking is through the **Open Systems Interconnect (OSI) model** developed by the International Organization for Standardization (ISO) that uses a seven-layer model, which maps to the TCP/IP four-layer model. The OSI model was described in detail in Chapter 9. Both models perform the same functions; however the tasks are further divided in the OSI model. The diagram in Figure 11–1 depicts the OSI model and maps the TCP/IP conceptual model to the OSI model.

FIGURE 11–1   *TCP/IP and OSI models*

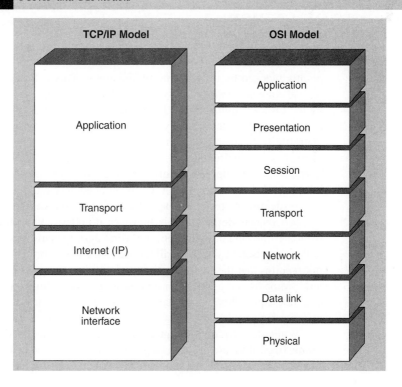

Whether you prefer to think of TCP/IP networking in a four-layer conceptual model or the seven-layer model of OSI, systems are still subject to the inherent risks. These include such vulnerabilities as TCP hijacking, IP spoofing, network sniffing, etc. Correctly designed firewalls will help organizations protect their internal systems from some of the inherent weaknesses of the TCP/IP protocol.

The risk of security breaches exists at any of the four basic layers. For example, data snooping can occur at the **network or link layer.** An example of a risk at the network (IP layer) is the **hijacking** of the IP connections. This type of attack must typically be conducted from the actual server site because access to the direct connection stream is necessary. An IP hijacker can use software (such as IP Watcher), download tools from the Internet, or create his or her own devices. The hijacker obtains a list of open connections as messages are flowing to and from the server. The data that are flowing through these connections can be intercepted. An IP hijacker can place the user "on hold" and take over the data transmission. Because of the speed with which data flows and the occasional delay that computer users experience and consider to be normal, many of these attacks do not raise suspicion by the users whose messages are being intercepted. Experienced network administrators have monitoring devices that can help them detect hijacking attempts.

Because of the potential dangers that hijackers present, businesses need to diligently examine the security procedures taken by their Internet Service Providers (ISPs) to protect all of their customer groups (businesses and households). If the ISP does not have good, consistent security precautions, a hacker can compromise the system by hijacking connections between customers and the businesses, and, unknown to the user, the hijacker can view the data transmitted via e-mail and Web browser forms. If the data are strongly encrypted, however, the viewed data are meaningless to the hijacker.

COMPONENTS OF A FIREWALL

Firewalls can be placed into two categories: static and dynamic. **Static firewalls** usually work in one of two ways. Static firewalls allow all traffic except that which is explicitly blocked by the firewall administrator. This is known as **default permit.** The second, known as **default deny,** denies all traffic except that which is explicitly allowed by the firewall administrator. In general, default deny is considered more secure than default permit. In default deny, only necessary traffic must be specified, and if a type of traffic is accidentally omitted, the worst that can happen is that some necessary traffic is accidentally blocked. Of course the accidental omission of necessary, critical traffic is undesirable, but the greater the degree of importance of the data, the greater the likelihood that its omission will be noticed very rapidly. Once an accidental omission is identified, efforts can be made to remedy the situation.

When using default permit, however, if undesirable traffic is accidentally omitted from the firewall configuration, the worst-case scenario involves unauthorized access to the very resources the firewall was implemented to protect. Furthermore, default permit requires that the list of explicitly blocked traffic must be continuously updated as new protocols and application types that are not authorized are created. Default deny does not require this strenuous, continuous environment scan for new, unauthorized application types.

While static firewalls are preconfigured as either default deny or default permit, **dynamic firewalls** manage the configuration in a more fluid fashion. Dynamic firewalls allow both denial and permission of any service to be established for a given time period.

FIGURE 11–2   *Gates, chokes, and default deny filtering*

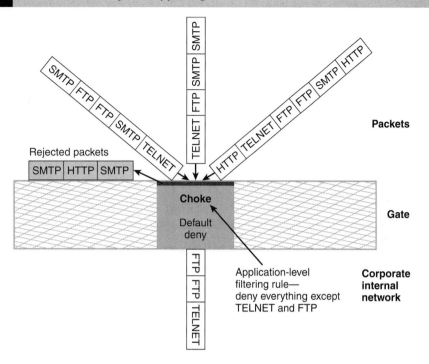

This type of firewall management requires greater human resources, but it also adds greater flexibility.

Firewalls are made up of two components: chokes and gates. **Chokes** limit the flow of packets between networks. **Packets** are small subsets of data that travel through networks. An e-mail message, for instance, might be broken up into hundreds of packets, each with the source address, destination address, protocol used, and part of the email text. Chokes read packets and determine, based on rules that the firewall administrator configures, if the traffic should pass. **Gates** act as a control point for external connections, similar to a typical gateway server. They receive connections and deal with them appropriately. Gates, chokes, packets, and default deny are illustrated in Figure 11–2.

An example of a service that runs on a gate machine is a proxy server. A **proxy** is a program that takes the place of another program. Typically, firewalls act as proxies for certain networking services. When internal users use TELNET, for instance, to connect to a host on the other side of the firewall, the proxy service accepts the TELNET request and forwards it on to the real TELNET service. The advantages of this approach are explained in the following section.

TYPICAL FUNCTIONALITY OF FIREWALLS

The definition of a firewall has changed over the years. While original firewalls consisted of a combination of chokes and gates, current firewall implementations are third-party software solutions that combine choke and gate functionalities, graphical administration, auditing, and monitoring capabilities into a single machine. Here is a list of common firewall characteristics; most firewalls employ a combination of two or more of these functionalities:

- Packet filtering.
- Network address translation.
- Application-level proxies.
- Stateful inspection.
- Virtual private networks.
- Real-time monitoring.

Packet Filtering

Packet filtering is perhaps the most critical function that firewalls perform. This is essentially what the choke performed in older implementations. Every packet that comes to the firewall is examined and either forwarded to its intended recipient or dropped. The level at which packets can be examined varies by firewall. Packet filtering can actually be performed by a router, firewall, or both. Figure 11–3 illustrates the level of filtering in relation to TCP/IP layers.

A **router** can be used for packet filtering by examining the destination network or host addresses and destination transport connection point and comparing them against access control lists. Packet-filtering routers can only limit traffic based on the transport level of the OSI network model, equivalent to the transport layer discussed in the preceding section. Typical transport-level protocols are TCP and UDP, both of which run on top of IP. These packet-filtering routers may block UDP traffic and allow TCP traffic. Because many types of inherent design weaknesses exist in networking application protocols (i.e., FTP), the packet-filtering routers may not provide the level of detailed filtering, commonly referred to as granularity, that certain entities require.

FIGURE 11–3   *TCP/IP layers and filtering*

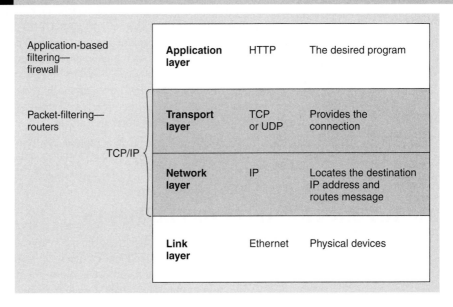

Many third-party firewall software packages provide traffic filtering at the IP and transport levels and provide application-level protocol checking at the application level. TELNET, FTP, HTTP, and SMTP are examples of application-level protocols. (These protocols were discussed in detail in Chapter 9.) TELNET and FTP may be allowed while HTTP, SMTP, and all other TCP protocols may be denied. TELNET and FTP are discussed in detail later in this chapter. **Proxies** are used to control network traffic at the application layer. This technique is much more robust than packet-filtering routers, because traffic can be examined in more detail before it is forwarded to a recipient. Of course, firewall software is much more expensive than routers.

Other third-party firewall solutions provide traffic filtering at the IP and transport layers and provide connection state checking at the application level. These solutions are typically known as stateful firewalls. Both proxies and stateful inspection firewall applications use the important concept of packet filtering as a control structure, but add application level controls on top. Proxies and stateful inspection are now discussed in more detail.

IP spoofing occurs when an attacker disguises his or her originating host server or router as that of another host or router. The highlights of a famous IP spoofing attack are presented in the box entitled "Mitnick Released for his Notorious IP Spoofing Attack." Depending on the attack, collaboration with the intermediate routers or hosts to accept routing table updates may also be needed to assist in IP spoofing. An external hacker may gain access to an internal network by disguising him- or herself as an internal system and bypassing a firewall that does not filter out incoming packets with an internal IP source address. The preventive measure is to filter out all packets that originate on an external network but appear to be coming from an internal address. A detective device is to monitor audit logs for messages received from an external interface that have both an internal source and destination IP address, because external networks should not be the source of internal systems.

To help prevent IP spoofing attacks, organizations should protect their internal address space by not publishing it to other networks, such as the Internet. Application-level (proxy or stateful inspection) firewalls can translate the source and destination addresses of network traffic sent to and received from these external networks to protect internal network addresses. These application-level proxies can also implement controls that deny traffic received on the external interface but have a source address of the internal corporate network, because this indicates some unauthorized user is attempting to initiate an IP spoofing attack. Security groups recommend that firms use this technique as a responsibility measure to reduce the risk of spoofing attacks being launched from their business sites.

Network Address Translation

Another typical capability of firewalls is **network address translation.** In many organizations, workstations do not have IP addresses that are unique in relation to the Internet. Each machine may have a unique address within the corporate network, but these addresses may already exist on the Internet. Obtaining IP addresses with a .com extension is becoming more difficult and expensive, so many companies may only apply for a small number of Internet-unique addresses. When employees want to access the Internet, however, their machines must have an Internet-unique address. Many application-level firewalls actually replace the workstation IP address with another, Internet-unique IP address when accessing other Internet hosts. This method can reduce an organization's IP addressing costs.

E-Commerce in Practice

Mitnick Released for His Notorious IP Spoofing Attack

In one of the most highly publicized pursuits and apprehensions of a computer hacker, Kevin Mitnick was arrested by Federal Bureau of Investigation agents on February 25, 1995, in an apartment building in Raleigh, North Carolina. In March 1999, more than four years after his arrest, Mitnick finally entered into an agreement that included a guilty plea to 5 of 25 charges. He was released in January 2000 after serving five years and paying $4,000 is restitution. This amount pales in comparison to the estimated millions of dollars in damage he caused. He is not allowed to use computers or access computer networks for three years. After his release, he attempted to sell his prison identification card, but it was pulled by three major auction sites.

When arrested, Mitnick was still prohibited from accessing computer networks from a previous conviction in 1989. The penalty for that violation added 14 months to his then-current sentence of 54 months. He had already served 49 months when he got his sentence.

The Crime

Mitnick has been credited with breaking into hundreds of business, personal, and university computers. He was accused of many counts of computer networking transgressions, but the ones mentioned here involve the trick of IP spoofing. On Christmas Day 1994, Mitnick began the activities that led to his capture. He began the attack by commandeering a Loyola University of Chicago computer and masquerading as a trusted source to gain access into a network that had access to Tsutomu Shimomura's home computer.

Shimomura, a cybersleuth and employee of the San Diego Supercomputer Center (SDCC), was apparently the wrong person to target. Mitnick gained access to his computer and electronically stole hundreds of files, containing software and sensitive files that would be useful in planning an attack on computer networks and cellular phone systems. (Mitnick liked to use cellular phones to conduct many of his break-ins.) To add insult to injury, Mitnick left a voice-altered, digitized message for Shimomura.

Shimomura rose to the challenge and began to work diligently on identifying and capturing the intruder. The logs kept by one of Shimomura's computers were routinely mailed to another, "safe" computer, which proved to be a very helpful detective device. These logs resulted in an automatic red flag that was seen by the SDCC, which then set off an alarm. These logs also allowed Shimomura to recreate the attack.

A helpful piece of information was brought to Shimomura's attention on January 28, 1995, by Bruce Koball, a computer programmer who was also an organizer for a group called Computers, Freedom, and Privacy. Koball had received a strange message from the group's ISP, The Well, notifying him that the group's site had recently stored way too much data. Koball thought this was odd because the organization's storage needs were very low. After checking the directory, he realized the files were not the property of his organization. About that time, Koball had read an article mentioning the attack on Shimomura's computer. After informing The Well that the files were not his, Shimomura was called in and identified the files as the ones stolen from his computer.

In an effort to help the FBI and Shimomura catch the perpetrator, The Well purchased a new server to begin round-the-clock monitoring. Eventually the monitoring activities were transferred to another ISP, Netcomm Communications Inc., which provided nationwide local access numbers to its customers. These monitoring activities, led by Shimomura, allowed the investigators to watch the intruder's every keystroke as he stole computer files from major companies, copied credit card account numbers, and took over telephone company switching centers.

By using the records of telephone companies, the investigators were able to narrow down a phone number. The calls had been looped so that GTE thought the call originated from Sprint and vice versa. Thus, neither company had an identifying number for the cellular phone. Finally, the calls were identified as originating from the vicinity of the Raleigh-Durham airport. Shimomura and a Spring technician circled the area in a car with a cellular-frequency-direction-finding antenna. Within half an hour, they had the apartment building located. On February 14, 1995, FBI agents took over and arrested Mitnick.

Protecting details of its network topology is a critical security measure taken by many organizations. Another important benefit of network address translation involves security of the network. Because the firewall replaces workstation IP addresses with an Internet-unique address, attackers cannot examine traffic to gain information about an organization's internal network.

Application-Level Proxies

Application-level proxies substitute the firewall's service for the normal service. For instance, when a user wants to use TELNET to access a host on the other side of the firewall, the firewall runs a TELNET proxy service that accepts the request and analyzes it against a rule base. An improperly configured rule base is illustrated in the box entitled "Misconfigured Firewall."

E-Commerce in Practice

A Misconfigured Firewall

Firewalls are usually implemented to limit connectivity between networks. Protecting a corporate network from the Internet, for instance, is a classic example of a firewall installation. In this example, a dual-homed system (a system with two network interfaces, and hence two IP addresses) is used with one interface attached to the internal network and one connected to the external network. The firewall machine is supposed to control the flow of data from one network to the other.

Today, many firewall vendors exist who distribute software that makes limiting connectivity fairly easy. Graphical user interfaces, precoded proxy services, and intrusion detection all make firewall implementations quicker and easier.

Analyzing network topologies to determine the risks that certain types of traffic introduce, however, is still a sometimes difficult, yet critical, step. Without fully understanding how networks are configured and determining what types of traffic should be allowed and denied, a firewall implementation is doomed to failure. What follows is a real-life example of a firewall that was configured inappropriately.

The Client

The client, which we will call XYZ Company, is a *Fortune* 1000 consumer products company specializing in cosmetics. With headquarters in New York and offices around the world, the firm is recognized as a global leader within its industry. Recently, the company started selling cosmetics over the Internet. This introduced a number of risks, so management hired PricewaterhouseCoopers to perform a general network controls review. This review included analyzing a sampling of routers and, most importantly, the corporate firewall, which was implemented to protect the corporate network from the Internet. Unfortunately, two miswritten rules compromised the integrity of the firewall.

The Problem

A firewall implements a security policy by following a set of rules that the administrator creates. These rules are a series of allow/deny commands that specify source and destination IP addresses and protocols. For instance, a rule might be written to limit the use of TELNET into a private network. The rule might look something like this:

Allow/Deny	Source IP Range	Destination IP Range	Protocols
Deny	10.1.1.0	10.192.1.0	TELNET

(continued)

E-Commerce in Practice

A Misconfigured Firewall—Continued

This rule would disallow TELNET traffic from any host in the 10.1.1.0 network to any host in the 10.192.1.0 network. Other protocols, however, would be allowed through the firewall.

The two rules that created a security exposure on the XYZ Company's firewall are listed here:

Allow/Deny	Source IP Range	Destination IP Range	Protocols
Allow	10.1.75.1	10.1.75.0	TELNET, FTP, HTTP, GOPHER, SMTP, REALAUDIO
Allow	10.1.75.1	"Universe"	TELNET, FTP, HTTP, GOPHER, SMTP, REALAUDIO

As illustrated in the accompanying network diagram, the first rule allows many types of sensitive traffic to travel from the external interface of the firewall to the corporate network. The second allows these same types of traffic to pass from the external interface to the "Universe," an alias that represents *any* IP address, internal or external.

XYZ Company's Network

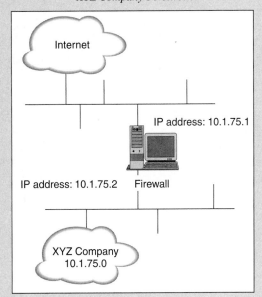

Clearly, this firewall is not providing any protection from Internet traffic. When PricewaterhouseCooper's penetration team attempted to add TELNET and FTP to the firewall, it was able, in both cases, to access any internal system without authenticating to the firewall! Below is a copy of the TELNET session.

```
# telnet 10.1.75.1
Trying 10.1.75.1 . . .
Connected to 10.1.75.1.
Escape character is ' ^ ]'.


XYZ Company. This is a secured network
violators will be prosecuted.
Hostname:
```

The company made two major mistakes:

- First, it allowed TELNET access to the firewall machine without authentication. From that point, any traffic was allowed to the internal network.
- Second, it put the company name in the legal notice message. An intruder could potentially use that information to penetrate the network.

Access to the firewall should generally be denied, but if access is allowed, users should always be required to authenticate. This will prevent unauthorized users from accessing the system, and it will provide auditing to monitor which users are performing certain actions.

The Solution

The short-term solutions recommended to the client were to remove the two rules from the firewall rule base and to remove the company name from the legal notice. These actions reduce the corporate network's exposure.

Going forward, any new rules added to the rule base must be thoroughly analyzed to ensure that they are not exposing the company to unnecessary risks. The purpose of a firewall is to limit connectivity to protect selected networks. Every rule should help achieve this goal.

The implementation of this rule base and its functionality is specific to the design and vendor of the firewall, but most support similar functionality. Because the connection originates from the user's system and terminates at the firewall, the data within the connection can be analyzed. An example of this includes a Web page request by a user in which the packet header includes the Web server's address (e.g., *www.microsoft.com,* translated to IP number format) and the data include the file requested (e.g., */misc/ privacy_security.htm*). The firewall, once it receives this request, can analyze the rule base and act appropriately. This may include requesting the user to authenticate himself to the firewall application prior to forwarding this request. At this point the user would be prompted to enter an ID and password, which would be verified against the firewall user database. If successful, the firewall may then check the rule base again to see if this user is authorized to view this type of file on this Web server. If so, the firewall would then initiate a connection from the firewall server to the destination Web server and request the same file the user requested. The Web server would then pass this information to the firewall, which would then verify that the information can be passed back to the user. This may include such checks as virus scanning or searching for risky Java programs. Throughout this entire process, the firewall may maintain detailed log records of the entire transaction.

The concept of proxies can be thought of as two separate and distinct connections, one originating from the user and ending at the internal interface of the firewall and the second originating from the firewall and ending at the destination system. This provides robust controls since the firewall has full control of every packet and all data as it transfers between these two connections. This also allows the firewall to control subsequent connections, such as FTP data connections, that originate from external systems and are destined for internal systems. Because granular controls can be placed on access to services, proxies are considered a robust solution.

Stateful Inspection

The features of **stateful inspection** are similar to those described in the application-level proxies section, because they too can control traffic passing to and from internal and external systems. "State" refers to connection information. Certain protocols (such as TCP) are connection based, and some are not (such as UDP). A stateful inspection firewall receives all packets destined for internal or external systems and then checks the rulebase to determine if this connection is authorized. In most stateful inspection firewalls, users make requests from their system directly to the end system, whereas in proxies, users make requests first to the proxy and then ask the proxy to make a request to the end system. As information passes through a stateful inspection system, it is halted and examined against a rule base. This could include requiring users to authenticate themselves, then checking the destination server to see if it is authorized, and then checking the type of file requested, etc. Thus, it supports similar functionality as the application-level proxies; however, it differs once the connection is authorized. In the stateful inspection, the firewall does not initiate a new connection, it merely modifies the existing connection (such as performs network address translation) and passes it on to the destination system. The stateful inspection application also places an entry in the state table, indicating this is an authorized connection. This means that all subsequent packets passed back and forth through this connection are only verified to make sure the state of the connection has not changed. If the state has not changed, the packets are forwarded. Again information throughout this whole process can be logged; however it is more difficult to implement virus scanning, Java program scanning, and other application-specific controls. Because packets are examined, as opposed to duplicating connections as in proxying, stateful inspection provides robust security with low performance degradation.

Virtual Private Networks

Some firewall vendors provide the function of a **virtual private network (VPN)** that creates a "tunnel" through an untrusted network, such as the Internet, to allow secure communications to and from external systems. This might include employees who are using remote access, for instance. In its simplest form, remote clients (such as sales professionals) can be provided with client software, which requests connections from an external Internet location to an internal network location. The application-level firewall (proxy or stateful inspection) would stop the request and ask the remote client to authenticate themselves through an encrypted message. Because the firewall has been preprogrammed to be able to decrypt the message, the user's authentication process can be verified. Once the user is authenticated, he or she can then send all information to the firewall encrypted, and the firewall can decrypt it. This protects the confidentiality and integrity of information passed over public networks, such as the Internet. VPNs have the advantage of being relatively lower in costs than using a leased, private line. The box entitled "Possible S&P Security Holes Reveal Risks of E-Commerce" discusses how the VPN of one organization, Standard & Poor's, may have been compromised by a hacker, although the hack of the VPN may not have been the problem. This box illustrates the security issues that arise when too much weight may be placed on an insecure VPN.

Real-Time Monitoring and Intrusion Detection Systems

Most firewalls provide the important function of **real-time monitoring.** Packet-filtering routers typically do not have robust auditing and monitoring capabilities; however, in application-level firewalls (proxies and stateful inspection) events that fail the rule base check can be automatically flagged. This process could include notifying administrators via e-mail, pager, audible alert, etc., after a certain threshold (e.g., a number of failed attempts from the same location). These types of patterns typically indicate an unauthorized person is attempting to circumvent the firewall controls. In addition to alerting, most firewalls have logging capabilities (sometimes called **audit logs**) that can track the details of all successful and failed connections made through the firewall. This could include information such as the Web servers and specific pages each user viewed when "surfing" the Web. This information should be retained and reviewed regularly to identify potential inappropriate activity and attempts to circumvent firewall controls. Firewall administrative logs should also be created and reviewed. These logs should track all changes made to firewall rule bases and configuration settings.

Much of this functionality is classified as an **intrusion detection system (IDS).** This functionality provides real-time monitoring and, in some cases, automated response to intrusion attempt patterns. Intrusion detection devices are included in some commercially available firewall packages, or they may be purchased as add-on devices to firewall software. A primary function of an IDS is to identify when ports are being scanned by outsiders. Such scanning is typically conducted by would-be intruders to identify the services being run by the server. Many IDS packages, such as PENS Dragon Server, place all identified incidents into a central database. The database is

E-Commerce in Practice

Possible S&P Security Holes Reveal Risks of E-Commerce

Alleged security flaws in an online service offered by a unit of Standard & Poor's financial Information Services highlight the risks companies sometimes face as they use the Web to connect with external partners.

Stephen Friedl, an independent security consultant in Tustin, Calif., last week reported security problems with S&P's Comstock service to Bugtraq, a security mailing list.

S&P Comstock is a subscription service that aggregates financial information from more than 140 sources and pumps it to Linux-based clients that sit at each subscriber location.

The problem is that a lack of adequate security controls on those boxes—and, more important on one of the virtual private networks (VPN) they are hooked up to—makes it relatively easy for hackers to gain access to the networks of some other Comstock subscribers, said Friedl. An earlier report on the problem was posted on Bugtraq in March.

Freedom to Snoop

Such access would give intruders the freedom to snoop around other subscribers' systems and networks, Friedl said. He claimed that while conducting a security audit for a Comstock subscriber, he exploited the vulnerability and detected the networks of other subscribers to show how easy it was to do.

Not all S&P Comstock subscribers are vulnerable. The problem affects only those hooked up to a VPN belonging to San Jose–based Concentric Network Corp.

David Brukman, vice president of technology at S&P Comstock, last week acknowledged that the firm's Linux-based client-side processors could be relatively easy to hack into.

But since the systems are hooked to a secure VPN, "they are not designed to be as secure as devices that would be on a public network," Brukman said. He challenged Friedl's assertion that the holes in the VPN allowed hackers to access systems belonging to other subscribers.

"It is possible that at some point in the past, the consultant may have found some flaw in the network, but the latest audit indicates the network is secure," Brukman said. S&P is shoring up security on its client-side processors and following up with the network provider to ensure total security in the future, he added.

Concentric declined to comment on the matter.

Need for Protection

Incidents such as this highlight the need for companies to protect themselves not just against hackers, but also from the security lapses of business partners they are connected with over the Web, said Ryan Russell, manager of information systems at SecurityFocus.com. The San Mateo, Calif.–based firm moderates Bugtraq.

"The main problem is that you are extending the trust of your enterprise to somebody else, who may have a very different idea of protection," Russell said. "Whether it is a link with a supplier, service provider or a business partner, you need to treat it as a hostile entity" from a security perspective.

Source: Jaikumar Vijayan © *Computerworld Online*, May 29, 2000. *www.computerworld.com*

then "mined," that is, relationships are sought out that might identify a certain type of attack. The 2000 CSI/FBI report indicated that 50 percent of firms currently use such devices. Because of lessons learned from security breaches and additional testing, each generation of intrusion detection software packages is better able to identify real intrusion incidents from regular traffic, although identifying distributed denial of service attacks is still a challenge (as discussed in Chapter 7). These capabilities allow unauthorized traffic to be identified and appropriate action to be taken immediately. The box entitled "Firm Nabs Cracker with Intrusion Detection Tool" describes a situation in which an IDS helped a firm to identify an attack, the attacker, and have the necessary documentation (logs) to support their request to have the attacker's account closed by his ISP.

E-Commerce in Practice

Firm Nabs Cracker with Intrusion Detection Tool

New Generation of Security Software Traces IP Address, Provides Legal Evidence

In January, system administrators at Rockliffe Systems Inc. in Santa Clara, Calif., discovered their mail and Web servers were under attack.

Using Black ICE, an intrusion detection system from Network ICE Corp., the company tracked the attacker's IP address, blocked his attack, and forced his provider to shut him down.

That's significant: Black ICE is an example of a growing breed of security tools that can track an attacker's IP address.

"It's a new concept to hunt down these hackers and take legal action," said Dan Arndt, Rockliffe's vice president of operations.

Rockliffe, which produces MailSite (e-mail and list server software), first noticed its Microsoft Corp. IIS server, running Windows NT 4.0 with Service Pack 3, was locking up under a TCP synflood and port scan attack. Synflood attacks bombard servers with data packets; port scans look for vulnerable ports that can serve as entry points.

Barrage during Beta

In April, the company became a beta site for San Mateo, Calif.–based Network ICE's Black ICE. Rockliffe also upgraded to Service Pack 4.

On June 22, the same invader launched a barrage of attacks: another TCP synflood and port scan, an HTTP get-data probe for open shares (which uses a known security hole to gain access to systems), and another exploit that looked for ways into the company's file system.

Rockliffe Was Ready

Arndt said the Black ICE tool detected the attacker's IP address within four hours, while the Black ICE Defender tool blocked further traffic from that location.

Rockliffe then contacted Global1.net, the attacker's network provider. The attacker turned out to be in Brazil and called himself "Marco Jr." Rockliffe sent Global1.net a copy of its attack logs, and the provider immediately shut down Marco Jr.'s account.

That's important because Internet providers are gun-shy about closing accounts unless the evidence is overwhelming. Arndt said Global1.net was impressed with the level of detail in the logs.

"This product is giving government agencies and investigators, or even users, the ability to pinpoint [attackers] and pursue them," Arndt said.

It's Against the Law

Rockliffe is now exploring legal action. The information provided by Black ICE also allowed Arndt to remotely log into Marco Jr.'s Web server. He discovered the attacker was running an evaluation copy of MailSite whose free-use limit had expired. "He just wanted to hack into the system and . . . not spend $2,000 for the product," Arndt said.

Arndt suggested that other companies look for intrusion detection tools that reveal the attacker's IP address. "If you take an active role in tracking these people down, these hackers will realize that they are not anonymous anymore," Arndt said. "Hopefully, that will be a deterrent."

Source: Ann Harrison, ©*Computerworld Online,* August 23, 1999, *www.computerworld.com*

PERSONAL FIREWALLS

As workers are increasingly telecommuting, they are remotely logging in to their employer's computers. In many cases, this remote log-in is the weak link that hackers are targeting. Further, home computers in the United States are increasingly connected through dedicated Internet lines with 24-hour-a-day continuous connectivity. The vast majority of telecommuters do not have personal firewall software installed on their computers.

The box entitled "Home Workers Imperil Systems" describes how Microsoft was a victim of weak personal computing security by one of its employers.

E-Commerce in Practice

Home Workers Imperil Systems

The theory that hackers reached Microsoft Corp.'s product development servers via a home-based employee's computer demonstrates why it's critical for companies to ensure that their remote employees aren't stepping-stones into the corporate network.

Attackers using a server in Russia penetrated Microsoft's corporate network in a high-profile security breach that was made public. . . .

Meanwhile, on Friday, another hacker claimed to have penetrated the company's Web servers, and Microsoft confirmed that at least one server had been breached.

Microsoft initially said some of its source code may have been stolen during the incident. Officials later said it appeared that the hackers may have only viewed portions of the code for products that are still under development.

Microsoft claimed that it knew about the hacker for at least 12 days—during which the company apparently tracked the person's every move within the network.

So far, Microsoft hasn't yet offered any public explanation as to how the hackers may have gained entry into what should have been a bulletproof network.

Several analysts said they believe the attackers used a Trojan horse program known as QAZ to break in.

Trojan horses [such as] QAZ usually enter a victim's system as e-mail attachments or are hidden in pornographic files and downloadable games.

Once inside a system, the programs broadcast their location to the hacker, who then takes administrative control of the system without the user's knowledge. He is then able to do the same things the authorized user of the computer would be permitted to do.

The odds of such programs being downloaded on a home computer are much greater than for an office-based one because home security is frequently less stringent and harder to monitor, said Russ Cooper, an analyst at Reston, Va.–based security firm TruSecure Corp.

An employee opening e-mail from an insecure service or using a work computer to log in to a personal Internet account could, for instance, unwittingly download a malicious program that could then infiltrate a corporate network. Similarly, unauthorized users—such as an employee's child—could use an office system to download games that contain viruses, Cooper said. "It's been a problem for quite some time, and with more people working from home, the threat is increasing," Cooper said.

In Microsoft's case, the hack could have also originated with an office-based employee downloading and opening a file containing malicious code, said Jeffery V. Johnson, CEO of Metases, an Internet security consulting firm in Atlanta and an affiliate of Meta Group Inc. in Stamford, Conn.

But increasingly, "people are breaking into home-based systems and using them as pivot points" into corporate networks, according to Johnson.

It's precisely this concern that prompted insurance and finance company Lutheran Brotherhood in Minneapolis to install firewalls on notebooks belonging to its 1,800-strong field force earlier this year, said information security manager Jay Dybdahl.

Such firewalls "become very critical when a home user is always connected to the Internet via [Digital Subscriber Line] or some other [persistent] connection," Dybdahl said.

"The fact is, if we're going to allow access to corporate networks from staff at home, there are going to have to be new procedures followed that protect those processors," said Cathy Hotka, vice president of information technology at the National Retail Federation, a retail trade association in Washington.

Controlling home users is a matter of faith, said Rick Waugh, a product manager at Telus Corp., a telecommunications company in Burnaby, British Columbia. "You put rules in place and hope they follow them," he said.

Source: Jaikumar Vigayan and Carol Sliwa, © *Computerworld Online*, November 6, 2000. *www.computerworld.com.*

Businesses need to consider the personal computers of their employees as part of their security responsibility if the employees are encouraged or even allowed to either remotely log-in or take digital files home to be loaded onto their home computers.

Many personal firewall packages are now available, some are free (e.g., zonealarm.com and Sygate at zdnet.com) and the others are available for purchase at a relatively low cost (e.g. McAfee and Norton). The functions that should be performed by a **personal firewall** include

- Programmable times for denying Internet access.
- Port probing monitors with reports.
- Ability to deny services from remote users.
- Tracking of all Internet connections.
- Ability to filter out requests stemming from denial of services and Trojan horse–type attacks.

Systems are only as secure as their weakest link, and companies should include in their risk analysis and information technology security plans an assessment of the vulnerabilities of telecommuters. In comparing the risks with the costs, the cost to purchase such personal firewall packages is low—approximately $50 per computer plus installation cost if the employee needs assistance.

NETWORK TOPOLOGY

The physical architecture of the systems that an organization implements is called its **network topology.** The topology is crucial to the successful protection of company resources. In general, a firewall should not be the only entity separating an internal network from external networks. Figure 11–4 illustrates a standard topology that many organizations choose to install. Note that, in addition to the firewall, two routers pro-

FIGURE 11–4   *Standard network topology*

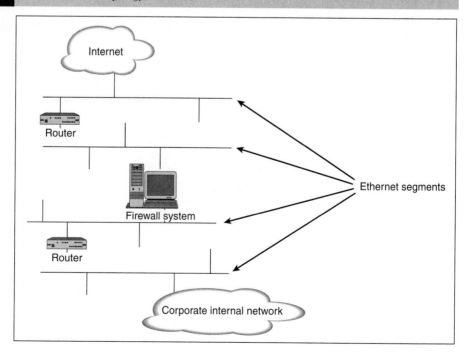

tect the internal network from the Internet. These routers sometimes contain packet-filtering rules to further limit traffic passed along by the firewall. Network performance is another criterion that determines what functionality will be utilized. Firewalls that employ strong authentication devices and screening can be very secure and yet flexible enough to accommodate a wide range of remote access users.

DEMILITARIZED ZONE

A subnetwork that is located neither inside the internal network, nor outside as part of the Internet is called a **demilitarized zone,** commonly referred to as a **DMZ.** A DMZ is illustrated in Figure 11–5. Technically, a DMZ is any area in which access is controlled, but not prevented, by firewall technology. It can lie between two firewalls or off of a separate segment from one firewall. In either case, the types of access to and from DMZ servers is controlled and should be limited to a small group of people or networks. The firewall technology generally provides this control; however, host security issues on these DMZ servers should also be adequately addressed. DMZ servers can provide multiple functionalities, such as e-commerce servers, Web servers, FTP servers, etc. These servers are subject to vulnerabilities based on the services allowed to access them through the firewall. As a result, the traffic that originates from these servers and is destined for internal systems should be limited and controlled. This may include using robust message authentication, such as data encryption, to pass information from DMZ servers to internal servers. Overall, DMZs add an extra, potentially rich layer of security to firewall configurations, but they increase the cost of the system and can increase processing time.

FIGURE 11–5   *Demilitarized zones*

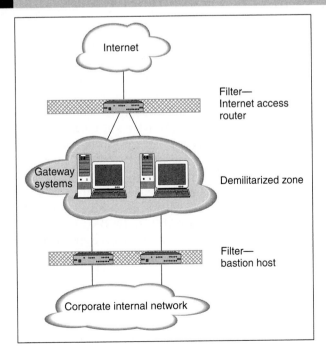

SECURING THE FIREWALL

Because the firewall acts as the connection point between a company's internal network and other external networks (the Internet, business partners' networks, customers' networks, etc.), configuring the system properly and ensuring that it is resistant to attack is critical. This section discusses some items to consider in securing a firewall:

- Policy.
- Administration.
- Services.
- Internal firewalls.
- Authentication.
- Operating system controls.

Policy

Before a firewall is designed or implemented, it should be guided by a well-thought-out and explicitly formulated and documented computer resources security policy. Keep in mind that firewalls are just one component of overall security techniques. The computer resources security policy encompasses all facets of computer security, including the security of any stand-alone, nonnetworked personal computers and the data and programs housed on them. The International Computer Security Association (ICSA) identifies two levels of network security policy:

- Network service access policy.
- Firewall design policy.

These network security policies are a subset of the overall computing resources security policy as illustrated in Figure 11–6.

Network Security Access Policy

This security policy is a higher-level policy than the firewall design policy. It addresses network security issues from a big picture, while still defining issue-specific policies. Services that will be allowed or denied are clearly defined. For services that are allowed, the manners in which these services may be used should be clearly defined. If any exceptions to allow or deny policies are to be permitted, they should be clearly stated. In addition, all of the necessary procedures that must be followed for the exception to become qualified and authorized should be documented. This last item is particularly important in security design and implementation. Defined policies must be adhered to if they are to be effective. If users are allowed to disregard these rules on an ad hoc basis for what they consider to be a good purpose, then the security of the system begins to unravel quickly. System administrators may need to run tests, reconfigure systems, etc., and may need to perform tasks, for valid reasons, that contradict stated policies, but these actions should be documented and authorized and fall under the category of acceptable exceptions to the stated policies.

Firewall Design Policy

After the network security access policy is clearly formulated and network services and access policies are clearly defined, then the firewall design policy can be drafted. This policy addresses *how* the denied services will be restricted and *how* the permitted ser-

FIGURE 11–6   *Security policies*

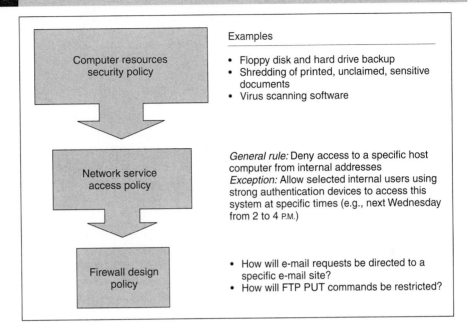

Examples

Computer resources security policy

- Floppy disk and hard drive backup
- Shredding of printed, unclaimed, sensitive documents
- Virus scanning software

Network service access policy

General rule: Deny access to a specific host computer from internal addresses
Exception: Allow selected internal users using strong authentication devices to access this system at specific times (e.g., next Wednesday from 2 to 4 P.M.)

Firewall design policy

- How will e-mail requests be directed to a specific e-mail site?
- How will FTP PUT commands be restricted?

vices will be allowed. The specific filtering techniques and configuration of firewall servers are clearly detailed. For example, if the security access policy states the files kept on an Internet server may be read or downloaded, but not altered, the firewall design policy needs to clearly define how the firewall will prevent these files from being altered.

Administration

An extremely important requirement in maintaining up-to-date firewalls is good administrative policies and procedures. The number one reason cited in the 1998 CSI/FBI report for firewall breaches is mismanagement. The box entitled "Microsoft Stung by Hack Attack" illustrates how even a large, security-conscious firm such as Microsoft may have security administration issues and the problems they can cause a firm.

Slightly more than one-half of the firms reported that mismanagement was the reason for firewall breaches, while another 42 percent reported that the firewall breach was a function of mismanagement and product weakness. Thus, 93 percent of reported firewall breaches were blamed, to some extent, on poor administration practices. As stated earlier, many third-party vendors provide firewall software packages that use graphical administration to configure traffic filtering rules. These rules may be reviewed periodically to ensure that they serve a business purpose and that they are technically correct. In addition, administration procedures should be documented and followed at all times. These procedures should take into account the sensitivity of the system. For instance, many systems are administered remotely through TELNET sessions or remote log-in (rlogin) sessions. If sessions are unencrypted, any user on the network can use a network sniffer to capture and view data as they are transmitted from the system administrator's remote computer to the server. These transmitted data might include passwords and/or traffic filtering rule changes, both of which could be employed by malicious users

E-Commerce in Practice

Microsoft Stung by Hack Attack

Microsoft Corp. today confirmed that its internal computer network was hacked by malicious attackers who were able to view—but apparently not modify—some of the software vendor's source code.

The incident, which security experts said could potentially have serious repercussions for Microsoft, was discovered by the company on Wednesday and reported to the FBI yesterday, according to a spokeswoman. The attack, which is now being investigated by the FBI, was believed to have been initiated in St. Petersburg, Russia.

Microsoft, in a statement released this afternoon, said the incident "appears to be much narrower" in scope than it originally feared.

"Our investigation shows no evidence that the intruder gained access to the source code for our major products, such as Windows Me, Windows 2000 or Office," Microsoft said. "Although the hacker apparently was able to view some source code under development for a future product, the investigation confirmed that there was no modification or corruption of any source code."

Company executives "are confident that the integrity of Microsoft's intellectual property remains secure" and don't think any customers were affected by the intrusion, the statement added.

Microsoft noted that it's working with law enforcement officials "to address this deplorable act of industrial espionage." An FBI spokesman said only that the agency's investigators "are aware of the matter and are looking into it."

Graham Cluley, a security expert at U.K.–based security software vendor Sophos Anti-virus, said it appears that the attackers used a worm known as QAZ to break into Microsoft's network, although he noted that reports vary about whether Microsoft has confirmed that fact.

"That's what it looks like it would most likely be," Cluley said. "[But] there's really a garbled message coming out now [from Microsoft]." However, an attack with a worm such as QAZ "shouldn't have been possible" if Microsoft had properly configured its firewall and antivirus software and kept them updated, he said.

Cluley said QAZ—also known variously as Troj.QAZ Worm.QAZ or QAZ.Trojan—is the fifth-most reported worm to the Sophos help desk and has been in circulation for several months. Trend Micro Inc., another antivirus software vendor, rates QAZ ninth on the list of the top 10

viruses and worm programs it's tracking, with a medium-level risk to users.

But companies such as Sophos, Trend Micro and Finland-based F-Secure Corp. previously updated their antivirus packages to detect QAZ. And the descriptions of the worm that are posted on their Web sites include steps users can take to protect themselves from QAZ.

According to Trend Micro's description, the QAZ worm functions as a backdoor tool that gives remote users control of an infected PC. The worm then disguises itself as a NOTEPAD.EXE file and can be spread through a LAN's shared resources, Trend Micro said. In addition, attackers can use QAZ to upload and execute other malicious programs.

Cluley said an attacker wouldn't "have to be a genius" to use the worm. But Ira Winkler, a security analyst at Internet Security Advisors Group in Severna Park, Md., said the Microsoft hack "appears to be a very complicated and successful attack." The attackers "did a lot of work to do this without getting detected," Winkler added.

To protect themselves from the same kind of attacks, Winkler said, companies should make sure they have a firewall installed, do regular updates of their antivirus software and have a security administrator in place to review system logs to determine if any machines have been penetrated by unauthorized outsiders.

Eric Hemmendinger, an analyst at Aberdeen Group Inc. in Boston, said the attack against Microsoft is ironic because so many of the vendor's applications have included unintentional security holes that have been exploited by virus writers. The tables "appear to have been turned on Microsoft here," Hemmendinger said.

Mikko Hypponen, antivirus research manager at F-Secure, said in a statement that QAZ makes it relatively easy for an outsider to gain access to confidential data. "We've been forecasting that worm-based industrial espionage would happen for quite some time, and it looks like now it has happened big time," Hypponen said.

In its statement, Microsoft said there are regular attempts to break into its network. Security managers at the software vendor "actively address these issues and . . . are working aggressively to isolate this problem and ensure the security of our internal network," the company added.

Source: Todd R. Weiss and Linda Rosencrance, ©*Computerworld Online*, October 27, 2000. *www.computerworld.com*

to compromise the system. In general, the number of administrator accounts on the system should be limited to a few individuals, and administration should either be done at a dedicated administrator's station or with the use of one-time passwords for authentication and encrypted network connections for privacy of transmitted data.

Services

The **services** that are run on the system are often the target of attackers. Only approved vendor software, if it is being used, should be running on the system. Unnecessary and potentially sensitive services such as TELNET, FTP, Finger, and HTTP, etc., are considered dangerous and should be disabled. Vendor software usually includes application-level proxies that replace any standard networking services that would be running. In this way, users can still employ these services to access other hosts, but access is limited by firewall configuration rules. Also, attacks against the system are limited since vulnerabilities in the services cannot be exposed by attackers.

TELNET and FTP Security Issues

Remote log-ins can be made via an Internet protocol called **TELNET,** which stands for terminal network emulation. This provides users with command line character-based access to remote systems, which is similar to obtaining a remote Microsoft DOS shell on a PC but not being able to obtain a Windows interface on this remote system. This type of log-in is particularly useful for performing remote system administration; however, this administration method may also expose the remote systems to attack. Many other legitimate uses of remote log-ins exist, such as the sharing of information with guests to the system.

Because the TELNET protocol allows remote users to log-in, severe vulnerabilities exist if unauthorized users gain access to a system. For this reason, "strong" passwords should be required for users to access systems. Strong passwords possess certain characteristics, such as the requirement that they are a combination of both character and letters and that they are at least six characters in length. This makes it difficult for hackers to use automated tools to guess users' passwords. Because so much information can be gathered about individuals via data stored on the Internet and through social engineering techniques, passwords should be checked by password software to ensure that they are strong. Passwords should be encrypted for data storage and transmission purposes so they cannot be read while they are residing in memory devices or transmitted across networks. Passwords may also be linked to prespecified terminal locations or remote locations from which the user may access the system. This security device prevents unauthorized remote log-ins by hackers using a password that is only valid if it originates from a specific list of locations.

If guests are allowed to log-in, then their sessions should be limited to a very short time period that can allow them to reasonably accomplish a typical information search expected by guest users. Further, if no input commands are issued by a remote user for a prespecified amount of time, the session should be terminated to protect against hackers' access to dormant connections.

A popular protocol used to transfer files from location to location is the **File Transfer Protocol (FTP).** Because of the potential theft of data that can occur if a hacker logs in to a system's FTP server and gains access to sensitive directories, a proxy FTP server should be used. A DMZ may be used to funnel both TELNET and FTP requests to a proxy server located in the DMZ area. A router channels all FTP and TELNET requests to the application-level firewall server (proxy or stateful inspection). Requests for file access may be authenticated here or may be passed directly to the appropriate FTP or TELNET server on the DMZ. This method has the advantage of being able to mask the host name of the DMZ server; the user only has to name the proxy server/gateway's host name. The proxy also provides the ability to log monitor connection attempts and control the types of files transferred to (PUT) or retrieved from (GET) DMZ servers. If anonymous FTP log-ins are considered to be a serious threat, then a different FTP or TELNET server may be used for anonymous log-ins that denies all PUT commands used to upload files to the server. This configuration prevents anonymous guests from writing files to the system.

Finger Service Security Issues

Finger is a program that maintains a database of the mail addresses of local users. This service is considered to be dangerous in systems connected to the Internet or Extranets because of the multitude of information that can be gleaned from Finger commands, such as

- Log-in status of a particular user, including whether they are currently logged in, how long they have been logged on, and the last time they logged in.
- Determination of a user's full name.
- Determination of whether a user has unread mail in his or her mailbox.
- Determination of system usage rates.

This list is not comprehensive, but it paints the picture of the types of information a potential hacker could gain access to and use in future attack schemes. Access to such a service should be blocked by the firewall.

Internal Firewalls

Another important use of firewalls involves **internal firewalls.** Many organizations have their internal networks divided into subsections. This might occur because the entity has many subsidiaries, or perhaps the company keeps its research and development network separate from its financial network. Invariably, these separated networks are joined together by some type of backbone. Internal firewalls can be used to protect one area of the corporate network from other areas. This way, if one area is compromised by an intruder, the other areas are not automatically exposed. In addition, limits can be placed on employees of the company. For instance, a research scientist might not need access to the financial data of the firm. Firewalls can be used to limit access to corporate resources.

Authentication

Authentication techniques are not always placed under the firewall umbrella. However, the benefits and usefulness of authentication techniques in screening users for specific applications and data is a very important security aspect that can significantly enhance the overall security program. Authentication techniques allow *deny or permit* privileges to be individualized rather than globally administered. This type of custom-tailored access privilege is a key component to designing and managing effective Web-based applications.

Operating System Controls

Operating system controls are essential in all systems but even more so in firewall systems. The two most prevalent systems used for firewalls are UNIX and Windows NT. Appropriate controls for these platforms are critical. These include, but are not limited to,

- User and group settings.
- File and directory permissions.
- Remote file system access (UNIX, Network File Service, or Windows NT shares).
- Operating system initialization files.
- Scheduling of jobs.
- Other core operating system settings (Windows NT registry or UNIX Kernel).
- Trusting relationships (allows users from "trusted" application gateways to use predefined, basic services locally).
- Networking services monitor.

FACTORS TO CONSIDER IN FIREWALL DESIGN

This section summarizes the information presented in this chapter and presents a list of minimum—meaning necessary—but not sufficient, features that should be considered when designing or configuring firewalls, as identified by the ICSA:

- *Deny capability.* The firewall should be able to support a "deny all services, except those specifically permitted" policy. The firewall should not necessarily be configured to perform this task, but it should have the capability to perform it if the need arises.
- *Filtering.* The ability to judiciously and dynamically employ filtering techniques, such as permit or deny services, for each host system is crucial to a good firewall design.
- *Security policy.* Developing a security policy is a precursor to designing and implementing effective firewalls. The firewall design should support this policy, not mold it.
- *Dynamic.* Networking environments are fluid, and the firewall design should allow agility and be responsive to changing requirements.
- *Authentication.* The firewall design should utilize strong authentication devices and be continually updated to incorporate the most advanced and feasible authentication devices that emerge.
- *Flexible filtering.* The firewall should employ a flexible, user-friendly IP filtering language that can filter on as many attributes as is deemed necessary, such as
  - IP source address.
  - IP destination address.
  - Source and destination transport connection (TCP/UDP ports).
  - Inbound and outbound interfaces.
- *Recognize dangerous services.* The firewall design should identify potentially dangerous services and either disable them for outside users or use proxy services in DMZs to reduce exposure from such services.
- *Filter dial-in access.* The firewall design should incorporate the ability to filter dial-in access and limit the access ports.

- *Audit logs.* The firewall design should include mechanisms for logging traffic and suspicious activity, and this information should be displayed in an easy to understand format.
- *Current version.* Firewalls that require operating systems should have the most secured version of the operating system installed with any known patches to known problems installed as well.
- *Good documentation.* The firewall development process should be implemented in a fashion that provides checkpoints and a verifiable log of actions taken during its development, implementation, and maintenance.

IN-HOUSE SOLUTIONS VERSUS COMMERCIAL SECURITY SOFTWARE

After all requirements of the firewall design have been carefully and explicitly stated, an organization has to decide whether to build its own firewalls or purchase one of the many commercial firewall software packages available. One of the primary factors to consider is the availability of in-house expertise to build a well-designed firewall system from scratch or to coordinate and integrate purchased firewall component parts. If the expertise is available, then in-house solutions can prove to be very effective and flexible. However, if the firewall design is not well-documented and the designer(s) suddenly becomes unavailable, then maintenance of the system can be a real security problem.

Commercially available software offers firms without the time or the expertise to build their own solution with a viable alternative. When choosing a vendor, the following items, at a minimum, should be carefully examined:

- The reputation of the vendor—request references and check them.
- Does the software meet the requirements as set forth in the network service access policy and firewall design policy?
- Does the vendor have 24-hour, 365-day-a-year support? How reliable is this support?
- Does the vendor provide training?
- How frequently has this vendor released updates and patches to known security holes in the past? What is their commitment to do so in the future? What support do they provide in installing security patches?
- How does this software fit in with future networking expansion plans?

Another point to consider is the operating system the organization will purchase, because many vendors offer their product on both Windows NT and UNIX. In some cases the functionality is different, but in others it is identical. The main point to consider is the skill set the organization has to support each environment. If the implementation team is not intimately aware of the type of operating and firewall system chosen, chances are it may make a configuration error, which exposes the firewall to attack. The team should choose the system with which it is most comfortable, and if this vendor does not support the functionality required, the team should choose another vendor.

One mistake to avoid is selecting a package solely because "XYZ Company uses it, so it must be good." Different organizations have different needs and software packages need to be assessed on how they meet a specific organization's needs. Many firewall

E-Commerce in Practice

Du Pont Adopts Central Security Monitoring

Security managers at large companies must often monitor a collection of multivendor security software and other security devices without the ability to conduct real-time surveillance of their far-flung systems from a single location.

Evaluating data from individual intrusion-detection systems or firewalls can drain staff resources, reduce response time and create unexpected security gaps or blind spots. The fragmentation of proprietary security products frequently requires labor-intensive administration aggravated by uncoordinated security information overload.

Some firms, such as Du Pont Co., are trying to solve these problems by adopting an integrated security platform to tie products together and provide real-time graphical displays on a centralized console. The need for a highly scalable common security infrastructure was especially critical at the sprawling Wilmington, Del.–based company, which operates in 65 countries and maintains 135 manufacturing facilities and more than 100,000 clients on its network.

According to Robert Paszko, Du Pont's incident response and vulnerability manager, most security operations are centralized at the company's main data center in Newark, Del., which is managed by Computer Sciences Corp. in El Segundo, Calif. But Du Pont was searching for a way to unite existing security systems and expand network surveillance for central and regional data centers.

Paszko said the company chose e-Security Inc.'s Open e-Security Platform (OeSP), which provided a framework for integrating network hardware and software point products. The platform gives security manager real-time views of security events as they occur and are noted by various devices such firewalls, intrusion-detection systems and application logs.

Last month, Naples, Fla.–based e-Security announced that it had extended integration with 29 more products in 10 categories. E-Security said its OeSP allows log information from various products to be collected into a single database and monitored from one console. It also gives customers the ability to monitor response to security incidents against agreed-upon service levels.

Paszko said OeSP's agent technology and engineering support from e-Security allowed Du Pont to integrate 10 to 20 security sensors per week without having to build its own custom system. He said the company is now using the platform to monitor extranets and will continue to roll out OeSP agents throughout the network. Last year, the Washington-based System Administration, Networking, and Security (SANS) Institute announced that e-Security was the only company offering a product suite that fit the SANS designation for Real-Time Security Awareness. "Real-Time Security Awareness provides a real-time, holistic view of enterprise security that allows security managers to monitor, understand, and respond to security events," according to Daragh Carter, operations director at the SANS Institute. Such capabilities, Carter said, offer "meaningful operational benefits."

Paszko said the e-Security suite, which was installed in October, satisfied the company's extensive experience in process controls. "The OeSP product ties together all disparate products in the marketplace, takes feeds from all these products, communicates with them, and reports in one common fashion," Paszko said. "It has helped us concentrate our efforts and focus them on high-level alarms and accordingly we are able to quicken our response."

OeSP core software is priced at $32,995, with additional pricing structures for OeSP components.

Source: Ann Harrison, ©*Computerworld Online*, February 14, 2000. *www.computerworld.com*

packages are available on the market and most of them make strong claims about the security provided. A firewall purchaser needs to carefully scrutinize the claims and the features of each package considered. If necessary, advice from an independent security consultant may be necessary to make a good selection. The box entitled "Du Pont Adopts Central Security Monitoring" discusses the issues faced by Du Pont and the security platform they purchased.

LIMITATIONS OF THE SECURITY PREVENTION PROVIDED BY FIREWALLS

Firewalls are an important component of enterprise security. They are essential for protecting internal networks from all external connections, such as vendors' networks, business partners' networks, customers' networks, the Internet, and remote users. These systems have evolved from simple dual-homed (a system with two network interfaces, and hence two IP addresses) UNIX machines that provided proxy services to users, to today's systems that perform packet-filtering, network address translation, and robust auditing and monitoring functionality in addition to proxy services.

In the marketplace today, a seemingly unending list of choices for firewall software is available. Many software companies claim their firewall packages provide complete enterprise security to their customers. When reviewing these packages and their claims remember that firewalls are a *component* of security, not a complete solution by themselves.

Many types of attacks for which firewalls are not appropriate can occur. For instance, firewalls, in general, provide authorization control: They control who may access what. Firewalls do not always provide authentication controls: Is a user who he or she claims to be? Therefore, if an attacker can successfully masquerade as an authorized user, such firewalls provide no security over resources. Furthermore, firewalls do not protect systems that allow access into the system behind the firewall protective devices, such as direct modem connections to a local area network (LAN) located behind the firewall, which may house remote access security devices. Equally important is the fact that firewalls are neither intended nor designed to protect the organization from abuses inflicted by its own employees who have direct connections to the systems behind the firewall. These types of issues should be identified and mitigated by additional security measures, such as authentication controls, as previously discussed in Chapter 10.

Some application-level firewalls support virus scanning; however, macro viruses (self-executing commands) attached to "legitimate" files sent from "legitimate" sources may pass through firewall detection devices, and additional security devices should be implemented in the internal network. The security devices to detect and prevent havoc from these types of attack need to be placed "behind" the firewall to prevent the possible malice associated with viruses of this type.

When implementing security controls, the designers need to keep in mind the number of resources required by the system to implement the security features. This is the art of designing good, efficient, security-conscious systems that address the needs of the organization without imposing an overly cumbersome system that does not provide users with ease of use or adequate response times.

IMPLICATIONS FOR THE ACCOUNTING PROFESSION

Increasingly, the security of the internal control function cannot be sufficiently examined without considering the security of the networking devices and firewall technologies. Accounting professionals conducting traditional assurance functions increasingly need to conduct thorough analyses, not just of the overall security policies, but also of the network security access policy and the firewall design policy. The security and integrity of the underlying accounting information system may be vulnerable to any weaknesses in such policies. The placement of accounting transaction data in the network topology (e.g., behind what type of firewall) needs to be clearly understood by the accounting professional. To make this assessment, the accountant, both internal and external auditors, must audit through the network and the firewalls, not around them. The performance of these tasks requires a thorough understanding of network and firewall technologies. Thus, the role of the accountant is expanding and so is the necessary skill-set. Three relatively new areas of services for accountants are explored here.

Penetration Testing and Risk Exposure

Penetration testing refers to a systematic examination of the vulnerability of a system from unauthorized, external individuals. Because data reliability and integrity can be compromised by unauthorized access, accountants must consider the risks imposed to accounting information systems from unauthorized intruders. Technically, an accountant does not have to perform penetration testing; the task can be outsourced to a security specialty firm. Accounting firms, however, can extend their practices to include such services. To do so, additional technological skills beyond the traditional accounting and auditing technical skills acquired in most accounting degree programs and tested on the Certified Public Accountant (CPA) exam are necessary. An in-depth understanding of major hardware platforms and their operating systems, Internet network protocols and services, firewall configurations, and the latest trends in hacking tools is a necessity in order to perform penetration testing.

Accountants must understand the safety of data, especially data that directly impacts the financial statements. In Figure 11–7, several financial accounting data and programs are clearly behind a firewall, but another path may be traversed from the Internet to the server via the research and development (R&D) server that has a direct connection to the Internet and an indirect connection to the inventory and order processing server. Complex interconnections of internal and external networks may exist, but they have to be identified to determine if even one path can be traversed by a hacker to obtain access to the financial transaction databases or programs.

FIGURE 11–7   *Network security and internal controls*

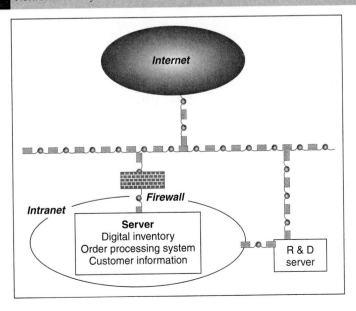

If an accounting firm is to properly conduct its internal control analysis function on electronic commerce systems, it must

- Know the exact number of Intranets and servers.
- Be aware of the data and processing methods contained on each Intranet.
- Decide which Intranets contain data and processing methods within the domain of the audit engagement.
- Understand the configuration and internetworking infrastructure.
- Assess the security methods employed over data accessible by the Intranets, including protection methods and policies against malicious programming code.

Only by knowing this information can the audit team begin a systematic check of entry points to data.

Provider of Network Solutions

Aside from the revenues that can be generated from penetration testing services, the performance of such services generally generates a great deal of attention from top management, especially if the penetration tests result in proof that a system was penetrated. Helping a firm to remedy poor or incomplete system security and choose, install, or configure a firewall is a natural extension of service for the same firm that performed the penetration testing. Again, this area is not one in which a client has to choose an accounting firm, but they certainly can. In terms of providing network solutions, accounting firms have the opportunity to provide solutions that can be integrated into other services provided by them, such as internal control assessment. As with penetration testing, the skill-set necessary to provide network solutions requires that accounting firms have employees with the requisite knowledge, similar to the skill-set mentioned for penetration testing.

Forensic Accounting and Intrusion Investigation

Penetration testing is used to determine if a would-be hacker can penetrate a system. **Intrusion investigation** is conducted *after* a perpetrator has infiltrated a system. **Forensic accounting** is a service provided by accountants that involves investigation of fraud, typically affecting the accounting transaction processing cycles, with a focus on gathering legal evidence to help support the prosecution of the perpetrator. As illustrated in a box presented on page 354, "Mitnick Released for His Notorious IP Spoofing Attack," much investigative work was necessary to catch Kevin Mitnick, a top-notch hacker. Tsutomu Shimomura, a computational physicist, and an FBI team were finally able to locate and apprehend Mitnick. Does an opportunity exist for forensic accountants to engage in investigation on security breaches that involve financial data? Already, other groups have formed to perform such services, such as the Intrusion Management and Forensic (IMF) Group, a division of Sanda International Corp. IMF offers four main services for intrusion management: avoidance, assurance, detection, and investigation. Forensic accountants with a technological background, because of their in-depth knowledge of investigative accounting work, are uniquely positioned to enter this line of work, if they acquire the requisite technological skills. Again, the skills mentioned throughout the chapter are a good basis for performing such services.

Summary

The final piece of the primary security issues is discussed in this chapter: firewalls and their use in controlling access to the organization's data. Understanding firewalls and their configurations is an important component to understanding how to assess the security of Internet-based e-commerce systems. The basic components of firewall and router technologies are presented. The typical functions that a firewall can and should support are reviewed. A good security policy to guide the design of the firewall is necessary, as well the administration of policies and the maintenance of the firewall. Items to consider in securing a firewall and making the decision whether to build the firewall in-house or buy commercially available software are discussed. A final reminder to the student: Firewalls are just one piece of overall computer security. It is a very important piece, but it is just one piece, nonetheless!

Key Words

application layer
application-level proxies
audit logs
chokes
default deny
default permit
demilitarized zone (DMZ)
dynamic firewall
Finger
firewall
File Transfer Protocol (FTP)
Forensic accounting
gates
hijacking
internal firewall
intrusion detection system (IDS)
intrusion investigation
IP layer
IP spoofing
link layer
network address translation
network layer

network topology
Open Systems Interconnect (OSI) model
operating system controls
packets
packet filtering
penetration testing
personal firewall
physical/network layer
proxy
real-time monitoring
router
services
stateful inspection
static firewall
TELNET
Transmission Control Protocol/Internet
  Protocol (TCP/IP)
TCT/IP stack
transport layer
Universal Resource Locator (URL)
User Datapram Protocol (UDP)
virtual private network

Review Questions

1. What is a firewall? What characteristics should it possess?
2. Identify the four basic layers of TCP/IP. Give an example for each layer.
3. What is hijacking?
4. Distinguish between static and dynamic firewalls.
5. Define default permit.
6. What is default deny?
7. What is a choke?

8. What is a gate?
9. Define a proxy.
10. Define a packet.
11. What is a router?
12. Explain IP spoofing.
13. How does network address translation help provide network security?
14. What is stateful inspection?
15. What is a personal firewall?
16. Explain a virtual private network.
17. What is real-time monitoring?
18. Define an audit log.
19. What is an intrusion detection device?
20. What is a network topology?
21. Define a DMZ.
22. What is a security zone?
23. Identify the three policy levels. Give an example of each.
24. What is a service?
25. Distinguish between TELNET and FTP.
26. What is Finger?
27. List the seven operating system controls relevant to network security.
28. What is an internal firewall?
29. Identify four factors to consider in firewall design.

Discussion Questions

1. Why are organizations finding it difficult to completely isolate their networks?
2. Why do businesses need to include an assessment of their ISP in their security analysis and ISP choice?
3. Which is easier to maintain, default deny or default permit?
4. Are proxies an inefficient use of resources? Why are they used?
5. How do current firewall techniques differ from original firewalls?
6. How does packet filtering at the application level provide more robust techniques than the transportation-layer filters?
7. Why should a firm care about IP spoofing attacks that originate from its site but do not pose a threat to its own computer security?
8. Compare stateful inspection with application-level proxies.
9. How can a matching technique enhance stateful inspection methods?
10. How are audit logs used in real-time monitoring?
11. Why do you think nearly one-third of firms reported their dissatisfaction with intrusion detection devices?
12. Why spend additional funds to buy servers and place them in a DMZ? Do they increase efficiency?
13. How important is it that a security policy be constructed before the firewall design? Why?
14. What role does administration play in firewall security?
15. What are some potentially dangerous services and why?
16. What purpose do internal firewalls serve? Are they less important than Internet firewalls?

17. What role does authentication play in firewall security?

18. Why should a firewall be able to support a "deny all services, except those specifically permitted" policy if this policy is not expected to be used?

19. Why should a firewall design allow agility? How should an agility feature be incorporated without losing control over the security of the firewall?

20. Discuss the relative merits of developing firewalls in-house or buying commercial firewall software.

Cases

1. Personal Firewall Security

   If you work in a corporate business environment, answer these questions for your own business. If you do not, interview someone who works in a corporate business environment.

   a. Do you have remote access to your company's computer? If so, what kind of applications can you remotely access?

   b. Do you have a personal firewall installed on your computer?

   c. Do you keep business records, word processing documents, spreadsheets, databases, drawings, etc., on your home or laptop computer? If so, list what types of items. Next to each item, list any exposures if a competitor or other outsider got this information.

2. XML and Data Security

   The eXtensible Markup Language (XML), fully supported by Microsoft's Internet Explorer 5.0 and Netscape's Communicator 5.0, is causing concern to some security analysts. XML is a data format for Web page documents, but because users will be able to extract certain pieces of data of interest to them, new problems are created for server management:

   > It might be possible for a document to contain secure and unrestricted information, and a server handing out pieces would need to be able to figure which pieces were which . . . [One possible set up is to create] a new XML-based information firewall, which provides more depth to current firewalls and therefore additional security. Existing firewalls do things on a port basis by user, and that's not granular enough.
   >
   > (*Jeff Walsh, "XML May Cause Security Risk," PCWorld, June 26, 1998*)

   a. Give an example of data in a single XML Web page document that may be considered (1) secure (private information) and (2) unrestricted (public information).

   b. How can encryption and authentication be used to increase security in this scenario?

   c. How does the use of the XML format affect a default permit firewall that was designed before the use of XML?

3. Intrusion Detection

   The Computer Emergency Response Team Coordination Center identified the following four areas of intrusion detection practices:

   - Integrity of intrusion detection software.
   - Integrity of file systems and sensitive data.
   - System and network activities.
   - Physical forms of intrusion.

   For each of these areas recommend at least one practice that can help to either prevent or detect network intrusion. Specify whether the technique is a detective or preventive technique.

4. Website Security

The Computer Emergency Response Team Coordination Center identified the following three areas of public website security:

- Selecting public server technology.
- Configuring server technology.
- Operating the server.

For each of these areas recommend at least two practices that can help to either prevent or detect network intrusion.

5. Commercial Firewall Package Comparison

Here are some features that a firewall server may perform:

- Provide a secure mail server.
- Provide an anonymous FTP server.
- Provide a Finger server.
- Provide a separate Web server.
- Provide a graphical user interface used for configuration, setup, and maintenance.
- Provide the ability to hide internal IP addresses.
- Apply packet-filtering rules in a flexible manner.
- Provide the ability to use strong authentication techniques, such as one-time passwords, for incoming access.
- Provide audit logs.
- Provide real-time monitoring of systems with alarms.

Identify two firewall server packages and compare them on these features.

References and Websites

CERT. "Detecting Signs of Intrusion." 1997. *http://www.cert.org/ security-improvement/ modules/m01.htm.*

_____. "Security for a Public Web Site." 1997. *http://www.cert.org/ security-improvement/ modules/m02.htm.*

Cheswick W. R., and S. M. Bellowin. *Firewalls and Internet Security.* Addison-Wesley, 1994.

Computer Security Institute. *"Computer Security Issues and Trends—Information Security Market for 1998."* Winter 1997/1998.

Goncalves, M. *Firewalls Complete.* McGraw-Hill. 1998.

Information Factory. *"Introduction to TCP/IP."* 1994.
http://www.informationfactory.com/ifc3.htm.

International Computer Security Association. *"NCSA Firewall Policy Guide, Version 2.0."*
http://www.ncsa.com /fpfs/fwpg.htm.

Information Management and Forensics Group. *http://www.imfgroup.com.*

Markoff, J. "How a Computer Sleuth Traded a Digital Trail." *The New York Times,* February 15, 1995.

Ranum, M. J., and M. Curtin. "Internet Firewalls FAQs." 1998.
http://www.clark.net/pub/mjr/pubs/fwfaq.

The Well. "The January 25 Systems Intrustion," *http://www.well.com/intrusion.html.*

ZDNET. "Mitnick Plea Accepted," March 26, 1999. *http://www.zdnet.com.*

12   ELECTRONIC COMMERCE PAYMENT MECHANISMS

Learning Objectives

1. To distinguish between alternative electronic payment mechanisms.
2. To understand the underlying structure of the SET protocol.
3. To understand the role of digital certificates and smart cards in electronic payment processes.

INTRODUCTION

The primary payment mechanisms for traditional commerce are cash, checks, credit cards, debit cards, and electronic funds transfer. This chapter explores alternative payment mechanisms for electronic transactions that will supplement and may surpass traditional payment mechanisms early in the twenty-first century. Some of these alternative electronic payment mechanisms are variations on traditional commerce payment methods, while others are substantially different. Many different electronic commerce payment mechanisms are emerging, and consumers will ultimately decide which form of payment they prefer. The payment mechanisms discussed in this chapter include credit cards, magnetic strip cards, smart cards, electronic checks, debit cards, and electronic cash. Some of these payment mechanisms are not being used solely for Internet applications; they are being marketed and used as alternatives to carrying physical cash. Further, a protocol, Secure Electronic Transaction (SET), which was designed with secure data transmission as its primary objective is discussed. Included in this discussion is the role of certificate authorities, a topic previously covered in Chapter 10. The box entitled "The Speed of Money" reveals some of the concerns of the financial industry regarding payment infrastructures, including digital certificates and authentication. This chapter explores some solutions to secure electronic payments.

THE SET PROTOCOL

This chapter begins with a discussion of the protocol as it applies to credit card payments. The **Secure Electronic Transaction (SET)** protocol was developed jointly by MasterCard and Visa with the goal of providing a secure payment environment for the transmission of credit card data. The SET specification Version 1.0 was published in

---

E-Commerce in Practice

The Speed of Money

The Internet is bringing about massive changes in the way capital flows, which could translate into an economic boom of global proportions.

The road from paper to virtual money has been blocked at every turn by cultural and technological barriers. But a new spirit of both cooperation and competition between fast young start-ups and traditional financial institutions is beginning to push some of these barriers aside.

Within five years, the vast majority of business-to-business transactions is expected to be electronic, analysts say, leading to faster payments, lower costs and, potentially, less fraud as stringent identity authentication and credit risk-assessment procedures become easier and less expensive.

These savings, combined with faster collections, integration with back-end procurement and financial systems, and access to a larger supplier and customer base, could expand the U.S. economic boom to the rest of the world, analysts say.

"Money is always in search of the place where it gets the best return," says Thornton May, until recently a futurist at Cambridge Technology Partners Inc. in Cambridge, Mass., and an occasional *Computerworld* columnist.

The increased access to market information made possible by the Internet, along with the ease of making electronic payments, will make it possible for companies to change suppliers or distributors in real time on a global scale.

"You will be able to exit bad resource allocations more quickly, which is really what's driving much of the New Economy right now," he says. "It's almost real-time feedback: That didn't work; stop; try again."

Security Barriers

While virtual transactions are gaining steam, the vast majority of payments are still made with checks.

According to Stamford, Conn.–based Gartner Group Inc., 14% of business-to-business payments are made electronically. But that figure is expected to grow to 50% by 2009, says Gartner analyst Avivah Litan.

The biggest reason for the resistance to virtual payments is security, according to May. Companies, particularly those making large transactions, are concerned about the integrity of financial information that travels over the Internet, he says.

"Companies are going to spend more on digital security [than Y2k]," says May. "Probably one and a half times more."

The threat isn't only from hackers breaking into sensitive systems. Fraud is also a possibility: Persons or companies passing themselves off as someone or something else.

"There's very little done now to validate the identity of the person making an inquiry," says Elizabeth Achorn, an analyst at Newton, Mass.–based Meridien Research Inc.

But both banks and start-ups are beginning to address the problem. Digital Signature Trust Co., a subsidiary of Salt Lake City–based Zions Bancorp., serves as a digital signature clearinghouse for banks. Other companies, including start-ups like Mountain View, Calif.–based VeriSign Inc. and major credit card companies, also offer online identity verification and digital certificates. And the American Bankers Association recently initiated its own digital signature program, called TrustID.

But the process of using a digital certificate is still cumbersome and unattractive to consumers, says Litan. Businesses are more likely than individuals to use digital signatures, she says, because they have more to lose from fraud.

Source: Maria Trombly, *Computerworld* © Online, August 14, 2000. *www.computerworld.com*

May 1997. Since the release of Version 1.0, eight extensions (enhancements) to the protocol have been made. MasterCard and Visa once again joined forces in December 1997 to form SETCo to lead the implementation and promotion of the SET specification. The enhanced version of the SET protocol is projected by some industry members[1] to become the standard specification of secure transmission of e-commerce payment mech-

---

[1]Dave Potterton and Sarah Ablett. "Online Fraud: Almost SET," Meridien Research. April 4, 2000. www.meridien-research.com.

anisms, although some skeptics[2] disagree with the need for the SET protocol. In the last couple of years, an increased acceptance and use of digital certificates has occurred and is predicted to continue. Accordingly, an increase in the use of the SET protocol is beginning to occur as well; the number of SET users has increased by 300 percent since 1998. Specifically, the features of the SET specification, Version 1.0, are

- Confidentiality of information through the use of encryption.
- Integrity of data through the use of digital signatures or message digests.
- Cardholder account authentication through the use of digital signatures and certificates.
- Merchant authentication through the use of digital signatures and certificates.
- Interoperability through the use of defined protocols and message formats.

SET versus SSL

The initial version of the SET protocol, version 1.0, is considered to be a stronger security mechanism than other transmission protocols, such as the **Secure Sockets Layer (SSL)** protocol because of its stronger authentication features. SSL is good at providing confidentiality during the transmission of sensitive data, but alone it does not authenticate either the sender or the receiver of the message. If mutual authentication is used (through the use of **personal digital certificates**), authentication of the client is possible, but this is not a standard practice today. In this case, the authentication of the customer is only as strong as the criteria for issuing the certificate to the customer and the personal safeguards that the customer affords access to the certificate.

A comparison of the SET protocol and SSL was illustrated in Chapter 9 in Figure 9–13. Both protocols provide confidentiality of data transmitted over the Internet via encryption. The SET protocol mandates the use of digital certificates that are tied to the purchasers' financial institutions to help identify authorized purchasers and their accounts. It also uses digital certificates that are tied to the merchants' financial institutions and their accepted methods of payment brands. The SET protocol has the capability to use dual signatures to allow the purchaser to transmit only necessary information to the merchant, which is not always inclusive of credit card account information. Also included in the SET protocol are methods to track individual merchandise and transaction totals, as well as merchant credit policies. Thus, the SET protocol has greater capabilities than SSL, but these additional features cannot be implemented without additional infrastructure and processing capabilities, as discussed later. As e-commerce waddles out of its infancy stage, this infrastructure is beginning to take shape.

Version 1.0 and Its Enhancements

The strong authentication provided by the SET protocol requires some mechanism for identification and verification of the customer, merchants, and banks. The SET protocol requires that all parties involved in the transaction hold a valid **digital certificate** and use either digital signatures or message digests. This means that both the buyer and seller must have a registered certificate from an approved certificate authority. SET was originally criticized for not adequately addressing interoperability issues. **Interoperability**

---

[2]Matthew Friedman, "Future in Doubt for SET Protocol," *The Gazette (Montreal),* March 4, 1998.

issues are being addressed, and eight large vendors have engaged in interoperability efforts: Brokat, Entrust, Globeset, GTE, IBM, Trintech, and Veri-Sign.

The approved extensions that have been made to Version 1.0 are as follows:

- Allows information from a B0' card (issued exclusively in France) to be included in the payment instructions generated by a cardholder.
- Allows information collected from a hardware token to be included in the payment instructions generated by a cardholder.
- Allows a cardholder and merchant to exchange information related to payment options available for Japanese domestic transactions.
- Allows a merchant to use SET messages for authorization and capture for orders that were placed by the cardholder using a transmission method other than SET.
- Allows **personal identification numbers (PINs)** and related information to be included in the payment instructions generated by a cardholder.
- Provides a means for transporting chip card data in the purchase request message.
- Provides a means for transporting track-2 data in the purchase request message.
- Allows the purchase request message to carry additional card verification data such as Visa's Card Verification Value 2 (CVV2), MasterCard's Card Verification Code 2 (CVC2), and American Express's Four-Digit Batch Code (4DBC).

A simplified depiction of the SET credit card purchase model is illustrated in Figure 12–1. Five entity types are included in this model: cardholder, merchant, payment gateway, certificate authority, and certificate trust chain. **Cardholder** is defined as the

| **FIGURE 12–1** | *Simplified SET credit card purchase model* |

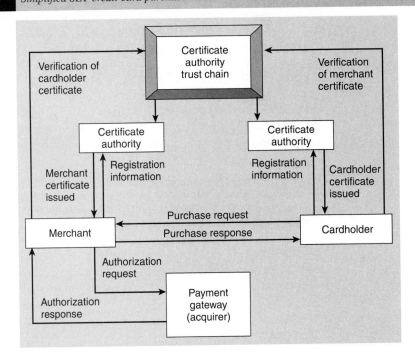

purchasing entity using the designated credit card. **Merchant** is defined as the business accepting the transaction. This model illustrates a general model of certificate issuance, purchase initiation and response, authentication of merchant and cardholder, and authorization of transaction by the credit card company. This model does *not* illustrate the actual transfer of funds from the transaction acquirer to the merchant nor the billing statement from the customer's credit card issuer to the cardholder.

Branding is also allowed within the SET model. By SETCo's definition, a **brand** is a financial institution with its own distinct logo that issues and accepts payment cards (or accounts) and processes these transactions using an entity that issues payment cards with its own distinct logo. The SET Root certificate authority, discussed later, issues digital certificates to financial institutions that meet SETCo's brand requirements. Once a brand is issued its certificates, it has the ability to sign certificates for cardholder certificate authorities, merchant certificate authorities, and payment gateway certificate authorities.

Payment Gateway

An acquirer or some other designated third party is necessary in order to authorize and process the transaction. The party that performs these functions is called the **payment gateway.** Some credit card services that are owned by financial institutions may perform more than one role, such as issuing the credit card and cardholder certificates and serving as the acquirer/payment gateway. Some institutions may outsource some of these functions to a third party. Thus, many different models are available.

Certificate Issuance

The two certificate authorities depicted in Figure 12–1 demonstrate the scenario in which the merchant and customer's certificates are signed by different certificate authorities; however, the cardholder and merchant could have received their certificates from the same certificate authority. The credit card company or a third-party agency representing the credit card company issues certificates to the cardholders that are digitally signed by a financial institution (**certificate authority**). The account number, expiration date of the card, and a secret value determined by the cardholder, similar to a personal identification number (PIN), are encoded in the certificate using a one-way hashing algorithm so that the information cannot be revealed by looking at the certificate. The information contained in the certificate can be verified, however, if the recipient provides certain data.

The merchant must also obtain a certificate that must be approved by a financial institution, called an **acquirer,** in order to participate in SET transactions. The acquirer processes the merchant's credit card authorizations and payments. A merchant will have to obtain a certificate for each credit card brand that it accepts. The merchant's certificate is an indication to the consumer that the merchant is authorized to accept that credit card brand as payment, similar to a store or restaurant that displays a credit card replica on its storefront. The certificate also allows the cardholder to verify the authenticity of the merchant.

Certificate Trust Chain

A **hierarchy of trust** is used to verify the certificates used in SET transactions. This **certificate trust chain** is traversed to locate the next appropriate certificate authority for authentication. Figure 12–2 illustrates how the hierarchy of trust chain may be used to traverse from a cardholder's signature to the brand signature signed by a root key certificate. The same sort of verification process is used for merchant signatures and payment

FIGURE 12–2   *Hierarchy of trust chain of certificates*

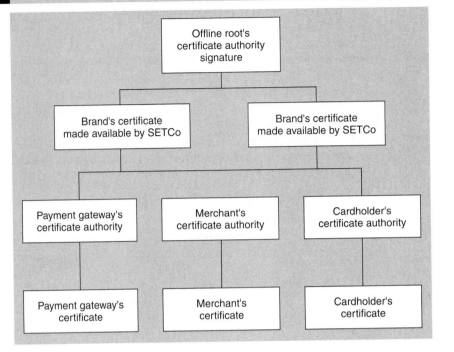

Adapted from SETCo's Specification, Version 1.0.

gateway signatures. SETCo makes the root key certificates available to approved software. The SET **root certificate authority** is offline and performs four main functions:

- Generate and securely store the SET root certificate authority's public and private keys.
- Generate and "self-sign" the SET root certificate authority's certificates.
- Process brand certificate requests, and generate SET brand certificate authority certificates.
- Generate and distribute certificate revocation lists.

  (*Setco, 1999*)

SETCo self-signs its own certificates because it is the "end of the chain." The processing of approved brand certificate authorities requires that representatives from the company physically travel to SETCo's root certificate authority facilities where a "signing ceremony" takes place. The company representing the brand physically receives the digitally signed certificates to take back to its facilities.

Cryptography Methods

The SET protocol uses both randomly generated symmetric keys and public-private key pairs. As discussed in Chapter 10, the combination of these two methods is frequently used to combine the efficiency of symmetric key encryption for the encoding of messages and the power of public-private keys to provide authentication. The customer's payment message is encrypted using a randomly generated symmetric key. Because the random key is needed to decrypt the payment information, it is encrypted using the public key of the merchant's acquirer. Both the encrypted message and the encrypted key are sent from the customer to the merchant in what is called a **digital envelope.** The integrity of the digital envelope is protected using a **message digest.** The customer signs the envelope with his or her private key. This combination of methods

- Ensures message confidentiality during transmission.
- Ensures that only the intended recipient can decode the digital envelope.
- Authenticates the sender.
- Ensures message integrity.

Dual Signatures

The SET protocol uses a unique application of dual digital signatures as illustrated in Figure 12–3. **Dual signatures** incorporate the use of the generation of two messages, one for the acquirer and one for the merchant. Each message contains only the information that is essential to that particular party in order to protect privacy of as much information as possible. Consider the following scenario. Sharon, the bidder in Figure 12–3, sees a rare painting for sale in an online auction. She wishes to make a bid for the item. She does not want any party other than the auction house to know that she is bidding, or ultimately purchasing, this painting, not even her own financial institution. She submits her bid to the auction house, the merchant. The message to the auction house reveals the item that is desired and the bid amount, along with identification data. Simultaneously, a message to Sharon's financial institution, the acquirer, is generated. The message to the acquirer contains account information and payment authorization in case the auction house accepts Sharon's bid.

Both messages are encrypted, and a message digest is created for each message. To provide an authentication procedure, both of the message digests are encrypted with Sharon's private key. The acquirer is also sent the dual signature. The dual signature is cre-

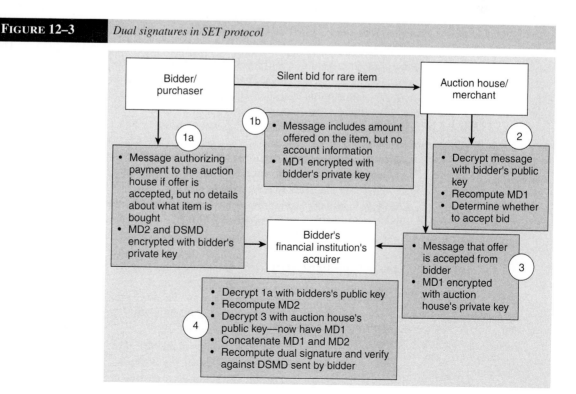

FIGURE 12–3   *Dual signatures in SET protocol*

ated by combining the two message digests and creating a new digest, the **dual signature message digest (DSMD).** The new digest is also encrypted with Sharon's private key.

The merchant receives the encrypted message digest one (MD1), along with the actual encrypted message, and decrypts it with Sharon's public key. The merchant then verifies the integrity of the message by recomputing MD1 and comparing it with the received MD1. If Sharon's bid for the item desired is accepted, then the merchant forwards MD1, *not the actual message,* to the acquirer for payment processing. Before forwarding MD1, the merchant encrypts it with its private key.

The acquirer receives the encrypted MD2 and DSMD, along with the actual encrypted message, from Sharon and decrypts the MD2 and DSMD with her public key. The acquirer then verifies the integrity of the message by recomputing MD2 and comparing it with the received MD2. Upon receipt of MD1 from the merchant, the acquirer decrypts it with the merchant's public key for authentication. At this point, the acquirer has three important pieces of information:

- The message from Sharon authorizing payment to the merchant.
- MD2.
- MD1.

Note that the acquirer does not have the actual message sent from Sharon to the merchant containing information about the items bought. The acquirer has MD1, from which it cannot reveal the meaning of the underlying message. The acquirer then verifies the dual signature by combining MD1 and MD2, recomputing the DSMD, and comparing it with the DSMD received from Sharon. If the DSMDs agree, the acquirer can be confident that MD1 sent from the merchant is valid and proceeds to process the payment to the merchant. Thus, the dual signature method allows the purchaser to send information on a need-to-know basis to the acquirer and the merchant and provides controls to verify the information sent from the merchant to the acquirer requesting payment for goods sold or services rendered.

This example is used to illustrate the dual signature process. In practice, two additional encryption techniques are used that are not illustrated in Figure 12–3. The messages sent to the acquirer and merchant would be encrypted with a randomly generated key. The randomly generated key would then be encoded with the recipient's public key to ensure that only the intended receiver can recover the key to decode the message.

The SET Logo

SETCo has a logo that they allow software vendors to display if they apply for and receive compliance testing approval for specific software products. Website merchants that use SET-compliance-approved software may also use the SET logo, but only if the site uses SET functionality features of the software for e-commerce transaction processing.

Compliance Testing

Compliance testing is required for all products bearing the SET mark. SETCo currently uses an external contractor, Tenth Mountain Systems, to conduct compliance tests. The main element in compliance testing is the submission of results of test cases. A **test case** data set contains sample transactions. Tenth Mountain Systems, also known as the SET Compliance Administrator (SCA), reviews the software capabilities and the accuracy of performance of the essential functionalities of the SET protocol using this data set of test cases. Figure 12–4 provides an overview of the compliance process. The test data are also tested using 40- and 56-bit DES and up to 2,048-bit RSA encryption. (DES and

FIGURE 12–4	*SET compliance testing process*

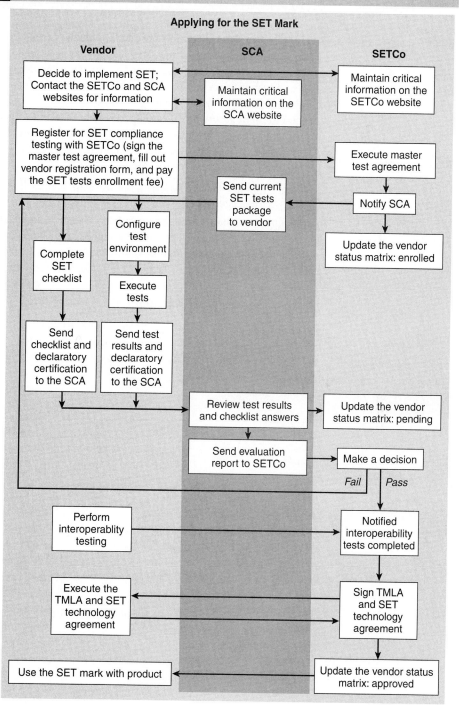

From SETCo, 2000.

RSA encryption are discussed in Chapter 10.) SETCo requires that each operating system family be tested separately (e.g., the test cases must be run for each family). Derivatives of an operating system family do not have to be tested separately (e.g., Windows

98 and Windows NT), but in-house, voluntary testing is strongly encouraged. Compliance testing is necessary for each SET component. The four SET components are as follows:

- **Cardholder wallet.** This "wallet" holds the cardholder's digital certificate and card account information. This component performs the authentication of the cardholder and provides secure transmission of cardholder data.
- **Merchant server.** This component performs the authentication of the merchant and its accepted payment brands.
- **Payment gateway.** This component provides the security of data transmission to/from the acquirer and processes the payment request and authorization procedures.
- **Certificate authority.** This component issues and manages the cardholders', merchants', and root key certificates.

Once the SET logo is awarded, the software vendor must resubmit test case results for annual reviews using SETCo's most recently issued test cases. If SETCo receives reports of noncompliance or software failures, the software vendor may be required to undergo an audit of its system. If noncompliance is determined, SETCo can revoke the SET award and require that the logo be removed. At that point, the vendor will have to begin the entire process over again to reobtain the logo award.

Status of Software Implementation

As of the beginning of 2001, 14 software vendors had received their software-compliance award: Brokat, CyberCash, Entrust, Fujitsu, GlobeSet Inc., Hitachi, IBM, Oasis Technology, PrivyLink, ProfiTrade 90, Samsung, Trintech, VeriFone, and VeriSign. The

FIGURE 12–5	*Visa and MasterCard branded merchants by country*

Country	Number of Merchants
Finland	122
The Netherlands	65
Spain	42
Germany	25
United Kingdom	25
Canada	21
Norway	15
Switzerland	14
Denmark	13
Singapore	12
Taiwan	12
Hong Kong	8
Sweden	8
Austria	5
Italy	4
Australia	1
Czech Republic	1
Hungary	1
Japan	1
Malaysia	1
United States	1

Note: Table does not include merchants branded by American Express Company, Cyber-COMM, JCB Company Limited, Maestro, Nippon Shinpan Company Limited, and PBS International A/S/Dankort.

number of merchants registered with either Visa or MasterCard is listed by country in Figure 12–5. Merchants that are registered under other "brands" are not included in these numbers. The current SET brands as of January 2001 are American Express Company, Cyber-COMM, JCB   Company Limited, Maestro, MasterCard International, Nippon Shinpan Company Limited, PBS International A/S/Dankort, and Visa International.

Why has the implementation of the SET protocol been so slow relative to the implementation of other protocols such as SSL? One reason is the required underlying infrastructure and its related costs. The banks issuing cards and the payment gateways used by them have to establish the mechanism for issuing digital certificates to both the cardholders and the merchants. Establishing these mechanisms and receiving SET certification is an expensive endeavor; estimates are approximately $3.00 per cardholder. Because this infrastructure development to support the SET protocol took several years to implement, SSL was widely used in conjunction with other security techniques during this time. Now vendors that have had success with these other techniques are asking the question: Do we need SET, and is it worth the extra money? As the SET protocol is becoming stronger and more versatile with its extensions, it is being adopted by an increasing number of financial institutions.

MAGNETIC STRIP CARDS

A **magnetic strip card** is a small plastic card that has some form of magnetically encoded strip or strips on its exterior. Magnetic strip cards are widely used for applications such as bank debit cards; credit cards; telephone cards; employee identification cards; and cards for building and machine access privileges, vending machines, and copy machines. To the extent that these cards are used as an "electronic purse" allowing the cardholder to use the card to purchase goods or services, these cards support a form of e-commerce. Prepaid phone cards have become very popular worldwide, although not all cards are magnetic strip cards (some are optical cards and smart cards). Prepaid phone cards allow a customer to buy units of time on a card at a prespecified price, allowing the customer to avoid feeding money into a pay phone or being charged an unknown amount on his or her phone bill. Magnetic strip cards have been used for more than a decade to allow students and other library patrons to easily pay for photocopies in university libraries without having to feed change into the machines.

Magnetic strip cards typically have one magnetic strip on them that contains two or three tracks of information. The encoding of this information is usually done in accordance with an ISO standard (e.g., ISO 7810, 7811, or 7813). Magnetic strip card readers are necessary to both read and encode the cards. The data that are encoded onto the card may be encrypted, making it difficult for potential thieves to decode or copy the information onto another card.

On their own, magnetic strip cards are vulnerable to compromise because the information is magnetically encoded and stored on the exterior of the card and can be copied, forged, or altered. If the data are encrypted, then the security of the information is enhanced, but the ability to exactly copy the encoded data and create a forged copy of the card is still a threat. Another drawback is that the magnetically stored data is vulnerable to inadvertent damage if the card is placed close to a magnet (some purses and wallets have very small magnets in the snaps to help them more easily close) or to another magnetically encoded device. The magnetic strips are also vulnerable to scratches. These drawbacks have not been a deterrent to the adoption and use of magnetic strip cards, but they are a drawback to be considered.

Magnetic strip cards are typically one of three types: online strip, offline strip or a smart card hybrid. **Online magnetic strip cards** are used to read customer information from the strip. The information is then used to access information about the cardholder from a central computer. These types of cards are commonly used for debit cards, credit cards, library cards, and building and machine access. **Offline magnetic strip cards** actually store information that can be interpreted by the card reader and altered. For example, vending machine and telephone cards often use this technology to store the amount of money or call units to the card. As the card is used to purchase products, make photocopies, or place a call, the value of the product or service is deducted by the reader and the updated amount encoded back to the card. The card reader rewrites data to the

FIGURE 12–6   *Lehigh University's magnetic strip card system*

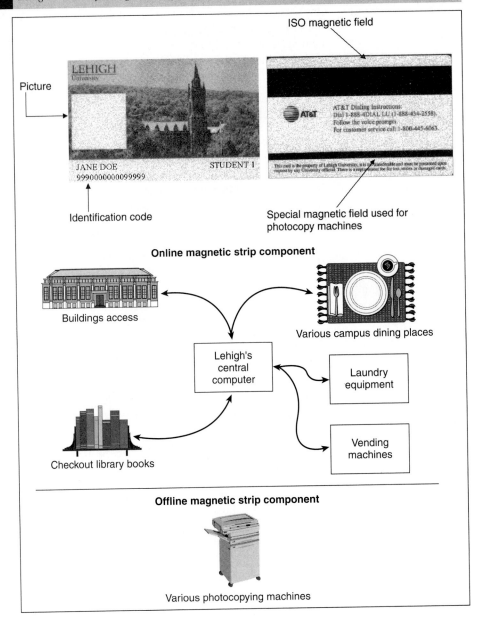

strip reflecting the transaction (i.e., a debit of value on the card). Some magnetic strip cards serve both online and offline purposes. Lastly, magnetic strip cards that are combined with smart card technology are called **hybrid cards.**

Figure 12–6 illustrates a magnetic strip card with both online and offline functions used by Lehigh University. The card is a multipurpose card designed to be more convenient for students, faculty, and staff. The card contains two magnetic strips. The top strip is used for online access to account information and is stored in accordance with ISO 7811. The bottom strip is used for offline access to on-campus photocopying machines. At Lehigh, the second strip is necessary because of interoperability issues with the ISO strip and reader devices used on the campus photocopy machines.

An online use of the card is to allow faculty, staff, and authorized students after-hours access to certain buildings. This feature is online because a central database needs to be accessed to verify the authorization of the user to enter the building. If the authorization code were stored directly on the card and the card was lost or stolen, then the card could be used by an unauthorized user to gain entry to the building. The online feature allows the user to report the card missing and for the central database to be immediately updated to deny entry to the possessor of the lost or stolen card.

Other online services available include checking out library books, purchasing food at any of the university dining facilities, purchasing goods from on-campus vending machines, and using on-campus laundry machines. The students can place additional money in their accounts throughout the semester. Many parents favor this system because they can place money on the student's account and know the specific uses for which it can be spent.

SMART CARDS

A **smart card** is a small plastic card that looks similar to a credit card, but it contains a microprocessor and a storage unit. Smart card technology is an innovation that overcomes most of the limitations mentioned in the previous section to which magnetic strip cards are susceptible; however, they are more expensive to issue. The stored data are not externally exposed to physical damage, such as scruffs and scratches, and are not vulnerable to damage from magnetic fields. Further, smart cards can store at least 100 times more data than magnetic strip cards.

Historically, smart cards have been predominantly used in Europe, but they are beginning to make their way into use in the United States. One reason for the slower adoption in the United States is the estimated $6 billion cost of switching from the older magnetic strip card readers to the newer smart card readers. However, the added security of smart cards is expected to cause their usage rates to increase to approximately 67 million smart cards in the United States by 2004, up from 14 million in 1999. Giga Research estimates that 40 percent of U.S. corporate employees will use smart cards by 2003, up from 2 percent in 2000. As much as 80 percent of U.S. commercial banking customers will use them by 2003, up from 10 percent in 2000. The use by U.S. consumers is expected to rise from 1 percent in 2000 to 20 percent in 2003. On the other hand, the European financial industry was very quick to widely adopt smart card technology. In France, every Visa debit card (25 million) has an embedded chip on it. In Germany, the number of smart cards issued is even higher: approximately 45 million banking smart cards and 80 million (including Austria) health care smart cards. Figure 12–7 highlights some of the many uses of smart cards throughout the world.

Smart cards can be divided into two categories: memory smart cards and "intelligent" smart cards. **Memory smart cards** contain less information and have lesser processing capabilities than microprocessor smart cards. They are typically used to record a monetary or unit value that the cardholder can spend. Memory smart cards rely on the

Examples of some of the many uses of smart cards

Loyalty Programs	
Boots Advantage	More than 10 million cards
Shell	More than 5 million cards
Health Care Programs	
Gemplus-Belgian Social Identity cards	More than 11 million cards
Slovenian National Health Insurance cards	More than 2 million cards
Financial	
Germany GeldKarta	More than 40 million cards
French Chip Card—GIE Carte Bancair	More than 25 million cards
Telephony	
Mobile Telephone Industry	More than 250 million smart cards in use worldwide
Mass Transit	
Motorola and Amtrak	Expected to be more than 10 million smart cards
Education	
U.S. College IDs	More than 1 million smart cards

card reader for their processing. **Microprocessor smart cards** have the additional feature of being able to add and process a wider variety of information components than a memory smart card, and they also have greater processing capabilities for programmed decision making necessary for multiple application requirements. Smart cards can either require contact by inserting the card into a reader or they can be contactless. **Contactless smart cards** require only require that the card be waved rather than inserted. Such applications are good for mass transit situations, where drivers or passengers can just wave their cards at a reader and have the fare deducted from their electronic purse.

The term **electronic purse** is used to refer to a monetary value that is loaded onto the smart card's microprocessor and that can be used by consumers for purchases. Merchants accepting smart cards as a form of payment must have a smart card reader. Many smart card readers are compatible with magnetic strip card readers. Smart cards were discussed in Chapter 8 as a technological tool that can help to improve the security of access control and authentication through one-time-use passwords. Most of these smart cards can be read directly from a reader placed in either the PCMCIA slot or USB port, which are standard features of most modern laptops and personal computers. Mondex, a very popular smart card used in Europe, allows the electronic purse to be divided into five different pockets, allowing up to five different currencies to be held on a single card. Money can be transferred from an account using a kiosk, over a telephone line, or over the Internet. The microchip keeps a record of the last 10 transactions. For security purposes, the **electronic cash** can be locked by entering a special code chosen by the user. The Mondex card can be used for payment to merchants or between individuals. Users in the United Kingdom can also purchase airtime over the Internet for their mobile phones.

Smart card technology may be used in either an online or offline mode, as with magnetic strip cards. Offline smart card technology can be used in countries lacking a good or reliable telecommunications infrastructure, required for real-time authorizations, or in remote locations. An example of an offline smart card technology implementation is Visa International Inc.'s Chip Offline Preauthorized Card (COPAC), which was pilot tested in Russia at the end of 1997. The card works similarly to a debit card, but placing

E-Commerce in Practice

Remote South Africans Get Banking Services for the First Time Thanks to Smart Card Technology

Advanced smart card technology developed in the United Kingdom is to allow South Africa's most remote region to be linked to banking services for the first time in a program designed to overcome one of the country's most severe social exclusion issues.

The Venda region of the Northern Province is the first to join the national program to combat social exclusion of South Africa's 36 million long-term disadvantaged. U.K.–based smart card firm Mondex International Limited (MXI) has designed the electronic cash and banking system to be adopted and incorporated through the South African Post Office's 2000 Post Bank counters.

Huge numbers of people living in remote regions of South Africa do not have access to a bank account or any other financial services because traditional identification such as a passport is required to set up an account, something which is practically nonexistent in these communities. The need for credit history and references is also a major inhibitor to access to most financial services.

The problem comes when those without bank accounts are paid—either through work or benefits. Most payments are made by check and in the absence of a bank account must be cashed. The recipient loses up to 40 percent in fees when cashing a check at an exchange bureau or post office—a particularly significant loss given the extreme poverty in many of these regions. Exchanging checks also results in people carrying large amounts of cash, making them vulnerable to crime.

This new smart card–based project, developed by Mondex International, will enable people to set up pseudo-bank accounts, with biometrics technology enabling fingerprints to provide reliable identification.

The e-bank accounts can be used in a variety of ways. When a cardholder has paid in his [or her] benefits or wages, he [or she] can then choose to transfer direct payments to organizations such as the Church (in most regions, community members pay a regular subscription to the Church). Alternatively they can set up savings "pools" where they store pots of money they are saving to pay for something specific. These "pots" can then be used for a variety of expenses such as education. Although all the money is held on the same smart card, the different pots enable people to take a more planned approach to their finances than ever before, and the direct payment facility provides guaranteed transfer of funds without inappropriate and costly intervention.

Head of Business Development, EMEA at MXI Alison Greensmith said the need for programs [such as] this is a requirement for real change in the country.

"Access to banking services for the majority of South Africans has always been difficult. Apart from the simple logistics of remoteness from the larger towns, it has been dependent largely on culture. In the past, the need for a minimum salary guarantee, credit reference, formal identification, as well as previous banking history essentially ruled out 36 million South Africans," Mrs Greensmith said. "We're delighted to be helping to change that."

The smart card operating system being used, MULTOS, can manage a number of other applications on the card in the same way a PC is equipped with applications [such as] word processing, spreadsheet, and e-mail.

"It's this multiapplication environment that means the card can hold numerous applications— in this case three including electronic identification (name, ID number, and biometric data such as fingerprints), membership information, and of course the Mondex e-purse. The new system simply checks to see whether the 'live' fingerprint matches the stored 'fingerprint template' on the card," Greensmith added.

The MULTOS-based cards equipped with Mondex e-cash are provided by Xpress Connect, which developed the biometrics identification technology. The first users of the e-bank kiosks will be members of the UAAC Church, which has [more than] 3.5 million members. 2001 will see the beginning of a national rollout with kiosks situated at each post office, enabling far greater access to these new banking services.

Source: *Catherine Spaul, Mondex Press Release.* November 10, 2000. *www.mondex.com*

the chip on the card is necessary because the telecommunication links were not readily available or reliable to merchants in Russia at that time. A more recent example of how smart cards are helping areas lacking in reliable telecommunications infrastructures is in remote areas of South Africa. The box entitled "Remote South Africans Get Banking Services for the First Time Thanks to Smart Card Technology" explains how this technology is being implemented and should result in great savings to the users since they will not have to pay commissions to have paychecks and other checks cashed. Biometric devices are used for authentication. In 2000, Mondex launched another program, this one in the Philippines, and it projected a cardholder base of at least 800,000. In this region, it is implementing 500 Mondex loading stations (kiosks) and at least 15,000 commercial establishments with card readers.

A general model of how offline smart cards may operate is illustrated in Figure 12–8. The consumer loads money to the smart card by visiting a machine and putting in cash, credit card, or checking account information along with the amount desired to be loaded onto the smart card. Another variation not illustrated in Figure 12–8 is to download the money directly from a personal computer if the smart card issuer has software available for such downloads and if the user has a smart card slot. The user can then use the smart card for any purchase at a location where the merchant accepts the smart card. The user then does not have to carry any cash.

The consumer inserts his or her smart card into the smart card reader, enters a valid password, and the amount of the purchase is deducted from the balance on the card. The smart card reader computes a running total of the sales amounts deducted from the customers. At the end of the day, or at any time interval desired by the merchant, the merchant inserts its own smart card into the reader along with a valid password and is able

FIGURE 12–8   *General model of offline smart card implementation*

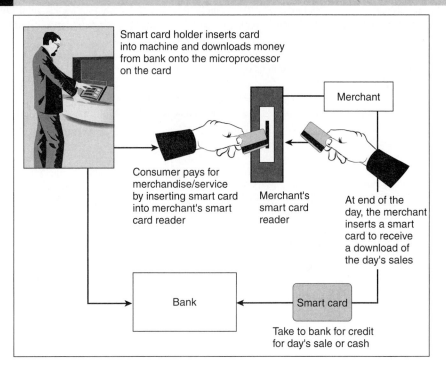

Smart card holder inserts card into machine and downloads money from bank onto the microprocessor on the card

Consumer pays for merchandise/service by inserting smart card into merchant's smart card reader

Merchant

Merchant's smart card reader

At end of the day, the merchant inserts a smart card to receive a download of the day's sales

Bank

Smart card

Take to bank for credit for day's sale or cash

to download the amount of the sales that have been recorded since the last download. The smart card can then be taken to the bank for immediate cash payment. One option not shown in Figure 12–8 is the merchant's use of a networked personal computer and banking software. If the merchant has such components, it may insert the smart card and transfer the amount on the smart card directly into a bank account. If telecommunication lines are not reliable, it may not be feasible to rely on them every time a customer wishes to make a purchase. Obtaining a connection once per day may be feasible, however, to transfer funds. If the connection cannot be made, the merchant can still physically take the smart card to the bank for cash redemption.

Why not just carry cash? Cash is easily used by a thief. Smart cards with identification pictures on them and passwords that must be entered into a key pad make them less of a target by a thief because their reusability value is substantially lower (particularly if passwords are required for purchases.) Unfortunately, many smart card systems do not employ the use of PINs for purchases. An advantage of smart cards over cash is that they provide an electronic record of purchases and the ability to print out transaction data that can serve, in some cases, as business receipts. This feature provides convenience to the business traveler who traditionally has to keep track of many receipts for small purchases.

Why not just use a credit card or a bank debit card? Credit cards may also have identification pictures on them, but this does not prevent their use for fraudulent online or phone purchases if the card is stolen. Also, many credit card merchants require a minimum purchase amount for credit card transactions because of the commission fee that is required to be paid to the issuing credit card company. Smart cards can be used for any size purchase; they are virtually the same as cash to the merchant. If fees are charged to the merchant, they are generally smaller than for credit cards because of the reduced risk of fraud. Currently, bank debit cards are in wider use in the United States than in Europe and may help to account for the disparity between the use of smart card technology between the United States and Europe. One distinct advantage that smart cards have over bank debit cards is their ability to be used in an offline environment. Bank debit cards require that a good, reliable telecommunications infrastructure is in place.

Smart cards, when used with strong cryptosystems, such as elliptic curve cryptography discussed in Chapter 10, store the cardholder's digital signature very securely and provide strong authentication and repudiation. Smart card technology with this type of security feature is being implemented by the banking/credit card industry in conjunction with the SET protocol to allow the secure purchase of goods and services on the Internet (e.g., CyberComm's smart card based on the SET protocol).

Smart card technology also provides another mechanism for authentication and nonrepudiation for Internet transactions. If the purchaser has either a personal computer or a telephone device with a smart card slot, then verification via smart cards is possible for Internet transactions. Further, the most recent generation of automated teller machines is incorporating smart card technology. Figure 12–9 illustrates the relatively new American Express Blue Card with a chip on it that has been introduced into the United States. The Blue Card has both a smart chip for Internet purchases and a magnetic strip for use as a traditional credit card. The smart chip contains an electronic purse with the following features:

- Purchasing history.
- Shipping and billing data.
- Card number.
- Automatic completion of online forms.
- User ID and password recording/entering at many merchants.

FIGURE 12–9	*Illustration of American Express's Blue Card smart card*

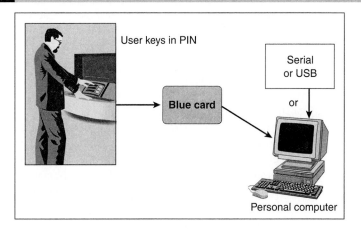

A smart card reader is necessary to use a Blue Card. The USB and serial port card readers were initially given away for free (a $25 value). An optional keyboard with an integrated card reader, manufactured by Compaq, could be purchased for approximately $59 initially. The Blue Card is available to both businesses and consumers. On the chip is stored a digital certificate that must match the PIN number to use the electronic purse. Thus, this electronic purse uses two-factor authentication—something you have and something you know. Visa also has a smart credit card similar to American Express's that it launched in 2000.

Some people are concerned that smart cards may be getting too smart and storing too great an amount of personal data. Despite privacy concerns, the future of smart cards appears bright, but it rests on the ability of standard setters and industry members to solve interoperability issues that result from proprietary systems and countries currently using slightly different formats.

SMART CARDS AND MOBILE COMMERCE

Telephone manufacturers, both traditional and cellular, are introducing smart card phones that can be used for a variety of purposes. The phones contain a smart card slot that can be used to

- Pay for items purchased over the phone (providing stronger authentication of purchases for the issuing financial institution).
- Download money from bank accounts to a smart card.
- Transfer balances between accounts.
- Check bank account balances.

The number of smart phones in use are expected to surpass the usage of conventional wireless phones in 2003 as illustrated in Figure 12–10. Further, the number of users of wireless financial services is expected to reach almost 2 billion by the year 2005, as illustrated in the bottom half of Figure 12–11. Personal digital assistants (PDAs) are becoming integrated with cellular phones. With the Palm Pilot VII, users can conduct e-commerce transactions with their credit cards. In 2000, one company, Funge Systems,

FIGURE 12–10	*Wireless, smart card phone growth*

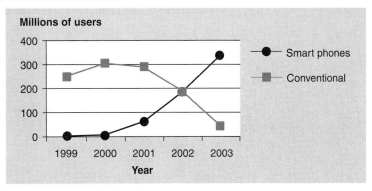

DataComm Research

FIGURE 12–11	*Projected users of wireless financial services*

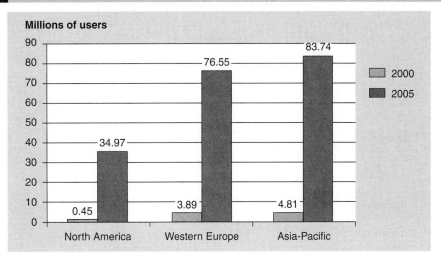

Tower Groups, Wireless Financial Services

launched its Open Transaction Platform (OTP) for smart card transactions. Funge developed smart card readers with multiple chips for cell phones and the integration of mobile phones with PDAs and card readers. Their platform enables customers to choose any operating system, smart card manufacturer, encryption, back-end process, or financial settlement institution for their e-payment or mobile commerce infrastructure. It also has a **secure authenticated counter (SAC)** that authenticates and secures payments by a screening process that uses prespecified business rules to examine cards, terminals, and users. This screening process should be helpful in reducing fraudulent transactions. Secure mobile commerce must rely heavily on the encryption techniques discussed in Chapter 10 to be secure during transmission of account and transaction data.

Mobile devices basically work in one of three ways for conducting e-commerce: Store the electronic purse onto a smart card that inserts into a wireless device such as a phone or PDA, store the electronic purse directly onto a chip in the wireless device, or remotely store the purse on the financial institution's server.

ELECTRONIC CHECKS

Another mechanism for Internet payments is the electronic check. With **electronic checks,** the **payor** (either an individual consumer or a business) instructs its financial institution to pay a specific amount to another party, the **payee.** The Boston Consulting Group (BCG) predicts that by 2008, banks worldwide could lose as much as half of their $300 billion in annual fees. These losses would occur from the loss of fees of processing checks and other payments as consumers switch to electronic and mobile payments. As of the beginning of 2001, banks process about 70 percent of all payments. The BCG reports that banks are evaluating the risk online services and cell phone makers pose and how to move into the virtual payments space. Furthermore, BCG expects banks to see a drop in the volume of traditional payments in the next few years, with the growth of e-payments and banking.

Electronic Billing Methods

Financial EDI systems have performed an electronic payment function for years using private communication circuits, such as the value-added networks (VANs) discussed in Chapter 6. The new generation of electronic checks provides Internet websites with the ability to perform the following functions:

- Present the bill to the payor.
- Allow the payor to initiate payment of the invoice.
- Provide remittance information.
- Allow the payor to initiate automatic payment authorizations for a prespecified amount or range of amounts.
- Interface with financial management software and transaction processing software.
- Allow payments to be made to new businesses with which the payor has never before transacted; for example, no paper-based, preestablished trading partner agreements are necessary.

The last item, in particular, distinguishes traditional financial EDI payment systems from the new generation of electronic check systems. The new electronic checks should be viewed as an EDI enhancement, not replacement. Electronic payment systems can be viewed from two perspectives: the payor and the payee. A general overview illustrating a general Web-based electronic check payment system from both of these perspectives is depicted in Figure 12–12. The top half of the diagram illustrates the most convenient scenario from the perspective of the payor and is a general model of home banking systems for the consumer side.

An **electronic bill** contains the same information as a hard copy bill transported to the payor through the postal system. Having an electronic bill sent directly from the payee to the payor's electronic checking e-mail account without having to visit the payee's website is more convenient to the payor than having to visit each payee's website to retrieve the bill. An electronic bill does not have to be received, a payor can make payments for bills received through the postal system. If an electronic bill is not received and a postal bill is used for an electronic payment, however, the remittance advice information may not be in a format as desirable to the payee. For example, the payee may still send paper bills and process cash receipts using optical character recognition (OCR) technology to read accounting information from the preprinted remittance advice. The

FIGURE 12–12   *Electronic check systems*

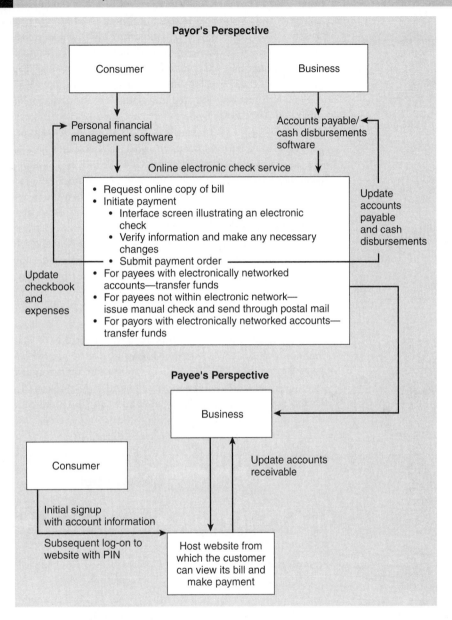

same information can be provided to the payee, but not in a format that the payee is configured to easily handle. Over time, more and more companies are expected to migrate to systems that will not only receive electronic check payments, but also automatically process the remittance advices. Once the bill is paid from the payor's software management system, its accounting records can be automatically updated to reflect the issuance of the electronic check.

Most electronic check systems can accommodate situations in which the payee does not have an account at a "participating" financial institution, since many electronic check service providers will produce a hard-copy check for these types of payments. Because of this feature, most online electronic check services require that the payor initiate all payments at least three to five days in advance of the due date regardless of whether the service can electronically transfer the amount or must write a manual check. A consumer who has a bill due tomorrow, in most cases, will not be allowed to jump online and have an electronic check payment issued that will be guaranteed to reach the payee by tomorrow's due date. As consumers and businesses use electronic check services to a greater extent and greater competition among services arise, this five-day notification process for electronic payments should be reduced as consumers demand greater flexibility and reduced lead times.

The bottom half of Figure 12–12 illustrates the optimal payment structure for the payee. This scenario is called a **biller presentment system:** The biller allows its customers to visit the biller's website, view the bill, and submit payment. In most cases, the customer will be required initially to sign up for this service and to use a personal identification number every time he or she logs on to use this service for making a payment to this payee. From the customer (the payor) perspective, this is not as convenient as having the bills centrally located for payment, nor does it always automatically update the customer's own transaction processing records. Some electronic check software packages provide electronic purses for their customers that enable them to write electronic checks at any website location and automatically record the check in the financial management software.

In some cases, people may wish to purchase online, but they may not have a credit card or may just wish to pay by an electronic check. The box entitled "PayByCheck.com Holiday Sales Statistics" reports the upward trend in electronic checks experienced by on online check service for the 2000 holiday shopping season. The successful electronic payment methods will continue to incorporate the strongest possible methods of security measures such as encryption, digital signatures, and authentication. The use of smart cards to help provide stronger authentication and nonrepudiation of signatures is on the rise.

E-Commerce in Practice

PayByCheck.Com Holiday Sales Statistics

The Holiday Season of 2000 versus 1999

PayByCheck.com, a leading provider of electronic check technology, released its annual holiday sales statistics of e-tailers that accept payment by electronic check from their websites:

- This year 62 percent more merchants accepted checks from their online customers than in 1999.

- The average check transaction was up 89 percent from last year to $172.15.

- Merchants who accepted checks saw an average increase in revenue of 36 percent over those who only accepted credit cards.

- The average savings to merchants were $4.08 per transaction.

"Customer demand for payment methods beyond credit cards was evident, and successful e-tailers were ready to embrace checks this year. 2001 will be 'the year of the check,'" according to Ron Ehli, CEO of PayByCheck.com. "Two years ago we were educating merchants about the benefits of accepting checks. Today it is widely understood that in order to be successful you need to offer your customers a payment choice."

Source: *PayByCheck Press Release.* December 26, 2000. *www.paybycheck.com*

From the biller's perspective, the biller presentment system is extremely beneficial because it brings the customer to its website for payment, from which it can automatically interface with its accounts receivable/cash receipts transaction processing systems for automatic update. A white paper prepared by CyberCash estimates that such biller-driven websites can cut processing costs by approximately 50 percent, even if paper bills are still sent out in addition to hosting a biller presentment, payment-capable website. The main cost reductions are in the handling of remittance advices and checks and posting to accounts, all of which can be performed automatically for electronic payments initiated from its own website. Many utility and phone companies currently offer biller-presentment payment systems.

Another option for billers is to use a **bill concentrator,** which is a third-party service that performs the functions of bill presentment and payment acceptance. This form of outsourcing is more costly to the biller and may result in less flexibility in posting procedures to the biller's accounts receivable system. While this method saves the firm money over traditional paper systems, the costs/benefits to the biller are not as great as the biller presentment system. Banks that offer their customers electronic payments services, such as BankOne, are basically serving as bill concentrators. For example, BankOne provides unlimited electronic checks for a monthly flat fee of $4.95 for its account holders. The services it provides are the ability to

- Receive invoices electronically from selected billers.
- Pay anyone in the United States.
- Automatically schedule payments for recurring bills.
- Schedule payments up to 365 days in advance.

Not all recipients have the capability to receive the funds electronically, so BankOne still requires that five days' notice be given just in case it has to issue a physical check and mail it.

Consumer-to-Consumer Electronic Check Services

New markets for consumers to trade their goods have resulted in new settlement mechanisms. One such mechanism is BillPoint used by eBay traders to buy and sell items. The buyer is charged nothing and can pay by either credit card or electronic check. The seller is charged either nothing (small item sellers) or lower transaction fees for the use of electronic checks than for credit cards by the buyer. Regardless of the payment mechanism used by the buyer, the seller receives the funds by direct deposit into its designated checking account. Further, eBay provides 100 percent insurance against electronic checks after it has gone through a confirmation process by Wells Fargo (typically a three-day process). At this point, the seller receives a confirmation of funds, and if the electronic check "bounces," the seller still gets its money. Clearly, the seller should not ship any items to the buyer until the confirmation is received. PayPal is a similar service that provides electronic cash services in addition to auction settlement services. Electronic cash and PayPal are discussed later in this chapter.

DISPOSABLE CREDIT CARD NUMBERS

Toward the end of 2000, two credit card companies, American Express and Discover, responded to consumers' fears about their credit card numbers being intercepted and used fraudulently by offering disposable credit card numbers. **Disposable credit card**

FIGURE 12–13	*American Express's one-time-use credit card number*

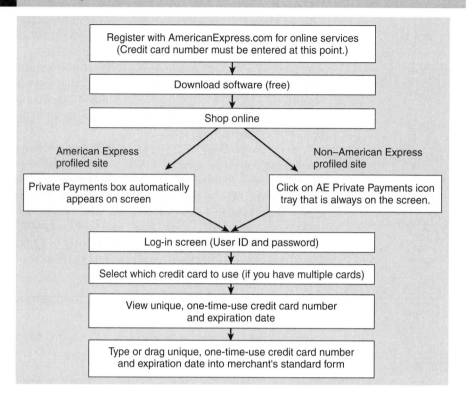

numbers are one-time-use credit card numbers. Thus, if the disposable credit card numbers are intercepted or hacked, the user should not be able to purchase anything with the intercepted number if they have already been used once. American Express's numbers expire after 30 to 67 days, but Discover's disposable numbers do not. The process for setting up and using American Express's Private Payments systems is illustrated in Figure 12–13. The cardholder's monthly statement looks the same as it would with the use of a regular card. The merchant sees only the one-time credit card number and not the credit card number that is being billed. American Express admits that the usage has a few caveats since the card cannot be reused:

- Disposable credit card numbers should not be used for recurring charges since they can only be used once.
- Disposable credit card numbers should not be used for charges that are pending past 30 days (e.g., a hotel reservation for four months from now) since the number will expire.

The popularity of disposable credit cards is yet to be determined, but one thing is certain: It requires an extra step beyond using a smart card credit containing an electronic purse.

ELECTRONIC CASH

Electronic cash is a term that is used to refer to a prepaid, stored value that can be used for electronic purchases in lieu of cash. By this broad definition, payment mechanisms already discussed such as magnetic strip cards, smart cards, and even electronic checks can be classified as forms of electronic cash. Indeed, the Mondex system of stored monetary values on smart cards is considered to be electronic cash. In this section we consider a few additional forms of electronic cash not covered previously in this chapter. Now, *electronic cash* is defined as a form of stored value that is easily exchangeable in an electronic format and is tamper resistant. If the phrase "in an electronic format" is removed, the definition fits a description of paper-backed currency and checks and coins. One additional feature of paper-backed currency, **anonymity of payor,** when applied to electronic cash makes the entire system much more challenging to implement, especially when no physical storage device is available, such as a magnetic strip card or smart card that can be inserted into a reader. This issue is predominantly a consumer, not a business, concern. In this section, an electronic cash service, PayPal, is discussed. After that discussion, an anonymous electronic cash payment, Manneta's ecash Prepaid card, is examined.

PayPal was introduced in the electronic checks section for auction settlements, but it is mentioned again here because it can be used to send money to anyone in the United States with an e-mail account. The money can be sent from a checking account, PayPal account, or credit card. The recipient receives an e-mail and can claim his or her cash minus a commission by having it deposited into a bank account, requesting a hard-copy check be mailed, or keeping it in a PayPal account that can be used to pay others.

PayPal works well for transferring funds between individual and merchants, but it is not anonymous. The Manneta ecash Prepaid card by Digicash is, however, an anonymous electronic cash payment. (Digicash offers an entire suite of many different electronic cash products; only the Prepaid card is examined in this section.) When an individual makes a purchase with cash, the merchant generally does not ask questions about his or her identity (unless the purchase is for items such as alcohol, firearms, tobacco, or real estate). The desire by American consumers, thus far, to make anonymous online purchases has not been great, and thus anonymous electronic cash transactions on the Internet are very, very small and primarily conducted in Europe. The basics of anonymous electronic cash for Internet purchases are presented because they are used somewhat in Europe and may become popular in the United States as privacy concerns escalate.

If an individual has electronic cash, how does he or she spend it and maintain his or her anonymity? DigiCash's model developed by David Chaum and used for their ecash™ transactions is used to illustrate anonymous electronic payments on the Internet. (Again, Digicash offers an entire suite of many different electronic cash products, but only its Prepaid card is examined in this section because of its feature to provide anonymity.) Because the electronic cash needs to be verified as authentic, some system of tracking the electronic cash must be implemented, similar to serial numbers on paper-backed currencies. The challenge is for the bank to have the ability to track authentic electronic cash notes and coins without linking the purchases made to the individual who bought the electronic cash from the bank.

The basic technique used is illustrated in Figure 12–14. The bank customer, Alice, generates a blank coin randomly by using special software. She then sends this blank coin in a digital envelope to the bank to have the value of $1.00 added to it. The "embossment" process does not record any information linking Alice to this particular coin or digital envelope. The bank deducts the $1.00 from her account and embosses the digital envelope and coin simultaneously with its validating signature. The "embossment" transcends the digital envelope to the coin so that the coin also has the bank's validating signature. When Alice receives the coin from the bank, she removes it from the digital envelope and is free to spend it anonymously. The merchant receiving the coin sends it to the bank for authentication, and the bank, recognizing its own validating signature, honors the coin. Mathematical equations are used to enable Alice to randomly generate the coin and for the bank to add a validating signature to it.

FIGURE 12–14	*Anonymous electronic cash*

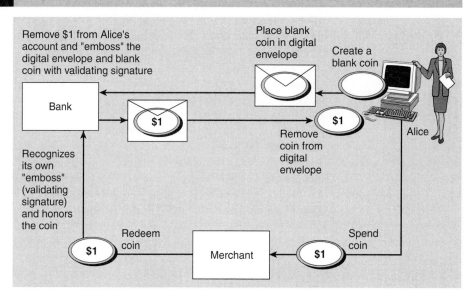

IMPLICATIONS FOR THE ACCOUNTING PROFESSION

Electronic payment mechanisms are at the heart of the revenue and expenditure cycles of businesses. This is an exciting time for the development and implementation of new and improved payment technologies made possible by the Internet infrastructure. Because the accounting profession serves as consultants and reviewers of revenue and expenditure cycles, its members must stay at the forefront of understanding these emerging payment mechanisms. The related security issues must be clearly understood, as well as the use of these devices to help businesses operate as efficiently as they possibly can given current technology. Further, some of these technologies may be used strategically to help some companies achieve closer customer relationships. The accounting profession must be prepared to provide these advisory services to their clients and be on the cutting edge of technological methods, such as new payment services such as PayPal and BillPoint.

Audit Implications

Verification of the cash, accounts receivable, sales, and cash disbursements accounts are a vital component of any financial audit engagement. The integrity of underlying transactions must be assessed. A sampling of transactions need to be traced. The only method that can be used to trace an electronic transaction is to understand the underlying programs and digital methods that are used to create the transaction. More than ever, accountants must audit through the computer, and as this phrase implies, understanding what goes on inside the computer is necessary.

Accountants also perform a stewardship role over a client's assets, such as cash and accounts receivables. Audit techniques that employ periodic testing and sampling methods may not be adequate for electronic payment systems as these approaches may result in too great a lag between unauthorized or erroneous transactions and their detection. The longer the lag exists, the longer the fraud or erroneous processing can occur. Continuous, real-time audit modules that perform checks of transaction validity and authentication of merchants and customers are necessary. Further, monitoring systems that can detect suspicious activity and alert internal auditors or other managers are important. Just as brick-and-mortar merchants do not want to accept counterfeit bills for payment, neither do e-commerce firms want to accept digital counterfeit (e.g., forged magnetic strip cards) for payment.

Electronic Bill Presentment and Payment Systems

Firms may choose to outsource some of their e-commerce payment systems to third parties, just as some firms have been doing with their payroll and cash disbursements for years. Accountants are uniquely positioned to provide such services because they have a reputation for providing similar services. Because of the technology involved and the potentially lucrative nature of providing such services, non-accounting-based firms are emerging to provide electronic bill presentment and payment systems. Traditional financial electronic processing firms need to actively update their skills and technologies to remain a competitive force in this market. Further, accounting firms with the resources could take this opportunity to develop proprietary software solutions for such systems.

Summary

More and more payment options are becoming available to both businesses and consumers. Many of these options are discussed in this chapter—magnetic strip cards, smart cards, electronic checks, and electronic cash, as well as the SET protocol. These technologies and specifications are emerging and need to gain both consumer and business acceptance. The ultimate benefits to be derived from such systems include reduced processing costs, reduced lead times for making payments, increased interoperability, and increased flexibility in choosing a payment mechanism. To the extent that businesses and consumers perceive these benefits to be worthwhile, the new payment mechanisms should flourish over the next few years. As with any emerging technology, some products will become mainstream and other products will wither on the vine.

Key Words

acquirer	electronic cash
anonymity of payor	electronic check
bill concentrator	electronic purse
biller presentment system	hierarchy of trust
brand	hybrid card
branding	interoperability
cardholder	microprocessor smart card
cardholder wallet	magnetic strip card
certificate authority	memory smart card
certificate trust chain	merchant
compliance testing	merchant server
contactless smart cards	message digest
digital envelope	offline magnetic strip card
disposable credit card numbers	online magnetic strip card
dual signatures	payee
dual signature message digest (DSMD)	payment gateway
electronic bill	payor

personal digital certificate	Secure Electronic Transaction (SET)
personal identification number (PIN)	Secure Sockets Layer (SSL)
root certificate authority	smart card
Secure Authenticated Counter (SAC)	test case

Review Questions

1. What is the SET protocol?
2. Why was SETCo established?
3. Distinguish between the SET protocol and SSL.
4. List the main enhancements of Version 1.0 of the SET protocol.
5. Explain the role a certificate authority plays in the SET specification.
6. What is an acquirer?
7. Explain the hierarchy of trust concept.
8. Identify the four main functions the SET root certificate authority performs.
9. What is a dual signature?
10. How is a dual signature message digest created?
11. Explain compliance testing.
12. List the four SET components for which a firm can be compliance tested.
13. What is a test case data set?
14. Define magnetic strip card, and list some popular uses of such cards.
15. Distinguish between online and offline magnetic strip cards, and give examples of each.
16. What is a hybrid card?
17. What is a smart card?
18. What is an electronic purse?
19. Give some examples of appropriate uses of contactless smart cards.
20. How many currencies can be stored on one Mondex card?
21. What smart card is based on the SET protocol?
22. What are the features of American Express's Blue Card?
23. How are smart cards being used for mobile (wireless) commerce?
24. What are the three main configurations of smart card mobile phones and PDAs?
25. Identify two electronic check services.
26. List some functions smart card phones can provide.
27. What is an electronic check?
28. Distinguish between a payor and a payee.
29. Identify some functions the new generation of electronic checks perform.
30. What is an electronic bill?
31. Distinguish between a biller presentment system and a bill concentrator.
32. What is a disposable credit card?
33. What is electronic cash?

Discussion Questions

1. Why would two competitors such as Visa and MasterCard collaborate, as in the formation of SETCo?

2. Why has the SSL protocol prevailed over SET in the past? Do you think it will continue?

3. Why must a merchant obtain a certificate for each credit card brand that it accepts?

4. Why does the SET protocol use both symmetric keys and key pairs?

5. What role do message digests play in the SET protocol?

6. Why are dual signatures preferred over single signatures in the SET protocol?

7. Why would a software vendor subject itself to SETCo's compliance testing process?

8. Why is it necessary to require firms to use SETCo's test case data set rather than the firm's own transaction data set when performing compliance testing?

9. Why are some SET approved vendors using both SET and SSL?

10. Why do some magnetic strip cards have more than one magnetic strip?

11. Review the options available and describe which method you feel is most appropriate and convenient for placing long-distance telephone calls from a pay phone.

12. What advantages do smart cards have over magnetic strip cards? Why are hybrid cards sometimes used?

13. Explain how smart cards are "reloaded." Is this convenient or a nuisance compared with other payment forms?

14. Explain why the biometric authentication was considered a necessity in the implementation of smart cards into remote areas of South Africa.

15. How can smart cards enhance smart cards?

16. Why can BillPoint comfortably provide 100 percent insurance against electronic checks it processes?

17. Is it better for disposable credit cards to expire like American Express's or not to expire like Discover's?

18. Why have smart cards been used substantially more in Europe than in the United States?

19. Is electronic cash preferable to ordinary cash? Why or why not?

20. Why are telephone manufacturers offering smart card phones? Do you predict they will be successful?

21. Why are some citizens concerned about smart cards infringing upon their privacy rights?

22. Are electronic checks different from traditional EDI systems? Explain.

23. Explain the relative costs and benefits to both the consumer and the biller of biller presentment systems and e-mailed electronic bills.

24. Why have electronic cash services with the feature of anonymity of the payor not been a much demanded service in the United States? Will this trend continue?

25. What happens to the traditional EDI market as a result of these new payment features?

Cases

1. Disposable Credit Cards
   Using the Internet, research the usage rates of disposable credit card numbers for Internet purchases. Find some usage rates if possible. Also try to locate at least one article critiquing this method.

   Assess whether you think the solutions offered by American Express and Discover help consumers to either *be more secure* in their online transactions or *feel more secure* in their online transactions.

2. Electronic Checks versus Credit Cards

   Visit two sites, such as BillPoint.com or PayPal.com, that process credit and electronic check payments for online merchants and complete the following using these assumptions:

   - The company processes 12,000 credit card transactions a month.
   - The average bill processed is $74.72.
   - The company has a large college student customer base, and it is estimated that 10 percent of sales are lost due to college students who have a checking account, but no credit card.

   a. Identify the website.

   b. Calculate the monthly cost of credit card processing versus electronic check processing for each service. Determine whether it is feasible to use both services or whether just one is preferable.

   c. Determine whether the difference is enough to give incentives to customers to use one method over the other.

3. Smart Cards and Privacy

   The Malaysian government has implemented a single smart card containing the following items:

   - National identification code.
   - Driver's license (and possible driving history).
   - Immigration details.
   - Health details.
   - Electronic cash.
   - Bank accounts details.
   - Credit card.

   In the United States the Smart Card Forum was formed in 1993 to promote the widespread acceptance of smart cards in North America. Below are some excerpts from a document it prepared entitled "Consumer Privacy and Smart Cards—A Challenge and an Opportunity":

   - . . . successful unauthorized attempts to access or alter data in a smart card system are unlikely because of the prohibitive costs of those efforts.

   - . . . the greatly increased levels of security possible in smart card designs should remove consumer concerns that access to a financial function, for example, could provide access to a health care function. This technical capacity to securely segregate functions on the card itself can be supplemented by ensuring that the device that reads the card is programmed only to perform the particular function being used. Depending on the application and the level of privacy protection appropriate for that application, the consumer will be able to further protect data on the card by personal passwords or PINs unique to each compartmentalized application.

   a. Do you agree with these statements made by the Smart Card Forum? Are they presenting a balanced view of the merits of smart technology?

   b. What are the benefits of using a single smart card to

   - Businesses?
   - Consumers?
   - Government agencies?

   c. For each of these groups, identify any disadvantage of using a single smart card. Give specific examples to explain any disadvantages mentioned.

   d. Do any of the Smart Card Forum's comments listed help to alleviate any of the disadvantages mentioned earlier?

    e. If such a system were to be implemented in your country, what kind of authentication devices would you advocate?

    f. What happens if you lose your smart card? Where would the backup data reside? How would you get a new smart card issued?

4. The Future of ATMs

   The technology is now available to download cash from a smart card phone or a PC using the Internet. At the same time, ATM manufacturers have already upgraded their new ATMs to be smart card compatible.

       a. Are these technologies in competition with one another, or are they complements to one another?

       b. How might ATMs differ in three to five years?

       c. Do you think, in the next three to five years, that the use and location of ATMs will grow, decline, or remain steady. Why?

5. Electronic Payment Design

   Your consulting firm has been hired to design a new enterprise system for a hospital system that oversees four hospitals, all located within a 15-mile radius. Your specialty is electronic payment mechanisms, and thus you have been assigned the following design tasks:

   - Cash disbursement payment mechanisms.
   - Customer billing and collection processes.
   - Payroll tracking and payment processes (both salaried and hourly employees).
   - Vending machine payments.
   - Cafeteria payments.
   - Tracking of photocopy usage by various cost centers for allocating costs.

       a. Outline a plan for the payment mechanisms to be used. Discuss whether they are online or offline solutions.

       b. In designing your solution, remember that you are just one member of a larger team. With this in mind, make a list of any activities not included in your assigned tasks that may be integrally related to your proposed design solutions.

References and Websites

Anonymous. "Smartcard Technology Added to Mobile Phones." *Financial Times (London),* April 29, 1998.

Crone, R. K. "Opportunity on the Line." *TeleTimes,* No. 3. 1998.

CyberCash. "Billers: Introduction." *http:// www.cybercash.com/cybercash/billers/wp/ banking_wp.htm.*

Dalton, G., and B. Davis. "Bank of America Readies Net Credit Card Payments." *TechWeb News.* May 1, 1998.

Davis, B. "Electronic Checking Pilot Begins," *TechWeb News.* July 1, 1998.

Dempsey, M. "A Fresh Lease of Life for New-Look 'Cash Machines,' " *Financial Times (London),* July 1, 1998.

Digicash. "How ecash Works Inside." *http://www.digicash.com/ecash/docs/works.*

Financial Services Technology Consortium. "FSTC Electronic Check Project." *http://www.fstc.org/projects/echeck/ eckfaq.htm.*

_____. FAQs. *http://www.fstc.org/projects/ bips/public/BIPSFAQ21a.htm.*

Fraser, Cecily. "Smart Cards Lack Brain Power in the U.S." *CBS Market Watch,* July 14, 2000. cbs.marketwatch.com.

Friedman, M. "Future in Doubt for SET Protocol." *The Gazette (Montreal),* March 4, 1998.

Gruman, G. "E-commerce not Ready for SET." *Computerworld,* June 29, 1998.

Kerstetter, J. "Visa Bets Smart Cards Revolutionize the Way We Pay," *ZDNet,* September 12, 1997.

Manuel, G., and G. Schloss. "Privacy Watchdog Raises Fears over Smart ID Cards." *South China Morning Post.* March 23, 1998.

Morningstar, K., and C. Federman. "First Experimental SET Secure Electronic Transaction Pilot Approved by SETCo Incorporated End-to-End Use of Certicom's Security Technology." *Business Wire.* July 8, 1998.

Paquette, P. "Smart Cards: The Dawn of the Cashless Society." *http://www.Hightechcareers.com/ doc198e/smartcard198e.html.*

_____. "Smart Cards: Are Fears of Privacy Invasion Warranted?" *http://www.hightechcareers.com/ doc198e/fears.html.*

Peirce, M. E. "Electronic Cash, Tokens and Payments in the National Information Infrastructure." *http://ganges.cs.tcd.ie/ mepeirce/Project/Pro/ToC.html.*

Power, C. "Credit Card Firms Back Security System." *The Irish Times.* May 22, 1998.

SETCo. "First SET Compliance Marks Awarded: Four Vendors Successfully Complete SET Testing; Others in Queue," *PR Newswire.* June 4, 1998.

_____. *"SET Secure Electronic Transaction Specification: Book 1: Business Description."* Version 1.0. May 31, 1997. *http://www.setco.org.*

_____. "Vendor Status Matrix." *http://www. setco.org/matrix.htm.*

_____. "SET 2.0: Overview of Proposed Enhancements." *http://www.setco.org.*

_____. "SET Compliance Testing." Presentation, November 29, 1997. *http://www.setco.org.*

_____. "SET Open Vendor Global Meeting." Presentation, February 3, 1998. *http://www.setco.org.*

_____ and G. Garon. "SET Debit: Proposed Architecture." Presentation, February 3, 1998. *http://www.setco.org.*

Smart Card Forum. "Factoids." *http://www. smartcard.com/info/more/Factoids.htm.*

_____. "What Is a Smart Card?" *http://www.smartcard.com/info/whatis/whatis.htm.*

13   INTELLIGENT AGENTS

Learning Objectives

1. To understand the nature of intelligent agents and agent societies.
2. To identify potential applications of agent technologies.
3. To understand the limitations of agent technologies.

INTRODUCTION

This chapter introduces a technology, that of intelligent agents, that falls within the field of artificial intelligence. Two common problems that this classification of technology generally face are (a) the overuse or misuse of the term for marketing hype and (b) the over-promising of the benefits and results that the technology can deliver. Robots, expert systems, and neural networks are examples of previously introduced artificial intelligence technologies that faced these problems during their initial phases. All three technologies are still alive and growing in their relevant application areas, and most of the media hype has subsided. This chapter explores this media-grabbing field and attempts to separate *currently* feasible applications from unrealistic ones. The relevance of intelligent agents to electronic commerce is discussed, and examples of some current applications of intelligent agents are presented.

DEFINITION OF INTELLIGENT AGENTS

The Internet can be viewed as a large, distributed information resource, with connecting systems that are designed and implemented by many different organizations with various goals and agendas.[1] The growth of the Internet and the correspondingly vast amount of information it holds, presents a problem to users—**information overload.** One may reasonably argue that this is a nice problem to face, but if relevant information cannot be efficiently located, what then is to be gained from such a system? Information overload occurs when individuals receive so much information that they cannot adequately process all of it; as a result, much of the information is discarded or processed in a

---

[1]Jennings and Woolridge, 1998.

suboptimal manner. Many Internet enthusiasts hope that intelligent agent technology will be able to help users overcome information overload. Further, they hope that agent technology can be used to aid the future growth of e-commerce by more efficiently matching buyers and sellers. The top half of Figure 13–1 illustrates the traditional user–computer interactive mode: The user issues commands to the computer, which the computer then performs. The bottom half of Figure 13–1 illustrates a different interactive mode that is more indicative of the manner in which users and computers are beginning and will continue to interact in the future. The user, in addition to issuing some commands, will also delegate many tasks to the computer to perform. Intelligent agents conduct many of these tasks. With this paradigm in mind, one can define intelligent agents as follows:

> An **intelligent agent** is software that assists people and acts on their behalf. Intelligent agents work by allowing people to **delegate** work that they could have done to the agent software. Agents can, just as assistants can, automate repetitive tasks, remember things you forgot, intelligently summarize complex data, learn from you, and even make recommendations to you.

> (*Don Gilbert—IBM,* 1997)

In addition to making recommendations to the user, agents can also make decisions and perform acts based on those decisions. As discussed later, many agent purists consider this last factor to be a distinguishing feature of "true" intelligent agents.

The communication and multilateral directives between these systems need to operate without constant human supervision and guidance. Although *constant* human

---

FIGURE 13–1   *Traditional computing environment versus intelligent agent computing environment*

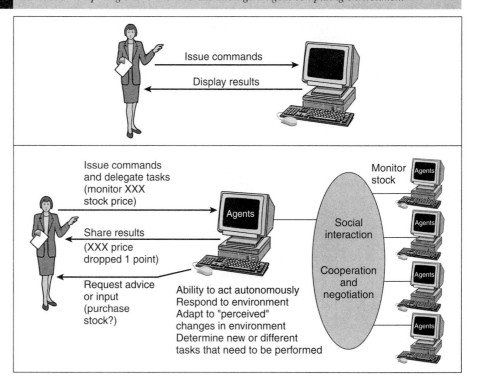

supervision should not be necessary in an agent setting, interaction between the computer and the user in a cooperative sense can be desirable in many situations. Rather than have computer users issue command by command to a computer, "smarter" systems will allow the user to delegate some tasks to the computer.[2]

> Agents are seen as a way of supplying software that acts as the representative of the user's goals in the complex environment. Agent software can provide the glue between the applications, freeing the user from the complexity of dealing with the separate application environments.
>
> *(Lieberman and Maulsby, 1996)*

A **single-agent system** is one in which the problem domain is encapsulated within the system. Single-agent systems are not configured to interface with other agents. **Multi-agent systems,** on the other hand, are much more complex to design and test, but they provide greater potential for e-commerce applications because the interaction between agents of multiple systems is possible. A multi-agent environment necessitates that cooperation between agents exists. **Cooperation** involves the "handling" of directives between agents. The manner in which agents request and pass data, which may include use of executable files, is programmed into each agent module. Security is a concern in multi-agent systems, and this issue is further explained later in this chapter.

Why is agent technology useful? For a new technology to be considered valuable and useful to the marketplace, it needs to possess at least one of the following two characteristics:

- The ability to solve problems that have hitherto been beyond the scope of automation—either because no existing technology could be used to solve the problem or because it was considered too expensive (difficult, time-consuming, risky) to develop solutions using existing technology.
- The ability to solve problems that can already be solved in a significantly better (cheaper, more natural, easier, more efficient, or faster) way.

(Jennings and Woolridge, 1998)

Agent technology is being implemented and further developed to provide both of these requirements. Specific features of agent technology are discussed in the following section.

CAPABILITIES OF INTELLIGENT AGENTS

Agent Dimensions

Intelligent agents can perform many functions. One definition lists three primary dimensions: agency, intelligence, and mobility.[3] The intelligence dimension can denote multiple characteristics and is further broken down into three subcategories:

- **Agency.** The degree of autonomous action that can be taken; that is, actions performed without the need for direct human intervention or intervention by other agents. The agent should have control over the actions performed within its system (i.e., not have actions imposed by other agents). Actions can be requested by other agents, but the agent itself decides whether to approve and allow the action.

---

[2]Negroponte, 1995.
[3]Gilbert, 1997.

- **Intelligence.** The extent to which an agent can understand its own internal state and its external environment. The level of intelligence is further classified according to its ability to respond, to adapt, and to take initiative:
  - **Respond.** Agents should "perceive" and "respond" to their environments.
  - **Adapt.** Agents should have the ability to detect changes in the user's environment and the relevant external environment.
  - **Initiate.** Agents should be able to determine when new or different "goal-directed" behavior is necessary by first recognizing a developing need to achieve that goal.
- **Mobility.** (Also refers to the **sociability** of the agent.) Agent mobility refers to the ability of software to travel from machine to machine and perform tasks or processes on foreign computers. When necessary, agents should be able to interact with other agents and humans, both to perform their own activities and to help other agents and humans with theirs.

All agents will not necessarily exhibit all of these characteristics.

> All possible intelligence, however, is not simply thrown into all possible agents, and there is no single all-knowing intelligent agent. It is the building in of the right kind of intelligence for the right purpose that is the key to successful design.

(Peter Fingar, 1998)

Some agent purists, however, categorize any agent system that does not possess all functions as "agent-like" rather than as a "true" agent as illustrated in Figure 13–2. The box entitled "Website Helps Hunt Down Pirates" illustrates a search engine application that can be classified as agent-like rather than a true agent because it does not initiate or adapt. It is used to detect improper and/or unauthorized use of logos. In addition to its detection task, the agent also sends correspondence to the site and continues to periodically check for compliance.

FIGURE 13–2   *Characteristics of intelligent agents*

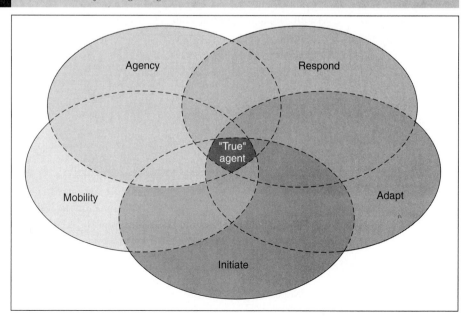

E-Commerce in Practice

Website Helps Hunt Down Pirates

As the realm of the Internet increases, corporations and individuals are searching for ways to protect their images and logos from being improperly used. A San Francisco company has created a search engine to scan the Internet for images and to help firms and individuals in tracking their intellectual property.

The search engine is now available from ImageLock Inc., and the company has signed up Federal Express Corp. and small individual clients for the service, said Bennett Smith, ImageLock's president.

ImageLock is working with Landor Associates Inc., a San Francisco branding firm, to reach agreement with other firms, but Smith declined to say who they are.

The Internet currently has 160 million images available, and ImageLock has 100 million images indexed, said Ken Belanger, the company's chief technology officer. The company is expected to have the remaining images indexed in the coming weeks, Belanger said. In the next two to three months, the Internet will have 200 million images, he added.

ImageLock's search engine constantly searches 3 million domain names and newsgroups for images, logos, and other items, Belanger said. Searches can be done on exact items or ones that have been modified, he said. Once completed, the search informs how many sites are using the image, where it can be found and contact information for the site, Belanger said.

The search engine can be used for general purposes, as well as to ensure images are being used properly. A large credit company is using the search engine to ensure all its old logos have been removed, that reproductions of the new logo are of good quality, and that its logo is being used properly, Belanger said. A jewelry company is using the search engine to ensure other sites aren't posting images, he added.

If a site is using an image without a company's approval, ImageLock sends an e-mail out requesting they ask for permission, Belanger said. ImageLock checks back one week later and if the image hasn't been removed, a second e-mail is sent, he said. By the third time, the company that owns the logo is asked to get involved, Belanger said.

One observer had mixed reactions to the value of an image search engine. It has most applicability to adult sites, according to Paul Hagen, an analyst at Forrester Research Inc. in Boston, because much of the legal wrangling over image copyrights on the Internet has involved adult sites such as Playboy. "The value is marginal with other visual content," Hagen added.

2001 Update:

- ImageLock serves many large companies including BBBOnline, VeriSign, and TRUSTe looking for unauthorized displays of seals.

- ImageLock reports that it has found numerous incidents of unauthorized issues of its seals for many of its clients.

The online options and reports available to its clients include:

- Programmable tracking. (Select the digital assets you want to track within a given date range.)

- Listing of all instances where each file copy or reference link is identified.

- Links to each Web page where each media asset or text target is identified.

- The reference link used for each identified incident.

- A date stamp indicating when each incident is identified.

Source: Kathleen Ohlson, *Computerworld Online*, February 17, 1999. © Computerworld, Inc.

Systems exhibiting "intelligence," such as expert systems and neural networks, have been developed for many business applications, such as loan approvals and audit risk assessment. Intelligent agents differ from other intelligent systems primarily because of their mobility or social nature, and to some extent, their degree of agency. The preceding list of characteristics can be viewed as an ideal toward which to strive in developing true agent systems.

Another characteristic that intelligent agents may possess, but that is not generally considered to be a "characteristic" of intelligent agents, is the ability to express **emotion** or **personality.** This feature is contained primarily in the user interface, whereby the agent interacts with the user in a manner that may be considered human. The challenge to developers is that the emotion expressed or personality traits exhibited by the agent may be viewed as pleasing to one user and annoying or condescending to another user. Microsoft attempts to address this potential conflict by offering a variety of "office assistants" to its users for download, such as Mother Nature, Kairu the Dolphin, the Genius, and Scribble the Cat. These office assistants do have some characteristics of agents, but are not of the category of true intelligent agents.

Persistence is yet another attribute that has been offered in describing intelligent agents. A persistent agent is one that "never sleeps" and is continuously running. Continuously running does not necessarily mean 24 hours a day, 365 days a year; rather it can refer to the relevant time frame for the problem domain. For example, an agent that performs stock-related tasks regarding U.S. stock exchanges may not need to run around the clock, while stock-related tasks related to international exchanges need to continuously run around the clock.

Level of Agent Sophistication

The degree to which agent systems possess certain characteristics may be referred to as their level of sophistication. Figure 13–3 illustrates a categorization of agent systems as identified by Jennings and Woolridge. The lowest level categorization is that of a **gopher agent** that can function in a well-defined domain in which specific rules and assumptions can be clearly identified. The tasks that can be carried out are relatively simple.

FIGURE 13–3   *Level of sophistication of agents*

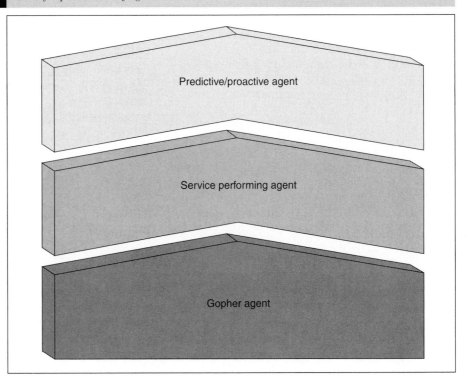

Some of the tasks carried out by gopher agents are similar to tasks that have been carried out by another field of artificial intelligence, expert systems. Gopher agents can be distinguished from expert systems by their mobility capability. An example of a gopher agent is one that can search a specific website for requested information/products given and make recommendations to the visitor based on the visitor's profile.

The second level of categorization is that of a **service-performing agent,** which also functions in a well-defined domain but has the capability of carrying out more cumbersome tasks that may require some negotiation or cooperation with another agent. Consider an agent that can help a student select appropriate courses for his or her major given an academic record, prerequisites, the list of classes that are available, and the list of classes and sections that have already been filled.

The most sophisticated level of agents is the **predictive/proactive agent** that is able to function more autonomously by assessing the environment and choosing a course of action. These agents are able to act in a much more flexible manner and to exercise a greater range of judgment than the gopher or service-performing agent. An example is an agent that is able to retrieve the prices of requested raw materials; continuously monitor prices and availability of raw materials; and make purchasing decisions based on projected inventory levels, production schedule, optimal pricing strategies, and inventory storage costs.

At the beginning of this chapter, in the bottom half of Figure 13–1, the user is depicted as delegating tasks to the agent. The nature of the task delegated and the corresponding level of autonomy given to the agent can vary by application. As mentioned previously, the task may be merely to gather information and make recommendations based on the information gathered or to make the actual decision based on the information gathered.

AGENT SOCIETIES

Multi-agent systems are comprised of agents that interact with one another. To perform their duties effectively, these interoperating agents must be designed so that they are able to achieve their own goals and accommodate other agents in achieving their goals. A system or environment in which multiple agents work together to achieve multiple but interdependent goals is called an **agent society.** Agent societies need to be designed with at least the following five features in mind:

- Openness.
- Complexity of society.
- Interfacing techniques.
- Negotiation.
- Internal control methods.

The first feature, **openness** of a system, refers to the capability of the system to dynamically change in response to its environment. Given the evolutionary nature of the Internet, agent societies must be agile or they will quickly become outdated with their worth diminishing over time. **Complexity of society** involves the manner in which tasks are decomposed into manageable units, similar to objects in object-oriented design. This typically entails designing **modular agents** for specialized task performance. Such a design requires cooperation between the agents in order to properly manage interdependencies. The complexity of the society encompasses both the structure of the internal agents that must interact with one another and agents that are external to the system that must interact with one another.

Interfacing techniques help the various agents in the society to connect and communicate. Autonomous or semiautonomous agents, or nodes, in a society must employ some agreed-upon interfaces. Four levels of agreement were identified by the External Interfaces Working Group of the DARPA Knowledge Sharing Effort as necessary for agents to interoperate:

- **Transport**—the manner in which agents send and receive messages.
- **Language**—the meaning of the message.
- **Policy**—the manner in which agents structure their dialogues.
- **Architecture**—the manner in which systems are connected employing protocols.

As agent technology begins to converge in methods used at each of these levels, **interoperability** of agents will increase. Popular communication representation languages are the Knowledge Query and Manipulation Language (KQML) and Knowledge Interchange Format (KIF). A Java KQML (JKQML) has been developed and used in mobile agents written in applets, called **aglets.**

Negotiation between agents is a key component of societies, and the method used to negotiate can affect the quality and optimization of decisions made by agents. Negotiation between agents refers to the ability of agents to communicate and propose courses of action to one another. Any course of action proposed by one agent may be accepted or rejected by the other agent. If rejection occurs, either agent may propose another course of action; this process continues until a mutually acceptable course of action is proposed or all acceptable alternatives are exhausted. Zeng and Sycara[4] propose that using a sequential decision-making process allows a dependent sequence of decision-making points. Thus, the agent can update its knowledge base after each decision is made and before it makes its next decision. Within a society, negotiation techniques that provide the best solution for both parties involved are necessary. This may include performing the negotiations efficiently (e.g., without too many iterations) such as for complex, but very time-sensitive financial transactions.

Figure 13–4 adds another dimension to Zeng and Sycara's price negotiation model, quantity. Consider the scenario in which a buying agent is searching for a supplier from which to buy a specific item. The buying agent will have certain price and quantity threshold levels above and below which it will not buy the item. The agent may adjust these parameters in order to adapt to its environment, but at a given point in time, the agent will either be given threshold levels or determine them. The selling agent will also have its threshold levels. Each agent knows its parameters, but not the threshold levels of the other agent. The agents negotiate by submitting proposals to one another until an agreement can be made that falls within the threshold levels of both. As depicted in Figure 13–4, the zone of agreement is a space with many different price and quantity levels. Each agent should strive to negotiate a solution that is as far away from its uppermost boundaries as possible. The challenge is designing a system that can negotiate well, but efficiently, without too many iterations; although most designers agree that a negotiated solution as close to the optimal solution is the overriding goal. Modelers of agent negotiation processes frequently rely on game-theory models in their design.

Internal controls over the data used by agents and the actual knowledge base contained by the agent are another feature of agent societies. Controls over data used in systems connected to the Internet and the WWW were covered in Chapters 8 and 9. The same control issues apply in the case of agent technologies, with one difference: The data

---

[4]Zeng and Sycara (1997).

| **FIGURE 13–4** | *Price-quantity agent negotiation* |

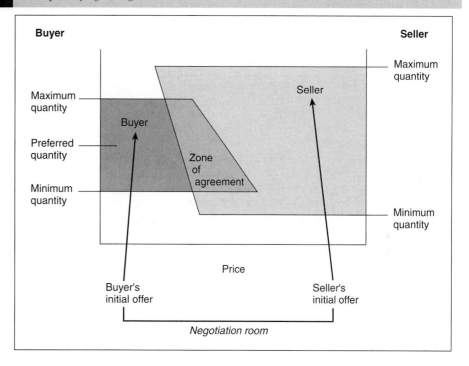

are frequently requested by an external entity, the agent. Safeguards need to be incorporated to ensure that the data are accessed by and passed to the external agent in a safe method. Another issue is the security of the knowledge base that is stored in the coding of the agent software since mobile agents frequently travel from machine to machine. The knowledge base needs to be secured so that its contents cannot be revealed to malicious sites, other agents, or individuals.

INTELLIGENT AGENTS AND ELECTRONIC COMMERCE

Intelligent agents have the potential to affect e-commerce in a variety of ways:

- Help entities to more effectively and efficiently reach their targeted customers, for both marketing purposes and delivery of products or information services.
- Help customers to more effectively and efficiently gather product information and conduct price and product feature comparisons.
- Provide greater customization of services for customers.
- Help businesses to more effectively and efficiently conduct environment scans to keep abreast of new developments.
- Open new geographical markets for business.
- Help the speed and efficiency of electronic transaction negotiations.

The progress made thus far in the implementation of actual agent systems is occurring more rapidly in some areas, such as with those agents responsible for searching online content and information and those agents charged with determining user profiles based

Focus on Air Products

The Challenges of Using Search Agents to Perform Research on the World Wide Web

When mining the World Wide Web for "nuggets" of relevant information, researchers can employ a variety of search engines, or agents. Although search engines have improved in the past several years, their capabilities have yet to match the sophisticated search and retrieval functionality provided to the users of commercial database services for the past 25 years. The primary difference is that data on the Web is unstructured, as opposed to the structured information found within commercially produced databases. However, no matter how information is found, human beings evaluate the results of any search as being "relevant," "close enough," and "not on target." realistically, a search engine that delivers either zero "hits" or 30,000 "hits" is not of much use to the searcher attempting to find the proverbial needle in the haystack.

Structured versus Unstructured Searching

Commercial databases, and the sophisticated search-retrieval interfaces designed to make their contents usable, apply many of the same indexing techniques librarians have used for years. By being able to define, or limit, the search to fields such as "title," or "author's name," a searcher increases the precision of recall. Professional online searchers are also able to specify the word order (proximity), enabling them to differentiate stories about "oil wells in New Mexico" from those about "new oil wells in Mexico." Search agents for these databases usually give the searcher the option to select a keyword from a predefined authority list.

The power of a well-designed search interface applied to a highly indexed database becomes apparent, when, for example, a single keyword such as "manager" retrieves all related content without requiring the searcher to anticipate possible synonyms, such as "white collar workers," or "supervisors," etc. The most effective search agents permit any combination of natural language, word proximity, and concept searching.

This sort of organized searching has many advantages, but it lacks the serendipity one encounters when searching the Web, with its many links to related information. It is interesting to recall that many of the Internet search engines began as hierarchical lists of websites categorized as having similar content, and that these hierarchies were created by humans.

No Single Search Engine Covers the Web

The Internet has made vast information available to the public, but that does not mean John Q. Public has the tools to search it completely or even efficiently.

Unfortunately, with the explosion of free-text, free-form information on the Web, a variety of advanced options have been added to many of the more popular search engines. Yet, most of these search engines fail to take into account that data created for the Web often lacks spelling checks, is incomplete, out of date, undated, and too often leaves the authority open to question. Dates more likely to refer to Web page creation rather than to the origin of the data itself, and an out-of-date website might appear first in a list of results simply because the frequency of the search words was higher on that particular page.

The simplest searches performed by search agents match words or strings of characters. Searchers soon learn the technique of entering their most unique word first in any search box. Unfortunately, most Internet search agents cannot differentiate between something written "about" George Bush from those items written "by" the former President. They cannot sort through items mentioning other individuals with the name. Pity the Internet searcher at-

upon behaviors, than other areas, such as business-to-business negotiation agents. Employees of Air Products and Chemicals Inc. use sophisticated search-retrieval services to pull important, relevant information. In the box entitled "The Challenges of Using Search Agents to Perform Research on the World Wide Web," Air Products' supervisor of its Corporate Business Information Center discusses the challenges of using search agents.

Ultimately, intelligent agents have the potential to affect every phase of the value chain as illustrated in Figure 13–5. The framework illustrated views the intelligent agents as object-oriented devices that are the "glue" to holding together the new e-commerce domain. Intelligent agents are used by buyers and sellers that engage in e-business transactions. Sellers might use intelligent agents to interact with suppliers of tempting to separate information about Texas Governor George W. Bush, from former President George Bush.

One could deduce from the advertising campaigns among the most popular search engines during the past several years that there has been, if not a war, at least a campaign to capture the accolade as "favorite" among Internet searchers. In highlighting their new features, search agent promoters mention relevancy ranking, the ability to search for phrases, and expansion of Boolean logical operators ("and," "or," "not") with a "find more like this" option.

Few attempts have been made to use artificial intelligence to enable a searcher to enter a request in the form of a question such as "What is the outlook for the consumption of plastic bottles in the United States?"

There is so much content to search now, that even the most sophisticated search engines can search across a fraction of what is available. Searchers tend to become wedded to their favorite search engine, without realizing that some engines are updated much more frequently than others. They are not interchangeable.

Research has shown that researchers depending on a single search agent are, at the least, missing content. A study in *Science* reports that no search engine covered more than one-third of the Web, and searching with six different search engines still covered only about 60 percent of the indexable Web. (a) A cottage industry has grown up around newsletters that detail the characteristics of various search agents and guide researchers to sites that have been evaluated for authenticity, currency, and ease of use.

Some searchers use metasearch tools to find and sort results from more than a dozen different search engines, often with mixed results. New Internet search tools keep track of sites, and alert the user when something new has been added or updated. Some Internet management tools can organize links to websites that have been useful in the past, so that the path to them can be re-created on demand.

Ultimately, whether something is right on target, or only slightly interesting, remains in the eye of the beholder.

While it is certainly legitimate to browse to see "what's out there," more often a searcher needs to maximize research time by finding sites that contain information that is highly relevant to their specific needs.

Good Information (Usually) Is Not Free

It's a myth that "it's all out there for free on the Internet." One commercial database vendor named Dialog provides access to databases with 50 times the content found on the Web. Their appeal is that they have organized information that will never appear for free on the Internet, coupled with search agents to assist users in finding information efficiently.

Portals Are the Next Big Thing

One of the more interesting developments is the advancement of Internet portals. Integrators package content along with a search interface to help the searcher navigate to specific information, such as journal articles and newswire stories. In theory, this minimizes the probability that a search will include results from an enthusiastic third-grader's personal Web page. Some firms have capitalized on the demand created by those willing to pay extra to employ search agents with screens uncluttered by advertisements and to provide their subscribers with the ability to locate highly-desirable, relevant content, albeit for a fee.

It is ironic that too much information without the power to search it efficiently represents an exercise in futility for most and an economic opportunity for entrepreneurs attempting to cash in on the new currency of our lives—information.

(a) Steve Lawrence and C. Lee Giles, "Searching the World Wide Web," *Science*, vol. 280, no. 5360, April 3, 1998, pp. 98–100.

Source: Michelle Burylo, Supervisor, Corporate Business Information Center © Air Products and Chemicals, Inc.

raw materials and outsourced component parts, wholesalers, retailers, and customers. Figure 13–5 represents a goal that will not be reached overnight but that is certainly conceivable within the next few years.

Companies need to first determine what their role should be in an electronic market place and then begin a formal system design process that matches the needs of the company. Many companies are now realizing that e-commerce may be beneficial to them, but are not yet sure in what manner. Once companies determine whether they have a need to engage in some form of e-commerce, they must then determine what form they will use. Only then can a company realistically expect to be successful in implementing an e-commerce system employing technology such as intelligent agents.

FIGURE 13–5   *E-commerce using intelligent agents*

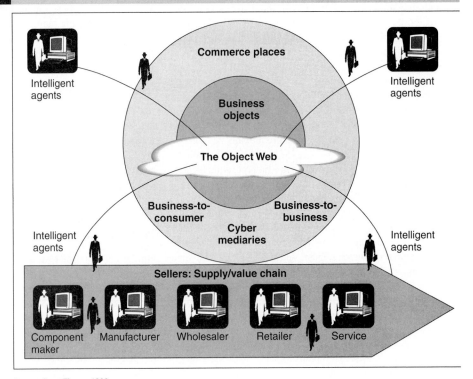

Source: Peter Finger, 1998.

The technology for building an e-commerce society is available. A lack of standards and interfacing mechanisms, however, is still a deterrent. New types of businesses focused on Internet-specific business applications have generally used intelligent agents. Businesses that provide customized news services or other personalized content, as well as many Internet-only e-commerce companies have employed intelligent agents in order to differentiate their online storefronts from traditional businesses. Traditional businesses are, for the most part, still assessing and planning their entrance to the e-business realm. Proper planning and assessing are vital precursors to proper implementation of this technology. Analysis paralysis, on the other hand, can cause a firm to miss out on the potential opportunities of electronic commerce. Here is some advice offered by Peter Fingar:

> Competitive pressure and markets will demand that each step taken toward the fully open digital market economy will place increasing competitive pressure to take yet the next step. Since the ultimate digital economy is not a single end-state, corporations are in for a long journey. Those that will succeed will do so not with the systems they have in-place today, but with a solid enterprise architecture that has the central design goal of *agility.*

> *(Peter Finger, 1998)*

The following sections outline a number of potential effects that intelligent agents have for specific e-commerce functions. Examples are given of intelligent agents that are currently being deployed in these areas.

| **FIGURE 13–6** | *The online information chain* |

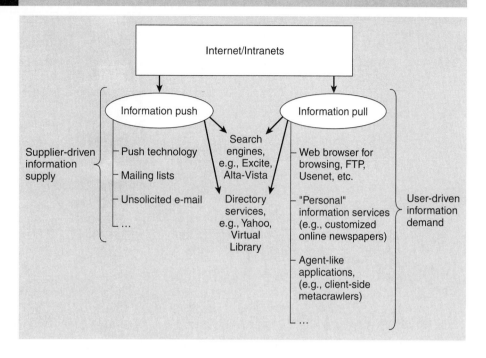

The Online Information Chain

The distribution of information between suppliers and customers is one of the greatest benefits of the Internet. As illustrated earlier in Figure 13–5, the sharing of information and interacting societies of intelligent agents is a driving force of e-commerce. Figure 13–6 illustrates the **online information chain.** The two main concepts of the online information chain, push and pull technologies, are discussed in the following sections.

Push Technology and Marketing
Firms are using agent technology to more effectively and efficiently reach customers who are connected to the Internet. Push technology is supplier driven, and it sends customized information directly to the customer. Unfortunately, push technology has already been abused and has received much criticism and bad press regarding junk e-mail, or spam mail, that clogs e-mail boxes and furthers the problem of information overload. **Push technology**, when implemented responsibly, professionally, and considerately can foster good customer relations.

A well-designed system can benefit the supplier by reducing inventory carrying costs and marketing costs, and it can benefit the customer by offering special discounts not available to the general public. One example of intelligent agent push technology is illustrated in Figure 13–7. Intelligent agents can be used to help businesses "unload" specific inventory items by determining which customers are more likely to be interested in purchasing the items, perhaps at a discount. Chapter 14 more extensively covers push technology, the information chain, and the use of intelligent agents to enhance contact with customers in reference to marketing.

FIGURE 13–7   *Example of push intelligent agents*

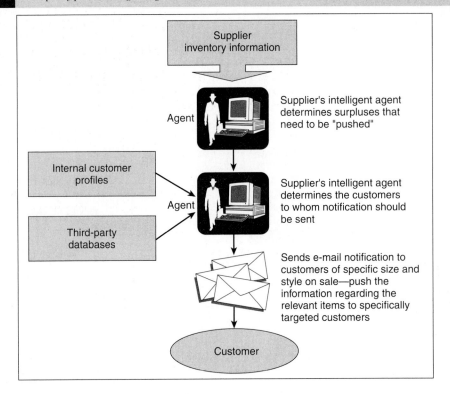

Pull Technology and Demands of Information and Services

Customers and businesses use **pull technology** to help alleviate the information overload problem and to more efficiently and effectively compare product/service information. Figure 13–8 illustrates several potential uses of intelligent agents by consumers. The first use is that of web **search agents** located on the Internet that can help users to narrow down the number of sites that contain the desired information. Search agents are frequently referred to as **bots,** short for robots. A majority of frequent Internet users rely on search engines to locate websites. Intelligent **metasearch agents,** such as BullsEye2, Copernic, and LeviBot, are now available that can consult multiple search engines simultaneously for the user to allow a wider, yet more efficient, net to be cast in an information search. Multitudes of comparison shopping intelligent agents also exist (see *www.botspot.com* for a detailed list). Specialized agents, such as BestBookBuys for locating the best price for a given book, are readily available, as well as more general personal shopping agents, such as Excite's Jango. MySimon is a personal shopping agent that allows the shopping results to be sorted by price or merchant rating. The site also provides reviews of the online merchants it searches for merchandise. Shopping agents that help customers more easily locate a product at the best price and then transfer the customer to the appropriate website are a great enabler of e-commerce because they bring buyers and sellers together.

Another manner in which customers make use of intelligent agent services is to use or subscribe to a service that provides customized news or other information content. The Morning Paper (*www.boutell.com/morning*) is an example of an intelligent agent (fee based) that visits users' favorite websites each morning and summarizes any

FIGURE 13–8	*Example of pull intelligent agents*

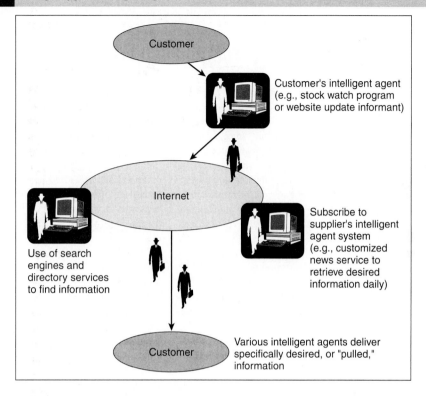

changes to the site from the previous day into a newspaper format. Thus, users, after pre-specifying the sites, merely have to check their "morning paper" to see any new items or developments from their favorite sites. Ananova.com, a British website that provides global news, allows its viewers to request personalized news topics about which they would like to receive regular e-mail or WAP phone alerts (wireless application protocol—discussed in Chapter 9). It also has video reports generated by a computer-animated reporter.

Another product/service that can be downloaded for a fee is NetReaper. NetReaper helps to search for information and store it. NetReaper's site suggests that it can be used for the following:

- Extract prices from a competitor's website and store these in a database for reporting or comparisons.
- Scan local e-mail files from Netscape or another mail program and extract names or e-mail addresses into a text file.
- Retrieve public news headlines and automatically generate an HTML page for your website.
- Get stock quotes from a public website and store daily or weekly prices in a tab delimited file for use in a charting application.

Law Enforcement Uses of Intelligent Agents in Electronic Commerce
Because fraudulent acts occur on the Internet as in any other market place, the Federal Trade Commission (FTC) is building a special lab to help detect fraud and deception

E-Commerce in Practice

Microsoft in Hot Pursuit of Software Pirates

In the past [few] weeks, Microsoft Corp. has ordered 7,500 websites and Internet auctions to stop selling counterfeit Microsoft software. Another 600 notices were sent out Tuesday. The software giant's secret weapon in combating piracy: an Internet monitoring tool that, according to the vendor, sniffs out Net fraud 24 hours a day, seven days a week.

"[Microsoft has seen an] increasing volume of complaints related to fraudulent materials and both the distributing and posting of illegal downloads," said Tim Cranton, a corporate attorney with Microsoft's antipiracy group. "Customers are getting ripped off, paying good money for bad products."

Microsoft is leasing the tool, an intelligent Web crawler, from the software's developer, a third-party vendor that Cranton didn't identify. Microsoft has been using the tool to detect counterfeit versions of its Windows 2000 operating system since November [1999], he added.

Since February [2000], the tool has been programmed to search for all counterfeit versions of Microsoft products, resulting in the discoveries that spurred Tuesday's announcement of both the software vendor's campaign to fight fraud on the Net and its subsequent filing of several lawsuits in the United States.

The tool is capable of detecting the illegal distribution of all copyrighted material, including books, movies, and music, and is able to do so in different languages, Microsoft said. The automated online scanning tool simulates a search that someone looking for fraudulent material would run. The software is capable of searching the content of every website and each site's links.

"It is a solution for all content creators because it can protect all sorts of content online . . . [Microsoft's] goal is to create an honest marketplace where [customers] can get trusted Microsoft content online," Cranton said.

So far, Microsoft's campaign has generated 64 criminal raids and resulted in 17 civil lawsuits being filed in 15 countries. In the United States, where more than 3,000 Internet auction postings were taken down in July, Microsoft recently announced five lawsuits and two settlements. One of the lawsuits is against New York–based Copy USA.

To date, Microsoft has shut down 600 postings on the company's auction site. The settlements are related to college students who had been selling illegal copies of Microsoft's software through auction sites out of Sacramento, Calif., and Chicago.

The Business Software Alliance (BSA) in Washington, a nonprofit trade group of which Microsoft is a key member, said it supports the software giant's actions. However, the BSA is not using its power of attorney to take legal action against fraudulent parties.

"This is Microsoft's own action," said Karine Elsen, the BSA's director of marketing. Many of the raids have been led or supported by the BSA, whose involvement is instrumental to Microsoft's success, Cranton said. The industry body has been criticized in the past for having an overly close relationship with Microsoft.

Source: Anna Scott, *Computerworld Online*, August 2, 2000.
© *www.computerworld.com*

on the Internet. Ultimately, the lab will employ search agents that scan Internet advertisements 24 hours a day. Specifically, the agent will be trained to look for what is considered to be dubious, deceptive, or illegal marketing or business practices. A key component of this lab is the collection of evidence. The agent will capture and save what it believes to be fraudulent or deceptive material. This is important because websites change and delete material constantly, and preserving evidence is very difficult in many cases after the fact of the incident. Microsoft has taken the job of identifying instances of fraudulent uses of its products and illegal downloads into its own hands using agent technology as mentioned in the box entitled "Microsoft in Hot Pursuit of Software Pirates."

Intelligent agent software can also be developed by the user or downloaded from sites for personal use. Downloadable intelligent agents, such as NetProphet, are available that perform such tasks as gathering stock price information for user-specified stocks and displaying quotes. Another service that intelligent agents can perform is website update information, such as CyberAlert, javELink, and Minder, which allows users to prespecify websites that they wish to monitor for changes. These agents continuously monitor the sites and indicate when a site has changed. This type of agent allows a user to monitor sites without having to physically revisit them throughout the day.

Businesses can also use intelligent agent technology to continuously conduct environment scans. Such agents can alert management to changing conditions and events in their environment. For example, an attorney who specializes in patent law can use pull technology to continuously monitor multiple sites and alert him or her to any developments such as new patent-related court cases or court decisions. If the attorney needs to perform a specific legal search, he or she may use an intelligent metasearch agent such as Legal Seeker, which combines 40 legal search engines into a single search. Thus, customers and businesses can customize the retrieval of information and services received. Many of the pull technologies that are of value to customers and businesses are not free services; fees are charged. Pull technologies employing intelligent agents are creating new offerings of electronic products and services.

New Geographical Markets

Intelligent agents can help businesses market their products to a wider geographical market for two simple reasons:

- Intelligent agents can work around the clock in different time zones.
- Intelligent agents can converse in any language in which they are programmed.

These benefits allow businesses to market and sell their products without the necessity of having around-the-clock sales and support staff who can speak multiple languages. Further, small businesses can compete on a more level playing field with large firms because of the ease and low cost of marketing on the Internet. The deployment of international intelligent agents (other than search and metasearch agents) has been low thus far, but the potential is great.

Business-to-Business Transaction Negotiation

The near-term horizon does not appear to offer much promise for widespread implementation of Internet-based intelligent agents that will negotiate business transactions as depicted earlier in the chapter in Figure 13–4. Researchers are actively working on simulated models, but the primary technological deterrent is the lack of standards for intelligent agent development. Three factors will significantly affect the adoption of intelligent agent based business-to-business transaction negotiations:

- Development of intelligent agent interfacing mechanisms.
- Security over data access by external intelligent agents.
- Adequacy and trust of negotiation models used by intelligent agents.

The last item may prove to be a deterrent after advances are made in the other areas. Even the most forward-thinking management teams may have reservations about turning the task of transaction negotiations over to a computer program, as sophisticated as the program may be. For this to happen, a cultural change will have to occur, and such changes typically do not happen very rapidly.

LIMITATIONS OF AGENTS

Agents are not a panacea for integrating distributed systems for problem-solving tasks. Champions of agent technology tend to offer overly zealous illustrations of potential agent applications, at least for a short-term horizon. These champions tend to paint the somewhat unrealistic picture that humans will be able to rely on agents to do most, if not all, of their work for them. Human intermediaries will continue to be needed, but their role will likely be to perform intelligence-requiring tasks, while the agents will perform more information gathering and updating tasks. This is not to say, however, that the agents are not able to perform some tasks with features of intelligence. They do, and they will continue to do so, but only in limited and structured domains.

As promising as agent technology appears, some limitations have been identified.[5] Three such limitations of the agent paradigm are listed here:

- No overall **system controller.** Agent technology may not be appropriate for systems
  - In which global constraints have to be maintained.
  - Where a real-time response must be guaranteed.
  - In which deadlocks or livelocks[6] must be avoided.

- No **global perspective.** The local state of the agent determines the agent's action. From a global perspective, the agent may make suboptimal decisions because of the agent's "tunnel vision." Multi-agent systems will need to work on cooperation and negotiation techniques to promote more optimal global decisions.
- **Trust** and **delegation.** Individuals must trust the underlying technology of the agent and the actual knowledge base of the agent in order for them to comfortably delegate tasks to an agent. Further, the boundaries of the tasks performed by the agent need to coincide with the comfort zone preference of the user. The agent must strike a balance between needlessly consulting the user and exceeding its authority by not consulting the user enough.

Further, testing an agent in a simulated environment does not necessarily provide adequate feedback as to how well the agent will perform in a real-time, multi-agent environment. Thus, diagnostic testing and refinement of the agent can sometimes only occur after flaws are discovered during its use in the real environment.

Before societies of interacting agents will be realized, developments to overcome two hurdles need to be made. One hurdle is the lack of standards used in agent development that will allow agents to seamlessly interact. Underlying this problem is another problem, which many agent developers consider to be more significant: the unwanted access to databases by other agents participating in multi-agent societies. This issue is further discussed next.

IMPLICATIONS FOR THE ACCOUNTING PROFESSION

To provide assurance over systems, accountants need, at a minimum, to thoroughly understand the systems—which includes the use of intelligent agents by companies in their transaction processing systems. Further, accountants have the opportunity to help

---

[5]Jennings and Woolridge, 1998.

[6]A livelock occurs when a system devotes all of its resources to processing interrupts.

their clients in the development and control of agents that are used in their e-commerce applications.

Continuous Reliability Assurance

Continuous reliability assurance is the type of assurance service that accountants can perform over real-time, computer-based systems. As its name implies, continuous reliability assurance is an around-the-clock monitoring and detection system that is designed to foster data and transaction processing integrity. The American Institute of Certified Public Accountants (AICPA) asserts that CPAs need to provide assurance about both the customer and supplier's systems reliability in e-commerce applications. One mechanism for achieving continuous reliability assurance is the use of ubiquitous sensors or software agents:

> Evaluating controls over real-time systems must be computer based. It is impractical, or impossible, to do it after the fact based on paper transaction trails. Data flowing through the system will be monitored and analyzed using CPA-defined rules. Exceptions to these rules trigger real-time warnings to call the CPA's attention to potential problem areas and issues that need immediate resolution.
>
> Electronic sensors and software agents (some of which may be owned or controlled by the CPA) will be introduced at key checkpoints throughout the preparer's set of business activities.
>
> Sensors will lead to early and automatic identification of transactions, events, and/or relationships that are unusual and therefore demand immediate consideration. Redundant sensors would not demand any human consideration; they would simply override defective sensors. Assurers will use audit software agents to search for unusual patterns and/or corroborative patterns in transactions.
>
> The CPA may provide general parameters to the software agent, such as industrial, macroeconomic, and technological factors, but give the software agent discretion to add other factors or information appropriate in the circumstances. Agents may have adaptive, quasilearning algorithms embedded to adjust to a constantly changing model.

(*AICPA Special Committee on Assurance Services, 1998*)

Thus, what is described is the use of a semiautonomous, adaptive agent. Accounting professionals need to understand agent technology from two perspectives: enhancing traditional assurance services through the use of intelligent agents and helping clients to develop agents used in e-commerce applications. The understanding of the latter will help accountants perform the assurance function.

Agents and Security

Agents are characterized as mobile, and this mobility presents security problems. Mobile agents that require program execution on the remote computer present a challenge to security systems. The danger of malicious code being present in the agent module is present. Accountants need to be aware of the risks to systems that allow agent societies to operate. If properly configured, systems can only allow "authorized" agents to enter the local agent society residing on a company's host computer. This authorization means that some form of authentication process is necessary for agents. The possibility exists that agents can hold digital certificates from a trusted third party similar to individuals and businesses. Until the appropriate infrastructure is in place that allows for screening and authentication of agents, accountants should cautiously assess agent societies of their clients.

Summary

Intelligent agents are a mechanism that users can employ to help them to work more productively by delegating certain tasks to the computer. Intelligent agents used in electronic commerce applications have the potential to dramatically affect the supply value chain. Some significant hurdles, however, must be overcome before multi-agent societies can truly thrive and reach their full potential (e.g., agent interfacing mechanisms, data security, and trust of agents). Members of the accounting profession should learn to take advantage of agent technology in order to adequately perform the assurance function over agent applications that affect the financial status of a company. Further, agent technology is a technology that accountants can themselves use to enhance continuous reliability assurance functions.

Key Words

adapt	metasearch agents
agency	mobility
agent society	modular agents
aglets	multi-agent system
architecture	negotiation
bots	online information chain
complexity of society	openness
continuous reliability assurance	persistence
cooperation	personality
delegate	policy
emotion	predictive/proactive agent
global perspective	pull technology
gopher agent	push technology
information overload	respond
initiate	search agents
intelligence	service-performing agent
intelligent agent	single-agent system
interfacing techniques	sociability
interoperability	system controller
internal controls	transport
language	trust

Review Questions

1. Define information overload.
2. What is an intelligent agent?
3. Explain what is meant by "delegating work" to the computer.
4. Differentiate between a single agent and a multi-agent system.
5. List two characteristics that make technology valuable and useful to the marketplace.
6. Identify the three primary functions performed by intelligent agents.
7. List the three categories of intelligence.
8. Distinguish "agent-like" systems from "true" agents.
9. What is meant by a persistent agent?
10. Explain what is meant by an agent's level of sophistication. List the three levels of sophistication.

11. List the four features that should be considered in the design of agent societies.
12. Why are agents typically designed in a modular form?
13. List the four levels of agreement identified by DARPA.
14. What is an aglet?
15. Explain the "negotiation of agents" concept. Why is this important?
16. In agent societies, what are the objects of concern for internal controls?
17. List four ways in which intelligent agents can positively affect e-commerce.
18. Explain the online information chain.
19. Distinguish between a search engine and a metasearch agent.
20. How can agents be used to conduct an environment scan?
21. How can agents be used to help businesses market their products to a wider geographical market?
22. Identify some factors that need to be overcome before intelligent agents are widely used in business-to-business transaction negotiations.
23. List three limitations of the agent paradigm.
24. In what way can accountants use intelligent agents to perform the assurance function?

Discussion Questions

1. How does the intelligent agent computing environment differ from the traditional computing environment? Which mode do you think most users will prefer? Why?
2. Would you be comfortable letting the computer make a decision, any decision, on your behalf? If so, give an example of a decision. If not, explain why.
3. Why is multi-agent technology significantly more difficult to design and implement than single-agent technology?
4. How can agents be expected to "adapt" to their environments? Give an example.
5. Is it necessary for intelligent agents to exhibit all defined characteristics of agents? Why or why not?
6. How can a software module, such as an agent, exhibit emotion or personality? Is this desirable? Why or why not? Give an example.
7. Which sophistication level of agents are you most likely to use for personal reasons? For business purposes? Give examples.
8. Does the zone of agreement contain a unique solution? If so, how is it realized? If not, how is a solution ever reached?
9. How can intelligent agents affect the supply/value chain? Give an example.
10. Between push and pull technologies, which method do you think consumers prefer? Why?
11. Discuss why cultural changes may need to occur before the use of intelligent agents by businesses is widely accepted.

Cases

1. Detective Agents
   a. Does the kind of policing that Microsoft is conducting hold up in court? Do you think it will be supported by law enforcement agencies?
   b. What implication does it have for the recording industry?

2. Intelligent Agents and Price Comparisons

 Some merchants have been put off by search agents' capabilities to search their sites and display their products and prices in price comparisons on other sites.

 a. Why do you think a merchant would block the search agent's access?

 b. Research this topic using the Internet and report your findings.

3. Intelligent Robotic Guides

 Motion Factory has developed a new technology tool, Motivate, that allows three-dimensional, interactive showrooms to be placed on websites. The intent of the product is to allow salespeople to "greet" the customers at the door, show the various products and model in three-dimensional images, and close the sale.

 a. Do you think such agents will help to increase "trust" in negotiations?

 b. What impediments currently exist to impede widespread implementation of agents?

4. Intelligent Agents and Potential Price Wars

 A 1998 research study conducted by IBM's research center that simulated the use of broker and consumer agents reported that heavy use of agent technology resulted in dramatic price wars. Further, customers with low volume were not serviced by the broker agents because it became unprofitable.

 a. Do you think this model realistically predicts what will happen?

 b. What factors may have been omitted from the model that may cause a different result?

 c. Do you think studies such as these will deter companies from developing or participating in agent technology?

References and Websites

Angehrn, Albert. *The Strategic Implications of the Internet. http://www.insead.fr/CALT/ Publication/ICDT/strategicImplication.htm.*

Barker, Don. "Let Mata Hari Spy for You!" *Best of the Bots,* October 15, 1998. *http://www.botspot.com.*

_____. "Hit a Bullseye Every Time," *Best of the Bots,* July 17, 1998. *http://www.botspot.com.*

_____. "Excite Yourself by Shopping with Jango," *Best of the Bots,* 1998. *http://www.botspot.com.*

Chislenko, Alexander. "Some Thoughts on Multi-Agent Systems and 'Hyper-Economy,' " 1997. *http://www.lucifer.com/~sasha/articles/hypereconomy.htm.*

DARPA. "Specification of the KQML Agent-Communication Language." *http://www.cs.umbc.edu/kqml/kqmlspec.html.*

Fingar, Peter. "A CEO's Guide to eCommerce Using Intergalactic Object-Oriented Intelligent Agents." July 1998. *http://home1.gte.net/pfingar/eba.htm.*

Firefly Network Inc. *http://www.agents-inc.com.*

Gartner Group (ECS team). "How to Create an Electronic Marketplace." 1996. *http://www.networking.ibm.com/nnn/nnn3emk.htm.*

Geocities. "Software Agents: Coming to Terms with Software Agents." *http://www.geocities.com/ResearchTriangle/Thinktank/4633/Agents_definition.htm.*

Gilbert, Don. "IBM Intelligent Agent White Paper." May 1997. *http://www.networking.ibm.com/iag/iagwp1.htm.*

Guilfoyle, C., J. Jeffcoate, and H. Stark. "Agents on the Web: Catalyst for E-Commerce." April 1997.

Hamilton, Annette. "Online Travel Explosion Reveals Secrets of Ecommerce Success," *ZDNet,* 1998, *http://www.zdnet.com.*

Hermans, Bjorn. "Information Brokering, New Forms of Using Computers, Agency, and Software Agents in Tomorrow's Online Market Place: An Assessment of Current and Future Developments." May 1998. *http://wdww.hermans.org.*

IBM Corporation. "The Role of Intelligent Agents in the Information Infrastructure." *http://www.dcc.unicamp.br/~euzebio/Agents/eight-applications.htm.*

Jennings, N. R., and M. Woolridge. *Applications of Intelligent Agents.* Springer Verlag/Berlin/Heidelberg, 1998.

Levin, Rich. "RAD Tool Finds Business APPs for VR," *InformationWeek,* October 13, 1998.

Lieberman, H., and D. Maulsby. "Instructible Agents: Software That Just Keeps Getting Better," *Systems Journal,* 1996. *http://www.almaden.ibm.com/journal/sj/mit/sectiond/lieberman.htm.*

Moltzen, Edward. "Web Saves Cisco $550 Million Annually," *TechWeb,* October 13, 1998. *http://www.techweb.com.*

Petrie, Charles. "Agent-Based Engineering, the Web and Intelligence," *IEEE Expert,* December, 1996. *http://cdr. standford.edu/NextLink/Expert.htm.*

Salnoske, Karl. "Testimony before the Subcommittee on Telecommunications Trade and Consumer Protection Committee on Commerce." May 21, 1998.

Toft, Dorte. "FTC to Set Up Internet Fraud Lab," *Computerworld Online,* June 25, 1999. *www.computerworld.com.*

U.S. Department of Commerce. "The Emerging Digital Economy." April 1998. *http://www.ecommerce.gov/danc1.htm.*

Ward, Mark. "Wired for Mayhem," *New Scientist,* July 4, 1998. *http://newscientist.com.*

Zeng, D., and K. Sycara. "Benefits of Learning in Negotiation," *Proceeding of AAAI-97,* 1997.

14 WEB-BASED MARKETING

Learning Objectives

1. To understand the effect of the World Wide Web on business and marketing strategies.
2. To apply the four marketing Ps to the World Wide Web.
3. To understand the importance of personalization.
4. To learn and categorize Internet marketing techniques.

INTRODUCTION

The World Wide Web (WWW) provides an exciting and powerful new distribution channel for marketers. BizRate reports that consumers spent approximately $6 billion online during the 2000 holiday season, up from $3.75 billion in the previous year. During the five-week holiday season leading up to Christmas, more than 52 million online orders were placed. Web-based electronic commerce is providing marketers with an exciting new marketing channel. Innovative uses of the WWW are being launched every day by creative marketing professionals and website entrepreneurs. The Internet Advertising Bureau (IAB) reported that Internet advertising revenues totaled nearly $2 billion for the third quarter of 2000, which is up 63 percent from the same period in the previous year. Not all online merchants have been successful, however. For many dotcoms, 2000 was the year of going under; at least 210 Internet companies shut down during the year, causing as many as 15,000 layoffs according to Webmergers.com. The amount of capital invested into these firms was estimated at $1.5 billion. This chapter discusses the necessity for alignment between a firm's Web-based strategy with its overall strategy in order to be successful. No longer can Web entrepreneurs assume "If you build it, they will come." This chapter also presents some techniques used on the Internet to promote goods. Website design issues for creating an effective and efficient site are examined. The chapter closes with a discussion of the implications of Web-based marketing on the accounting profession.

THE SCOPE OF MARKETING

This book explores many facets of business applications on the Internet and the WWW. This chapter is concerned with those activities considered to fall under the domain of marketing. What is marketing? The concept of marketing conjures up many images, such as people sitting around trying to create a catchy slogan or phrase, print advertisers laying out the page of a new glossy advertisement or billboard, or perhaps a roomful of telemarketers placing phone calls to direct-sell a good or service or to collect questionnaire data. The WWW presents a new venue for marketers to use, and with it comes new guidelines. Many of the old rules and guidelines still apply, but some rules need adaptation to appropriately apply to this new environment. In other words, new rules and guidelines are needed for such radically new environments as the Internet and WWW. Even so, the definition of marketing and what it encompasses has not changed in essence as a result of the use of the WWW as a new marketing channel. According to the American Marketing Association, **marketing** is

> The process of planning and executing the conception, pricing, promotion, and distribution of ideas, goods, and services to create exchanges that satisfy individual and organizational goals.

These tasks are often considered as precursor activities to the actual engagement in business transactions, and indeed they often are. However, many marketing activities, such as the distribution of ideas and services, may not result in an immediate financial business exchange, especially with marketing techniques available on the WWW. For example, SesameWorkshop.org is a website that creates a community for the distribution of a service (free children's activities). Does this type of activity qualify as a marketing technique? Does the free distribution of ideas (such as projects for children) and services (such as story time for children) qualify as creating satisfying exchanges for individual goals? Many parents and children would agree that the exchange is satisfying. In Chapter 1, virtual community space was mentioned as one important aspect of e-commerce. This type of activity is a great example of virtual community space.

Further, marketing activities may also encompass postsale processes, such as service to the consumer after the sale is placed. The WWW offers an unlimited opportunity for businesses to service their customers after the sale. Such service activities may fall into either the virtual information or the virtual communication space. The crayola.com website provides this feature by providing Crayola users with methods for cleaning the many Crayola products off numerous surfaces, a valuable service to many parents who have purchased Crayola products for their children.

While reading this chapter, consider two issues regarding the use of Web-based marketing. First, determine whether Web-based marketing is (a) *evolutionary* (altering an existing firm's business model) or (b) *revolutionary* (forming a new organization to realize the opportunity of marketing on the Web). Second, consider how the various Web-based marketing techniques can supplement current marketing initiatives or how traditional marketing techniques can supplement Web-based marketing, even for revolutionary ventures. For example, should an evolutionary firm consider Web banners in addition to or in place of current print advertisement? Should a new Web-based firm consider marketing the site on television? These issues are explored in this chapter. To start this exploration, examine the table in Figure 14–1. This table illustrates the increasing importance of branding. Six of the top 10 sites with the highest percentage traffic growth are well-known brands. MySimon is a shopping search agent that is most useful when a shopper knows what brand product they want, and this site helps them to find it at the lowest price. Well-known brands are increasing by gaining ground on the web. The importance of branding is discussed in the box entitled "Revving Up E-Commerce."

FIGURE 14–1	Top 10 gaining retail sites for 2000 holiday season

		Average Daily Unique Visitors		Year-over-Year Percent Increase for the 5-Week Average
Rank	Site	Weeks 1–5 1999	Weeks 1–5 2000	
1	WALMART.COM	50,000	370,000	640.0%
2	MYSIMON.COM	88,000	283,000	222.0%
3	BESTBUY.COM	82,000	249,000	203.2%
4	AMERICANGREETINGS.COM	216,000	538,000	149.1%
5	DEALTIME.COM	74,000	175,000	137.0%
6	STAPLES.COM	50,000	117,000	134.8%
7	HALLMARK.COM	97,000	218,000	124.3%
8	SEARS.COM	107,000	210,000	95.9%
9	800.COM	68,000	114,000	67.1%
10	BIZRATE.COM	310,000	510,000	64.6%

Source: Media Metrix.

E-Commerce in Practice

Revving Up E-Commerce

IT leaders are busy with the next generation of websites, which must handle more customers, enhance the brand, and make a profit.

Shailendra "Shelley" Nandkeolyar has a full plate this year. He's vice president of e-commerce at Williams-Sonoma Inc., a San Francisco–based upscale store for kitchen and cooking items. Ann Delligatta, chief operating officer at Autobytel.com Inc. in Irvine, Calif., is also booked with new projects. So are Kas Naderi, senior vice president of emerging technologies at Bass Hotels & Resorts Inc. in Atlanta, and most other high-level information technology executives in the United States. Having conquered the date-rollover demons of Y2K, these IT leaders have turned their attention to a flurry of e-commerce projects. In fact, 81 of the *Computerworld* Premier 100 IT Leaders say that working on "electronic-business infrastructure" is a mission-critical project for the next 12 months.

The stakes are high for their companies.

The pure dot-coms, such as Autobytel.com, realize that growth in revenue and earnings won't mean much without delivering a positive bottom line for shareholders.

Likewise, brick-and-mortar businesses such as Williams-Sonoma understand the need to advance their brand in the electronic space as well as through traditional sales channels—or lose market share.

And all companies—be they business-to-business or business-to-consumer, buyer or seller—are recognizing the cost-saving benefits of online procurement of supplies. The high-level IT leaders of these aggressive companies offer valuable, and often surprising, insights into e-commerce project strategies.

From Naderi's perspective, for example, Bass Hotels is as much about information as it is about hotel and resort accommodations. Bass Hotels is really in the business of providing information to customers, making it easier for customers to discover and utilize the services provided by company-owned and franchise properties.

Naderi says he's also in the business of providing electronic procurement for the hotels and leveraging IT to help ensure that franchisees follow a corporate code of quality.

Although brand recognition will remain important in e-commerce, just as it has in other marketing venues, "consumers are getting flooded with so many brands," he says. In his business, Naderi says, the brand concept will ultimately be overshadowed by intelligent-agent technology. He says consumers will go to portals that serve up the specific information they're seeking, instead of looking for a particular brand.

That's why he's pushing e-commerce that offers a total travel experience: hotel, car, and airline tickets, all in one

---

E-Commerce in Practice

Revving Up E-Commerce—continued

package. "We are focused on making our website more of an alliance instead of a brand site," Naderi says.

Designing for Customers

Delligatta says, "We have always designed our system from the customer backward." And this year, she says, she wants to expand the customer relationship management features of the Autobytel.com site so customers can connect with "live human beings."

Those customers aren't necessarily located in the United States, because Autobytel.com has set its sights on overseas markets, too.

"We have been the car-buying service that has put the stake in the ground internationally," Delligatta says. "We've been doing a lot of sharing of best practices in other countries, including the United Kingdom, Sweden, Japan. We'll move very quickly across Europe."

Because the business model and e-commerce are intertwined, Delligatta says there's one question that keeps coming up: "Do the projects reflect changes in thinking about the business model of the company?"

"Our No. 1 challenge," she says, "is to stay the leader."

Source: James Cope, Excerpt from © *Computerworld Online,* May 8, 2000. *www.computerworld.com*

BUSINESS, MARKETING, AND INFORMATION TECHNOLOGY STRATEGY CONGRUENCE

How do you evaluate a technology that has completely captured the public's imagination? A technology perceived as so rich in promise that thousands of articles in newspapers and magazines explain its workings to their readers. A technology that has come to indicate innovativeness, where failure to appreciate it is taken as a sure sign of belonging to the wrong side of a generational divide. Which has led, almost overnight, to the creation of new companies, brands, industries, and fortunes. One that commentators claim will revolutionize not only public culture, but also education and commerce. And, in moments of excess, a technology hailed as the best new chance for creating a peaceful world.

(*Ward Hanson, 1998*)

This quote refers to the effect of wireless radio technology. The radio industry took the world by storm in the early 1920s. It was truly the original WWW (World Wide Wireless, RCA's logo from 1920 to 1927.) Much can be learned from the lessons taught from the introduction of this revolutionary information dissemination and marketing medium. The left side of Figure 14–2 illustrates Ward Hanson's radio euphoria cycle; this model is adapted for today's WWW on the right side of the figure. As with radio, the novelty and ease of use made the WWW instantly popular. The number of subscribers to the Web has grown at exponential rates. In response to the overwhelming demand for WWW usage, the number of Internet Service Providers (ISPs) has grown as well. Further, existing ISPs continue to increase their infrastructure to accommodate an increasing number of users.

Missing from Figure 14–2, however, is the clarification between business-to-consumer and business-to-business applications. Figure 14–3 adjusts the diagram to reflect the entrance of business-to-business uses of the WWW relative to the entrance of business-to-consumer uses. In its initial growth phase, the uses of the WWW were primarily for business-to-consumer applications, and the emergence of well-known Internet merchants, such as Amazon.com and eBay.com, was seen. These businesses were created

FIGURE 14–2	*World Wide Wireless and World Wide Web*

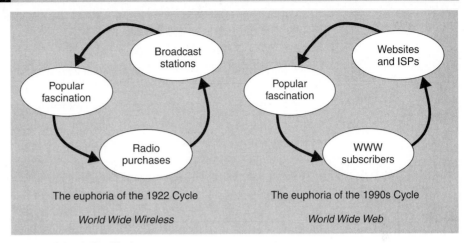

The euphoria of the 1922 Cycle   The euphoria of the 1990s Cycle

World Wide Wireless   *World Wide Web*

Source: 1992 Cycle—Ward Hanson.

FIGURE 14–3	*Business-to-consumer versus business-to-business*

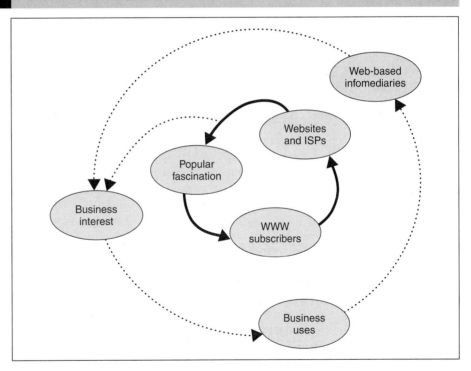

solely to operate on the Internet in order to directly market their goods to consumers. Other new types of businesses emerged as well, such as America Online, an ISP that provides a "community" of services to its subscribers, and Doubleclick, a marketing firm specializing in WWW marketing services.

The outer circle of Figure 14–3 illustrates the entrance of already established businesses that believe the WWW can be used to connect in some fashion with their existing business partners or by possibly increasing market share through market development. Although total B2B sales dwarf B2C sales, this type of application has lagged behind business-to-consumer applications for several reasons:

- Initial views of WWW as a recreational device or merely as a fancy e-mail device.
- Security concerns over access to information and data transmission.
- Legal concerns surrounding internationally inconsistent laws.
- Uncertainty regarding how to best utilize the WWW to help achieve its corporate mission.

Initial uses of the Internet were not perceived by many businesses that do not sell their products directly to the consumer as beneficial for transacting or interacting with their business partners. Further, because of the newness and openness of this technology, many firms felt extremely uncomfortable using this medium for their business applications. In many cases, this feeling of discomfort stems from the longstanding use of their internal systems or traditional, planned EDI networks with which their comfort level over security is quite good. Further, as discussed in Chapter 5, many legal issues surrounding transacting on the Internet exist because of its global reach. Many businesses stalled launching business-to-business sites because of the lack of understanding of the legal ramifications and security issues, some of which are a result of encryption import/export rules.

One final reason for the lack of WWW-based applications is the confusion or uncertainty as to how the use of such a technology fits into the overall corporate mission and goals (e.g., does the technology support or enhance the mission?). A study by the Cambridge Information Network found that more than one-third of firms studied did not believe that their company successfully implemented its e-commerce initiative. Further, one-fourth of these firms attributed their lack of success to a failure to connect the e-commerce effort with the goals of the business. Why is this issue explored in this chapter devoted to Internet marketing? As will be explained in the following section, marketing encompasses many aspects of the firm's operations, and the Internet is largely a marketing device for many businesses. The marketing plan and Web-based commerce plan must be in congruence with the overall business mission and strategy in order for the firm to reap the greatest amount of benefits. Figure 14–4 illustrates the hierarchy of mission development. Established businesses, the ones that have traditionally been slower to launch websites, already have corporate-level mission statements.

Does new technology require that the **mission statement** be changed? Maybe—maybe not, but to the extent that new technology affects the business' environment, it may need to adjust either its corporate mission or its marketing mission or both. The information technology (IT) department may need adjustment of its mission as well. For example, Barnes & Noble faced a different business environment due to the popularity of the Internet and the emergence of Amazon.com. Amazon.com opened for business in mid-1995; in 1998, Amazon's sales reached $610 million, and it was the number one on-line retailer of books. They reported that more than 60 percent of their shoppers were repeat buyers, an indication of satisfaction. This certainly changes the competitive environment for other book retailers such as Barnes & Noble. Not surprisingly, in May 1997, Barnes & Noble launched its own website selling books directly to consumers. In October 1998, Barnes & Noble sold 50 percent ownership to Bertelsmann A.G. Then, in March 1999, stock was sold to the public, leaving Barnes & Noble owning 40 percent

FIGURE 14–4   *Corporate and Web-based mission congruence*

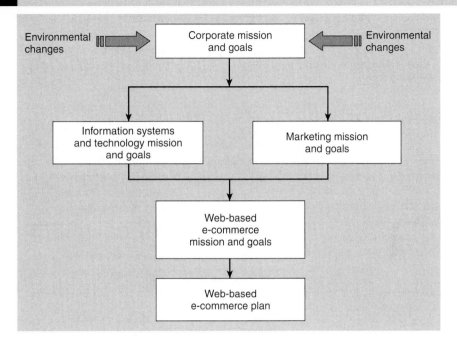

and Bertelsmann owning 40 percent. The following statement, issued in its 1999 Annual Report, illustrates BarnesandNoble.com's focus on the use of multiple distribution channels in recognizing that the brick-and-mortar stores provide it with a well-known brand-name and presence:

> B&N.com has pursued a strategy of focusing on the sale of a broad range of knowledge, information, education, and entertainment related products. Since opening its initial on-line store in March 1997, B&N.com has sold products to over 4.7 million customers in 224 countries. B&N.com has created a model for e-commerce based upon a compelling value proposition. B&N.com's suite of online stores is anchored by its online bookstore, and also includes online stores offering software, magazines, music, prints and posters, and related products, all seamlessly integrated within B&N.com's website located at www.bn.com.

(Barnes and Noble.com, 1999 Annual Report)

Thus, Barnes & Noble plans to capitalize on all of its marketing channels. In fact, they recently changed their policy to allow books purchased online to be returned to their brick-and-mortar establishments. For the first three quarters of 2000, sales were $215.5 million, up 83 percent from $117.5 for the same period in 1999. Although, the site has been rated number one by Forbes.com as the best bookselling site on the Internet two years running and its music store was named as its favorite online music site, the company has (as of the beginning of 2001) yet to show a profit. Only time will tell if this dot-com will make it into the black.

Increasingly, businesses are examining their environments and their corporate missions to determine whether Web-based commerce is appropriate for them. As businesses conduct formal analyses and determine appropriate uses of Web-based commerce, including marketing methods, more of the established, larger businesses will migrate some

E-Commerce in Practice

Tupperware to Sell on the Web

The party ain't over, but the venerable plastics vendor sees need to try new channels. There will still be parties, but Tupperware Corp. by year's end also will be selling its plastic food containers directly over the Web.

Besides the Web, Orlando, Fla.–based Tupperware will use TV infomercials and shopping mall kiosks—along with the traditional home parties it has used as a marketing tool since the 1950s—to sell its products.

Analysts said Tupperware's about-face on direct sales points to a challenge most manufacturers face today: finding a way to satisfy customers who want to buy online from the manufacturer while not ignoring traditional distribution channels.

Tupperware has had a website for the past few years (*www.tupperware.com*), but it was established mostly for brand awareness purposes and as a means of locating the closest salespeople, said Christine Hanneman, vice president of financial relations at the company. Tupperware has never sold products over the Internet and has kept a tight leash on regional distributors who tried to do so. The idea is not to undercut the local distributors, said Franca Celli, a Tupperware consultant in Canada.

By using the Web, the company plans to reach out to customers "who don't know how to find our products or sales representatives in their areas and who don't want to go to the parties," Hanneman said.

Bigger Audience

Tupperware can reach a broader audience over the Internet, said Lisa Fontenelli, an analyst at Goldman, Sachs & Co.

in New York. The question is how it will standardize pricing for different products in different regions over the Internet, she said.

"Tupperware needs to find a way to respond to the market demand for e-commerce and help make it a plus for their distributors—such as referring follow-on business to a customer's local representative," said Cliff Allen, president of GuestTrack, a Web-personalization software company in Los Angeles.

Source: Roberta Fusaro © *Computerworld Online,* February 8, 1999. *www.computerworld.com*

Update 2000: Tupperwares's strategy appears to be paying off. In October 2000, it announced an incredible growth in profit. For the quarter ended September 30, 2000, its net income increased 71 percent to $6.0 million from $3.5 million in 1999 excluding reengineering costs.

"We're quite pleased to have achieved a double-digit sales increase in local currency this quarter," said Rick Goings, Tupperware chairman and chief executive officer. "These results help to validate the approaches we've been using to take advantage of our growth platforms of increasing the size of our sales force, integrating new sales channels, and enhancing the contribution of new products. In particular, the dramatic sales growth in the United States is evidence that our integrated access strategies—mall showcases, the Internet, and TV shopping—are working together to build the core business."

Source: Quote from Tupperware's 10-23-2000 Press Release.

of their applications to or develop new ones for the WWW. As mentioned in the box entitled "Tupperware to Sell on the Web," businesses may see potential, but they must first examine the business implications of selling their products on the Internet. Will Internet sales cannibalize (serve existing customers) sales from its sales representatives if customers are allowed to place orders on the Web? What role will local sales representatives play in the new structure?

What will happen to the newly created Internet-specific firms as well-established businesses migrate to the Web? If Barnes & Noble's relatively late entry into the WWW market is any indication, the outlook is good for traditional businesses—especially as they enter into strong and interesting new business relationships. In the box entitled "BarnesandNoble.com, Yahoo, and Barnes & Noble Inc. Unite," one such new

E-Commerce in Practice

BarnesandNoble.com, Yahoo, and Barnes & Noble Inc. Unite

In the fall of 2000, BarnesandNoble.com, Barnes & Noble Inc., and Yahoo! Inc. announced a landmark marketing relationship that leverages the online and offline resources of the three companies. In addition, Barnes & Noble superstores and Yahoo! are teaming with Spinway Inc., a leading Internet marketing infrastructure company, which provides a premium cobranded ISP offering, to develop a free Internet service for Barnes & Noble customers.

Under the agreement, BarnesandNoble.com will be the premier bookseller featured throughout the Yahoo! ® directory and a featured merchant on Yahoo! Shopping, recently ranked the No. 1 portal shopping destination on the Web (Neilsen/Netratings, June 2000). This Yahoo! Fusion Marketing program unites two of the most recognizable brands on the Internet and will feature BarnesandNoble.com graphic links on every search results page in the Yahoo! directory and book category pages in the Yahoo! directory.

The in-store retail component of the agreement teams Barnes & Noble Inc. and Yahoo! with Spinway Inc. to develop a free cobranded Internet service for Barnes & Noble retail customers. The service, which is expected to launch in October, will be promoted extensively in 551 Barnes & Noble stores across the country and will include the distribution of CDs to facilitate registrations. By working with Spinway and Yahoo!, Barnes & Noble is able to offer consumers one of the highest-rated Internet access services available with fast, reliable connections; 24-hour customer support; and thousands of local access numbers nationwide. The service is designed to be easy to use, as millions of consumers using Spinway's service are accessing the Internet for the first time.

"Barnes & Noble and Yahoo! consider retail customers as key to the future of the Internet," said Steve Riggio, vice chairman of BarnesandNoble.com. "This agreement provides Yahoo! with access to the tens of millions of upscale, educated Barnes & Noble retail customers, who are among the most sought after demographic groups in the country.

In addition, BarnesandNoble.com will have access to a massive audience of Internet users, as Yahoo!'s reach represents a significant portion of people online today. The rollout of a cobranded free ISP brings terrific value to our retail customers as well as providing a new marketing channel for BarnesandNoble.com."

"By choosing to work with BarnesandNoble.com and Barnes & Noble Inc., we are entering into a broad relationship that leverages the strengths of our combined online and offline assets and provides consumers with a trusted merchant integrated deeply throughout the network and our Yahoo! Shopping platform. Together we are offering consumers comprehensive access to a leading multichannel merchant and the ability to find and purchase resources online that are relevant to them," said Jeffrey Mallett, president and chief operating officer, Yahoo! "This agreement emphasizes Yahoo!'s ongoing strategy to create unique Yahoo! Fusion Marketing programs for leading brand name merchants that achieve their marketing objectives. Working with BarnesandNoble.com and Barnes & Noble Inc. displays our continued commitment to offering convenient, quality resources and services to our millions of users."

"We are pleased to work with Barnes & Noble and Yahoo! to develop a closed loop marketing infrastructure that will drive customer traffic both on- and offline," said Steve Seabolt, chairman and chief executive officer, Spinway Inc.

In addition to placements on all Yahoo! search results and book category pages, BarnesandNoble.com will be a featured merchant within Yahoo! Shopping *(http://shopping.yahoo.com)*. As well as placement on the Yahoo! Shopping front page, BarnesandNoble.com will be featured throughout individual categories in Yahoo! Shopping. BarnesandNoble.com's placement in the directory and throughout the Yahoo! network will direct shoppers to the BarnesandNoble.com site within Yahoo! Shopping.

Source: Excerpts from Press Release—*BarnesandNoble.com.* September 19, 2000.

cobranding opportunity is discussed. Partnering with Yahoo may turn out to be just what BarnesandNoble.com needs to bring it out of the red: During the first half of 2000, Yahoo "directly enabled" transactions worth more than $2 billion. Only time will tell, however, which firms will be the winners and losers in each industry as the dot-com shakeout continues.

THE FOUR Ps APPLIED TO INTERNET MARKETING

Chapter 1 introduces a customer-oriented value chain that places the customer as the center of attention, with information flows passing from a business to its customer for all facets of its operations, except for its own procurement procedures, where the firm interfaces with its suppliers. However, to the extent that a procurement process affects production or delivery of a good, information may be shared with the customer. For example, Insight Enterprises Inc. is electronically linked to nine of its own suppliers. When one of Insight's customers requests the availability of an item not stocked by Insight's warehouse, Insight checks the inventory availability of its suppliers in real time. All of this occurs seamlessly to the customer, who merely receives inventory availability data displayed to it by Insight's computer.

In this section, the four Ps of marketing—product, pricing, place, and promotion—are examined and discussed within the context of the customer-oriented value chain and Internet marketing. Figure 14–5 illustrates the relationship between the customer-oriented value chain and the four Ps and a fifth P—personalization. In essence, the **customer-oriented value chain (COVC) model**, because of its focus on serving the customer during all phases, necessitates the synthesis of marketing techniques into virtually all business processes. Increasingly, firms are concerned with **customer relationship management (CRM).** The information system that brings together the customer and the business with all facets of every business process involved in serving the customer is considered the CRM. In Figure 14–5 the information system in the COVC is considered to be the CRM.

FIGURE 14–5	*The relationship of the five Ps and the customer-oriented value chain*

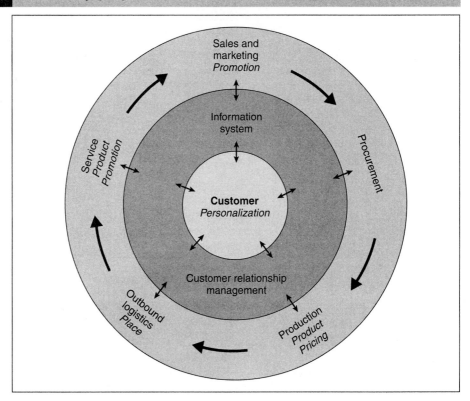

Product

A **product** is a good or service that a business offers to its customers. Without some sort of viable product to offer, a business cannot survive. The product component frequently mentioned in the marketing literature is placed in the production section of the customer-oriented value chain. Traditional **physical goods** generally have a physical, tangible presence and include items such as automobiles, grocery items, and printed newspapers. Traditional **service products** generally involve the performance of a task for the customer; examples include work performed by doctors, accountants, hairdressers, and actors.

The Internet has allowed the creation of new virtual service offerings, such as online news and real-time stock quote services. Distinguishing between goods and services is not always easy (e.g., how do you categorize the output of a movie theater?). The delineation between the two product types becomes even more difficult as new products and variations of old products are created and sold on the Internet. Is an electronic greeting card categorized as a physical good or service product? If the recipient prints the card upon receipt, classifying it as a physical good may seem reasonable. If the recipient merely views it, smiles, and then deletes it, classifying it as a service product may be reasonable. Labeling a product as a physical good or service product is not all that important. Clearly defining the attributes of a product or service and the corresponding benefits that it provides to the consumer is vitally important.

Service provided to the customer *after* the sale is also an important component of the total value of the product to the consumer and may actually be bundled with the product when it is sold. Examples of such bundling include the guaranteed, 24-hour roadside service that accompanies the purchase of a new automobile or the six months' worth of free product upgrades for a virus scanning software package. Postpurchase service to reduce cognitive dissonance (anxiety after purchase) is considered, in some cases, to be part of the actual product sold. The WWW allows new opportunities for after the sales followup and feedback. Software companies offer support bulletin boards, discussion groups, and/or answers to frequently asked questions. Food makers offer recipes and prominently display their website on their products. To the extent a firm builds the service component into prepurchase marketing devices, it can be considered part of the product the customer is buying.

Pricing

The **pricing** of a good refers to the processes involved in determining the amount to charge for a specific physical good or service. Pricing models are typically used to determine a firm's price. The firm's strategy typically dictates the type of pricing model chosen, such as a high-volume, low-price penetration strategy. Physical goods are frequently discounted if a large enough quantity is ordered.

Web-based marketers are already producing interesting pricing strategies. Some sites provide free services for visitors in order to create a community in which it can sell advertising space, such as Parenthood.com discussed later in the chapter. A more dramatic move is for a site to pay customers to use its services. For example, AllAdvantage.com pays its customers to place its viewbar with advertisements at the bottom of its Web browser. New revenue generating models such as this have emerged on the Internet.

Frequent purchase systems are also being used to help strengthen customer loyalty and encourage repeat buying. Because of the development of search engines, discussed in Chapter 13, consumers are easily able to compare prices of many goods offered for sale on the Internet. Online auctions are a popular method for selling items on the Internet. Low minimum prices are typically set, with bidders typically bidding the prices up to a fair price. An interesting method of pricing goods on the Internet is through offers made by consumers. Priceline.com allows buyers to request their own price for airline tickets, hotel reservations, cars, and financing. To filter out nonserious shoppers, requests are binding if they are accepted. Thus, Priceline.com's pricing mechanism is its product!

One question raised by the increased use of the Internet for price comparison is this: Will prices be forced down to the lowest possible point? Clearly, increased competition and consumer buying power will force prices down somewhat, but other items are also important in the purchasing decision (i.e., service, availability, reliability of vendor, and incentives). Further, differential pricing schemes present a challenge for Web-based e-commerce sites. Tupperware Corporation is an international business that sells its products in the U.S., Europe, Asia Pacific, and Latin America. As mentioned in the box on page 442 one of Tupperware's Web commerce design issues is how it will standardize its prices. Thus, price is an extremely important factor in purchasing decisions, but firms engaging in WWW e-commerce must also develop value-based pricing strategies, which "call for increasing perceived value and then setting the price at a level compatible with that value."[1] Those businesses that charge a premium have the challenge of providing their WWW customers with premium service and possibly premium products. As mentioned in the update to the box, Tupperware is achieving success in a premium marketplace.

Place (Distribution)

Place is frequently referred to as outbound logistics or distribution. The **distribution** task entails moving the product from the producer to the customer. The product may travel directly from the producer to the consumer or it may be channeled through intermediaries, such as wholesalers, warehouses, and/or retailers. Tupperware's distribution channels have changed as a result of the changes to its business strategy to incorporate Web-based sales. Inventory items can now be shipped, if desired, directly to the consumer without the necessity of first being delivered to its local distributors.

E-commerce involving the sale of physical goods can be very useful in exchanging information between businesses and delivery companies. The interfacing of sales or purchasing systems with delivery companies enables faster pick up of goods from warehouses and shop floors for faster delivery to the customer. Insight Enterprises Inc. has formed a strategic alliance with Federal Express, so that FedEx performs a valuable service by providing timely deliveries direct from its own suppliers to its customers, bypassing the need to warehouse many items.

The physical Internet itself is also a delivery channel for digital products. **Digital products** are goods that are comprised of digitally encoded software, data, or multimedia files. Delivery of such products can occur instantaneously in real time. It is 2:00 A.M., and a customer needs a software package to translate a business document into Spanish. The stores are closed and a physically shipped product will not arrive for 18 hours. The customer can go to an online store that, upon digital receipt and verification of credit card information, downloads a copy of an English-Spanish business document translation software package. Sale and distribution are both completed in less time than it would take to drive to a store (if the store was open!). Some Internet merchants, such as online news services, electronic greeting cards, and stock trading systems, digitally de-

---

[1]W. Keegan, S. Moriarty, and T. Duncan, *Marketing,* 2nd Ed. Prentice-Hall, 1995.

liver their products. This electronic distribution channel opens up vast new markets for sellers of digital products. These sellers have a very cheap, fast channel to distribute their products anywhere in the world connected to the Internet. The only potential impediments are theft of digital data, such as unauthorized copies of music and movies, and international legal issues as discussed in Chapters 5 and 6.

Promotion

The sales and marketing function is a separate entity in the customer-oriented value chain, and the activities performed in this capacity fall under the traditional marketing category called promotion. The successful **promotion** of a product requires that, at a minimum, a positive message be received by potential customers. This message may be communicated in many ways:

- Paid advertising channels.
- News stories and press releases.
- Word of mouth.
- Consumers' personal experiences.
- Packaging.

The first technique, **paid advertising channels,** is a common method used by companies. Typically a firm will have an advertising budget, and the funds are allocated among many competing advertising media, such as newspaper, magazine, direct-mail, television, radio, billboards, special events, etc. Using the Internet to create an awareness of products is a relatively low-cost and increasingly effective medium. Internet marketing firms are aggressively selling their services to businesses. These marketing firms, discussed later in the chapter, provide the service of attracting WWW users to specific client websites.

Because paid advertising requires cash outlays, marketing groups attempt to track the success or effect of the marketing funds spent. As illustrated in Figure 14–6, these types of tracking mechanisms are often very difficult to perform with any precision because of the simultaneous use of multiple media. The ability to specifically identify which mechanism(s) caused the consumer to buy the product or service is a challenging, and sometimes impossible, task.

The advertising channels in Figure 14–6 are labeled as either one-way or two-way channels. **One-way channels** send a message to the potential customer, but do not provide a direct mechanism for communication to the business. Examples of one-way communication include radio, roadside bulletin boards, television, magazines, newspaper, and most direct mail. **Two-way channels** send the message to the potential customer and provide a direct mechanism for communication from the potential customer to the business. Examples of two-way channels include some direct mail via phone responses and inquiries, infomercials via phone responses and inquiries, telemarketing, website advertising via forms-based input, e-mail with hypertext links to interactive websites or via a reply function, and Web banners that link to interactive websites.[2]

Just because two-way channels have the capability for two-way communications does not necessarily mean that they are always designed as such. For example, some websites are solely information providers and do not allow the visitor to do much other

---

[2]Inserts with mail-order forms or 800 numbers in newspapers and magazines are also examples of two-way communication.

| **FIGURE 14–6** | *Alternative paid marketing channels* |

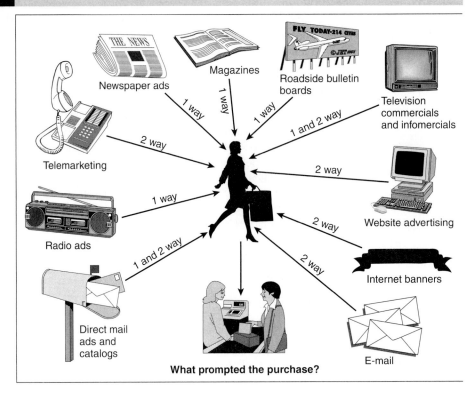

What prompted the purchase?

than read a few pages of printed matter and view a few pictures. When taking full advantage of highly interactive two-way channels, such as websites, the potential customer can receive advertisements in a more personalized fashion, as discussed in a later section. This is a way to track effectiveness that was never before possible.

In addition to the paid advertising mediums, three additional, very powerful advertising mechanisms are available: **news stories, word of mouth,** and **consumers' personal experiences.** The message sent out by these mechanisms can be positive or negative. Negative messages can be very detrimental to a company's success, while positive messages can help to strengthen a company's reputation and sales base. Controlled advertising mechanisms are important because word of mouth is not controllable, and the Internet allows both to occur with a new speed and reach.

Companies that decide to use the Internet are using a new advertising channel. If the website is poorly designed, not user-friendly, lacking in information, or slow to respond to visitors' commands, this reflects negatively on the business. Some businesses have rushed to open a website, just because it seemed the fashionable thing to do and is relatively cheap compared with other advertising channels. Unfortunately, these sites wind up disappointing the visitor and leave some business executives doubting the power of the Internet as an effective marketing channel. These same business executives would not consider placing a poorly designed commercial on television or photograph in a magazine, yet the same attention has not always been given to website design. In some cases, the mistakes made in website design are merely due to inexperience in website design issues. In fact, traditional print rules and guidelines do not necessarily translate to good website design, and they can actually be quite different. Thus, **digital packaging** becomes very important to the message being conveyed.

Other aspects of the promotion function exist outside of the traditional sales and marketing function as illustrated in Figure 14–5. The *service* that accompanies a product can be used to promote an item. If the service component becomes an integral component of the product over time and becomes expected by the customer, it can arguably be categorized as part of the product. How do you categorize a virus scanning package that allows unlimited software upgrades during a six-month period via the Internet for newly found viruses? Is this a service provided by the software company to promote its software? Is this type of service expected by consumers buying scanning software? In this case, the answer to both questions is yes. Initially, this type of service was provided to promote the sale of virus scanning software, but over time, it has come to be expected by consumers.

Another aspect of promotion is the sharing of information with customers. Businesses are increasingly informing customers beyond inventory availability, price, and product details. Customers are receiving information regarding the shipping status of products, and the sharing of such information is often used as a promotional tool. FedEx pioneered this concept by allowing its customers to track the progress of the delivery of their packages. Many online merchants, such as Amazon.com and Wine.com, keep their customers informed of the status of their orders and send messages to the customer informing them when the items are actually shipped and when they can expect to receive them.

THE FIFTH P—PERSONALIZATION

The Internet is leading marketers to a fundamental paradigm shift from mass marketing to personalized marketing. Databases, cookies, and telecommunications technology make it very easy and cost efficient to mass market personalized services. Although "mass marketed, personalized service" sounds like an oxymoron, it is not. **Personalization** on the Internet refers to the ability of customers to receive personalized information (e.g., sales advertisements or coupons) or visit a website with a home page customized for them (e.g., their favorite stock quotes prominently displayed by their browser software.) Personalization crosses the boundaries of two of the marketing Ps, product and promotion, because it has the potential to affect and enhance both. Because personalization is automated and it is at the core of many Internet marketing methods, it is deemed important enough to hold its own category. In Figure 14–5, personalization is placed in the domain of the customer because it is defined and controlled by the customer.

Most of the examples of Internet marketing given in the following sections are examples of such mass-marketed, personalized services. Hallmark has a successful website from which it provides free e-mail greeting cards, as well as hard-copy cards that can be sent. It mass markets its products, but through the use of databases it is able to store information about its visitors and provide a personalized, free service for them: reminding individuals of important events, such as birthdays, anniversaries, and graduations. Greetings can be prearranged months in advance of the desired send date so that the customer does not have to worry about forgetting an important occasion. Increasingly, websites greet return visitors by name and suggest items for them to examine based on prior preferences. Additionally, some sites allow the user to configure his or her own home page for its site that best suits the visitor.

Toffler's Powershift—Knowledge as Power[3]

Personalization represents simultaneously the extreme challenge and opportunity present in the form of Internet medium. Personalization of marketing-related tasks and activities on the Internet can take numerous forms, but clearly the most intriguing form of personalization enabled by the Internet is the proactive format, sometimes referred to as **manual customization.** This is the category of transaction in which the consumer assumes the initiative for the bulk of information, communication, transaction, and distribution activities.

Viewed in the context of the traditional producer–consumer relationship, the consumer has not only acquired additional power but also enhanced the nature of this power. A review of Toffler's[4] three sources of power—force, wealth, and knowledge—helps to explain the power shift consumers are currently realizing. The emphasis in our discussion is on the latter source of power. The true power of today's consumer is knowledge. At the core of this knowledge lies the universe of information now available to consumers— quite literally at their fingertips. At any hour of the day or night, for example, consumers can log onto the Internet and obtain a vast amount of information on literally any topic.

What separates this approach from traditional consumer information acquisition is the scope and, in many cases, the relative objectivity of the information. Previously, consumers were very limited in their ability to access this level of unbiased marketing information (non-marketer-initiated) except for a select number of situations, such as acquiring information on a potential auto purchase by calling a *Consumer Reports'* reader service number and requesting information via fax.

This illustration is a mere microcosm of an Internet-enabled information search process that is currently available and that will soon precede transactions of all shapes and sizes. The demand for such information is undoubtedly an outgrowth of changing demographics and advanced technologies. However, while the consumer's penchant for value has remained constant, his or her perception of value has been shaped by an abundance of information and a chronic lack of time. Since 1969, the annual work hours of employed Americans have risen by 140 hours.[5] With more households consisting of one or both parents working outside the home, the buying public's lack of time has translated into a desire or, perhaps more aptly, a demand for convenience and service. Consumers want increased control over their consumption choices, and they want a reliable, quality product specific to their needs. Moreover, time constraints have forced consumers to demand immediate fulfillment of their needs. The union of these forces of demographics, information, and control has formed the backdrop for the rise of personalized consumer power.

Marketing Implications of the Consumer Power Shift

Building Relationships through Database Marketing

What does **consumer power shift** mean, and what are the implications for globally networked firms? The power pendulum swinging clearly toward the consumer represents a fundamental shift from a consumer–producer relationship of the past toward a marketing exchange relationship today. In the past, marketing was essentially driven by a single trans-

---

[3]James Maskulka, D.BA., Associate Professor of Marketing, Lehigh University, contributed to this section. This section and the one that immediately follows were adapted from a manuscript entitled "Consumer Driven Marketing: Riding the Interactive Wave," by James Maskulka and Karen L. Mackrides.

[4]Alvin Toffler, *Powershift.* Bantam Books, 1990, p. 17.

[5]Coopers & Lybrand. Response Analysis Corporation and Arlen Communications Inc. "Electronic Access: A Multi-Company Study." New York, 1994, p. 6.

action. Today, the focus has shifted toward repeated transactions, or building a consumer relationship. Futurist Joel Arthur Barker has identified the growth in consumer power, along with environmentalism and personal computers, as a leading paradigm shift that has occurred since the 1960s.[6] For marketers, this transformation means listening instead of telling and asking instead of acting. Service and customer satisfaction come to the forefront of the marketing focus. Indeed, marketing trends have already begun to reflect this growing emphasis on the consumer. Industry trends captured by terminology such as micromarketing, mass customization, smart selling, and smart products, reflect a growing corporate awareness aimed at understanding a specific customer's needs and responding effectively to meet those needs. It is basic marketing with a new, but very important twist: an increased focus on information gathering, data warehousing, consumer purchase behavior monitoring, and future purchase patterns predictions through modeling.

Customer-Oriented Marketing: Emergence of the Personalized Transaction Domain

A fundamental shift is occurring between producer and consumer; technology-enabled consumers are actively participating in activities, tasks, and decisions that were once the sole domain of the marketer. The basic premise is that actionable knowledge is power, and the current technology has provided the consumer with this missing component. The term coined to capture this emerging paradigm between consumer and producer is the **personalized transaction domain.** In the past, consumers' decisions were primarily limited to purchase and consumption; today, through the enabling power of technology, consumers are able to design products from their homes and store and access information at their convenience. From the marketer's perspective, this reduction in the traditional value-enhancing opportunities fundamentally alters the way marketers will interact with consumers.

Customer-Oriented Marketing—The Relentless Search for Value

While the typical consumer has always had an intuitive sense of value, he or she has become far more discriminating as to what actually constitutes value. The power over the traditional transaction domain that consumers now savor has been driven by their comprehension of their ability to convert information into value. This added dimension of information into the value equation signifies not only a paradigmatic shift in power, but also a fundamental change in the nature of consumer power—a **value sphere.** In this context of perceived value, Barker's paradigm shift, Toffler's powershift, and the personalized transaction domain coalesces into a **customer-oriented value sphere** that is characterized by three dimensions:

   • Consumers are not merely limited to existing assortments, but now have the ability to create choices by reconfiguring information disseminated by producers.
   • Consumers increasingly have the ability to participate at their discretion in the degree of value creation as it relates to the exchange transaction and at any point in the customer-oriented value sphere.
   • Consumers have become increasingly proactive in initiating transactions. Timeliness and context of the offer have assumed an elevated prominence in the creation of value. Absolute time has the most inelastic demand curve of all commodities.

Thus, consumers are increasingly initiating, shaping, and controlling the terms of a transaction in an emerging Internet paradigm called the customer-oriented value sphere.

---

[6]J. S. Collins, "The Business of Paradigms," *Business and Economic Review,* January/March 1992.

INTERNET MARKETING TECHNIQUES

As mentioned earlier in this chapter, the Internet provides a new advertising medium, but to categorize it as a single medium is not really accurate. Many different advertising mechanisms exist on the Internet, each varying in its cost and ability to reach targeted customers. Figure 14–7 illustrates a continuum of Internet marketing techniques, ranging from passive to aggressive. In this section, a range of Internet marketing techniques that fall along this continuum are discussed.

Internet marketing techniques are considered to be **passive advertising** if they require visitors to seek out the site. In a pure sense, passive techniques are considered to be those methods that require the user to "pull" the information from the website. Conversely, Internet marketing techniques are considered to be **aggressive advertising** if the site actively seeks out potential customers and initiates contact with them. In a pure sense, aggressive techniques are considered to be those techniques in which the website "pushes" the information onto the consumer, regardless of whether the consumer is interested or not. Most techniques fall somewhere in between true passive and aggressive techniques. As mentioned in the previous section, personalized service is a key component to many effective WWW advertising techniques. Figure 14–8 illustrates how an individual may use Web-based systems throughout the day for both personal and business use. The activities illustrated in Figure 14–8, for the most part, fall into the middle portions on the continuum in Figure 14–7. How commercial e-mail is sent, passively or aggressively, is important. According to The eMail Marketing Report conducted by eMarketer.com, solicited, commercial e-mail message volume reached approximately 64 billion in 2000, accounting for 12 percent of total U.S. email. In the United States, e-mail accountholders are predicted to receive 31 of these per week by 2003.

| **FIGURE 14–7** | *Internet marketing continuum from passive to aggressive* |

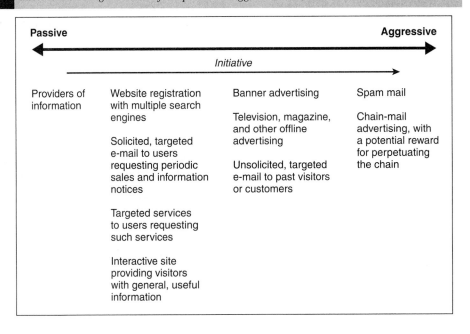

FIGURE 14–8 *Internet marketing and pull and push technologies*

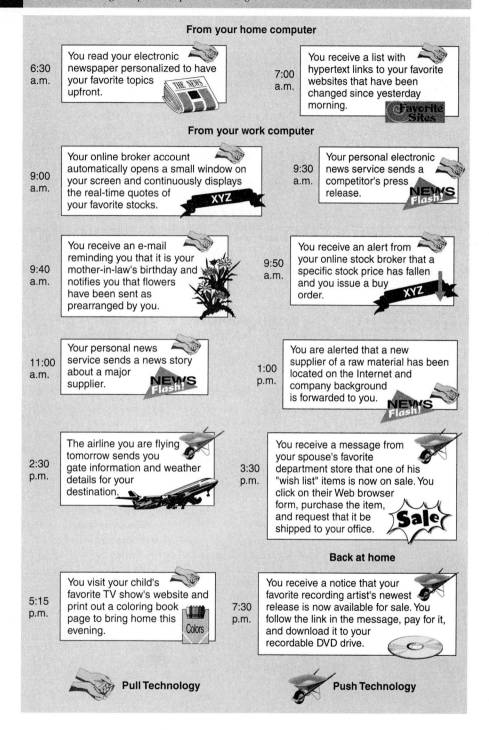

Passive Providers of Information

Lying on the far side of the continuum, closest to the passive end, are websites that build a site and do not actively promote it by registering with a directory or search engine or by using any other online advertising technique. Inevitably, these sites will be picked up by search engines. These types of websites may be created to provide a corporate presence on the Internet for those individuals seeking out information. Established businesses sometimes enter the WWW launching this type of website. They are not seeking out customers or visitors, but they want the site to be present if current or potential customers wish to locate information about their company or products. Generally, this type of site indicates that the company has not yet identified a strategic use for Web-based commerce. These are typically low-cost sites that generate little interest or enthusiasm by visitors.

Search Engine and Directory Registration

Moving along the continuum are firms that take more initiative to either attract visitors to their site or to interact with them. One way that firms can attract visitors to their informational site is to register with directories and search engines. A discussion of search engines and directories and their registration processes and methods are presented later in this chapter. An example of such a site is a legal practice's site, legalcounselor.com, that provides information about its law practice and attorneys and provides some articles written by its attorneys, as well as phone and e-mail contacts for interested potential clients.

Solicited, Targeted E-Mail

E-mail marketing has become a popular medium because of its relatively low-cost and the ability to send HTML messages containing full-color pictures of products, as well as links to order form pages. The transmittal of a message to a **solicited, targeted e-mail** list is a method used to attract visitors to a website that requires acts by both the website and the visitor. This mechanism allows a business to maintain regular contact with customers and drive traffic to websites or other products. These types of arrangements are mutually beneficial and can be a great information source for customers/users and a wonderful advertising mechanism to help businesses unload unwanted inventory or notify interested parties of requested information. These types of relationships are typically initiated by the business offering an information service to its visitor. If the visitor is interested, he or she can sign up for the service. The amount of information required to register can vary by site. Typically, the more information required, the fewer interested parties a site can expect to receive.

Because the user requests the information, this type of Internet marketing technique is considered to be "pulled" by the consumer with the help of the website. From the website's perspective, it can also be considered to be a "soft push," since the site encourages the distribution of information and provides it. Examples of these types of activities can be found in Figure 14–8: e-mail reminding the user of a family member's birthday, an alert from an online stock broker of a specific stock position, and notification that a specific merchandise item has gone on sale from your spouse's registered wish list. Some other specific examples include

- News "pull" services offered by ananova.com, computerworld.com, and numerous other services.

E-Commerce in Practice

DoubleClick to Buy NetCreation in $191 Million Stock Deal

DoubleClick Inc. announced today that it was acquiring Net-Creations Inc. for $191 million in stock. The Internet marketer hopes to expand its base with the purchase of the "opt-in" e-mail marketing company, also based in New York.

NetCreations has had an impressive beginning despite being "a little off with their revenue projections" recently, said analyst Christopher Todd at Jupiter Communications Inc. in New York. NetCreations is one of the leaders in e-mail marketing, he said, along with Andover, Mass.–based CMGI Inc.'s Yesmail.com and Lifeminders Inc.

The stock-for-stock transaction will give DoubleClick access to 22 million e-mail addresses and give NetCreations access to DoubleClick's international business and sales operations. "It's absolutely a great deal for DoubleClick," Todd said. "They've been struggling for about a year trying to put out an e-mail product."

NetCreations has a "double opt-in" system, which is used by some of its clients, such as ABC's Sportsline.com.

For example, users sign up for updates from Sportsline and receive an e-mail. They must reply to the e-mail to confirm that they want the updates and to be registered for the mailing list, or they can "unsubscribe."

The NetCreations program also allows users to sign up for other general interest areas, which are then confirmed via e-mail.

Once NetCreations has a user signed up for those interest areas, it can then rent the list to companies that sell products and services in those categories.

Then the initial site, such as Sportsline, gets a fee for NetCreations' access to site visitors, a fee for attracting a user to the network or some combination of the two, depending on how the deal is structured.

DoubleClick has operations in more than 20 countries.

Source: Jennifer Disabatino, © *Computerworld Online,* October 23, 2000. *www.computerworld.com*

- Product update information offered by many software and hardware vendors, such as McAfee Virus products.
- Company press releases, such as those offered by Hershey's corporate page.
- Specific shopping news for out-of-stock items, such as that offered by Amazon.com.

Similar to the preceding example is an Internet marketing technique in which a site offers a service to its visitors or customers. In many of these cases, these services are provided for a fee, but some sites have services they provide to existing customers for free. An example of this from Figure 14–8 is the notification of a news story about a pre-specified competitor. The box entitled "Doubleclick to Buy Netcreation in $191 Million Stock Deal" explains the magnitude of such solicited, targeted e-mail services.

Interactive Sites

Some sites may exhibit initiative to attract initial and subsequent visitors to their site by providing general information in an interactive fashion, typically with the hope of generating goodwill with the visitor so that he or she may use the site's services either on or off-line. An example of such an **interactive site** from Figure 14–8 is the ability to visit a website and choose a page from a coloring book to print for one's child such as that provided by crayola.com. Another example, not found in Figure 14–8, may be an attorney who has a Web page with frequently asked questions about certain kinds of legal services. The attorney may not sell anything tangible on the Internet, but the site may allow visitors to receive "free" legal definitions that may help them to better understand their own situations and determine whether they may or may not need an attorney. Also, sites that allow the customer to configure and view his or her own product fall under this category, such as customizing a car at Ford.com or Honda.com.

Banner Advertising

Moving along the continuum to slightly more aggressive advertising techniques are those that use online banner advertising, offline advertising, and targeted, but unsolicited e-mail. Online banner advertising, a service sold by Internet marketing firms, can be very effective. Firms pay these companies a fee to flash advertising banners with links to a business' site across the pages of other sites. These services can be relatively costly compared with the methods discussed thus far in this section, but they can yield results. A major advantage is that the banner's effectiveness, in terms of attracting visitors to a site, is easily monitored. Such companies as Ameritrade and Microsoft use banner advertisements. Banner advertising is discussed in more detail later in this chapter.

Offline Advertising

Another method used to promote web sites is **offline advertising,** such as television, radio, and print. These advertising mechanisms are also relatively more costly than previously mentioned methods in this section. In the 1999 Super Bowl, Victoria's Secret made history by logging an unprecedented 1.5 million viewers to its site. Intimate Brands heavily invested in television, print, and online ads to promote its first Victoria's Secret website live fashion show. In addition to many national and local televisions slots, Intimate Brands invested in the highest priced advertising event of the year—the Super Bowl. Additionally, they placed advertisements in many highly regarded newspapers, such as *The Wall Street Journal, USA Today, Barron's* and *The New York Times.* In fact, approximately 75 percent of the advertising dollars spent promoting this online event went toward offline advertising. The advertising was considered a success since many more visitors than expected attempted to view the live fashion show. In fact, the offline advertising blitz was such a success that many would-be visitors never got connected to the site and many of those that did experienced delays. In October 2000, Victoria's Secret's executives announced that they expect their Internet sales to triple for the year. They have continued the integrated marketing approach, primarily using offline advertising.

Unsolicited, Targeted E-Mail

Another method of on-line advertising that entails the web site business taking initiative is **unsolicited, targeted e-mail advertising** to past visitors or customers. This type of advertising is somewhat aggressive in that the visitor or customer does not specifically request additional sales or promotion items. When conducted properly, these methods can be effective (e.g., sending only a few advertisements to past customers and discontinuing the e-mails if the former customer does not return to the site during that period). The use of cookies enables the tracking of customers' responses to such e-mail advertisements. When abused, these methods can result in an irritation factor. For example, if a previous customer is continuously bombarded with e-mail sales promotions, he or she may find it annoying and even begin to block such incoming messages. According to Jupiter Communications, the average yearly messages per consumer is expected to reach approximately 1,600 by 2002. Thus, marketers need to realize that users will begin to screen more and more e-mail because of the increased volume. From a financial cost perspective, the site sending the messages may say "so what," but from a customer relations perspective, this type of action can generate negative attitudes on the part of the customer toward the business. The challenge is to send e-mail that will get attention and not to send too much of it!

Spam Mail

Even more aggressive tactics to attract customers is the sending of unsolicited e-mail advertisements to individuals or businesses that have never visited the site. The e-mail addresses may be purchased or traded with another business. Another method of obtaining e-mail addresses is use to software robots to scan the WWW and collect addresses from public sources such as Usenet postings. Direct-mail advertisers have used this method for years, flooding the postal mail boxes with what many term "junk mail." The online equivalent of junk-mail that is sent out repeatedly is referred to as **spam mail.** Spam is referred to as "postage due marketing" because the thousands of messages (even millions) sent reside on the recipients' host computers until they are deleted, and the storage of such messages cost businesses money. Multitudes of software packages exist that allow users to filter out mail from sites known to send spam mail. Other methods of filtering are to filter mail with certain words, such as "for only $" or "free" that are typically found in promotions. Of course, a legitimate message may contain those words and would be filtered as well. Spam mail is viewed negatively by the public and groups such as the Coalition Against Unsolicited Commercial Email (CAUCE) and the Responsible Electronic Communication Alliance have emerged in the United States, Europe and Australia, as well as other countries to fight for spam mail regulation. In July 2000, the U.S. House of Representatives passed a bill that, if passed into law, would make it illegal to send e-mail messages to recipients who asked not to receive such mail. The European Union is considering similar regulation. Additional spam mail regulatory issues were covered in Chapter 5.

ONLINE ADVERTISING MECHANISMS

Attracting visitors to websites is a key component to a successful Web-based commerce site. Because e-mail advertising has already been discussed, this section discusses the remaining primary online mechanisms for promoting sites and attracting visitors: directories, search engines, banners, sponsoring, and coupons. New mechanisms for delivering products and services online are continuously emerging, such as "free PCs." However, you never get something for nothing; the recipient must view a prespecified amount of targeted online advertising in exchange for the "free" computer, most of which are e-mail and banner advertisements.

For businesses that provide a service, such as online news, online magazines, search engines, and Web browsers, their sites are supported by advertising revenues, and these revenues are crucial to these sites. The most common sources of revenue come from allowing advertisers to pay for banners on their sites or to be listed as a site sponsor. The following sections review advertising options available to businesses wishing to promote their site. Keep in mind, however, that many services provided on the Internet rely on the advertising revenues from businesses willing to pay to promote their sites from these popularly visited "service" sites. The box entitled "ParenthoodWeb" illustrates the advertising and sponsorship opportunities offered by ParenthoodWeb.com, an online community for parents and expecting parents. The information in this box is the actual information provided by this company to potential advertisers, and it illustrates the selling of banner space; sponsorships; and targeted, solicited e-mail lists.

Directories

Directory services on the WWW provide an index that lists and provides links to websites. The sites may be listed in one of many ways: alphabetically, or by subject, category, or region, such as the directories found on Yahoo.com. For those indexes listed by category, the registrant of the site specifies the category. The correct choice of a category is important because the user navigates through the directory and may not find the site if it is categorized differently than expected by the visitor. Unfortunately, many directory services have multiple categories that can accurately depict many businesses.

Currently, websites can be registered at no charge to a number of directory services, such as Infoseek, Internet Mall, The Yellow Pages, and Yahoo. Other directories, such as Galaxy, may charge a fee (currently $25). Registering with multiple directories is important in order to cast as wide a net as possible and because users are traversing the net using many different directories. Many ISPs that serve as website hosts register the sites with many of these directories as a service. A waiting time of two to three weeks is typical because many of the directory services screen the new sites for illegal or illicit material, such as pornography.

E-Commerce in Practice

ParenthoodWeb

The ParenthoodWeb family, including ABC's of Parenting, RecipeXchange.com, and eSafety.com, offers advertisers a unique opportunity to reach a targeted audience of parents and expecting parents. Our extensive and informative pages take visitors through a guide to parenting—from tracking the growth of their unborn baby from conception to birth, naming their new child, talking with experts on sleeping habits, and other parenting issues—to finding an appropriate daycare. (Visit our Site Map for more details.) And that's only the beginning.

ParenthoodWeb has been recognized by respected industry sources as a must-visit site on the Internet and a definite resource for parenting and childcare information. Articles and television features in *Newsweek, Redbook, Better Homes and Gardens,* Microsoft Network, NBC, ABC, and CNET have chronicled our site. Other websites such as NetGuide Live, Webcrawler, and Excite have given ParenthoodWeb their highest ratings.

Thousands of parents spend as long as an hour every day on ParenthoodWeb to seek and offer advice, learn from our panel of experts, and compare experiences with other parents. Learn how our targeted niche can help your company gain valued customers through a customized advertising campaign at ParenthoodWeb.

Demographics

A recent survey of our visitors showed the following results regarding our audience demographics:

- 87 percent of ParenthoodWeb visitors are women.
- 75 percent of the women are mothers.
- 30 percent are currently pregnant.
- 91 percent of ParenthoodWeb visitors are parents.
- 83 percent of our audience is between the ages of 18 and 44.
- 78 percent have children under the age of 6 or are expecting children.
- Of our visitors with children, 71 percent of these children are between the ages of birth to age 6.
- 91 percent of our audience is college-educated.
- Our visitors' mean income is $62,431.
- 41 percent have a household income over $80,000.

Traffic

October 2000 site traffic on ParenthoodWeb shows

- Number of hits to site: 52,306,366.
- Monthly page views (impressions): 3,509,944.
- Average hits per day: 1,687,301.
- Unique users per month: 546,565.
- Average length of stay: 21 minutes, 54 seconds.

Rates

Our standard rate card is as follows for 468 × 60 sized, run-of-site, top-of-page banner ads:

Three-Month Order:

Impressions	CPM	Price per Month
100,000	$25	$2,500
150,000	20	$3,000
200,000 +	20	$4,000

Rates are also available for one- and two-month orders.

The number of impressions delivered is guaranteed. There are many options advertising on ParenthoodWeb. Let us put together a customized package for you. Pricing generally varies depending on content, placement, and length of the campaign.

Banner Sizes/Media Types

ParenthoodWeb supports standard GIF banners, animated GIF banners, HTML/form-based banners, and Java-enhanced and Enliven rich-media banners. We prefer banner sizes be no more than 11k.

We have the flexibility to work with advertisers on different sizes of banners. Pricing of these packages vary depending on the exact placement, the size of the ad, and the specific pages the ad appears on.

Banner Size	CPM	Description
468×60	$35	Traditional
156×356	50	Did you know box
125×125	25	Square button
120×60	20	Right-side bar button
234×60	10	Half-banner bottom-of-page

List Your Website on Our Shopping Channel

The ParenthoodWeb Shopping Channel is growing. We currently have 11 different categories within this channel.

To post a listing in one of these categories costs $500 per month. Discounts may apply with a year commitment; be sure to ask one of our sales representatives for details. A category listing includes a 120×60 logo along with a 100-word-or-less description of the website in one of the categories, as well as a listing in the Quick Picks by Store pull-down menu on the Shopping page. For an additional $50 per month, an individual product may be listed on the Quick Picks by Product pull-down menu. An additional $200 per month will list a website under Recommended Picks on the home Shopping page. This link may be graphic (234×60) or a text link.

Tracking and Reporting

All ParenthoodWeb ads are served through Doubleclick, one of the leading third-party ad serving companies in the industry. We are also willing to work with advertisers and their ad agencies to accommodate special ad delivery requests. We furnish comprehensive reports detailing impressions and click-thru performance on a weekly basis, or clients can choose to have online access to their campaigns via DoubleClick.

Sponsorship Opportunities

We also offer unique sponsorship opportunities, promotional contests, and custom mini-sites. Be sure to outline your needs when you contact us.

Newsletter Sponsorships

The ParenthoodWeb Newsletter is distributed every Saturday to approximately 55,000 (and rising) parents and parents-to-be who have requested to join our weekly mailing list. The newsletter features articles, poll results, recall information, and many summaries from the ParenthoodWeb website. The newsletter is fully HTML-enabled (the newsletter looks just like a web page) and offers advertisers a terrific opportunity to reach our target audience for a fraction of the cost of standard banner ads. Not only do we feature your 468×60 banner (see allowable media types above), but we will also feature a two- to three-sentence advertising message directly in each mailing. The rate for one of our weekly newsletter sponsorships is $1,000. Only one sponsor appears in each weekly newsletter distribution.

The ParenthoodWeb Newsletter is a great investment for your company. But don't just take our word for it. A review from Ad/Insight at ChannelSeven.com stated, "After reading [the newsletter], I was interested in visiting the site again."

E-Commerce in Practice

ParenthoodWeb—continued

Targeted E-Mail Lists

Many ParenthoodWeb visitors have chosen to join a popular service called "opt-in" mailing lists. Visitors tell us what kind of information they would like to receive from advertisers such as you. Requested topics include family, clothing, catalogs, flowers, cooking, children's products, the outdoors, computers, automobiles, as well as hundreds of other topics. We rent out these lists for a very reasonable cost (10 to 30 cents per name, including list rental, e-mail delivery, and merge/print) and will handle all aspects of the mailing for you. This is not spam! All of our list members have requested your mailings. What's more, targeted e-mail distributions have proven to offer advertisers the highest response rate of any type of direct marketing. To learn more about this unique opportunity be sure to visit our list management partner, PostMasterDirect, by contacting www.postmasterdirect.com.

Source: This information was taken from the following site. Additional rates are available on the site that are not listed here.
http://www.parenthoodweb.com/parent_cfmfiles/mediakit_ratecard.html

---

Search Engines

Using search engines is a more popular method of finding sites than the use of directories. Specifically, web **search engines** take user-defined strings and boolean expressions (such as AND and OR) and return a list of closely matched websites in the order of the closeness of match. The search engines periodically "crawl" through the Internet looking for new pages and update their existing databases. The frequency with which these engines perform updates and the range of their crawl (the number of locations examined) affects the number of sites indexed and the currency of the sites listed.

When designing a Web page, certain features can increase a site's hit rates and ranking. Understanding what these terms mean and how to design a site with them in mind is important. **Hit rates** are the number of matches found between user requests and a web site, while **ranking** is the assigned relevancy score given by the search engine. This score directly affects the order of the listing of a site relevant to other sites meeting the criteria. The further down the list the site is located, the less likely the user will find the site. If they cannot find the site, they cannot visit it! Discussed here are some criteria by which search engines index sites and rank them. Each search engine works a little bit differently and that is why different search engines yield slightly different results. Increasingly, search engines are charging a fee for premium listing of sites for search results. For example, Go.com charges $199 per URL.

Before each of these methods is discussed, three common Hypertext Markup Language (HTML) tags are explained that may affect a site's ranking. The **keyword tag** is used to identify key words for search engines that use this information. The **description tag** is the body of text that is returned by the search engine to describe the contents of the web site and may be used for ranking as well. The **title tag** is typically returned at the top of the listing returned by the search engine and also may be used for ranking. An example of the relevant source code found on Crayola.com's home page follows:

Keyword Tag:
```
<meta name="Keywords" content="art, crafts, creativity, imagination, projects,
activity, activities, coloring, colouring, lesson plans, creative fun, art ideas, art edu-
```

cation, curriculum, family fun, family activities, activity pages, crayon, e-cards, electronic cards, free email, e-mail, chalk, color, coloring book, crayons, draw, paint, Drawing, Educational, mark, markers, paint, paint, painting, painting, pen, pencils, pens, pens, post, pre-school, early childhood, artists, printable pages, curriculum ideas, web cards.">

Description Tag:

<meta name=“Description” content=“Kids, parents and educators find creative solutions, colorful ideas and fun development ideas at crayola.com”>

Title Tag:

<title>Crayola Creativity Central</title>

Note how coloring is spelled two ways in the keyword tag: coloring and colouring. This is done because of the differences between the U.S. way of spelling and the British way of spelling. A site would not want to miss out on visitors because of societal differences in spelling. Some search engines consider a word to be very important for that site and thus cause its rating to be high for searches using that word if it is repeated frequently throughout the page. Caution must be exercised, however, because some website designers have abused this feature and caused search engine designers to take this abuse into account. These abuses are called **search engine spamming** and can be accomplished in a number of ways. One way is to list the word consecutively, time after time, in the keywords section. Repeating a word only a few times is not generally considered spamming, as in the crayola.com example. The occasional repetition of a few words, such as crayola and "family activities" scattered throughout the keywords section is generally accepted. Family activities is surrounded in quotes so that these words when entered into a search engine together will result in a higher score than if they are considered as separate words.

Another method of search engine spamming is to repeat a word all over the page using the same color text as the background so the visitor will not see the word, but the search engine will. This type of activity is generally not rewarded any longer and can result in the site being dropped from the indexes or severely downgraded in its relevancy ranking. The best advice is to find ways to legitimately repeat key words in the keyword tag, description tag, title tag, and the text contained in the body of the page. Finally, most search engines will index linked pages as well as the home page, so additional submissions for each page are not generally necessary.

Some search engines place weight on search words that are found in the HTML keyword and **metatags,** such as those illustrated above in the crayola.com example. Sometimes more importance is given to words in the title tag than the keyword or description tag.

Banners

Historically, the most popular form of online advertising used to attract visitors to a site has been banner advertising, approximately 53 percent according to the Internet Advertising Bureau (IAB) in 1999. The eadvertising Report, however, predicts that figure will decline to 26 percent of web advertisement sales in 2001 as firms switch to other online advertising methods, most notably sponsorships. Typically rectangular in shape, **banner advertisements** contain text and graphics that are placed on the screens of search engines, Web browser software, and websites to attract the attention of WWW users. These banners are typically about 60 pixels high and 360 pixels wide (roughly 1 inch by 5 to 6 inches). They are generally **click-through advertisements,** meaning they contain hypertext links to the site about which the banner is advertising. The banners can contain static text or animation. Not all advertisements are click-throughs because some sites that allow banner advertisements to be placed on their sites do not wish to encourage the exodus of their visitors to other sites. Thus, some sites have links to a followup page that provides more information about the advertised company or product without having the user exit the site.

Click-through advertising is like no other form of advertisement in that the advertising can lead the potential customer directly to a transaction location, close the sale, and record the direct link between an advertisement and its resulting sale. Banner advertising is typically measured and priced according to two features. One feature is the **cost per thousand impressions,** called the **CPM.** An **impression** refers to each time a page is viewed that is displaying the banner. Browsers can be set by their users to filter out graphics, and hence most banners. If a user does this and the banner is not seen by the user although it is technically displayed, it is still counted as an impression. The range of advertising rates quoted per CPM is quite wide, ranging from as low as $10 to as high as $80. The wide variation is primarily due to the nature of the sites bearing the banner. More specialized services that deliver the banners to users more likely to be interested in the product/services being offered in the banner will, as a general rule, charge more.

The other feature that is important in advertising rates, is the **click-through rate,** called the **CTR.** The click-through rate is considered to be more important by many advertisers because it measures the number of users "delivered" to a site. For example, if a business purchases a service that delivers its banner to sites at a rate of $20 CPM and the click-through rate is 1 percent (a common click-through rate for nontargeted banners), then it can expect that for every 1,000 viewers that see the banner, 10 will arrive at the site. This example yields a cost of $2 to deliver each visitor to the site via banner advertising. If, on the other hand, a business pays a little extra for a more targeted method of placing the banner across the screen (e.g., $ 40 CPM), then a higher CTR is to be expected (e.g., 4 percent). In this case, the cost to deliver a visitor to a site is $1, and this gives the business trying to promote its site more "bang for its buck."

Firms are also very interested in tracking whether visitors stay for a while and navigate through multiple pages and also whether they make a purchase from the site. **Fulfillment** is a term used to track whether a product or service was sold as a result of the advertisement. Software tracking devices are available for tracking such items, but they are very imperfect and imprecise due to the following items:

- The use of computer-sharing by individuals.
- Network servers and ISPs that serve as gateways that make it difficult or impossible to count each individual user.
- The ability of users to disable their cookie features of their browser.
- The prevalence of intelligent agents or "bots" and Web crawlers to peruse the WWW and update indexes.

Banner advertisements may be placed by subscribing to a network, such as that offered by DoubleClick. These types of firms use cookies to track visitors who visit sites within their network and then target specific types of banner advertisements based on what it has "learned" about each user. Another option is to join one of the many banner exchange networks that will display a business's banner on other sites in the exchange program based on some prespecified ratio of how many banners are displayed on the business's site.

One word of caution when choosing any advertising service or exchange service, however, is to investigate the types of businesses that may have advertisements flashed across the screen that may be either inappropriate or in direct competition with the site. Another method is to buy advertising time directly from a website, as illustrated in the Parenthoodweb.com box. Some guidelines given by DoubleClick for designing effective banners are:

- Target the banner to specific industries, appropriate regions, and user interests.
- Pose a question as a teaser to entice people to click-through.
- Use bright colors. As a general rule, research has shown that blue, green, and yellow are most effective, while white, red, and black are least effective.
- Post banners to the most appropriate page(s) of a site, which may not be its home page.
- Place the banner at the top of the page.
- Use animation; this can help increase the click-through rate by as much as 25 percent.
- Use a cryptic message that intrigues; this can help increase the click-through rate by as much as 18 percent.
- Use phrases that call the user to an action, such as "Enter Here." These types of statements can help increase the click-through rate by as much as 15 percent.
- Avoid banner burnout; research has shown that people tend to "tune-out" a banner after they have seen it four times.
- Measure beyond the click-through; fulfillment is also important.

(Adapted from DoubleClick.com)

Sponsorships

Sponsorships are another popular online advertising method (predicted by emarketer.com to rise to 58 percent of online advertisement expenditures in 2001.) **Sponsorships** are similar to banners in that a business gets to display a message, typically just a logo, on a site, and click-throughs may be allowed. What distinguishes a sponsorship from a banner are two features:

1. Sponsorships typically allow the firm's banner to stay on a site for a longer period of time, perhaps during prespecified time slots or for a certain number of days.
2. Sponsorships send a message that the advertising firm believes in the company behind the website.

Sponsorships are a good mechanism for generating brand recognition. Firms sponsoring a website may pay a flat rate, but require a minimum number of CPMs or click-throughs.

Portals and Infomediaries

A **portal** is referred to a site that serves as the "port of entry" onto the Web. Portals are designed to give Web users the information they need as they first enter the WWW. Customized pages are an option, as well as customized news items and stock quotes.

E-Commerce in Practice

AllAdvantage Launches AdvantageGrams

Personalized, Paid Opt-In E-Mail to Its U.S. Members

Infomediary company AllAdvantage.com and NetCreations Inc., the leader in 100 percent Opt-In® e-mail marketing, today announced the launch of AdvantageGrams, paid opt-in e-mail messages sent to AllAdvantage's U.S. members with information about self-selected interest categories. The service uses AllAdvantage.com's double opt-in e-mail addresses, which are managed by NetCreations in its PostMasterDirect.com database, and marks a further step toward a personalized online experience for AllAdvantage.com's members.

AllAdvantage members who opt in are rewarded for surfing the Web based on their individual profiles, all in a way that maintains their privacy. They "opt-in" to receive personalized offers on the company's Viewbar™ software, a two-way communication tool they install on their desktops and use as they browse the World Wide Web. Members in the United States may now also opt-in for the e-mail product, AdvantageGrams, where they can choose to receive advertising messages on subjects of interest to them. Members will receive payments for each click-through to sponsored websites.

Membership response to this initial AdvantageGrams message has been high. Within the first month, during the prelaunch phase of the program, more than 120,000 members signed up, reflecting the growing popularity of opt-in e-mail.

"This is a further development of our infomediary services," AllAdvantage Spokesperson Gregg Stebben noted, "increasing our ability to help members take advantage of some of the great deals offered on the Web. We know from surveys we've conducted that our members are highly active Internet consumers, with 93 percent shopping online."

"We are delighted to be working with AllAdvantage.com on a new e-mail product that rewards a responsive audience and delivers results for marketers," said Rosalind Resnick, chairman and CEO of NetCreations. "AdvantageGrams will be another secure way for marketers to reach consumers effectively."

AllAdvantage.com's Stebben added that this announcement is one in a series of "infomediary at work" announcements by AllAdvantage.com this month. It follows on the heels of AllAdvantage.com's agreements with Net2Phone Inc. to deliver free PC-to-PC and discounted PC-to-phone services, and with Ecount Inc. to deliver online payment accounts.

Source: Press Release. *AllAdvantage.com*. August 15, 2000. *www.AllAdvantage.com*

Further, search indexes and engines are typically available. Portals typically sell advertising space on their sites and take a percentage of sales made by customers that arrive at an e-tailer (electronic retailer) site from the portal. Portals are available for business-to-business applications as well (e.g., WIZnet's eCommerce Portal is designed "exclusively for business-to-business commerce" and has full catalog content for more than 20,000 suppliers). **Infomediaries,** information consolidators and distributors, are similar to portals and very important in electronic marketplaces. Infomediaries add value to the customer by helping to assess what the consumer or business wants or needs and helping that person or business locate it quickly and at the best price. *Infomediary* is one of those terms that is currently being used rather loosely by businesses involved in any aspect of online servicing of customers and businesses in their purchase decisions. The box entitled "AllAdvantage Launches AdvantageGrams" describes how one infomediary uses personalized offers and solicited e-mail (opt-in) to serve its customers.

Online Coupons

Another way for firms to advertise is to use **online coupons.** Online coupons may be redeemed online, printed for use in stores, or requested and sent via postal mail for use in stores. A leading drug chain, Longs Drug Stores, is using an Internet site to advertise its coupon savings. Once the visitor expresses the products in which they are interested, the drug store mails the coupons to them. This type of direct targeting can raise redemption rates and lower printing and mailing costs of coupons. Online coupons are also distributed from sites that specialize in distributing such coupons for businesses that subscribe to their services. Coolsavings.com allows registered users to choose both online and offline coupons and print them or redeem them online free of charge.

In the spring of 1999, BarnesandNoble.com looked to coolsavings.com to start an online promotional campaign. Barnes & Nobles's brick- and-mortar stores had previously used coolsavings.com to help kick off a program designed to drive brick-and-mortar store traffic for grand openings through the use of targeted printable coupons and promotions. BarnesandNoble.com decided to go with the same type of program to help increase online traffic. Thus, the future of online coupon services appears to be promising for those industries in which coupons are used, such as the supermarket, food, book, and other retail industries. (Coolsavings.com hopes to show a profit in 2001.)

WEBSITE DESIGN ISSUES

Entire books are available that address the issue of how to design effective websites. This section presents the basic design concepts and some generally accepted rules of thumb for designing good websites. Sites with different objectives will obviously have different needs. Moreover, individuality and uniqueness of websites are also valued features. With that in mind, these guidelines are offered as a starting point for developing good Web design skills, not as a formula that should be followed point by point.

Page Loading Efficiency

The temptation to overload a page with graphics should be resisted. A few well-chosen graphics are fine, but too much on a page and the visitor may become frustrated with the required **page load time**, and "click, click" they are off to another site. Frames also increase the loading time, and if the site sells or exchanges advertising space in which banners will appear, these items will also slow down the load time. Website designers should review the load time periodically from an offsite connection with a connection speed that is comparable to a reasonably low connection speed. Graphics and videos should be an option to visitors, not opened automatically. Also, all important information should be available in an alternative, text format so that users with slower Internet connections do not lose any information. For these slower-connection users, the website should be designed with a **text-only option,** which displays text in lieu of graphics and contains the same hypertext links.

Simplicity

Avoid clutter on Web pages. If the business has a lot of information to convey, organize it well and spread it out over multiple pages. Unlike printed advertisements, website hosting costs are so low and competitive that the number of pages is typically not a significant cost factor. Do not go overboard, however, and place so little information on each page that the user must click to advance to the next page after reading only three or four sentences. A guideline is to use about 60 characters per line. Also, avoid long pages that require a lot of scrolling. Again, organizing the material well can preclude excessive scrolling from being necessary.

Wise Use of Space

Do not ramble on; make each statement count. Just because Web space is relatively cheap does not mean that visitors want to weed through hoards of verbose commentaries and other non-value-added information to find the items desired. Kernels of information that are succinctly worded and have impact are best. (Note the shortness of this paragraph!)

A Reason to Return

Once a visitor comes to the site, give them a reason to return. Suggest they bookmark the site—it works! Some suggestions for items that may cause the visitor to return:

- Daily or weekly specials.
- Daily or weekly updates to the site that are clearly labeled, such as editorials, current events, projects, and recipes.
- Frequent buyer programs.
- Contests.
- Events, such as hosting a chat session with a guest celebrity or public figure.

Framing

A **frame** is a section of the viewer's computer screen. A screen can be split into multiple sections that can load different Web pages, even those from other sites. The use of frames has it benefits and its drawbacks. Framing is useful, for example, for providing a directory of options in one frame and the contents of each option in another frame. It helps the visitor to know where they are and where they have been, through the use of highlighted hypertext links. The drawbacks are that they slow the load time, not all browsers support frames, and most search engines cannot read the hypertext links in the frames. Over time, these drawbacks will most likely be non-issues.

Tables and Fonts

Tables are useful for providing structure to text that will not be lost due to the size of the visitor's screen and the size of the viewing window, which is affected by the viewer's Web browser. Whenever possible, avoid using all uppercase letters as they are more difficult for the eye to follow. Further, the use of fancy fonts may look good on the Web designer's screen, but the fonts displayed to visitors are limited to those that are available on their own computer. The Times and Helvetica fonts are good fonts for readability on websites. As mentioned earlier, try to keep line lengths less than 60 characters per line.

Graphics

Graphics can enhance a website when used properly. Attempt to use images that are no larger than 70k, or the load time may annoy visitors. Fortunately, many image software packages allow the user to view the image in different storage sizes and indicate the approximate load time for each size. The larger the image, the better the image, but a slightly less vivid image that loads faster may pay off in terms of retaining visitors. If picture clarity is important, (e.g., for inventory items), allow the user to choose to view a bigger, clearer picture by clicking on the smaller picture.

Interlaced Graphics

Images that gradually appear sharper are called **interlaced graphics.** Not everyone appreciates these pictures, and some people find them annoying. Designers that use interlace graphics contend that the visitor is able to see the picture faster, albeit fuzzy, and has something to view while the remainder of the picture is loading and sharpening.

GIF versus JPEG files

Either format can be used. The primary difference between the two file types is the compression technique used. GIF files are typically more efficient for solid-color images, such as logos, or images with large regions of solid color. JPEG formats will typically yield better results for multicolored images or photographs in terms of best quality for the size.

Purchasing Information

Sites that sell their products/services online should clearly post policies in an easily found place regarding these items:

- Tax rates.
- Shipping rates.
- Shipping schedules.
- Return policy.
- Privacy of transaction.
- Security of data that are transmitted.

Further, items selected for purchase (placed in a shopping cart) should be easily reviewed at any point. The total bill, including taxes and shipment cost, should be displayed to the user before asking for payment information, such as credit card data.

Tracking Data

To analyze the success or contribution of a site, certain data need to be tracked. Some useful information includes

- Number of different visitors (not repeat visitors).
- Number and frequency of repeat visitors.
- Location of site prior to visit, including the search engine used to locate the site, if applicable.
- Length of time of visit.
- Pages visited.
- Items examined by visitors.
- Domain names of visitors.
- Country codes of visitors.
- Purchases made, if applicable.

Cookies may be necessary to avoid double counting. The examination of correlations between some of these items can provide useful information, such as the correlation between the location of prior site and length of time visited or purchases made. For example, a site selling infant clothing may notice a strong correlation between prior site and length of visit if a significant portion of its visitors are arriving via an advertising banner placed on a site similar to ParenthoodWeb.com. Obviously, a great deal of analysis of such data is necessary before any conclusions should be drawn and used to make future decisions; however, such data contain a wealth of information if collected and analyzed properly.

INTELLIGENT AGENTS AND THEIR EFFECT ON MARKETING TECHNIQUES

Intelligent agents were defined and discussed in Chapter 13. Marketers need to seriously consider the use of such agents by consumers. Through the use of agents, consumers can filter out unwanted sites. This filtering means that banner advertising directed at catching the consumers' attention, similar to point-of-purchase displays in retail stores that are used to increase impulse buying, may not be as effective. The increased use of agents may mean that consumers spend less time wandering around the Internet, thereby enabling them to spend time more productively at targeted sites recommended by agents. Further, consumers can and are becoming more brand loyal because it is extremely easy to use an agent to price compare and shop for a specific brand.

Online store sites may lose some of their identity or never strongly develop it because of the lack of a physical environment. The challenge to marketers is to develop a mechanism that not only catches the attention of the agent but convinces it to recommend the site to its "master," the customer.

Also, using intelligent agents to keep customers at a site by increasing the personalization experience is also a potential application. The box entitled, "Manna: Real Time Becomes Reality" explains how one company is developing such a product using artificial intelligence to better serve customers once they arrive at a site.

IMPLICATIONS FOR THE ACCOUNTING PROFESSION

Customer-oriented firms integrate their marketing activities into virtually all phases of the value chain, except perhaps for their own procurement activities. As information systems increasingly serve customers and information is directly passed to them, through channels such as the WWW, many marketing tasks and core business processes are merged. Accounting firms provide assurance services that are concerned with the effectiveness and efficiency of business processes. Because of this increasing integration of marketing tasks into core business processes, accountants need to be well versed regarding the nuances of different marketing methods.

Furthermore, as accounting firms expand the boundaries of their profession toward increased business consulting, the knowledge of specific marketing tactics becomes important, including the assessment of the effectiveness and efficiency of marketing dollars spent on various marketing tools (the marketing mix). Also, accountants need to assess the integrity and reliability of marketing systems, especially if such systems provide mission-critical and financial reporting data. Providing the assurance function for Web-based commerce requires a different skill-set than for providing the assurance function for a traditional manufacturing or service firm. Activity-based costing models are very

E-Commerce in Practice

Manna: Real Time Becomes Reality

FrontMind Updates Websites to Suit Surfers' Tastes—On First Visit

A customer asks a salesclerk for gum. "We're out," says the clerk, not looking up from his book. Candy? "Sorry." The customer walks out empty-handed, and the clerk shrugs: The next time that guy comes in, he'll want gum.

Fat lot of good that'll do if the customer doesn't come back.

That's the problem Newton, Mass.–based Manna Network Technologies Inc. wants to solve. Using tools from the world of artificial intelligence, its first product monitors site visitors' actions and immediately alters a website's presentations to match what it thinks a customer wants—before that customer leaves.

With most of today's Web personalization tools, the next visit, not the current one, results in a more personalized offering. Because it's all too easy for visitors to look elsewhere on the Web, the site that can't satisfy the customer on the first try has probably lost the chance.

Sure, today's personalized websites keep a watch on visitors' actions, segregate them into groups, then pour the appropriate content into dynamic Web pages. Amazon.com, for example, recommends new books based on the ones you're browsing.

But personalization tools are barely out of the custom development project category. They are generally based on Java, Microsoft Corp.'s Active Server, and other dynamic Web technologies that need hard-to-come-by Web developer talent to update.

The programming foundation for those systems can be tough to build; the rules that keep them going swell to hundreds or thousands when the site's in active use, making scalability a problem. That also makes a system tough to alter quickly when inventory or customer preference data dictates a change.

Worse, a new rule's debut is often on the live site. The slow reaction time of an unwieldy personalization system could annoy—and thus cost the business—hundreds of potential customers.

Manna's Java- and Extensible Markup Language-based FrontMind for Marketing, scheduled for a June 14 debut, puts a wizardlike Web front end on the rules creation and editing process that requires little training to use. It also "stages" the rule by simulating its effects before it goes live, so inexperienced users can see the results before unleashing a potential disaster on the live site.

Business managers can fine-tune online sales presentations or add special offerings quickly, without an intermediary from the information technology department. The feature may ultimately prove the most valuable for corporate e-commerce because giving managers control of their online product presentations speeds the site's reactions to changing market conditions. It also shifts that responsibility from resource-stretched IT managers to the people who sell the product.

FrontMind can develop demographic reports to help managers refine strategies. A manager whose inventory is overstocked can ask the system to profile the customer most likely to buy that product, then use the profile to create a rule that presents a special sale price on that product only to the customers most likely to buy.

The system can offer buying hints to customers it detects are unfamiliar with the product category, recommending best-fit products. It can be easily stretched to accommodate information from other parts of the corporation; a customer on record as being kept waiting for technical support could be offered a free gift by the commerce site.

Of course, all that capability doesn't come cheap. Artificial intelligence systems are expensive to build and maintain, and FrontMind is no exception at a base price of $250,000. The high cost is liable to restrict the product to areas where extreme personalization pays off: huge corporate commerce sites that carry a wide range of very diverse products at relatively high profit margins.

Still, FrontMind is definitely a glimpse of things to come in website personalization.

Source: Cynthia Morgan, © *Computerworld Online* May 24, 1999. *www.computerworld.com*

different from those of manufacturing firms. The relevant "activities" of many Web-based firms are the underlying marketing techniques used to draw customers to the website. Hence, the types of marketing tracking data mentioned in the previous section will enter into an accountant's analysis of cost drivers.

Summary

The marketing potential of the WWW makes this an exciting period for those individuals in the field of marketing. Innovative and creative energies are flowing. One thing that firms and marketers must keep in mind, however, is that Web-based applications must be in alignment with the organization's overall business goals. In some cases, an organization may need to reassess its goals and adjust them to environmental changes. In many situations, businesses will find that the presence of the WWW and its uses are an important environmental change to which they must adapt.

If a firm decides that the WWW can help it achieve its mission, the next step is to determine how it should proceed. A very important, if not crucial, piece of the plan is the marketing plan. Included in the plan should be a well-thought-out use of the various marketing techniques discussed in this chapter. Because the WWW is still in its infancy, new marketing techniques will undoubtedly arise; however, the methods discussed in this chapter should provide a good starting point for understanding the various marketing channels available on the WWW.

Key Words

aggressive advertising	one-way channel
banner advertisements	online coupons
click-through advertisements	page load time
click-through rate (CTR)	paid advertising channels
consumer power shift	passive advertising
consumers' personal experiences	personalization
cost-per-thousand impressions (CPM)	personalized transaction domain
customer-oriented value chain model (COVE)	physical goods
customer-oriented value sphere	place
customer relationship management (CRM)	portal
digital products	press releases
directory	pricing
distribution description tag	product
frames	promotion
fulfillment	ranking
hit rates	search engine
impression	search engine spamming
infomediaries	service products
interactive sites	solicited, targeted e-mail
interlaced graphics	spam mail
keyword tag	sponsorship
manual customization	text-only option
marketing	title tag
meta tag	two-way channel
mission statement	unsolicited, targeted e-mail
news stories packaging	word of mouth
offline advertising	

Review Questions

1. What is marketing?
2. Did business-to-business or business-to-consumer applications spread first on the WWW? Why?

3. Did the number of ISPs or the number of users contribute most to the increased use of the WWW?
4. Why is it important for a firm to align its marketing and Web-based strategies with the overall corporate mission?
5. What is customer relationship management?
6. Identify the traditional four marketing Ps. What is the fifth P introduced in this chapter?
7. Distinguish between physical and service goods. How are these types of goods sold over the WWW?
8. How do the five Ps integrate into the customer-oriented value chain?
9. What is a digital product?
10. Distinguish between one-way and two-way advertising channels and give two examples of each. Why does the WWW provide a promising two-way channel?
11. Is all media attention good?
12. What is meant by mass-marketed personalization?
13. Distinguish between a passive and an aggressive online marketing strategy.
14. Distinguish between a directory and a search engine. Which method produces a larger number of sites from which to choose?
15. What is online banner advertising? How is it priced?
16. Explain the difference between solicited, targeted advertising and unsolicited, targeted advertising.
17. Why can spam mail be costly? To whom is it costly?
18. Distinguish between a portal and an infomediary.
19. What is an impression?
20. What are keyword and metatags? How are they used by search engines?
21. List four reasons visitor tracking devices for websites may result in imprecise information.
22. What is banner burnout?
23. What is a text-only option, and why use it?
24. In Web page design, is it better to place as much information as possible on a page or to keep it simple? Why?
25. What are interlaced graphics?
26. What types of data can be helpful to track if done properly?

Discussion Questions

1. Has the field of marketing changed as a result of the WWW?
2. How is the introduction of the WWW similar to the introduction of the wireless radio? How is it different?
3. Why didn't many large businesses initially flock to the Internet for marketing purposes?
4. Do you think all businesses really implement their Web-based marketing strategies from the top-down perspective presented in Figure 14.4? Why or why not?
5. Once established businesses begin to extend portions of their business to the Web, do you think they will take market share from startup companies designed specifically to do business on the Web? Specifically, discuss Tupperware's and BarnesandNoble.com's experiences?
6. How is the WWW creating new pricing models?
7. Can personalized service be mass marketed? Why or why not? Give an example to support your answer.
8. How important is it to register a site with a search engine?
9. How can the contents of a Web page and its HTML code affect the results produced by search engines?

10. Discuss the relationship between online and offline advertising. Has this relationship changed over time?

11. How can the effectiveness of banner or sponsorship advertising be measured?

12. Discuss the issues to be considered in page loading efficiency and why judgment has to be used.

13. Why should accountants be concerned with marketing techniques of Web-based systems?

Cases

1. Online Marketing of Pharmaecutical Products
   Identify two online pharmacies, one in the United States and one in either Canada, Mexico, or Europe.

   a. Research any two prescription drugs (U.S. prescription) you wish and compare prices.

   b. Explain the process or inhibitors to shipping to another country.

   c. Summarize your findings with any suggestions about the process.

2. Infomediaries
   Identify an infomediary not discussed in this chapter.

   a. List the services provided.

   b. Mention any services charges.

   c. Identify at least one competitor.

   d. Specifically explain how this infomediary plans to make money. Give details about past financial performance.

3. Spam Mail
   In summer 2000, the U.S. House of Representative approved an anti-spam bill. Specifically, the act makes it illegal to send unsolicited, bulk e-mail. The European Union is considering similar legislation

   a. Research whether this bill or any similar bills have been passed at the federal level.

   b. If one country passes such a bill and others do not, discuss the implications.

4. Assessing the Five Ps of a Website
   Visit Wine.com and categorize each of its activities into the following categories: product, price, place, promotion, and personalization.

5. Assessing the Communication Effectiveness of a Company Website
   The objective of this exercise is to assess the communications value of the Internet as a *complementary* communication medium. Select two websites from one of the following categories:

   - Air travel.
   - Travel other than airlines' sites.
   - Book, CD sales.
   - Online trading.
   - News services.
   - Automobile.
   - Hardware and software sales.
   - Children's sites.
   - Auctions.

   Because this exercise is concerned with the use of the Internet as a complementary advertising mechanism, do not choose firms that solely market their goods on the Internet, such as Amazon.com. The firms must have alternative sales and distribution channels.

   a. Use the rating sheet that follows to assess each of the websites. Do not use just the home page. You may have to navigate through many pages.

   b. Provide an overall summary of the effectiveness of each of the websites.

   c. Prepare a memo to the VP–Marketing, with a copy going to the CIO, indicating any proposed enhancements you would recommend. Specifically indicate which of the five Ps are affected by these enhancements.

Rating Sheet for Case 5

Category of Website_____

URL_____

Circle the Appropriate Response

Evaluation Criteria	Poor						Excellent	NA

Page Layout

Overall effect of home page	1	2	3	4	5	6	7	NA
Simple, uncluttered display	1	2	3	4	5	6	7	NA
Presence of corporate symbols, logos, etc.	1	2	3	4	5	6	7	NA
Appealing and readable color scheme	1	2	3	4	5	6	7	NA
Appropriate use of banner advertising	1	2	3	4	5	6	7	NA

Interactivity

Opportunity to interact	1	2	3	4	5	6	7	NA
Incentive to interact	1	2	3	4	5	6	7	NA
Reason to return to site again	1	2	3	4	5	6	7	NA
Effectiveness of prompts	1	2	3	4	5	6	7	NA

Business Policies

Privacy statement	1	2	3	4	5	6	7	NA
Secure data transmission	1	2	3	4	5	6	7	NA
Return policy	1	2	3	4	5	6	7	NA
Tax policy	1	2	3	4	5	6	7	NA
Shipping and handling policy	1	2	3	4	5	6	7	NA

Value or Offer

Current information	1	2	3	4	5	6	7	NA
Provision of useful information	1	2	3	4	5	6	7	NA
Availability of e-mail updates	1	2	3	4	5	6	7	NA

Action Requested

Offline purchasing only	1	2	3	4	5	6	7	NA
Online purchasing available	1	2	3	4	5	6	7	NA
Ability to review entire contents of shopping cart	1	2	3	4	5	6	7	NA

Product Support

FAQs	1	2	3	4	5	6	7	NA
E-mail	1	2	3	4	5	6	7	NA
Search feature	1	2	3	4	5	6	7	NA
Online support literature	1	2	3	4	5	6	7	NA

Search Logic of Hypertext Links

Topically relevant links	1	2	3	4	5	6	7	NA
Appropriate number of links	1	2	3	4	5	6	7	NA
Ability to go to home page from any page	1	2	3	4	5	6	7	NA

NA = Not applicable.
Source: Evaluation form developed by James Maskulka.

References and Websites

Adresource. "Web Advertising Terminology, Traffic, Statistics and Usage—An Advertising Primer." *http://www. adresource.com/html/advertising_terminology.html.*

American Marketing Association. "Definitions." *http://www.ama.org/about/ama/markdef.asp.*

Barnes & Noble. Press Release, February 19, 1998. *http://www.shareholder.com/bks/news/021998e.htm.*

_____. Annual Report 1997. *http://www. shareholder.comj/bks/outlook.htm.*

Coalition Against Unsolicited Commercial Email. "Welcome to CAUCE." *http://www.cauce.org.*

Cobalt Systems. "Website 101." *http://cobaltsystems.com/advice/.*

Coolsavings.com. "BarnesandNoble.com Attracts New Customers with Targeted Online Coupons and E-mails." Case Study.

Diederich, Tom. "Coupon Craze Continues." *ComputerworldOnline,* February 17, 1999.

Do, Orlantha, Eric March, Jennifer Rich, and Tara Wolff. "Intelligent Agents & The Internet: Effects on Electronic Commerce and Marketing." *http://bold.coba.unr.edu/odie/paper.htm.*

DoubleClick Inc. "Utilize Your Unsold Inventory." *http://www.doubleclick.com/publishers/utilizing.*

Fusaro, Roberta. "Tupperware to Sell on the Web." *ComputerworldOnline,* February 8, 1999.

Gimeniz, Syliva. "Dot Com—Going, Going, Gone." *Emarketer Estats,* January 5, 2001. *www.emarketer.com.*

Gurley, J. William. "How the Web Will Warp Advertising." *Fortune,* November 9, 1998, p. 119–120.

Handley, Ann. "Editorial vs. Advertising," *ClickZ Network.* *http://www.searchz.com/Articles/0216991.shtml.*

Hanson, Ward. "The Original WWW: Web Lessons from the Early Days of Radio." *Journal of Interactive Marketing,* Vol. 12. No. 3, Summer 1998.

Helm, Leslie. "The Cutting Edge; Special Report: Electronic Commerce; Buying into E-commerce; Web Is Reshaping How Firms Deal with Each Other." *Los Angeles Times,* February 15, 1999.

Hof, Robert D. "Now It's Your Web." *Business Week,* October 5, 1998, pp. 164–178.

Internet Advertising Bureau. *IAB.net.*

Johnson, Marc. "Winning Long-Term Consumer Attention." *Online Advertising,* December 1998. *http://www.webtrack.com/research/ oas/excerpts/oa9812.htm.*

Macaluso , Nora. "Report: E-Holiday Sales Topped $6B." *E-Commerce Times,* December 29, 2000. *www.ecommercetimes.com.*

Niccolai, James. "Government to Compile Online Shopping Stats." *ComputerworldOnline,* February 8, 1999.

Ohlson, Kathleen, "Pay to Play: New Service Pays Users to Surf." *ComputerworldOnline,* March 30, 1999.

Pascuzzo, Peter. "Three Elements of a Good Website Maintenance Program." *The Northtown Gazette,* Issue 15, June 15, 1998. *http://www.northtown.com/gazette/issue16.htm.*

Rafter, Michelle. "Stop Spam." *CNET*, December 19, 1996. *http://www.cnet.com/Content/Features/Howto/Spam/Index.htm.*

Reuters Limited. "DoubleClick Predicts Rapid Ads Growth." Februry 10, 1999. *http://www.news.com/News/Item/0,4,32270,00.html.*

Sullivan, Danny. "How Search Engines Rank Web Pages." *Search Engine Watch.* *http://searchenginewatch.internet.com/webmasters/rank.htm.*

_____. "Search Engine Design Tips." *Search Engine Watch.* *http://searchenginewatch.internet.com/webmasters/tips.htm.*

Unplugged Software, Inc. "Great Website Design Tips." *http://www.unplug.com/great/.*

Welch, Mark. "Web Publishers' Advertising Guide." February 1999, *http://www.Adbility.com/WPAG/.*

Willman, John. "Consumer Profiles Made to Measure." *Financial Times (London edition),* November 5, 1998, p. 16

ABA - American Bar Association, 168

ACAP - Application Configuration Access Protocol, 293

ACH - Automated Clearing House, 194, 195

ACK - Acknowledgement, 224, 348

AES - Advanced Encryption Standard, 314

AHSC - American Hospital Supply Company, 182

AICPA - American Institute of Certified Public Accountants, 47, 96, 123, 429

AIS - Accounting information system, 111

ANSI - American National Standards Institute, 181, 189, 275

ARP - Address Resolution Protocol, 348

ASC - Accredited Standards Committee, 189, 275

ASEC - Assurance Services Executive Committee, 102

ASP - Application service provider, 53, 67, 72

AVNET - Aviation Network project, 192

B2B - Business-to-business commerce, 25, 62

B2C - Business-to-consumer commerce, 61

BBB - Better Business Bureau, 123

BCG - Boston Consulting Group, 398

BGP - Border Gateway Protocol, 348

BSA - Business Software Alliance, 426

CA - Certification authority, 328

CA - Chartered Accountant, 95, 128

CAUCE - Coalition Against Unsolicited Commercial Email, 457

CC - Communication channel, 70

CDT - Center for Democracy and Technology, 220

CEFACT - United Nations Center for Facilitation of Procedures and Practices for Administration, Commerce, and Transport, 277

CEO - Chief executive officer, 97

CERT - Computer Emergency Response Team, 244

CERTC - Computer Emergency Response Team Coordination Center, 281

CFO - Chief financial officer, 97

CIAC - Computer Incident Advisory Capability, 244, 283

CICA - Canadian Institute of Chartered Accountants, 47, 123

CITP - Certified information technology professional, 138

COPAC - Chip Offline Preauthorized Card, 392

COPPA - Children's Online Privacy Protection Act, 154

COSO - Committee of Sponsoring Organizations of the Treadway Commission, 107, 263

COVC - Customer-oriented value chain, 111, 444

CP - Certificate policy, 331

CPA - Certified public accountant, 95, 373

CPM - Cost per thousand impressions, 462

CPS - Certification practice statement, 329

CR - Certificate repository, 328

CRL - Certification revocation list, 328, 329, 334

CRM - Customer relationship management, 13, 49, 444

CSI/FBI - Computer Security Institute/Federal Bureau of Investigation survey, 18

CSRC - Computer Security Resource Clearinghouse, 283

CSTC - Computer Security Technology Center, 283

CTR - Click-through rate, 462

DARPA - Defense Advanced Research Projects Agency, 7, 280

DDoS - Distributed denial of service attacks, 225

DES - Data Encryption Standard, 296

DFSC - Defense Fuel Supply Center, 193

DHTML - Document HTML, 291

DMV - Texas Division of Motor Vehicles, 173

DMZ - Demilitarized zone, 363

DoD - Department of Defense, 197, 215, 282, 294

DoJ - Department of Justice, 158

DOM - Document Object Model, 291

DOS - Denial of service attack, 224–225

DSA - Digital Signature Algorithm, 324

DSMD - Dual signature message digest, 386

DSS - Digital Signature Standard, 324

DSS - Distributed Sniffer System, 231

DTD - Document type definition, 202, 288